THE

ANNUAL REGISTER
VOL. 174—FOR 1932

THE

ANNUAL REGISTER

A REVIEW OF PUBLIC EVENTS
AT HOME AND ABROAD

FOR THE YEAR

1932

EDITED BY

M. EPSTEIN, M.A., Ph.D.

NEW SERIES

LONGMANS, GREEN AND CO. LTD.
39 PATERNOSTER ROW, LONDON, E.C. 4
NEW YORK, TORONTO, CALCUTTA, BOMBAY AND MADRAS

SIMPKIN, MARSHALL, LTD., LONDON, E.C. 4
JOHN MURRAY; J. & E. BUMPUS, LTD.
BICKERS & SON, LTD.; WHELDON & WESLEY, LTD.; BURNS, OATES & WASHBOURNE, LTD.

1933

MADE IN GREAT BRITAIN

CONTENTS.

PART I.

ENGLISH HISTORY.

CHAPTER I.

THE GENERAL TARIFF.

v   a*

CONTENTS.

CHAPTER II.

THE BUDGET AND THE CONVERSION LOAN.

CHAPTER III.

THE OTTAWA AGREEMENTS.

CHAPTER IV.

THE AMERICAN DEBT PAYMENT.

CONTENTS.

IMPERIAL HISTORY.

FOREIGN HISTORY.

PART II.

PREFATORY NOTE.

THE Editor of THE ANNUAL REGISTER once again expresses his thanks to *The Times* for permission to make use of matter published in its columns.

Mr. Ramsay MacDonald's Second National Ministry.

(TOOK OFFICE NOVEMBER 6, 1931.)

Cabinet Ministers.

Prime Minister and First Lord of the Treasury . . .	Mr. Ramsay MacDonald.
Lord President of the Council .	Mr. Stanley Baldwin.
Lord Chancellor . . .	Lord Sankey.
Lord Privy Seal . . .	{Lord Snowden (till September 28). / Mr. Stanley Baldwin (from September 29).
Chancellor of the Exchequer .	Mr. Neville Chamberlain.

Secretaries of State :—

Home	{Sir Herbert Samuel (till September 28). / Sir John Gilmour (from September 29).
Foreign	Sir John Simon.
Colonies	Sir Philip Cunliffe-Lister.
Dominions . . .	Mr. J. H. Thomas.
War	Lord Hailsham.
India	Sir Samuel Hoare.
Air	Marquess of Londonderry.
Scotland . . .	{Sir Archibald Sinclair (till September 28). / Sir Godfrey Collins (from September 29).

Presidents :—

Board of Trade . . .	Mr. Walter Runciman.
Board of Education . .	{Sir Donald Maclean (till June 15). / Lord Irwin (from July 16).
First Lord of the Admiralty .	Sir Bolton M. Eyres-Monsell.
Minister of Health . . .	Sir E. Hilton Young.
Minister of Agriculture and Fisheries	{Sir John Gilmour (till September 28). / Major Walter Elliot (from September 29).
Minister of Labour . . .	Sir Henry Betterton.
First Commissioner of Works .	Mr. W. Ormsby-Gore.

Ministers not in the Cabinet.

Chancellor of the Duchy of Lancaster	Mr. J. C. C. Davidson.
Minister of Pensions . .	Major G. C. Tryon.
Postmaster-General . . .	Sir H. Kingsley Wood.
Minister of Transport . .	Mr. P. J. Pybus.
Attorney-General . . .	{Sir William Jowitt, K.C. (till January 24). / Sir Thomas Inskip (from January 27).
Solicitor-General . . .	{Sir Thomas Inskip (till January 27). / Sir Frank Boyd Merriman (from January 27).
Paymaster-General . . .	Lord Rochester.
Civil Lord of the Admiralty .	Captain D. E. Wallace.
Financial Secretary to the Treasury	{Major Walter Elliot (till September 28). / Mr. Leslie Hore-Belisha (from September 29).
Financial Secretary to the War Office	Mr. A. Duff Cooper.
Secretary for Mines . . .	{Mr. Isaac Foot (till September 28). / Mr. Ernest Brown (from September 29).

Under-Secretaries of State :—

Air	Sir Philip Sassoon.
Colonies	{ Sir Robert Hamilton (*till September 28*). { The Earl of Plymouth (*from September 29*).
Dominion Affairs . . .	Mr. Malcolm MacDonald.
Foreign	Mr. R. A. Eden.
Home	Mr. Oliver Stanley.
India	{ Marquess of Lothian (*till September 28*). { Mr. Richard Austen Butler (*from Sept. 29*).
Scotland	Mr. A. N. Skelton.
War	The Earl of Stanhope.

Parliamentary Secretaries :—

Admiralty . . .	Lord Stanley.
Agriculture and Fisheries .	Earl De la Warr.
Education . . .	Mr. H. Ramsbotham.
Health	{ Mr. Ernest Brown (*till September 29*). { Mr. Geoffrey Shakespeare (*from September 29*).
Labour	Mr. R. S. Hudson.
Pensions	Lt.-Col. Cuthbert M. Headlam (*till Sept. 29*).
Post Office . . .	{ Mr. Henry Graham-White (*till September 28*). { Sir Ernest Bennett (*from October 22*).
Board of Trade . .	{ Mr. Leslie Hore-Belisha (*till September 29*). { Dr. Edward Leslie Burgin (*from Sept. 29*).
Overseas Trade . .	Major D. J. Colville.
Transport	{ Earl of Plymouth (*till September 29*). { Lt.-Col. Cuthbert Morley Headlam (*from* *September 29*).
Treasury . . .	Mr. H. D. Margesson.

SCOTLAND.

Secretary of State . . .	{ Sir Archibald Sinclair (*till September 28*). { Sir Godfrey Collins (*from September 29*).
Under-Secretary of State .	Mr. A. N. Skelton.
Lord-Advocate	Mr. Craigie M. Aitchison.
Solicitor-General . . .	Mr. Wilfrid G. Normand.

ANNUAL REGISTER

FOR THE YEAR
1932.
PART I.
ENGLISH HISTORY.

CHAPTER I.

THE GENERAL TARIFF.

AT the opening of the year, the supreme question confronting
the Government was whether the national accounts would balance
at the close of the financial year on March 31. Any serious
deficit would, it was feared, weaken foreign confidence in Great
Britain's financial stability, and so bring about a collapse of the
currency and a dislocation of the economic life of the country.
The Budget of October, 1931, balanced on paper, but whether
it would balance in fact depended now to a preponderating
extent on the amount of revenue which would flow into the
Exchequer from income-tax payments in the interval. In its
extreme anxiety to collect the money which it required, the
Government at the end of 1931 took the unusual step of issuing
an appeal to the public to come to its assistance by meeting their
income-tax obligations without evasion and with the utmost
despatch.

To this appeal the public made a magnificent response. Heavy
as were the demands upon them—on account both of the high
rate of the tax itself and of the enactment by which this year
three-quarters of it fell due in January instead of a half, as previously—they were met with a promptness and even eagerness
the like of which had never before been witnessed. From the
first day of the year there was a veritable rush to the income-tax
offices, which were literally besieged by persons anxious to settle
their account and so help the nation in its emergency. Many
persons in order to raise the money required sold securities or
postponed other payments almost equally urgent. The results
to the Treasury were highly satisfactory. For several weeks the

A

receipts from income tax were materially higher than in the corresponding period of the previous year, and before long the equilibrium of the Budget was practically assured.

Economically, the year 1932 opened under slightly better auspices than its predecessor, not because the country was better off—the reverse was the case—but because it seemed to be on the upward grade. The last unemployment return for 1931 had stated that on December 21 of that year there were 2,572,602 unemployed persons on the register. This was nearly 100,000 more than at the end of 1930, but considerably less than in September, before the country abandoned the gold standard. The improvement had been general, affecting nearly all trades except those which normally suffered a decline in the winter season ; it had been most marked in the textile industries. As compared with the beginning of the year, wages had fallen by the end of 1931 by a weekly average of 400,000*l*., or over 2 per cent., but during the same period the index number of the cost of living as compared with 1913 had fallen from 58 to 47. The actual number of persons in employment at the end of 1931 (9,409,000) was nearly 400,000 less than at its commencement.

It was announced at the beginning of the year that henceforward unemployment totals would be published not once a week as hitherto but once a month, and that the published statement would contain information which was necessary for the correct understanding of the figures, and which it was not possible to obtain more than once a month. This change had been recommended as far back as July, 1929, by the Association of British Chambers of Commerce, and had had the approval of successive Ministers of Labour, but political considerations had prevented it from being carried out until now. One of its chief objects was to remove certain misconceptions as to the state of British industry which, based upon a mistaken interpretation of the previous returns, were prevalent abroad, and were thought to be injurious to British trade interests. The first return under the new system was issued on February 8, and showed that on January 25 the number of unemployed had been 2,728,411, or over 200,000 more than in December.

On January 8 the Prime Minister returned to London from Lossiemouth, where he had been spending the Christmas recess, and immediately took in hand the preparations for the International Conference on German reparations which had been arranged provisionally to meet at Lausanne on January 18 (*vide* ANNUAL REGISTER, 1931, p. 116). A Committee of the Cabinet had already drafted a report on the subject, and on January 8 Sir Frederick Leith-Ross, a Treasury expert, left London for Paris in order, if possible, to make a preliminary arrangement with the French authorities as to the line to be adopted. Difficulties being raised by the latter, the British Government proposed that the date of the conference should be fixed for January 25 instead of the 18th, though it would have preferred the earlier date, so as to allow Ministers more time to prepare for the opening of Parliament. On January 9 Dr. Brüning, the German Chancellor, stated publicly that it would be impossible for Germany to continue political payments. Mr. MacDonald thereupon, on January 11, issued a statement in which he said that Dr. Brüning's declaration rendered the conference more necessary than ever, since it was impossible to leave things as they were.

The French view was that if a preliminary agreement could not be reached between France and England, it would be useless to hold the conference. Redoubled efforts were accordingly made from the British side to effect such an agreement with M. Laval's first Government, but without success; and the fall of that Government on January 18 seemed to place it out of the question, at any rate for the time being. Nevertheless, the British Government persisted in regarding the conference as being merely postponed, and continued its conversations with the other Governments concerned.

Reporting to Parliament on the state of the negotiations on February 2, Mr. Chamberlain expressed the British Government's concern at the postponement of a settlement. Believing as they did that a speedy solution was necessary, which could be best reached by general cancellation, they had suggested an immediate conference upon receipt of the Basle Committee's report. Having found this to be impracticable, they had proposed to defer the conference till May or June, and conclude a provisional one year's agreement to begin at the expiration of the Hoover moratorium. Negotiations with the French Government had shown that a general agreement in advance of a conference was unattainable, and probably therefore nothing could be done till the conference in May or June, although the Basle Report had shown clearly that the existing arrangements could not stand.

If the postponement of the proposed conference on reparations was a disappointment to the public, it could still entertain good hopes for the success of the Disarmament Conference which was about to be held at Geneva. On January 14 the Lord Mayor of London convened a meeting of Lord Mayors and Mayors of England and Wales and Provosts of Scottish burghs to emphasise the importance of the conference. Sir John Simon, who was unable to be present, wrote a letter to the meeting in which he warned it not to expect anything spectacular from the conference, and expressed the opinion that it might well prove to be but the first of a series. The meeting was addressed by Mr. Eden, the Parliamentary Under-Secretary for Foreign Affairs, who said that the British Delegation would enter the conference with a clear conscience in the knowledge that successive British Governments since the war had constantly striven to set the

world an example in disarmament. Almost alone among the
Great Powers of the world they had not increased their expenditure on armaments during the past five years. Their Army was
little more than a police force ; their Navy had been successively
reduced ; and they were only fifth among the air Powers. This
country therefore could make no further contribution to unilateral disarmament ; other nations must now do their share.

On January 9 the Foreign Office issued a *communiqué* setting
forth British policy with regard to Manchuria, and explaining
why England had not associated herself with the Note recently
addressed by the United States to Japan on the subject.

The British Government, it stated, stood by the policy of
the open door for international trade in Manchuria which was
guaranteed by the Nine-Power Treaty at Washington. Since
the recent events in Manchuria, Japanese representatives had
stated at the Council of the League of Nations at Geneva on
October 13 that Japan was the champion in Manchuria of the
principle of equal opportunity and the open door for the economic
activities of all nations, and on December 28 the Japanese Prime
Minister had stated that Japan would adhere to the open-door
policy and would welcome participation and co-operation in
Manchurian enterprise. In view of these statements the Government had not considered it necessary to address any formal
Note to the Japanese Government on the lines of the American
Government's Note, but the Japanese Ambassador had been
requested to obtain confirmation of these assurances from his
Government. This explanation did not satisfy the critics of
the Government, who continued to call for stronger action.

On January 12 the Burma Round-Table Conference, which
had opened on November 27, 1931, was wound up with a statement from the Prime Minister indicating the length to which
Britain was prepared to go in granting self-government to Burma,
supposing she elected to sever herself from India. In that case,
it was the intention of the Government to place responsibility
upon her Legislature for the administration not only of the
subjects which would fall within the range of Provincial Governments in India, but also of those which would be administered
in India by the Central authority. In order, however, to maintain the stability of the realm, certain important powers would
have to be reserved to the Governor, including the regulation,
subject to responsibility to the Legislature, of Defence and
Foreign Affairs, the administration of the Shan States, certain
branches of supply, direction of monetary policy, and the right
of veto on proposed legislation. The announcement was not
received with any show of enthusiasm by the delegates, nor
were they greatly cheered by Mr. MacDonald's promise that the
Government would endeavour to ensure that the reserved powers
should not prejudice the advance of Burma to full self-government.

Throughout the Christmas recess, the Committee of the Cabinet which had been appointed to consider ways and means of redressing the adverse balance of trade had been hard at work examining the facts relating to this question. As a result of its investigations, it had come to the conclusion that the " invisible " exports of Britain in 1931 had been considerably less than in the previous year, and that therefore it was essential to resort to some means of restricting imports. A general tariff naturally suggested itself as the readiest instrument for effecting this object. The Conservative members of the Committee—Mr. Chamberlain and Sir P. Cunliffe-Lister—of course needed no conversion to this idea. Mr. Runciman and Sir John Simon, in spite of their Free Trade proclivities, were prepared to adopt it as a temporary expedient. Sir Herbert Samuel and Lord Snowden, however, could not be brought to assent to such a step, the latter declaring that, on account of the fall in the value of the pound, even a 10 per cent. duty would be no longer a revenue tariff, as it might have been when first considered by the Labour Government, but a purely protective tariff.

The Committee was thus unable to come to a unanimous decision, and had to content itself with submitting to the Cabinet a report embodying the recommendations of the majority. The chief of these were that a 10 per cent. tariff should be immediately imposed on a very wide range of manufactured and semi-manufactured goods, and that a Tariff Commission should be appointed to go through the list of articles in the schedule with a view to deciding whether any of them could be regarded as non-essential, in which case the duty could be increased subsequently. This plan was regarded as evidence of great moderation on the side of the Conservative members of the Committee, but it still went much too far for the more ardent Free Traders ; and the long-prophesied clash within the Cabinet on the subject of tariffs became inevitable.

The Committee's memorandum was laid before the Cabinet on January 21. Four members—Lord Snowden, Sir Herbert Samuel, Sir Donald Maclean, and Sir Archibald Sinclair—declared themselves inflexibly opposed to the imposition of a general tariff on manufactured goods. Others were equally insistent on its necessity. Prolonged discussion failed to produce any reconciliation of the opposing views, and the unity of the Government was gravely jeopardised. The four Free Trade members sought to break the impasse by offering their resignations to the Prime Minister, but this course was strongly deprecated on all sides, and strenuous efforts were made to effect a compromise.

The difficulty was at length solved by a remarkable expedient. When the Cabinet resumed its sitting next day (Jan. 22) it was decided, on a proposal of Lord Hailsham, that the recommendations of the Committee should be adopted, in accordance with the will of the majority, but that those Ministers who found themselves unable to support the conclusions of the majority on the subject of import duties and cognate matters should be at liberty to express their views by speech and vote. This strange decision, involving a breach with the usual Ministerial practice and with the long-established principle of collective Cabinet responsibility, was justified on the ground of the paramount importance of maintaining national unity in presence of the grave problems confronting both England and the rest of the world. Being essentially united on all other matters of policy, the Cabinet was able to flatter itself that by this special provision it was best interpreting the will of the nation and adapting itself to the needs of the time.

The action of the Government was naturally the cause of no small surprise among the public, but it was generally considered to be wise in the circumstances. Only in two quarters was it actively condemned. The extreme protectionists complained that the Government had made far too great concessions to its Free Trade element, and objected strongly to the continued presence in its midst of the dissenting Ministers. The Labour Party also suddenly became great sticklers for constitutional propriety, and called for the resignation of a Government which had abandoned the doctrine of collective responsibility.

On January 23 Sir H. Samuel issued a statement explaining and defending the course which had been taken by himself and his associates. When differences arose in the Cabinet over the question of the tariff recommendations of the Committee, there were, he said, four possibilities. The four Free Trade Ministers might have subordinated their opinions on the ground that larger issues predominated. This they were precluded from doing, as they had undertaken at the time of the General Election to exercise their own judgment on the questions involved, and not to do so would be inconsistent with political sincerity. For analogous reasons it was impossible that the other members of the Cabinet should defer to the views of the minority. There were really therefore two courses open. One was to accept as inevitable the break-up of the National Government. This would have been most regrettable and would most certainly have been deplored by the nation at large. It would also have made untenable the position of the Prime Minister, whose resignation was desired by none. It remained therefore frankly to suspend in this instance and for the time being the rule of the collective responsibility of Ministers, to allow Ministers and Members of Parliament latitude to express dissentient views by speech and vote without withholding their general support from the National Government as such. Whether the arrangement would work remained to be seen. But at any rate it deserved a trial.

In an address to his constituents a few days later (Jan. 29), Mr. MacDonald vigorously defended the Government's action. Criticism of it, he said, seemed to be based on Lord Melbourne's well-known remark to his Cabinet on a famous occasion, that it did not matter what they said so long as they all said it together. This, he admitted, was a fundamental axiom in the practice of party government. When there was one party in power, the Cabinet could not be disunited, not for constitutional but for party reasons. They should not, however, lift party expediency into constitutional principle. If by sacrificing Lord Melbourne's axiom he had helped to keep the National Government from crumbling, he was proud of his achievement. He was most grateful, and the nation and every party which joined in the creation of a National Government should be most grateful to the colleagues who assisted him to effect a very desirable end.

There was one protectionist impost which the " agreement to differ " did not touch. On January 12 the Minister of Agriculture, had met representatives of the millers, merchants, and farmers to discuss with them finally his project for instituting a quota for home-grown wheat. The millers now abandoned their former demands for a duty on imported flour and a levy on home-milled flour, and agreed that the Minister's scheme was workable, with certain modifications, which he accepted. The revised scheme was laid before the Cabinet, and accepted by all the Ministers, including Sir Herbert Samuel and the other Free Traders.

A kindred matter to which the Government devoted its attention during the recess was the Imperial Conference to be held at Ottawa in the summer. On January 27 Mr. Thomas stated that the Government was attaching great importance to it, and would send a strong delegation, including experts and representatives of trade and industry. Mr. Thomas also repeated a statement already made by the Chancellor of the Exchequer, that the Government would enter into no commitments to foreign countries which would prevent free and unfettered discussion, and, if possible, agreement at Ottawa.

On January 24 a disturbance which the Home Office described as " somewhat serious " took place at the Dartmoor Convict Prison, where some hundred of the prisoners got out of hand and kept the prison staff at defiance for a couple of hours. They were eventually brought under control with the help of police from Plymouth and Exeter. Some twenty of them were injured, but none seriously, and none escaped. The outbreak caused a widespread feeling of uneasiness in the country, and the Home Secretary commissioned the Recorder of Bristol, Mr. Herbert du Parcq, to institute an inquiry into the circumstances.

On January 24 Sir William Jowitt resigned the office of Attorney-General, which he had held for nearly three months without having a seat in Parliament. In spite of the active assistance of the Prime Minister, who was most anxious to retain him in the Government, he had been unable during that time to find a constituency which would nominate him as a candidate in a by-election. Conservatives looked askance on him as a Socialist, and among Liberals resentment was still felt at his change of party in 1929 (*vide* ANNUAL REGISTER, 1929, p. 54). He was succeeded by the Solicitor-General, Sir T. Inskip, a Conservative, who had been Attorney-General in the last Conservative Government. Sir F. Boyd-Merriman, also a Conservative, became Solicitor-General.

Public confidence in the Government was greatly strengthened by the announcement on January 25 that the Bank of England intended on February 1, the date of maturity, to complete the repayment of the credit of 50,000,000*l.* gold which the Government had raised in August in France and the United States in its efforts to save the pound. 20,000,000*l.* of this sum had been repaid on October 21, and the balance renewed for three months. In making the previous payment, the Bank had shipped 15,000,000*l.* of gold, but on this occasion it made no gold shipment. Its ability to meet its obligations in this way, and without even stipulating for a renewal of the loan, if required, was taken as a sign that the National Government had succeeded in at least one of the objects which it set out to attain.

On January 27 the Government finally broke off the negotiations which had been proceeding perfunctorily for a couple of years with the Soviet Government for a settlement of the claims of British citizens against Russia, The reason given was that the Soviet Government had failed to make the definite proposal which it had repeatedly promised, and had merely put forward the wholly unacceptable suggestion that any satisfaction of claims of British citizens should be linked with the grant of a loan or credit to the Soviet Government. When asked in Parliament whether this policy was likely to produce more fruitful results than the former one, Sir John Simon drily remarked that it could hardly produce less.

The outbreak of hostilities between the Japanese and Chinese at Shanghai on January 28 was viewed with grave concern by the Government, and a Cabinet Committee was appointed to watch events in the Far East. Military and naval reinforcements were immediately sent to Shanghai for the protection of British life and property there. In concert with the United States, and subsequently with France and Italy, the Government instructed its representatives at Tokio and Nanking to lay certain proposals before the combatants with a view to restoring and maintaining peace ; and Sir John Simon, who about this time went to Geneva to attend the Disarmament Conference, exerted himself to the same end there also.

Parliament reassembled on February 2, and the House of

Commons immediately gave a second reading to the Town and Country Planning Bill, the chief object of which was to confer on local authorities greater power to prevent the destruction of local amenities by injudicious building. The Bill was substantially identical with the one of the same title which had been introduced by the Labour Government in the previous year, and its Socialist parentage was made a matter of charge against it by a number of Conservative speakers. A more serious objection raised in the debate was that local authorities could not be trusted to carry out the intentions of the Bill, but this was not the view taken by the majority of the House.

On the next day (Feb. 3) the House by a large majority approved the third Order made by the President of the Board of Trade under the Abnormal Importations Act of December 17, 1931. In submitting the resolution, Mr. Hore-Belisha, the Under-Secretary of the Board, gave an encouraging account of the results of the Act up to date. Imports of the articles included in the three Orders had been reduced by over 5,000,000*l*., and British purchases from abroad of Class III. goods had declined by no less than 10,000,000*l*. in one month. Exports and re-exports, instead of declining concurrently, had actually increased in December ; more people were employed and the cost of living had not risen. Thus so far the prophets of evil had been completely falsified.

Having disposed of these preliminary matters, the Government now (Feb. 4) proceeded to lay before the House the new fiscal policy which it had adopted at its historic meeting of January 22 and 23. Before a full House and a distinguished company of strangers, the Chancellor of the Exchequer moved a money resolution providing that as from March 1, there should be charged on all goods imported into the United Kingdom a duty of 10 per cent. of their value, save for such as should be subsequently exempted by Act of Parliament. After remarking that they were at last settling down to the main business which had brought them together, Mr. Chamberlain went on to explain at some length the reasons which had led the majority of the Government to this decision. It was true, he said, that if they compared the present position of the country with what it was when the Government came into office in November, they had no cause for dissatisfaction. They were on the highway to balancing the Budget ; the cost of living had not risen ; sterling had remained stable ; and in certain quarters there was a definite improvement in trade. Also there was a more hopeful feeling abroad, as evidenced by recent speeches of prominent bankers, industrialists, and others. Nevertheless, they were by no means as yet out of their troubles. International trade was being hampered by a multiplication of restrictions ; the problems of war debts and reparations were still unsettled ; and a new source of anxiety had arisen in the Far East. Unemployment was still very high, and the basic trades were still stagnant ; nor could they expect the taxpayer to repeat the heroic effort of this year.

Some of their problems, he proceeded, were international in character, and could only be solved by the willing co-operation of other nations. But others were within their own control, and therefore, in accordance with the undertaking of the Speech from the Throne, they had devoted themselves to the consideration of the problem of the balance of trade, or rather of payments, which for Britain was of the very first importance. The results of their investigations into this matter had been disquieting. A credit balance of 100,000,000*l.* in 1929 had become an adverse balance of 113,000,000*l.* in 1931. The change was due to a decline of 186,000,000*l.* in invisible exports and of 38 per cent. in visible exports, on the basis of comparable prices. Imports on the other hand had not really declined at all. These figures, he thought, established the vital necessity for any action which it was in the power of the Government to take for restoring the balance of payments to the right side. The Government in these circumstances had set itself to evolve a policy which should serve seven objects : first, to correct the balance of trade ; secondly, to raise revenue, without placing undue burdens on any section of the community ; thirdly, to prevent an unchecked depreciation of currency ; fourthly, by means of moderate and scientific protection, to transfer to their own fields and factories work which was being done elsewhere ; fifthly, to encourage industrial efficiency ; sixthly, to obtain a bargaining counter for use in negotiations with other countries ; and seventhly, to encourage reciprocity within the Empire.

For these purposes the specific proposals of the Government were as follows. A general *ad valorem* duty of 10 per cent. would be imposed with the double purpose of raising a substantial contribution to the revenue and of putting a brake on the total value of the imports coming into the country. Articles already subject to the McKenna and similar duties would not be subject to the new duty, and there would be a short free list, including wheat, meat, and other articles. On the basis of the 10 per cent. flat rate would be built a superstructure of additional duties to be imposed on articles which were non-essential, in the sense that they were either luxuries or could be produced at home in sufficient quantity. These duties would be imposed by Order of the Treasury, but only on the advice of an independent Advisory Committee. The Committee, which would consist of two to five members with a chairman, would be salaried, and would be expected to devote its whole time to its duties, and would be instructed to consider the interests of industries which were consumers as well as those which were producers of goods. The Treasury would have power to revoke or vary such Orders, and all Orders would require confirmation by the House of Commons. Finally, Mr. Chamberlain announced, amid loud applause, that none of the new duties would apply to goods from the Dominions, at any rate till after the Ottawa Conference. This concession, he said, which was purely voluntary, was a gesture intended to mark their desire to approach the conference in the true spirit of Imperial harmony and unity.

In the debate which followed, Mr. Attlee, on behalf of the Opposition, moved the rejection of the resolution, while Mr. Amery, as a high protectionist, welcomed it as at least bringing the day of deliverance from Cobdenism. Sir Herbert Samuel, making full use of his liberty to differ from his colleagues on the tariff issue, stated with great force the arguments against the Government's proposals. He first pointed out that the Government had pledged itself to adopt tariffs, if needs be, as a means of redressing the adverse balance of trade, but the Chancellor had declared that his policy had many other objects besides this, and had stated the case for a permanent and scientific system of Protection. The 10 per cent. duty would tax 100 per cent. of imports in order to exclude perhaps 8 per cent., while as to the other 92 per cent. it could only be justified on the grounds of taxation or of Protection. This was totally different from the Abnormal Importations Act, where they had heavy prohibitive duties deliberately and successfully intended to shut imports out. Neither was this 10 per cent. a temporary measure. The Chancellor might say that it was an emergency measure and that this was an additional reason for it, but he did not say that when the emergency was over it could be repealed. It was obviously meant to be permanent, since upon it was to be based a series of bargains or arrangements with the Dominions. If these were once made, they would not be free later on to say that they intended for reasons of their own to repeal any of these duties. Sir Herbert then went on to adduce the usual Free Trade arguments on the adverse effects of tariffs on the export trade and on the cost of living. He also pointed out that the new tax would be no lever to secure the efficiency of industry, because the privilege of Protection was to be accorded to all alike, without conditions, and that it was no weapon for bargaining with foreign countries, because it was to be the basis of commercial treaties with the Dominions which would preclude concession.

After Sir Herbert Samuel had made his protest, further debate, as Major Elliot pointed out, was unnecessary, as the House had obviously already made up its mind. The Home Secretary's speech, however, constituted a challenge which could not be disregarded to those supporters of the Government's proposals who still called themselves Free Traders. It was taken up by Mr. Runciman, who was really no less responsible for the proposals than Mr. Chamberlain himself, and who now gave his own justification of them, differing in material respects from that given by Mr. Chamberlain. He based it on the proposition that the paramount consideration for the moment was the need for consolidating the internal financial position—in other words, for maintaining confidence in sterling at home and abroad. For this purpose it was absolutely necessary for them to keep their revenue up to the level of their expenditure, or their expenditure down to the level of their revenue. It was no longer possible by the ordinary operation of the foreign exchanges and so forth to secure an automatic adjustment of their payment balances abroad. Other means had to be sought, and one of the things they could do was to prevent imports coming into the country and by that means put an impediment in the way of those who would use their purchasing capacity abroad for things which were not necessary to their national or individual existence. If the Orders under the Abnormal Importations Act were a kind of surgical operation, the policy he was now recommending could be described as a slimming process. Another motive which influenced him was his anxiety to raise more revenue. He calculated that the new tariff, even with all the exemptions that would be made, would provide nearly 30,000,000*l.* of revenue, which would be a contribution of the greatest value to them. He was of opinion, too, that this could be done without increasing the cost of living.

Unlike Mr. Chamberlain, Mr. Runciman made no claim for the tariff that it would benefit industry, whether by securing for it the home market or stimulating exports. On the other hand, he accepted the Conservative thesis that it would furnish a means of bargaining with other protectionist countries. It had already been called a tariff *in terrorem*, but he preferred as a negotiator of long experience to have a tariff in being. In regard to the additional duties which were to be imposed on the recommendation of the Advisory Committee, Mr. Runciman spoke with less assurance, but he managed to defend them on the ground that they would provide shelter for struggling British industries—an object which Sir Herbert Samuel had also declared to be desirable, though he sought to attain it by somewhat different methods.

Mr. Baldwin, in concluding the debate, deprecated the idea that the present tariff should be regarded as permanent. It was an experiment which had to be justified by its success. The country demanded that the experiment should be made, and therefore he pleaded that for the sake of the country all should try to make it a success. And he warned industrialists that if they tried to use tariffs as a shelter for inefficiency, idleness, and profiteering, the whole experiment would stand condemned.

In the division, the resolution was carried by 452 votes to 76, the Liberals being about equally divided.

The vigour of Sir Herbert Samuel's criticisms of the tariff proposal had taken the House by surprise, and was resented by a number of Conservatives who thought that he was presuming unduly on his " liberty to differ." Among those also who approved of the matter of his speech, there was a feeling that he had made his position in the Cabinet untenable. In a speech delivered at Manchester on February 5, he defended himself on both counts. He laid stress on the importance to Europe of political unity in Britain, mentioning that many Continental statesmen had said to his colleagues and himself that this unity gave a widespread sense of security, and its ending would be universally regretted. When therefore his three colleagues and he himself were invited to remain in the Government in spite of their disagreement on the protectionist proposals, they had been placed on the horns of a dilemma. If they stayed, they would be attacked for conniving at a policy of which they disapproved. If they resigned, they would be attacked for deserting their responsibilities and leaving others to wrestle with the difficulties of the time. They preferred to face the former charge, and therefore they accepted the invitation to remain, but on the clear understanding that they should retain liberty of speech and vote, liberty to speak, not to mumble or whisper. And he had used that liberty because it was essential that the House of Commons should know clearly the points on which they disagreed and the reasons.

On February 9 the Labour Party moved a vote of no-confidence in the Government for " violating the long-established principle of constitutional responsibility." Mr. Lansbury in moving it made it clear that the Labour Party were not opposed to members of the Government having freedom of action, and that they would be prepared to support very drastic changes in the methods and procedure of the House. Their complaint was that the present Government had no intention of asking Parliament to change the present practice, and yet had acted in defiance of it. Mr. Baldwin in reply quoted a number of precedents from British history for the " agreement to differ," and pointed out that the attacks upon it all came from quarters where the desire to see the National Government split was strong, but it was approved by the broad common sense of the man in the street. It was difficult to say what was constitutional in the conduct of a National Government. What they were doing was an experiment, and its success would depend on the spirit in which it was worked.

The view of the dissentient Ministers was expressed by Sir Donald Maclean. He pointed out that the " agreement to differ " really dated from the time when the Prime Minister issued his manifesto before the General Election. The crisis which had happened had been foreseen, and though the solution adopted was without proper precedent, it was not incompatible with the flexibility of the British Constitution. This flexibility was possible because the Constitution was on the whole worked by men of public spirit and a high sense of responsibility in all parts of the House. As to their own procedure, he promised that they were determined that their conduct should be governed by the same considerations of honour and public responsibility as had led to the creation of the experiment. They must use their own discretion as to when they should speak and vote upon these proposals ; but they would always be mindful of their responsibility as Ministers.

The vote of censure was negatived by 438 votes to 39.

The Cabinet "agreement to differ" was discussed by the House of Lords on February 10, and a motion condemning it produced a piquant alliance between the extreme Conservatives, represented by Lord Banbury, and the Labour Peers, represented by Lord Ponsonby. Lord Snowden defended his action on lines similar to those followed by Sir Herbert Samuel, and reserved to himself no less emphatically the right to speak his mind on Protection on all occasions. Nevertheless, he expressed the belief that the "agreement to differ" would be justified, because there was complete unanimity in the Cabinet on all other questions. The motion was rejected by 73 votes to 7.

The resolutions for imposing a tariff having passed through Committee without alteration, on February 11 the text of the Import Duties Bill was issued to members of the House of Commons. The list of exemptions proved to be considerably longer than Mr. Chamberlain's speech of February 4 had led members to expect. It included gold and silver bullion and coin, wheat in grain, meat, live quadrupeds, fish of British taking, tea, raw cotton, flax and hemp, cotton seed, rape seed and linseed, raw wool and rags of wool, hides and skins, newspapers and printed books, newsprint, wood-pulp, raw rubber, iron ore, scrap iron and steel, iron pyrites, tin ores, wooden pit-props, sulphur, phosphates of lime, unset precious stones, and radium compounds and ores. For the rest, the Bill corresponded closely to the description already given by Mr. Chamberlain. The cost to the Customs and Excise Department was estimated for the year 1932-33 at not more than 500,000*l*., and the expenditure on the Advisory Committee for the same period was put at 50,000*l*.

Concurrently with the publication of this Bill, the Minister of Agriculture gave a brief outline in Parliament of the Government's policy for assisting agriculture. This consisted partly in steps to be taken immediately, and partly in plans for a more distant future. Under the former category came the subjection of all agricultural and horticultural produce, with the exception of wheat, meat, and wool, and a few other items, to the general 10 per cent. tariff which would be imposed by the Import Duties Bill, and to the additional duties which might be recommended by the Advisory Committee. The long-range policy included

the improvement of the marketing of milk and milk products
through a Reorganisation Commission ; a scheme for the reorganisation of the bacon industry ; a scheme, if desired by the
growers, to reorganise the marketing of the home potato crop ;
and further action to help the fishing industry, in addition to
the assistance it would receive through the new import duties.

The second reading of the Import Duties Bill was debated
by the House of Commons on February 15 and 16. Major Elliot,
in moving it, naturally had little to add to what had already been
said by Mr. Chamberlain and Mr. Runciman, but he used with
some effect an *argumentum ad hominem* against the Opposition
by pointing out that both Liberals and Socialists had in various
ways subscribed to the principles underlying the Bill. In the
course of the debate, Sir Archibald Sinclair joined his voice to
that of the other three Ministers who had already availed themselves in Parliament of their right to criticise the Government.
Mr. Chamberlain, in summing up, said that the free list must
finally be shaped by experience, as the Bill provided, but he
hinted that if the list were to be much extended, the Tariff Committee would have to be given power to take items out as well
as to put them in.

Throughout the debates on fiscal policy, the Prime Minister
had been unavoidably absent from Parliament. After suffering
eye-trouble for some time—due to overwork—he was advised
by his doctors on February 2 that an immediate operation was
necessary on his left eye, and that he would have to rest for some
time afterwards. He was thus prevented from attending the
Disarmament Conference at Geneva as he had intended, and it
was for this reason that the British proposals there were made
by Sir John Simon, who had not intended to go until later.

The report of Mr. du Parcq on the mutiny at Dartmoor prison
was published on February 7. His conclusion was that the
outbreak would not have taken place had not the convicts been
assisted beforehand by one or more of the prison staff. For this,
however, no blame attached to the Governor. Dartmoor, on
account of its isolation, was declared to be an unsuitable place
in which to confine prisoners of the dangerous modern type ;
there was ground for suspecting that persons outside had been
able to get into touch with some of the convicts with a view to
helping them to escape. In Mr. du Parcq's opinion, the disorder
was not to be accounted for by any recent change in the prison
administration, either in the direction of severity or of leniency.
The prisoners had no substantial grievances, and those which
they had would not have led to disorder, had not the more dangerous characters played upon the feelings and fears of the others.

Referring to the report in Parliament on the next day, the
Home Secretary said that no pains would be spared to obtain all
available evidence with a view to appropriate action against

the small number of officers who were mentioned in the report as being suspected of grave misconduct. Criminal proceedings would also be instituted in open Court against those prisoners whose offences had been too grave to be dealt with as mere breaches of prison discipline. The remarks of the report on the disadvantages of Dartmoor as a place of detention for dangerous characters confirmed a view which had already been formed at the Home Office. On November 19 last a scheme had been decided upon for making a very large reduction in the population of the prison so soon as alternative arrangements could be devised, and the admission of fresh cases had been discontinued since that date.

On February 12 the House of Commons gave an unopposed second reading to a Bill amending the existing law in regard to young offenders, so as to bring it more into harmony with the spirit of the age. The new Bill widened the scope of the juvenile courts, made stricter provision to prevent the young from being brought into contact with adult offenders, and set up a selected panel of magistrates interested in the care of the young. It also empowered the Lord Chancellor to prescribe rules which would make the procedure of juvenile courts less formal and more easily understood by young persons, and prohibited such courts from being held in a police station or a place used as a court of trial for adults. The age up to which young people were to be subject to the jurisdiction of juvenile courts was raised from 16 to 17. It was laid down that reformatories and industrial schools should cease to be known under those names and should be officially described as Approved Schools. The period of detention in them would no longer be specified by the Courts, but would be automatically three years for a child under 14, or until it reached that age, and three years also for young persons, but in any case not beyond the age of 19. The age up to which street trading was prohibited was also raised by the Bill from 14 to 16.

The continued efforts made by Great Britain after the setback in January to bring about an International Conference on Reparations (vide p. 3) did not remain fruitless. On February 14 it was announced by the Foreign Office that the exchange of views between the British and French Governments had at last resulted in a basis of agreement being reached. Sir John Simon had accordingly communicated with the countries principally interested, with the result that the Governments of Belgium, France, Germany, Italy, Japan, and the United Kingdom, after having taken note of the Basle experts' report, had agreed to recommend to the other Governments concerned the adjournment of the Lausanne Conference to the month of June. The object of the conference would be to agree on a lasting settlement of the questions raised in the report of the Basle experts, and on the measures necessary to solve the other economic and financial difficulties which were responsible for, and might prolong, the present world crisis.

On February 16 Mr. Runciman announced in the House of Commons that the French Government had consented to exempt British coal from the 15 per cent. surtax which it had imposed in November to correct the effect of sterling depreciation, and which had caused so much irritation in England (*vide* ANNUAL REGISTER, 1931, p. 112). Conservative members saw in this step the first-fruits of the new bargaining power which tariffs were conferring on the Government, and cheered the announcement with great vigour.

On February 23 the Government appointed a Committee to make a thorough and impartial examination into the character and organisation of the Post Office, and to consider whether any changes might with advantage be effected in its constitution. A persistent agitation for transferring the Post Office to private control had for some years been carried on by Lord Wolmer, who had been Assistant Postmaster-General in the last Unionist Government, and towards the end of 1931 a memorial, signed by 320 members of Parliament, had been presented to the Prime Minister asking for an impartial inquiry. The Committee consisted of three members, with Lord Bridgeman as Chairman.

On February 17 the Labour Party moved a vote of censure on the Government for its treatment of the unemployed. There were two main grounds of complaint. One was that the provision of employment through public works had been greatly diminished. The other was that the administration of the " means test " was putting vast numbers of the unemployed in the position of paupers. The Minister of Labour made a vigorous defence of the Government on both counts. Since 1924, he said, the amount spent on public works to relieve unemployment had been 700,000,000*l.*, while local authorities had in the last nine or ten years increased their indebtedness by nearly as much. The result was that just in those very areas which were most distressed and most wanted help, there was a burden of rates which made it almost impossible for industry to revive. The Government had no mind to continue this vicious circle, and would consider only such schemes as would increase the national income. In regard to the means test, he reminded the Opposition that transitional payments were not insurance benefits but State maintenance for those who had exhausted their benefit. They had no right to pay away public money to people who had no insurance claims without inquiring whether they needed it or not ; such a course would be highly unfair to the small taxpayers, who were in many cases little better off than those who were claiming and drawing benefit. In regard to the administration, he affirmed that every possible means was taken to obviate what was called the stigma of the Poor Law. The censure motion was eventually rejected by 415 votes to 39

B

The proceedings of the Japanese at Shanghai at this time gave great concern to the Government and strengthened the anti-Japanese feeling in the Labour Party. Unable to obtain facilities for a debate in the House of Commons, they raised the subject in the House of Lords. On February 18 Lord Ponsonby pressed for a more extended statement of the Government's policy than had hitherto been given. He criticised the Government for not associating itself with the American Note to Japan, and with merely urging that country to observe the open-door policy, which looked as if they regarded British trade in China as the foremost interest. He also charged Sir John Simon with having shown lukewarmness in the cause of the Covenant, and blamed Great Britain for not having given the League of Nations a stronger lead. Lord Hailsham in reply said that the situation was causing the Government grave anxiety, both on account of the immediate danger to British interests in Shanghai, and because it was difficult to reconcile the position there with the Pact of Paris and the Covenant of the League of Nations. So far as the protection of Shanghai was concerned, they had increased their naval and military forces there, and would be prepared to advise the evacuation of their nationals if necessity should arise. In regard to the international situation, he deprecated any disposition to prejudge the case against Japan, or to form any opinion as to where the responsibility lay until an opportunity had been given for either the Council or the Assembly of the League to determine that issue. The reason, he said, why Britain had adopted a different course from the United States was because she was a member of the League of Nations and the United States was not ; but he assured Lord Ponsonby that she was working in the very closest touch with that country. Britain certainly was sparing and would spare no effort to bring about peace between the disputants.

A few days later (February 22) Mr. Lansbury managed to raise the question in the House of Commons, and Sir John Simon gave him a similar assurance. The policy of the Government seemed to be justified by the news that on March 2 hostilities at Shanghai had ceased ; and Mr. Eden, the Under-Secretary for Foreign Affairs, in informing the House of Commons of the fact, drew loud cheers when he ascribed a large share in the improvement of the situation to the efforts of Admiral Kelly and Sir Miles Lampson in China and Sir John Simon at Geneva.

So large a number of amendments were handed in for the Committee stage of the Import Duties Bill that the Government deemed it advisable to lay down a time-table in order to ensure that the Bill should become law by March 1, when they desired the new duties to come into force. Discussion, as was natural, centred on the free list, the consideration of which was not reached till February 23, after the substantive clauses of the Bill had been passed without alteration. By a ruling of the Chairman, amendments were allowed both for adding to and subtracting from the list. Great pressure was brought to bear on the Government by stock-raisers not to hinder the free import of maize, which was an important feeding-stuff, and to tax imported meat. The Government was at first strongly opposed to removing the proposed duty on maize, at any rate until after the Ottawa Conference. Finally, however, it yielded to the representations of a deputation from the small farmers of Northern Ireland, and decided to put maize on the free list, at an estimated loss to the Treasury of 1,000,000*l*. per annum. Other articles which were at the same time placed on the free list were animal hair, wool waste, esparto, semi-precious stones and pearls, platinum, whale oil and products produced in British floating factories, coal and coke, unwrought copper, and various fertilisers. The Government, however, to the great disappointment of a number of Conservative members, firmly refused to tax meat, on the ground that the cost of living had to be very carefully watched.

After a brisk discussion, hemp was taken off the free list, in order to give a better chance to the sisal growers of East Africa. An attempt was made by a group of Conservative members to remove newsprint (paper for newspapers) from the free list, on the ground that the home mills were capable of satisfying all requirements. On the other side it was pointed out that the foreign importation, though small, was necessary in order to prevent the acquisition of a monopoly by the " Press lords " who controlled most of the paper output in Great Britain. The Government, out of extreme zeal for the liberty of the Press, adopted, not without hesitation, the latter view, and the amendment was defeated by 317 votes to 69.

In the debate on the last stages of the Bill, which were taken on February 25, the Government stated that the duties would not apply to articles manufactured or produced 100 years before the date of importation, such as works of art, and undertook somewhat vaguely to consider the question of allowing the free entry of all works of art. The free list was enlarged on the Report stage by the addition of soya beans, cork, and undressed ramie, and after a very brief debate the third reading was passed by 442 votes to 62.

The Import Duties Bill was passed through all its stages in the House of Lords on February 29. In the course of the debate on the second reading, Lord Snowden reiterated his objections to tariffs, and maintained that the stability of sterling discounted the theory of an adverse trade balance ; to which Lord Hailsham replied that sterling remained steady only because the Bill had been introduced. Besides recording his protest, Lord Snowden hinted that the Free Trade Ministers would resign if the revenue derived from import duties was in the Budget devoted to the relief of the direct taxpayer. In the division on the second reading, twelve peers voted against the Bill. On the same night the Bill received the royal assent, and on the next day the general tariff came into force, and England, after eighty years of Free Trade, became again a protectionist country.

On the same day the constitution of the Import Duties Advisory Committee was announced. The Chairman was Sir George May, who had given his name to the now so well-known Economy Report. There were two other members—Sir Sydney J. Chapman, hitherto Economic Adviser to the Government, and once known as a staunch Free Trader, and Sir G. A. Powell, Chairman of the Food Council. The salary of the Chairman was fixed at 5,000*l*. a year and of the other members at 3,000*l*. a year. Sir Sydney Chapman was succeeded as Chief Economic Adviser to the Government by Sir Frederick Leith-Ross.

On February 22 a deputation of the Amenities Group of Members of Parliament urged the Home Secretary to take steps for bringing under effective Government control the recently perfected invention of " sky-writing " so as to prevent its abuse as an advertising medium. The Minister declared himself to be entirely in sympathy with the object of the deputation, but thought it prudent not to proceed to legislation till an inquiry had been made into the subject by a Select Committee ; and he suggested that the inquiry should also embrace the subject of " sky-shouting," which seemed to him to threaten even worse possibilities. The deputation concurred in this view, and shortly afterwards a Committee for this purpose was set up under the chairmanship of Sir A. Steel-Maitland.

The Civil Estimates for the coming financial year, which were issued on February 24, totalled 330,210,320*l*. This was over 12,000,000*l*. more than the corresponding Estimates for the previous year. The increase, however, was more apparent than real, being due to the fact that there was to be no further borrowing this year for the Unemployment Insurance Fund or the Road Fund, and that all charges on these Funds were to be met out of current revenue. In consequence, the Estimate of the Ministry of Labour had risen from 44,866,000*l*. to 64,458,000*l*., and there was an item of 2,750,000*l*. for the Road Fund which had not appeared in the previous year's Estimates. But for these two items, there would have been a substantial reduction, as certain heavy cuts had been made, notably of nearly 5,000,000*l*. in the Board of Education Estimate and nearly 3,000,000*l*. in that of the Ministry of Pensions. On the other hand, there were some large automatic rises, *e.g.*, of 1,546,000*l*. for old-age pensions and of 1,000,000*l*. for widows' and orphans' pensions.

The Estimates for the three defence Services which were published a little later (March 3) showed a total saving of over 5,000,000*l*. on those of the previous year. The Navy Estimate was for 50,476,300*l*., as against 51,605,000*l*. in the previous year ;

the Army Estimate for 36,488,000*l.* as against 39,930,000*l.* ; and the Air Estimate for 17,400,000*l.* as against 18,100,000*l.* The Estimate for Customs and Inland Revenue collection was, owing to the tariff, over a million more than in the previous year ; and the Post Office Estimate was also nearly a million higher. Altogether the Estimates of Expenditure, excluding provision for the National Debt payments, amounted to 506,392,495*l.*, as compared with 497,245,572*l.* in the previous year—an increase of over 9,000,000*l.*

On February 29 the Secretary for India, Sir S. Hoare, gave a review to the House of Commons of the situation in that country. At the end of last year, he said, a storm had burst in India of which they were still feeling the reverberations. The leaders of the Congress Organisation had decided to renew their war with the Government of India, and tore the Delhi pact to pieces. At the same time a menacing situation arose on the North-West frontier. The Indian Government therefore felt itself obliged to assume emergency powers in order to combat the pretensions of Congress and to render the repetition of such events as the Cawnpore massacre impossible. He had no hesitation in saying that those powers had been used with moderation and discretion, and the bulk of the people of India itself had regarded them as necessary. In consequence of the firm action of the Government, the situation on the whole was very much better than it had been at the beginning of the year. The Red Shirt movement on the North-West frontier was beginning to collapse, and the " no-rent " movement in the United Provinces was also coming to an end. There was still some terrorism in Bengal and some picketing in Bombay, but there also the position had improved. There had fortunately been of late a marked improvement in the economic and financial condition of India which rendered the task of the Government easier. In spite of what had happened, he said, the Government were just as anxious for co-operation with representative Indians as they had been in the past—a fact of which the Committees now working out the details of the Indian Constitution in India were the outward sign. The emergency powers taken by the Indian Government did not at all mean the end of the policy of co-operation ; they were but the bulwark of any Government against anarchy and revolution, and were as much needed for Indian constitutional progress in the future as for the avoidance of strife and bloodshed in the present.

The Minister's statement was warmly applauded by a number of Unionist speakers, and even the Labour criticism was somewhat perfunctory. In closing the debate, he assured Mr. Lansbury that there had been no reversal of policy, but with the best will in the world he was unable to give any date for the coming into being of the new Indian Constitution, for the reason that there were many factors in the problem outside their control altogether.

On March 6 the Minister of Agriculture moved the second reading of the Wheat Bill, by means of which the Government sought to fulfil its undertaking given in the previous November, to come to the rescue of the cereal industry. This problem, he said, had engaged the attention of the previous Government also, and he had derived material assistance from the investigations made by his predecessor, Dr. Addison, though the scheme contained in the Bill was no doubt different in many respects from that which would have been put forward by the Opposition. After long negotiation, he had succeeded in drawing up a scheme which was agreed to by all parties concerned, that is, farmers, millers, and merchants. The Government had throughout insisted that four conditions should be fulfilled : first, that the wheat-growers should obtain an enhanced price for their product ; secondly, that there should be a secure market for home-grown wheat of millable quality ; thirdly, that there should be no subsidy from the Exchequer ; and fourthly, that there should be no encouragement for the extension of wheat cultivation on land unsuited to the crop. Under the Bill, the first object, to enhance the price for the wheat-grower, was to be secured by giving him a deficiency payment, that is, the difference, reckoned in his certified sales, between the ascertained average price of home-grown millable wheat and the standard price, which was fixed for the present at 10s. per cwt., equivalent to 45s. a quarter of 540 lb. at the farm. The money required for the deficiency payments would be obtained from quota payments to be made in respect of all flour milled in the country or imported, so that no charge would fall on the Exchequer or on the local rates. To provide a secure market for the wheat-grower, the Bill enacted that in June of any year after the present, the Minister of Agriculture might order the Flour Millers' Corporation to purchase stocks of home-grown millable wheat remaining unsold at the end of the cereal year. Finally, to prevent the extension of wheat growing to unsuitable land, the Minister was to prescribe each year the quantity which he anticipated would be sold by the growers during that year, and on which alone the full bonus would be paid, with the proviso that the estimate must not in any case exceed 6,000,000 quarters. The machinery for operating the Bill would consist of two bodies, both to be appointed by the Minister— a Wheat Commission, which would be responsible for the payment of the bonus and for the issue of certificates to the growers, and a Flour Millers' Corporation, which would collect the quota payments from the millers and flour importers.

Although the consumers had not been represented in the negotiations preceding the Bill, the Minister maintained that their interests had not been forgotten. With wheat at its present price, the increase in the cost of bread would, he calculated, be not more than one farthing on the two-pound loaf for eleven weeks in the year. This, he thought, was a sacrifice which the town-dwellers of England, where bread was cheaper than in any country in the world except, perhaps, Belgium, might well be called upon to make on behalf of the wheat-growers who found themselves facing a very disastrous position, chiefly because the United Kingdom was the world's greatest free market for wheat.

The Bill was criticised by Opposition speakers on the ground that it was an attempt to bolster up an unremunerative form of agriculture by State assistance, and that, in spite of the assurances of the Minister, it would inevitably make bread dearer. By the great majority of the House, however, including Sir A. Sinclair, who spoke for the other Free Trade Ministers also, it was very favourably received, and the second reading was passed by 428 votes to 55.

On March 7 the First Lord of the Admiralty, Sir Bolton Eyres-Monsell, in introducing the Naval Estimates to the House of Commons, candidly admitted that, as an ex-naval officer, he was unable to regard the provision which was being made for the safety of the nation and the protection of its trade as at all satisfactory. Nevertheless, as a member of the Government, he loyally accepted treaty limitations and bowed to the overwhelming necessity of economy. The saving of 1,128,700*l*. was really much greater than it seemed, as automatic increases to a total of over 3,250,000*l*. had had to be met by counterbalancing economies, so that the real saving was not 1,128,700*l*. but 4,500,000*l*. This had been secured by postponing the 1931 construction programme for six months at the cost of grave difficulties to the shipyards, by cuts in pay and pensions, and by various administrative economies. It would be impossible, he thought, to reduce the Estimates further until disarmament became more general, and his contention that Britain had gone as far as she could in the direction of unilateral disarmament was not seriously challenged even by the Opposition.

Similar regrets were expressed by Mr. Duff Cooper, the Financial Secretary to the War Office, in introducing the Army Estimates on March 9. They were not, he said, what the Army required, but were the product of the crisis. They were written all over with economy, and must not be taken as providing a standard to which in future the Army must always conform. In particular he pointed out that the saving of a million pounds by holding no Territorial camps could not be repeated, as two years without camp would be almost equivalent for the Territorial force to disbandment. It was announced that the cadet corps, from which recognition had been withdrawn by the Labour Government, would be reinstated in their former condition.

In introducing the Air Estimates on March 10, Sir P. Sassoon, the Under-Secretary for Air, said that the reduction of 700,000*l*. made in them, which was very heavy in comparison to their total, had been achieved only with the help of a number of admittedly makeshift measures which it would be impossible to repeat in another year. It had also entailed the making of sacrifices in directions in which in happier times the maintenance or even the increase of expenditure would have been desirable. Instances were the decision to break up the R100, the sister airship to the ill-fated R101, and the cancellation of the 33-ton flying boat which had been designed for passenger and mail service over the Mediterranean. The Minister dwelt on the pioneering work performed by military aviation in the opening up of routes for civil and commercial purposes, and also referred to certain minor activities of the Air Force, such as searches for parties lost in the desert and conveyance of medical assistance to remote stations, which were helping to maintain the prestige of the British flag and the good name of Britain in all parts of the world. After paying a tribute to all who had been concerned in the winning of the Schneider trophy, he remarked that though in size the Royal Air Force took only fifth place among the air forces of the world, there was no other better equipped or where the standard of training and efficiency was so high. He warned the House, however, that to maintain that standard they would require in future years much more money than they were now asking for. With regard to civil aviation, he said that the process of enabling civil air transport to dispense with State assistance was obviously going to take much longer than they had at one time hoped; nevertheless, few lines, if any, could show so satisfactory an approach to a commercial basis for their operations as the civil air lines of the British Empire, the mileage of which now exceeded that of any country except the United States.

In the course of February, a remarkable change took place in the financial position of the country. At the beginning of the month, a strong demand for gold arose in Holland and other countries, inspired, it was thought, by the Bank of England. The public awoke to the fact that it had an opportunity of disposing of its gold coin and other articles such as might never occur again, and hastened to seize it. For several days dealers in precious metals in London and elsewhere were besieged with customers, and the offer of 27s. and more for a sovereign brought hundreds of thousands of these coins out of the hoards in which they had lain for years. The " gold rush " lasted nearly three weeks, and materially contributed to restore the financial stability of the country.

So much, in fact, had the position by now improved that the Treasury decided at the beginning of March to pay back more than half of the 80,000,000l. which it had borrowed in August from the United States and France in its last efforts to save the pound. The original loan had remained intact and was still available for the repayments. For the purposes of the repayment it was necessary to acquire foreign currency at a fairly high premium, but the loss incurred in this was offset by the enhanced value of the British stock of gold, and no burden was therefore placed on the current revenues of the Budget. The Government also now judged it safe to remove the embargo which had been laid upon the purchase of foreign exchange six months before.

This action on the part of the Treasury, following on the similar action of the Bank of England a few weeks earlier, made a great impression on foreign observers, and led to a revival abroad of confidence in British finance. Flattering as was this feeling to British self-esteem, it was not without its dangers to British industry. Partly for speculative purposes and partly in a search for security, money began to flow back to the Bank of England almost as rapidly as it had been withdrawn in the previous summer. The result was that early in March the gold value of the £ rose by more than a 1s. in a few days. Exporters immediately took alarm, fearing that they would lose all the benefits which the depreciation of the £ had given them, and suspicions were aroused that the Bank of England was pursuing a radically wrong policy.

In spite of the rise in sterling, the Government deemed it advisable to renew the emergency powers which it had assumed six months before both for safeguarding the currency and for preventing profiteering in food-stuffs. In moving the second reading of the Bill, on March 11, Mr. Hore-Belisha, the Parliamentary Secretary to the Board of Trade, explained how it was that the Government had had no occasion to interfere with food prices. He observed with great satisfaction that the prognostications which had been made at the beginning of the winter of a great rise of prices accompanied by exploitation had not been fulfilled. One reason was that a number of countries with whom they dealt had also decided to go off the gold standard, the percentage of food and drink imported from such countries, excluding Canada, being 59. Not only so, but so powerful was their purchasing power abroad that even gold standard countries had to accommodate themselves or adjust themselves in some measure to their purses. The result was that on an average wholesale prices had remained lower in Great Britain than in 1930, and food prices were lower than the average of 1930 by 10 per cent.

The Bill was non-controversial, and members utilised the debate to air their views on the currency question. Amid a great diversity of opinion, there was general agreement that a further rise in the £ would be disadvantageous. In reply to inquiries as to the Government's intentions, Mr. Chamberlain said that it did not desire to see the £ forced up to a rate which might be injurious to industry. As to the manner in which this was to be ensured, he could give no sure indication. Speaking for himself he said he was not attracted by the idea of a managed currency. He thought that, sooner or later, they would find that they would have to link their currency to a metallic basis, though he could not say whether it would be gold or gold in combination with something else. He agreed with the conclusion of the Macmillan report that if there was to be management, it should be in the hands not of the Government but of a central banking institution. Shortly afterwards the Bank rate was considerably reduced, and sterling was effectively " pegged " at a gold value of about 15s.

In a public address delivered at Ilford on March 15—not long before Parliament broke up for the Easter recess—Mr. Baldwin took stock of the Government's achievements, and found much cause for congratulation. They were now certain, he said, that the Budget would be balanced. Borrowing on current account had been stopped—he hoped, for ever. Foreign money was pouring into the country, showing that they had regained the confidence which had nearly been shattered six months before. In a winter remarkable in many ways, the most remarkable feature had been the steadiness of retail prices. Even their export trade was not without signs of hope ; the volume of world trade was still declining, but relatively they were better off than their competitors. Altogether he was more hopeful than he had been for several years.

The undoubted improvement in the financial position of the country was interpreted in some quarters, whose motives were perhaps not above suspicion, as a sign that the emergency was over and that there was no longer need for the rigid economy of the last few months. Speaking at Birmingham on March 18, the Chancellor of the Exchequer strongly discountenanced such assumptions. The damage, he said, was far from being repaired yet. Those who talked about a surplus should remember that a large part of next year's revenue would be based on the trading results of a period which until lately had been one of almost unrelieved depression. They should therefore beware of jeopardising what they had so hardly won by any premature relaxation of their efforts.

On March 22 Mr. Lansbury again raised the question of the situation in Manchuria and Shanghai in the House of Commons, the disquietude of the Labour Party having been intensified by statements made in the course of the discussions on the Service Estimates that within another year it might be advisable to increase expenditure on British armaments. Sir John Simon in reply defended at length the policy which he had pursued at Geneva during the previous two or three months, and for which he had been accused in some quarters of weakness and even poltroonery. The British policy, he said, had been, first, to hold the scales fairly in a very difficult controversy and to carry out faithfully the principles of the League of Nations, and secondly, to co-operate with the other Powers especially interested in Shanghai. The question had presented itself how the League of Nations could most properly act in a case like this. From the time when he first studied the question, his own view had been that this was a case where the League was most likely to be useful as a mediating force, and in which it was advisable to keep its coercive powers in the background. This course had not led to any weakness in the pronouncements made by the League. On the contrary, the resolution carried by the special Assembly on March 11 contained some extremely strong expressions, and they were expressions which Great Britain meant to stand by. It declared that it was incumbent on the members of the League not to recognise any situation, treaty, or agreement which might be brought about by means contrary to the Covenant of the League or the Pact of Paris. The reference to the Pact had brought them the co-operation of the United States. The resolution further affirmed it to be contrary to the spirit of the Covenant that the settlement of the Sino-Japanese dispute should be sought under stress of military pressure on the side of either party. It was significant that there had since been a withdrawal of Japanese troops from Shanghai. With regard to Manchuria, Sir John uttered a caution against condemning Japan before her case had been presented, but he assured Mr. Lansbury that the alleged new Administration in Manchuria was not one which any country was likely prematurely to recognise. In conclusion, he claimed for British policy that it had kept them on terms of perfectly friendly relations with both China and Japan, that it had satisfied the smaller States in the League, who often did not see eye to eye with the larger, and that it also had the full support of the United States—three things which it was by no means easy to reconcile.

On March 23 a private member, Sir W. Davison, asked leave in the House of Commons to introduce a Bill for legalising lotteries under State supervision, for charitable, scientific, and artistic purposes. Nearly twelve months before the same member had failed to obtain a first reading for a similar Bill of a somewhat narrower scope. In the interval money to the amount of millions of pounds had poured out of England in the purchase of tickets for the sweepstakes run by the Irish Free State on behalf of the Irish hospitals ; the perfunctory endeavours made by the British Government to stop the traffic had merely brought derision both upon itself and upon the law. Whether because its personnel was different or because it had learnt from experience, the House of Commons on this occasion showed itself more tolerant than in the previous year, and passed the first reading of the Bill by 176 votes to 123. This convinced the Government that it ought itself to take action in the matter, and soon afterwards it

resolved to appoint a Royal Commission to consider the state of
the law on sweepstakes and lotteries.

The names of the British delegates to the Lausanne and
Ottawa Conferences were announced by the Prime Minister on
March 17. The delegates to Lausanne were to be Mr. MacDonald,
Mr. Chamberlain, Sir John Simon, and Mr. Runciman, with the
addition, should it be found advisable and possible, of Sir Herbert
Samuel, Sir Samuel Hoare, and Sir Hilton Young. The Ministers
chosen for Ottawa were Mr. Thomas, Sir Philip Cunliffe-Lister,
and Mr. Runciman, with the possible addition of Mr. Baldwin,
Mr. Chamberlain, and Lord Hailsham.

The national accounts for 1931-32 were closed on March 31
with a surplus of 364,000l. The magnitude of the effort made
by the taxpayer was shown by the fact that income tax produced 287,367,000l., or over 15,000,000l. more than the estimate
of Mr. Snowden's revised Budget in September, and surtax
76,700,000l., or over 3,000,000l. more than the estimate. The
whole of this excess, however, was needed to counterbalance
the shortage in the receipts from estate duty and stamps, the
former being 18,000,000l. and the latter 3,000,000l. behind the
estimates. The revenue from Customs and Excise exceeded the
estimate by some 3,000,000l., of which about 2,000,000l. came
from the new duties under the Abnormal Importations Act, the
Horticultural Products Act, and the Import Duties Act. While
total revenue corresponded fairly closely to the estimate of
September, it had been found possible to make a saving of about
12,000,000l. on the estimated expenditure, chiefly on account
of the lessened requirements of unemployment benefit. The
reason why this sum did not appear in the surplus was because
the Dollar Exchange Account was raided to the extent only of
12,000,000l. instead of 23,000,000l. as originally contemplated,
which meant a reduction in the revenue figures of 11,000,000l.
The sinking fund was maintained at the level originally fixed
of 32,000,000l. The total revenue was put at 770,963,000l., as
against 784,700,000 estimated, and the total expenditure at
770,559,000l., as against 783,179,000l. estimated.

In the early part of the year, friction again arose in the
Lancashire cotton industry over the more-looms-to-a-weaver
question. At the end of January, strike action was threatened
by 25,000 operatives in the Burnley district on account of the
policy of certain employers in introducing the system. Negotiations were opened between representatives of the two sides, as
a result of which a tentative agreement was reached early in March.
Meanwhile some 4,000 weavers had actually struck. The agreement was rejected by the General Council of the Weavers' Amalgamation a fortnight later, but no immediate step was taken by
either side.

Throughout the session, the five Independent Labour Party

members had maintained themselves in Parliament as a separate group. Efforts made by them to procure a change in the Standing Orders of the Labour Party, which demanded obedience to the Whips from all the members, had proved unavailing. A strong movement, led by Messrs. Maxton and Buchanan, had in consequence arisen within the I.L.P. for complete disaffiliation from the Labour Party. A proposal to this effect brought forward at the I.L.P.Conference at Blackpool on March 28 was defeated by 183 votes to 144. On the other hand, a proposal for continued affiliation without terms was defeated by 214 votes to 98 ; and the Conference by 250 votes to 53 decided to make an attempt to retain affiliation on conditions acceptable to the party. For this purpose the National Council was instructed to open negotiations with the Labour Party once more, although there was no reason for expecting that any concession would be made by that body.

Towards the end of the session, Irish questions once more began to engage the attention of the Government and Parliament. Relations between Great Britain and the Irish Free State had been uniformly harmonious so long as Mr. Cosgrave was President, but they underwent a change for the worse as soon as he was replaced by Mr. de Valera, as a result of the elections held in the Free State in February. Scarcely was the Republican Party installed in office when the High Commissioner of the Free State in London informed the Secretary for the Dominions that his Government intended to lay a Bill before the Free State Parliament for abolishing the Oath of Allegiance laid down in the Treaty of 1922. Mr. de Valera at the same time made a statement in the Irish Senate that his Government intended to retain in their own hands the Land Annuities which hitherto had been regularly paid to the National Debt Commissioners. The British Government considered that the former step would be a violation of the Treaty of 1921, and the latter a breach of a most formal and explicit agreement between the two countries, and consequently took a most serious view of the Irish Government's intentions. A statement to this effect made by Mr. Thomas in the House of Commons on March 23 was loudly applauded.

In accordance with this statement, a Note was immediately despatched to the Free State Government, emphasising the British Government's contention that the Oath was an integral part of the treaty " hitherto honourably observed on both sides," and that failure to pay the Land Annuities would be a " manifest violation of an engagement binding in law and honour on the Irish Free State." Further than this the Government did not care to go for the present, hoping that Mr. de Valera might be induced by an appeal to reason to alter his policy. In this they were disappointed. In a long reply which he despatched on April 5, Mr. de Valera showed himself as intransigent as ever.

He characterised the Oath as an intolerable burden to the people of the Irish Free State, and declared that its removal was a matter of purely domestic concern and was required for the peace, order, and good government of the State.   With regard to the Annuities, he disclaimed any knowledge of the " formal and explicit " Irish undertaking to which Mr. Thomas had referred, though he promised that any just and lawful claims would be scrupulously honoured.   Not content with this, he even hinted at the possibility of a repudiation of the whole settlement of 1921, as involving " the consummation of the outrage of Partition."

Mr. Thomas, in his reply, sent on April 9, again endeavoured to be at once firm and conciliatory.   He reminded Mr. de Valera that under the Settlement, the Free State had participated in the constitutional development of recent years by which the Dominions had become equal members with the United Kingdom of the British Commonwealth of Nations.   He reaffirmed the Government's view that the Oath was an integral part of the Treaty Settlement, and asserted once more in unmistakable language that they stood absolutely by that Settlement.   He quoted the Free State undertaking with regard to annuities given in the heads of the " Ultimate Financial Settlement " ; and, while expressing the hope of continued friendly relations, warned the Free State that such relations could not but be impaired by any failure in the complete fulfilment of obligations deliberately undertaken.

Referring to the question of partition raised by Mr. de Valera, the Note said that, in the Government's opinion, there could be no conceivable hope for the establishment of a united Ireland except on the basis that its allegiance to the Crown and its membership of the British Commonwealth should remain unimpaired. This passage created some alarm in Northern Ireland, suggesting as it did that Ulster might be sacrificed to Mr. de Valera if he would consent to retain the Oath of Allegiance.   Lord Craigavon, the Prime Minister of Northern Ireland, hurried to London to make representations on the subject, and he was assured by Mr. Thomas and Sir Herbert Samuel that his fears were quite groundless.

During the Easter recess an unsuccessful attempt was made by the Government to solve the Danubian problem.   On March 12 Sir John Simon had gone to Paris to attend the funeral of M. Briand, and while there he discussed with M. Tardieu, the French Premier, the question of a Federation of Danubian States.   On March 22 Sir John suggested in a letter to M. Tardieu, that before a Danubian Conference was called, there should be a preliminary meeting of representatives of Great Britain, France, Germany, and Italy, and that this also should be preceded by a personal exchange of views between M. Tardieu and Mr. MacDonald, for which the latter was known to be anxious.   M. Tardieu consented, and it was arranged that the Four-Power Conference should meet in London on April 6. On April 3 M. Tardieu himself came over to London with M. Flandin, and on the next day an exchange of views took place at 10 Downing Street.

The Four-Power Conference opened a couple of days later (April 6), with Mr. MacDonald as chairman. The first question to be discussed was the number of States which should be invited to the coming conference of Danubian countries. Great Britain and France desired that the conference should be restricted to the five Danubian States ; Germany and Italy that the four Powers of the present conference should take part as well. After two days of discussion, it was found impossible to reconcile the opposing views on this question. Further deliberation was held to be useless, and it was decided on April 8 to adjourn the conference indefinitely, each of the four Governments undertaking to address to the other three as soon as possible a considered statement of its views on the points reserved and on the best mode of further advance.

CHAPTER II.

THE BUDGET AND THE CONVERSION LOAN.

PARLIAMENT resumed its sittings after the Easter recess on April 5. On April 7 the Wheat Bill, which had already emerged from Committee without much alteration, passed through its remaining stages, the third reading being carried by 398 votes to 58.

On the next day (April 8) the Government brought forward a Bill to continue transitional payments to the ever-growing number of unemployed who had exhausted their insurance rights. Labour Opposition speakers in the debate, while naturally in complete sympathy with the object of the Bill, complained loudly of the retention of the means test and demanded that the contributory system also should be abolished. The Minister of Labour, in reply, pointed out that the need for economy was still urgent, and therefore they could not afford to dispense with the means test, which, as he had previously informed the House, enabled a saving to be made on unemployment insurance at the rate of 7,500,000l. a year. The Government, he said, would not consent to diminish contributions or increase benefits until some way could be found of making the Insurance Fund—which was still incurring a deficit of 200,000l. to 250,000l. a week—self-supporting. He did not deny that the system needed to be reformed, but he deprecated taking any steps in that direction until the Royal Commission which was examining the subject should have issued its report. The second reading was carried without a division, and the Bill became law in due course.

Great interest, both in Parliament and outside, was taken in the next measure brought forward by the Government (April 13) —the Sunday Performances (Regulation) Bill, commonly known as the Sunday Cinemas Bill, which had been formally introduced before Easter. The Bill was substantially the same as the one with the same title which Mr. Clynes had moved a year before (*vide* ANNUAL REGISTER, 1931, p. 37), only it embodied certain amendments which had been carried while the Bill was in Committee ; the chief of these was that urban district councils could pass resolutions stating whether or not they desired Sunday entertainments to be given in their area, such resolutions to be binding on the licensing authority. As on the previous occasion, the Government sponsored the measure, but left the decision to a free vote of the members, including Ministers also.

The second reading was moved by Mr. Oliver Stanley in a speech to which no exception could be taken on religious grounds. He laid stress on the fact that the challenge to the Sunday opening of cinemas, which had been tolerated for years in spite of the law of 1780, had come not from those zealous for Sunday observance, but from rival entertainers who were not treated with the same indulgence. The challenge having been given and having been upheld by the Courts, it was no longer possible to ignore the law of 1780, and for that reason the Government last October had passed a temporary measure legalising the *status quo* for one year. That Act, however, would expire on October 7, and if between now and then there was no fresh legislation, on the following Sunday, and all succeeding Sundays, every cinema and concert hall throughout the country would remain closed.

Whether this would be a good or a bad thing, or whether it would do more harm than good, was the real issue raised by the Bill. Opinion on the matter proved to be more evenly divided in this House of Commons than in its predecessor, and, a division being taken, 235 members voted for the second reading and 217 against. The voting did not follow party lines, but there was a majority of Conservatives for the Bill and of Liberals against, while Labour members were about equally divided.

The point in the Bill to which special objection was taken was the fact that it provided for the Sunday opening of cinemas in districts where hitherto it had been forbidden. In order to prevent this, the opponents of the Bill declared themselves ready to accept a compromise on the following terms : that picture galleries, zoological gardens, and debates should be removed altogether from the scope of the 1780 Act ; that local authorities should be empowered to grant or refuse licences for Sunday concerts without going through the procedure of ascertaining whether it would be in accordance with a substantial demand in the locality ; and that the Sunday opening of cinemas should continue in the ninety or more areas where it was at present permitted, but should not be permitted in other areas without a special enabling Bill. These proposals were considered on April 26 by the supporters of the Bill, and were rejected on the ground that they would penalise those authorities who desired Sunday cinema performances but had hitherto refrained from breaking the law.

The Standing Committee to which the Bill was referred was almost equally divided between those who had voted for and against the second reading, so that the measure was regarded as doomed from the outset. Two or three meetings of the Committee were in fact sufficient to show that it would be quite impossible to pass the Bill into law in its present form before the summer recess. The members of the Government, therefore, realising that matters could not be allowed to drift, determined to sink their differences and to produce an agreed measure which should have Government backing. Accordingly it was announced on May 11 that the present Bill would not be proceeded with further, and that a new measure to take its place would be introduced without delay.

Another social problem which urgently claimed the attention of the Government was the continued widespread disregard of the law in regard to sweepstakes and lotteries. The subject, however, presented so many difficulties that the Government still hesitated to act, and in order to obtain some guidance appointed a Royal Commission, with Sir S. Rowlatt as Chairman, to examine whether any changes should be made in the existing law.

The introduction of the Budget, which was fixed for April 19, was preceded as usual by debates on certain Estimates which produced some statements of interest from the Ministers concerned. In the discussion on the Estimate for the Board of Trade on April 14, Mr. Runciman laid before the House of Commons a number of facts and figures which went to show that the effects of the measures taken in the previous November and December to restrict imports had been so far highly satisfactory. The Abnormal Import Orders of last winter appeared to have kept down imports by at least 8,000,000*l*. directly and 16,000,000*l*. or 17,000,000*l*. indirectly. This was all to the good, as it enabled the country to reserve its purchasing power abroad for the most pressing needs, and at the same time it gave the home industries such an impetus as they had not received since 1921. Judging by exports alone, Britain had suffered less from the shrinkage in world trade than any other country. In the first three months of the year the trade of the United States had declined by 34 per cent., of Germany by 21 per cent., of France by 33 per cent., and of the Netherlands by 34 per cent., while British trade had declined by only 11 per cent. It was gratifying to record that

C

since September there had been an increase in the number of persons employed of nearly 250,000, whereas in the period from September, 1930, to March, 1931, there had been a decline of over 250,000. A feature specially deserving of mention was the eagerness shown by foreign firms to start operations in England, and by British firms to seek the aid of foreign experts in order to open new lines. Most of this industrial extension was taking place in the area round London, but efforts were being made to attract it to the older industrial districts in the North and Midlands.

Dealing with the question of future policy, Mr. Runciman first remarked on the grave harm done to international trade by quotas and similar restrictions, specially mentioning the restriction which had recently been placed by Germany on the import of British coal. As the prospect of extending the country's markets in Europe became smaller, the Government naturally turned to the possibilities of trade within the Empire, where the people of this country could place themselves on a far more self-sufficing basis than other countries dared to aspire to. Ministers would go to Ottawa with sentiment strongly in favour of Imperial action, and with the intention of combining the interests of those who lived in the British Empire with the sentiment which bound them together. That, however, was to be but the first step ; the next would be to enlarge the area of their world trade among those who were also ready to confer advantages on them, and so extend their trade along freer channels throughout the whole world.

In the debate on the Home Office Estimate on April 15, Sir Herbert Samuel dealt at some length with the question of the increase of crime, which was causing great concern to the authorities and the public. The number of indictable offences, which had been 2,700 for every million of the population in the year before the war, had in 1930 risen to 3,700. There had been also a serious increase in the number of burglaries in London, and in the number of " smash-and-grab " raids, which had risen from a monthly average of 11 in 1925 to 31 in March, 1932. Statistics showed the common opinion, that a wave of murders was sweeping over the country, to be false ; but juvenile crime was on the increase, though yet not so prevalent as before the war, in spite of the growth of population. The reasons for the increase in crime Sir Herbert found in the breaking up of family life during the war, the economic depression, and the aid brought by the motor-car to criminals ; but he was emphatically of opinion that the oft-abused cinema did more good than harm. He paid a tribute to the zeal and efficiency of the police, and scouted the idea that they were hampered by the new restrictions on investigation and interrogation.

In the debate on the Estimate for the Ministry of Health, the Opposition charged the Government with unduly restricting the public health services for the sake of economy. The charge was vigorously rebutted by the Minister, Sir Hilton Young, who declared that the Government regarded public health as a matter of urgent national importance, to neglect which would be false economy. This was proved by the increase in the provision for tuberculous patients and in the number of infant welfare centres and ante-natal clinics. He referred with special gratification to the beneficial effects which were being produced by the transforming of Poor Law hospitals into municipal hospitals under the De-rating Act of 1929—a point in which Mr. Lansbury fully concurred with him.

When the Estimate for the Board of Education came to be considered (April 18), the Minister, Sir Donald Maclean, greatly disappointed a large number of Labour and Liberal members by laying down that any expansion in the field of educational work was for the present out of the question. He himself did not find this prospect so serious, as he thought that after a period of rapid expansion, education would be none the worse for an interval of stocktaking. He pointed out that even after the cuts which they had suffered in their salaries, English teachers were still the best paid in Europe, and unemployment among them was very slight. He estimated the total cost of education for the year at nearly 100,000,000*l.*, which was far greater than in any other European country, and in fact more than half the whole of the national expenditure in 1913-14.

The Estimates having been disposed of, Mr. Chamberlain on April 19 introduced the Budget. Commencing as usual with a survey of the year just closed—which he described as one of " anxiety, difficulty, and hardship, relieved only by a glimmer of hope at the end "—he dwelt with satisfaction on the fact that they had on the whole more than realised the expectations of the 1931 emergency Budget, a performance, he said, which had produced a profound impression on instructed opinion in all parts of the world. The result was all the more remarkable, seeing that the death duties, always an uncertain factor, had fallen so lamentably short of expectation. The deficiency of 21,000,000*l.* on death duties and stamp duties would have been sufficient to wreck any ordinary Budget. Their salvation was due to the self-sacrificing efforts of the tax and surtax payers, combined with the assiduity of the tax-collecting officials.

Coming to his own Budget, Mr. Chamberlain first informed the House that he was including no receipts for reparations and Allied war debts, and no outgoings for their own war debt payments. He was, in fact, proceeding on the assumption that the Hoover moratorium would remain in force for an unspecified period. This seemed in the circumstances to be the safest plan, though of course the future position was really dependent on the issue of the Lausanne Conference. Similarly, he had decided to omit any estimate of receipts from the Dominion war debts, the service of which had been suspended for a year on July 1 last (*vide* ANNUAL REGISTER, 1931, p. 53), although these were on a different footing from Inter-Allied war debts. This decision would deprive him of some 10,000,000*l*. which had been included in the forecast of revenue in the previous September, when it had been assumed that after the expiration of the Hoover moratorium the previous position in regard to reparations and war debts would be restored.

The expenditure for the coming year had been fixed at 766,000,000*l*., including 32,000,000*l*. for Sinking Fund, and excluding the two self-balancing items, the Post Office and the Road Fund. This meant that, as compared with the estimate of the preceding year, expenditure was being cut down by no less than 79,000,000*l*., or 9,000,000*l*. more than Mr. Snowden had contemplated when he brought in his emergency Budget in September ; and this in spite of the fact that concessions had been made on pay cuts to the amount of 3,500,000*l*. a year, and 1,250,000*l*. would be necessary for extra income-tax collection and for work entailed by the Import Duties Act. A large part of the extra saving was based upon the anticipation of a continued diminution in the figures for unemployment. But, thanks to the assistance of those in charge of the spending departments, he had been able to make reductions over all Departments of State larger than those which were forecast in the previous autumn.

In his endeavours to raise the revenue for meeting this expenditure, he was faced with the difficulty that the yield from income tax and surtax, being based on the profits of the year just past, was bound to be much lower than that of the preceding year. Keeping the taxes at their present level, he did not feel justified in reckoning on more than 260,000,000*l*. from income tax and 66,000,000*l*. from surtax. On the other hand, he thought it reasonable to reckon on 6,000,000*l*. more from stamp duties and 11,000,000*l*. more from death duties than in the year just past. The old Customs and Excise duties also (*i.e.*, those on beer, tobacco, etc.) he reckoned would give 10,000,000*l*. more than last year on account of the increases in them imposed in September. Still with all these increases he could not see his way clear to raise more than 731,275,000*l*., leaving him still 34,750,000*l*. to find. From where was he to get it ?

To Mr. Chamberlain the question presented little difficulty. The means for raising this sum were ready to hand in the tariffs which had been imposed by the National Government, and especially the 10 per cent. general tariff, which, considering that they had had no experience to guide them, had proved to be extraordinarily well adapted to their needs. He counted on receiving from this source a sum of 27,000,000*l*. The other duties, including the higher ones which would be imposed shortly on the recommendation of the Tariff Advisory Committee, would bring in an additional 6,000,000*l.*

This left the Chancellor still with a deficit of 1,750,000*l.* which he increased to 2,800,000*l.* by certain concessions to sugar producers both at home and in the Colonies. The whole of this sum, with 796,000*l.* in addition, he proposed to raise by once more taxing tea, to the extent of 4*d.* a pound on foreign tea and 2*d.* on Empire tea. Apart from this, taxation during the forthcoming year was to remain practically unaltered.

In addition to explaining the provisions of the Budget proper, Mr. Chamberlain informed the House of a proposal which he intended to embody in the Finance Bill for the purpose of stabilising the exchange. There was a danger, he said, that the money which had flowed so rapidly into the Bank of England in the last few months might as rapidly be withdrawn, with serious results to British currency. He had therefore come to the conclusion that it was essential for them to hold adequate reserves of gold and foreign exchange, in order to be able to meet a sudden withdrawal of gold and short-dated capital, and to check and repel speculative movements. For this purpose he proposed to ask for powers to borrow up to 150,000,000*l.* in order to form an Exchange Equalisation Account of gold, sterling securities, and foreign exchange, which would enable the Bank of England, or the Exchequer (which in this matter was the same thing), to deal far more effectively than they had done hitherto either with an unwanted inflow of capital or a sudden outflow. He admitted that they stood to lose by the transaction if they eventually returned to gold when the £ stood at a higher gold value than it did when the purchases of foreign exchange were made ; but he thought that the prospective benefit justified the risk.

It could not be said that Mr. Chamberlain, previously to introducing the Budget, had raised any false hopes ; he had indeed done his best to prepare the public mind for continued hardship. Nevertheless, there was a general feeling of disappointment that he had not seen his way to lighten the burden imposed by his predecessor in a single particular ; nor did the manner of his presentment—clear and precise but somewhat bald and unsympathetic—make the matter of his speech less unpalatable. Still, it was generally recognised that he was the victim of circumstances over which he had no control ; and it was accounted to him for righteousness that he had fostered no illusions and resorted to no questionable devices. Criticism, therefore, in the debate on the Budget resolutions, was directed rather to faults of omission than of commission. Labour speakers complained that nothing was to be done to relieve unemployment ; others, led by Sir R. Horne, that there was no hint in the Budget

speech of further economy in national and local expenditure,
and no clear indication of a monetary policy.

One provision of the Budget, however, was definitely challenged. This was the retention of the additional duty on beer
which had been imposed in the last Budget. Numerous representations on the subject had been made to the Chancellor of the
Exchequer while he was preparing the Budget, and when he
stated in the course of his speech that the increased duty had
caused a great falling off in consumption, members confidently
expected that he would go on to announce its removal. When
he failed to do so, therefore, the disappointment was all the
more acute. Other matters of complaint were that instead of
taxing the profits of co-operative societies—whose exemption
had for years been a sore point with the Conservative party—
he had merely referred the matter to a Commission ; that he had
only suspended, instead of abolishing, Mr. Snowden's Land Tax,
and that he had not reduced the tax on raw silk, so as to assist the
silk trade.

The debate was signalised by the reappearance in the Parliamentary arena of Mr. Churchill, after an interval of several months,
during which he had been lecturing in America. He was able
to inform the House on the strength of his experiences that
Britain, which at the time of his former visit three years before
had been looked upon by Americans as decadent and outworn,
was now regarded by them with admiration not unmixed with
envy. Along with a number of other speakers, both Conservative
and Labour, he expressed regret that the duty on beer had not
been lowered. Mr. Chamberlain, in reply, said that he had
approached this question in a sympathetic spirit, but had found
on going into it that no substitute for the increased duty could
be found. For beer to produce the same revenue with a lower
duty, its consumption would have to be increased by 40 per cent.,
which he thought was beyond the capacity of the nation in the
course of a single year.

Immediately after the introduction of the Budget, a White
paper was issued representing the first-fruits of the work of the
Advisory Committee which the Government had set up to assist it
in framing a tariff. The Committee had had no time as yet to
make a detailed examination of every class of imports with a view
to determining the duty exactly appropriate for each, and it
contented itself therefore with recommendations based merely
on general information already available, but covering as wide
a field as possible. It was aware that this method might involve
errors both of omission and commission, but it was anxious to
put an end to the period of uncertainty, and it made provision
for rectifying errors as promptly as possible.

The general scheme of the Committee was to impose a uniform
rate of additional duty on fully manufactured goods, with a lower

rate for some products where special considerations arose, and higher rates for luxury commodities. For most manufactured goods an additional duty of 10 per cent. was recommended, making 20 per cent. in all. This category included canned vegetables, most pottery and glassware, metal furniture and a number of iron and steel products, the more finished kinds of non-ferrous metal manufactures, cutlery, machinery and tools (other than agricultural), electrical goods, manufactures of wood (except builders' woodwork), textile manufactures (except yarns), apparel, boots and shoes, a number of chemical products, saddlery and harness, paper and manufactures of paper, brooms and brushes, and a variety of miscellaneous goods. For agricultural machinery and tools, and a considerable range of building materials, a total duty of 15 per cent. was considered sufficient. Luxury or semi-luxury articles which were to bear a total duty of 25 per cent. included fruit pulp, sensitised paper, leather trunks and bags, pipes, guns and ammunition, and sports goods and games ; while a duty of 30 per cent. was recommended for shell-fish, oysters, caviare, artificial flowers, beads, furs, and jewellery.

These rates signified in many cases not a raising but a lowering of the existing duties, because they were to take the place of the 50 per cent. duty imposed under the Abnormal Importation Act, which was to lapse as soon as they came into force. The Committee, however, declared itself ready to receive representations with a view to recommending a higher duty in appropriate cases, while on the other hand it disclaimed all intention of recommending changes in a downward direction, save in special cases, for twelve months.

The Committee found that iron and steel presented peculiar difficulties, partly because they entered as material into so many other industries, and partly on account of the intense competition to which semi-finished goods of this material were exposed. It was still undecided as to the precise tariff treatment required by the industry, but it was convinced of the necessity of stopping abnormal importations, and for this reason it recommended a total duty of $33\frac{1}{3}$ per cent. on semi-finished steel for a period of three months, when it hoped to be in a position to submit a more permanent scheme.

Along with the recommendations of the Committee was issued a Treasury Order bringing them into operation as from midnight on April 25, subject to subsequent confirmation by the House of Commons. An outcry was immediately raised against them not by Free Traders, but by those industries which were being deprived of their 50 per cent. protection and given only 20 per cent. in exchange. The Yorkshire textile manufacturers were particularly loud in their complaints, protesting that even with a 50 per cent. duty they could hardly meet Italian competition in certain lines. Some members of Parliament approached Mr. Baldwin and Mr. Runciman on their behalf, but were referred by them to the Advisory Committee. This body, however, refused to listen to them, on the ground that, as it was not a political body, members of Parliament had no *locus standi* for dealing with it. It was thereupon approached by representatives of the industry itself, but after hearing their arguments decided that a case had not been made out for increasing the duty.

In the course of his Budget speech, Mr. Chamberlain had said that if any industries felt that their interests were not sufficiently protected by the new duties, they should make representations to the Advisory Committee and not to the Government. An exception, however, was made in the case of the silk industry, the position of which was peculiar, since it had lost its protection under the Abnormal Importations Act and had gained nothing in exchange. The Committee had recognised that it was entitled to a substitute, but had nevertheless abstained from providing one because duties were already levied on silk goods under the McKenna Act, and the Committee did not care to interfere with these. The Government recognised that the silk industry had a legitimate grievance, especially as its raw material was also taxed, and promised to afford it redress in the Finance Bill.

At this point the House of Commons was deprived for a few days of the presence of Mr. Runciman for a very curious reason. A legal gentleman in revising Lord Halsbury's " Laws of England " noticed that according to an Act of 1909, the Presidency of the Board of Trade was a " new office of profit under the Crown," and that therefore, by an Act of 1707, the holder of such an office could not sit in Parliament without presenting himself for re-election. Presidents of the Board of Trade since 1909 had been unaware of this, since they relied on an Act of 1826 which declared the Presidency of the Board of Trade to be not an office of profit under the Crown. As this Act, however, had itself been repealed by the Act of 1909, they had been unwittingly breaking the law. This point had been completely overlooked when the Act of 1909 was drafted, but was now brought to the notice of the Law Officers. The matter was quickly put right by an Indemnity Bill which passed through all its stages in a single sitting.

The trend of the Government towards Protection placed a severe strain on the loyalty of a number of its supporters in the Liberal Party, and caused great searchings of heart in the section which followed Sir Herbert Samuel. Strong expression was given to their feelings at the annual conference of the Liberal Federation held at Clacton on April 28 and 29. Resolutions were passed affirming the independence of the party and its continued adherence to Free Trade principles, and the question was then raised whether the Liberal Free Trade Ministers in the Government should be called upon to resign. Mr. Ramsay Muir drew a comparison between the present condition of the Liberal Party and that of twelve years before, when the majority of Liberals in the country were distressed and bewildered because Liberals and the majority of their representatives in Parliament were supporting a Coalition Government. Speaking as one who had had exceptional opportunities of feeling the pulse of the party, he said he was convinced that there was only a small minority which was willing to go on supporting the National Government, and that the vast majority had had their confidence undermined by the way in which the Government had used their mandate, so much so that there was a large element which wished to denounce and repudiate not only the National Government but any Liberal who had anything to do with it. Between the extremists was the great mass of the party who earnestly desired to be dissociated from a Government pursuing a policy which they believed to be wrong and mischievous, but who did not want to do anything to slight or criticise leaders whom they respected and trusted. He was against imitating the bad precedent of the Labour Party in trying to issue orders from outside to responsible Cabinet Ministers, and he therefore moved a resolution thanking the members of the Government and of Parliament who had done their best to defend the cause of Free Trade when it was overthrown by an abuse of the mandate given to the National Government, and declaring that the Liberal Ministers, having helped to form a National Government in a time of crisis, must themselves be the best judges of the extent to which their support of the Government should be carried. After an animated discussion, this was carried. Addressing a public meeting on the same night, Sir Herbert Samuel stated that it would be a relief to him and his colleagues when the present situation could be ended, but it must be ended on clear grounds of public interest.

The resolution creating the Exchange Equalisation Account—the feature of the Budget which had aroused most interest and curiosity, both at home and abroad—was moved on April 25 by Major Elliot, the Financial Secretary to the Treasury, in the absence of the Chancellor of the Exchequer on account of illness. Major Elliot explained that the nucleus of the Account would be the 25,000,000*l.* still left from the Dollar Exchange Fund created for a similar purpose during the war, and that it was proposed to add to this up to 150,000,000*l.* Large as this amount was, it was, he said, by no means out of scale with the gigantic movements which had taken place in liquid capital during the last few months in the exchanges of the world. The mass of capital was extremely timid, and moved from place to place at a breath of rumour, no longer subject to the ordinary rules of trade or commerce. In such a situation, the creation of the Account could be compared to the erection of bulkheads in a ship to make sure that no sudden lurch in the vessel would cause the cargo to shift from one side to the other and give the ship a list from which it might not easily recover. In other words, the Account could be used to counteract the effect of any sudden withdrawals from the Bank of England such as had precipitated a crisis in the previous summer. Members were eager to know whether the Account would be used for the purpose of stabilising the currency at any particular level, but on this point the Minister refused to say a word. He assured them, however, that it would be always regarded strictly as capital, and would in no circumstances be "raided" for purpose of revenue.

The new import duties were not discussed by the House of Commons till May 4, the debate having been postponed for over a week on account of the illness of the Chancellor of the Exchequer. In asking the House to approve the Order imposing the duties, Mr. Chamberlain characterised them as being on a moderate scale, and reminded Sir Herbert Samuel that he had anticipated a rate of something like 50 per cent. instead of the actual 20. The chief reason why food-stuffs had not figured in the recommendations of the Committee was that they had been unwilling to make any proposals on this matter until it had been discussed at Ottawa. The country, he thought, was behind the proposals, and was determined to give a fair trial to a system of moderate Protection such as was embodied in the Order. Despite this assurance the Opposition went through the formality of moving the rejection of the motion, and Sir Herbert Samuel once more stated the Free Trade case, only to be told by Mr. Churchill that, like the Duke of Orleans on a famous occasion, he "had missed a very fine occasion for keeping quiet." Mr. Runciman also maintained in opposition to him, that England, in spite of the new duties, could still be counted a low-tariff country. The motion for approving the duties was carried by 405 votes to 70.

To meet the grievances of the silk industry, Mr. Chamberlain on the next day (May 10) brought forward a resolution imposing duties of 10 per cent. or over on various classes of silk goods, in addition to the existing duties. This, he explained, was only an interim arrangement, and would be replaced by a more scientific tariff when the Advisory Committee should have had time to investigate the conditions and needs of the industry, which was a very complicated one. The representatives of the industry declared themselves satisfied with this as a first step, and the resolution was agreed to by 275 votes to 36. The industry also desired the duty on raw silk to be remitted, but Mr. Chamberlain declared this for financial reasons to be impossible.

At the same time, further pressure was brought to bear on the Chancellor of the Exchequer to reduce the beer duty. The agitation was carried on by the Conservative Agricultural Committee, and had the support of several members of the Government. On May 5 a largely attended gathering called by the

Committee met the Chancellor and laid before him the arguments
for a remission. Mr. Chamberlain did not attempt to minimise
the force of these arguments, but he pointed out that financial
considerations made it absolutely imperative to retain the duty,
in spite of the burden which it would inflict on many industries
and on agriculture. He convinced the meeting that there was
no alternative to the tax in existing circumstances, and it contented itself with urging that a reduction in the duty should
be made at the earliest possible moment consonant with the
public good.

The situation in the coal-mining industry at this time began
to cause the Government anxiety. On April 7 a joint committee
had been formed of members of the Mining Association, representing the mine-owners, and of the Miners' Federation, representing the workers, to consider the situation which would arise
on the lapsing on July 8 of the existing Coal Mines Act, passed
in the previous July (*vide* ANNUAL REGISTER, 1931, p. 55). In
default of new legislation, the seven-hour day would then automatically once more come into force, and the wage rates fixed
by the Act would terminate, leaving the owners free to make
fresh arrangements. Of this liberty they threatened to make
full use, to the disadvantage of the men, if the seven-hour day
should once more be enforced. Much as they desired a shortening
of hours, the men were willing to retain the seven-and-a-half-hour
day, provided that no reduction were made in their wages, or
alternatively, that national machinery were set up for fixing
wages. The owners would not accept these conditions, and
a deadlock ensued.

The Government on its side realised that fresh legislation
would soon be necessary, and was anxious to draft it in such a
manner as would satisfy both parties. Mr. Runciman accordingly
approached representatives of both and induced them to resume
negotiations. The mine-owners now went so far as to offer to
guarantee the maintenance of existing wage rates, for a seven-
and-a-half-hour day, for twelve months, but not for longer, nor
would they hear of the setting up of national machinery for
fixing wages. The men still insisted either on a guarantee of
existing wage rates for as long as the seven-and-a-half-hour day
should continue to be worked, or on the national, as opposed to
district, fixing of wages. As the owners would not hear of this,
negotiations came to an end on May 5.

A somewhat gloomy picture of the condition of the coal
industry at this juncture was drawn by Mr. Foot, the Secretary
for Mines, in the debate on the Departmental Estimates on May 3.
In respect both of production, export, and the number of men
employed, the industry was now considerably smaller than it
had been in 1913. The decline was due chiefly to the more
economical use of coal, to trade depression, and to increased foreign

competition. But over and above these the British coal industry had had to suffer lately from the quotas and restrictions enforced in Belgium, France, and Germany, which, along with certain other factors, had deprived it of the advantages which it might have derived from the fall in the pound. The Board of Trade, he said, had made strong representations concerning these restrictions to the Governments concerned, but so far without effect.

On April 29 the Secretary of State for India gave in the House of Commons a review of the position in that country, chiefly in order to show that the firm policy recently pursued by the Viceroy there was being justified by its results, and that in spite of the 26,000 persons in prison the condition of the country as a whole was definitely improving. This view was cordially endorsed by Mr. Churchill, who congratulated the Government and Parliament on having, all too late, adopted the policy formerly advocated by himself at the cost of so much odium and unpopularity. Sir S. Hoare, in a concluding speech, declared that there had been no change in the policy of the Government on the dual problem of law and order and constitutional advance in India. If the emergency continued, the emergency Ordinances would have to be renewed in whole or in part ; there could be no question of making a bargain with Congress as a condition of its co-operation.

On April 20 Mr. MacDonald left for Geneva to attend the Disarmament Conference, a step to which his medical advisers consented with great reluctance, on account of the condition of his right eye. They insisted that while at Geneva he should take at least three hours complete rest daily. In spite of this precaution, the condition of the eye grew steadily worse, and when he returned to London on May 3, the doctors declared that an operation was imperative. It was successfully performed on May 5, but Mr. MacDonald was not able to resume his duties for some time afterwards.

On May 7 the report was issued of the Committee appointed in 1929 to examine the use made by heads of Government Departments of the very considerable powers of legislation and judicial function delegated to them of recent years by Acts of Parliament. The Committee owed its creation to the alarm aroused in certain quarters by the growing practice of Parliament, especially in the sphere of social legislation, of drafting laws in somewhat wide terms, and leaving Ministers to frame regulations at their own discretion for applying the law in practice to points of detail. Attention was called in Parliament early in 1929 to the rapid growth of such regulations, and fears were expressed lest they might constitute a serious encroachment on public liberties and subject the country to the domination of a bureaucracy. The danger was also trenchantly exposed in a book published in the summer of that year by Lord Hewart, the Lord Chief Justice, which had a wide circulation.

In regard to the practice of delegation itself, whether of legislative power or of judicial functions, the Committee came to the conclusion that not only was it constitutionally legitimate, but that in the complex conditions of modern life it was highly desirable for a number of reasons, *viz.*, to relieve the pressure on the time of Parliament and allow that body to concentrate its attention on general principles rather than on minor details, often of a highly technical character ; to meet unforeseen contingencies ; to create greater flexibility and opportunities for experiment ; and to provide for emergencies calling for immediate legislative action. The problem was to keep these powers within the limits consistent with the proper exercise of parliamentary control. While of opinion that Parliament had been right to delegate certain powers to Ministers of the Crown, the Committee found that the methods by which those powers had actually been delegated were open to serious criticism. Parliament, it said, did not seem to have fully realised how extensive the practice of delegation had become, or the extent to which it had surrendered its own functions in the process, or how easily the practice might be abused. It acquitted the Civil Service of any arbitrary misuse of its power or conscious desire to extend its bureaucratic authority unduly ; nevertheless, it noted as significant the fact that after the agitation of 1929, the tide of statutory orders and regulations had ebbed back to a pre-war mark.

To prevent abuses in the future, the Committee recommended that Parliament should amend its ways in various directions. In the first place, it should pay more attention to its terminology, and be careful not to use different words in the same sense or the same word in different senses—a fruitful source of confusion and error. Further, in delegating power, it should always clearly define in the statute the limits of the power delegated, and should not delegate powers of the exceptional type—*i.e.*, powers to legislate on matters of principle or to impose taxation—save on exceptional grounds and after the most careful consideration. In the matter of judicial functions, Parliament, in all but the most exceptional cases, should be careful to preserve the jurisdiction of the Courts of Law to decide whether a Minister in purporting to act under powers given to him by Parliament had in fact acted within the limits of those powers, and the process of appealing against his decisions should be simplified. Full publicity should also be given to cases under this head. Finally, the Committee expressed the opinion that the time had come to establish in each House a Standing Committee charged with the duty of scrutinising, first, every Bill containing proposals for conferring legislative powers on Ministers, as and when it should be introduced ; and secondly, every regulation made in the exercise of such powers and required to be laid before Parliament, as and when it should be laid. The Committee would have no need to go into the merits of the powers delegated or of the individual regulation, but it would supply members with such information as would enable them to form a judgment for themselves.

As a contribution to the policy of reducing public expenditure, the Minister of Health, on May 6, issued the text of a Bill the object of which was to make certain changes in the National Health Insurance scheme for the purpose of restoring it to a position of financial stability. In an explanatory memorandum it was stated that the balance between income and expenditure under the scheme had in recent years been seriously upset by two main causes—heavy expenditure on sickness and disablement benefits of insured women, particularly married women ; and a serious loss of contribution by reason of widespread unemployment among insured persons. According to reports received by the Government, the claims of women, both unmarried and still more married, under the scheme had increased progressively in recent years, so that the total amount of sickness and disablement benefit paid to women during the period covered by the last quinquennial valuation was nearly 4,000,000l. in excess of the actuarial provision. Further, under the Act of 1928, arrears of contributions due to genuine unemployment were excused without involving any loss of benefit, and this was placing on approved societies a burden of over 2,000,000l. a year, which was altogether beyond their capacity. To relieve this financial strain, the Bill proposed, on the one hand, to reduce the rate of disablement benefit for unmarried women from 7s. 6d. to 6s. a week, and to fix the rate of sickness benefit for married women at 10s., and of disablement benefit at 5s. a week ; and on the other hand, to excuse arrears due to unemployment in future to the extent only of one-half.

The Bill itself was brought up for second reading on May 11. The Minister of Health, after pointing out the loss caused to the Insurance fund by the heavy claims made by women, said that it had to be made up either by increasing the women's contributions or by decreasing their benefit. The first method seemed inappropriate in a time of depression, and he had therefore chosen the second ; but even after reduction, the benefits would still be above pre-war level. In regard to the unemployed who had fallen into arrears, the hardship inflicted on them by the Bill would be mitigated by various concessions, such as allowing them to draw medical (though not cash) benefit till the end of 1933, and preserving their pension rights till 1935. After some criticism from the Labour benches, the second reading was carried by 245 votes to 43.

The second reading of the Finance Bill was moved on May 9.

As in the debate on the Budget, Ministerialists took the opportunity to urge upon the Government the adoption of a more
constructive and comprehensive policy for meeting the economic
situation, and their tone was now all the sharper for the deterioration which had taken place in the interval. Sir Robert Horne
again assumed the rôle of chief mentor. He reminded the Government that production was being carried on at the cost of actual
losses and dwindling reserves, and pointed out that in these
circumstances a Budget which clearly relied on some industrial
recovery would not balance. Tariffs, though they would produce
revenue and save some of the home market for British industry,
would not outweigh the blighting effects of world depression.
The way to make the Budget balance and tariffs successful was
to raise prices to some level at which producers could make a profit
given their present costs. The Government apparently looked
to international agreements to bring this about, but without
disparaging these factors he held that it could do something
independently to raise sterling prices : first by making the Bank
of England lower its rate to 2 per cent., and then by publishing
its intention of raising sterling prices to a certain level—a step
which they could take without resorting to any dangerous inflation,
their reputation for honesty having been re-established and
belief in the power to manage their currency being universal.

Sir Robert Horne's advocacy of a controlled inflation was
echoed by a number of other speakers, including Mr. Churchill,
who, however, laid more stress upon the extreme importance
of securing the co-operation of the United States in monetary
policy. Mr. Chamberlain, in replying to Sir Robert Horne,
agreed with him so far as to admit that some attempt to guide
sterling would be valuable to the whole area which followed
sterling. The Government, he said, did aim at a rise in wholesale
prices, though not to the same extent in retail prices, and they
did not desire to see sterling rise higher than about its present
level ; and he also looked forward to a period of cheap and abundant money. Further than this, however, he would not commit
himself. Major Elliot, to whom it fell to reply to Mr. Churchill,
declared that any advance from any great country wishing to
work on parallel monetary lines would be welcomed, and more
than welcomed by the Government—a hint which, as subsequent
events proved, was not lost on the United States.

Another field in which the supporters of the Government demanded from it a greater show of activity was the retrenchment
of public expenditure. The time had come, in the opinion of
some speakers, for major changes in policy which would effect
far greater savings than the mere elimination of waste. Mr.
Chamberlain, while insisting that no economy was too small,
admitted that something more drastic than parings would be
needed to save enough to reduce taxation. He claimed credit

for what had already been accomplished, and asked the House to have patience until the Government should have disposed of the very serious business immediately ahead, after which he promised "hard thinking" on economy with satisfactory results.

On May 10 the Chancellor of the Exchequer, in a speech to the British Bankers' Association, somewhat amplified the remarks which he had made the day before on the subject of economy in the House of Commons. The Government, he said, was not insensible to the cry of the over-burdened taxpayer, and was aware that the only way in which relief could be provided to him was by reductions in national expenditure. Great as were the economies which the Government had already made, it might be possible to add to them by continuous and day-to-day attention. But any attempt to give effective relief to the taxpayer would involve changes in national policy going far beyond anything that had yet been contemplated. And such changes might prove to be necessary, not to relieve the taxpayer, but to preserve the equilibrium of the Budget. In fact, before the year was out, the Government might find it necessary to call for further sacrifices from the public in order to maintain financial stability.

In the prevailing state of the public mind, the Chancellor's words were taken as a prophecy of evil, and produced a depressing effect in many quarters. This was accentuated by a speech delivered a few days later by Mr. Ormsby-Gore, the First Commissioner of Works, in which he remarked that the country was about to enter a phase of the crisis even more difficult and acute than any they had yet experienced. On May 25, in Parliament, a Labour member tried to turn this into an admission by the Government that it had failed in its endeavours. Mr. Baldwin, in reply, pointed out that his colleague had been referring to world conditions, on which the British situation naturally depended to a large extent. The Government, he maintained, in spite of this dependence had made good progress in dealing with the national problems, and he declared that while the situation was one of gravity, there was no excuse for the wave of hysteria which was visible in certain quarters in the country.

One of the causes of the general depression was an announcement made about this time that Great Britain was about to sign an agreement binding her to repay to the United States in the near future the instalment of the debt which had been suspended by the Hoover moratorium. This was interpreted to mean that the United States was pressing for repayment of the money, and fears were entertained that by so doing she was gravely prejudicing the prospects of the forthcoming conference at Lausanne. These apprehensions were allayed by a statement of Sir John Simon in the House of Commons on May 25, in which he pointed out that when the moratorium was instituted, it had been on

the understanding that the arrears incurred through it should
be made up as soon as payments were resumed, by means of ten
equal annuities as from July 1, 1933. The new agreement was
therefore only a formal step which was necessary in order to
give legal effect to President Hoover's proposal, and implied no
decision on any question of principle. On June 5 the British
Ambassador at Washington signed an agreement on behalf of
the British Government to repay the sum of $159,530,000 over
a period of ten years at 4 per cent., the first payment to fall due
in December.

On May 10 tributes were paid in both Houses of Parliament
to the memory of M. Doumer, the President of the French Republic
who had just been assassinated, and it was resolved to present
an Address to the King conveying to His Majesty their deep
sorrow and indignation, and praying him to express their abhor-
rence of the crime and their sympathy with the French Government
and the people of France.

Before it adjourned for the Whitsuntide recess on May 13, the
House of Commons heard a statement from the Foreign Secretary
on the work of the Disarmament Conference at Geneva. Sir
John Simon explained to the House why he thought that qualitative disarmament was more feasible than quantitative, but he
admitted that there were grave difficulties in the way of this
method also, and he could not give an assurance that any practical
decisions would be reached by the conference. Nevertheless,
he was not without hopes, and his determination was as strong
as ever to pursue good results. Mr. Lansbury described his
speech as one of the most disheartening on the subject that
he had ever heard, and prophesied that disarmament would
never be brought about till each nation fairly faced the question,
" Against whom are you arming ? " Mr. Churchill went further,
and saw in the proceedings at Geneva a proof that disarmament
conferences in the present state of the world were futile, and
were in fact likely to do more harm than good. To this gloomy
forecast no rejoinder was forthcoming.

By this time the British Government had received informal
intimations from all the Governments concerned that they
accepted June 16 as the opening date for the Lausanne Conference
on Reparations. They also expressed their willingness that
Great Britain should act as their mandatory in the matter, and
accordingly formal invitations were sent out by the Foreign Office
(May 11). The British Government was also responsible for the
proposal, which was likewise accepted by all the others, that the
conference should proceed by three stages—German reparations,
other reparations, and general questions—that is to say, in the
words of the Foreign Office announcement of February 13, " the
other economic and financial difficulties which are responsible for
and may prolong the present world crisis." The countries to

D

which invitations were sent were, besides Germany, France, Italy, Belgium, Japan, Czechoslovakia, Rumania, Yugoslavia, Poland, Portugal, Greece, Hungary, and Bulgaria.

Not content with convening a European Conference, Mr. MacDonald at the end of May inquired of the United States Government whether it would be willing to take part in an International Conference to consider methods for stabilising world commodity prices, such as had been suggested by Mr. Churchill in the debate on the Finance Bill. He received a favourable answer through Mr. Mellon, the United States Ambassador in London, and it was immediately assumed in many quarters that such a conference had been actually decided upon. Sir John Simon, however, stated in the House of Commons, on June 1, that this assumption was premature. The matter, he said, had not yet advanced beyond an informal and preliminary stage, and there had not yet been an opportunity of consulting the other Governments concerned. He promised, however, that the Government would lose no time in conferring with the Governments represented at Lausanne as to the form which the proposal to America should take.

On May 13 the trial of the men charged in connexion with the mutiny in Dartmoor prison on January 24 was concluded, after a hearing of sixteen days. Twenty-one were found guilty, and received sentences of penal servitude to follow the terms they were already serving. The prisoners were distributed among various prisons throughout the country, and none of them was taken back to Dartmoor.

During the Whitsuntide recess, unrest became acute in the Lancashire cotton industry. In March the weaving operatives, after once more considering the more-looms-to-a-weaver system, had definitely rejected it. Thereupon the employers in the manufacturing section sought to obtain the consent of the workers to a reduction of wages, but without success. Accordingly, on May 10, they gave one month's notice to terminate the existing agreements relating to wages and hours, thus bringing to an end the *modus vivendi* which had subsisted between them and the operatives since 1919. In this they were following the example of the spinners, who had similarly terminated their agreements with the workers at the end of the previous year (*vide* ANNUAL REGISTER, 1931, p. 115). The gloomy prophecies called forth by that action had so far not been realised ; matters had gone on in the spinning section very much as usual, in spite of the absence of any binding agreement. Nevertheless, the operatives saw in the action of the manufacturers a preliminary to a piecemeal reduction of wages, and they denounced it bitterly as a blow to the principle of collective bargaining. The Executives of their amalgamations met to consider the situation on May 19, and resolved to ballot the whole membership of the unions, about

200,000 in number, on the question of declaring a strike as a protest against the employers' action.

When the ballot was concluded on June 6, it was found to have yielded majorities for both a strike and negotiation, and the issue was referred back to the Executives of the various amalgamations. A second ballot was then taken, which again yielded an indecisive result, 48·4 per cent. of the voters being for strike action and 38·1 for negotiations. The Executives did not feel themselves justified in calling a strike by these figures, and decided to continue negotiations. Meanwhile the notice given by the employers to terminate the existing wage agreement duly took effect on June 11, and the outlook for the industry became grave.

Parliament reassembled on May 23, after the Whitsuntide recess, for a short but strenuous session. In addition to the Finance Bill, its programme included the final stages of the Town and Country Planning Bill and of the Health Insurance Bill, a Bill dealing with Sunday entertainments, and legislation for the coal industry. Members were also anxious for debates on Ireland and economy.

In the debate on the Committee stage of the Finance Bill, a vigorous attack was made by the Opposition, assisted by some Liberals, on the clause allowing the Import Duties Advisory Committee to advise the removal of articles from the free list. Such a clause, they declared, giving the Committee power to tax wheat and meat, was a breach both of constitutional usage and of election pledges. Major Elliot, who was in charge of the Bill, replied that, after a definite fiscal policy had been sanctioned, it was neither necessary nor desirable that Parliament should retain control over every detail, and that it was sufficient if the Committee should thoroughly examine the case for and against every duty. No Government, he added, would attempt far-reaching changes unless it were reasonably sure of Parliamentary sanction. After a long discussion, the clause was approved by 341 votes to 61.

In spite of previous rebuffs, a number of Unionist members determined to renew their endeavours to procure a reduction in the beer duty. Their first attempt ended in a fiasco which covered them with no little ridicule. An amendment for reducing the duty on beer was put down in the name of six Unionist members for May 26. Through the rapid despatch of other business, this clause was reached much earlier than was expected, and when the amendment was called not one of the members responsible for it was in his place, and it was accordingly passed over. However, it was duly brought forward on the Report stage on June 8 by Sir William Wayland, who claimed to express the deep resentment of the working classes at a tax which had put a healthy pleasure out of their reach. As an alternative means of raising revenue, he suggested a tax of 1s. a pound on rubber and 1d. a pound on sugar. Mr. Chamberlain did not deny that the tax might be injurious in many ways, even to the future prospects of the revenue, but he pointed out that this year at any rate it would probably bring him in 10,000,000l., which he could not raise in any other way, and he again made the question one of confidence. In spite of an appeal from Mr. Churchill, who was himself one of the strongest critics of the duty, the motion for reducing it was taken to a division, and found 71 supporters, against 301 for the Government.

The determination of a large number of back-bench members to keep a stricter watch on Government spending was whetted by a speech made in the debate on the Finance Bill (May 24) by Sir Vivian Henderson, the chairman of the Estimates Committee, in which he pointed out that the House controlled in detail only about one-sixth of the total civil expenditure. An analysis of the Civil Appropriation Accounts for 1930-31 showed that of a total of 335,000,000l. voted only 51,000,000l. was expenditure over which the House had detailed control, that is to say, the power to approve or reject a particular item without opposing or rejecting the whole sum. Over the rest, amounting to 283,769,000l., and made up chiefly of various block grants, pensions and grants in aid, and unemployment benefit, along with the beet sugar subsidy, the House of Commons had little or no detailed control.

In the debate on the clause of the Finance Bill providing for the establishment of an Exchange Equalisation Fund (May 25), a storm of protest was directed from all sides of the House against the proviso contained in the clause, that the Account should in any event be wound up not later than six months after the date on which certain sections of the Gold Standard Act of 1931 ceased to have effect—in other words, after Britain should have returned to the gold standard. Members saw in this a clear indication that the Government intended sooner or later to return to the gold standard at the old value of gold, and a number of speakers denounced any such intention in no measured terms. Major Elliot assured them that the Government had no intention of returning to the gold standard as long as gold was behaving as it did, but he could not pacify the House until he had promised to recast the clause for the Report stage.

The next day (May 26) the Government came in for some hard words from its supporters for merely suspending the Land Value Tax instead of repealing it altogether. Mr. Baldwin admitted that if he had been a private member he also would have advocated repeal. He pointed out, however, that Lord Snowden had rendered valuable services to the National Government, and explained that it was out of consideration for his feelings that the tax had not been abolished but had been left in a state of coma, from which he himself thought it would never emerge.

On May 23 the text was issued of the new Sunday Entertainments Bill which was to be laid before Parliament as a Government measure to be carried through with the assistance of the Whips, if necessary. It was largely on the lines of the compromise which had been rejected by the Standing Committee. It removed from the purview of the Sunday Observance Acts, 1625 to 1780, musical entertainments, museums, picture galleries, zoological and botanical gardens, aquariums, and debates. In regard to cinemas it laid down that any authority which had power to grant licences under the Cinematograph Act of 1909, and which had allowed Sunday cinematograph entertainments within the period of twelve months ending October 6, 1931, might permit Sunday opening in its area, provided that no person was employed on Sunday who had been employed in connexion with a cinematograph entertainment during the previous six days of the week, and provided that the whole of the profits, or such proportion as might be determined by the authority, should be given to charity. Thus the *status quo* was preserved for London and those other areas which had Sunday cinemas within the twelve months ending October 6, 1931. In other areas, if a majority of the inhabitants desired the Sunday opening of cinemas, they could call upon the local authority to authorise it by special draft order, but all such orders before becoming effective had to be laid before Parliament and approved by resolutions of both Houses.

The second reading of the Bill was moved on May 27 by the Home Secretary, who had himself been one of the staunchest opponents of the previous Bills. He professed to see in this measure more adequate safeguards against the secularisation of Sunday—an argument which did not seem to carry great weight with the House. From the tone of the debate it was clear that had the decision been left to a free vote of the members, this Bill would have fared not very much better than its predecessors. With the backing of the Government Whips, however, it obtained its second reading by 237 votes to 31.

The problem of the coal industry was tackled by the Government with equal decision. After his failure, on May 5, to bring about an agreement between the owners and the miners, Mr. Runciman, having ascertained the views of both sides, proceeded to draft a Bill which he thought would ensure peace in the industry, and which was approved by the Cabinet on May 25. It contained only two provisions. One was that Part I. of the Coal Mines Act of 1930, which established the quota and was due to expire in December, should be continued for another five years. The other was that Section 1 of the Coal Mines Act of 1931, which fixed the working day at seven-and-a-half hours and was due to expire on July 7, should continue in force until such time as it could be replaced by the draft international convention of the International Labour Organisation of the League of Nations of June 18, 1931, which limited the hours of labour underground to seven-and-a-quarter. The Bill contained no stipulation whatever about wages.

In moving the second reading of the Bill, on May 30, Mr. Runciman expressed his deep regret that it should have been necessary for Parliament once more to step in because of the failure of the two sections of the industry to agree. His recent experiences, he said, had driven him to the conclusion that the coalowners were the hardest and most practised bargainers in the country, with the exception of the Miners' Federation. The one thing on which the two sides would agree was that the settlement proposed by a third party was unsatisfactory. Nevertheless, he claimed for the Bill that it was an honest endeavour to save the industry from drifting into a crisis, and that it protected the miners' interests as far as the economic situation would allow. It was generally agreed that it would have been disastrous to slip from a seven-and-a-half to a seven-hour day on July 8. The Bill therefore established a seven-and-a-half-hour day without definite time limit. He gave the word of the Government, however, that hours would be reduced when the Geneva Convention was ratified by the seven coal-producing countries, and that every effort would be made to secure this general ratification. The second point in favour of the miners, for which he took some credit to himself, was that the owners in every district had given a guarantee that all elements in wages governed by the Act of 1931 would be continued for twelve months at 1931 rates. Seeing that wages in foreign coal-fields and in other British industries had fallen substantially since June, 1931, he thought such a guarantee worth having. The guarantee was not put in the Bill because the Government held strongly that the enactment of wages was undesirable, and would involve undesirable consequences both political and economic. On the other hand, the quota had been continued because maintenance of the quota meant maintenance of prices, and so gave substance to the guarantee of wages.

In the debate which followed, supporters of the Government expressed disappointment that the opportunity had not been taken to make certain changes in the 1930 Act, relating to quotas and other matters, which experience had shown to be desirable if not even necessary. Miners' members on their side clamoured for the reorganisation of the industry on a national basis, and showed themselves somewhat sceptical with regard to the guarantee of wages. Mr. Foot, the Minister of Mines, tried to allay their suspicions by a solemn assurance that the Government stood behind the guarantee, and he also promised the owners' representatives that their suggestions would be considered in due course. The second reading was eventually carried by 391 votes to 58.

While the Bill was being debated in Parliament, the question of its acceptance if and when it became law was being discussed by a national conference of the Miners' Federation. On May 31 the conference passed a resolution condemning the Bill. On the same day the Executive Committee saw Mr. Runciman, and in virtue of the assurances which he gave them were able the next day, not without difficulty, to bring about a change in the temper of the conference. By a small majority—278,000 votes to 239,000 on a card vote—it was resolved that the Bill should be accepted, and that meanwhile the Executive Committee should be empowered to negotiate with the Government on the question of strengthening the Coal Mines National Board so as to meet the circumstances of the industry at the end of twelve months. Thus a crisis in the industry was narrowly averted.

On June 1 the House of Commons considered a Money Resolution submitted to it by the London County Council for the purpose, among other things, of obtaining powers to take down the existing Waterloo Bridge across the Thames and replace it by a wider one. It had for some time been known that the bridge was commencing to give way, and there could be no doubt that it was no longer adequate to the traffic demands upon it. The question was therefore whether it should be underpinned and widened or taken down and rebuilt. After long and heated discussions, the London County Council had by a small majority decided in favour of the latter and more expensive course. Built in 1816 by the engineer Rennie, and named after the victory which was then fresh in all men's minds, Waterloo Bridge was celebrated far and wide as a work of art and one of London's proudest ornaments. Hence the proposal to demolish it caused a great outcry, and numerous petitions were addressed to the Government by artistic and learned bodies to prevent such an act of vandalism.

Three months before, when the question was raised in the House of Lords, the Government had declared that it would be loth to interfere with the London County Council in the discharge of its own responsibilities. On this occasion the Minister of Transport, speaking unofficially, went further and maintained that the Council had done all in its power to save the bridge, and had been driven by sheer necessity to the course which it had adopted. The majority of the House, however, attached more importance than the Minister to financial and æsthetic considerations, and the scheme of the Council was rejected by 222 votes to 154.

On June 4 the Import Duties Advisory Committee, as a corollary to the step which it had taken six weeks before of recommending a temporary protective duty of $33\frac{1}{3}$ per cent. for the iron and steel industry, appointed a National Committee to work out, in conjunction with district sub-committees and a small Executive Committee, appropriate schemes for the reorganisation of the industry. For years representatives of the industry, both employers and workers, had recognised the need of such reorganisation, but had protested that it could not be carried out effectively without protection against foreign competition. The Advisory Committee had admitted the justice of this view, and had also acknowledged the efforts which the industry had already made, under a severe handicap, to set its house in order. On the other hand, as Sir George May, the Chairman of the Committee, reminded its representatives, the industry had to consider the needs of the other industries—mostly exporting—which used their products, and for which it was essential to get from the iron and steel industry the requisite material of the right quality at the lowest possible price. Hence it was necessary that reorganisation should proceed concurrently with the granting of an adequate protection in the home market, and in fact be a condition of such protection. The representatives of the iron and steel producers, when they met the Committee on June 3, recognised the justice of this view, and assured it of a whole-hearted response on the part of the interests which they represented to the Chairman's call for a national effort.

When the Town and Country Planning Bill was in Committee, an amendment was inserted, under Conservative pressure, to remove to a large extent from the scope of the Bill areas already built up. In the opinion of many this change was calculated to weaken seriously the effectiveness of the Bill, and protests were made against it by a number of town-planning authorities. Along with certain other concessions to the landlord interest, it was strongly condemned in the discussion on the Report stage (June 7) by Mr. Greenwood, who, as Labour Minister of Health, had first introduced the measure, and who had lately been returned to Parliament at a by-election. A motion to delete the obnoxious clause was, however, rejected by 305 votes to 50.

In the debate on the third reading of the Finance Bill (June 10), the Chancellor of the Exchequer took occasion to deny certain rumours which had become current, that he intended to bring in a new Budget in the autumn and that he regarded increased taxation as inevitable. He admitted that unemployment relief was making rather larger demands on the revenue than they had anticipated, and that revenue was coming in rather slowly, but he denied that there was as yet any cause for alarm. Much, of course, would depend on the issue of the negotiations at Lausanne, but even if these should prove fruitless, he was not sure that there would be any necessity for imposing new taxation. There was, he pointed out, another way of meeting financial difficulties, namely, by reducing expenditure. This statement was received with loud Ministerialist cheers, but Mr. Chamberlain, as on a previous occasion, somewhat discounted its effect by adding that before embarking on any serious changes in policy, it was necessary that there should be a good deal of " hard thinking." Another idea which was naturally always present to his mind was that of a great conversion loan, but for this also it was necessary to await the suitable opportunity. A Labour amendment to reject the third reading was defeated by 409 votes to 34.

Before the debates on the Finance Bill were concluded, a number of Conservative members of the House of Commons formed themselves into an unofficial Committee, with Sir G. Rentoul as Chairman, to inquire into the whole subject of national economies. Such was the interest taken in the movement that in a very short time more than a hundred members offered their assistance towards the prosecution of the inquiry. Being thus amply provided with workers, the Committee set up five sub-committees to deal with various aspects of the problem, *viz.*, local government, including education and housing, defence services and Government departments, transport and roads, National Debt and the preparation of the Estimates, and Pensions, National Health Insurance, and Unemployment Insurance. The sub-committees commenced work without delay, intending to report by the autumn even if for this purpose they should have to sit during the recess.

The efforts of the House of Commons Committee were reinforced by a debate in the House of Lords on June 23 and 29, on a motion calling on the Government to secure a further reduction of public expenditure and a corresponding reduction of taxation. The motion was brought forward by a Conservative peer, Lord Hunsdon, but it also had the support of Lord Reading, who saw no reason why the Government should be unable to accept it. Lord Snowden, with some reserve, adopted the same view. He reminded the House of the efforts which the Government had already made in the direction of economy, and he defended the principle of taxing the well-to-do in order to increase the spending power of the poor. Nevertheless, he admitted that high taxation had a bad psychological effect in discouraging enterprise, and that income tax on the lower ranges of income was a real hardship, and he therefore agreed that it was very desirable that income tax should be brought down to a lower rate.

The Chancellor of the Exchequer explained his own views on the subject of economy in a speech which he made to the House of Commons on July 11. He gave a cordial welcome to the formation of an unofficial Committee of private members, of which he had only just heard on account of his absence at Lausanne. One of the great difficulties of Chancellors of the Exchequer in the past, he said, when they had tried to effect economies, had been that they had had to address themselves to an uninformed House ; the fact that so large a body of members intended themselves to take up the study of this question would mean, he had no doubt, that when the Government put forward its proposals for economies or reductions of expenditure there would be a much larger proportion of the House fully equipped to understand both the difficulties and the possibilities of the situation. He deprecated the idea that the Government were less keen on economy than the members themselves ; they realised, however, that economies, if they were to be substantial, had to be weighed in all their bearings before they were embarked upon. Mr. Chamberlain proceeded to give an analysis of the public expenditure from which he drew the conclusion that, while minor economies could be found in various directions which added together might make a substantial sum, really big reductions of expenditure could be effected only in the fields of pensions and insurance among the nationally administrative services, or in grants to local authorities. He assured the House, in conclusion, that in the mind of the Government the question of economy was one of the most important that remained to be dealt with that year.

On June 6 Mr. Thomas, accompanied by Lord Hailsham, crossed over to Dublin, at the invitation of the Irish Government, to discuss with Mr. de Valera the questions outstanding between Great Britain and Ireland. They returned a couple of days later, and on June 10 Mr. de Valera came over to London to continue the conversations. The tone was friendly, but Mr. de Valera would make no concession with regard to the Oath, and in the absence of such concession the British Government adhered to its decision to enter into no trade treaties with Ireland at Ottawa. Hence no result was achieved by the discussions beyond the establishing of personal relations between the British Ministers and Mr. de Valera.

On June 17 Mr. Thomas gave to the House of Commons a full account of the transactions which had passed between himself and Mr. de Valera since the latter's entry into office. The last item was a despatch which he had received from Mr. de Valera only a couple of hours before, and which showed that he had not departed an iota from his original position. In these circumstances Mr. Thomas could only repeat that the Government would adhere to the policy which it had already laid down. It would not countenance for a moment the breaking of agreements. It would never attempt to force Ulster against her will. It would not renew the preferences at present enjoyed by Ireland when they lapsed in November. It would continue to repay the loan raised on the security of the land annuities, but it would take steps to recoup itself from the Free State Government.

On behalf of the Labour Party Sir S. Cripps tried to make out a case for Mr. de Valera, and while admitting that Mr. Thomas had held out a velvet glove to Ireland, remarked that it seemed to conceal a somewhat mailed fist. The debate was signalised by the first speech made in the present House of Commons by Mr. Lloyd George. Mr. George recalled that eleven years before, when consulted with regard to the treaty then being negotiated, Mr. de Valera had put forward the demand that Ireland should be a sovereign State, having the same relation to England as Belgium and Holland to Germany or Portugal to Spain, and he thought it was obvious that he had not departed in the least from that position. Much more, therefore, was at stake than the Oath or the annuities, and he considered that the Government had acted judiciously and with circumspection. On the Ministerial side, support of the Government's action was naturally unanimous.

Mr. de Valera, in his latest Note, had declared that the Free State Government accepted the British proposal for referring to arbitration the question of the land annuities, and agreed that a tribunal of the general character outlined in the report of the Imperial Conference of 1930 would be suitable, but he would not consent to the personnel of the tribunal being limited to citizens of States of the British Commonwealth. The Cabinet, after considering the Note on June 22, sent a reply in which it expressed satisfaction at Mr. de Valera's admission that the question of the annuities was a suitable one for arbitration, but declared itself unable to accept the suggestion that the personnel of the tribunal should not be limited to citizens of the British Commonwealth ; and matters accordingly remained *in statu quo*.

When July 1 arrived Mr. de Valera, in accordance with his threat, withheld from the British Government the sum of 1,500,000*l*. due to it on account of the land annuities. In spite of this the Government paid the holders of the Irish Land Stock their dividends as usual, but it resolved to take steps to recoup itself as best it could from the Free State. For this purpose it drafted a resolution giving power to the Treasury to make Orders imposing duties on any imports from the Free State up to 100 per cent. over and above any existing Customs duties. Mr. de Valera's reply was to announce that he intended, in the absence of such arbitration as he proposed, to withhold further payments due to England amounting to about 1,800,000*l*. a year, of which the chief item was 1,000,000*l*. a year for pensions for the Royal Irish Constabulary.

This left Mr. Thomas no option save to move, " with deep regret," in the House of Commons on July 4, the financial resolution for taxing Irish imports. The terms of the resolution had been drawn very widely in order, as he said, to give the Government every facility for recovering not only the sum at present involved, but also any further sums the Free State Government might withhold ; on the other hand, he promised that the duties would be remitted as soon as the requisite sum had been collected, and that every care would be taken to use them for revenue only,

and not for protective purposes. He admitted that the task was
difficult and unpleasant, but it was not to be tolerated that
other people should be allowed to make free with the British
taxpayer's money. The Opposition moved a number of amendments to limit the application of the duties, but the motion was
finally carried in its original form by a large majority.

Two days later, in moving the second reading of the Bill
imposing the duties, Mr. Thomas made a final appeal to Mr.
de Valera, offering to accept any form of tribunal agreeable to
the Irish Free State, provided only that it was an Empire tribunal.
The Opposition blamed the Government for standing too much
on its Imperial dignity, and challenged a division, which resulted
in the second reading being carried by 321 votes to 41. As
Mr. de Valera made no response to Mr. Thomas's offer, the Bill
duly became law, and the duties were imposed on July 12. Mr.
de Valera lost no time in retaliating, and thus England and the
Free State found themselves engaged in an open tariff war on the
eve of the conference which was to cement Imperial unity.

In view of the near approach of the Imperial Economic
Conference to be held at Ottawa, Mr. Thomas, as the Minister
responsible for the preparations on the British side, on June 16
made a statement to the House of Commons on the steps which
the Government had so far taken and the policy which it intended
to pursue. The object of the conference was, he said, to break
down as far as possible the trade barriers between the different
members of the British Empire. Considering the great diversity
of their interests and the complete freedom enjoyed by each of
the Dominions, he admitted that this was a very difficult task.
The Government would not for a moment assume that the
Dominions had no right to develop their secondary industries,
nor on the other hand would they be prepared to sacrifice the
interests of British industries and agriculture. If they had been
called upon to reconcile such differences with foreign countries,
he would frankly have regarded the task as impossible. The
one factor which gave him hope of the present conference was
that they would be meeting the representatives of their own
kith and kin, and therefore they started with a fund of good-will.
Mr. Thomas spoke with some pride of the pains which the Government had taken to ascertain the views and desires of all trades
that were likely to be affected, but he did not say whether the
information thus elicited was likely to make the task of coming
to an agreement with the Dominions any easier. In regard to
the policy of the Government, all he would say was that they
were going to the conference free and unfettered, with an open
mind prepared to examine every question on its merits.

Mr. Thomas's statement did little to dispel the doubts of
Labour and Liberal members as to the possibility of the conference
achieving any useful result, or their fears that it might even produce

positive harm ; while Mr. Amery on his side declared that it was useless for Britain to take part in the conference unless they were prepared to tax wheat and meat.   Mr. Baldwin, in closing the debate, did not minimise the difficulties in front of the conference, but he pointed out that the Empire had come to the parting of the ways, and that they must either have closer fiscal relationship or drift apart.   England, he said, had set a splendid example to the Dominions by embodying the principle of Free Trade within the Empire in the Import Duties Act, which was specially designed to lead up to Ottawa.   In so far as the conference followed that system, he believed it would do something to help not only the members of the British Empire but also the trade of the whole world.

The moving of a vote of censure on the Government by the Opposition, on June 23, gave the Ministerial following an opportunity of demonstrating its still unbroken solidarity, the motion being defeated by 446 votes to 47.   Mr. Lansbury blamed the Government for the continued prevalence of want and unemployment, and the decline in world trade—facts which in themselves could not be gainsaid.   Mr. Baldwin, in reply, said that whatever might be the state of other countries, Britain was still holding her own, and he drew the inference that tariffs were proving increasingly useful, though they were still only in the experimental stage.   He protested against Britain being blamed for the growth of obstacles to trade set up by foreign countries, and he claimed that the British policy at Lausanne was the first step on the road to commercial sanity.

On June 23 the Committee on Sky-writing, appointed in March, presented its report to the House of Commons.   The conclusion of the Committee was that " sky-writing " should be allowed in all towns and cities with a population of more than 20,000, but in rural areas not without the specific permission of the local authority, and then only for special occasions.   It was further suggested that " sky-writing " should be prohibited entirely in the neighbourhood of military works, aerodromes, and lighthouses.   The Committee thought that the regulation of the practice might for the present be entrusted to the industry itself, and that the Home Office should assume control only if this arrangement proved unsatisfactory.   It was of opinion that " sky-shouting " should be prohibited absolutely.

On June 28 Sir S. Hoare informed the House of Commons of some important decisions which the Government had taken with regard to India.   One was that most of the Ordinances affecting civil disobedience would be renewed when they expired on July 3, though they would be put into operation only where necessary. A second was that, in default of any agreement between Hindus and Moslems, the British Government would announce their own decision on the communal question in the course of the summer. The third was that the Government would thereupon proceed to active steps for conferring on India a Constitution. It would consult the Consultative Committee in India, lay its proposals before a joint Committee of the two Houses of Parliament, and finally bring in a Bill with provisions both for provincial autonomy in India and for an All-India Federation, though the former would probably take effect some time before the latter. The announcement was very favourably received by the bulk of the House, even Mr. Churchill declaring himself not dissatisfied ; a motion by the Opposition to reduce the India Office Vote was defeated by 242 votes to 28.

On June 11 the Prime Minister, accompanied by Sir John Simon, left London for Paris in order to visit M. Herriot before proceeding to Lausanne to take part in the Conference on Reparations. The other British delegates to Lausanne were Sir Herbert Samuel, Mr. Chamberlain, and Mr. Runciman, who left on June 14. The Opposition had made arrangements for a preliminary debate in the House of Commons on the subject of the conference, but at the request of the Prime Minister deferred it. Thus Mr. MacDonald left with his hands completely unfettered. It was generally understood, however, that he would follow the lines laid down by Mr. Chamberlain in his statement to the House of Commons on February 2, and work for the complete cancellation of both reparations and war debts.

Mr. MacDonald returned to London on July 11 with an agreement which fell considerably short of this objective. Nevertheless, the part he had played in the Lausanne Conference won general commendation in England, and on his arrival at Victoria Station he received an ovation from a large gathering. The outcome of the conference was received by the public with a sense of relief which was all the more profound on account of the fears which had prevailed at one time of a breakdown. Some misgivings, however, were caused by the announcement a few days later that a " gentleman's agreement " had been made between the creditor Powers not to ratify the agreement until they had themselves come to an arrangement with their own creditors. Expression was given to this feeling by Mr. Churchill in a debate in the House of Commons on July 11, in which he tried to make out that British interests had been sacrificed by the Lausanne Treaty, and that the " gentleman's agreement "—about which a great deal of secrecy was still being preserved—had made it more difficult for Britain to approach her own creditors.

On the next day (July 12), Mr. MacDonald gave the House of Commons a report on the proceedings at Lausanne, in the course of which he dealt with the allegations of Mr. Churchill. He claimed for the conference and its results no more than that it could lead to a settlement of the question of reparations which lay somewhere about the root of every economic trouble that had overtaken the world since the war, and had done so much to throw every national economy out of gear. If members doubted the value of their achievement, he asked them to exercise a little imagination and picture to themselves what would have happened if they had come back from Lausanne without an agreement. He recalled the alarming picture of the state of Europe which had been drawn by the Basle Committee in its report issued in the previous December. The gap between that date and the calling of the Lausanne Conference on June 1 was no credit to anybody, but Britain could not act earlier because she had to wait for the French and German elections. There was an election pending in America also ; but they could not possibly wait for that. Fortunately, American speeches and other expressions of American opinion led them to believe that if Europe decided on a settlement which it deemed practicable for itself, America would consider carefully the part which she in equity could play. As for the " gentleman's agreement," there was nothing secret or under-handed about it ; and he challenged Mr. Churchill to say how he could have acted differently in the circumstances. Per-sonally he believed that although America had never uttered a pledge so far as he knew nor indicated in any way how far she was prepared to meet them, there was no nation in the world more prepared to lend a hand in straightening out the entangle-ments and troubles with which they were surrounded. Mr. MacDonald then proceeded to explain and defend the arrange-ments which had been made at Lausanne. The British Govern-ment, he said, stood for " cancellation all round," which would have been by far the simplest plan. As, however, they could not obtain agreement on this, they had to put up with something less satisfactory. He described as " highly ingenious " the scheme by which the Bank for International Settlements was to be left, after a moratorium of three years, with the decision on placing the German bonds on the market. They had at any rate put an end to reparations, and though this meant a nominal loss to the creditor nations, it would really be a great boon to them by allowing industry a chance to recover.

After the Prime Minister had spoken, Mr. Lloyd George, like Mr. Churchill on the previous day, belittled the work of the conference. He blamed the British representatives for not holding out for complete cancellation of war debts, and said that the results actually secured could have been obtained just as well months before. He failed, however, to carry the House with him, and Mr. Chamberlain was greeted with loud Ministerialist cheers when he asserted that the British delegation by its work at Lausanne had made a long step forward towards the restoration of the confidence which the world so urgently required. In response to an inquiry by Mr. Lloyd George, it was stated that there was no objection to the publication of the " gentleman's agreement," provided other Governments consented, and it was actually made public a few days later.

On the next day (July 13), Sir John Simon informed the House of Commons of a sequel to the Lausanne Treaty in the shape of a new accord between the British and French Governments. In the declaration which formed part of the final act of the Lausanne Conference, the signatory Powers, he said, had declared their intention to make every effort to resolve the problems existing at the present moment or which might arise subsequently in the spirit which had inspired the Lausanne Agreement. In that spirit the British and French Governments had themselves decided to give a lead by announcing their intention, first, to keep one another informed and to exchange views with complete candour on any questions coming to their notice similar in origin to those which had just been settled at Lausanne ; secondly, to work together to find a solution of the disarmament question which should be beneficial and equitable for all the Powers concerned ; thirdly, to co-operate in the preparation of the world economic conference. In these three respects the agreement was to be open to all other nations which cared to join it. In addition, France and England had declared that, pending the negotiation at a later date of a new commercial treaty between them, they would avoid any action in the nature of discrimination by the one country against the interests of the other.

Towards the end of June, while the issue of the Lausanne Conference appeared to be still in suspense, the Government judged the conditions favourable for launching the great conversion operation which every Chancellor of the Exchequer was known to have had in mind since the time when the 5 per cent. War Loan first became repayable in 1929. Preparations having been made, on the morning of June 30 the Bank rate was reduced to 2 per cent., the lowest figure which it had touched for thirty-five years, and 4 per cent. lower than the figure in February. This was a kind of signal to financial circles, among which rumours of conversion had been rife for some time ; and on the same day Mr. Chamberlain returned to London from Lausanne, where he had been attending the Reparations Conference, in order to make the first announcement to Parliament, timing it so that it might be known in America before the close of business hours, and published and commented on in the British Press the next morning.

Having secured without difficulty the adjournment of the current business, Mr. Chamberlain gave the House his chief reasons for deciding to convert, and for choosing that moment. The first was to effect a saving in the national expenditure by reducing the interest charge on the debt. In the second place, he anticipated that from a general reduction in the level of interest charges great benefits would flow to industry, which would be enabled to obtain more easily the capital it needed, and on better

terms.   There was a general consensus of opinion that the continued existence of a vast body of British Government stock
yielding a 5 per cent. return was an artificial obstacle to a fall
in interest rates to a lower level at which they would otherwise
naturally stand.   Thirdly, they were in the fortunate position
that the relative merits of British Government securities by
comparison with all other investments, British and foreign,
had never been more amply recognised by the world at large than
at that moment ;   and this was a vital factor in the success of
such an operation.   Fourthly, while they were in a position to
secure such important results as he had indicated immediately,
he did not consider that further delay would be justified either
by the prospect of small additional savings or by any hope that
the operation would become any easier with the lapse of time.
Finally, the strongest argument for immediate action was to be
found in the spirit of the country.   After a long period of depression they had recovered their freedom in monetary matters.
They had balanced the Budget in the face of the most formidable
difficulties, and had shown the strongest resistance of all countries
in the world to the general troubles affecting world trade.   He was
convinced, therefore, that the country was in the mood for great
enterprises, and was both able and determined to carry them
through to a successful conclusion.

With regard to the details of the scheme, Mr. Chamberlain
stated that the dividend of December 1 next would be paid at
the rate of 5 per cent., but thereafter interest would be paid at
the rate of $3\frac{1}{2}$ per cent., without deduction of income tax, and
that the loan would not be redeemable till 1952.   As an inducement
to stockholders to convert, and to convert quickly, a bonus of 1*l.*
on every 100*l.* of stock was promised to all who undertook to do
so by July 30.   Those who did not wish to convert could demand
redemption of their stock in December.   As the total amount of
the loan was over 2,000,000,000*l.*, the saving in interest charge,
if the whole of it should be converted to the lower rate, would
amount to about 30,000,000*l.* per annum, which, allowing for a reduction in the yield of income tax and surtax, would mean a net
budgetary saving of 23,000,000*l.* per annum.

The announcement was received both by Parliament and the
public with an enthusiasm which augured well for the success of
the scheme.   In order to leave no stone unturned, the Government
on the same night sent a letter to all the holders of War Loan
stock, nearly three millions in number, urging them both on
financial and on patriotic grounds to convert their holding and
not to redeem it.   It was pointed out that, though the lower
rate of interest which would be payable after June of next year
would bear hardly on some holders whose income came chiefly
from the loan, yet the change was inevitable.   No one, it said,
could reasonably expect to enjoy the right to 5 per cent. interest

E

when the national credit justified a much lower rate and the country was strong enough to overcome any difficulties attendant on a conversion operation. If holders were called upon to make a sacrifice, they should recognise that there was no section of the community from which sacrifices were not being asked in that time of trouble—sacrifices which were being resolutely borne. Another step which the Government took to ensure the success of the loan was to make a request—which was equivalent to a command—that no new capital issues should be floated until further notice.

While making this effort to reduce national expenditure, the Government did not overlook the importance or the possibilities of economy in local expenditure also. Since the issue in the previous September of the appeal by the Minister of Health (*vide* ANNUAL REGISTER, 1931, p. 76), local authorities had not been inactive in the matter, but the Government now felt that further action was necessary, and accordingly, on July 1, it sent a letter to the London County Council and to the associations representing the local authorities in England and Wales and Scotland asking them to set up committees to consider the whole field of local expenditure, with a view to submitting their views and recommendations by the end of October. The Government promised to assist in every way by furnishing information, providing accommodation for meetings, and so forth. The bodies approached consented to co-operate with the Government in the manner desired, and a main committee on the lines suggested was formed by July 13 and began its labours immediately.

The response of the British Government to the disarmament proposals issued by Mr. Hoover at the end of June was made in a statement delivered by Mr. Baldwin to the House of Commons on July 7, and repeated almost at the same time at Geneva. The Government, said Mr. Baldwin, cordially welcomed President Hoover's declaration alike because it called for a really substantial measure of disarmament and because it sought to apply the two principles of quantitative and of qualitative limitation. They agreed with President Hoover that reduction should be carried out not only by broad general cuts in armaments, but also by increasing the comparative power of defence through decreases in the power of attack, and they desired to contribute all that they could to the practical application of this conception. They had therefore advanced wide suggestions of their own for an agreed general programme, suggestions which, while differing in some important respects from those of President Hoover as to method or measure, were inspired by the same purpose, and covered a substantial area of common ground.

Mr. Baldwin then proceeded to give an outline of the United Kingdom's proposals under the three heads of military, naval, and air disarmament. In regard to land forces, they were at one with President Hoover in advocating the reduction of effectives to the lowest level consistent with national safety—they had themselves already carried out a measure of land disarmament which more than conformed to his standards—and the abolition of chemical warfare and the prohibition of specifically offensive weapons, among which however, they did not reckon tanks of less than 20 tons. In the field of naval armament they had put forward for immediate adoption proposals which included the fixing of the maximum size of any future capital ship at 22,000 tons and the maximum calibre of guns carried by them at 11 inches, of the maximum size of cruisers hereafter constructed at 7,000 tons and the maximum calibre of guns carried by them at 6·1 inches, and of the maxima for aircraft carriers at 2,200 tons with 6·1 inch guns ; and the abolition of submarines. In regard to air forces, they had proposed the complete prohibition of all bombing from the air, save within limits to be laid down as precisely as possible by an international convention ; a strict limitation of the unladen weight of military and naval aircraft ; and a restriction in the numbers of all kinds of military and naval aircraft. Mr. Baldwin's statement was received by the House with loud applause.

When the Sunday Entertainments Bill was in Committee, the Government accepted an amendment proposed by Mr. Buchan, that 5 per cent. of the profits of Sunday film exhibitions should be devoted to the establishment of a National Film Institute, similar to those which existed in some foreign countries for the purpose of improving the quality of the films shown. As a good deal of opposition to the proposal developed, the Government, when the Report stage of the Bill was taken, withdrew its sanction and left the matter to a free vote of the House. After an animated debate, the proposal was adopted by a majority of 16. A proposal to allow the Sunday opening of theatres was not accepted by the Government and was rejected by the House.

The Bill dealing with young offenders was altered in the House of Lords by the insertion of an amendment permitting the punishment of whipping to be inflicted in certain cases. The House of Commons at first threw out the amendment, but when the Lords insisted on retaining it, gave way. On July 12 the Bill received the royal assent, along with the Town and Country Planning Bill and the Sunday Entertainments Bill, and on the next day Parliament adjourned till October 27.

The long-drawn quarrel between the National Labour Party and the Independent Labour Party came to a head in the course of this session. In accordance with the resolution taken at the conference in March, the Administrative Council of the I.L.P. once more appealed to the Parliamentary Labour Party to amend its standing orders in such a way as to allow more liberty of speech and action to Labour members of Parliament. The Parliamentary

Labour Party replied that alteration of its standing orders was neither desirable nor necessary in present circumstances, and that revision should be postponed till the time came for the creation of the next Labour Government. The I.L.P. Council thereupon, as a last resort, appealed to the Executive Committee of the Labour Party not to endorse this decision, threatening that if it did so, they would summon a special conference and recommend disaffiliation. The only reply of the Executive was to inform them that if the I.L.P. desired the amendment of the standing orders of the Parliamentary Labour Party, they should first join that party.

Early in July the " National " Liberals, the group led by Sir John Simon and Mr. Runciman, who had improvised an organisation at the time of the General Election in 1931, decided to form a permanent organisation under the name of the Liberal National Council. The policy of this body was for the present to be wholehearted support of the National Government. It claimed to represent the bulk of the Liberal Party, and invited the adhesion of all who called themselves Liberals.

CHAPTER III.

THE OTTAWA AGREEMENTS.

BEFORE Parliament rose, the British delegation to the Imperial Economic Conference at Ottawa had already left England. It consisted of Mr. Baldwin, Mr. Chamberlain, Lord Hailsham, Mr. J. H. Thomas, Mr. Runciman, Sir Philip Cunliffe-Lister, and Sir John Gilmour. They were accompanied by a very large body of experts and representatives of industries and industrial bodies, including the Trade Unions Congress. A number of industries also sent unofficial advisers to Ottawa.

In his speech at the opening meeting on July 22, Mr. Baldwin outlined the policy which he desired that the British delegation should pursue. The real importance of the conference, he said, was that it marked a point where two roads diverged, one leading to the development of purely national interests and the other to closer Imperial unity and mutual co-operation in trade. A definite choice of the latter road was of greater importance than the actual distance progressed at the conference. While complete Empire free trade was impossible, there were opportunities to-day of securing trade within the Empire and with groups outside which could not be reached if each Government acted alone. The first aim of the conference, then, should be to clear the different channels of trade among the members of the Empire. Each member should approach the problems with a view to seeing how much each could contribute to the common stock without detriment to national interests, but without assessing too closely the relative advantages. The conference, he said, should not only maintain the existing preferences, but should find ways of increasing them. This could be done either by lowering barriers within the Empire or by raising them against others. The British Government held that they should endeavour to follow the first rather than the second course, since no nation could live in isolation amid depression and impoverishment.

These last words struck the keynote of Mr. Baldwin's policy, to which he adhered throughout the conference. Rumours were at times current that some of his colleagues were at variance with him on this point, but they turned out to be incorrect, and, somewhat to the general surprise, complete harmony was maintained within the British delegation, a fact which contributed not a little to the ultimate success of the conference.

As a result of their deliberations at Ottawa, Mr. Baldwin and his colleagues brought back with them a number of agreements which they had made with the representatives of all the Dominions—excepting Ireland—and of India for the purpose of encouraging trade between their respective countries. With this end in view, the existing preferences enjoyed by Britain in the Dominions and by the Dominions in Britain were not only to be confirmed, but to be widened in various particulars. Thus, besides maintaining the existing duties of at least 10 per cent. *ad valorem* on timber, canned and fresh fish, canned meat, leather, tallow, lead, zinc, castor seed, and ground nuts, Britain undertook to impose new or increased duties on a number of other articles in which one or other of the Dominions was specially interested, including butter, cheese, raw and canned fruit, condensed milk, eggs, and rice. For the benefit of the cattle-raisers in Australia, New Zealand, and South Africa, an arrangement was made for regulating the supplies of meat imported into England on an agreed programme for the next eighteen months, during which time there would be consultations with a view to devising a more permanent scheme for the orderly marketing of supplies on the British market. For the benefit of Canadian wheat-growers, it was agreed to impose a small duty of 2s. per quarter on foreign wheat, on condition, however, that the duty might be removed at any time if Empire producers were unable or unwilling to offer their wheat to Britain at prices not exceeding world prices and in quantities sufficient to supply British needs. The tobacco preference was to be stabilised for ten years, the tea preference maintained, the preference for coffee increased to 9s. 4d. a cwt., and on light wines to 2s. a gallon, while the duty on certain dried fruits was to be increased from 7s. to 10s. 6d. a cwt. To allay the apprehensions of Canada with regard to Russian " dumping," a clause was inserted in the agreement between Great Britain and that Dominion providing that if either Government was satisfied that preferences were being frustrated by State action on the part of any foreign country, steps would be taken for the prohibition of the importation from that country of the goods concerned.

In return, England secured certain advantages for some of her manufacturing industries—especially iron and steel—the precise extent of which was not disclosed for the present, but which at the highest estimate of those who were immediately interested were not likely to assist British trade very materially. Of more importance, perhaps, to British manufacturers than any of the actual preferences secured at Ottawa was an undertaking given by Canada and Australia that their Tariff Boards, before which British manufacturers would be free to appear, should review the position so as to ensure that within a reasonable period the protective duties should be reduced to a " level which should give United Kingdom producers full opportunity of reasonable competition in the Dominion markets on the basis of the relative cost of economical and efficient production." It was also laid down that protection in those countries should be afforded only to industries which were reasonably assured of sound opportunities for success.

Mr. Baldwin and the majority of his colleagues in the British delegation returned to Southampton on August 26, and immediately on their arrival issued a statement setting forth the main results of the conference. The agreements, they said, marked a degree of success far beyond anything that was expected before they left England. This did not mean success for them at the expense of the Dominions nor gains for the Dominions at their expense : such a result would not have meant success, for it would have left behind it the seeds of future friction. On the contrary, each part of the Empire had made its contribution to a policy which they believed would eventually lead to closer Imperial unity, based on the recognition of the advantages of mutual co-operation in trade. They were confident that the arrangements made would lead to increased trade between the several parts of the Empire and to increased prosperity, which could not fail to exercise an influence far beyond the borders of the Empire itself. In this way the Ottawa Conference marked a further step, along with the Lausanne Conference and the success of the Conversion Loan, in their progress away from the area of deep depression, and left them prepared to play their full part in the approaching World Economic Conference.

The reference to the Conversion Loan was fully justified by the course of that venture during the absence of the Delegation from England. Even before he left for Ottawa Mr. Chamberlain had had the satisfaction of knowing that its success was assured. From the outset holders of the stock, both great and small, daily notified their assent in large numbers, and throughout the month of July the officials of the Bank of England were kept working at high pressure dealing with applications. On August 15 the Treasury announced that the amount converted up to July 31, and so carrying the benefit of the cash bonus, was approximately 1,850,000,000*l.* This was almost 90 per cent. of the total amount of the loan, and exceeded the most optimistic forecasts. It was already certain therefore that the amount of cash to be found by the Treasury in December for redemption would not unduly strain its resources, and that the annual saving to the State in interest would be very considerable. Thus this operation completely eclipsed the famous pre-war conversion of Goschen in 1888, when out of a total of 558,000,000*l.*, 514,000,000*l.* was converted.

On his return from Lausanne after the Reparations Conference, the Prime Minister, after a brief rest, devoted himself to the task of working out, in conjunction with those of his colleagues who had not gone to Ottawa, a scheme for the representation of the various communities in British India in the Provincial Legislatures, in accordance with the statement made earlier in the year by the Secretary for India. The scheme was completed on August 4, and on August 17 was made public simultaneously in England and India. The Prime Minister issued an accompanying statement in which he reminded the Indians once more that the Government had never wished to intervene in the communal controversies of India, and that they only did so because of the failure of the communities to agree amongst themselves. They would, he said, be only too glad if at any stage before the Bill became law the communities could come to an agreement. But on the strength of past experience they were convinced that no further negotiations could be of any advantage, and they would be no party to them. Still, they would be willing to substitute for their scheme any scheme, either in respect of any one or more of the Governors' Provinces or in respect of the whole of British India, that should be generally agreed upon and accepted by all the parties concerned.

On July 30 the Independent Labour Party held a conference at Bradford to consider the National Administrative Council's recommendation of immediate disaffiliation from the Labour Party. After some discussion the motion for disaffiliation, which was moved by Mr. Brockway and seconded by Mr. Jowett, was carried by 241 votes to 142. The leaders of the minority, Messrs. Wise and Dollan, maintained that they represented half the movement, and announced their intention to organise the dissenting branches in a new association maintaining affiliation with the Labour Party.

On August 8 Treasury Orders were issued substituting a permanent scale of duties for the emergency duties imposed on market garden imports, *viz.*, fresh fruit and vegetables, flowers, and trees and shrubs, by the Horticultural Products Act of 1931. In recommending the Orders, the Import Duties Advisory Committee stated that, while it would be premature to draw final conclusions from the experiment represented by the Act, they were satisfied that one of its results had been to encourage the home producer to enlarge his operations. They were therefore of opinion that the experiment ought to be continued with certain modifications, and they thought that the protection of the home grower when his crops were ready for market could be best achieved by the imposition of duties not subject (as the existing duties were) to seasonal variations of rate, and by extension of the periods of the duties. At the same time they emphasised the importance of improvements in marketing methods, and stated that they would not hesitate to recommend the immediate removal of any of the additional duties, should it appear to them that, through lack of effective organisation or otherwise, the home products fell short of what might be properly expected in quality, quantity, and reasonable price.

Immediately on his return from Ottawa, Mr. Chamberlain was pressed from various quarters to raise the embargo which had been placed on the floating of new issues while the conversion of War Loan was being carried out. He recognised that a certain hardship was being inflicted on investors by the action of the Government, but before giving them relief, determined to carry out another financial operation for the benefit of the Treasury while the conditions were still favourable, *i.e.*, while it was able to borrow money at unprecedentedly low rates. On August 30 notice was given to holders of Four-and-a-half per cent. War Loan, 1925-1945, and Four-and-a-half per cent. Treasury Bonds, 1932-1934, that these loans would be repaid at par on December 31. The holdings of the former loan amounted to 12,804,341*l.*, and of the latter to 140,418,035*l.* Thus the saving in annual interest, supposing the Treasury could borrow at 2 per cent., was likely to be about 3,000,000*l.*

The report of the Committee appointed in the spring to consider whether any changes should be made in the constitution of the Post Office was made public on August 22. The Committee came to the conclusion that on the whole the Post Office performed its work with remarkable efficiency, and that a change in status to that of a public utility company or statutory authority was not desirable. It discovered, however, a serious defect in organisation in over-centralisation at headquarters, and held that the domination of the secretariat had resulted in a too rigid bureaucracy. To correct this fault, it advised that a Board of Control should be appointed to direct policy. In regard to finance, it recommended that a fixed sum should be taken annually by the Treasury, and any surplus used for improving the postal services. It found the telegraph service to be on the decline, and urged that it should be amalgamated with the telephone system.

The Government at this time once more turned its attention
to the question of the dangers arising from motor traffic on the
roads. A Return of Street Accidents caused by Vehicles and Horses,
issued at the end of May, showed that so far there was little sign
of the beneficial effects which the new Highway Code had been
expected to produce. The number of persons killed in such
accidents in Great Britain in 1931 had been 6,691, which, though
some 600 less than in the preceding year, was still appallingly
high ; and this decrease was offset by an increase of over 24,000
in the number of persons not fatally injured, which amounted
to 202,119. Correspondence in the Press showed that the public
was deeply agitated on the subject, but also that opinion differed
on the question whether in order to reduce the number of accidents a change in the law was necessary or whether it would
be sufficient to administer more strictly the existing law. The
Government thought that the latter course should at any rate
first be tried, and at the end of August the Home Office addressed
a circular to all magistrates in the country calling their attention
to the figures of the Return, and suggesting that they should
make freer use of their power to suspend motor licences in order
to bring home to drivers generally the need for improvement
in the standard of care and consideration for other road users.

Another aspect of the motor problem, which engaged the
attention of the Government to an equal, if not greater degree,
was the competition of road and rail transport. In spite of the
permission which they had obtained in 1930 to engage themselves
in road transport, the railways continued to complain that they
were being deprived by the motor lorry of traffic which should
legitimately belong to them and that motor traffic was being
unfairly subsidised at their expense. In response to their
representations, the Minister of Transport in March called together a conference of representatives of the railways and
commercial road users to consider what would be a fair basis of
competition between rail and road transport of goods. In its
report, which was submitted at the end of July and published
on August 17, the conference unanimously recommended higher
taxation of commercial motor vehicles and regulation of this
form of transport by a system of licensing to enforce payment
of reasonable wages and good conditions for employees and
the maintenance of vehicles in a state of fitness ; also that the
Minister of Transport should be empowered to prevent the
transference of certain classes of goods from the railways to the
roads.

The recommendations of the conference were attacked with
some bitterness by representatives of the motor interests, but in
other quarters they were considered fair and impartial. Lord
Buckmaster saw in them a means of reducing the appalling
mortality on the roads, and on that ground moved in the House

of Lords, on November 8, that the report of the conference ought to be carried out without delay. He also called upon the Government in impassioned language to take further steps to control the motor traffic, which was endangering the life and limb of all wayfarers, besides ruining the amenities of the country. Lord Plymouth, on behalf of the Government, admitted that there were directions in which improvements, mainly of an administrative character, were possible and desirable, and that the existing law might be more strictly enforced. He announced that a full investigation into the causes of accidents was being embarked on, and he suggested that it would be unwise to introduce further legislation until they had the results of the inquiry before them. Lord Buckmaster's motion was then carried without a division.

The sixty-fourth Congress of the Trade Unions opened at Newcastle on September 5, the Chairman being Mr. J. Bromley, of the Associated Society of Locomotive Engineers and Firemen. Since the last Congress the membership of trade unions had declined somewhat, but not nearly so much as had at one time been feared, and it still stood at about 3,600,000. Politically the General Council of the Congress was now in closer touch with the Labour Party than ever before, thanks to some new machinery for co-ordination which had been introduced after the political crisis of last year ; and it was now satisfied that there was little danger of a conflict of policy between the Congress and the Labour Party.

The chief business of the Congress was to consider two reports, published a couple of months before by the General Council, dealing at length with the subjects of fiscal policy and the control of industry. Both reports contained features which marked a new departure in trade union policy, or at any rate the abandon-ment of old watchwords. The report on fiscal policy was remark-able for its emphatic repudiation of *laissez faire* in trade policy, and for the open-mindedness with which it approached the vexed question of regulating foreign trade. It pointed out that although trade union leaders fell under the influence of the Manchester School in the nineteenth century, the trade union movement had never at any time in its history adopted whole-heartedly the *laissez faire* theory. On account of the extremely delicate and complicated character of the mechanism of international trade, control of foreign trade, it said, should be undertaken with extreme caution. There were circumstances in which a high degree of imports or exports might be necessary, but no general principle could be laid down and each case should be dealt with on its merits. Even where a decision had been taken to regulate imports it could not be laid down that tariffs were the best method to use, nor again that import boards or quotas or licences or subsidies were always preferable. In regard to tariffs, however, the report went so far as to say that they were so liable to become merely a form of indirect taxation, and their administration was so liable to abuse, that they were a pro-tective device which should be adopted only with the greatest reluctance. It forbore to make any pronouncement on the present fiscal policy of the country on the ground that it was an experiment which it was still too early to judge.

The report on the Control of Industry, issued early in July, definitely repudiated State Socialism, and favoured instead the establishment of public corporations, like the Electricity Board, for the direction of industries which were ripe for socialisation. This method, it held, ensured greater flexibility and better manage-ment on the one hand, and freedom from party political domination on the other. In regard to the Boards for managing such under-takings, the personnel of which should of course be appointed by the Government, it held that, while the members should be drawn from different classes of the community, particular interests—including Labour—should not nominate members, but should rather be represented on advisory or consultative Boards. As a general rule, there should be no State assistance for industries so controlled, and each one should be required to stand on its own feet financially. In some cases the State could become a share-holder in concerns that in other respects remained private enter-prises, but in such cases it should have a real share in the control. For industries still left in private hands, Government control could be achieved by the setting up of legislative standards. Fair compensation should be paid in respect of any undertakings taken over by the State.

In his presidential address, Mr. Bromley challenged the theory, prevalent among the employing class, that the troubles of industry were largely due to the " rigidity " of wages, and maintained that the right policy, in present conditions, was to strive to maintain and improve wages and conditions, to increase consumption, and not to curtail production. As a remedy for unemployment, he ad-vocated the reorganisation of industry on the basis of a shortening of the working day and week without reduction of wages. Refer-ring to the Ottawa Conference, he said that its result, whatever it might be, could only be of a temporary character, as the capitalistic system of society required much more than patching ; and he referred with satisfaction to the fact that the efforts made to induce Britain to place an embargo on its imports from Russia had so far not been successful.

Although the reports of the General Council contained much that was controversial from a Labour point of view, they provoked comparatively little discussion. The Congress duly registered its protest against the means test, and passed a comprehensive resolution calling for the abolition of war debts, the provision of employment, the public control of banking and monopolistic industries, and the taxation of land values, but again with very little discussion. Only on two occasions were the proceedings marked with any show of animation. One was when a request was sent in to the Congress to receive a deputation from a body of unemployed who had marched up to the hall. The Council was against complying with the request on the ground that the procession had been organised under Communist influence. In spite of this fact, a number of speakers urged that the deputation should be admitted, and it was found necessary to settle the matter by a card vote, in which the Council was upheld by 1,577,000 votes to 963,000. The other occasion was when Mr. Lansbury addressed the Congress as fraternal delegate from the Labour Party, and roused it to enthusiasm by denouncing the " Frankenstein monster of the money market of the City of London " and calling on it not to reform but to revolutionise the capitalistic system. The Congress also listened sympathetically to a speech from Mr. Henderson on disarmament, and passed a resolution in support of the Hoover plan. On the Ottawa Conference, like the Chairman, it reserved judgment.

The Congress devoted no little attention to the industrial struggle then proceeding in Lancashire. On the first day it passed an emergency resolution expressing sympathy with the strikers, and instructing the General Council to organise all possible moral and financial assistance on their behalf. The Council, in response, opened a fund for them with a subscription of 1,000l. Its example was soon followed by a number of trade unions, and before the Congress closed it was announced that over 10,000l. had been promised.

The trouble in Lancashire was the natural, if regrettable, result of the strained relations which had for some time prevailed between employers and employed in the textile industry. During July and August the friction became steadily worse. The weaving manufacturers were not slow to take advantage of the liberty of action which they had obtained on June 11, and many of them reduced the wages of their employees. Some had even done so before the agreement terminated, dismissing those of their workers who would not accept the new rates. The operatives became greatly embittered, and in the Burnley district most of them struck work.

The Executive of the weavers' amalgamations reopened negotiations with the employers early in July, with a view to framing a new wage agreement. The discussions were far from harmonious. Both sides were agreed that it was necessary to reduce costs of production in the industry. But while the employers desired to secure this end by reducing wages, the operatives insisted that it was first incumbent on the employers to see what economies they could effect by means of better organisation. This contention seemed to be justified by the fact that on June 23

Sir Kenneth D. Stewart had resigned the chairmanship of the
Lancashire Cotton Corporation, Ltd., the body which had been
formed two years before to produce a greater centralisation of
effort in the industry, on the ground that he could see no sign of
any progress in that direction. Nevertheless, the men's representatives did not exclude the possibility of wage reductions, and
after some weeks of bargaining an agreement seemed to be in
sight. At that point, however, early in August, they introduced
an entirely new issue, demanding the reinstatement of the men
who had been dismissed for not accepting reduced wages before
June 11. The employers would not promise more than to take
them back as vacancies arose. The men were not satisfied with
this, and on August 9 the negotiations broke down.

From this point the more militant section of the men obtained
the upper hand, and on August 15 a general strike of the weavers
was proclaimed to take effect on August 27, " failing sufficient
action on the part of the employers." A week later the Deputy
Mayor of Manchester succeeded in once more bringing the parties
together, but again the negotiations proved fruitless. Appeals
were made to the Minister of Labour to intervene, but he declared
that it would be useless to do so till a spirit of good-will was more
clearly discernible on both sides. On August 27 the strike notices
duly took effect, and within a week over 150,000 workers were idle.

The strike lasted just over four weeks, and was ultimately
settled through the mediation of the Ministry of Labour. The
stoppage had not been in force many days when a change of temper
showed itself on both sides. The Minister of Labour took advantage of this to address, on September 5, a letter to both sides
suggesting a new approach to the problems of the industry through
the appointment of joint committees to examine them, and offering
the assistance of the Ministry, though without suggesting mediation. Both sides caught at the hand thus held out, and expressed
their willingness to enter into a conference presided over by a
representative of the Ministry. The Minister thereupon sent to
Manchester Mr. F. L. Leggett, an official of the Ministry, and a conference under his chairmanship opened on September 13. Negotiations were conducted in a spirit of good-will, but progress was
not rapid. However, on September 16, proposals were adopted
for restoring the principle and strengthening the machinery of
collective bargaining, which had been more or less in abeyance in
the industry for three years ; on September 23 wages reductions
equivalent to over 1*s*. 8*d*. in the pound were agreed to ; and on
September 25 the thorny question of the reinstatement of the
dismissed workers was settled in a manner agreeable to both sides.
The agreements having been ratified by the main bodies of the
employers and employed, work was generally resumed on September 28.

No sooner had the weavers in Lancashire returned to work

at the end of September than the prospect of a strike in the spinning section of the industry became imminent. Following the example of the manufacturers, the spinning employers had in August called upon the operatives to accept a reduction equivalent to 2s. 9d. in the pound. Negotiations had thereupon been opened as a result of which they reduced their demand to 2s. 2d. This was far more than the operatives were willing to concede, and the negotiations were broken off. On October 3 the Wages Committee of the Cotton Spinners' Associations recommended that notices of a reduction equivalent to 1s. 8d. in the pound should be posted on October 10, and this step was generally taken. This time the Ministry of Labour was not slow in its offer of mediation, which was made on October 11. The offer was immediately accepted by both sides, and Mr. Leggett again essayed the task of restoring peace to the industry. He was no less successful than on the previous occasion, but only after efforts even more unremitting. Both sides bargained with great stubbornness, and had to be brought together by slow steps. Not until the evening of October 22—the very day on which work at the old terms ceased—was an agreement reached. In the end, the operatives consented to accept a reduction equivalent to 1s. 6½d. in the pound, and in return the employers consented to restore the agreement relating to the 48-hour week which had been abrogated in December of the previous year. Both sides also consented to the restoration of collective bargaining, and to the setting up of a new Conciliation Committee. Thus the result of the two struggles in the textile industry was to bring relations between employers and employed into a healthier condition than they had known for some time.

The settlement thus made did not come into effect as quickly as had been expected. A delegate meeting of the Operative Spinners' Amalgamation, in a burst of ill-will, on October 29 refused to ratify it. The employers announced that they would on no account reopen negotiations, and the Executives of the workers immediately prepared to take a ballot of their trade unions. Meanwhile the vast majority of the spindles remained idle. The result of the ballot, declared on November 5, was that in one amalgamation, according to the official statement, " an insufficient majority had voted in favour of continuing the dispute," while in the other a small majority declared themselves in favour of accepting the settlement. Work was accordingly resumed on November 7, and on the next day the agreement was formally ratified.

The War Loan Conversion offer closed on September 30, and on the same day the Treasury announced that, out of the total amount of the loan outstanding on June 30, viz., 2,085,000,000l., about 1,920,000,000l. had been converted, leaving 165,000,000l., or about 8 per cent. to be redeemed in cash on December 1—about the same proportion as in the Goschen plan, forty years before. At the same time, the Chancellor of the Exchequer raised the embargo on the flotation of new British issues, still, however, retaining the restrictions on replacement issues and on foreign issues.

The Labour Party opened its annual conference at Leicester on October 3. In preparation for this event, a number of prominent ex-members of the Independent Labour Party, who in August had opposed the decision of that body to disaffiliate itself from the Labour Party (*vide* p. 71), met in Leicester on October 2, and formed themselves into a new organisation, to be known as the Socialist League, under the chairmanship of Mr. E. Wise. The object of the new body was to perform the same service for the Labour Party which had formerly been rendered by the I.L.P. —to strengthen and assist the party in the heavy tasks with which it was confronted. Thus while pursuing their own path, they would work within the Labour Party, and the fighting of elections would not be a primary object with them.

The report submitted to the conference by the National Executive Committee of the party opened with a vigorous denunciation of the Government, both for the means by which it had obtained office and for the policy which it had pursued while in office, and which was held to prove its essentially Tory character. The Chairman of the conference, Mr. George Lathan, of the Railway Clerks' Association, devoted a great part of his opening address to the same topic.

The chief business of the conference was to consider four reports issued during the summer by the Executive Committee on currency, banking and finance, on the land and the national planning of agriculture, on the reorganisation of the electricity supply, and on the national planning of transport. These were meant to convey a more or less authoritative statement of Labour policy for the next General Election, and to take the place both of the " Labour and the Nation " pamphlet and of the Scarborough resolutions of the previous year. Mr. Henderson informed the conference, however, that in the event of the Labour Party being returned to power in the course of the coming year, the Government would not proceed to put this policy into practice before convening a new conference.

The report on banking advocated that the Bank of England should be brought under public ownership and control, that a National Investment Board should be appointed to regulate capital issues, and that emergency powers should be taken to deal with any attempt by private financial institutions to obstruct a Labour Government, damage national credit, or create financial panic. Sweeping as was this resolution, it did not go far enough for a section of the delegates, and Mr. Wise moved that the resolution should be extended to include joint-stock banks and acceptance houses. The amendment was supported by Sir Stafford

Cripps, and was carried against the Executive by 1,241,000 votes to 984,000.

A similar fate befell the resolution submitted by the Executive on the question of transport. Its proposal was to nationalise the means of transport as far as possible and to place them under the control of a National Transport Board to be appointed by the Minister of Transport. As in the debate on the same subject at the Trade Union Congress, a number of delegates protested that no provision was made for the all-important factor of workers' control, and so strong was the feeling manifested on this point that the Executive found it advisable to withdraw the resolution for further consideration.

Even this was not the worst rebuff suffered by the Executive. On October 4 Sir Charles Trevelyan moved that the leaders of the next Labour Government and of the Parliamentary Labour Party should be instructed by the conference that on assuming office, whether with or without power, they should immediately promulgate definite Socialist legislation, and that the party should stand or fall in the House of Commons on the principles in which it had faith. Mr. Henderson protested energetically against the resolution, on the ground that it was a profound mistake in this way to tie the hands of a Labour Government. His objections, however, were over-ruled, and the motion was carried by a large majority.

Soon after the conference, Mr. Henderson resigned his position as Leader of the Labour Party—not on account of the proceedings of the conference, but because he regarded his prospects of re-entering Parliament as " rather remote," and also to relieve himself from pressure of work. His place as leader of the party was taken by Mr. Lansbury.

The annual conference of the Conservative Party was also held on October 6 and 7 at Blackpool. On the motion of Sir H. P. Croft, the leader of the extreme protectionist wing in the party, the delegates congratulated the Government on the success of the Ottawa Conference, and recorded their view that the agreements there concluded advanced the cause of Imperial economic unity and would result in substantial and increasing advantages to British industry and agriculture. On the question of India the conference did not show itself so favourably disposed to the Government. On behalf of Mr. Churchill—who was prevented by illness from attending the conference—a resolution was brought forward stating that the attempt to force a democratic system upon a great and mainly primitive and illiterate electorate would conduce neither to Indian nor to British welfare. Any doubts as to the purpose of the resolution were removed by Lord Lloyd, Mr. Churchill's associate in Indian matters, who expressly stated that it was meant as a warning against the Government's policy. On behalf of the Government, Sir S. Hoare, the Secretary

for India, appealed to the conference not to pass a resolution which would make the task of the Government in India
more difficult than it need be, and he promised that no step
would be taken before it had borne the full light of comment and
criticism, both in Parliament and outside. From the reception
given to the various speeches, there could be little doubt that
the feeling of the conference was in favour of the resolution, but
out of deference to the Minister it passed an amendment which,
without supporting the Government, at least implied no censure
on it. The conference also urged the Government to tax foreign
imported meat and to lower the beer tax.

The conference did not fail to discuss the subject of economy,
and passed a resolution demanding drastic reductions in public
expenditure. Mr. Chamberlain attended the debate on this subject, and, while dwelling on the savings already effected by the
Government, promised that further economies would be made
from time to time with the least possible disturbance of national
efficiency. After the conference, Mr. Baldwin delivered an
address to a mass meeting in which he emphasised the importance
and necessity of a strong and stable Executive for democratic
government, and claimed that the National Government ensured
that form of Executive. He declared that the storm which raged
a year before was not yet over, and that, having undertaken
to stick to the Prime Minister till the sky was clear, he would
stick to him. It was, he held, still the duty of the Tory Party
to carry on in the letter and the spirit their part of the National
Government.

A new phase in the Anglo-Irish dispute was opened when at
the beginning of October Mr. de Valera, who was then at Geneva
presiding over the Assembly of the League of Nations, wrote
to Mr. Thomas suggesting that on his way back to Ireland he
should meet representatives of the British Government in order
to discuss the possibility of reopening negotiations on the
questions at issue between the two countries. Mr. Thomas
accepted the offer with alacrity, and the interview duly took place
on October 5. It was arranged that a delegation should come
from the Free State in ten days' time to London to discuss the
land annuities and other subjects of dispute. As Mr. de Valera
had taken the initiative in opening the negotiations, hopes were
widely entertained that he was now prepared to modify his
attitude and that progress would be made towards a settlement.

These hopes were doomed to disappointment. Mr. de Valera,
it is true, came to London on October 13, with some of his Ministers,
and on the next day began to confer with Mr. Thomas and other
British Ministers on the subject of the land annuities. Instead,
however, of moderating his demands as had been expected, he
simply restated them in an even more peremptory form than
before ; among other things, he demanded compensation for the

F

over-taxation of Ireland since the Act of Union in 1801. The
British Ministers listened to him with courtesy and patience,
and made a show of continuing the negotiations for a couple of
days. They were convinced, however, almost from the outset
that the proceedings were little more than a waste of time.
Without troubling, therefore, to open any other question they
broke off the discussions, leaving matters *in statu quo.*

By this time a great change had been made in the composition of the Government as a result of Liberal dislike of the
Ottawa Agreements. Any hopes entertained in 'Government
circles that the Liberals as a body would accept the *fait accompli*
were dispelled by a pronouncement made on September 11 by Mr.
Ramsay Muir, the Chairman of the National Liberal Federation,
that the agreements ought to be opposed tooth and nail, for three
reasons : first, because Liberals objected to food taxes ; secondly,
because they insisted on the power of regulating their own taxes
and not putting them under the control of the Dominions ; and
thirdly, because the agreements were a barrier to the progress
of the world and endangered the friendship on which the British
Empire rested. Mr. Muir's appeal found a ready response in
Liberal quarters, and the Liberal Press commenced to agitate
strongly for the resignation of the Liberal members of the
Government. A meeting of the National Liberal Federation,
on September 21, utterly condemned the Ottawa Agreements,
and while not in any way trying to force the hand of the Liberal
Ministers, plainly intimated that it would welcome their resignation
from the Government.

The Ottawa Agreements were fully discussed by the Cabinet
at a long meeting on August 27, presided over by the Prime
Minister. No dissentient voice was raised against the proposals,
though Sir Herbert Samuel and his Free Trade colleagues were
present. The only question considered was how to get them
through Parliament. It was necessary to ratify them before
November 15, the date when the existing preferences would
lapse. As many of them would entail fresh legislation, the
question was raised whether Parliament should not be convened
earlier than October 27, the date originally fixed, in order to
ensure that there would be sufficient time. After some discussion, the matter was left to the discretion of the Prime
Minister ; and a fortnight later it was announced that Parliament
would be summoned to meet on October 18.

Whether as a result of pressure from their supporters or of
more mature reflection, Sir Herbert Samuel and his associates
soon began to doubt whether the Ottawa arrangements could be
brought under the cover of the " agreement to differ." After
consulting with his Free Trade colleagues in the Government
and with other prominent Liberals, Sir Herbert early in September
had submitted to the Prime Minister proposals for certain modi-

fications in the Ottawa Agreements. These Mr. MacDonald found himself quite unable to accept, anxious as he was to avoid a split in the Cabinet. Sir Herbert and his colleagues thereupon began seriously to contemplate the possibility of resignation, a step to which they were strongly urged by the Liberal Press, while the voices raised against it were feeble by comparison. They decided, however, to reserve their ultimate decision till the next meeting of the Cabinet, which was fixed for September 28, the earliest date at which it was possible to obtain a full meeting. Sir Herbert was present at the meeting of the National Liberal Federation on September 21, and gave an account of the steps he had taken, but he still kept his counsel, nor was any direct pressure brought to bear upon him by the meeting. For some days, however, before September 28, it was generally regarded as a foregone conclusion that he and several other Ministers would resign, and Mr. MacDonald made active preparations to fill their places.

The fateful Cabinet meeting of September 28 brought no surprises. Sir Herbert Samuel duly handed in his resignation, and his example was followed by nine other Ministers. Two of these were of Cabinet rank, *viz.*, Lord Snowden and Sir Archibald Sinclair (the fourth Free Trader in the Cabinet, Sir Donald Maclean, had died in June, and his place as Minister of Education had been filled by Lord Irwin, a Conservative). The principal junior Ministers who resigned were Lord Lothian, Under-Secretary for India, and Mr. Isaac Foot, Minister for Mines.

At the same time that they handed in their resignations, the Liberal Ministers sent a joint letter to the Prime Minister justifying the step they were taking. It was their view that, after the National Government had accomplished the most urgent tasks for which it was elected—to balance the Budget, to stop borrowing for unemployment allowances, to save the pound and to re-establish the national credit—its next task should have been to assist by every possible effort in freeing the world from the network of tariffs, quotas, and all kinds of restrictions which were hindering a return to prosperity. Instead, the Government had built up an immense and intricate system of similar restrictions, intended to be lasting. The measures now about to be taken as a result of the Ottawa Agreements were in their opinion open to even graver objections than the earlier measures. On the other hand, while undoubtedly there were still grave difficulties facing the country both at home and abroad, it would not be true to say that there was now any acute and imminent danger such as existed a year before, and even, though in a less degree, eight months before. " We do not therefore," they went on, " consider that there is any longer an overriding national duty to maintain the present political combination notwithstanding the fundamental differences on great issues which divide us." At the same time they undertook to give full support to the Government in carrying into effect its general policy in regard to India, in fulfilling the obligations of the Covenant of the League of Nations and the Pact of Paris, and in promoting international disarmament.

Lord Snowden, as a member of the National Labour Party, sent in his own letter of resignation, similar in tenor to that of the Liberals, but couched in more vigorous language and striking a more personal note. His arguments were devastating. He had, he said, taken his part in forming the National Government, and so sacrificed the associations of a political lifetime, on the assurance given by the Prime Minister and Mr. Baldwin that such a Government would work only in the national interests and would not be used for party purposes and policy. He was still prepared to support a National Government which adhered to those conditions. But for some time past it had become increasingly clear that the protectionist section in the Government and the House of Commons were determined to carry through a full protectionist policy, using them as their instruments. The Ottawa Agreements he denounced as a policy of national humiliation and bondage in which Free Traders could not be expected to acquiesce even passively. The " agreement to differ " did not meet the situation, as, if he were to yield now, he would be inescapably committed to the support of the whole future policy of the Government. Therefore he went at once.

Among those who aligned themselves with Sir Herbert Samuel in this controversy were the three " elder statesmen " of the Liberal Party—Lord Crewe, Lord Reading, and Viscount Grey of Fallodon. In a letter issued to the Press on September 29, they said that they regarded his retirement and that of his Free Trade colleagues from the Government as inevitable, and the only honourable course open to them. The difference now was too great to be covered by the " agreement to differ " which served its purpose some months before. They hoped, however, that there would still be harmony on other questions.

The Prime Minister, on his side, on behalf of himself and his National Labour colleagues, also issued a statement, in which he said that the work they had taken up twelve months before was not yet finished, and could not be finished until, one way or another, there was a Reparation and Debt settlement and a World Economic Conference had been held. They would therefore go on until those things were done, and they made the same appeal to the electors as they had done twelve months before, maintaining that the nation needed a non-party Government, and that purely party considerations would weaken Britain's influence in the world, and would be a blow to the movements for world recovery. The members of the Liberal National Group also reaffirmed their belief that the continued existence of the National Government

was vital in face of the grave problems with which Britain and the
world were confronted. The National Labour members of both
Houses of Parliament also expressed their unabated confidence in
Mr. MacDonald's leadership and their determination to support
the Government in the future, as in the past. Thus the Government continued to command such support as justified its title of
" national," though in many quarters it was held that it was in
reality overwhelmingly Conservative in character, and the Liberal
secession did not make Mr. MacDonald's position untenable, as it
might have done had it taken place a few months earlier.

The gaps left by the resignations were filled by Mr. MacDonald
with great expedition, and with a minimum of disturbance to
existing arrangements. Sir Herbert Samuel's place at the Home
Office was taken by Sir John Gilmour, the Minister of Agriculture,
who was himself succeeded by Major Walter Elliot, the Financial
Secretary to the Treasury. Mr. Baldwin took over the office of
Lord Privy Seal, combining it with the one he already held, without increase of salary. The post of Secretary of State for Scotland,
vacated by Sir A. Sinclair, was given to Sir Godfrey Collins, a
National Liberal. As a result of these changes, the number of
Cabinet Ministers was reduced from 20 to 19, and was composed
of 13 Conservatives, 3 National Labour members, and 3 National
Liberals. In the appointments to the junior posts, which involved
a good deal of reshuffling, the number of National Liberals was
increased from two to five—a fact which gave rise to no little
comment. The opportunity was also taken at the same time, on
grounds of economy, to suppress the post of Under-Secretary of
Pensions.

The concessions offered to Britain by the Dominions under the
Ottawa Agreements were made public on October 12. They
hardly bore out the statements made by some of the delegates,
that the Dominions had made important tariff reductions in favour
of Great Britain. What they had done in perhaps the majority of
cases, was to increase the duties on imports from countries outside
the British Empire, and so establish a preference in favour of Britain.
While such a procedure might give advantages to British trade,
from the Free Trade point of view it was highly unsatisfactory.

On October 17, the day before Parliament was due to meet,
Mr. MacDonald was entertained by the National Labour Party to
a luncheon at which all the members of the Cabinet were present
save one or two who were not in London. Mr. MacDonald took
the opportunity of affirming his determination to continue the all-
party national effort until the country had emerged from its
present condition. He referred humorously to the sentence of
" excommunication " passed on him—along with Lord Snowden
and Mr. Thomas—at the recent conference of the Labour Party,
and declared that he had no intention whatever of seeking for
readmission. He deplored the action of Sir Herbert Samuel and

his colleagues in leaving the Government, as it was tantamount to a declaration that the time had now come to stop trying to make a national effort and to go back to party politics. Whatever others might do, those who belonged to the National Labour section would not desert the plough until the furrow was completed.

The House of Commons met on October 18, and lost no time in getting to grips with the Ottawa resolutions. The first debate on the subject took place on a resolution brought forward in Committee by the Chancellor of the Exchequer to give effect to the agreements. Mr. Chamberlain devoted himself to considering the question whether the agreements as a whole presented a result which it was desirable for the House to approve. While pointing out that they had brought back from Ottawa preferences which in course of time and even immediately would prove of substantial benefit to British industry, he asked them to judge of the results of Ottawa rather by the broad tendencies of the agreement. Supreme among these he reckoned the effect it would have in preserving the unity of the British Empire. For many years there had been a tendency for the constituent parts of the Empire to drift apart, as witnessed by the extent to which Canada had become dependent on American finance, and by the South African trade agreement with Germany. He was confident that the Ottawa Agreements had stopped that drift, and by instituting closer trading relations between the different parts of the Empire had opened up a prospect of attaining a new strength and new security for all the countries of the Empire.

The resolution was opposed by Mr. Lansbury on behalf of the Labour Party and by Sir H. Samuel on behalf of the Liberals. The former laid stress on the fact that Mr. Chamberlain had failed to specify any branch of employment which would benefit by the agreements, and he could see no prospect in them of new work for the people. Sir Herbert Samuel dwelt on the constitutional impropriety of imposing what was virtually taxation for a period of five years, and moved an amendment that the duties should be terminable at six months' notice.

The Prime Minister also took part in the debate, now for the first time declaring himself openly in support of the agreements. He criticised the seceding Ministers with some asperity, pointing out that the National Government when it went to the country had expressly reserved to itself the right to bring in protective duties should it find them advisable after due study and consideration. He admitted that there might have been grounds against holding the Ottawa Conference in the first instance, but once it had been decided upon it could not possibly be allowed to fail. He was willing to face the International Economic Conference with the Ottawa Agreements, but failure at Ottawa would have made it impossible to do this. The speech was cheered enthusiastically by the Ministerialists.

Later in the debate, Sir John Simon replied to Sir Herbert
Samuel on the constitutional issue. He had, he said, been
assured both by the Foreign Office and the Board of Trade that
it was the usual practice for the Government to make commercial
treaties, even when imposing duties, having validity for a number
of years. He recalled the fact that in 1860 Conservative members
had opposed Cobden's Anglo-French Treaty on precisely the same
grounds as those now brought forward by the Liberals, and they
had been overruled. The distinction which Sir Herbert Samuel
tried to draw between imposing duties and taking them off he
declared to be quite unknown to the Constitution.

In the division the voting followed strictly party lines, the
Liberals and Labour members voting solidly against the resolution
and the other groups for. The resolution was passed by 451
votes to 84.

One of the undertakings given by the British delegates at
Ottawa was to prohibit the importation into England of goods
which, being produced under sweating conditions, could be sold so
cheaply as to render the preferences accorded to the Dominions
of no avail. This stipulation was avowedly aimed at Russia, and,
as a first step towards making it effective, the Government on
October 17, denounced at six months' date the temporary commercial agreement made with the Soviet Government on April 16,
1930. At the same time, however, the Government declared that
it was anxious for the furtherance of trade with Soviet Russia,
and was prepared to enter into a discussion for the promotion
of this end at the earliest moment. When questioned on the
subject in Parliament on the next day, Mr. Thomas stated that
the Government had come to their decision on two grounds. One
was that, having entered into an obligation to give preferences
within the British Commonwealth, they must see that no country
should frustrate that object by dumping sweated goods ; and the
other was that the Government, having given that intimation to
the Dominions at Ottawa, desired also to make it clear that it
need not interfere with legitimate and common-sense trading
agreements between the two countries.

The Ottawa Agreements Bill proper was brought before the
House of Commons for its second reading on October 26, by Mr.
Thomas. In the course of the debate, Mr. Runciman for the first
time justified his support of the agreements, which Free Traders
had found not a little bewildering. He treated them purely as
a business transaction, from which he expected that Britain
would derive considerable benefit. While, however, he laid stress
on the fact that Canada and New Zealand were reducing many of
their duties, he made no reference to the fact that England was
about to do the opposite. That the agreements crippled their
action in regard to foreign treaties he would not admit for a
moment ; so far from being hampered, the Government had in

fact entered into and were carrying on negotiations for trade agreements with foreign countries.

The Government majority on the second reading was 347. In the Committee debates, a determined effort was made by the Opposition, on November 1, to nullify the clauses which were aimed at Russia. They proposed among other things that the " State action " against which the Imperial preferences were to be secured should not include " economies effected in production by reason of the elimination of rent, interest on capital, and other overhead charges, but should be applied to subsidies, bonuses, or remissions of taxation." To this Mr. Hore-Belisha replied that the correct definition of " State action " was any action which frustrated the Ottawa Agreements, whether taken by Russia or any other country. The Bill eventually passed through Committee without alteration, and on November 3 the third reading was carried by a majority of 348.

The House of Lords held a preliminary discussion on Ottawa on October 26, in the course of which Lord Hailsham maintained that the conference had been a " great success." This idea was vigorously controverted by Lord Snowden in the debate on the second reading on November 9. He declared roundly that the Dominions had come to the conference for what they could get, and in particular for what they could get from the Mother Country, and that the conference would have broken up but for the concessions of Great Britain in the matter of food taxes, which had been expressly ruled out after the conference of 1930. He laughed to scorn the idea that the Dominions had become less protectionist, and pointed out that foreign countries had sought to make reciprocal trade agreements with Britain even before Ottawa. Finally, to refute Lord Hailsham's contention that they had done " great things," Lord Snowden triumphantly quoted the frank confession of Mr. Baldwin in the House of Commons a few days before that if asked what they had got out of it all, he was bound to answer " I do not know."

Lord Snowden's tirade was not calculated to shake the Ministerialists in their support of the Bill, and the result in the House of Lords was a foregone conclusion, as in the Lower House. The Bill passed its third reading on November 15, and on the same day received the royal assent. Immediately afterwards the Treasury issued an Order giving effect to the Act, so that the existing preferences were continued and most of the new ones came into force within twenty-four hours.

At the beginning of September, the British Government was consulted by the French Government on the claim just put forward by Germany for " equality of status " in the matter of armaments. The Government gave its views in a statement published on September 18. It deplored the raising of a political controversy of such magnitude at a moment when attention and energy should be concentrated on efforts to restore the productive and commercial prosperity of the world ; and declared that whatever Germany might say, Part V. of the Treaty of Versailles was still binding, and could only cease to be binding by agreement. Nevertheless, it recognised the justice of the German contention that the limitation of Germany's armaments contained in the treaty was intended to be, and announced to be, the precursor of a general limitation by others. It deprecated, however, any attempt on Germany's part to re-arm, and pointed out that the purpose of the Disarmament Conference was to frame a Convention which would create equality of status by subjecting the armaments of every country to the same kind of control.

The withdrawal of Germany shortly afterwards from the Disarmament Conference at Geneva was regarded by the British Government as a great blow to the cause of peace, and it considered that no efforts should be spared to bring Germany back to the conference. With this end in view, it entered into communication with the Governments of France, Germany, and Italy in order to ascertain whether they would consent to exchange views on the difficulties which had arisen from the withdrawal of Germany from the conference, suggesting London as a meeting-place. Italy declared herself willing, but difficulties were raised by France and Germany, especially the former. As a result, instead of the conference being held on October 11, as Mr. MacDonald had desired, M. Herriot, the French Premier, came over to London on October 12 to discuss matters with Mr. MacDonald, and see if the French objections to the proposed conference could not be removed. The conversations, which lasted two days, produced the desired effect, and on October 14 it was announced that the French and British Ministers were agreed in considering that the proposed Four-Power Conference should take place, and that the best place for it would be Geneva.

Taking advantage of the continued cheapness of money, the Government on November 1 floated a loan of 300,000,000*l.* for the purpose of repaying 165,000,000*l.* of unconverted War Loan and various other debts. The loan was at 3 per cent., issued at 97, and repayable between 1948 and 1953. A month earlier the Government had raised a loan of 150,000,000*l.* at 2 per cent., repayable in five years, for a similar purpose. Both loans were over-subscribed almost immediately. This was the fifth conversion operation undertaken in the course of the year, and it brought the total amount of saving in interest up to about 40,000,000*l.* Besides bringing relief to the Treasury, the success of the loans had an excellent psychological effect on the Stock Exchange and the public, and greatly strengthened the position of the Government.

On November 2 Lord Ponsonby in the House of Lords called the attention of the Government to the Lytton Report on

Manchuria, and after speaking of it in terms of high praise, urged them to press it upon the acceptance of the League of Nations. He was supported by Lord Lothian and Lord Cecil, and Lord Lytton himself also expressed the hope that the Foreign Secretary would take it as his brief at Geneva. Lord Hailsham, in reply, expressed his admiration and that of the Government for the report, but deprecated the request that they should define their attitude to it or to any of its proposals before it had been considered by the Council of the League of Nations. Their object at Geneva, he said, would not be to focus attention on their own initiative, but to find a policy which might fairly be described as that of the League as a whole.

One effect of the ratification of the Ottawa Agreements was to free the hands of the Government to open tariff negotiations with foreign countries (*vide* p. 7). The Scandinavian countries and the Argentine had expressed a desire for such discussions some time before, but the Government had asked them to wait till the Ottawa Conference was over. So soon as it knew where it stood with the Dominions, it invited these countries to enter into conversations on tariff matters, and soon afterwards they all sent representatives to London for the purpose.

CHAPTER IV.

THE AMERICAN DEBT PAYMENT.

WHATEVER might be the benefits in store for Great Britain from the Ottawa Agreements, it was certain that they would not accrue till some time had elapsed. Meanwhile two important classes of the population were crying out for immediate relief. A vast army of unemployed was facing the approach of winter with grave apprehension, and as a result of enforced idleness was drifting into an ever more hopeless and helpless condition. And a large number of farmers, after struggling with adversity for a succession of years, now found themselves reduced to ruin by the sharp decline in prices which had taken place in the summer. The Government realised its obligation to take action on behalf of both these classes ; but at the same time it had to take into consideration the taxpayer, who, while resigned to bearing a little longer his existing burdens, was insistent that they should on no account be made still heavier.

The discontent of the unemployed was aggravated by the means test, which they alleged was administered in many places in such a way as to degrade them to the rank of paupers. Their resentment against this measure gathered strength during the summer and ultimately found vent in outbreaks of violence at

various places.   These culminated in a serious riot at Birkenhead
on September 17, for the suppression of which police had to be
called in from Liverpool ; in fact peace was not restored until
the local authorities had promised to attend to the grievances
of the unemployed.   Police inquiries showed the disturbances
to have been instigated in every case by a body calling itself
the National Unemployed Workers' Movement, a Communist
organisation in close touch with Moscow.   On October 18 the
Movement organised a demonstration in South London which
came into conflict with the police, and in the struggle which ensued
thirteen demonstrators and thirty-seven police were injured.

In their protests against the means test the unemployed had
the support of a number of local authorities, especially in mining
districts.   In two places, Durham and Rotherham, the Public
Assistance Committees openly set the law at defiance and refused
to administer the test ; and in others they did so under protest.
The representations of the Government had little effect upon the
recalcitrant bodies, and at Durham the Minister of Labour
eventually found himself obliged to supersede the Public Assistance Committee by officials from the Ministry.

On October 19 Mr. Lansbury called attention in Parliament
to the demonstration which had taken place in South London
on the previous day, and charged the police with having used
high-handed methods on various occasions.   He also dwelt on
the fact that after the trouble at Birkenhead a great concession
had been made to the unemployed and that the same thing had
happened at Belfast.   He warned the Government of the danger
of allowing an idea to grow up that concessions could be extorted
by force and rioting, and urged them, if they were going to do
anything for the unemployed, to act at once on their own initiative.

The Home Secretary, in a lengthy statement, maintained that
the police had always shown great self-restraint, and charged the
National Unemployed Workers' Movement with deliberately
fomenting trouble.   The Prime Minister admitted that the
policy of making concessions after disorder instead of before
was a thoroughly bad one, and in answer to an appeal from Sir
S. Cripps, promised that the Government would very quickly
make a statement on the subject of the means test.   Meanwhile
he appealed to Labour members not to find excuses for rioting
or to facilitate matters for those whose object was not to help
the unemployed but to create trouble.

The *tour de force* of the National Unemployed Workers'
Movement was to organise a demonstration of " hunger marchers "
from all parts of the country who were to meet in London on
October 27—the day originally fixed for the opening of Parliament—and then proceed in a body to the House of Commons
and protest against the means test.   The " marchers " found
numerous sympathisers in most of the towns through which they

passed, and duly arrived in London, by no means hungry, on the date fixed. As had been anticipated, before long they came into conflict with the police, with the result that several persons were injured and some damage was done to property in the neighbourhood of Hyde Park—mostly, however, by London roughs, and not by "marchers." The Home Secretary gave an account of the affair the next day in Parliament, but the Labour leaders did not see fit to raise a debate on the subject. After spending a few days in London and causing a number of minor disturbances, the "marchers" returned to their homes by train. Their attempt to invade the House of Commons proved a fiasco. Shortly afterwards the two principal organisers of the "march" were brought to trial, and sentenced to terms of imprisonment for inciting to disturbance.

On October 25 the Labour Party moved a vote of censure on the Government for its economic policy in general and for its imposition of the means test in particular. The Prime Minister in defending the Government reminded Mr. Lansbury that he also had declared himself against giving State money to those who had means to maintain themselves ; but he admitted that the administration of the means test might be improved. In regard to the general economic situation he pointed out that under the National Government the increase in unemployment had been far less than under the Labour Government which preceded it, and that the cost of living had actually gone down a couple of points and was now far lower than it had been three years before. Sir Herbert Samuel stated that he and his followers would oppose the motion, as they had no desire for a change of Government, though they did demand from this Government resolute and effective action. Mr. Lloyd George, on the other hand, supported the motion, on the ground that the Government had no constructive policy for dealing with unemployment. The vote of censure was eventually rejected by 462 votes to 55.

Although this victory was decisive enough, the Government could not possibly regard it as an endorsement of their handling of the unemployment problem. The Prime Minister therefore readily accepted a suggestion of the Leader of the Opposition that there should be a non-party debate on this subject in which members should pool their ideas with the single object of assisting the Government. The debate began on November 4 and was continued through three days, the House of Commons on this occasion making its nearest approach to becoming the "Council of State" once visualised by Mr. MacDonald. Mr. Lansbury opened with a temperate speech on a motion that the House would welcome "all proper measures for dealing with unemployment," which he described as a plague or disease the victims of which they had to help. He urged the Government to hasten the Economic World Conference, and to reconsider the

question of public works, and by means of national planning
to prevent districts from becoming derelict. Naturally, he said,
his party desired that the remedy should be found on Socialist
lines, but he called upon the Government to " reorganise in any
way so long as they did reorganise."

The Minister of Labour, in order to put the House in a position
to judge the value of any proposals that might be laid before it,
gave a comprehensive survey of the state of unemployment and
of the schemes which had been suggested for combating unemployment. Of these he enumerated no less than seventeen,
of which the principal were relief works, emigration, and systematic short time. Examining these three in detail, he showed
that they were all inadequate, and might indeed do more harm
than good. The late Labour Government at the cost of a vast
expenditure had found work for 220,000 men during a period
when the number of unemployed rose by a million and a half,
leaving a great burden to be borne by national and local revenue
during the next thirty or forty years. Emigration on a large
scale was not to be thought of till the Dominions themselves were
more prosperous and able to absorb immigrants. A limitation
of the working week to forty hours without reduction of wages
could only be brought about by international action of which
there was little prospect at present. Thus in dealing with the
positive side of the question the Minister was not encouraging.
On the other hand, he cautioned the House against taking too
gloomy a view of the situation. The number of persons in
employment, after declining considerably between 1929 and 1931,
had during the past twelve months remained practically stationary.
In the previous period there had been an increase in unemployment practically every industry, but during the past twelve
months there had been a decrease in the great majority, including
some of the most important, the chief exceptions being coal,
the building trades, public works, contracting, and local government services. England was now in a far less unfavourable
position in the matter of unemployment than other countries,
such as the United States, France, Germany, and Belgium, where,
up to 1929, there had been no unemployment. The main reason
for the difference, he conceived, was that none of these countries
had balanced its Budget. The Government therefore had
rendered a supreme service to the country and the working-
classes by balancing the Budget and putting the finances on a
sound basis.

On the second day of the debate (November 7), the Prime
Minister indicated, not indeed an actual policy from the side of the
Government, but the manner in which it was approaching the problem. He began by ruling out definitely an extension of public relief
works. This method, he said, had been given the fullest possible
trial by the late Labour Government, and its results had been

disappointing, since for the expenditure of every million pounds they had been able to keep not more than 4,000 men in work. In any case the country could no longer afford to spend money on schemes the permanent value of which was doubtful. The one course open to them, he thought, was to concentrate all their powers of thought upon finding out how they could stimulate trade, so that the demand for labour would be a natural demand. That was the only hope he could hold out for the unemployed. Their success, he thought, would depend largely on the result of the International Economic Conference, because the economic troubles of this country could not be separated from those of the world in general. He was hoping that the preparatory work of the conference would be completed by Christmas, and the British Government at any rate would be no party to unnecessary delay.

In any scheme for relieving unemployment, Mr. MacDonald continued, land would have to play a much greater part than hitherto. So far, it was true, land settlement had been a very expensive experiment, but they were learning from experience and securing far better results than formerly. He paid a tribute in this connexion to the work done by the Society of Friends, which he thought this generation could never adequately thank. In conclusion he declared that the winter would be a hard one, and he appealed to the great outside authorities and organisations who were in a position to give work to offer a generous helping hand.

The Prime Minister's speech did not make a favourable impression, and Mr. Lloyd George was generally felt to be hardly too severe in describing it as "full of confusion, hesitation, and bewilderment." Mr. George himself pinned his faith to the extension of small allotments. Other speakers advocated other remedies, such as slum clearance and inflation. Mr. Chamberlain, in summing up the debate, promised that the Government would consider and examine carefully all the suggestions made, not forgetting the lessons learnt from the experience of past years, and taking care that in trying to solve the problems of to-day they were not multiplying the problems of to-morrow. In the meantime he bade his hearers not to be too pessimistic about the present situation, because there were signs in many quarters that the effect of the measures they had taken was beginning to show itself—one sign being that the number of unemployed in October, a month which usually witnessed an increase, had fallen by nearly 250,000.

The long-awaited report of the Royal Commission on Unemployment Insurance appointed in 1930 was presented on November 7. It consisted, in fact, of two reports—a Majority Report signed by the Chairman and four other members, and a Minority Report signed by two members. The chief feature of the Majority Report was that it advocated the institution of a relief system side by side with that of insurance, so that henceforth insurance would be restricted to those who had paid contributions, and relief would be for those who had exhausted insurance benefit rights or who were in uninsured trades. The relief scheme was to be under the control of the Minister of Labour and to be administered by local authorities. The Poor Law would remain for persons not able-bodied and for persons able-bodied not satisfying the conditions of the assistance scheme or in need of disciplinary or deterrent treatment.

In regard to insurance, the report proposed that contributions should remain as at present, but that the principle of relating the period of benefit to the record of insurable employment over a recent period should be restored. It proposed further that the age of entry into insurance should be made to correspond with the school-leaving age ; that the income limit of non-manual workers should be raised from 250*l.* to 350*l.* ; and that an earnings test should be instituted for workers employed less than a full week.

The chief features of the proposed relief scheme were that the recipient must not refuse an offer of suitable employment ; that assistance should be subject to proof of need, which should be judged after assessment of the needs of the household ; that the amount of relief must be definitely less than wages ; and that the whole of any homogeneous industrial area should as far as possible be treated on uniform principles.

The Majority Report also dealt at length with the vexed question of the means test. It proposed among other things that a proportion of the earnings of the applicant should be ignored, so as to preserve the inducement to work ; that a reasonable proportion of the earnings of other members of the household should also be excluded from the assessment of the household resources ; that no account should be taken of capital assets of less than 50*l.* ; that house property belonging to a member of the household should be treated as a capital asset ; that half the amount of disability pensions should be ignored, or more in special cases, and that a discretionary allowance should be made of the amount received as workmen's compensation.

For financing the new service the report proposed that for the first year the local authorities should levy a 4*d.* rate, and that the liability of the Exchequer, with the number of unemployed at 3,000,000, should be 58,000,000*l.* per annum, the Exchequer contribution to be distributed among local authorities in whose areas the cost should exceed the product of a 4*d.* rate. All the debt of the insurance fund (at present 115,000,000*l.*) should be transferred to a separate account and provision made to amortise it.

The Minority Report was signed by two Labour members of the Commission, and followed closely the lines laid down by the General Council of the Trade Union Congress in 1931 (*vide*

ANNUAL REGISTER, 1930, p. 41). It advocated higher benefits, was against the application of a means test, and rejected the idea of discriminating between insurance benefit and relief. It also favoured the extension of the insurance scheme to agriculture and domestic service. It gave no detailed estimate of the cost which would be involved by its proposals.

With this report before it, the Government had no longer any excuse for delaying its promised legislation with regard to the means test, and on November 9 the Minister of Labour did in fact submit to the House of Commons a money resolution which was meant to prepare the way for a new law on the subject. In this proposal the recommendations of the Commission were followed fairly closely. It was laid down that in estimating the means of an applicant for transitional benefit, wounds or disability pensions should be treated as if they were reduced by a half, and workmen's compensation payments as if they were reduced by a half ; that savings up to 25*l*. should be disregarded, and between 25*l*. and 300*l*. should be treated as equivalent to an income of 1*s*. for every 25*l*. ; and that the interest of any person in the house in which he resided should be disregarded. The same rules were also to be applied to applicants for Poor Law relief. The Minister explained that the allowances laid down were to be regarded as minima, and could be increased at the discretion of the Public Assistance Committees. He gave some striking instances of persons with good incomes applying for benefit, and maintained that the abuses which a means test was intended to prevent were even more flagrant than those dealt with by the Anomalies Act. The resolution was opposed by Mr. Greenwood on behalf of the Labour Party on the ground that the concessions were empty, but was eventually carried by 267 votes to 43.

In addition to retaining the means test the Government in the course of the session effected three other economies of importance. In September the Ministry of Education addressed a circular to all education authorities instructing them not to assign free places in secondary schools save to pupils whose parents could not afford to pay any fees, and also to raise the fees in certain cases. On October 24 the Government decided to make a further cut in the pay of the police, in accordance with the condition which had been laid down a year before, when part of the cut originally made was remitted. And on October 30 the Postmaster-General announced that, after consultation with the Chancellor of the Exchequer, he had decided to suspend the opera subsidy (*vide* ANNUAL REGISTER, 1930, p. 94) for the next year.

The proposal to reduce the number of free places in secondary schools was regarded in many quarters as a retrograde step in educational policy, and called forth vigorous protests. In the House of Lords on October 28, Lord Sanderson, a Labour Peer, declared that the circular would be regarded in many quarters as a class challenge and would be bitterly resented. The Minister of Education, in reply, denied that the circular would in any way make it more difficult for the children of poor parents to obtain secondary education. What it would do, he hoped, would be to rectify, to some extent at least, three features in the present arrangements which it was hard to justify—the fact that there was a substantial gap between payments made by parents and the average cost to public funds, that many children of comparatively well-to-do parents received free education, and that there was a surprising differentiation of fees and practice between adjacent and comparable districts. In addition it would effect a saving in the neighbourhood of 400,000*l.* a year, and so appreciably lighten the burden of taxpayers and ratepayers.

Lord Irwin's defence did not satisfy his critics, and pressure was brought to bear on him both in Parliament and without to withdraw the circular, but without success. As a last resort, the Opposition on November 16 brought forward a motion in the House of Commons condemning the circular on the ground that it sought to raise or restore secondary school fees, restrict the number of free places, and introduce a harsh means test. On behalf of the Board of Education it was pointed out that the object of the new plan was to secure payment from parents who could afford to pay and relieve those who could not, and it was therefore preferable to the existing haphazard, confused and inequitable system. The circular was in fact a step in the right direction. In the debate which ensued the motion received a certain amount of support from Liberal and Unionist speakers, but in the division it was negatived by 353 votes to 53.

The plight of agriculture after the summer constituted a national problem hardly less grave than that of unemployment. In the middle of September the president of the National Farmers' Union addressed a letter to the Prime Minister in which he pointed out that the collapse in the prices of several major agricultural commodities during previous weeks had created an extremely serious position for the industry, and pressed for some action to alleviate the immediate financial straits of the farmers, who on a declining income had to pay wages fixed by statute. The Government was unwilling to reduce the level of wages, but it was in hopes that the meat quota scheme drawn up at Ottawa would raise the prices of livestock, which was the most urgent requirement for the farmers. In the course of the debates on the Ottawa Agreements, however, the scheme was criticised by a number of Ministerialists, especially Mr. Amery, as being quite inadequate for the needs of the British farming industry.

As prices continued to fall, on November 1 a deputation from the Parliamentary Agricultural Committee, including representatives of all the parties supporting the Government,

G

waited on the Prime Minister to urge further action. The deputation pointed out that owing to the fall in livestock prices the plight of the British farmers was desperate, and that while the Government's scheme might be commendable as a long-term policy, some immediate action was needed to tide the agricultural industry over the present emergency. The Government recognised the force of these representations, but much to the disappointment of the deputation did not announce any definite step.

A large number of Conservatives would have liked to see a duty of 4d. per pound imposed on all meat imports, with a preference of 2d. to the Dominions. To this plan, however, Mr. Runciman was known to be inflexibly opposed, and in deference to him the Cabinet did not so much as consider it. In order to attain the object in view, this Minister adopted a method more in consonance with his fiscal opinions. He entered into negotiations with representatives of various countries for the purpose of bringing about a voluntary curtailment of meat imports on the part of foreign and Dominion producers. These efforts soon met with a considerable degree of success. In the course of the debate on unemployment on November 7, the Minister of Agriculture was able to inform the House of Commons that on that morning the importers from the River Plate had consented to put into effect at once a cut of 20 per cent. in the supplies of mutton and lamb, and of 10 per cent. in those of chilled beef, and a similar promise was made the next day on behalf of the importers from Australia and New Zealand. Soon after similar concessions were made by the countries which exported large quantities of bacon and ham to England, notably Holland, Denmark, Sweden, and Latvia. The arrangements were made in the first instance for a period of two months.

The withdrawal of Germany from the Disarmament Conference and the Lytton Report on Manchuria caused a great perturbation of public opinion in England, and led to renewed pressure being brought upon the Government to take active steps in the cause of peace and disarmament. The most noteworthy manifestation of this feeling was a deputation representing the Protestant Churches and led by the Archbishop of Canterbury which waited on the Prime Minister and Sir John Simon on October 20. The purpose of the deputation was first to express the very great disappointment of Christian people in the country at the lack of progress made at the Disarmament Conference, and then to urge that when the Conference resumed, the British Government should immediately declare a definite policy of disarmament, based upon equality of status among all members of the League of Nations.

The Archbishop said that the deputation represented a very great volume of Christian public opinion throughout the country ; he had rarely known any subject which had roused such unanimity

and depth and earnestness of conviction as disarmament. They
were there to express deep and growing concern at the international situation and the present position of the Disarmament
Conference. Their main concern was with the moral issues
involved. They felt a moral obligation that the promise given
by the Allied Powers after the war should be fulfilled, and they
thought it would be morally wrong to acquiesce in anything less
than a wide and general reduction of armaments. The Government would have their enthusiastic support in fulfilling their
declared willingness to give to Germany a place of equality among
other nations, and in making disarmament and not re-armament
the keystone of their policy ; and also of course in maintaining
as close a co-operation as possible with the United States. They
believed that the British Government was in a position to give
a really effective lead, and they confidently hoped for such a lead
and prayed for its success.

Sir John Simon in reply declared that the deputation was
very valuable for the Government, because it came avowedly
to urge a moral duty and to emphasise a moral claim, and that
aspect of disarmament was one which was always present to
Ministers' minds. The proof was that the real object of his
recent Note, which had been greatly misunderstood in many
quarters, was to insist that Germany's claim upon the consideration of other nations was essentially a claim in the moral
and not in the legal sphere. He admitted that it was not sufficient merely to dwell upon what England had already done
since the war in the name of disarmament, but on the other hand,
he warned his hearers that to belittle that achievement might
actually damp the desire of the British people for more disarmament. He went on to complain that Britain was sometimes
unfairly criticised from Geneva, instancing the fact that he
himself had been represented in the Swiss Press as dismissing
President Hoover's disarmament proposals with somewhat scant
courtesy, whereas he had in fact laid stress from the outset on
their profound importance.

The Prime Minister also cautioned the deputation not to be
too impatient for results. He pointed out that if the peace-
maker wanted to do his job properly he had to consider other
issues besides the moral ; and consequently he himself had to
proceed more slowly than perhaps he would like. If they had
been successful in securing co-operation with America, it was
because they had done their work patiently and without parade.
There was, however, a danger that the politician might lose himself in matters of detail, and therefore he hoped that the Churches
would continue to exercise pressure upon them and to keep before
their eyes the " big thing."

Soon afterwards (November 3) the Prime Minister and Sir
John Simon received a deputation from the General Council of

the Trade Union Congress and certain affiliated unions which came to draw their attention to the resolution on disarmament passed by the Trade Union Congress in September. This contained three demands—the application to land, naval, and air armaments of the proposals of President Hoover; a drastic reduction of expenditure on armaments; and a strict international control of the manufacture and sale of armaments. The deputation expressed disquiet at the slow progress of the Disarmament Conference, and called attention to the difficult position in which this placed the trade unionists of Germany, who were adamant against the re-armament of that country. The Prime Minister in reply informed the deputation that they were now negotiating with the American authorities a settlement which they hoped would ultimately become general. With regard to the manufacture and sale of arms, he promised to bring the views of the deputation to the notice of those dealing with the subject at Geneva.

A few days later Major Attlee, on behalf of the Labour Party, brought forward a motion in the House of Commons calling on the Government to work for reduction of armaments on the basis of equality of status for all nations, and to support the League of Nations by upholding the finding of the Lytton Commission. He charged the Government with having been weak and evasive over the Manchurian question, and " unhelpful, obstructive, and pettifogging " in regard to disarmament. In spite of these harsh epithets, Sir John Simon refused to regard the resolution as a vote of censure, saying that, subject to certain reservations, it was couched in terms which would appeal to the whole House. With regard to Manchuria, he said it would be difficult to praise the Lytton Report too highly, but he pointed out that Japan had promised to submit her observations upon it, and it would be unfair to take any action till these had been received. Dealing with the question of equality of status for Germany, he said that Britain's desire was to see a Disarmament Convention framed which would meet that claim. If any hesitation had been shown in working for that end, it proceeded not from any desire to inflict upon Germany permanent inferiority of status, but from anxiety as to the use which might be made of the new situation and from fear of the resulting dangers to the tranquillity of Europe. To remove that anxiety, they suggested that, side by side with the fair meeting of Germany's claim, the European States should join in a solemn affirmation that they would not in any circumstances attempt to resolve any present or future differences between them by resort to force. If some such assurance were given, they would advocate that the Article of Part V. of the Treaty of Versailles which at present limited Germany's arms and armed forces should be superseded by a new Disarmament Convention which should include both Germany and other nations;

also that the new limitations to be applied to Germany should last for the same period and should be subject to the same methods of revision as those of other countries. They were also willing to see embodied in the new Convention the principle that the kinds of arms permitted to other countries ought not to be prohibited to Germany. This principle, however, could not be realised in practice all at once. It was necessary that confidence in its application should be gradually built up, and the Government therefore conceived that what was needed was a practical programme of stages, each step being justified and prepared for by the proved consequences of what had gone before. A similar principle could of course be applied to Austria, Hungary, and Bulgaria.

The Foreign Secretary's speech was warmly commended by Sir A. Chamberlain as " a new factor for good in the situation," and an amendment approving it was moved from the Unionist side. Mr. Lansbury, however, refused to withdraw the Labour resolution, on the ground that the Opposition could not discover any contributions which the National Government and Sir John Simon had made to disarmament. On a division being taken, the resolution was defeated by 402 votes to 44, and the amendment was then agreed to.

In addition to the Government's statement of policy, a noteworthy feature of the debate was a speech by Mr. Baldwin on aerial disarmament, which made a profound impression both in Parliament and outside. Mr. Baldwin declared that all questions relating to disarmament were dwarfed by the menace of bombing from the air. He held that what the world was suffering from was a sense of fear, a want of confidence ; and there was nothing more responsible for that fear than the menace from the air. It was useless to talk of the reduction of the size of aeroplanes, the prohibition of the bombardment of the civil population, or even the prohibition of bombing altogether. All these safeguards would be swept away by actual warfare. The one thing was to abolish the air forces of the world altogether. Even then there would be civil aviation providing potential bombers, and therefore in his view it was necessary for the nations of the world to devote the whole of their mind to the question whether it was possible so to control civil aviation as to make such disarmament feasible. In conclusion he pointed out that this was a question essentially for the younger men, for the instrument was in their hands. There were some instruments so terrible that mankind had resolved not to use them ; he knew at least of three such proposed for use during the last war. If the conscience of the young men should ever come to feel the same in regard to this instrument, the thing would be done. But if not, they, and not the old men, would be responsible for the wiping out of European civilisation.

The Government was not slow in endeavouring to translate into act the various undertakings it had given in the matter of disarmament. When Sir John Simon left to attend the next meeting of the Disarmament Conference at Geneva, he took with him a comprehensive scheme which the British Government proposed as a " first stage " in general disarmament. The proposals were issued on November 17—at the same time that they were stated by Sir John Simon at Geneva—as a White Paper under the title of " Declaration of Policy of His Majesty's Government in the United Kingdom on Disarmament in connexion with Germany's claim to equality of rights," and made a good impression on Ministerialists. It was not, however, thought necessary that there should be any debate on the subject in the House of Commons.

The efforts of the Prime Minister to bring about a Four-Power Conference for the purpose of inducing Germany to return to the Disarmament Conference proved unavailing. In another quarter, however, he found some compensation for this disappointment. Mr. Norman Davis, the principal delegate of the United States to the Disarmament Conference, was in London at the end of October, and Mr. MacDonald had a number of conversations with him as a result of which good progress was made towards reconciling British and American views on naval policy.

On November 8 Mr. Thomas asked the House of Commons to endorse a new Order of the Treasury increasing the duties on many classes of imports from the Irish Free State. He stated that the yield of the duties during the fifteen weeks ending October 29 had been 674,000l., but that during the last four weeks of this period the average weekly receipts had increased from 44,000l. to 74,000l., the reason being that the Free State Government had given a bounty to their people on exports sent to England. The 5,000,000l. due from the Free State was not likely to be recovered out of the duties imposed in July, and the Government had decided to raise the rates because they were determined that the British taxpayer should not bear the burden. The policy of the Government was criticised by the Opposition as likely to embitter feeling and make peace between the two countries impossible, but the duties both new and old were approved by the House by a large majority.

On November 14 the Minister of Labour brought in a Transitional Payments Bill embodying the provisions regarding the means test laid down in the resolution of November 9, and after some debate the second reading was passed by 344 votes to 45. On the next day it was passed through its remaining stages in the House of Commons and through all its stages in the House of Lords. The enactment of this measure, along with the Ottawa Agreements Bill, completed the business of the Session, which had commenced on November 3, 1931, and Parliament was prorogued on November 17.

The Ministerial speech at the Guildhall banquet on November 9 was delivered for the seventh time by Mr. Baldwin, Mr. MacDonald having absented himself on grounds of health. Dealing with international affairs, Mr. Baldwin expressed his regret that the success which had attended the Lausanne Conference on reparations had not also attended the Disarmament Conference, and exonerated England from any part of the blame. The same characteristics which had helped to make Lausanne a success had also made Ottawa a success, namely, patience, forbearance, sympathy, and the sense of one another's position, requirements, and interests. They were now looking to the meeting of the World Conference in London, failure of which would be a disaster. He offered a warm welcome to the representatives of various foreign Governments who were coming to England to enter into trade negotiations with the Government, and expressed gratitude to the bacon-exporting countries in Europe and to Argentina for the way in which they had come forward to discuss with Britain her agricultural difficulties. He described the conversion of the Five per cent. War Loan and the operations following as a " marvellous achievement," and said that the Government looked to the provision of cheap and abundant supplies of credit as a most potent influence in industrial recovery. The unemployment situation was giving the Government anxiety, but he believed the tendency was to improve.

On November 10 the report was issued of the Committee which, under the chairmanship of Lord Salisbury, had been considering the reform of the House of Lords. It was in favour of a Second Chamber with power to veto general legislation, but insisted that such a Chamber must adequately represent non-Conservative parties. To this end it proposed that the Second Chamber should be composed of 150 members elected by the hereditary peers out of their own number, 150 members elected by county and county borough councils (or, alternatively, nominated by members of the Privy Council, and ultimately by the Prime Minister), and about 20 other members. For deciding what was a Money Bill, a joint authority of both Houses was recommended.

Lord Salisbury's scheme created some alarm in Labour and Liberal quarters, where it was feared that the Government might now, under Conservative pressure, proceed to strengthen the House of Lords. Their apprehensions, however, were soon set at rest. On November 30 a Conservative member brought forward a motion in the House of Commons urging the Government to deal at once with the reform of the House of Lords. The Solicitor-General in reply refrained from expressing any opinion on the recommendations of the Salisbury Committee, and contented himself with pointing out that it would be absolutely impossible during the present session for Parliament to find time for dealing with so difficult and contentious a subject.

On November 11 the Committee which had been appointed to consider the procedure of the House of Commons for the conduct of public business also presented its report. The Committee had been set up as a result of complaints that the machinery of the House of Commons was no longer suitable for modern requirements, but it came unanimously to the conclusion that this charge was not justified and that in fact the machinery was pliable enough to deal with any unexpected emergency, as was proved by the fact that, for instance, the Bill dealing with the departure from the gold standard was passed in a single day. The chief direction in which a change might, in the opinion of the Committee, with advantage be made was in giving the House a more direct and effective control over expenditure. For this purpose the Committee proposed that the work of the Estimates Committee and the Public Accounts Committee should be linked more closely together, and that definite opportunities should be given to the House to discuss the reports of those Committees every session. It also recommended that the Estimates Committee should be enlarged and provided with technical advisers. Suggestions were also made for expediting the handling of amendments and questions, and for a better utilisation of private members' time. The report was issued as a White Paper on November 18.

The Committee of Conservative members of Parliament which had been formed on June 2 to inquire into the whole field of national expenditure and to make suggestions for effecting economies (*vide* p. 57) completed its labours just before Parliament rose. The sub-committees which considered the various heads of public expenditure made a number of more or less drastic proposals which, if adopted in their entirety, would have meant a saving of about 100,000,000*l*. In the opinion of a large number of the members of the Private Members (" 1922 ") Committee— the parent body from which the Economy Committee had been formed—these proposals should have been kept for the eye of the Chancellor of the Exchequer, but the Chairman of the Economy Committee, Sir Gervais Rentoul, who was also Chairman of the parent body, decided to publish the reports of the various sub-committees even before these had had an opportunity to confer and collate their conclusions. This proceeding called forth strong protests from members of the 1922 Committee, and many of them hastened to dissociate themselves from the reports, which they were afraid might create a very bad impression in the constituencies. By this time, too, the zeal even of Conservative members for economy had somewhat cooled, on account of the adverse effect which the restriction of public expenditure was seen to be exercising on the spending power of the people. Sir G. Rentoul soon after paid the penalty for his temerity by failing to secure re-election as Chairman of the 1922 Committee.

On November 25 the report was issued of the Committee which had been appointed in July to go into the question of local expenditure in England and Wales. The Committee made an exhaustive survey of the whole field of local expenditure, particularly in regard to education, housing, roads, public health and public assistance, and put forward a number of recommendations which they believed, in combination with the economies already effected by the Government and local authorities, would enable local expenditure falling on rates and grants to be reduced within three years by from 35,000,000*l.* to 40,000,000*l.* below the expenditure for 1930-31. At the same time the Committee which had been appointed to review local expenditure in Scotland submitted recommendations which it estimated would enable a yearly saving to be made in Scotland of over 3,380,000*l.*

Parliament reassembled on November 22 after a recess of only five days, nominally to commence a new session. The break, however, was hardly perceptible, and the King's Speech gave prominence to two subjects which had engaged the greater part of the attention of the House of Commons during the closing stages of the last session—unemployment and agricultural depression. With regard to agriculture, the Speech expressed the hope that the measures recently taken to check the imports of meat and other products had been of real assistance to producers, and announced that the Government would take further action upon investigations which had just been concluded or were still proceeding. As to unemployment, it was stated that the Government intended to bring forward measures dealing comprehensively with unemployment insurance and with the treatment of those unable to find work, with the object not only of affording them material assistance, but also of maintaining their morale and their fitness to resume work when opportunity offered. The legislative programme was also to include Bills dealing with rent restriction, with London passenger transport, and with Scottish affairs.

The vagueness of the references in the Speech to legislation for dealing with unemployment caused general disappointment, and was strongly animadverted upon by the Leader of the Opposition. The Prime Minister in endeavouring to defend the Government was once more much clearer as to its negative than its positive intentions. While, he said, they would encourage every normal expansion of municipal enterprise, he warned the municipalities that rates and taxes could not be drawn upon extravagantly. The chief anxiety of the Government was for the large section—especially the younger people among them—which, owing to improvements in machinery, could not be absorbed in industry even if trade revived. The problem was a new one, and all that he could say was that the Government was considering it and would produce its proposals at the earliest possible moment, some certainly during the present session. He would, however, point out that the revival of agriculture was an essential part of the plans they were working out, and that they were aiming at putting a much larger percentage in direct contact with the land than had been the case during the development of the factory system.

The Opposition moved a somewhat academic amendment advocating the adoption of a " socialist policy " for attacking the fundamental causes of the poverty problem. This, of course, was overwhelmingly defeated. But a number of Conservative speakers in the course of the debate also expressed the opinion that the resources of the Government were not being utilised to the full extent for the stimulation of enterprise and industry, and some declared themselves ready to accept drastic measures, though they did not specify what precisely they had in mind.

An entirely new line was struck out by Mr. Churchill, who, in one of his best oratorical efforts, called into question that aspect of the Government's policy which hitherto had been immune from criticism—its internationalism. For one thing, he threw on the Government the blame—at any rate in part—for the postponement of the World Economic Conference till April. This showed, he thought, that the Prime Minister had been completely out of touch with what was going on, and appeared to indicate a lack of thoroughness in the day-to-day conduct of public business. Dealing next with the pacifism of the Government, he expressed the opinion that not too much attention should be paid to the disarmament schemes of the League of Nations, which he considered wholly impracticable. France's military predominance, he thought, was the chief guarantee of peace and stability in Europe, and England's best policy was, while trying within the restricted limits now open to prevent war, to make sure that she herself was not involved in a war, and above all to make sure that if war broke out among other Powers, the King's Dominions could be effectively defended.

A part of the debate was by agreement given up to a discussion among members for Scotch constituencies on the question of Home Rule for Scotland. A movement in favour of such a step had lately been gathering force, being fostered by the belief that it would conduce to a more effective treatment of the problem of economic distress in Scotland. Opinion on the subject proved to be sharply divided, and the Secretary of State for Scotland declared that so far as the Government was concerned, the question was an academic one, and he had not even asked his colleagues to consider it. In his opinion a separate Parliament for Scotland would be a definite handicap to the trade, industry, and well-being of Scotland, and would be a retrograde step. Scotland to-day was well able to safeguard her interests and

control her destiny, and at the same time to exercise her due
weight in the Imperial Parliament.   He hoped, however, to introduce certain improvements in the present system of Scottish administration, the broad effect of which would be to secure that
a greater proportion of Scottish private legislation should be
examined in a Scottish atmosphere in Scotland.

The first actual step taken by the Government for the relief
of unemployment was to give official recognition to a body calling
itself the National Council of Social Service, a voluntary organisation, which for some years had been carrying on ameliorative
work among the unemployed.   In January, the Prince of Wales,
as patron of the National Council, had addressed a meeting at
the Albert Hall at which he appealed for voluntary service on
behalf of the unemployed, and he had since followed up his
appeal by visits to some of the areas where unemployment was
most severe.   The Government now encouraged the Council to
undertake a great extension of its work by appointing a special
committee of men prominent in the industrial, commercial, and
educational life of the country which should be the central body
for furthering help for the unemployed, and promised to make
a grant towards the increased cost of organisation which such
work would entail.   Among the means envisaged for assisting
the unemployed were the establishment of occupation centres,
the provision of facilities for physical training and for work on
allotments and constructional schemes, and the fostering of
educational activities, including music and the drama.

Before the Government could take any further steps for the
relief of unemployment, the whole of its attention was demanded
by a problem of even greater gravity and urgency.   The Hoover
moratorium, which included the suspension of England's war
debt payment to America, was due to expire on December 15,
and on that date it would be incumbent on Great Britain to pay
to the United States the next instalment of the debt, amounting
to over 19,000,000*l.* at par, unless fresh arrangements were made
in the meantime.   The whole of Britain's financial arrangements
for the year, including the Lausanne settlement, had been based
on the assumption that the United States would not demand
any war debt payments on this scale.   For a time hopes were
entertained that an arrangement to this effect would be reached
at the projected World Economic Conference.   When it became
clear, however, that the conference would not meet before Christmas, the only course open was to request the United States
Government to prolong the moratorium.   So long as the presidential campaign was in progress in the United States, Britain
forbore from opening the subject, in order not to embarrass
the candidates.   But no sooner was the election over than she
lost no time in trying to come to an understanding with her
creditor.

On November 10 the British Ambassador in Washington presented to the United States Secretary of State a Note (which was not issued for publication till three days later) setting forth in a somewhat formal manner the views and desires of Great Britain with regard to the debt. The Note began by pointing out that the hopes which were at first raised by the initiative of President Hoover in June, 1931, had not been realised, and that the economic troubles which it was designed to alleviate had not come to an end. His Majesty's Government were therefore of opinion that further remedial measures must be sought. On the nature of those remedies they had frequently expressed their view, and they saw no reason now for changing it. They believed that the regime of inter-governmental financial obligations, as now existing, ought to be reviewed ; and therefore they earnestly hoped that the United States Government would see its way to enter into an exchange of views on the subject at the earliest possible moment. The immediate objective of the present Note, however, was of a more limited nature—to ask for a suspension of the payment due from them on December 15 for the period of the discussions now suggested, or for any other period that might be agreed upon. This course, it was pointed out, would be in accordance with the precedent set at Lausanne, when the execution of the payments due to the participating Powers was reserved during the period of the conference.

In official circles in England little doubt was at first entertained that the British request would be complied with. Not only was it thought to be eminently reasonable in itself, but it was fully in accord with numerous authoritative statements which had been made at various times in the United States, and in fact could be regarded as a logical corollary of the Hoover moratorium. Feeling became somewhat less optimistic as the days went by and the opposition to the British request in America became more vocal. Nevertheless, it was still thought that the better sense of America would prevail. Speaking on November 23 on a recent decline in the exchange value of sterling, Mr. Chamberlain took occasion to combat the suggestion that one reason was uncertainty as to the outcome of their recent communication to the United States regarding the debt. He himself refused to see any ground for anxiety or fear on that account, because he could not believe that America would be so unreasonable as to reject Britain's proposal. He pointed out that the suspension of reparation payments during the Lausanne Conference had had an immediate effect in steadying public opinion in all the financial centres of Europe, and that the confidence born of the settlement made there had continued to increase, and he had no doubt that America would bear in mind these considerations, which were not less important for herself than for the nations on this side of the Atlantic.

Scarcely had Mr. Chamberlain uttered these words when they were completely belied by a statement made by the United States President on the subject of war debts at Washington. The proposals to postpone the payments due on December 15, said Mr. Hoover, "did not appear to him to carry weight." No facts had been presented by the debtor Governments which would justify postponement of payment under principles hitherto laid down by the United States. As to the effect of demanding payment on the proposed World Economic Conference, he thought that discussion would proceed under more favourable conditions if the debt obligations were paid than if they were suspended prior to discussion. The only concession he would suggest was the creation of an agency to discuss war debts further. Shortly afterwards a Note was received from Washington to the same effect.

Mr. Hoover's statement was a great disappointment to the British Government, but they refused to be disheartened and resolutely put upon the statement the most favourable construction possible. Speaking on November 24, Mr. Chamberlain drew comfort from the fact that President Hoover had recognised that the request for a fresh discussion on the subject was reasonable, and that he was apparently not averse from some means by which it might once more be made the subject of conversations. He also thought it well to abstain from hasty conclusions as to the final attitude of the American Congress either on the question of the suspension of payments next month or on the larger question of the debt itself. And on the same day Mr. MacDonald declared that if a real effort were made, if each side tried to put itself in the other's place, he could not believe for a moment that a solution would not be found before December 15.

If Mr. Hoover's statement had not deprived Britain of hope, it had at any rate shaken her out of her complacency. Now for the first time the Government and the public began seriously to face the question what was to be done if America after all insisted on her due. Actual payment seemed at the first blush out of the question. Goods and services America would not take ; dollars England had not the means to purchase ; and though there was a stock of gold in the Bank of England, yet to deplete it by the amount claimed by America might have reactions on the currency which could not be contemplated without the gravest apprehension. As was only natural, the idea of defaulting began to be actively canvassed. It found favour with some members of the Government, including, according to rumour, the Chancellor of the Exchequer, but it was strongly deprecated by two speakers in the debate on the Address, Sir Robert Horne, and Mr. Amery—by the former because of the blow which a default on the part of Great Britain would strike at the whole credit structure of the world, by the latter because of the excuse which such a step would give to Ireland not to pay her debt to England. The Cabinet were at first divided on the question, but they were agreed that a new Note must be sent to America reiterating Britain's request and setting forth the British case with the utmost force and cogency possible. To the preparation of this Note the Cabinet devoted the major part of its energies during the next few days.

The text of the Note was finally approved by the whole Cabinet on November 30, and despatched to Washington and made public on the next day. It was a document of about 5,000 words, and set forth in detail the reasons for the two requests made in the previous Note—for a reconsideration of the whole question of war debts and for a suspension meanwhile of the instalment due on December 15. By far the greater part of the Note was devoted to the former question, and no effort was spared to make the British case as convincing as possible. The arguments adduced were familiar to those who had studied the subject, but were set forth with a clearness and force which made the document a classical exposé of the effects of war debts on world economy. The Note pointed out that the system of inter-Governmental debts was undermining confidence and preventing the inter-national monetary mechanism from functioning properly ; that the policy of the creditors in refusing to take payment in goods had rendered intolerable the peculiar burden of war debts ; that the endeavours of the debtor countries to pay in gold led to a great decrease in their purchasing power and so to a diminution of world trade, with disastrous results to the creditor countries also ; that even a partial recovery of business activity in the creditor countries as a result of the removal of the abnormal conditions would compensate their Exchequers many times over for the loss of revenue involved in the revision of the war debt settlements ; that in fact the payment of war debts had been proved to be inconsistent with the present economic organisation of the world, and that any resumption of them was bound to accentuate gravely the present crisis and to compromise fatally all efforts to counteract it.

Dealing more particularly with the case of England, the Note called attention to the past record of the United Kingdom in the matter of inter-Governmental debts, to the financial efforts which she had made and the amounts which she had forgone, pointing out that while the British share of the total indebtedness to the United States was only 40 per cent., 80 per cent. of the total debt payments made had come from Great Britain—a fact which, in the opinion of the Government, constituted a strong claim on her behalf to consideration on the part of the United States. Mention was then made of the increase in the burden of the debt due to the depreciation of sterling in terms of gold and to the adverse effects of the American tariff on Anglo-American trade, and it was pointed out—in language which almost amounted to a threat—that insistence on further debt payments would still further impair Britain's power to purchase American farm products and so react unfavourably on the United States producer.

In regard to the instalment of the debt due on December 15, the Government expressed the conviction that its proposal to suspend this payment would in no way affect any ultimate settlement, and was necessary in order to create the conditions favourable to a successful issue of the subsequent conversations. Any attempt to make the transfer in present circumstances would raise doubts and anxieties which would distract the attention of peoples and Governments and prevent an objective and systematic approach to the problem to be solved. If England paid at all, she would have to pay in gold, and this would involve the sacrifice of a considerable part of the gold reserves of the Bank of England, which were widely regarded as no more than sufficient for the responsibilities of London as a financial centre.

The general opinion in England was that the Note had presented the British case in a way which was " unanswerable." Nevertheless, from the outset no great confidence was felt that it would have the effect desired. Reports which continually arrived as to the state of opinion in America gave the impression that the majority in Congress had inflexibly made up its mind not to forgo the December payment and was not open to argument on the subject. This discovery was a bitter pill for the British public, but was swallowed by it with characteristic fortitude. Even before the Note was sent, Mr. Baldwin in a public speech pointed out that America was in a difficult position, and appealed for the exercise of restraint in passing criticism upon her. The appeal met with a loyal response from the bulk of the Press, which not only studiously refrained from fanning anti-American feeling but did its best to present sympathetically the American point of view.

It was as well that the public prepared itself for a disappointment, because President Hoover's reply to the British Note, received on December 8, again insisted on payment of the December instalment. The only concession it contained was to repeat a suggestion of the President, that Britain should offer to make deposits of sterling to be guaranteed as to dollar value and to be transferred at such time as would not interfere with the stability of exchange. The British Government had already declined this suggestion on the ground that the existence of a large sum of sterling awaiting transfer would probably affect the exchange markets almost as seriously as actual purchase of exchange. The Note also controverted in detail a number of the statements made in the British Note, as for instance that the payment of debts to the United States had drained the gold reserves of other countries. With regard, however, to the first request of the British Government, for a reconsideration of the whole question of inter-Governmental war debts, the President showed himself much more accommodating than formerly. It was clear, he said, that these debts had a very definite relation to the problem of recovery, in which both the British and the American people had so vital an interest, and he was prepared, through whatever agency might seem appropriate, in co-operation with the British Government, to survey the entire situation and to consider what means should be taken to bring about the stability of currencies and exchange, the revival of trade, and the recovery of prices.

The British Government now resigned itself to the inevitable, and prepared to pay, not, however, without a final effort to secure some advantage. In a reply dated December 11, it referred to the criticisms made by Mr. Hoover on its Note of December 1, and said that it saw no reason to modify the general conclusions there set forth. It expressed regret that the President had not seen fit to recommend to Congress the solution there proposed, but stated that, since he insisted on payment, Britain would pay on December 15 the amount due under the Funding Agreement of 1923. In the view of the Government, however, this payment was not to be regarded as a resumption of the annual payments contemplated by the agreement, but as a capital payment, of which account should be taken in any final settlement. Such a procedure, it said, must obviously be exceptional and abnormal ; and it therefore urged on the United States Government the importance of an early exchange of views so that a new arrangement might be made before June 15 next, and the danger of a general breakdown of existing inter-Governmental agreements might be obviated. The payment this time would be made in gold, as being the least prejudicial of the methods open to them.

The offer to pay in gold was immediately accepted by the United States Government, but with the caveat that it had "no authority to accept any conditions of payment other than those contained in the Debt Agreement, which Congress alone had power to alter." To this the British Government replied by once more placing on record its own point of view, and the exchange of Notes then ceased.

On December 15 some 20,000,000l. worth of gold in the vaults of the Bank of England was duly transferred to the possession of the United States, and shortly afterwards was shipped across the Atlantic in a number of steamers. For the time being the country remained entirely unaffected by this drain of the precious metal which had been so much dreaded. Sterling, which had lately commenced to rise again after falling to a record low level of 3.12 dollars to the pound, continued to advance until at Christmas it stood at 3.32 dollars to the pound. Government stocks also remained fairly steady. Thanks to the resource-

fulness of England's banking chiefs, the payment which a few weeks
before had seemed impossible was effected almost with the ease
and smoothness of an ordinary banking transaction.

So long as the exchange of Notes with the United States
Government was going on, the subject of the American debt
was barely mentioned in Parliament. This did not by any
means indicate that all members were satisfied with the Government's proceedings, and as soon as the exchange was closed, a
desire was expressed in certain quarters for a division on the
subject. To this the Government would not consent, and the
demand was not pressed. On December 14, however, the adjournment of the House was moved in order to give members
an opportunity of expressing their views. Mr. Chamberlain
opened with a long and spirited defence of the Government's
action. He pointed out that from the outset Britain had
consistently and on every occasion advocated the complete
cancellation of war debts, and that her proposals to the United
States were in complete accord with that policy. Other nations,
he said, had gradually been coming round to the British view,
and the Hoover moratorium itself was an admission that the
old arrangements were no longer binding. Strictly speaking,
therefore, Britain was not bound to pay the December instalment,
but they had decided to do so, because to refuse, on however good
grounds, would have been equivalent to a default, and such an
action on their part might have produced incalculable harm.
They had, however, exercised their right so far as to declare that
the payment they were making was not to be taken as implying
a revival of the old system, but as anticipatory of the new regime
which they expected to result from their discussions with the
United States Government.

Speakers from all sides of the House expressed their approval
of the Government's decision to pay, and to pay in gold. If there
were any members who thought otherwise, they did not make
themselves heard in the debate. The chief critic of the Government was again Mr. Churchill, who held that the course of events
had justified the strictures which he had passed on the Lausanne
arrangements at the time when they were made—a view which
still did not find much acceptance in the House. Sir Robert
Horne also dealt with the past, and made a vigorous defence
of Mr. Baldwin against aspersions cast upon him for the part he
had played in bringing about the American debt settlement in
1922. Mr. Chamberlain, in summing up the debate, laid stress on
the friendly tone of the American Notes, and drew from it a favourable augury for the impending negotiations.

While Sir Robert Horne was speaking, and again after he
had finished, he was charged by Mr. Lloyd George with having,
as a member of the Cabinet, been opposed in 1923 to the Balfour
Note. Sir Robert denied the charge, and the two speakers, in

H

the course of their altercation, brought up their recollections of a certain Cabinet meeting at which the matter was decided. Mr. George was so bent on proving himself right that he suggested that the minutes of the meeting should be made public. The Prime Minister, however, decided that this was not in the public interest.

The incident gave no small concern to many responsible politicians, and the need for keeping Cabinet proceedings secret was strongly emphasised in a debate in the House of Lords on December 21. Lord Rankeillour, who as Mr. Hope had for many years been Deputy-Speaker of the House of Commons, introduced a motion on the subject, and hinted that both Mr. Lloyd George and Sir Robert Horne had come very near to breaking the oath of secrecy which they had taken as Privy Councillors. Lord Hailsham took the same view, and pointed out that such conduct was not only a breach of tradition but was punishable by law. He thought that any relaxation of the existing rule was most undesirable, as it would make the position of Cabinet Ministers intolerable—a view which was strongly supported by the Lord Chancellor.

While the debt negotiations were proceeding, good progress had been made in Parliament with the Government's legislative programme. On November 29 the House of Commons commenced the discussion in Committee of the Bill for regulating London transport, which had been originally drafted and introduced by Mr. Morrison as Transport Minister in the Labour Government in 1931. After passing its second reading and receiving a number of modifications in a Joint Select Committee, this measure, in spite of its Socialist origin, had been taken over by the National Government, but time had not hitherto permitted the consideration of it to be resumed in Parliament. In order that the labour spent on it should not be wasted, the Government had twice taken the precaution to obtain the consent of the House for carrying it over to a new session. Hence it was now taken up at the point at which it had been dropped in 1931.

In addition to the changes which had already been made by the Select Joint Committee, the Government had put down three new amendments of importance—one, that the appointments to the Board which was to co-ordinate passenger traffic should be made by trustees, and not by the Minister ; a second, to make the Railway Rates Tribunal the arbiter over facilities and fares, instead of the Minister ; and the third, to incorporate in the Bill the agreement which had in the meantime been reached with the Metropolitan Railway Company. A number of members maintained that with these amendments the Bill would be practically a new measure, and demanded a fresh second reading debate ; to this, however, the Government would not consent. The Bill even in its amended form was not popular with the Conservative Party on account of its Socialist leanings and parentage, and it met with determined opposition from the Ministerialist benches. The revolt, however, did not spread far enough to endanger seriously the prospects of the Bill.

After finishing the Committee stage of the Transport Bill, the House of Commons began the consideration of two Bills laying down a new policy in regard to housing. One, the text of which was issued on December 2, dealt with the matter of rent control. It divided houses into three classes : those with a rateable value of 45*l.* in London, or 35*l.* in the rest of England and Wales, and 45*l.* in Scotland ; those with a rateable value between 20*l.* and 45*l.* in London, or between 13*l.* and 35*l.* in the rest of England, and 26*l.* 5*s.* and 45*l.* in Scotland ; and those with a rateable value lower than these figures. Houses of the first class were to be decontrolled within three months ; those of the second class were to become decontrolled as they became vacant, as at present ; and houses of the third class were, save in a few special cases, to remain under control for another five years. The Bill also contained provisions for preventing the exploitation of sub-tenants, and for giving facilities to landlords to obtain possession of their property.

The second Bill, published on December 8, abolished the subsidy granted to municipalities under the Acts of 1923 and 1924, and instead empowered local authorities to extend additional facilities, subject to the approval of the Minister of Health, to building societies for the purpose of stimulating private enterprise in building. The subsidy for slum clearance under the 1930 Act was, however, to be maintained at its present level.

The Rent Control Bill came up for its second reading on December 12. The Minister of Health, in explaining the reasons for its provisions, stated that since 1920 the supply of houses of the two more expensive classes mentioned in the Bill had increased by 60 per cent., and it had been found that rents had not materially increased when houses of these types had been decontrolled. There was therefore every reason for quickening the process of decontrol in respect of the first class and at least not retarding it in the case of the second. With regard to the third, the poorer type of houses, the case was different. Here supply had not kept pace with demand to the same extent, and the result was that where houses of this type had been decontrolled —the proportion so far was one-sixth—rents had been increased on an average by 35 per cent. more than the rents of controlled houses in the same class. There was therefore a clear case for retaining control of these houses, at least for a period of years, in the interest of the poorer class of tenant. Mr. Greenwood, on behalf of the Labour Party, approved of the Bill in the main, but pointed out that recently a number of middle-class tenants in the more expensive types of houses mentioned in the Bill had fallen on hard times and also deserved consideration.

H 2

The other, so-called Housing Bill, came up for its second reading on December 15. The Minister of Health described it as the second and last step in the adjustment of housing policy to changing conditions. The time when subsidies had to pump capital into housing was, he said, past, and the Government believed that capital could now be normally and naturally attracted into the building of small houses of the type contemplated by the Act of 1924, which could be let at 7*s.* 9*d.* a week, exclusive of rates. He had been assured by the National Federation of House Builders that, if there were no competition from subsidised municipal building, the whole demand for this type of house could be supplied. Mr. Greenwood bitterly attacked the Minister's scheme, as a " capitulation to private enterprise," and the Liberal Party was not enamoured of it, but it obtained its second reading by 238 votes to 42.

On November 30 a debate was started in the House of Commons by a private member on the question of naval disarmament, and the First Lord of the Admiralty, Sir B. Eyres-Monsell, took the opportunity to protest emphatically against a propaganda which was being carried on to create and foster the impression that Great Britain was standing in the way of naval disarmament. He pointed out that the total tonnage of the British Fleet, which in 1914 was 2,160,000, would in 1936 be only 1,150,000, a decrease of 47 per cent., whereas in the same period America had increased her naval tonnage by 29 per cent., and Japan by 37 per cent. Vital as was the Navy to Great Britain, he was not opposed to further reductions, but only on condition that they should not be unilateral.

Towards the end of the session the Government, through no fault of its own, found itself in hot water with that section of Parliament and the public which was jealous for the preservation of London's architectural amenities and which had seen in the Town Planning Bill the sign of a new æsthetic conscience. Some time in November it transpired that the Commissioners of Crown Lands, as the ground landlord of No. 4 Carlton Gardens in London, a house formerly occupied by Lord Balfour, had in the summer leased that building to a manufacturing firm to be used for commercial purposes, at the same time giving it permission to make certain structural alterations which would considerably change the outside appearance. A cry was immediately raised in various quarters that one of London's finest residential sites and most beautiful façades was in danger of being spoilt, and efforts were made to save it. On December 5 a memorial, signed by a large number of members of Parliament, was presented to the Prime Minister protesting against the proposal to erect a high block of buildings on the site of No. 4 Carlton Gardens as " an act of vandalism totally unwarranted." On December 13 the matter was discussed in the House of Lords, and the Government was pointedly asked why Nash's admirable work should be destroyed to provide commercial offices when there was a large area available for the purpose on the other side of the Thames. On behalf of the Government it was stated that the cost of maintaining the building was 200*l.* a year, and as there seemed to be no prospect of letting it as a private residence the Crown Lands Commissioners had accepted the offer of a commercial firm, with the stipulation that the plans for the new building should be shown to the Fine Art Commission. As the Commission had been asked to pronounce an opinion only on the merits of the proposed building itself and not on its relation to the block as a whole, this explanation entirely failed to satisfy the critics of the scheme. A few days later, questions were asked on the subject in the House of Commons, and it was discovered that the Government, however much it might desire, no longer had any power to prevent the rebuilding plan being carried out, if the new owner insisted, as the Commissioners for Crown Lands were not responsible to Parliament. The incident led to a strong agitation for bringing the Commissioners under Parliamentary control before they could do any more mischief.

On December 19 the House of Commons voted a supplementary estimate of 18,010,000*l.* for the Ministry of Labour. Of this sum, 12,600,000*l.* was required for transitional payment, and the bulk of the remainder for balancing the Insurance Fund. The Minister of Labour ruefully confessed that his estimate of unemployment figures made earlier in the year had been unduly optimistic, but as usual he drew comfort from the fact that Great Britain was holding its own in world trade, and almost alone among nations was maintaining its position in the midst of the general deterioration. The odd 10,000*l.* was a contribution to the voluntary movement for assisting the unemployed (*vide* p. 107).

Among the other proceedings of Parliament during this session was the continuance for one year of the Dyestuffs Act (*vide* ANNUAL REGISTER, 1930, p. 108), and the granting of an authorisation to the Government to guarantee Britain's share of the new loan promised to Austria at Geneva in July (December 20). Both steps were taken by the House of Commons somewhat unwillingly, and only under pressure from the Government. On December 20 the House also voted a Supplementary Estimate to make good the default of the Irish Free State. It was stated that the special duties on Irish produce were expected to realise about 2,500,000*l.* by the end of the year, which was about 1,500,000*l.* less than the amount in default.

On November 17 what was described as "the third session of the Indian Round-Table Conference" was opened in London by the Prime Minister, who acted as Chairman. The object of the conference, according to Mr. MacDonald, was particularly

to fill in the gaps so far left in the discussion of the Federal
Constitution by examining definite points in a businesslike way.
The conference remained in session till Christmas and came
to decisions on a number of important points. Speaking in the
House of Commons on December 23, the Secretary for India
asserted that its discussions had been useful and on the whole
satisfactory. He also declared that the situation in India itself
was definitely better than it had been six months before, and that
the beginning of a new chapter had been reached.

The year 1932 was, like its predecessor, a bad one for the
railways, and as it drew to its close the Companies felt that it
was imperative for them to make further economies on a large
scale. A reduction in labour costs naturally suggested itself as
the readiest means, and on September 30 the Companies laid
their position before the representatives of the employees and
proposed to them that the deductions of $2\frac{1}{2}$ and 5 per cent. made
in the previous year should be replaced by a general reduction
of 10 per cent. The men would not hear of any further reductions,
and after some wrangling the matter was referred to the National
Wages Board. This body commenced its hearings on November 29,
and the Companies and the men proceeded to repeat the arguments which they had submitted to the Board on a similar
occasion in the previous year (vide ANNUAL REGISTER, 1931,
p. 8). The hearings were concluded before Christmas, and the
Board announced that it would give its decision early in the
new year.

As the largest shareholder in the Anglo-Persian Oil Company, the Government was directly affected by the action of the
Persian Government in cancelling, on November 27, the concession
held by the Company in Persia. The British Government
immediately made energetic representations at Teheran and
threatened, if the cancellation were not withdrawn, to refer the
matter to The Hague International Court. Persia, however,
refused to recognise the matter as a subject for the jurisdiction
of the Court, and Britain thereupon appealed to the League
of Nations. The Persian Government consented to accept
the League's mediation, and relations between the two countries,
which had been disturbed for a time, again became amicable
[vide Persia].

At the same time a minor contretemps of a familiar character arose between Britain and the Soviet Government. On
November 28 the Foreign Secretary demanded an apology for
statements in the Izvestia that the British Foreign Office had
instructed their agents to furnish documents, genuine or forged,
to establish a connexion between the Soviet and the Third International. The Russian reply was that the Izvestia was not an
official paper, and that the Soviet was not responsible for statements made by it. The Government at first refused to accept

this, but on receiving an admission from the editor of the paper that he had been misinformed, it declared the incident closed. At the same time representations were made at Moscow with regard to instructions given by the Third International to Communists in England and India, but rather to pacify Conservatives at home than in the hope that they would be effective.

The end of 1932, like its beginning, found England anxiously waiting for an international conference which should clear away the barriers to world trade. For twelve months, it is true, she had weathered existing conditions better than most other countries, and had lost little, if any, ground in industry and commerce. At the same time internal prices had remained stable ; by some economic miracle, she had reaped the benefits of a depreciated currency without suffering its drawbacks. But it was not to be expected that this state of things could continue indefinitely. The Ottawa Conference, whatever might be its value, had shown clearly that the day was still far distant when the British Empire could become a self-contained economic unit. For Britain, therefore, an improvement in foreign trade was still a vital requirement ; and while her own efforts might contribute to this, they could not carry her very far without a change in the policy of foreign nations, especially America.

IMPERIAL HISTORY.

CHAPTER I.

IRELAND.

NORTHERN IRELAND.

ONE of the outstanding events of the year was the opening by the Prince of Wales of the new Parliament Buildings at Stormont, on the outskirts of the city of Belfast, on November 16.

No first-class legislative measures were passed by the Ulster Parliament during the year, though a number of Bills for the improvement of industrial conditions within the Province became law. An Act was passed which virtually prohibited the importation of the musk-rat into Northern Ireland. The Government reduced the subsidy on the building of working-class houses to 25l. per house, with the result that the erection of such dwellings dwindled almost to nothing. The Government also ceased to sanction schemes for the erection of labourers' houses in rural areas. A Bill for the Revaluation of the Province was passed during the Spring session ; the Nationalist members of the House of Commons walked out of the House (May 11) as a protest against not being permitted to discuss Imperial questions reserved to the British Government—financial matters dealing with the Post Office, Customs, and so forth. They did not return during the remainder of the year, and took no part in the ceremonial opening of the new Parliamentary Buildings at Stormont.

For over ten years both Houses of Parliament had met in the Presbyterian College in Belfast, and as the lease had expired, they assembled for the last time—before going into their new Stormont home—in the City Hall (September 30), and it was here that Mr. J. Beattie, the only Socialist member, seized the Mace and threw it on the floor, because he was not permitted to break the procedure of the House. He desired to discuss the unemployment question, but it was not on the Order Paper and it was not allowed. The incident ended quietly enough and the session was closed in the traditional manner. On December 20 the royal assent was given to the various measures passed, and the House adjourned until February 28, 1933.

A deputation from the Ulster Government, headed by Mr. H. M. Pollock, Minister of Finance, attended the Dominion Conference at Ottawa.

In common with most other States, industrial and agricultural depression was very acute throughout the Six Counties, and in Belfast the City Corporation expended vast sums in providing employment by relief schemes. New roads were built, old thoroughfares reconstructed, and repairs carried out extensively in various districts. In order further to relieve depression, the Corporation in the beginning of winter embarked on an additional scheme of street reconstruction works, the gross cost of which amounts almost to 493,000*l*., the net cost to the Corporation— owing to Government grants—being about 285,000*l*.

On October 11 riots broke out in Belfast, and much damage was done to property. Two men were killed and many were wounded. Firm action was taken by the police authorities, and the rioting, ostensibly due to dissatisfaction with the curtailed unemployment relief, was quelled in a few days, and the relief was raised to a higher standard. There were also troubles in connexion with Roman Catholic pilgrims travelling from various centres in the Six Counties to attend the Eucharistic Congress in Dublin last June. Excursionists were interfered with going to and coming from trains, chiefly at Ballymena, Portadown, and Larne Harbour. Many of the offenders were severely dealt with by the Courts, and harmony between the people was restored.

The Belfast Fire Brigade received 219 calls during the year, of which 12 were maliciously given, while the salvage corps attended 164 calls, and the ambulance was summoned to give assistance on 3,408 occasions. The losses by fire during the twelve months amounted to 18,616*l*., while the estimated value of the property at risk was 2,437,351*l*.

IRISH FREE STATE.

The two outstanding events in the Irish Free State during the year 1932 were the General Election in February, which put Mr. De Valera in office for the first time and marked the beginning of strained relations between the Irish Free State and British Governments, and the International Eucharistic Congress in June, the first of these Roman Catholic assemblies to be held in Ireland.

For some months before the General Election it was becoming increasingly evident that a reaction against Mr. Cosgrave's regime, which had lasted for ten years, had set in. This was particularly noticeable among the rural community. Small holders were attracted by Mr. De Valera's declared intention, if elected, to withhold the Land Purchase Annuities and other sums hitherto paid, under agreement between Mr. Cosgrave's Government and the Government of the United Kingdom (which Mr. De Valera contended had never been ratified by either Parliament), amounting in all to 5,100,000*l*. per annum. Mr. De Valera's policy was to retain these moneys until the British Government established its claim to them, and if the claim could not, as he believed, be upheld by an impartial court, he promised to devote the money to the relief of the farmers from the burden of rates. Mr. Cosgrave stoutly maintained that these moneys were legally due to the holders, British and Irish, of Land Purchase Stock, and that it would be an act of dishonour and a damaging blow at the country's credit to repudiate the Inter-Governmental Agreement of 1925.

There were other factors which contributed to Mr. Cosgrave's defeat. His Government had taken a strong line against certain Republican and Communist organisations, which were proclaimed illegal, and had set up a Military Tribunal with large powers to deal with secret societies and sedition. A number of persons had been imprisoned by the Tribunal, and the Editor of Mr. De Valera's new daily newspaper was brought before the Tribunal some weeks before the election on a charge of seditious libel and fined 200*l*. These measures, however necessary, were not regarded with favour, and incensed the younger element, largely Republican in sentiment.

Mr. De Valera's denunciation of the Oath of Allegiance and of Partition won the support of the extreme Republicans though he refrained from seeking a mandate to set up a Republic as they had urged.

The election aroused far more interest than any held since the establishment of the Free State, and the total votes cast increased from 1,170,960 in 1927 to 1,274,156. Mr. De Valera's Party (*Fianna Fail*) won 72 seats, Mr. Cosgrave's 65, Independents 13, Labour 7, Farmers 4. The Labour group declared itself in favour of Mr. De Valera's policy, especially that part of it which promised to deal with unemployment by encouraging native industries, by equitable division of land, and by promoting increased tillage.

The new Dail met on March 9, and Mr. De Valera was elected President of the Executive Council by 81 votes to 68 for Mr. Cosgrave. Mr. Frank Fahy (*Fianna Fail*) was elected Speaker, and Mr. P. Hogan, a Labour member, Deputy-Speaker. Mr. De Valera announced his Executive Council as follows : Vice-President and Minister for Local Government, Mr. Sean T. O'Kelly ; Minister for Agriculture, Dr. J. Ryan ; Minister for Justice, Mr. J. Geoghegan ; Minister for Industry and Commerce, Mr. S. Lemass ; Minister for Lands and Fisheries, Mr. P. Ruttledge ; Minister for Defence, Mr. F. Aiken ; Minister for Education, Mr. T. Derrig ; Minister for Posts, Senator J. Connolly. Mr.

De Valera assumed the office of Minister for External Affairs. Mr. C. Maguire was appointed Attorney-General.

One of the first acts of the new Government was to release the men who had been imprisoned by the Military Tribunal. The released men were acclaimed by enthusiastic crowds in Dublin and elsewhere, and the Irish Republican Army, one of the bodies proscribed by the Cosgrave Government, began to hold public parades once again. The country was in a ferment of excitement, not unmixed with apprehension. Mr. De Valera made a declaration of policy on March 15 in which he stated that the Government were determined to maintain law and order and stood for one Government and one army.

In January preparations were already afoot in London for the Imperial Economic Conference at Ottawa. On January 13 two members of Mr. Cosgrave's Government, Mr. McGilligan, Minister for Industry and Commerce, and Mr. Hogan, Minister for Agriculture, had a meeting in London with Mr. Runciman, President of the Board of Trade, with the object of examining the trade relations between the United Kingdom and the Free State as a preliminary to the general discussion of inter-Imperial trade at Ottawa. During the election these Ministers expressed the fear that Mr. De Valera's policy if put into force would upset Anglo-Free State economic relations and would deprive the Free State of the advantages that would accrue to it from a successful outcome of the Ottawa discussions. These predictions were unhappily fulfilled.

When the new Government had clearly shown its hand, Mr. Thomas, Secretary of State for the Dominions, was questioned in the House of Commons on the situation. He stated that His Majesty's Government in the United Kingdom regarded the relations between the two countries as resting on the treaty of 1921. Shortly afterwards Mr. Thomas, having consulted the Free State High Commissioner in London on the policy of the new Government, made a further statement in the House. It was manifest, he said, that the Oath was an integral part of the treaty hitherto honourably observed by both countries. He also said that the Free State Government were bound by the most formal and explicit undertaking to continue to pay the Land Annuities to the National Debt Commissioners. Notes were exchanged between the two Governments setting out their respective views.

When the Dail met at the end of April Mr. De Valera introduced his Bill to remove the Oath of Allegiance from the Constitution, contending that it was not mandatory in the treaty, and that it would make for unity and peace in the country. It was passed by a majority of 8 votes. It was drastically amended in the Senate, and its operation, in accordance with the Constitution, was delayed for eighteen months.

The first *Fianna Fail* Budget imposed much additional taxation, the standard rate of income tax being increased to 5s. in the £. Tariffs were imposed on a wide range of imports, mainly manufactured goods from Great Britain, and the business community began to voice protests. There were several modifications in the course of the next few months. The Government explained that the increased taxation was unavoidable because of the large deficit left to them by their predecessors, and justified the import duties as necessary for the protection of Irish industries and home produce.

The Free State Government had accepted the invitation of the Canadian Government to participate in the Ottawa Conference, and Mr. O'Kelly, Mr. Lemass, and Dr. Ryan were appointed delegates. Mr. Thomas announced on June 2 that since the Free State Government repudiated an agreement entered into between the two Governments, the Government of the United Kingdom felt that no good purpose could be served by entering into trade discussions in preparation for Ottawa with the Free State Government until that Government was ready to observe an agreement.

Mr. De Valera having expressed his willingness to discuss the situation with British Ministers, Lord Hailsham, Secretary of State for War, and Mr. Thomas went to Dublin, and on June 8 had a talk with Mr. De Valera at which it was agreed that a discussion would take place in London on June 10. This discussion duly took place between Mr. De Valera and Mr. O'Kelly on the one side, and the Prime Minister, Mr. Baldwin, Sir H. Samuel (Home Secretary), and Mr. Thomas on the other. Arbitration on the moneys in dispute was discussed, but Mr. De Valera would not agree to the British Government's offer to have the questions at issue referred to an Empire Tribunal in accordance with the decision of the Imperial Conference of 1930, and the discussions were again fruitless.

The Eucharistic Congress was held in Dublin in the last week in June and coincided with the 1,500th anniversary of the landing of St. Patrick, and for the time being politics were put aside. The culminating ceremony was the open air Mass in the Phœnix Park which was attended by nearly a million people, representing many countries of the world. The only unpleasant incident in connexion with the Congress was the attacks made by irresponsible youths in certain parts of Northern Ireland on returning pilgrims. These attacks were strongly condemned by the Northern Ireland Government and leaders of the Protestant Church, but caused a good deal of sectarian bitterness in the North.

A half-year's instalment of the Land Annuities fell due on June 30, and Mr. Thomas introduced the Irish Free State (Special Duties) Bill, empowering the Treasury to impose duties on Free State imports with the object of making good the moneys with-

held.   The Bill was speedily passed, and a Treasury Order came
into force on July 15 imposing a duty of 20 per cent. on about
two-thirds of the Free State Exports to Great Britain, comprising
live animals, dairy produce, and meat.   The Free State Government replied by placing heavy duties on coal, cement, iron and
steel, electrical goods, and other imports from Great Britain.

On July 14 Mr. Norton, Leader of the Labour group in the
Dail, had a conference in London with Mr. Lansbury, M.P.,
Sir Stafford Cripps, M.P., Major Attlee, M.P., and Mr. Arthur
Greenwood, M.P., and was subsequently received at Downing
Street by the Prime Minister.   He offered a suggestion that the
matters in dispute should be the subject of direct negotiation or,
alternately, that a Commission of four, comprising two representatives from each Government, should examine and report
on the whole situation.   The result of this step was another
meeting in London, on July 15, between the Prime Minister and
Mr. De Valera.   The Lord Chancellor and the Attorney-General
also took part in the conversations, but again it was announced
that no agreement was reached.

On July 17 the Free State Government issued a statement
declaring their willingness to submit the questions in dispute
to arbitration, but insisting that the personnel of the arbitral
Tribunal should not be confined to the British Empire.   As
proof of their good faith they announced that the disputed sums
had been paid into a suspense account pending the final determination of their ownership.

The Free State delegates returned from the Ottawa Conference
without having secured any considerable benefits in the way
of trade agreements.   The only agreements they were able to
make were with Canada and South Africa, and these did not
promise any substantial expansion in Free State exports.

In September it fell to Mr. De Valera's lot to preside over
the Council of the League of Nations at Geneva.   His opening
speech, criticising the inactivity of the League, created widespread interest.   While at Geneva he appears to have had talks
with Sir John Simon, Britain's representative, on the Anglo-
Free State situation.   At any rate another meeting between
Mr. De Valera and Mr. Thomas was arranged.   This meeting
took place at Downing Street on October 5, and it was afterwards
announced that formal negotiations between the two Governments on the questions at issue would begin on October 14 in
London.   On that date Mr. De Valera, with Messrs. MacEntee,
Geoghegan, and Maguire met Mr. Thomas, Sir John Simon,
and other members of the British Cabinet.   The discussions
lasted two days, and nobody was surprised when it was announced
that they had again broken down.

On this occasion Mr. De Valera presented a claim for the
repayment to the Free State Government of the 30,000,000*l.*

already paid in respect of Land Annuities, and of something like 400,000,000*l.* in respect of alleged over-taxation of Ireland from the Act of Union to the establishment of the Free State.

The economic war went on. The Special Duties on Irish imports to the United Kingdom were increased to 30 per cent. and in some cases to 40 per cent. This increase was due to the fact that the 20 per cent. duty was not producing the equivalent of the moneys withheld. It was also intended to counter the effect of the bounties which the Free State Government were paying on exports of cattle, butter, and other produce.

The attitude of the new Free State Government to the Governor-General, Mr. James McNeill, was known to be un-friendly, and matters came to a head in July with the publication by Mr. McNeill of certain letters that had passed between him and Mr. De Valera concerning discourtesies shown to him by some Ministers.

In November Mr. De Valera made formal submission to the King that Mr. McNeill should be displaced and His Majesty accepted. The Executive Council advised the King to appoint Mr. Donal Buckley to the office. The appointment was duly made, and Mr. Buckley took the Oath in Dublin on November 6. It was decided that he should not reside at the Viceregal Lodge and a house was provided for him in a suburb of Dublin.

Late in November Mr. De Valera was again in Geneva, pre-siding over the League Council, but had to return hastily to deal with a threatened strike on the Free State railways. The strike was temporarily averted by the offer of a subsidy to the railway workers.

On December 20 the Government announced their intention of paying the loan raised among sympathisers in the United States during the Anglo-Irish troubles in cash and in Irish Free State Government securities.

Interference with meetings in support of Mr. Cosgrave's party led to the formation, towards the end of the year, of the Army Comrades' Association whose avowed object was to guarantee free speech. Members of the Association came into conflict here and there with *Fianna Fail* supporters, but nothing of a serious nature occurred. Mr. De Valera issued a prohibition against the public carrying of arms whether by the A.C.A. or the I.R.A., an edict which was welcomed by the public.

The British tariff proved particularly damaging to the Free State cattle trade, and the Board of Trade returns for the year showed a big reduction in the number of Irish Free State cattle imported into Great Britain. A further bounty was announced by the Free State Government in December on exports of poultry to Great Britain. Prices of animals and of dairy produce fell to extraordinarily low levels in the Free State throughout the year and fairs and markets were reduced to very small proportions.

CHAPTER II.

CANADA.

THE Third Session of the Seventeenth Parliament under the Bennett Conservative Administration was opened ceremonially at Ottawa by Lord Bessborough, Governor-General, on February 4. In his Speech from the Throne, read in English and French, Lord Bessborough referred to the universal economic disturbance and distress, which had created conditions beyond the control of the Canadian people, but adherence to policies designed for the welfare of the nation had minimised their adverse influence. Evidence of the fundamental soundness of Canada could be discerned in the over-subscription of the recent National Service Loan, in Canada's preservation of her high place in the world's commerce, and in the favourable balance of trade. But prosperity in full measure must await a satisfactory adjustment of accounts between debtor and creditor nations and a restoration of international monetary standards.

The Speech was brief and, after forecasting legislation to amend the insurance, patent, shipping and fisheries Acts, it laid emphasis on the determination of Ministers to maintain a policy of rigid economy consistent with the discharge of statutory and contractual obligations.

The main estimates for the fiscal year 1932-33, totalling 356,773,794 dollars, compared with 400,500,000 dollars for the previous year, were tabled in the House of Commons on February 15 by Mr. E. N. Rhodes, Minister of Finance, who, with Senator Arthur Meighen, Minister without Portfolio, had been sworn in as Cabinet members in January. Drastic cuts were made in nearly all Votes, the only substantial increase being the interest on the Public Debt by 13,000,000 dollars. These reductions included a cut of 10 per cent. in the salaries of Ministers, Members of Parliament, and all public servants.

Debates on financial matters in the House of Commons during March involved currency questions and the advocacy, principally by representatives of the Western agricultural constituencies, of the abandonment of the gold standard. Mr. R. B. Bennett, the Prime Minister, explained that while there had been a technical departure from the gold standard, the Dominion's foreign commitments, the interest and sinking fund payments due mainly in New York, amounting to about 1,000,000 dollars a day, would make the sudden abandonment of the gold standard and a reversion to unsound credit " an experiment the Government dared not sanction." The Canadian dollar had been driven considerably below par when the English sovereign left the gold standard, but if Canada followed a similar course the dollar, in the Premier's opinion, might drop as low as 25 cents, with disastrous effects upon Canada's credit.

The extension until May 1 of the legislation passed during the last session giving the Governor in Council extraordinary powers for unemployment and farm relief and enabling the executive " to take any steps considered necessary for expenditure or otherwise under the present economic conditions " gave rise to prolonged debate, the Liberals, led by Mr. Mackenzie King, strongly opposing the renewal of such powers while Parliament was in session.

On April 6 Mr. Rhodes introduced his first Budget. After a brief survey of events in international finance, he outlined the steps taken by the Government to meet the situation created by the depreciation of the Canadian dollar in New York, such as the arrangements for an extension of credits in New York, the prohibition of the export of gold except under licence, and the purchase of the output of the Canadian gold mines. Their efforts had been directed to preventing any flight from the Canadian dollar, to maintaining a reservoir of credit, and to meeting all external debts at the due dates. Canadians could look back with satisfaction on an accomplishment which had contributed greatly to a return of confidence, which was evidenced by the improvement of the position of the Canadian dollar and Canadian public securities. Mr. Rhodes placed the total revenues for 1931-32 at 334,750,000 dollars, compared with 356,000,000 dollars in the previous year, the main decline being in Customs and income tax. Ordinary expenditure had been 378,700,000 dollars, which was 19,000,000 dollars less than the estimates and 22,000,000 dollars less than the previous year, but to these must be added 17,000,000 dollars on capital account and special expenditure of 55,000,000 dollars, of which the wheat bonus accounted for 11,000,000 dollars and the unemployment relief programme 38,250,000 dollars. The Federal Treasury had also had to make loans of over 22,000,000 dollars to various provincial administrations. The total Federal expenditure for the year was therefore 454,246,000 dollars, which was 119,500,000 dollars (about 24,000,000l. at par) in excess of revenue. Setting forth the detailed balance sheet of the country, the Minister placed its total liabilities on March 31 at 2,832,000,000 dollars and its active assets at 451,000,000 dollars, which reduced the net debt to 2,381,000,000 dollars.

After announcing increases in corporation and personal income tax, as well as raising the rates of sales and excise taxes, Mr. Rhodes declared that as the near approach of the Imperial Conference made it undesirable to make any tariff changes affecting British preference, no major tariff adjustments could be made. Mr. Rhodes added that the sacrifices now being asked from the Canadian people might entail hardship, but in the long run they would be less than might befall from a less courageous policy.

Colonel J. L. Ralston, a former Cabinet Minister in the Liberal administration, strongly attacked the Government during the Budget debate for its practice of advancing loans to the Provinces, and criticised the leniency of income tax on the richer as compared with the poorer classes. The Government's trade policy, he contended, was a contributory factor in the country's financial difficulties. Since Canada had the necessaries of life to sell, she should be able to recover more quickly than any other country, but was having her foreign trade strangled by artificial barriers, particularly the fixing of valuation for Customs purposes. The avowed object of the Government's tariff policy, continued Colonel Ralston, was an increase in industrial employment, but this had not been attained. Official data showed that there was substantially less employment than two years ago in industries like textile manufacturing, which had been the largest beneficiaries of high protection. The " Canada First " policy had shut out imports, decreased employment, and maintained high prices.

Mr. Mackenzie King, the Opposition Leader, expressed regret that the Government had not made a friendly gesture in respect of preferential tariffs to Great Britain as a preliminary to the Imperial Economic Conference, and similarly complained that the Government had gradually fastened upon Canada a prohibitive tariff against imports.

After the defeat of a Progressive (Farmers) amendment urging the nationalisation of the credit system and stabilisation of currency on the basis of maintained and stable price levels, the Budget resolutions were carried by 108 votes to 72 on April 27.

In the same month the trade agreement between Canada and New Zealand, which had been the subject of protracted negotiations by cable since it was provisionally signed at Honolulu in January to replace a treaty abrogated in November, 1930, was brought before the House of Commons and ratified. Under this agreement Canada obtained preferential tariffs for exports of lumber, automobiles, certain canned goods, rubber products, and other manufactured articles, while New Zealand gained special tariff rates for wool, butter, and products receiving preferential treatment under the standing agreement with Australia.

Other subjects of debate were the constitution of a national system of broadcasting along the lines recommended (and subsequently adopted) of a Special Committee of the House, the St. Lawrence Waterway Scheme (culminating in the signing of an important treaty with the United States in July), transportation problems and trade affairs.

After one of the shortest regular sessions of recent years Parliament was prorogued by Mr. Justice Duff, in the absence on tour of the Governor-General, on May 26.

Immediately following prorogation Ministers became absorbed

I

in preparations for the outstanding event of the year—the Imperial Economic Conference.

Under the chairmanship of Sir George Perley, a Parliamentary Committee was formed to make plans for the reception of the Empire delegates. Briefs were invited by the Prime Minister from the Provincial Premiers, meetings of farmers, manufacturers, and industrialists were held, and a Governmental Committee appointed to consider representations made affecting the list of goods submitted by the British Government for which Britain considered an advantageous market might be developed in Canada. In this connection Sir William Clark, High Commissioner for Great Britain in Canada, proved to be a valuable liaison.

Delegates [1] from the Governments of the United Kingdom, Australia, New Zealand, South Africa, Irish Free State, Newfoundland, India, and Southern Rhodesia all arrived in Ottawa about the second week in July, accompanied in some cases by their wives and with advisers and secretarial staffs.

The conference opened on July 21 with an imposing ceremony in the Chamber of the House of Commons, which was filled to the utmost capacity.

Under the presidency of the Prime Minister of Canada (the original sponsor of the conference) speeches outlining in general terms the views and policies of their respective Governments were delivered by Mr. Bennett for Canada, Mr. Baldwin for the United Kingdom, Mr. Stanley Bruce for Australia, Mr. J. G. Coates for New Zealand, Mr. N. C. Havenga for South Africa, Mr. Sean T. O'Kelly for the Irish Free State, Mr. L. E. Emerson for Newfoundland, Sir Atul C. Chatterjee for India, and Mr. H. U. Moffat for Southern Rhodesia.

The decision was taken to allocate the work of the conference to five major committees, to deal with (1) Promotion of trade within the Commonwealth, (2) Methods of Customs administration, (3) Trade relations with foreign countries, (4) Monetary and financial questions, and (5) Methods of economic co-operation within the Commonwealth.

Of these subjects the promotion of trade ranked of first importance and the Anglo-Canadian trade negotiations overshadowed the discussions with other countries. Negotiations of the British delegates with the other Dominions and India presented comparatively few difficulties, except perhaps the claim from New Zealand and Australia for preferential taxes on meat which the British delegates were unable to accept, but who subsequently agreed to a plan of quantitative restriction with a view to the raising of

---

[1] The complete list of delegates, advisers, and staffs given in the published Report of the Conference (Cmd. 4175) gave the names of 294 persons officially attending the conference. In addition there were groups of industrial and financial experts representing various interests or unofficially connected with the several delegations. Canada's own Government delegates were drawn from a panel of the whole Canadian Cabinet as the subject required.

prices. In the Anglo-Canadian discussions, however, difficulties were less easily overcome and deadlocks occasionally threatened.

Mr. Bennett's dislike of the Soviet had been re-enforced by the pressure of different Canadian interests, notably the lumber men of British Columbia, Quebec, and New Brunswick, who were eager to find compensation for their recent exclusion from the American market in securing a guarantee of a large share of the British market for timber, and he was insistent in his demand upon the British delegates to consent to a complete embargo upon Russian wheat and timber, but this was refused. The British Ministers pointed out that they could not make an embargo upon Russian lumber effective unless it was extended to all the Baltic countries, to which it was a simple matter to ship Russian lumber surreptitiously ; that they had advanced large credit facilities for the promotion of trade to Russia which might be lost through an embargo, and that they did not want to commit themselves to a discriminatory trade war with Russia.

Canadian delegates, however, kept the question of unfair Russian competition to the forefront, and urged that unless it was checked, especially with regard to wheat and lumber, preferences in the British markets would be nullified. Eventually a formula was agreed upon that if any Dominion could demonstrate that preferences accorded to it were being vitiated by the trading activities of a foreign nation conducted under State control, adequate measures would be taken to rectify the situation. The object of the Bennett Ministry was to secure as generous preferential concessions for Canadian products as possible without making too serious sacrifices of the domestic tariff. The reciprocal offers of concessions to British exports were exhaustively examined and at length a series of agreements between Great Britain and all the Dominions and India (but excluding the Irish Free State) were concluded, in addition to bilateral agreements [1] between the different Dominions.

The gist of the agreements made by Great Britain was that, on the one hand, Britain agreed to continue the existing preferences to Dominion products and to extend them to other commodities such as wheat, meat, and certain minerals. On the other hand, the Dominions and India agreed to lower their tariff barriers against British goods in some cases and in others to widen

---

[1] Agreements signed at the conclusion of the conference were as follows :—

(i) United Kingdom —Australia.	(viii) Canada	—Irish Free State.
(ii) „ „ —S. Africa.	(ix) „	—S. Africa.
(iii) „ „ —New Zealand.	(x) „	—S. Rhodesia.
(iv) „ „ —India.	(xi) S. Africa	—Irish Free State.
(v) „ „ —Newfoundland.	(xii) New Zealand—S. Africa.	
(vi) „ „ —S. Rhodesia.		
(vii) „ „ —Canada.		

During the conference negotiations were commenced for agreements between other members of the British Commonwealth, and substantial progress was made.

the margin of preference for them and to carry out certain reforms in Customs administration by removing or investigating special regulations which had proved serious hindrances to British exports. Canada also agreed to appoint a Tariff Advisory Board, to whom British exporters could make representations. The goods specifically granted advantages by the Anglo - Canadian Agreement were wheat, apples, butter, bacon, and cheese. An undertaking by Britain of the removal of restrictions on the importation of Canadian cattle was also incorporated. The general lowering of tariff barriers, however, while ardently advocated by many of the delegates, was not whole-heartedly supported.

Proceedings of the other four Committees which had been working concurrently were harmonious and a number of difficult problems faced.

The report of the Monetary and Financial Committee, which had dealt with questions of inflation, bimetallism and a proposed common Imperial currency, supported in effect the financial policies recently pursued by the British Government and the Bank of England, and recorded an agreement that the British nations should work together at the forthcoming World Economic Conference.

The Committee on Customs Administration condemned the system of arbitrary valuations for Customs purposes and other administrative practices used for strengthening protective tariffs.

The Committee on Methods of Economic Co-operation was unable to endorse any plan for a permanent Imperial Economic Secretariat, which had been urged by certain delegates, and decided that the problem of co-ordinating the activities of bodies like the Empire Marketing Board should be the subject of further study by a committee to meet, probably in London, in the spring of 1933. The thorny problem of " Empire content " gave rise to sharp divergence of views about the scale which should be fixed, and was left for future consideration.

The Committee on Trade Relations with Foreign Countries met only a few times and its deliberations on the complicated question of the relation of preferences to " most-favoured-nation" clauses in commercial treaties with foreign countries resulted in a decision that each country must take its own course on such matters.

On the morning of August 20 the whole conference again assembled in the Commons' Chamber, where the agreements were signed and speeches delivered by each of the leaders of delegations. At this assembly the following resolution was unanimously adopted :—

" The nations of the British Commonwealth, having entered into certain agreements with one another for the extension of mutual trade by means of reciprocal preferential tariffs, this conference takes note of these agreements and records its convictions that by the lowering or removal of barriers among themselves provided for in these agreements, the flow of trade between the various countries of the Empire will be facilitated, and that, by the consequent increase in the purchasing power of their peoples, the trade of the world will also be stimulated and increased.

"Further, that this conference regards the conclusion of these agreements as a step forward which should in future lead to further progress in the same direction and which will utilise the protective duties to ensure that the resources and industries of the Empire are developed on sound economic lines."

The principal British delegates left Quebec for England on August 21.

Although it was recognised that immediate results on a wide scale could not be expected, the findings of the conference were generally welcomed in the Dominion as a fine Imperial achievement. Addressing the Annual Convention of Canadian Chambers of Commerce on September 14, Mr. H. H. Stevens, Minister of Trade and Commerce, expressed his belief that " marvellous opportunities " had been opened up for Canadian exporters through the Ottawa Agreements. But the benefits of the agreements, he said, could only be fully realised if Canadian exporters improved their methods and standards of overseas marketing.

Canadian railway difficulties, which had been intensified by prevailing economic conditions, were reflected in the Report of the Royal Commission presented to the Government on September 21. This Commission, appointed in November, 1931, under the chairmanship of Mr. Justice Duff, had made personal inspection of both the Canadian Pacific and Canadian National railway systems and exhaustively investigated all branches of their administration. The Commission found that the principal contributory causes of transportation difficulties were over-development of the railways beyond the immediate needs of the country ; aggressive and uncontrolled competition between the two transcontinental systems ; the reaction of world trade depression ; the competition of other forms of transport, notably by road ; inelasticity of freight rates ; contractual arrangements with labour organisations which established rigid wage scales and inflexible labour practices generally.

The Commission considered that the identity of the two systems should be maintained ; the management [1] of the Canadian National Railways should be freed from political interference and community pressure ; machinery should be provided for the co-operation of the two systems so as to ensure the elimination of duplicate services and the avoidance of extravagance ; there should be economies on a scale to reduce the burdens of the Canadian National lines to reasonable dimensions, and protection should be provided for the Canadian Pacific Company against arbitrary action of the C.N.R. which might prejudice its interests. To achieve this the Commission recommended for the Canadian

[1] Sir Henry Thornton had resigned his post as President in July.

National system the appointment of a Board of Trustees in which would be vested all the powers of the existing directorate.

Concluding their comprehensive Report, the Commission added a note of warning that the financial position of the State-owned system was a contributory factor of the first importance to transport problems.

The opening of the new Welland Canal by the Governor-General on August 6 marked an historic event in the development of Canada's inland shipping and, as a completed sector of the St. Lawrence Waterway Scheme, one of immense economic possibilities.

The landing (in September) of a shipment of Russian oil at Montreal in exchange for Canadian aluminium aroused some vigorous controversy in the light of Canada's strong stand at the Imperial Conference against trade with the Soviet.

The Prime Minister defended the transaction, which he said provided work for some 300 men, by pointing out that Russia originally wished to make payment in coal, which would have been damaging to Britain, but that oil was not included in the list of commodities upon which the Government had been empowered by Parliament to place an embargo.

At Winnipeg, during the same month, wheat reached the lowest price recorded, the October quotation being $49\frac{3}{8}$ cents a bushel against the previous lowest of 50 cents in December, 1930, when the Government intervened to check the decline.

In a speech at Seaforth, Ontario, on September 29, in support of Mr. W. H. Golding, the Liberal candidate for the South Huron by-election, who gained the seat against the Government candidate, Mr. Mackenzie King announced a new policy of the Liberal Party. This was the first revision of the Liberal policy since the National Convention of 1919. The Liberal Party, stated Mr. King, pledged itself to advocate while in opposition and to enact immediately on the attainment of power, the complete repeal of all exchange regulations, dumping duties, and "Order-in-Council tariffs." It further pledged itself to scale down the existing tariff to the level of the Dunning Budget of 1930—when the Liberals were in office—and to enact that no tariff against Great Britain shall exceed 50 per cent. of the general tariff rate. Mr. King emphasised the traditional Liberal policy of non-interference by one part of the Empire with the domestic affairs of the other, and declared that Canada must trade with the world as well as with the Empire.

The Liberal Leader gave fuller exposition of the party's policy during the debates of the Fourth [1] Session of Parliament, which was opened by Lord Bessborough on October 6. The principal business of this session was the ratification of the Anglo-Canadian Agreement made at the Imperial Conference.

---

[1] The strength of the parties at this session was: Conservatives, 139; Liberals, 88; Progressives and Labour, 18.

Sustained criticism of certain features of the agreement were
made by Mr. Mackenzie King, Mr. Malcolm, former Minister of
Trade and Commerce, Mr. Lapointe, former Minister of Justice,
and other Liberal members. They took strong exception to the
agreement as tending to interfere with British fiscal policy, to
tariff bargaining and to the diversion of trade into special channels
instead of " more business with the whole world."

Mr. Stevens, speaking for the Government, replied that the
agreements reached were the unanimous result of a conference
of representatives of all parts of the Empire and that a genuine
effort had been made to put into practical form the general desire
for closer economic co-operation between the members of the
British Commonwealth such as would strengthen the ties of
sentiment which already bound them together. There was
nothing in the agreement so far as Canada was concerned which
militated against world trading.

In moving the second reading of the Bill on November 9, Mr.
Bennett discussed the five-year clause of the agreement. It
was true, he said, that Canada had bound herself for five years
to maintain in a general way the tariff structure, but there was
a provision whereby, in the event of the British or Canadian
Governments desiring to vary the terms, consultation between
the Governments might take place. Mr. Bennett declared that
the Canadian textile industry had been saved by the regulations
preventing dumping from low-wage countries.

Concluding the debate—which had been lengthened by
continued opposition—the Prime Minister, quoting from many
speeches and records, maintained that the Liberal opposition in
contesting the agreement for reciprocal preferences from Britain
was going contrary to the whole political history of the party
since the days when Sir Wilfrid Laurier had advocated the return
of preference for preference.

Wheat marketing again came before the House in November.
After recounting the difficulties of the Wheat Pools and the circumstances which led to the appointment of Mr. John McFarland
as General Manager of the Central Selling Agency of the Pools
and explaining the process by which Western wheat was marketed,
the Prime Minister said that it had been found necessary two
years ago to guarantee bank advances to the Pools and to ensure
an adequate futures market in order to maintain prices.

Adjournment of Parliament took place on November 25.

The Ottawa Agreements Bill was assented to on the day of
adjournment, and other major matters dealt with by Parliament
were unemployment (for which Mr. Gideon, Minister of Labour,
had shown that the Federal Treasury had disbursed 115,000,000
dollars on direct and indirect relief), and the Decennial Redistribution Bill, for which a Committee was appointed to study
representation according to the census of 1931.

A new political movement known as the Co-operative Common-wealth Federation—formed at a Labour Convention in Calgary during August—created widespread attention. With Mr. J. S. Woodsworth (Labour, Winnipeg) as President, the new party invited all those who were dissatisfied with the current state of affairs and advocated a new economic system on Socialistic lines. Its programme appealed for financial nationalisation with a view to regulating credit and investment operation; abandonment of the gold standard and adoption of a policy of inflation; public ownership of public utilities; ownership by the State or co-operative organisation of facilities for the handling of farm products; measures designed to bring about the more equitable distribution of wealth; revision of the Constitution of Canada, and re-defining of the responsibilities of federal and provincial authorities; re-casting of tariff policies, and a non-party system of Government.

The United Farmers of Alberta decided to give the movement their support, and this was followed by the affiliation of the Farmer (Progressive) Party of Saskatchewan. Later, at the Annual Convention of the Ontario United Farmers at Toronto (December 2), the Ontario Farmers also voted unanimously in support of the new organisation, but decided to retain their own separate identity.

As a repercussion of this movement the Liberal Party—which, with all parties, had closely followed the course of the United States General Election in November—shortly afterwards provided a framework for the co-ordination of their activities by the constitution of a new National Liberal Federation, with Mr. Vincent Massey, formerly Canadian Minister at Washington, as President and with plans for a vigorous campaign throughout the country.

The continued agricultural depression naturally had political results in the Prairie Provinces, the most pronounced being the overwhelming defeat of the Conservative Party in the Provincial General Elections of Manitoba on June 14, when the Bracken Government, transformed into a Liberal-Progressive coalition, was returned to power despite its ten-year tenure of office. Dissatisfaction with the policies of the Ottawa administration was the principal reason.

In British Columbia Mr. S. F. Tolmie, the Provincial Premier, attempted to form a Coalition Government to hold office during the emergency period, but was unsuccessful.

In Nova Scotia, where coal-mining is one of the principal industries of the Province, drastic changes, involving the closing of unprofitable collieries, were recommended by the Duncan Commission early in the year.

In the Federal by-elections Liberals gained two seats from Government candidates (Mr. W. H. Golding for South Huron and Mr. J. F. McNeil for Summerside P.E.I.), both in October, the results of other by-elections being a Conservative victory (Mr. P. G. Davies, Athabaska, in March) and the retention of one Liberal and one Government seat (Mr. G. B. Jones, Royal, N.B., and Mr. J. Jean, Maisonneuve, Montreal), both in June.

The closing political events of the year were the raising of a two - year Federal Government loan of 80,000,000 dollars (16,000,000*l.* at par) ; the conclusion of a temporary Trade Agreement with Germany, and the negotiations by Mr. C. H. Cahan, Secretary of State, for a new Trade Treaty with France.

The operation of the Ottawa Agreements and other Anglo-Canadian affairs were taken up by Mr. Bennett during a short visit to London in the Christmas Recess.

CHAPTER III.

THE UNION OF SOUTH AFRICA—SOUTH-WEST PROTECTORATE— SOUTHERN RHODESIA.

THE UNION OF SOUTH AFRICA.

CONDEMNED at length even by the farming community, in whose interests its critics had averred bias at the expense of other industrial institutions, the Union Government found itself increasingly embarrassed as the year 1931 drew towards its close.

General Smuts (Leader of the Opposition), in a speech at Standerton (Transvaal), on January 6, summed up the position of the country as it appeared to the South African Party when he said that it had to face the alternatives of gold bankruptcy or sterling. Whatever position the Government took up the Union would have to leave the gold standard immediately, or after still greater struggles and sufferings.

Every public thought and action seemed to be dominated by the severity of the economic crisis. Moreover, its depressing influence was intensified by numerous public utterances directed to racial prejudices. Moderates of both white races despaired of the future, when even the possibility of general insolvency failed to reconcile clashing national ambitions. In order to counteract the influence of non-gold arguments in the agricultural districts the Government increased the export subsidies to meet losses on the exchange rate. Economists viewed the policy with apprehension. They agreed that while the subsidy system might temporarily pacify agriculture, it would eventually involve the country in financial commitments beyond its capacity of bearing.

Parliament met in an atmosphere of disillusionment and suspicion on January 27. The business of the session was overshadowed by gold and finance. The forces of the Government, already weakened by rumours of deflection, were concentrated on the defence of its gold standard policy. As soon as the House assembled, General Hertzog (Prime Minister) gave notice of motion for the appointment of a Select Committee to inquire whether the welfare of the country demanded the maintenance of the gold standard. The ensuing debate was one of the tensest in the history of the Union Parliament. It ranged widely—from Great Britain's anti-dumping regulations to the consideration of Germany's case at the Peace Conference—and at hardly any period of its three weeks' duration did prejudice allow a dispassionate examination of policy. Nor did the Premier further his case by the vehemence of his hostility towards the Opposition, particularly towards the Leader of the Opposition. His speech, listened to by a crowded House on February 22, was signally unimpressive as an exposition of policy, but it lost nothing in bitterness on that account.

Opposition objection to the appointment of the Premier's Select Committee was based on the argument that as the Government was determined to remain on the gold standard the recommendations of the Committee would be disregarded should they run counter to the Government's agreed policy. General Smuts' statement of the Opposition case was that South Africa's crisis was not due to world conditions. If the Union had abandoned gold and had taken advantage of her position as a gold-producer, so far from being in the same depressed condition as other countries, she would be enjoying a minor boom. General Smuts reminded the House that the Minister of Finance had admitted that if the Union were to leave the gold standard the mines would benefit to the extent of 13,000,000*l.*, and primary products to the extent of 5,000,000*l.*, which as additional income would make all the difference between deepest depression and real prosperity. General Smuts deplored the fact that when industry was almost at a standstill the Government had nothing to propose except an academic inquiry. Nevertheless, Parliament agreed to the appointment of the Committee by 76 votes to 60.

In the following May the Committee presented its report. It was its unanimous declaration that " the abandonment of the gold standard would confer no absolute benefit on the Union and would not increase our national wealth by one penny. . . . It would at best only temporarily alleviate the matter by bringing about a redistribution of wealth in the country, the full effects of which would be difficult to foresee." The report continued : " On the other hand, it would introduce absolute drawbacks in the uncertainty as regards the value of money, the shock to confidence, the impairment of economic machinery, and the substitution of an even more unstable measure of value when the chief evil we are suffering from is the instability of the present measure." The report considered that the Union had largely overcome the drawback incident on Great Britain's departure from gold, and such drawbacks as it was still suffering from were considered to be the result of general depression, not of that phase which forced Great Britain off gold. In conclusion it was stated that the " Union is in a position to maintain the gold standard ; and the maintenance thereof and the adjustment of its affairs to a new basis, which is proceeding, will leave it in a stronger position to face the future."

In reality this document was purely a Government report, for the Opposition refused to accept nomination to the Committee, and resigned after attending the first meeting.

General Smuts resumed his attack when the report came up for the consideration of the House. He described it as an academic ignoring of facts ; a repetition of predictions about the results of Great Britain going off gold which, made months previously, were still awaiting a scintilla of verification. The obstinate clinging to the gold theory was ruining the country, which, but for the gold mines, would already have collapsed under the strain. He said that all the most authoritative evidence given before the Committee—commercial banks, the gold industry, and chambers of commerce—was unanimous in recommending the abandonment of gold.

The Minister of Finance replied that General Smuts was exaggerating the difficulties of the country, and that his agitation against the gold standard was responsible for capital being sent abroad and not brought back. No country which was able to stay on the gold standard had abandoned it, and those compelled to go off gold were anxious to return to it.

Other disturbers of the harmony of the session were the disruptive rumblings emanating from within the Government party itself. Many prominent Nationalists became restive at the stubbornness of the adherence to gold, and at the resistance offered by the Minister of Finance to a system of devaluation. This policy was favoured by certain supporters of the Government because they regarded it as a reasonable alternative to the abandonment of gold. Further, it was more generally felt that Mr. Havenga's announced intention of introducing a Bill to provide for a new currency was ill-advised at such a juncture. This measure was to create three new coinage denominations, firstly, a coin to be known as a Rand, to be the equivalent of the sovereign ; secondly, a Florin, equal to the tenth part of a Rand ; and thirdly, a Cent, equalling one-hundredth part of a Rand. But before the Minister of Finance could proceed beyond a formal notice of motion, the Prime Minister was widely petitioned to postpone further action until the women of the Union, who would be affected by the proposed change to a far greater extent than men, should have an opportunity of recording their vote on the question.

Embodied in Mr. Pirow's Native Service Contract Bill,

a measure designed to bring about a more even distribution of labour supplies, there was what became known as the whipping clause. The adoption of this was fiercely contested during the procedure of a stormy debate. Its progress revealed serious differences in all ranks, especially between members of the South African Party. Those from the Cape registered disapproval of the Bill, an attitude denounced by the Transvaal and Natal members as destructive and ignorant. Outside Parliament, Church opinion strongly resented a measure which, it was asserted, would legalise what could only be described as thinly-disguised forced labour. A statement issued by the Bishop of Johannesburg said the effect of the Bill would be to drive thousands of natives down into a state of serfdom. Its passing would be contrary to the spirit of the Prime Minister's declared native policy.

There was a protracted debate on the Budget. The Minister of Finance asked for new taxation to raise 3,500,000l., and he recommended higher taxes on incomes, gold-mining profits and insurances, and an additional surtax on various imports. From a deepening anxiety concerning the country's financial position sprang a crop of rumours of pending political changes. For one thing, there was a growing belief that the Prime Minister, who was the recipient of birthday congratulations on April 3, would retire before the next General Election.

The Government had also to grapple with the financial troubles of the provincial councils. The Free State, on March 18, agreed without a division to the Administrator's motion to ask the Government to take over financial responsibility for the province, which was stated to be no longer able to carry on. The Government had repeatedly announced its desire to see the abolition of the provincial council system (ANNUAL REGISTER, 1931, p. 132), and Mr. J. H. Hofmeyer, in the House, had recently described their policy as one of insufficiency, ineffectiveness, and ineptitude.

In Natal, on the other hand, there was an influential movement for a greater measure of provincial control, failing which secession from the Union was suggested. In the Orange Free State and Transvaal the formation of other political organisations were further manifestation of dissatisfaction with the Government. The Natal movement quickly assumed formidable dimensions. It was stated on reliable authority that the secessionists numbered nine-tenths of the people of the province, who were actuated by a determination to fight the Government's policy regarding the councils, and to protest against its persistent and intensive campaign on behalf of Afrikaans and the Afrikaans people. The vital points of this movement were embodied in Article 2 of the Declaration to the Imperial Government which had been adopted by the Maritzburg Congress. It affirmed its intention of securing release from the present Union of South Africa, in order that the constitutional rights and liberties promised to Natal in

1909, but denied her by those since entrusted with the government of the Union, might be exercised in a fresh effort to secure racial co-operation in South Africa through a system of federation.

General Smuts' firm and diplomatic handling of a situation created mainly by members of his own party, saved a rupture, and eventually the Government appointed a Commission to report on what method of administration and local government should be substituted for the existing system.

The result of the Germiston by-election was a severe blow for the Government. The South African Party candidate had an absolute majority of 965 votes over his four opponents, and he obtained 1,181 votes more than the Nationalist nominee. General Smuts afterwards described the result as an emphatic protest against racialism and the gold standard policy of the Government. Germiston had given the Government notice to quit.

Severe as was this blow to the prestige of the Government, it was surpassed in dramatic intensity by a political development later in the year. In December, Mr. Tielman Roos, a former Minister of Justice in the Nationalist Government, resigned his position in the judiciary—he was senior member of the Appellate Division of the Supreme Court—in order to re-enter politics. Mr. Roos had been one of the most popular politicians in the country, with numerous friends among the Opposition, and the opinion became fairly general that his return to the arena paved the way for a coalition of Nationalist and South African Party moderates which would inevitably bring about the downfall of the Government.

Messrs. Havenga (Minister of Finance), Fourie (Minister of Mines), and Grobler (Minister of Lands) were the Union's delegates to the Imperial Economic Conference in Ottawa. Mr. Havenga, in the course of an interview at Cape Town, after the return of the party from Canada, said he was satisfied that the results of the conference were fair and reasonable, and that South Africa had every reason to be pleased with the result. "As between the Union and Great Britain," he added, "the balance of trade is considerably in favour of the latter ; it is therefore in our interests to make every effort to retain our share of the British markets by the stabilisation of existing concessions, and to extend that share by securing further concessions." Mr. Havenga expressed himself extremely pleased at the extension by Great Britain of existing preferences, and the part taken by Britain to develop the imports from South Africa of mutton, lamb, and chilled beef. As the agreements arrived at in Ottawa could be put into effect by administrative action, a special session of Parliament was not necessary.

SOUTH-WEST PROTECTORATE.

Early in the year the South-West Emergency Conference, attended by representative delegates from all parts of the country, met to consider possible remedial measures for the depressed state of commerce and industry, and to test the attitude of public opinion towards absorption in the Union, or the possibility of closer ties with it. Members of the United Party favoured some such policy, professing to see nothing but disaster in a continuation of the existing regime ; but the representatives of German-speaking interests, although pessimistic as to the outlook, declined to consider any suggestion savouring of amalgamation. They thought the country would be able to weather its difficulties, provided a loan of 200,000*l*. were forthcoming from the Union Government.

As an indirect outcome of the conference, the South-West African Farmers' and Labour Party came into existence, its policy being the abolition of the character of South-West Africa as a mandated territory, and its creation as an independent State with its own responsible Government. It further pledged itself to do everything possible to expedite the construction of the proposed Walvis Bay—Rhodesia railway.

SOUTHERN RHODESIA.

Mr. J. L. S. Jeffares, B.Sc., M.Inst.C.E., who conducted the Walvis Bay—Windhoek railway reconnaissance, recommended that in the event of the line being agreed to, the track should follow the Gobabis, Sandfontein, Eersterust, Botletle River Matetsi route. The total mileage from Gobabis to Matetsi would be 595, and the line would cost an average of 4,010*l*. per mile, making a total of 2,382,068*l*. He did not recommend a line from Plumtree to join up at 400 miles from Matetsi along the suggested route, as the cost would amount to 941,000*l*. In a second report Mr. Jeffares estimated that the traffic from Southern Rhodesia would amount to 700,000 tons per annum. In so far as the Union would be affected, the report saw no grounds for opposition from that source, as only 50,000 tons of coal and perhaps 5,000 tons of maize would be diverted by the new line.

Dr. A. E. Romyn, who was the official agriculturist attached to the survey party, reported favourably on the livestock outlook of the Gobabis-Matetsi section. Assuming that the line opened up a belt of country 150 miles wide, an area of 90,000 square miles would be available for development. The country could be settled either in small areas of 10,000 acres, or large blocks of 40,000 acres. Certain localities were suitable for dairying, once overseas markets were assured, and, given water (a comprehensive scheme for water development was considered a first step towards settlement), other districts possessed ranching possibilities. Except near the Botletle River and Matetsi the climate was stated to be healthy for Europeans.

Another interesting report was presented by the Geological expert, Mr. A. M. Macgregor, M.A. The possibility of developing the mineral industry in the surveyed area were regarded as small, as no deposits of commercial importance could be expected in the basalt country south-west of Matetsi. The granite country to the west of Plumtree might be found to carry veins of gold, or other metals, but no deposits appeared to be known. The discovery of alluvial diamonds in the overlaying Karroo beds was not impossible, but was unlikely in view of the nature of the deposits, which did not have the nature of far-travelled gravels in which a concentration of minerals was to be expected.

The Premier (the Hon. H. U. Moffat) was accompanied to Ottawa by the Minister of Finance (the Hon. P. D. L. Fynn). Prior to his departure from Salisbury he made an announcement regarding the future of the Premiership, and foreshadowed his retirement. This statement followed a ministerial crisis, which occurred soon after the Legislative Assembly met on March 31. In May the Premier suddenly tendered the resignation of his Cabinet to the Governor, who thereupon requested Mr. Moffat to form a fresh Ministry, and this he did by leaving out Mr. Fletcher, the Minister for Agriculture, whose portfolio was added to that of the Minister of Mines. This swift action was regarded as a consequence of Opposition attacks on Mr. Fletcher's policy. It was also understood that Mr. Moffat's retirement would take place after the next session of Parliament, which would be the last before the 1933 General Election.

Although there was a deficit of 18,000*l.* at the end of the financial year and extra taxation was sought to cover this and also the estimated deficit of 243,000*l.* in the current year, the country generally showed distinct signs of returning prosperity. No further progress was made with the proposed amalgamation of Northern and Southern Rhodesia, towards which the attitude of the Imperial Government was not regarded as encouraging ; but at the end of the year Mr. Moffat made a statement which indicated that the scheme was still in the forefront of Government politics as a practical ideal. The Premier considered that the door had been left open for a policy of amalgamation to be brought into effect. " I wish to say that not only has a great deal been done," continued Mr. Moffat in his Salisbury statement, " but that we have gone a long way on the road to the accomplishment of this policy, which will bring about the formation of a British Dominion in South Central Africa—a Dominion which is bound to have the very greatest influence on South Africa generally."

CHAPTER IV.

AUSTRALASIA.

AUSTRALIA.

THE political year opened in Australia with the installation of a National Coalition in office at Canberra, following upon the decisive defeat of Mr. Scullin at the General Election in December, 1931. The Ministry, headed by Mr. Lyons, was responsible for Commonwealth affairs throughout 1932, including Australia's representation at the Imperial Conference, Ottawa. During the year there were minor changes in the Ministry, including the translation of Mr. Stanley Bruce, the Assistant Treasurer, to London, as Minister without portfolio, representing the Commonwealth in the capital of the Empire. The change followed upon Mr. Bruce's successful leadership of the Commonwealth delegation at Ottawa. On October 5 Mr. J. E. Fenton, the Postmaster-General, resigned owing to disagreement with the tariff policy of the Lyons Ministry, consequent upon the agreement with Britain reached at Ottawa. Mr. Fenton regarded himself as pledged to a full protectionist policy, based upon the most generous development of primary and secondary industries in Australia, even if this involved hardship to British competitors. Apart from the tariff issue, Mr. Fenton continued his support of the Lyons Ministry. Mr. C. A. S. Hawker, Minister for Markets (Commerce), also resigned, differing from his colleagues upon a question of public expenditure. In particular, Mr. Hawker wished to reduce Parliamentary salaries from 750l. a year to 600l. The matter was debated in the House of Representatives on September 22. Mr. Lyons completed his Ministry by promoting Mr. R. A. Parkhill (Home Affairs) to the Postmaster-Generalship, and Mr. F. H. Stewart to the Ministry of Commerce, while Mr. J. A. Perkins took Mr. Parkhill's office. The most significant ministerial changes, however, could not be carried out. In October Mr. Lyons conducted negotiations with his allies of the Country Party, with view to the introduction of three Country Party members into the Ministry. He suggested that the choice of the members should rest with himself, and that he should remain sole head of the Government, with Mr. Latham as his deputy. The Country Party declined the offer, claiming full partnership, which Mr. Lyons rejected.

Following upon the General Election of December and the formation of the National Coalition Government on January 1, the thirteenth Commonwealth Parliament met at Canberra on February 17. It was noteworthy that the Mace and Speaker's wig, discarded during the Scullin regime, were restored. Sir

Isaac Isaacs, the Governor-General, in his Speech from the Throne, emphasised the necessity for ensuring Budgetary stability, and expressed concern at the failure of the New South Wales Government to conform to the financial scheme agreed upon between the Commonwealth authorities and the State Premiers in conference. As will be seen, this matter was to constitute an outstanding political problem during the rest of the year. Other legislation foreshadowed was a Bill requiring insurance companies to lodge deposits with the Commonwealth Government Treasury as a guarantee of stability. The Speech from the Throne also intimated that tariff changes would be introduced with view to preserving a satisfactory balance of trade, without unduly burdening certain departments of Australian production. In accordance with the latter promise, Mr. Gullett introduced a new tariff schedule on February 25. The reductions of duties were not so drastic as some supporters of the Lyons Ministry had hoped, but they represented a decisive reversal of the tariff policy of the Scullin administration, which had been designed to "encourage Australian industry," regardless of the adverse effects upon British trade, or upon Australian primary production. As Mr. Gullett pointed out, secondary industries, which extreme protection was designed to foster, languished directly the price of prime products fell. The Minister indicated that representatives of the Australian iron and steel industries had accepted his view, and acquiesced in the proposed reductions of duties upon many of their products. The chief criticism raised against Mr. Gullett's Bill was that of the Country Party, which dissented from the " terrific reduction " in the protection of the tobacco industry in Australia. The Government, however, held to its decision, pointing out that the new tobacco duties represented a saving of 1,000,000*l.* a year to the Australian exchequer. On May 11 a Commonwealth Bank Act Amending Bill was introduced, enabling the Commonwealth Bank to hold its note issue reserve either in gold or sterling, as seemed best. Another basic change from the policy of the Scullin Government was made when the Lyons administration abolished the rule giving preference in public works employment to trade union members, thus reversing a policy which had been in operation since 1930.

Throughout the year unemployment was rife in Australia, and a conference of Federal authorities and State Premiers met at Canberra between June 29 and July 9 to consider plans for relief. The original scheme was drawn up by an unofficial conference which published its conclusions on April 21, the idea being to raise 3,000,000*l.* to help tide the unemployed over the winter months. Already it was plain that the chief difficulty in carrying through the scheme would lie in New South Wales. This State had defaulted in connexion with certain of its loans during 1931, and bankers were not prepared to incur liabilities in respect of a defaulting State, even to provide monies to help its unemployed. The five other States, however, agreed to become responsible for 1,200,000*l*., in consideration of the Commonwealth Government contributing a similar amount, making a total of 2,400,000*l*., the remaining 600,000*l*. being the share of New South Wales, or rather the proportion which the Commonwealth Government was prepared to contribute if the Labour Government in New South Wales chose to come into the general scheme. Before the scheme was discussed in detail at Canberra, Mr. Lang, the New South Wales Premier, had been defeated, and his place taken by Mr. Stevens. The financial arrangements determined at the Premiers' Conference, therefore, covered all the States. Opening the conference Mr. Lyons stated that Treasury officials estimated the probable aggregate deficits facing all the Australian Governments in 1932-33 would be 20,000,000*l*., adding that the Commonwealth Bank could not promise assistance beyond a total of 6,000,000*l*. or 7,000,000*l*. to be divided among all the Governments. So drastic an announcement naturally aroused considerable dissent, and the State Premiers attempted to secure an increase in the amount set aside to meet Budget deficits, which the Treasury officials distributed among the several Governments in the following proportions : Commonwealth, 3,500,000*l*. ; New South Wales, 9,540,000*l*. ; Victoria, 1,950,000*l*. ; Queensland, 2,050,000*l*. ; South Australia, 1,770,000*l*. ; Western Australia, 1,360,000*l*. ; and Tasmania, 160,000*l*.

On behalf of the Commonwealth Bank it was pointed out that 31,000,000*l*. had been found to finance Budget deficiencies in 1931-32 and that 7,000,000*l*. was the limit which could be found for 1932-33, especially if the Budgets of Commonwealth and States were to be balanced by June, 1934, as was proposed. In the end the Commonwealth Government decided to balance its Budget without any aid from the banks, thus leaving the whole of the 7,000,000*l*. available for the State Treasurers, who agreed to reduce estimates by 9,000,000*l*. In addition, a 15,000,000*l*. loan was authorised on behalf of unemployment relief during the coming three years. The conference recognised that dole payments were uneconomic and destructive of the morale of the people, and decided that a substantial part of the loan should be diverted into profitable reproductive Government works, or used to stimulate semi-public or private enterprise. As a first instalment it was proposed to spend 7,000,000*l*. out of the 15,000,000*l*., upon a special relief works programme. Mr. Lyons gave details of the proposals in a ministerial statement published on July 9.

Throughout these financial discussions, which aimed at ensuring balanced Budgets within a reasonable period, as well as the provision of funds to meet the more urgent needs of a time of crisis, the basic trouble arose from the attitude of the State

of New South Wales.   Here Mr. Lang's prime endeavour was to
establish control over wages, wholesale and retail prices, and
industrial profits, which would amount to political control by the
Trades Hall group to which Mr. Lang belonged.   Mr. Lang and
his friends visualised a system of complete State control, obeying
the orders of a Labour Caucus.   By means of special boards and
commissions the New South Wales Government sought to interfere
with public and private services of all types, with view to the acceptance of Trades Hall control in general politics.   Such a policy
could not but arouse the angry dissent of opponents, as it aroused
the fears of leaders of industry and finance.   But if Langism was
dangerous in theory, it was also very expensive in practice, and
on February 2 Mr. Lang cabled to Mr. Willis, Agent-General
for New South Wales in London, instructing him to endeavour
to arrange with British bondholders for a suspension during twelve
months of all interest payments due in London by New South
Wales.   The action followed the refusal of the Commonwealth
Loan Council to approve of Mr. Lang obtaining further accommodation from the Commonwealth Bank.   Nominally, the State
was responsible for interest payments on its loans, but, in the
event of default, the Commonwealth Government was responsible
under a financial agreement negotiated in 1929.   Altogether,
interest payments aggregating 7,197,854*l.* were threatened by
Mr. Lang's action.   It thus became essential for the Commonwealth Government to interfere decisively.   As Mr. Lyons stated
on February 2, "The Commonwealth is entitled to compel New
South Wales to pay to the Commonwealth the interest due, and
will issue a writ to-morrow for the recovery of the amounts in default, and will take any other measures within its power to compel
New South Wales to honour its obligations."   On February 18
Mr. Latham, the Commonwealth Attorney-General, introduced
a Financial Agreement Enforcement Bill into the House of
Representatives at Canberra, based upon the principle which
had been recognised since 1929, that the credit of the Commonwealth was behind the public debts both of Commonwealth
and States.   Mr. Latham added that the Governor-General by
proclamation could retain monies received on behalf of the State
in order to meet liabilities under the financial agreement.   The
Bill passed the Senate on March 11.

In the course of the struggle with Mr. Lang's Government,
income tax, betting, totalisator and entertainment taxes, and
revenue from the New South Wales railways and trams were
attached by the Commonwealth authorities.   On April 11
notices were served on banks with headquarters in Sydney and
Melbourne requiring them to pay to the Commonwealth all
monies received on New South Wales account.   Mr. Lang
organised ingenious methods of obstruction to the Federal
collection of the State revenues, and matters arising from the

dispute were continually before the High Court at Sydney, the problem being complicated by the fact that the provisions of the Financial Agreement Enforcement Act necessarily covered other States of the Commonwealth. Thus Tasmania was anxious that the Act should be enforced against New South Wales in the existing crisis, but feared that certain provisions would make the maintenance of the Federal spirit difficult. The South Australian Government decided not to join Victoria and Tasmania in contesting the validity of the Act, taking the line that it would be " monstrous " to allow Mr. Lang's Government to treat the agreement between Commonwealth and States as a scrap of paper. Western Australia took a similar line. In the course of his struggle with the Commonwealth, Mr. Lang, on May 11, introduced a Bill into the New South Wales Parliament levying a 10 per cent. tax upon amounts secured by all existing mortgages ; failing payment, it was proposed that the mortgages should revert to the State. What Dr. Earle Page, a former Commonwealth Treasurer, described as " an outrageous tax " proved to be Mr. Lang's last gesture. On May 13 Sir Philip Game, the State Governor, dismissed the Lang Government from office. This followed upon a circular which the State Premier sent to the heads of New South Wales Government departments, instructing them not to pay money to the Commonwealth under the Enforcement Act. Mr. Lang's own description of Sir Philip Game's action was, " I'm sacked." The news of Mr. Lang's dismissal was received in Sydney with public demonstrations of delight which recalled Armistice Day, 1918. Mr. Lang was succeeded by Mr. B. S. B. Stevens, who associated himself with Mr. Bruxner, Leader of the United Country Party. The Coalition made an appeal to the State electors in the following month, thus destroying Mr. Lang's Parliamentary majority, and bringing New South Wales once more into line with public opinion in the rest of Australia. On May 17 proclamations under the Enforcement Act were suspended.

During the autumn Parliamentary proceedings at Canberra were largely concerned with matters arising from the Ottawa Conference. As Mr. Bruce had gone to London as High Commissioner, the task of explaining the Ottawa Agreement to Australia fell to Mr. Gullett, Minister for Trade, who returned to Australia on September 23. Mr. Gullett's explanation of the agreement signed by the Australian delegates was made to Parliament on October 14, the Minister claiming that it initiated a policy of reciprocal preferential trading between Australia and the rest of the Empire which would at once contribute to the dissipation of the depression. Mr. Gullett added that the benefits obtained for Australia exceeded in range those gained by any Dominion. Wheat, dairy produce, fruit, wine, and sugar were among the products which would benefit. As for British goods, where the British preferential duty stood at 19 per cent., a 15 per cent. margin of preference would be ensured in future. Where the duty was between 19 and 29 per cent., the margin of preference would be 17½ per cent. Where it was 30 per cent. and over, there would be a margin of preference of 20 per cent. Mr. Gullett explained that the tariff would be reviewed by the Tariff Board and Parliament on the principle that protective duties should not exceed a level giving British producers full opportunity for reasonable competition on the basis of relative cost of production, and that no protective duty would be imposed on British goods to an amount exceeding the Tariff Board's recommendations. The debate upon the Ottawa Agreement was renewed in the Canberra House of Representatives on November 3 in the absence of Mr. Gullett, owing to illness. Mr. Scullin, Leader of the Labour Opposition, was critical, maintaining that ties of kinship would not be strengthened by sordid bargaining or binding agreements. Mr. Scullin moved that the Ottawa Agreement Bill be withdrawn, and negotiations opened for a new agreement embodying concessions to Australian producers, and preferences to Great Britain on specified items, which would not endanger Australia's protective policy, or deprive the Australian Parliament of its power to give effect to the will of the people on general tariff policy. Mr. Lyons, countering Mr. Scullin's arguments, said that the amendment would be destructive of all the benefits achieved at Ottawa. Mr. Lyons pointed out that the value of the British preferences was shown by the fact that 95 per cent. of the wine, 90 per cent. of the butter, 76 per cent. of the meat, and 75 per cent. of Australia's fruit, found markets in Great Britain. Dr. Page, Leader of the Country Party, was also critical of the Ottawa Agreement, but on the ground that it did not go far enough. He described Ottawa as a lost opportunity. " The preferences were largely obtained by increasing foreign duties and leaving the British rate at an unnecessarily high rate." The House of Representatives passed the Ottawa Agreement Bill on November 16 without amendment.

Another important debate took place at Canberra on November 23, when Mr. Lyons announced remissions of taxation, totalling 1,300,000*l.*, among them being reductions in the land tax, and the removal of the sales tax upon books, magazines, and periodicals, and such semi-luxuries as jam, canned fruit, pickles, and sauces. At the same time Mr. Lyons announced that the Federal Government proposed to distribute 1,250,000*l.* for the relief of wheat-growers. During the first twelve months of office the Lyons Government was able to grant relief from taxation aggregating 2,100,000*l.*, and yet could announce to the people of Australia that there was a surplus of revenue over expenditure in current financial returns.

In general, the course of public affairs in Australia during

1932 brought it about that the more important public happenings were matters of Commonwealth, rather than purely State concern. The exception was New South Wales, where the Lang regime necessarily brought fundamental political issues to the fore. Apart from the financial troubles associated with the State public debt, Mr. Lang came into sharp conflict with his State Governor in connexion with the New South Wales Legislative Council. The Labour Government wished to abolish the Council, which constitutes the Upper House of the State Parliament, and consists of life members. In the course of the struggle Mr. Lang nominated sixty Labour members to the Council, charged with the task of outvoting the opponents of single-chamber government, but Sir Philip Game refused to accept the nominations. The Australian Courts had already decided that the House of Representatives had no power to abolish the Council without taking a referendum of the electors, and the matter came before the Privy Council in London on May 31, when the Lord Chancellor and four other English judges approved the decision of the Supreme Court of New South Wales dated December 23, 1930.

The matter of the Legislative Council was almost as decisive in bringing about the dismissal of Mr. Lang, as the action of his Government in connexion with State finances. The General Election on June 11 resulted in one of the biggest political landslides in Australian history. The Lang Party, which had 55 seats in the Old Parliament, came back with 21 representatives. The United Australian Party and the United Country Party, who constituted Mr. Stevens's supporters, had a majority of about 40 in a house of 90 members. The State Cabinet was reconstructed after the elections, Mr. Stevens being Premier and Treasurer ; Lieut.-Colonel Bruxner, Deputy Premier and Minister for Transport ; Mr. Manning, Attorney-General ; Captain Chaffey, Chief Secretary ; and Mr. Dunningham, Minister for Labour and Industry. The Cabinet included seven members of the United Australia Party and five of the Country Party. On July 10 Mr. Stevens announced that his Government proposed to spend 8,000,000l. during the year upon unemployment relief. On June 24 the Premier estimated the deficit in the State finances at 12,000,000l., instead of the 6,000,000l. estimated by Mr. Lang. The Budget presented on September 21, however, reduced the deficit in the coming year to 4,350,000l., in spite of a loss of 4,555,000l. upon the running of the railways. On September 21 the Legislative Council accepted the second reading of a measure for its own reform. In order to prevent deadlocks the Bill provided that, if the Council failed to pass a Money Bill approved by the Legislative Assembly, it should be presented to the Governor for his assent within a month. If the Council differed from the Lower House in regard to any other Bill, such a measure could not have the force of law until it had been approved by the New South Wales electors at a referendum. The reconstituted Council will consist of forty-five elected members with a tenure of office of six years, one-third of whom will retire at a time, thus ensuring that the Council will not represent a mere passing phase of public opinion.

In Victoria, the Labour Ministry, led by Mr. Hogan, was defeated at a General Election in May. A new Government took office on May 18 under the Premiership of Sir Stanley Argyle, with Mr. Macfarlan as Chief Secretary, Mr. Menzies as Attorney-General, and Mr. Allan as Minister for Agriculture. Included in Sir Stanley Argyle's Cabinet were eight members of the United Australia Party, three members of the Country Party, and Mr. Jones, Minister for Public Works, who represented a section of the Labour Party which withdrew its allegiance to Labour, in view of the urgent necessity for public economy. The Victorian Budget was introduced on September 16, when the deficit was announced as 851,000*l*., which was well within the figure agreed upon at the Premiers' Conference. In Queensland, there was also a General Election, and a moderate Labour Government, under Mr. W. Forgan Smith, took office on June 17. Mr. Moore, the outgoing Premier, was able to hand over to the incoming Administration a cash balance of 1,600,000*l*., after providing for all deficits, a notable conclusion to a term of office in times of such economic stress. Sir Leslie Wilson, the Governor, opened the new Queensland Parliament on August 15, when the legislative proposals of Mr. Forgan Smith's Government were disclosed. Mr. Hill, the South Australian Premier, made his Budget speech at Adelaide on October 6, the deficit revealed being 1,187,000*l*., compared with the maximum deficit of 1,215,000*l*., fixed in June at the Premiers' Conference.

NEW ZEALAND.

During 1932 the Dominion faced difficulties similar to those in Australia, both countries having to deal with the fall in world prices of their basic products, those of New Zealand being wool, meat, and dairy produce. The course of New Zealand history during the year was dictated by the fact that it had suffered a decline in national production during four years, amounting to something like 40,000,000*l*., and that national and private expenditure had to be curtailed to meet the changed situation. In particular, the value of farm produce had fallen from 82,000,000*l*. for the year ended June, 1929, to 54,000,000*l*. for the year ended December, 1931.

Throughout the year New Zealand politics and economics were controlled by Mr. G. W. Forbes and Mr. J. G. Coates, leaders, respectively, of the United and Reform parties, who had formed a Coalition Cabinet consisting of five members of each party, with Mr. Forbes as Premier, Mr. Coates as Leader of the House of Representatives, and Mr. Downie Stewart, of the Reform Party, as Finance Minister.

In view of the necessity for further curtailing public expenditure, a special session of the legislature met on February 23. Apart from cuts in public expenditure, it was essential to regularise Dominion overseas exchange, particularly with the Mother Country, seeing that New Zealand had to meet loan obligations during the year amounting to 8,000,000*l*., while 4,000,000*l*. of Treasury Bills were shortly due for payment in London. On December 24, 1931, a New Zealand Board of Trade order was promulgated forcing exporters to take out licences for all goods to be sold overseas and to have all credits obtained by the sale of such goods pooled under the control of the Associated Banks. Naturally, New Zealand farmers objected to these restrictions upon exchange, demanding that they should receive the full value of the exchange by means of a free market, as was the case in Australia. Replying to a deputation of primary producers on January 13, Mr. Forbes pointed out that the New Zealand banks were unable to guarantee the Government the funds necessary for the payment of overseas commitments unless the whole of the export trade was controlled. If the New Zealand exchange rose to 30 per cent., as in Australia, it would cost the Government a very large sum to transmit the 12,000,000*l*. due in London during 1932.

The matter touched so many interests that the Cabinet appointed a committee, under the chairmanship of Dr. James Hight, Professor of History at Canterbury College, to " examine the economic and budgetary position of the Dominion." The report was tabled in the New Zealand Parliament on March 4 and was followed by the interim report of a Commission of business men on March 11, which recommended budgetary savings during the coming year amounting to 2,976,000*l*. The final report of the National Expenditure Commission was tabled on September 30. These reports were the basis of the financial proposals which Mr. Downie Stewart placed before the New Zealand Parliament at the special session in the spring and of Mr. Forbes's Budget later in the year.

On the question of the exchange, the Government decided in favour of the low rate, in spite of the pressure exercised by the farming interests. The facts upon which the decision was made were as follows : Throughout 1931 the selling rate for telegraphic transfers on London had remained at 110*l*. New Zealand for 100*l*. London, the corresponding Australian rate being 130*l*. 10*s*. Australian for 100*l*. London, the Australian rate being reduced to 125*l*. at the end of the year. Naturally, every addition to the New Zealand exchange tended to discourage imports and helped to sustain export production by adding to the gross

returns made to primary producers. The committee of economists
came to the conclusion that at 40 per cent. exchange New Zealand's national income would be 112,000,000*l*., compared with
80,000,000*l*. at parity, and 90,000,000*l*. at the existing 10 per cent.
The economists were generally favourable to a high rate, but
Mr. Downie Stewart and the Government decided in favour of
maintaining the 10 per cent., and that rate persisted through
1932. As for the report of the Commission of business men,
though civil servants had experienced a cut in salaries and wages
of 10 per cent. in April, 1931, the Economy Commissioners proposed a similar cut in 1932, and reductions in pensions and cuts
in education costs were also proposed. Speaking in the House
of Representatives on April 27, Mr. Downie Stewart showed the
necessity for such further savings when he pointed out that,
though New Zealand expenditure had been reduced by 5,940,000*l*.
in the previous three years, and that a further reduction of
4,390,000*l*. was proposed for the current year, the deficit during
1931-32 would not be less than 2,000,000*l*. The Finance Bill
introduced in the House of Representatives on May 4 also diverted the proceeds of the petrol tax (500,000*l*.) from the High-
ways Fund to the general exchequer account, and extended the
life of the present Parliament by a year. Later in the year,
on November 2, a Government Bill was introduced providing
for quadrennial elections in all future Parliaments, in place of
the existing triennial Parliaments. The Labour Party strongly
opposed the extension.

Other matters considered at the Spring session of the New
Zealand Parliament were the amendment of the Mortgagors
Relief Act, and changes in the system of industrial conciliation
and arbitration. In view of the economic crisis the Government
decided that conditions and restrictions in the Arbitration Courts
militated against employment and made more flexible methods
essential. The second reading of the Industrial Conciliation and
Arbitration Amendment Bill was moved on March 10 by
Mr. Adam Hamilton, Minister of Labour, and the measure not
only aroused stern criticism from the Labour Opposition, but
led to five Government supporters, two of whom were ex-
Ministers, voting against the Bill. The second reading, however,
was carried on March 15 by 41 votes to 29. The point which
aroused most acute controversy was the Government's proposal
that, by Order in Council, it should be possible to exempt, either
wholly or conditionally, any industry from the operation of the
Act, and this proposal was eventually withdrawn. The Government, however, maintained its position that there should no
longer be automatic recourse to the Arbitration Court when the
parties could not agree. In future, the parties would have to
go, in the first instance, before a conciliation council. An angry
tone developed during the debates and the closure was enforced

no fewer than fifteen times. The Bill was finally carried in the House of Representatives by a majority of 15.

The Mortgagors and Tenants Relief Bill authorised the New Zealand courts to grant relief to lessees of farms and other property by way of reduction or remission of rent, the lessor being prevented for the time being from exercising his right of re-entry. Part III. of the Bill made a compulsory reduction of 20 per cent. in interest on all mortgages, including agreements for the sale and purchase of land and company debentures, and in all rents accruing between April 1, 1932, and April 1, 1935, with the provision that the net rate should not be reduced below 6½ per cent. in the case of mortgages of chattels, nor below 5 per cent. in respect of other mortgages.

The other outstanding measure considered during the Spring session was the Unemployment Amendment Bill, which imposed an emergency charge of 1s. in the £ on all wages and salaries, in lieu of an earlier 3d., and thus promised to bring in about 3,600,000l. to the New Zealand Exchequer for the relief of distress arising from unemployment. An Unemployment Board was charged with the task of assisting the unemployed with grants of food, clothes, or other necessities, by the payment of rent, or by the provision of land for the use of unemployed workers and their families. On June 15 Mr. Coates, Minister for Employment, stated that the small farm plan had been taken up with enthusiasm, the development of milking on the share system being a promising feature of the scheme. At this time the unemployed in New Zealand numbered about 50,000, but 66,400 were receiving relief in various forms from the Unemployed Fund, 17,000 being in subsidised employment on farms. Gold prospecting, land drainage, and land settlement were also absorbing a number of the unemployed. The Labour Party in the New Zealand Parliament was critical of the measures for the relief of unemployment, contending that the Government was pursuing a wage-reduction policy. On the contrary, not a few New Zealanders asked whether the Dominion could long afford to spend an amount equal to 25 per cent. of its Consolidated Fund revenue upon unproductive unemployment relief. On September 28 Mr. Hamilton stated that 3,750,000l. would be spent during the year upon unemployment relief, and that 73,000 unemployed men would profit during the winter. He added that most of the work was useful and was building up valuable assets for New Zealand, without increasing the national indebtedness.

In spite of these generous relief projects, New Zealand did not escape industrial troubles and there was serious rioting in Dunedin, Auckland, and Christchurch during April and May. Mob lawlessness, unfamiliar in New Zealand, aroused great anxiety. On April 15, in Auckland, there was window-smashing and looting of jewellers', tobacconists', and clothiers' shops.

More than 150 people were injured during the disturbances, and considerable damage was done to the Anglican Church of the Epiphany, which was set on fire by the rioters. The rioting at Christchurch on May 6 was associated with a tramways strike and was directed against free labour. Five hundred special constables were called on duty and dispersed the rioters without using their truncheons. In consequence of the disturbances the Government introduced a Public Safety Bill on April 19, sanctioning the proclamation of a state of emergency if public order were endangered, or if the community was threatened with the loss of proper food, water, fuel, light, or means of locomotion. The Bill followed the emergency powers taken by the British Government in similar circumstances.

The New Zealand Budget was introduced into the House of Representatives on October 4, when Mr. Forbes estimated the public expenditure for the coming year at 22,507,000*l.* and the revenue at 21,630,000*l.*, the deficit thus being 877,000*l.* The deficit for the previous year had been 2,140,000*l.* No additional taxation was proposed, Mr. Forbes holding that budgetary stability was a corollary to economic recovery, and that a respite from further taxation would encourage trade and industry and, therefore, hasten recovery. In spite of the decline in the values of primary products, there had been increased production, and New Zealand exports for the year ended June, 1932, were valued at 35,547,000*l.*, the imports being 23,060,000*l.*, and thus showing a favourable balance of trade. With a view to all possible economies the Government proposed to adhere to the policy of tapering off expenditure on all forms of capital works, a policy which was helped by the fact that a large proportion of the major public works in the Dominion were approaching completion. Mr. Forbes added that the earthquake in Hawkes Bay in February, 1931, had cost the Government 1,750,000*l.*, apart from 400,000*l.* which was publicly subscribed.

The public debt during 1932 totalled about 281,942,000*l.*, 56 per cent. being held in London, 117,000,000*l.* in New Zealand, and 4,175,000*l.* in Australia. Speaking in the House of Representatives on the no confidence amendment at the time of Mr. Forbes's Budget, Mr. Holland, Leader of the Labour Opposition, urged that New Zealand ought to take steps to secure a favourable arrangement of both principal and interest of these overseas debts. He said that the Dominion could not continue to pay the value of one-third of its exports to cover the interest upon its national debt, remembering that one-sixth of the exports sufficed to meet the interest bill two years ago. When asking Great Britain for a readjustment, New Zealand was entitled to keep in mind the readjustments made with other countries. Mr. Holland added that the policy of Labour, if returned to office, would be to cease borrowing overseas, except for conversions.

Mr. Coates and the delegation which represented New Zealand at the Ottawa Conference returned on September 20, and was entertained at a civic reception at Wellington, at which Mr. Forbes congratulated the delegates upon the success of their mission. Mr. Coates explained that New Zealand producers and consumers alike would benefit by the tariff concessions made to the Mother Country, as costs would be reduced, while New Zealand industries would not be subject to unreasonable competition. It was desirable that protection should only be given to Dominion industries which showed economically efficient production. The two-fold object to the Ottawa Agreements was to raise price levels to a figure remunerative to the producers and progressively to increase the Dominions' share in United Kingdom markets. The Ottawa Argeements were ratified by the House of Representatives on October 21. An Opposition amendment, moved by Mr. Holland, was defeated by 44 votes to 22. It proposed that the Ottawa Agreements should be ratified only on condition that there should be no interference with the measure of protection already accorded to goods produced in New Zealand, and that necessaries which could not be produced in the Dominion should be allowed in duty free.

A Customs Amendment Bill confirming the resolutions at Ottawa was introduced into the House of Representatives on November 2. For New Zealand, the most important provisions were those relating to the marketing of meat and dairy produce in Britain, and, in particular, the quota arrangement. The official attitude of New Zealand to a quota system was thus summed up by Mr. Coates in his opening speech to the Ottawa Conference :—

" In no case do we think the quota should apply to produce of the Empire, but the end can be best achieved by taking power to restrict the volume of foreign imports. This is an unusual course, but prevailing conditions are so abnormal that we are forced to regard it as necessary. New Zealand is concerned at the threatened flooding of the markets in which we rely ; and, in respect of dairy produce, meat, and fruit, we think that a quota on imports from foreign sources into the United Kingdom is urgently necessary."

Mr. Coates added that, at the appropriate time, New Zealand would be prepared to discuss the application of the principle of quota to selected articles of import into New Zealand. When the arrangements made at Ottawa were published in New Zealand public comment was generally favourable, though it was admitted that the working of any quota system was open to criticism. Thus the *New Zealand Herald* wrote : " As an effort to raise and stabilise price the quota may have practical merit. But it is a virtual invitation to South American countries to select for export to Britain only the highest quality, and thus to intensify, on a qualitative basis, foreign competition with the Dominions. It is well that the quota arrangements are subject to early review, with the expectation that the more stable effect of preference may be advantageously substituted." Of the conference as a whole, the *Star* (Christchurch) wrote, " Ottawa is a beginning, and the possibilities are limitless."

In inter-Dominion trade, a new reciprocal trade treaty between Canada and New Zealand was signed on April 23 and came into force on May 24. Canada thereby secured preferential rates for her exports of lumber, motor-cars, specified canned goods and certain manufactures, while New Zealand received special terms for her exports of butter, wool, and other products, these being similar to the privileges accorded to Australia in the Commonwealth's trade agreement with Canada. It may be added that a favourable report upon the condition of the New Zealand administration in Samoa was published in Wellington on October 4, when Brigadier-General Hart, the Administrator, returned to New Zealand to discuss business matters with Mr. Forbes

On May 10 Lord and Lady Bledisloe made a gift to the people of the Dominion of the historic estate, Waitangi, which was the scene of the signing, on February 6, 1840, of the treaty which established British sovereignty over the two islands, the Waitangi Treaty being also the Magna Carta of the Maoris. Lord and Lady Bledisloe chanced to visit Waitangi and found the property, which included the old British residency, in a state of neglect. Accordingly, they conceived the idea of purchasing and assuring its future possession to the New Zealand people. The Governor-General's act was only the last of a series of acts which have endeared himself and his wife to New Zealanders. On April 15 the Governor-General proposed to forgo 45 per cent. of his official salary, in view of the state of the Dominion finances, though the salary had already been voluntarily reduced by 1,062*l.* The office of Governor-General is itself a symbol of the affection which Dominioners have for the Mother Country, an affection which is nowhere more vital and assured than in New Zealand. An opportunity for expressing this affection arose when Great Britain was called upon to resume the payment of her war debts to the United States. The New Zealand Government at once offered to resume the payment of her own share of the debts, which had temporarily ceased under the Lausanne Agreement. The United Kingdom Government decided not to accept the offer, though deeply sensible of the unselfish loyalty which dictated it.

CHAPTER V.

INDIA.

PERSISTENCE was the keynote of Indian history in 1932—persistence of the third civil disobedience campaign renewed at the beginning of the year, and persistence of the Government, not only in fulfilling the elementary duty of fighting the challenge, but also in continuous work on proposals for a new Constitution transferring responsibility to autonomous provinces and an All-India Federation.

The year opened ominously with the decision of the Working Committee of the National Congress, sitting in Bombay under the chairmanship of Mr. Gandhi, to revive civil disobedience. This followed on the refusal of Lord Willingdon, the Viceroy, to discuss with him the Ordinances which Government had found it necessary to apply to Bengal, the North-West Frontier, and the United Provinces (*see* 1931 ANNUAL REGISTER). On January 4 the Viceroy promulgated four Ordinances of general application giving Government far-reaching special powers. On the same day Mr. Gandhi was arrested under a Bombay Regulation of 1827. The Congress Working Committee being declared an unlawful association, other members and helpers were arrested, but again and again their places were taken by associates. Through the year Government were engaged on the difficult and thankless task of wearing down an organisation which had established contacts not only in every town but also throughout the rural areas. Clashes of the police with processionists and picketers of shops selling British goods occurred in some of the large towns, and there were allegations of police brutality in *lathi* (bamboo cane) charges. The struggle was particularly severe in the city of Bombay, where business was in large degree paralysed by frequent *hartals* (days of mourning) and other efforts at Congress dictation. In May a petty quarrel between Muslim and Hindu youths led to guerilla warfare in the form of murderous assaults, pillage of shops, and incendiary fires. The disorder continued for many days, and before it was brought to an end by the troops and the police, nearly 3,000 casualties, including over 200 deaths, had occurred.

In the first two months of civil disobedience in British India, there were no less than 32,000 convictions, mainly for minor offences, and by the end of the year close upon 67,000 persons had been sentenced. The number still in prison was 14,815, of whom 610 were women. From various quarters Government were urged to open negotiations with Mr. Gandhi and others for a settlement. The invariable reply, notably by the Secretary of State in Parliament, was that there could be no question of co-operation with anyone associated with the civil disobedience movement, and that Mr. Gandhi and others could have their liberty at any time by its abandonment.

The Ordinances being valid for only six months, at the end of June they were modified and consolidated in Ordinance X. of 1932, comprising eighty sections, of which only eight were of general application. Very few of the other sections were applied in any province. Happily, further renewal at the end of the year was rendered unnecessary by the action of the Central and Provincial Legislatures in accepting proposals of Government to strengthen the ordinary law by inclusion therein of the more essential provisions of the Ordinance. Sir Samuel Hoare was able to state in the House of Commons on December 22 that such legislation had been passed without the vote of official blocs and by overwhelming majorities. He claimed that this showed that there was a great body of public opinion behind the Government, whether in the centre or in the provinces, in the efforts they had been making to maintain law and order.

While Government were able to maintain the initiative in the rest of India, the situation in Bengal continued intractable by reason of the determined activities of the terrorists. On February 7 Sir Stanley Jackson, the retiring Governor, when addressing the Convocation of the Calcutta University, was fired at five times by a young woman graduate, Bina Das, and narrowly escaped assassination. His successor, Sir John Anderson, late Permanent Under-Secretary for Home Affairs, gave the situation anxious attention in the light of his wide administrative experience, but there were few signs of amelioration. On May 1 Mr. Robert Douglas, Magistrate and Collector of Midnapore, was fatally shot while presiding over a meeting of the District Board. On August 5 and September 28 determined attempts were made to assassinate Sir Alfred Watson, editor of the Calcutta *Statesman*, who was wounded and had miraculous escapes. On the night of September 24, a whist drive was in progress at the Railway Institute, Pahartali, near Chittagong, when the premises were suddenly attacked on three sides by terrorists under a woman leader, armed with bombs, revolvers, and guns. One English-woman was killed and eleven other guests wounded, including four women.

At the beginning of the cold weather season two infantry brigades, comprising six Indian battalions and a British battalion, were moved to Bengal to assist the civil administration and encourage the populace to help to defeat terrorism. On expiry in May the Bengal Ordinance was renewed and in some respects strengthened, but towards the close of the year many of its provisions were incorporated in the ordinary law for a period of three years by the Provincial Legislature. In discussions on the menacing situation in the Legislative Council at the end of

September suggestions were made that Bengal should remain outside the proposed new Constitution, or that at least law and order should be " reserved " until terrorism had been overcome ; and prominent Muslim, Hindu, and European members of the Provincial Legislature made plans early in October for counter propaganda.

Amid these troubles the strength of the Government of India's dual policy was confirmed by the course of events in the North-West Frontier Province. The intention to raise that border country into constitutional parity with other provinces was formally announced in January, and on April 20 Lord Willingdon inaugurated the dyarchial system of administration with Sir Ralph Griffiths as the first Governor. The elections were held, not without disquieting moments, but on the whole with satisfactory results. Lord Willingdon, speaking to the Central Legislature in September, drew a moral favourable to constitutional reform which he said was not confined to the Frontier alone : " In place of dissatisfaction we have contentment, and the course is set fair for orderly and harmonious progress." Two other illustrations of the policy of meeting strong local aspirations were given by sympathetic investigation of the projected separation of Sind from Bombay in the West, and of claims for a distinct Orissa province in the East. At the closing meeting of the third Round-Table Conference on Christmas Eve the Secretary of State, Sir Samuel Hoare, announced the acceptance by H.M. Government in principle of the creation of these separate provinces.

In January three committees were sent out to India to carry out inquiries on the lines indicated in reports of the second session of the Round-Table Conference. The Federal Finance Committee, with Lord Eustace Percy, M.P., as Chairman, subjected to the test of figures the classification of revenues suggested at the Conference (Cmd. 4060). The Franchise Committee, under Lord Lothian, made recommendations increasing the aggregate electorate from 7 millions to 36 millions, including a notable advance whereby the voting strength of women would be raised to about one-fifth of the whole (Cmd. 4086). The Indian States Inquiry (Financial) Committee, under Mr. J. C. C. Davidson, M.P., laid down principles upon which it was held there might be equitable financial adjustments, between British India and the States for formulating the details of federation (Cmd. 4103).

Side by side with these investigations there were meetings at Delhi and Simla of a Consultative Committee of nineteen influential members and the Viceroy as deputy for the Prime Minister. Work was hampered both by the absence of statements of the policy of H.M. Government and by the intractable communal problem. Ultimately the Committee unanimously requested H.M. Government to implement the undertaking the Prime Minister had given on December 1, 1931, that in the event

of continued absence of Indian agreement thereon Government
would make a provisional Award. This Award, published on
August 17, was purposely confined to the two basic questions
of methods of election and proportions of representation in the
Provincial Legislatures. It maintained the principle of separate
communal electorates for Muslims, Sikhs, Indian Christians (in
selected areas), Anglo-Indians, and Europeans, but provided that
the arrangements might be revised by consent after ten years.
All others were entitled to vote in general (mainly Hindu) constituencies, but the Depressed Classes were to have in addition,
for a maximum of twenty years, the right to vote in special
constituencies for seventy-one reserved seats.

The Sikhs and Hindus of the Punjab expressed grave dissatisfaction with the Award as not giving due regard to their
claims as minorities ; but attention was concentrated upon the
provisions for the Depressed Classes, owing to a dramatic step taken
by Mr. Gandhi. The day following publication of the Award,
he wrote to the Prime Minister that he must resist these provisions with his life. From September 20 he would enter upon
a perpetual fast, abstaining from food of any kind, but the fast
would cease if during its course the British Government withdrew
their scheme of communal electorates for the Depressed Classes.
The Prime Minister replied that the Government decision stood,
and only the agreement of the communities themselves could
substitute other electoral arrangements.

Before the fast began there were anxious discussions between
some Hindu political leaders and Dr. Ambedkar who asked high
terms for the Depressed Classes. Negotiations were continued
at Poona with feverish zeal, and on September 24 Mr. Gandhi
approved a compromise providing for the absorption of the
seventy-one special constituencies in return for the reservation
to the Depressed Classes of no less than 148 general seats. H.M.
Government confirmed the agreement so far as it affected the
Award, and on the seventh day Mr. Gandhi renounced his fast.
By his action he had forced the hands not of H.M. Government,
but of the caste Hindus, who, in his own words, had consigned
the Depressed Classes for centuries to " crushing degradation."

There were strong undercurrents of opposition amongst the
more orthodox and conservative Hindus to the social implications
of the Poona settlement, and as time went on the reaction became
more practical and vocal. Mr. Gandhi in November threatened
to undertake another fast to death " if there is a manifest breakdown of the Yeravda (Poona) pact owing to the criminal neglect
of the caste Hindus to implement its conditions." The occasion
of the threat was the failure to throw open to Untouchables the
Guruvayur Temple in Southern India ; but later Mr. Gandhi
modified his attitude by announcing that the question of admission
to the temple might be settled by a referendum of the Hindus

L

of the neighbourhood. Yet a third time the Mahatma, late in December, resorted to this method of duress by announcing he would associate himself with a caste Hindu civil disobedience prisoner in Ratnagiri jail, who asked to be allowed to do scavenging work alongside Untouchables and threatened a hunger strike if, under prison rules, the request was refused.

A subsidiary consequence of the Poona settlement was the revival of attempts to devise a direct communal agreement between the Hindus and the Muslims. The outstanding figures in the effort were Pandit M. M. Malavaya on the one side, and Maulana Shaukat Ali on the other. A "Unity" Conference was held at Allahabad in November and again in December, and drew up an agreement accepting Muslim majorities in the Punjab and Bengal, and the separation of Sind on condition that the Sikhs were granted 20 per cent. of the representation of the Punjab Legislature and 5 per cent. in the Central Legislature. There was much bickering and controversy at the conference, and the presidency at one or two sessions of the Maharajah of Alwar, who was experiencing serious trouble with his Meo subjects (mainly Muslims) on quasi-communal lines, tended further to discount the movement. Well-known representatives of minorities refused to ratify the agreement, and no substantial results had been achieved at the end of the year.

An important question of procedure was settled by the announcement of Sir Samuel Hoare in the House of Commons on June 27 that Government had decided to endeavour to give effect to their policy in a single Bill providing alike for provincial autonomy and for the federation of Indian provinces and States, enabling new provincial constitutions to be set up, without necessarily awaiting the completion of all steps required for the actual inauguration of Federation. The Secretary of State further announced the intention of the Cabinet, after they had formulated their specific recommendations for Indian constitutional reform, to set up a Joint Select Committee of Parliament to examine these proposals in consultation with Indian representatives. He stated that H.M. Government held in the interests of speed that no further formal discussions would be necessary in London before these proposals were formulated, but they were prepared to arrange for such discussions if the deliberations in India of the Consultative Committee proved less conclusive than was hoped. The proposed change of procedure met with much criticism from important sections of co-operating opinion in India, mainly on the ground that by the time the Joint Select Committee was set up the principal points would have been settled without an opportunity for the exercise of the full weight of Indian opinion. There were resignations from the Consultative Committee and it ceased to function.

A few weeks later (September 5) Lord Willingdon announced

to the Indian Legislature that H.M. Government proposed to invite a small body of representatives of the States and British India to meet them in London about the middle of November. While the status of the Indian representatives would be the same as that of the delegates of the Round-Table Conference, the character of the discussions and the stages which had now been reached necessitated less formal and more expeditious procedure than that adopted at its two sessions. Government felt that this result would be best achieved by avoiding any public sittings and by working on a fixed agenda. The third Round-Table Conference accordingly met in London in November without representatives either of the Congress or the Opposition Labour Party. The latter preferred to hold aloof pending the setting up of the Joint Select Committee. The venue of the Conference was the House of Lords, and it was kept closely and usefully occupied until December 24, when it was brought to a close by a survey of conclusions and a declaration of Government policy in certain respects by the Secretary of State.

Meanwhile a new and unlooked-for obstacle to working out a scheme for All-India Federation had come into view. At the close of the Burma Round-Table Conference at St. James's Palace on January 12, the Prime Minister announced the Government's intention, in the event of Burma electing to pursue her political development apart from India, to place responsibility upon a bicameral Legislature for the administration not only of subjects which will fall within the range of provincial Governments in India, but also of subjects which will be administered there by the central authority. All indications pointed to the General Election, arranged for the month of November, giving a huge majority for separation. But intimidation and bribery were rife. The anti-separationists secured forty-three seats, the separationists twenty-eight, and neutrals nine. The leader of the anti-separationists, Dr. Ba Maw, explained that his party regarded the verdict as a mandate to work for full responsible government in Burma ; but he refused the invitation of the Governor to form a Ministry.

The Legislative Council met on December 6, and one of its first acts was to remove the new President, U Chit Hlaing, an anti-separationist, from office on the ground that he had not acted impartially in ruling out amendments when the question of separation came up for discussion. It was announced in the Council on December 17 that the Home Government was perfectly willing to permit Burma to remain part of India if she so desired ; but if Burma wished to separate, the Home Government would approach Parliament to grant a Constitution as outlined by the Prime Minister. Burma's representatives would be afforded the opportunity to express further views on the Constitution before it was finally enacted. The Secretary of State had intimated on November 16 that if Burma entered the Federation, she would remain a province of India, would be treated in exactly the same way as any other province, and would have no means at her disposal for withdrawing from Federation. On December 22, the day on which Sir Charles Innes was succeeded in the Governorship by Sir Hugh Stephenson, a motion was passed opposing separation on the basis of the Prime Minister's offer for a future Constitution and also permanent unconditional federation with India, but recommending Burma's entry into Federation under conditions, with the right of secession, and the calling of an early conference to consider the matter.

An important event of the year was the conclusion in August of a far-reaching Trade Agreement at the Imperial Economic Conference, Ottawa, between the British and the Indian delegations, the latter under the chairmanship of Sir Atul Chatterjee, late High Commissioner for India. The agreement was for reciprocal tariff preferences and other arrangements for the benefit of Indian trade in the United Kingdom and of United Kingdom trade in India. At the end of August, also, the protective tariff on non-British cotton goods was raised to 50 per cent. to enable the Bombay mill-owners to meet the growth of Japanese competition, which had been stimulated by the exchange depreciation of the yen.

Strong opposition to the Ottawa Agreement, based on political rather than economic grounds, was voiced in the special session of the Legislative Assembly in November and December to consider the question of ratification. This opposition was ably met by Sir Joseph Bhore, the Commerce member, and non-official members of the Indian Delegation. The agreement was referred to a Select Committee which reported favourably but recommended reconsideration in three years' time instead of five years. The instrument was ratified on December 6 by 77 votes to 25. The decision was the more welcome from the serious economic strain under which the country continued to labour, owing to low prices and small demand for agricultural products. One effect of the unfavourable international situation was the emergence from Indian hoards of vast quantities of gold under the stimulus of the high premium upon it, and close upon 53,000,000l. worth of the metal was exported during the year. The credit of the Government of India rose so steadily that while borrowings in June cost over $5\frac{1}{2}$ per cent., at the end of the year the rate was about 4 per cent.

FOREIGN HISTORY.

CHAPTER I.

THE LEAGUE OF NATIONS.

IT is not inept to describe 1932 as the *annus terribilis*. During the year the "economic blizzard," increasing in violence, completely overclouded the international horizon, and the resultant dislocation did much to counteract the normal development of co-operation between nations. Faced with dwindling trade balances and exchange difficulties, State after State resorted to all the paraphernalia of economic nationalism, such as tariffs, quotas, and import prohibitions and restrictions. Almost every nation seemed dominated by the sole idea of trying to snatch for itself such prosperity as could be found in a world threatened with adversity and chaos. Palliatives on a local scale could not be expected either to deal with the causes or to check the course of the depression. Information collected by the Economic Section of the League of Nations showed that international trade actually declined to less than 50 per cent. of its volume in 1929. There was abundant evidence that the majority of national measures, far from pointing the way to prosperity, had a malignant effect upon the general world economic situation.

As long as individual Governments ignored the repeated warnings issued since the World Economic Conference of 1927, the League of Nations could do little more than regularly call attention to the facts and carry out such research work as might ultimately facilitate a sane solution of these problems. Its "World Economic Survey" was acknowledged to be a masterly analysis of current economic tendencies.

The Economic Committee of the League, at its January session, drew attention to the fact that all economic relations were dominated by the problem of international debts. Owing to the specific nature of the reparations question, this was handled outside the League by the Lausanne Conference during June and July. But the Lausanne Conference decided to invite the League to convoke a conference on monetary and economic matters, not necessarily to meet at Geneva. After Mr. MacDonald had submitted this request to the League on August 30, a committee of qualified experts was set up to carry out the preliminary work.

During the year a valuable series of expert inquiries into the difficulties confronting leading industries was carried out under the auspices of the Economic Committee. At the consultation of coal experts in January, all factors of production were represented and were unanimous on the necessity for international agreement to remedy the chaotic state of distribution. Experts on hop production and trade, meeting the following month, decided that it would be to the advantage of producers in all countries to unite their efforts to combat the crisis. When the timber trade came under review in April, lack of balance between production and consumption was studied, while the automobile industry was the subject of similar investigations during May and June.

The Financial Committee devoted a great deal of its time to examining concrete proposals for improving the financial situation of Austria, Hungary, Greece, and Bulgaria. At the September session, Rumania appealed for technical assistance. Sixteen countries attended the Stresa Conference for the Economic Restoration of Central and Eastern Europe. In the final proposals, submitted to the League Commission of Enquiry for European Union, it was emphasised that " the crisis can be overcome only by continued co-operation among the countries of Europe." At the October session of the Council, the British Government presented the memorial drawn up by the League Loans Committee (London).

The Gold Delegation prepared its report in time for the Council to receive it in June. Surveying the recent breakdown of the gold standard, the experts were of the opinion that gold remained the best available monetary mechanism. Certain conditions, however, had to be fulfilled prior to a general return to gold, viz., freedom in the movement of goods and services, a solution of the debts problem, and agreement on the guiding principles of working the gold standard.

Among other economic activities of the League, progress was made with determining procedure for the friendly settlement of economic disputes. After further meetings in February and June, the sub-committee on the unification of Customs nomenclature completed its task. Three draft veterinary conventions were also drawn up with the intention of submitting them for approval to a conference in 1933.

The Disarmament Conference.—Sixty-four States, including the United States of America and the U.S.S.R., attended the First International Conference on the Limitation and Reduction of Armaments, which opened at Geneva on February 2. A precedent was created when representatives of the peoples of the world were allowed to submit petitions which had been collected by various national and international associations. During the general debate, much controversy was aroused by the French plan, which envisaged an international police force and the internationalisation of all civil aviation, and which stood for giving much more executive power to the League. The most drastic proposals were undoubtedly those coming from Italy. The draft convention, drawn up by the Preparatory Disarmament Commission, seemed generally acceptable as the basis of further negotiation.

Gradually a new idea—new, at least, in official circles—emerged from the speeches, that of abolishing the most aggressive weapons. The next move was to attempt to reach agreement as to which were primarily weapons of attack. The conference decided to seek the opinion of technical experts ; consequently committees were appointed to thrash out the different aspects of the problem. From this time, the dark days of the conference may be dated. The experts, it has been said, " lost themselves in the metaphysics of aggressiveness." By the fifth month of the conference, they had done little beyond registering their differences of opinion, without being able to brand any of the main types of armaments as particularly " offensive."

On June 22, in an effort to " cut through the brush," Mr. Hugh Gibson, the chief American delegate, announced the so-called " Hoover Plan." Reductions, he suggested, should be carried out by broad and general cuts of roughly one-third. Tanks, large mobile guns, chemical warfare, and bombing aircraft should be suppressed altogether.

The delegates, for the most part, adopted a cautious attitude towards the Hoover Plan, Signor Grandi of Italy being almost alone in accepting it unconditionally. Early in July Mr. Baldwin, in the British House of Commons, made alternative proposals for reductions in the maximum size of warships. No definite decision had been reached when, on July 23, the conference adopted a half-hearted resolution indicating a small measure of agreement on certain points, and then adjourned.

Disappointed by the slow rate of progress, the German Government demonstrated its impatience by launching a blunt demand for equality of armaments status and refusing to take any further part in the conference pending the recognition of this principle by other Powers. A long series of private negotiations, as delicate as they were complicated, began, involving at different times the Governments of the United Kingdom, France, the United States, Italy, and Germany. The British project for a Four-Power Conference on this question broke down through disagreement as to its *venue*. In November, M. Paul-Boncour, French Minister for War, exposed the outline of a fresh plan for disarmament and security, considerably in advance of any previous French proposals. A few days later, Sir John Simon presented a British scheme, intended not to rival but to supplement those of America and France.

Still it appeared doubtful whether these efforts would satisfy German objections, and the United States tentatively canvassed the idea of gathering together the meagre results already achieved into an interim treaty and virtually putting the Disarmament Conference into cold storage until 1936. On December 11, however, the Five Great Powers signed a declaration at Geneva recognising both the German claim to equality of status and the French demand for security. On the basis of this declaration, the German Government signified its willingness to resume its place at the Disarmament Conference. The responsible statesmen of the Powers concerned immediately joined in discussions with Mr. Henderson, President of the conference, in order that the Bureau and the General Commission of the conference might reassemble at an early date.

The Manchurian Dispute.—Throughout the whole of 1932, the appeal of the Chinese Government against Japanese military action in Manchuria, subsequent to the seizure of Mukden on September 18 of the previous year, continued to engage the attention of the League of Nations. Towards the end of January, with the outbreak of fighting at Shanghai, a diversion from the main issue occurred. Attempts to secure a cessation of hostilities were made through the good offices both of friendly Powers and of the League of Nations. After a special session of the League Assembly which opened on March 4, a basis for negotiations was established, and on March 24 a Sino-Japanese Conference began. Although, by this time, Japanese military and naval forces were being withdrawn from Shanghai, it was not until May 5 that a complete armistice agreement was ready for signature.

Meanwhile the Japanese had been methodically completing their occupation of Manchuria. On January 14 the League Council approved the composition of the Commission of Enquiry which it had appointed to investigate the situation in the Far East. The members were Lord Lytton (British), Count Aldrovandi (Italian), General Claudel (French), Major-General McCoy (American), and Dr. Schnee (German), accompanied by Chinese and Japanese assessors. Between February 29 and September 4 the Commission collected all available evidence in Japan, China, and Manchuria, and drew up its report at Peiping.

The Lytton Report was published by the League of Nations early in October. Its first eight chapters comprised an impartial examination of such matters as the background of the conflict, recent events in Manchuria, the establishment of the State of " Manchukuo," and the economic interests of China and Japan. In the last two chapters, the Commission concentrated attention on the future, outlining the principles and conditions of settlement and offering suggestions to the League Council. In the opinion of the members, the mere restoration of the *status quo ante* would be as unsatisfactory as the maintenance and

recognition of the existing regime in "Manchukuo," which
the Commission did not consider to be the outcome of a
spontaneous demand on the part of the inhabitants. A satisfactory solution, as proposed by the Commission, should be
compatible with the interests of both China and Japan ; should
conform to the principles of the Covenant, the Pact of Paris,
and the Nine-Power Treaty ; should recognise Japan's rights
in Manchuria ; should establish new treaty relations ; and should
secure Manchuria a large measure of autonomy consistent with
Chinese sovereignty. International co-operation in Chinese
reconstruction was considered to be an essential feature of a
final settlement.

Prior to the publication of the Lytton Report, the Council
agreed to Japan's request to postpone discussion for at least
six weeks, in order that the Japanese "observations" might
be brought to Geneva by a "qualified person." On August 25
Japan complicated the situation by officially recognising the
State of "Manchukuo," as the Lytton Commission had foreseen
would probably happen.

At the Council meeting, which opened on November 21, the
Japanese and the Chinese comments were heard, in the light of
which the Lytton Commission saw no reason to modify its
Report. In spite of obstructionist tactics by the Japanese
delegate, the matter went on to the full Assembly of the League,
at which twenty-three States supported the thesis of the Lytton
Report, two were non-committal and two sympathised with Japan.

Notwithstanding a general desire to define the principles of
the Lytton proposals, the British Government urged that conciliation by the Assembly's Committee of Nineteen should be
tried. It was suggested that the United States and the U.S.S.R.
should be invited to serve on this Committee. Ultimately a
special Committee, consisting of Great Britain, France, Czechoslovakia, Spain, and Switzerland, was appointed to frame a
suitable resolution, and a meeting of the Committee of Nineteen
was called for not later than January 16, 1933.

Political Action by the Council.—Whilst the Manchurian
question overshadowed all other political issues during the year,
the Council was called upon to deal with a number of other
disputes. In February the German Government called attention
to an alleged violation of the Statute of Memel by the Lithuanian
Government, but in view of the legal nature of the problem,
this was referred to the Permanent Court of International
Justice by the British, French, Italian, and Japanese Governments.

The claim of the Finnish Government against the British
Government respecting the use of Finnish vessels during the
Great War was again discussed at Geneva. On the question of
the Council's competence to deal with the matter, a special
Committee decided in the affirmative, but formulated two points

which should first be settled. After due consideration, the two parties informed the Council that they had agreed upon the means of settling them.

The Chaco dispute between Bolivia and Paraguay, considered by the Council on many occasions, proved difficult to handle satisfactorily, owing to the contradictory reports and explanations of the situation received from the disputants. On the President of the Council pointing out that the notes exchanged gave grounds for the view that the way lay open for pacific settlement, both Governments replied that they were in principle prepared to continue their efforts to reach such a settlement. The Council kept in close touch with the Washington Commission of Neutrals, and plans were made for the despatch of a military commission to the spot.

Following the steps taken by the Persian Government to cancel the concessions granted to the Anglo-Persian Oil Company, it was at first the intention of the British Government to submit this dispute to the Permanent Court of International Justice. In view of certain objections to this course raised by Persia, however, the matter was laid before the Council at its session on December 19, under Article XV. of the Covenant. A brief postponement was agreed upon in order to enable the Persian Government to prepare the necessary documentation and to send special representatives from Teheran. In the meantime, both parties agreed to refrain from any act or measure likely to aggravate or extend the dispute.

In the course of the year the Council dealt with various minority questions concerning the Ukrainian minority, the application of agrarian reform in Poland, the Polish minority in German Upper Silesia, a petition from the Prince of Pless regarding his father's property in Silesia, and complaints of discrimination against the Rumanian Government.

Arbitration.—Progress continued with the development of the system of arbitration and machinery for the peaceful settlement of international disputes. By the end of the year, forty States were bound by the " Optional Clause " mutually to accept the compulsory jurisdiction of the Permanent Court of International Justice in suitable classes of disputes. The General Act for the Pacific Settlement of International Disputes, covering other forms of quarrels not coming within the scope of the " Optional Clause," had secured the adherence of nineteen States. In the case of each of these agreements, this represented three additional ratifications during 1932.

The eleventh working year of the Permanent Court of International Justice, sitting in the Peace Palace at The Hague, proved to be the busiest on record. Meeting early in January, the bench remained in session until the end of December, with the exception of two short recesses at Easter and in the summer.

In the case concerning the treatment of Polish nationals in the Free City of Danzig, the Court ruled that, under the Danzig-Polish Convention of 1920, Polish citizens were entitled to treatment as favourable as, but not more so than, that administered to others by the authorities of the Free City. With regard to the effect of the Hoover Moratorium upon the " Molloff-Caphandaris " Agreement between Greece and Bulgaria, the Greek contention that emigration debts as well as reparations were covered was upheld.

A far more important case was that between France and Switzerland concerning the Free Zones of Upper Savoy and the District of Gex. On June 7 the Court, following on its preliminary decisions in 1929 and 1930, gave a final judgment upholding the Swiss contention. France accepted the adverse verdict and took prompt steps to settle the outstanding issues.

When four Great Powers brought an action in the summer under the Memel Statute, Lithuania contested the Court's jurisdiction. This objection was overruled. On the main issue, the Court substantially upheld Lithuania's views.

By its advisory opinion on the interpretation of the 1919 International Labour Convention on night work among women, the Court was able to remove doubts as to the meaning of this agreement and to pave the way for a possible revision.

With certain other cases the Court could not complete its work before the end of the year. An unusually large number of counsel and experts had to be heard in the dispute between Norway and Denmark regarding the ownership of parts of Eastern Greenland. This case was of special interest, owing to its having been raised under the " Optional Clause." The dispute over the property of the Prince of Pless was one of many which could not be heard until 1933.

Two new members were added to the League of Nations, bringing the total membership to fifty-seven States. A special session of the Assembly was held in July for the purpose of admitting Turkey. The admission of Iraq, the first country under mandate to attain independence, was an outstanding event of the Thirteenth Ordinary Assembly in October.

International Co-operation.—In spite of the economic depression co-operation between Governments, through the machinery of the League of Nations, produced excellent results during 1932. The Health Organisation continued to show its practical value in every continent. Progress was made with the reorganisation of public health services in China, while both the Chinese and the Siamese Governments received special assistance from the Malaria Commission. Inquiries were completed relating to the effect of the quinine shortage upon the prevalence of malaria. At its meetings the Health Committee at Geneva devoted special consideration to the repercussions of the economic crisis upon public health, and to the question of tuberculosis prophylaxis.

At the request of the Government of the Union of South Africa, the League organised a conference of directors of public health services from eighteen African countries and territories, which opened at Cape Town on November 15. The main object was to decide upon the application of the new Sanitary Air Convention in order to prevent the propagation of yellow fever, but such matters as the introduction of smallpox by vessels from India were also discussed.

With regard to the work of the Advisory Committee on Opium and the Permanent Central Opium Board, nineteen States intimated during the annual Assembly that they intended to ratify the 1931 convention for limiting the manufacture of narcotic drugs. An administrative model code was prepared as a guide to the operation of this agreement. The League's expert inquiry into the traffic in women and children in the Far East was completed. The Nansen International Refugee Office furnished assistance in Syria, Armenia, South America, and other countries.

After ten years of pressure from the British Government, the annual Assembly took an important step in the direction of providing the League with permanent machinery for securing the abolition of slavery. It approved the appointment of an Advisory Committee of experts to keep in constant touch with the situation. While the negotiations for assisting Liberia to stamp out slavery were in progress, serious civil war broke out between Government troops and native tribes on the Kru Coast. Dr. M. D. Mackenzie, who was immediately sent to the spot as special League Commissioner, succeeded in restoring peace and bringing about complete disarmament among twenty tribes.

On December 27, with the Persian Government's ratification, the 1929 Geneva Convention, setting up an International Relief Union to provide prompt assistance in cases of " public misfortunes due to *force majeure*," came into operation. By that date twenty-seven countries had acceded.

The League and Unemployment.—Unemployment, as in the previous year, was the principal problem upon which the International Labour Organisation of the League of Nations concentrated its attention. At the Sixteenth Session of the International Labour Conference, held at Geneva from April 12 to April 30, the possibility of shortening hours of work as a part remedy for world unemployment was tentatively discussed. In September, at the request of the Italian Government, a special meeting of the Governing Body met to investigate the subject of a forty-hour week. It was decided to call a Tripartite Conference early in 1933, with a view to putting this question on the agenda of the next International Labour Conference.

Nevertheless, the steady work of the Organisation developed in other directions. The annual conference adopted a convention on the age of admission of children to employment in non-industrial occupations, and held preliminary discussions on two questions, *viz.*, the abolition of fee-charging employment agencies, and invalidity, old-age, widows' and orphans' insurance. On December 31 490 ratifications of International Labour Conventions had been officially registered at Geneva, representing an increase of forty-one ratifications for the year.

During May the Organisation sustained a severe loss through the sudden death of its Director, M. Albert Thomas. His successor was Mr. H. B. Butler, the then Deputy-Director. Sir Atul Chatterjee succeeded M. Ernest Mahaim as Chairman of the Governing Body.

At the election of three non-permanent members of the League Council by the Assembly, Mexico and Czechoslovakia replaced Peru and Yugoslavia, and Poland secured re-election. In consequence of the approaching retirement of Sir Eric Drummond, the Assembly, at a later session, approved the appointment of M. Joseph Avenol as Secretary-General. Various changes were also made in the higher posts of the Secretariat.

Since so little progress was visible with any of the three major international problems (the economic crisis, disarmament, and the Manchurian issue), 1932 must be written down as a year of frustration for the League of Nations. Although a considerable volume of constructive activity proceeded in the background, aggressive nationalism prevented the League from achieving any striking successes and left the outlook for the future uncertain.

CHAPTER II.

FRANCE AND ITALY.

FRANCE.

REPARATIONS and Debts, Disarmament and the Budget—these were the problems with which France had chiefly to contend throughout 1932.

The unexpected death of M. Maginot, Minister of War, on January 3 aggravated the difficulties of the Laval Government. The question of a successor had already been considered during his illness, as it was hardly to be thought of that the Ministry of War should remain vacant on the very eve of the Disarmament Conference. Among the names considered were those of M. Painlevé, who himself did not seek the office, and of M. Paul-Boncour, who would undoubtedly have accepted it but for the objections raised by the majority of his friends of the Left. In the end M. Laval decided to resign with all his colleagues, and to reconstitute his Ministry leaving out M. Briand, the Minister of Foreign Affairs. The growing ill-health of M. Briand justified M. Laval in dispensing with his former leader and in turning his back, to a certain extent, on a foreign policy which had been discredited by the course of events, and against which certain sections of the majority inwardly chafed. M. Laval accordingly combined in his own hands the two offices of President of the Council and Foreign Minister.

On January 8 Chancellor Brüning, in reply to an inquiry from the British Ambassador whether Germany was disposed to accept the extension for a year of the Hoover moratorium, had declared that Germany would never be in a position to resume reparation payments. The Conference of Lausanne which was to submit to a new joint examination the question of war debts and frozen credits in Germany had been fixed provisionally for January 25. M. Laval, in his Ministerial declaration of January 19, still insisted on the letter of the agreements, basing his attitude on three main grounds—the opposition of America, the necessity of maintaining unimpaired the foundations of credit and confidence, and the necessity of protecting France against the expansion of a Germany relieved of all burdens.

At this juncture a certain tendency appeared towards a *rapprochement* with Italy, which seemed desirous of entering into conversations with France. But it was held in Paris that if the Franco-Italian entente was not first broached in the course of international negotiations, France could not expect much from one-sided concessions without any compensating advantage.

The second Laval Ministry was not destined to last long. The Senate was dissatisfied with financial conditions, especially with the manner in which the reflotation of the Compagnie Transatlantique had been carried out. A deeper and more serious motive for the discontent of the Senate was to be found in its attachment to the ideal of political concentration and its hostility to every form of cartel, whether of the Right or of the Left. On February 16 the Senate overthrew M. Laval. His period of office had been signalised by the presentation at Geneva, by M. Tardieu, of the French project of disarmament, before the Disarmament Conference which opened on February 2. In this scheme it was proposed to reinforce the power of the League of Nations, to place under its control both civilian and military aeroplanes, to create an international force, to organise peace by mutual assistance, to prohibit or internationalise offensive weapons and to impose new restrictions on armaments. The scheme was regarded at Geneva as a maximum difficult of attainment.

As it was the Left members of the Senate who had overthrown the Cabinet, Parliamentary procedure demanded that the President of the Republic should entrust to a member of the Left the task

of forming a new Government. Accordingly M. Doumer called
on M. Painlevé, a former President of the Council, who endeavoured
to form a Cabinet representing mainly the Left. The ostracism
of MM. Tardieu and Paul Reynaud, however, prevented him from
succeeding. M. Tardieu was then summoned, and he formed
a Cabinet differing little from that of his predecessor. On
February 23 he presented himself as Prime Minister before the
Chamber. Twelve days later, on March 7, took place the death
of Aristide Briand [see under Obituaries], which was interpreted
by every one as the eclipse, or, at any rate, the waning of the
policy of peace in Europe. The memory of the departed, who,
since 1925, had held almost uninterruptedly the post of Minister
of Foreign Affairs, who had been largely responsible for such pacific
instruments as the Locarno Agreements and the Briand-Kellogg
Pact, and had worked so hard for European co-operation, gave
a new impulse in France to all those who still placed their highest
hopes in the new methods of arbitration and of collaboration among
the peoples. Had not Briand desired to substitute for the alliance
of the victors a society of equal nations ?

Briand's death coincided with the opening of the electoral
campaign. In the Commission for Universal Suffrage, the
President, M. Mandel, tried hard to obtain the acceptance of
a new method of voting, which was secretly desired by the Government. By this method the second ballot would be eliminated,
and the candidate obtaining the largest number of votes at the
first ballot would be elected. M. Herriot sarcastically called
it " a drum with two notes " ; the voters would form part of a *bloc*
and vote in a *bloc !* However, the intrigues of M. Mandel were
doomed to failure. In the end the old system of voting by
arrondissements and of second ballots was retained, and so the
field was still left open for coalitions.

Meanwhile the members of the Left knew that the Treasury
was empty, that the fiscal reforms had been held up, that the
plans for national reconstruction had been cut down, that the
agricultural policy of the Government threatened to antagonise
the towns against the country, and that the high tariff punished
the consumer and, to the great injury of the producers themselves, kept up the high cost of living. The Budget presented
by M. Tardieu in the middle of March was criticised on these
lines. M. Caillaux estimated the real deficit concealed under the
apparent equilibrium at about seven milliards.

On April 6 M. Tardieu, the Prime Minister, delivered the first
great speech of the electoral campaign at Bullier, an old Parisian
hall. On the 16th, at Giromagny, he made an appeal for a combination from which only the Socialists were to be excluded—
a violently anti-Socialist combination which would break the
cartel of the Left and of which he could remain the head. On
the other side, M. Herriot, the Leader of the Opposition, made an

appeal for a combination—to which he gave no specific name—from which he excluded only the nationalist and clerical Right, and which would lean towards the Left. He avoided making any pronouncement on the relations of this coalition with the Unified Socialist Party, the support of which at the elections would be indispensable to the Radicals.

Among the organised parties, certain dividing lines could be traced. The old notion of laicity (Secularism) still served as a criterion. For laicity were the Unified Socialists, the French Socialists, the Republican Socialists, and the Radical Socialists. Against were the Republican Federation of France and the National Republican Party, and the Popular Democrats.

While these controversies were going on at home, conversations with regard to reparations were being carried on with foreign countries. The British Foreign Office had published a Note in which it declared that the problem of political debts was the one which most urgently required solution. M. Tardieu, who was congratulating himself on the agreement reached by M. Laval with the British Government (although this agreement only related to procedure), went to London to talk with Mr. MacDonald about the Lausanne Conference. Ostensibly, however, the main subject of the conversations was the assistance to be given to the Danubian States. The interviews, according to the official *communiqué*, were cordial, but led to no definite results.

M. Tardieu delivered another electoral speech on April 6. The result of the election was less easy to forecast in Paris than in the Provinces. The *bloc* of the Right parties, backed by superior financial resources, the support of the great industrial organisations, and the favour of a powerful Press, made a strong bid for Paris. On the other side, the parties of the Left possessed the advantages equally solid but less visible of an offensive position ; they stood to benefit by the swing of the pendulum due to the mistakes of the party in power, and by the moral and material effects of the economic crisis, of uncertainty and insecurity. M. Tardieu attempted once more to frighten the electorate and to break the cartel which was in preparation by calling up the spectre of the cartel of 1924 and the difficult times through which the country had passed up to 1926. M. Herriot made his final reply on May 7, reproaching M. Tardieu with leaving behind him an exhausted treasury and a deficit in the Budget.

M. Léon Blum, the Leader of the Unified Socialist Party, declared on his side at Narbonne (April 10) that he was ready to take office should the Left obtain a majority and the number of Socialist seats be larger than that of Radical seats. He laid down a minimum programme of which the main features were a drastic reduction of armaments, a national system of insurance covering unemployment, strikes, and agricultural risks, and the nationalisation of private insurance companies and of railways. And

while M. Tardieu appealed for union, his colleague, M. Paul
Reynaud, took it upon himself to address a final greeting which
was much commented upon to the Right.

On May 1 the first ballot took place. From May 2 the issue
of the battle was no longer doubtful, the swing to the Left being
evident. On May 6, two days before the second ballot, the
President of the Republic, Paul Doumer, was assassinated by
the Russian Gorguloff [see under Obituaries]. The murderer,
who, it appears, was attached to a small sect of Russian peasant
revolutionaries, had chosen his time well for creating a panic,
but he had under-estimated the good sense and sang-froid of the
French elector. All necessary steps were taken with the utmost
calm. The President having died at dawn on May 7, M. Tardieu
posted up a proclamation in all the communes of France expressing
the grief of the country and convoking Congress for the following
Tuesday. The elections for the Legislature took place on Sunday
the 8th. On Tuesday the 10th the old Congress met at Versailles
—since it was not possible to wait till the new Deputies should
take their seats for the election of a President, and the powers of
the old Congress did not expire till June 1—and appointed a successor to M. Doumer in the person of M. Albert Lebrun, President
of the Senate. The decision of M. Painlevé not to stand as
a candidate rendered a contest unnecessary.

M. Lebrun, a self-made man, formerly a mining engineer, and
once President of the Caisse d'amortissement and of the Senate,
was born at Mercy-le-haut, a small village of Meurthe-et-Moselle,
in 1871, of a farming family. His reputation for citizenship and
patriotism procured him a unanimous election.

The elections brought the parties of the Left a gain of about
a hundred seats. In the new Chamber a majority could be
formed in two ways, by a union of the Radicals with the Socialists,
or by a " concentration " of parties. The Radical-Socialists,
with 160 seats, occupied the centre of the Chamber, flanked on
their right by 77 Independent Radicals and on their left by
34 Independent Socialists. These three groups comprised 271
members, and so did not by themselves constitute a majority
in an assembly of 615. That was why the two majorities mentioned were possible. That of the Left, consisting of the elements
mentioned above along with 119 Unified Socialists, would consist of nearly 400 members, while a " majority of concentration "
would contain 330 to 350 members, excluding at its left the
Unified Socialists and the Communists, and at its right the Marin
group and the whole-hearted Conservatives.

Immediately after the election, a campaign was instituted
within the Socialist federations with a view to authorising the
Deputies of the party to participate in the Government. A
Government of participation also suited the wishes of numerous
Radicals, and to many seemed to be a logical corollary to the

M

electoral campaign, which, if it had not been conducted under the standard of the cartel, had in many cases been marked by a collaboration between the Radicals and Unified Socialists, to which the success of the Left candidates had been due in several constituencies. The Socialist Congress was held at Paris on May 30 and 31, and rejected the idea of participation pure and simple. Following its leader, Léon Blum, it considered that participation should only take place on the basis of a minimum and unalterable programme. Without entering into any argument with the Socialists, M. Herriot secured from the Executive Committee of the Radical Party a unanimous vote for a reply affirming the autonomy of that party.

Such were the circumstances in which the new Legislature met. As soon as the majority of the Deputies had had their elections ratified, the President of the Republic commissioned the head of the largest party to form a Government. In the night of June 3-4 M. Herriot formed a Government of Radical-Socialists along with a sprinkling of Independent Radicals, but without any Unified Socialists. He entrusted the vice-presidency of the Council and the charge of the Seal to M. René Renoult, an old campaigner of the orthodox Radical school ; the Ministry of War to M. Paul-Boncour, a deserter from the Socialist camp, who now belonged to no group in the Senate ; of finances to M. Germain-Martin, a member of the Centre, a professor in the Faculty of Law ; of the Colonies to M. Albert Sarraut ; and of the Air, the Navy, and the Interior respectively to MM. Painlevé, Leygues, and Chautemps, all former Presidents of the Council. On June 7 the ministerial declaration was approved by 384 votes to 115.

On June 16 the Conference of Lausanne opened. It had a double object : to settle the problem of reparations, and to decide upon the measures required for the reconstruction of Central and Eastern Europe. It had been delayed by the lack of agreement between France and England, but its meeting was now urgent, as the Hoover moratorium was to expire on July 1. The English wished to wipe out the debts altogether, on the ground that it was no use contending for an empty purse. The French had hitherto seemed to desire a provisional settlement, limited to the duration of the German crisis. The accession to power of the Radicals altered the atmosphere in which the negotiations were to take place. After three weeks of continuous negotiations, a " gentleman's agreement " between France and England was signed on July 2. This determined in advance of the agreements themselves how the two Governments would act in accord in the future in making the payment of their respective debts to the Government of the United States ; the reparations settlement was to be subject to the conclusion of an agreement between the United States and its debtors. Mr. MacDonald declared that if such an agreement were not concluded, it would be necessary to call another conference which would take as its starting-point a return to the Young Plan. The Churchill-Caillaux Agreement governing the payment of the French debt to England was also modified in such a way as to prescribe how these payments should or should not be made according as the Lausanne Agreements should or should not be ratified. The Lausanne Agreements were signed on July 9. France made an immense sacrifice, forgoing 35 annuities out of 37. Such was the result of the Hoover moratorium which, in 1931, had destroyed the Young Plan, if not technically at any rate in fact, and which was to have further reactions in the future. Finally, on July 13, there was signed at Lausanne a pact of friendship between France and Britain. This was not an alliance nor even an *entente cordiale*, but something which might be defined as a common atmosphere in which the two countries could survey the crisis, and breathe more freely and recover confidence.

Scarcely were the negotiations at Lausanne concluded when M. Herriot turned to the Disarmament Conference. Since February this body had been making slow progress ; its technical commissions were evolving an enormous mass of reports and of contradictory propositions. From the very opening of the Conference of Lausanne, M. Herriot had recognised that the two conferences, that of reparations and that of disarmament, would either succeed together or paralyse one another. On his arrival at Geneva, M. Herriot noted a number of disagreements and uncertainties among the delegates. He induced the representatives of Great Britain and the United States to try to find an agreement with France on a minimum programme. At this juncture, on June 22, Mr. Hoover published his sensational disarmament plan, recommending a quantitative reduction of about a third in existing armaments. A month later M. Herriot supported the Benes resolution which renewed for four months, as from November 1, 1932, the armaments truce which had been in force for a year. M. Herriot announced that at a later date he would submit a detailed project for the internationalisation of civil aviation. On August 29 came the bombshell of Germany's demand for equality of status for all members of the League of Nations. Germany's demand was equivalent to a threat ; if her continued presence at the Disarmament Conference was desired, it was necessary that Part V. of the Treaty of Versailles, which was responsible for Germany's inferior status, should disappear. The despatch of a German *aide-mémoire* to Paris, published on September 5, produced a serious tension between France and Germany. The French reply, dated September 10, called attention to the example given by France by voting a reduction of about 1,500 millions of francs in military expenditure. Scarcely had the German Government received this reply when it decided to withdraw from the conference (September 14). French opinion received the news without excitement.

On September 16 an extraordinary session of the Chamber was held to examine the scheme for the conversion of *rentes;* it was approved with an extremely large majority. After this *ad hoc* sitting of forty-eight hours, Parliament separated again, in order to allow the Senators whose term of office was expiring to canvass their constituencies. The partial renewal of the Upper House, affecting about a third of its members, resulted in a new accession of strength to the Radicals (13 seats). Thus the Senate was likely to be well disposed to the Government in power.

The Conference of Stresa, which was held September 5–10, under the presidency of M. Georges Bonnet, was meant to be a stage in the work of European reconstruction. Its object was to assist the States of Central and Eastern Europe in their difficulties. Its recommendations, which aimed particularly at raising the prices of cereals in Central and Eastern Europe and at improving the exchanges, were laid before the Committee of European Union at Geneva on September 30. Unfortunately the discussion at Geneva of the work prepared at Stresa was not marked by the same spirit of good-will as had inspired the conference.

When the question of disarmament was taken up again at Geneva, Great Britain, anxious to see Germany resume its place there, proposed with this end in view a discussion between four or five Powers at London. France objected, on the ground that the question at issue ought not to be discussed save under the auspices of the League of Nations. The first British project was replaced by an invitation from Mr. MacDonald to M. Herriot, who crossed the Channel and had some conversations with Mr. MacDonald on October 13 and 14. France and England agreed on an exchange of views between four or five Powers to take place at Geneva. Germany, however, still refused to participate, making its acceptance conditional on recognition of its equality of rights.

Between November 4 and 6 M. Herriot, during a brief visit to Madrid, carried the greetings of the French Republic to the Spanish Republic. In spite of all reports, this demonstration had no further significance.

On his return M. Herriot stopped at Toulouse in time to be present at the closing sessions of the Congress of the Radical-Socialist Party, after having made a striking statement with regard to Italy, from whom he seemed desirous of inviting a frank explanation.

Leaving on one side the problems of foreign policy, the Congress tackled the gigantic problem of the Budget for 1933, in which expenditure approximated to 55 milliards. One half of this

figure was claimed by the public debt, in one form or other ;
one quarter by national defence ; and one quarter by the Civil
services. The Congress seemed unable to make up its mind between a policy of stringent economy which would have to be at the
expense of Civil servants and ex-soldiers, and which might alienate
the support of the Socialists, and a policy of additional taxation
which might have to be put into effect by Socialist measures.
Thus the cleavage between the policies of cartel and combination
which had been foreseen at the elections of May, asserted itself.
In the succeeding weeks and months the financial question became more urgent and more acute than ever.

The new French plan for organising peace was at last made
public. Its novelty consisted in providing four guarantees for
the organisation of general security (and not merely of French
security). These were : (1) The American guarantee, to be based
on a strict interpretation of the Briand-Kellogg Pact outlawing
war, and a formal renunciation of the principle of the freedom
of the seas ; (2) the same guarantee to be given by Great
Britain and the British Empire ; (3) a pact of mutual assistance
to be concluded between all the European States or the largest
possible number of them, which in addition would be under obligation to adhere to the general Act of Arbitration ; (4) the guarantee
resulting from the international control of armaments. This
plan enabled M. Herriot to sign at Geneva, on November 11, the
agreement of the five Powers on the famous equality of rights,
which was to hold good in a regime conferring security on all the
nations. But while the equality of rights was defined with some
precision—the subjection of all armies to the same international
convention, that is to say, the suppression of Part V. of the Treaty
of Versailles—security was made conditional on the conclusion
of a European pact prohibiting recourse to force. Germany re-
entered the Disarmament Conference, Herr von Neurath interpreting this agreement as a decisive victory for German policy,
because it implied unequivocally the recognition of equality of
rights for Germany. It could also be reckoned a success for M.
Herriot, because it rescued France from the isolation into which
it had been plunged for months, and even for years, by the
controversies over armaments. In any case, the agreement
manifested the good-will of France and her profound desire for
peace. All the same, France remained anxious as to the results
of the agreement ; wondering whether " equality " would be com-
pensated by the conclusion of a new European pact, by mutual
assistance, and by firm guarantees of international security.

After wrestling for six months with the difficulties of reparations and disarmament, M. Herriot found himself in front of the
stone wall of the American debt. The 15th of December was
approaching, the date on which the payments suspended by the
Hoover moratorium were due to be resumed. The election of

Mr. Roosevelt on November 8 to the Presidency of the United States had roused in France new hopes. But repeated overtures made by France at Washington did not produce the desired effect, President Hoover deciding to reject the requests for a postponement. Note followed Note as the fateful day approached, and the relations between creditors and debtors seemed to grow more instead of less strained. Committees of both the French Chambers applied themselves to the problem. Among the public, discussion of the question became heated. The "man in the street," the ordinary Frenchman, had put up with the debt payments as long as they had consisted in the transfer of moneys received from Germany. But from the time when Germany had ceased to make these payments, on the instigation of the United States, he had thought that thenceforth he had nothing more to pay. Nevertheless, the United States were expecting from France the payment of 19 million dollars on the date mentioned.

The decision to be taken was one of the gravest since the war, and it gave rise to one of the most notable Parliamentary debates. By their Note of December 8 the United States definitely refused to allow a postponement, merely offering to examine the situation, without contemplating the possibility of cancellation. The French Government thereupon, at a Cabinet Council, drafted a Note to be submitted to Parliament at the sitting of December 13, and which meanwhile was laid before the Committees of Finance and Foreign Affairs. This document, while calling for fresh negotiations, declared that payment would be made, but informed the United States that France in the future would be unable to support the burden of a regime which could not be justified except by the discharge of reparations. At the actual sitting of the Chamber, however, M. Lamoureux proposed from the tribune another resolution which had been drafted by the Committees, and in which in spite of the expiry of the moratorium the Government was invited to defer payment. At this M. Herriot exclaimed : "I do not consent to dishonour the signature of France." Then, invoking the example of England, he added : "The peace of the world, the order of the world, the liberty of the world demand an agreement between these two great peoples, which, the one under a monarchical and the other under a republican regime, are to-day the two great defenders of private rights and public justice." In spite, however, of M. Herriot's energetic and eloquent appeals from the tribune, the Chamber at dawn on December 14 overthrew him by 402 votes to 187. His fall was due to a momentary coalition of the Right, the Centre, and the Extreme Left.

The President of the Republic first approached M. Herriot, whose popularity was still great with the Deputies, with a request to form a Government again, and on his refusal appealed to M. Paul-Boncour, formerly a member of the Unified Socialist Party,

who had succeeded Briand at Geneva as permanent representative
of France and who had been Minister of War in M. Herriot's
Cabinet. Paul-Boncour retained twelve of the eighteen Ministers
of M. Herriot, so that it could be said at Paris that the Herriot
Ministry continued in a decapitated form. As the debt negotiations
had been practically deferred till March, 1933, when Mr. Roosevelt
would succeed Mr. Hoover, the most urgent problem before the
new Government was that of the Budget. The Socialists opposed
all reductions of benefits and pensions, and demanded larger
reductions in the military credits. The parties of the Centre
and the Right wished to economise on all heads, save that of the
Army. Provision was made for two months by means of " provisional twelfths." Among the newcomers, M. Georges Bonnet,
President of the Conference of Stresa, was installed at the office
of Public Works; M. Pierre Cot, who during the discussion on the
debt had made a striking speech in favour of payment, became
Under-Secretary of State for Foreign Affairs, with the duty of
following the work of the League of Nations. The Treasury
was entrusted to the veteran Senator, M. Henry Chéron, who
seemed to have adopted a Poincarism tempered with Socialism.
On December 22 the declaration of M. Paul-Boncour was approved
by a very large majority, but there were good grounds for thinking
that, once the truce was at an end, the Government would find
itself in face of a very difficult task when it tried to balance the
Budget and to adapt the expenditure to the revenue on which
the nation could reasonably count. It would have to decide between seeking the support of the Socialists, which would mean
alienating the Senate, and resorting to " concentration," which
would be no easier for this Parliament than it had been for its
predecessor.

ITALY.

The outstanding events in Italy during the year 1932 included
the celebration of the Tenth Anniversary of the Fascist Regime
in October ; Italy's action at the Lausanne and Geneva Conferences ; the Ministerial changes in July ; and the striking results
of the wheat harvest.

Italy favoured a prompt settlement of War Reparations, War
Debts, and Disarmament. On January 13 Mussolini issued an
appeal in the *Popolo d'Italia* to the Nations urging them once
more to come to a decision to end the world crisis or to put an end
to conferences. When the Disarmament Conference opened on
February 8, Italy strongly insisted on effective reductions in
armaments, and proposed a plan of her own which met with
considerable approval.

The French proposal for an International Armed Force to
keep the peace was rejected by Italy at the outset, and the Press

treated it as chimerical and as a caricature of disarmament.
Italy was anxious to second any positive proposal for a real
reduction made by Great Britain or the United States, and on
February 10 Sig. Grandi, the Italian Foreign Minister, made
a concrete proposal on the following lines :—

(1) In the navy, the simultaneous abolition of ships of the line and submarines; the abolition of aviation transport ships.

(2) In land forces, the abolition of heavy artillery and of tanks of every kind.

(3) In aviation, the abolition of all bombarding aeroplanes.

(4) In all fields, the abolition of aggressive means of chemical and bac-
teriological warfare of whatever nature; a revision of the rules of warfare for the
purpose of ensuring the safety and most effective protection of the civilian
population.

Italy received with some suspicion the advances made to her
by France early in the year, considering that they were merely
intended to secure her support at the Disarmament Conferences.
She also felt aggrieved by the way in which, after the Lausanne
Conference, France and England concluded a Pact of Confidence
without consulting her ; but this did not prevent her from giving
her adherence to the Pact. She continued throughout the year
to cultivate the most cordial relations with Hungary, and in May
renewed for a further five years the Treaty of Friendship, Conciliation, and Arbitration with Turkey. Her relations with Yugoslavia
continued to be strained. A series of incidents in that State,
especially the destruction at Veglia, Arbe, and finally also at Trau
in Dalmatia, of certain historic emblems of Venetian rule, chiefly
the Lion of St. Mark's on public buildings, created considerable
ferment in Italy. Meetings were held in Vicenza and other places,
the students in Rome indulged in demonstrations, and finally,
in the Senate, on December 15, a series of interpellations took
place, and Senator Corrado Ricci criticised severely the action of
the Yugoslavs in destroying artistic and historic monuments, and
thereby offending Italian national sentiment. As a result Italy
entered a diplomatic protest at Belgrade.

The question whether Italy was to pay the second instalment
of her war debt to the United States on December 15 was a matter
of great interest, not only to Italy, but also to Great Britain and
France. Italy, some weeks before payment was due, declared
that she would pay the instalment, which she did on the date
fixed. The sum paid was 1,245,437 dollars, but a few days
previously the Grand Council had declared that it hoped that
before the next payment became due, some solution of the war
debt question would be reached.

Several new trade conventions were negotiated during the year
—with France, Germany, Spain, and Peru, and a commercial
treaty with the Hejaz.

One of the most memorable events of the year was the State

visit of Mussolini to the Pope on February 11, the third anniversary of the Lateran Treaty. This was the first occasion since the entry of Italian troops into Rome in 1870 on which an Italian Premier had paid an official visit to the Pope. This visit set the seal on the reconciliation between the Holy See and Italy, and marked the end of the conflict between them concerning the education and control of youth.

Internal administration was chiefly directed towards reducing as far as possible the effects of the general world crisis, which affected Italy very seriously, principally in the heavy fall in Italian exports, and in the conspicuous absence of foreign tourists. Unemployment was kept down in various ways, by stimulating normal industrial production wherever possible, by keeping open the factories and taking on unemployed men rather than making those actually employed work extra hours. The prosecution of vast schemes of public works gave employment to a large army of workers, but made heavy inroads on the Government finances, which had to take over a good part of the local expenditure of towns and communes whose receipts had fallen off owing to the suppression of the city tolls. Plans for great town improvements were nevertheless vigorously carried on, and Rome employed some 9,000 men on city works and improvements, Milan about 8,000, Turin and Genoa between 6,000 and 7,000, while the smaller centres also provided employment in proportion to their means.

The National Road Institute, an independent organisation controlled and financed by the State, employed 43,000 men at the beginning of the year, and this number was increased to 58,000 before it was concluded. The number of men employed on land reclamation schemes was increased from about 40,000 to 66,000, with the result that unemployment, which had risen to 1,150,000 at the beginning of the year, was reduced to 950,000 in the month of August, but at the end of December it had again risen to over a million.

The financial situation was unsatisfactory, the year 1931-32 closing on June 30 with a deficit of 2,124 million lire. For this situation extraordinary expenditure in connexion with the State railways was partly responsible. The continued fall in the export trade was a further factor in the deficit. Taxation returns were below the level of previous years.

On April 7 the Government called for a State Loan of 1,000,000,000 liras to redeem Treasury Bonds in October, and the sum was subscribed on the first day, while a few days later it was covered four times over. The Government decided to allocate 1 milliard liras to public works, and 2 milliards for a further issue of Treasury Bonds. The Public Debt thereby rose to 96 milliards, and the gold reserve in the Bank of Italy was increased to close on 5,800,000,000 liras. Rumours that Italy intended to depart from the gold standard were emphatically contradicted by the Government.

The composition of the various Ministries had remained unchanged since 1929, but on July 20 Mussolini announced the resignation of five Ministers : Sig. Grandi, the Foreign Minister ; Sig. Mosconi, Minister of Finance ; Sig. Giuliano, Minister of Education ; Sig. Rocco, Minister of Justice ; and Sig. Bottai, Minister of Corporations. Mussolini assumed the two Ministries of Foreign Affairs and Corporations himself, and at the same time he changed 11 Under-Secretaries of State. Sig. Guido Jung was made Minister of Finance ; Professor Francesco Ercole, Minister of Education ; and Sig. Pietro De Francisci, Minister of Justice.

These changes caused considerable surprise. In a country under normal Parliamentary Government the situation would have been described as a " Ministerial Crisis," but under the Fascist system, such a crisis is an impossibility, since the Head of the Government, by the terms of the new Constitution, alone decides upon changes and is accountable only to the King.

As in previous years, the economic policy of the country was largely concerned with agriculture as the best form of safeguard for a population of 43 millions. On September 25 Mussolini presided at the meeting of the Permanent Wheat Commission at Forli, his native district, and was able to state that the 1932 crop had reached 75,150,000 quintals, thus far exceeding that of 1931, which was 66,619,000 quintals, and that of 1929 which was 70,795,100 quintals. The excellent harvest was due in part to the untiring efforts of the Government to instruct, train, and enlighten the farming population in seed selection and in the use of fertilisers and in scientific methods of cultivation. All these points were conspicuous features in Mussolini's " Wheat Campaign " inaugurated in 1925, and still further developed during the last five years.

Reclamation work was carried on in every part of the Peninsula, and also in Sicily and Sardinia, by the " Opera Nazionale dei Combattenti " or Ex-Service Men's organisation, private enterprise, and the Government. On the low plains around Catania, in the once neglected district of Sibari in Calabria, and along the stretch of the coast railway from Naples to Reggio Emilia, thousands of workmen were employed in reclaiming lands, in re-afforesting the barren hill-slopes, and in controlling water courses. Vast areas of marshland between Gaeta and Caserta have been reclaimed by directing water courses through canals to the sea, and on the other side of the Volscian mountains in the Roman Campagna, the great expanse of the once unhealthy and malaria ridden Pontine Marshes was drained, the township of Littoria built, and numerous prosperous looking villages have come into being.

The celebrations of the Tenth Anniversary of the Fascist

Regime extended over three months, from September to November, reaching their climax during October.

On September 10, 50,000 young "Vanguard Fascists" ("Avanguardisti") were passed in review by Mussolini in Rome, in the presence of vast crowds of spectators. On September 18 another great rally took place in Rome, and 50,000 Bersaglieri, who had been brought in special trains from all parts of Italy, marched past Mussolini. On Sunday, October 2, the Intellectuals of Italy assembled to the number of 10,000 for a meeting in the Augusteo, where they were addressed by Mussolini. Almost every week great gatherings were held, and Rome swarmed with young Fascists, organised in a separate force, called the "Fasci Giovanili di Combattimento," and numbering 612,000 throughout Italy. On October 11 Mussolini opened at the Capitolium the meeting of the Association for the Progress of Science.

The new town of Mussoliniana in Sardinia was the centre of the decennial celebrations on October 12 for all the Sardinian people. The new town of Littoria, the centre of the reclaimed Pontine Marshes, was also the scene of demonstrations, although its formal inauguration was deferred until December. Its population had risen from 2,000 in 1931 to 18,000 by the end of 1932. In the next three years, two more towns, Sabaudia and Pontinia, will be established, and the reclaimed Pontine Marshes should have upwards of 50,000 inhabitants.

Italy's progress in shipbuilding was also associated with the celebrations. The maiden voyage of the 50,000 ton steamer *Rex* to New York stirred great interest throughout the country, and it was followed two months later by that of another great liner, the *Conte di Savoia*, of 48,500 tons burden, a product of Trieste shipbuilding. Meanwhile the *Oceania*, a third steamer of 20,000 tons, of the same type as the *Neptunia*, which had only just entered the South-American service, was launched, to be ready for South American traffic next year.

The official visit of Mussolini to Turin on October 23 produced a memorable demonstration, which was all the more noteworthy as that city had been regarded as an anti-Fascist centre. The Duce seized the occasion to deliver an address in which he laid down the main lines of Italy's foreign policy, pleading for collaboration between the four great Western Powers, and declaring against the formation of any hegemony whatever. He received similar ovations in Milan, Forli, Parma, Brescia, and other places.

The conclusion of the celebrations was reached on October 28, the actual anniversary of the Fascist march on Rome, when Mussolini formally opened the new "Strada Imperiale" or "Imperial Avenue" in Rome, between the Coliseum and the Piazza Venezia.

CHAPTER III.

GERMANY AND AUSTRIA.

GERMANY.

THE most significant feature in the internal history of Germany in 1932 was the spread of political extremism. The followers of Adolf Hitler, the National Socialists, became by far the largest single party, though the question whether the National Socialist movement had reached its peak or had already passed it was not possible to answer definitely. The Communist Party also registered striking successes. Through the growth of revolutionary forces on the Right and on the Left, and under the continuous pressure of the economic crisis, the stability of the Government was seriously shaken. A rapid succession of political changes weakened the authority of the State. Constitutional forms of government could not always be preserved, at times even the Constitution itself seemed to be in danger, and the political parties were doomed to impotence. However, the transference of the administration to the Conservative circles of the Right at least prevented the seizure of power by the National Socialists.

In the spring the term of office of President von Hindenburg expired. The parties of the Right were averse to giving him a new lease of power, and put up their own candidates, among them Adolf Hitler, for the presidentship. To prevent the election of the leader of the National Socialists, all the middle-class parties and the Social Democrats united and resolved upon the re-election of von Hindenburg. He, however, did not obtain an absolute majority, so that a second ballot was necessary. On April 10 von Hindenburg received 19,300,000 votes (53 per cent.), Hitler 13,400,000 votes (37 per cent.), and the Communist candidate 3,700,000 votes (10 per cent.). Thus after a hard struggle von Hindenburg, in his eighty-fifth year, was elected President of the Reich for another seven years through the votes of his former opponents, the middle-class parties and the Socialists.

The agitation carried on by the National Socialists became all the more unrestrained on account of their defeat. The Government at one time tried the effect upon them of concessions and indulgence, at another of force and severity. In February it was ordained that members of the National Socialist Party and the National Socialist militia should be eligible for the Reichswehr. Shortly afterwards, in April, the Government decided to disband all National Socialist defence organisations, as public insecurity spread more and more, and sanguinary encounters took place every day. This prohibition of the Hitler army led to sharp differences of opinion between Dr. Brüning and the President of the Reich, who called upon the Chancellor to treat the militias of all the parties in the same way as Hitler's army, and prohibit them also. With this request Dr. Brüning would not comply.

The Chancellor thus lost the confidence of the President, and at the same time National Socialists obtained notable successes in the spring elections in various districts. In Oldenburg, for instance, the Hitler party obtained 24 out of 46 seats. Although in May the Reichstag rejected a vote of censure on the Brüning Cabinet by 287 to 257 votes, yet at the end of May the Government felt compelled to resign. Professor Dr. Warmbold, the Minister of Economy, and the Defence Minister Groener had already given up their posts a few weeks before. The Brüning Ministry had been in office two years and two months.

It was now that, without the co-operation of the parties or of Parliament, certain circles which had for long been exercising a powerful influence behind the scenes, especially on the President, came to the front. On June 1 the President appointed Herr Franz von Papen, Chancellor ; Freiherr von Gayl, Minister of the Interior ; Freiherr von Neurath, hitherto Ambassador in London, Minister of Foreign Affairs ; Count Schwerin-Krosigk, hitherto Ministerial Director, Minister of Finance ; Dr. Gürtner, hitherto Minister of Justice in Bavaria, Minister of Justice ; General von Schleicher, Minister of Defence ; Dr. Warmbold, Minister of Economic Affairs ; Freiherr von Braun, Minister of Agriculture ; Herr Schaeffer, the President of the Reich Insurance Office, Minister of Labour ; and Freiherr von Elz-Rübenach, Minister of Posts and Communications.

The new Chancellor, von Papen, had hitherto taken little part in German home politics. At the beginning of the war he had been Military Attaché to the Ambassador in Washington, and had been recalled in consequence of a complaint of the American State Secretary Lansing in 1915. He had subsequently been Commander of a battalion on the Western front and Chief of the General Staff in the Turkish Army. He stood on the extreme right wing of the Centre Party, and had always strongly opposed any tendency of the Centre towards the Left. On assuming the office of Chancellor he left the Centre Party, which subsequently became sharply opposed to him.

The Government regarded as its chief task the " combination of all national forces." The Ministerial Declaration contained the following passage :—

" The German people must be informed of the condition in which the Government finds public affairs. The finances of the Reich, of Prussia, and of most of the other Provinces and of the municipalities are in utter disorder. None of the urgently needed reforms without which there can be no recovery has passed beyond the initial stages. The social insurances are faced with bankruptcy. The continually increasing unemployment is consuming the vitals of the German people. The post-war Governments thought that by State Socialism they could relieve both employer and employed of their material anxieties. They have

attempted to make the State into a kind of welfare institute. . . . The disintegrating influence of atheistic-marxist thought has penetrated far too deeply
into all cultural spheres of public life."

Simultaneously with the issue of this declaration of June 4,
the Reichstag, in which the von Papen Ministry could not hope
to command a majority, was dissolved. After the Landtag
elections in Prussia and in other Provinces the probabilities were
that a new election would bring gains of any consequence only to
the National Socialists. The Government openly expressed its
hope of being supported by Hitler. For one of its first steps after
the dissolution of the Reichstag was to permit again the formation
of the National Socialist militia which had been disbanded by
Dr. Brüning. The South German States, Bavaria and Baden,
feared that this measure would endanger public order, and they
therefore retained the existing prohibition, until the Chancellor,
by an emergency decree, secured the recognition of the Hitler
groups throughout the whole Reich.

From this point—from the middle of June—the streets in the
large towns of Germany belonged for some weeks to wearers of
uniform, and a civil war was imminent. Things came to such
a pass that the Oldenburg Government could venture for a time
to enrol members of the Hitler army in the State police. According to official statistics, there were in Prussia alone in the period
from June 1 to July 20 322 political assaults, in which 72 persons
were killed and 497 seriously wounded. In the course of the
whole year it is estimated that the victims of political unrest in
Germany numbered 250 dead and several thousand wounded.
A few weeks after his accession to office, von Papen, in view of
the deplorable consequences of the toleration of Hitler, felt compelled to forbid all public demonstrations. In August there was
issued a " Terror Emergency Decree," which directed summary
courts to be set up for dealing with political offences. Public
order was gradually restored, after five National Socialists in
Beuthen (Upper Silesia) had been condemned to death for killing a Communist workman. On hearing of this sentence, which
was afterwards commuted to imprisonment for life, Adolf Hitler
cried to the murderers : " Your freedom is a question of our
honour. . . ."

The elections to the Reichstag took place on July 31. They
brought to the National Socialists their greatest success so far, as
they obtained 37·3 per cent. of the votes. How keenly interested
the German people were in the political events of this momentous
summer is shown by the fact that 84 per cent. of the electors
registered their votes. To a Reichstag of 608 members there
were elected 230 National Socialists (in the last Reichstag 167) ;
37 German Nationals (41) ; 7 German People's Party (30) ; 2
Economy Party (23) ; 3 Christian Social Party (14) ; 22 Bavarian

People's Party (18) ; 75 Centre (68) ; 4 State Party (Democrats) (20) ; 133 Social Democrats (143) ; and 89 Communists (77).

In the second sitting of this Reichstag, on September 12, the Chancellor, von Papen, sought in vain to obtain a hearing before a vote was taken on the motion of censure on the Government. The President of the Reichstag, the National Socialist Göring, refused to allow the Chancellor an opportunity to speak, thinking thereby to prevent the dissolution of Parliament which was once more threatened, and to force the resignation of the Government. The members of the Government left the sitting and regarded the Reichstag as dissolved. Thereupon 512 members voted against the Government. Only 42, from the German Nationals and the German People's Party, voted for the von Papen Government. As in the eyes of the Government the Reichstag was already dissolved, this demonstration had no practical significance. The Government paid no regard to the adverse vote, and ordered a new election.

The elections of November 6, in which 80 per cent. of the electors recorded their votes, brought for the first time since 1930 a check to the National Socialist advance. The Communists, on the other hand, improved on their previous gains. Some of the middle class put more trust in the words of the Government than in the promises of Hitler. In the period which had elapsed since the July election, the von Papen Government had put forward an economic programme which, though strongly criticised, was regarded by large sections of the middle class as a sign of a return to sound methods of administration. Consequently, the National Socialists on November 6 obtained only 33·1 per cent. of the votes polled. Out of 584 seats the National Socialists obtained 196 (with 11,737,000 votes) ; the German Nationals, 51 seats (3,019,000 votes) ; the German People's Party, 11 seats (662,000 votes) ; the Economy Party, 1 seat (110,000 votes) ; the Christian Social Party, 5 seats (404,000 votes) ; the Bavarian People's Party, 20 seats (1,095,000 votes) ; the Centre, 70 seats (4,230,000 votes) ; the State Party (Democrats), 2 seats (336,000 votes) ; the Social Democrats, 121 seats (7,248,000 votes) ; and the Communists, 100 seats (5,980,000 votes).

Outside the ranks of the German Nationalists and the German People's Party, von Papen could even now find no sympathisers. His quick temper and off-handed manner were continually bringing him into conflict with Parliamentary conventions. Long and laborious conversations with the National Socialists had made it clear that the idea of a coalition with Hitler could not be seriously entertained. Hitler claimed the whole power in the Reich and in the provinces for himself ; he demanded, as he said, the same rights as Mussolini possessed in Italy. These demands were repeatedly rejected by the President of the Reich. Von Papen's consideration for the National Socialists turned out to be fruitless. On November 17 his Government resigned.

The most important, and also the most severely criticised step taken by von Papen was the *coup d'état* in Prussia. Hitherto Prussia had been regarded as a Social Democrat preserve ; since 1918 the Prussian Government had been without interruption in the hands of Social Democrats. Up to the summer of 1932 the rulers of Prussia saw in the National Socialists, equally with the Communists, revolutionaries and enemies of the State. Inspired as it was with such ideas, the policy of the Prussian Government could not be reconciled with the aims of the von Papen Cabinet.

As the elections to the Landtag on April 24 produced in Prussia also an overwhelming National Socialist majority, the Government resigned. Owing, however, to the difficulty of forming a coalition in the Landtag, the appointment of a new Prussian Government proved impossible. Consequently the Prussian Cabinet, led by the Prime Minister, Otto Braun (Social Democrat), and by the Minister of the Interior, Severing (also a Social Democrat), continued to conduct affairs. In the opinion of Chancellor von Papen, however, the acting Prussian Government was not in a position to maintain order in the critical days of the summer. On July 20 Braun and Severing were relieved of their offices. As the Prussian Ministers refused to withdraw, martial law was declared in Berlin and the Province of Brandenburg. A struggle between the Reichswehr and the Prussian police appeared to be by no means impossible. Eventually, however, the Chancellor had his way without resort to arms. All the Prussian Ministers were forced to resign, and in addition the heads of the Prussian and of the Berlin police forces were deposed. The administration of Prussia was taken over by the Chancellor in person. As his deputy he appointed Dr. Bracht, the Senior Burgomaster of Essen, and a political associate of his, at the head of the Prussian State, with the title of Commissioner.

The larger South German States protested against this " breach of the Constitution," and the Governments of both Bavaria and Baden associated themselves with the complaint which was laid by Prussia before the State Tribunal. But the legal discussions which followed on the admissibility of von Papen's procedure could not alter events. Unquestionably the Chancellor was wrong—so the Court held—in trying to justify his action on the ground that the Prussian Government had failed in the performance of its duty, in having opposed only the extremism of the Right, while displaying little energy against the Communists. For these assertions no proofs were adduced in the course of the proceedings in Court.

There was, however, another side to this " conquest " of Prussia by the Reich. Although the so-called " reform of the Reich " was taken in hand years ago, yet so far all efforts to simplify the complicated machinery of administration have made very little progress. In particular the dualism between the Reich and Prussia, the existence of two distinct Governments side by side in Berlin, had often caused trouble. This dualism was removed with one blow by a *tour de force*. The administration of Prussia was placed in the hands of a Commissioner appointed by the Reich. During the short period of his official activity, Commissioner Dr. Bracht carried the reform of the Prussian administration many steps forward. About 50 Rural Districts (Landkreise) were abolished, 60 District Courts (Amtsgerichte) lapsed, and the Prussian Ministry for Public Welfare was combined with the Ministry of Commerce. There were also several alterations in personnel. The Social Democratic influence in the police and in other branches of the Prussian administration was greatly curtailed. The rule which so far had been in force forbidding Prussian officials to belong to the National Socialist Party was cancelled.

In the Reich the situation was critical after the resignation of the von Papen Cabinet. As leader of the strongest party, Hitler was invited by the President of the Reich to form a Parliamentary Government. As in the summer, so now Hitler demanded full and unconditional powers for forming a " presidial Cabinet " which should be independent of Parliament. The negotiations were terminated with a letter from the State Secretary Meissner, which contained the following passage :—

"The President of the Reich thanks you for your willingness to become the head of a presidial Cabinet. He considers, however, that he would not be doing his duty to the German people if he handed over his presidential powers to the leader of a party which has repeatedly emphasised its exclusiveness and which . . . has taken up a preponderatingly negative attitude. In these circumstances the President of the Reich cannot help fearing that a presidial Cabinet conducted by you would inevitably lead to a party dictatorship bringing in its train a bitter aggravation of the conflicts within the German people, for becoming a party to which he could not answer to his oath and his conscience."

After the leader of the Centre Kaas had in vain endeavoured to form a Parliamentary Government, the President on December 2 appointed General von Schleicher, whose influence had already manifested itself under Dr. Brüning, Chancellor of the Reich. The Chancellor retained the Ministry of Defence. From the von Papen Ministry he took over the Minister of Foreign Affairs, Freiherr von Neurath ; the Finance Minister, Count Schwerin-Krosigk ; the Minister of Justice, Dr. Gürtner ; the Minister of Food and Agriculture, Freiherr von Braun ; the Minister of Economic Affairs, Professor Dr. Warmbold ; and the Minister of Posts, Freiherr Elz von Rübenach. The Ministry of the Interior was given to Dr. Bracht, who still remained Commissioner for Prussia, and the Ministry of Labour to Dr. Syrup, hitherto head of the Unemployment Insurance fund. A new Ministry for Settlement and Employment was created, and was filled by Dr. Gereke.

N

A place in the Cabinet as Minister without portfolio was also given to Dr. Popitz, one of the leading experts in German finance and taxation, who at the same time administered the finances of Prussia as Commissioner.

The von Schleicher Cabinet adopted in the main the programme of the von Papen regime, with the difference that it exerted itself to win the confidence of Parliament, which von Papen had thought he could dispense with.   On December 15 von Schleicher expounded his plans in a wireless message : " I am heretic enough to confess that I am an adherent neither of Capitalism nor of Socialism. . . . My programme consists of a single point—to create employment."

The attempt of von Papen to combat unemployment by offering prizes for the employment of additional workers had had only feeble success.   Von Schleicher therefore reverted to the view that unemployment could be reduced only by the official and artificial creation of work through the building of roads, canals, railways, etc.   A specially important point in the Government programme was the encouragement of land settlement, although previous large-scale endeavours in this field had not brought to the labour market the permanent relief which had been hoped.

The lowest point touched by the unemployment figures was 5·2 millions in October, which was still 1·2 million above the lowest figure of the previous year.   At the end of the year there were 6 million registered unemployed, who for the most part received a grant of only 7 marks a week (childless married pairs 15 marks).   Almost half of all the workless were supported by the municipalities, which for this purpose received only slender grants from the Government.   On this account a large number of German cities were no longer able to meet their obligations. Large municipalities like Cologne and Frankfort had even to cease paying the interest on their loans.

In pursuance of the policy commenced in 1931 of bringing banking under State control, all kinds of money transactions were subjected to drastic regulations.   Interest rates were lowered ; regulations were issued for the protection of distressed house-owners, to the prejudice of the mortgagees ; similarly, a far-reaching law for the stay of executions was passed for the benefit of agriculture.   In the period between March and September, the Reichsbank lowered its discount rate from 7 to 4 per cent., and its interest rate on deposits from 8 to 5 per cent., though this cheapening of money produced no revival of business.   Nor did the further cheapening of the cost of living by about 10 per cent. avail either to retard the shrinkage of production or to offset the decline in the income of large sections of the population.   A visible sign of the shrinkage in the volume of business was the decrease in the note circulation from 4,575 million marks in January, to 3,370

million marks in December, while in the same period the stock of
gold in the Reichsbank sank from 980 to 800 millions, and the
amount of securities from 162 to 117 millions.   The maintenance
of the mark exchange and the retention of the gold standard laid
heavy burdens on the German people.   Germany could not meet
her obligations to foreign countries, and had to request a prolongation and extension of the moratorium granted in 1931.   The
total debt of the Reich amounted at the end of the year to 12·2
milliards of marks.   In spite of far-reaching economies and reductions, the deficit in the Reich Budget increased in the course of
the year from about 1,690 to 2,070 million marks.   The financial
outlook was affected to an increasing degree by a perceptible
decline in the yield from taxation.   Between April 1, 1931, and
March 31, 1932, the revenue of the Reich was 7,787 million marks,
against 9,025 millions in the preceding year.   In the meantime the
best industrial concerns and companies, which hitherto had been
kept well going, showed losses on their working, while the Government's reconstruction plans had not advanced beyond the experimental stage, and a mitigation of the crushing burden of taxation
became more urgent every day ; so that the future financial state
of the country became a subject of deep anxiety.

For German foreign trade also the year was one of contraction
and decline, although in this field the balance was still favourable.
After the example of almost all European States, imports were
subjected to severe restrictions through tariff increases and quota
regulations.   Already in 1931 imports had declined by 3,560 and
exports by 2,400 million marks, though the excess of exports—
without reparations deliveries—still attained the imposing figure of
2,600 million marks.   In 1932 the excess of exports fell back to
the figure of 1930, and hardly exceeded 1,000 million marks.
Considering the height to which tariff walls had been raised, this
was a satisfactory result, which was only attainable because the
prices of German industrial products had fallen enormously, and
so they had been better able to compete in the world market than
formerly.   For German industry the foreign trade balance became
more and more important, as a large number of factories could be
kept running only so long as exports took the place of the almost
stagnant home market.   In particular trade with Holland and
Scandinavia was gravely prejudiced because the German Government in its solicitude for the native agriculture limited the
imports of eggs, butter, meat, etc.

The two attempts made during the year by the European
Powers to solve by joint action the world's problems—the
Lausanne Reparations Conference and the Geneva Disarmament
Conference—were considered by German opinion to be closely
connected with one another and with the economic crisis.   As
Dr. Brüning declared in Geneva on February 9 : " The econ-
omic distress of the world at the present moment is undoubtedly

due in the first instance to the political payments and to the excessive and unequal armaments."

The Lausanne Conference drew the logical conclusions from the verdict of the Advisory Committee of the Bank of International Payments in Bâle in December, 1931, on Germany's inability to pay. The Lausanne Agreements provided for a final payment by Germany of 3 milliards of marks in bonds and the ending of reparations, after 67,673 milliards of marks altogether have been handed over to the creditor States.

For her " equality of rights" in the matter of disarmament, Germany had to fight harder than for the cessation of reparations. If the negotiations finally resulted in a recognition of Germany's demand for equality, this was due in no small measure to the sympathetic understanding which Mr. Henderson, the President of the Disarmament Conference, showed for the German wishes. It was especially due to the efforts of Mr. Henderson and Sir John Simon that Germany withdrew her refusal to participate in the proceedings.

It was largely thanks to the transactions in Lausanne and Geneva that order was maintained in Germany, and that the Government was able, in spite of the alarming growth of revolutionary movements, to retain the rudder in its hands. The cause of public order and tranquillity benefited by the growing belief that the European Powers, acting in conjunction, would in time discover means to combat the economic crisis, and would carry them through in co-operation.

AUSTRIA.

Austria began the year in a serious economic plight and ended it worse off, though still surprising all who know the facts by her agility in avoiding complete economic collapse. In the political world she was fortunate in being spared to a large extent the threats or attempts at counter-revolution which have become a regular feature during recent years. Two Governments fell during the year, however, while the rise of the Hitlerite Party in Austria, following on its triumphs in Germany, caused considerable anxiety and unrest, more especially as Austrian Hitlerism has failed to produce any responsible leader. Hitlerism weakened the *Heimwehr* movement enormously, and although it is no more revolutionary or dangerous to the State, the Clericals are concerned lest it should possess itself of the enormous *Heimwehr* armoury. For while *Heimwehrism* is largely controlled by Clerical and pro-Habsburg wire-pullers, Hitlerism is largely anti-Clerical and controlled by wire-pullers in Germany to whom a return of the Habsburgs would be most unwelcome.

The irksome restrictions on financial transactions and foreign trade, imposed against the will of all the business and much of the banking community in a desperate attempt to bolster up the Austrian Schillinge, were maintained and in many respects tightened up. Towards the end of the year evasion of many of them by traders had become so common that in practice some relaxation was experienced, although the hindrance to trade continued. Foreign creditors and exporters to Austria continued to suffer, but the League of Nations and the banking interests behind it and its loans continued to tolerate or even encourage artificial propping of the Austrian and other actually depreciated currencies by means of financial restrictions so that the service of the League Loans should be met. Constant protests by business organisations did not avail to secure any but unimportant modifications.

On January 27 the Cabinet of Dr. Karl Buresch resigned, in consequence of the continued hostility of France towards the Foreign Minister, Dr. Johann Schober, who had never been forgiven for bringing forward the project of a Customs Union with Germany in 1931. Dr. Schober was to have gone to Geneva as Austrian delegate, but the Austrian Clericals, anxious to stand well with France, violently opposed the project. On January 29 Dr. Karl Buresch formed a new (minority) Cabinet consisting of a coalition between the Clerical (Christian Social) and Agrarian (*Landbund*) parties, the Pan-Germans declining to join out of loyalty to Dr. Schober, who was excluded. The coalition worked badly from the start, as the *Landbund* was anxious to pursue a conciliatory policy towards the Socialist Opposition (which consisted of the strongest party in Parliament). This was unpalatable to the majority of the Clericals, and constant bickering followed.

On May 6 the second Buresch Cabinet resigned. It had become obvious that the Hitlerites had secured the favour of many of those who had formerly supported the Buresch Cabinet. The unrepresented Hitlerites called for a General Election ; for varying reasons the same demand was made by the Socialists, Pan-Germans, and *Heimwehr* in Parliament. Dr. Buresch asked for the support of the *Heimwehr* members in an endeavour to avoid a General Election, but when they demanded a seat in the Cabinet and that the Government should follow an extreme reactionary course dictated by themselves, Dr. Buresch resigned rather than comply.

The *Heimwehr*, however, secured all and more than they asked. The crisis lasted until May 20, when Dr. Engelbert Dollfuss, Clerical Minister of Agriculture in the preceding Cabinet, formed a Cabinet, which included not only the *Heimwehrman*, Dr. Jakconcig as Minister of Commerce, but also the powerful patron of the Styrian *Heimwehr*, Dr. Rintelen, Governor of Styria, as Minister of Education. Herr Vaugoin, another powerful *Heimwehr* supporter, was retained as Minister of War, a post which he had occupied for over a decade. The *Heimwehr* were taken into the Cabinet after the demand of the Pan-Germans, as price of their collaboration, for a declaration of Austria's inability to continue the service of her loans and a guarantee for the State officials that their salaries would not again be reduced, had been rejected. The new Government, with its average majority of one vote in Parliament, was naturally weak, but despite —or perhaps because of—that fact, it made some play with the idea of being a " strong-hand " Cabinet. In the voting on the League Loan Bill on August 3, it was saved only by the death of Monsignor Seipel who had been home very ill and would have been unable to vote. His death enabled a substitute deputy to be nominated and sworn in, and the Dollfuss Cabinet was saved by him and other deputies brought from hospital on crutches or bandaged.

The vicious circle of decreasing revenue receipts, due in part to restrictions on financial and trading operations and necessitating further State economies which still further reduced incomes and so revenue receipts, leading to fresh attempts to restrict imports, operated throughout the year. On April 1 the Trade Treaty with Hungary was denounced. On May 23 the Government announced that a transfer moratorium would be proclaimed that week, but actually the half-yearly payments on the League of Nations Loan and the Federal Loan of 1920 were made with great difficulties. The Government declared on June 5 that the proclamation of a transfer moratorium could probably not be delayed much longer. On June 21 the Minister of Finance, Dr. Weidenhoffer, first revealed that despite new taxation and economies, the country would be faced with a deficit of 14,000,000*l.* on the 1932 Budget. The Government were sharply attacked for their guiding principle of placating the peasant at any cost to the townsman and worker by granting various agricultural preferences. On July 8, in a speech introducing new economy measures and increases in the turnover tax and certain duties, the Minister of Finance made a fuller statement on the financial situation. The service of the League and Federal Loans on June 1 had depleted the National Bank's reserve of gold deposited abroad by 10,000,000 Schillinge, and another 5,000,000 Schillinge worth of gold had had to be sold to strengthen the bank's holding of foreign exchange. Of the Budget deficit of 322,000,000 Schillinge (Herr Weidenhoffer said on July 8), 100,000,000 was due to the credit Anstalt troubles. Revenues had fallen short of the estimate by 82,400,000 Schillinge, including a big deficit on posts and telegraphs. He introduced schemes to save 81,000,000 Schillinge and to increase revenues by 62,500,000 Schillinge by taxation.

Throughout the summer Austria was occupied with a conflict over the question of ratifying the Lausanne Loan Protocol. The Protocol provided for a Loan to Austria from the B.I.S. of

9,000,000*l.*, guaranteed as to one-third each by the British and
French Governments, the remaining third being guaranteed by
smaller States. From the start the Austrian Government
shrouded the terms in mystery, and for a long time refused to
admit what everybody knew—that France had refused to let
Austria have this vitally necessary loan until she signed away
her economic freedom in respect of a possible Customs Union
with Germany for a further twenty years (the period of the loan).
3,000,000*l.* of the proceeds were ear-marked to repay the advance
made the previous year by the Bank of England. The remainder
had to be used by the Austrian Government to repay its debts
to the National Bank, so that the practical advantage of the
loan lay only in the moral strength which the granting of it
afforded to Austrian credit abroad. In addition to the political
condition made by the French (prohibiting Austria from concluding a Customs Union), the Government also promised various
financial reforms : to keep the Budget balanced, to accept financial
supervision by the League exercised through its representative
in Vienna, Dr. Rost van Tanningen, to bring together the official
and private rates of exchange, and to abolish the irksome exchange restrictions. Neither of the latter two promises had been
fulfilled by the end of the year. It was quite clear to foreign
observers that Austria was completely bankrupt before the loan
was made, and many people said that to make this loan was
throwing good money after bad. The dangers of a political up-
heaval with Austria as a centre, and the hope that a loan now
might possibly enable Austria at some distant date to liquidate
her earlier indebtedness, were decisive. At home Socialists, Pan-
Germans, and Hitlerites were unanimous in demanding that
Austria should reject the Protocol with its implied " enslavement
to France." The Clericals who supported the Protocol complained
that German industrialists were encouraging the opposition, and
thus interfering in Austrian internal politics. While the controversy was at its height—on July 29—the Austrian Government
officially announced its default in the previous month, on the Six
Per Cent. Guaranteed Loan of 1923, although the trustees had
funds to meet the interest due on December 1, and to provide for
the redemption of bonds up to May 31. On August 2 the Bill for
ratification received its third reading, and was sent to the Main
Committee of Parliament for further consideration. On August 7
further consideration of the Bill was postponed in the hope of
winning more support, but on August 17 it passed the National
Assembly by 1 vote only. It passed to the Senate, where it
was defeated by 27 votes to 23, and had to be returned to the
National Assembly, where amidst many protests that the Government had sold the country to France, ratification was passed by
2 votes only. The course of events in France caused anxiety, and
the opponents of Lausanne told the Government that they would

find France unwilling to pay them their " Judas Money " after all ; there was great triumph in Clerical circles when it was learned on December 29 that France also had ratified.

Another international agreement which caused much debate in Austria was the new Trade Treaty with Hungary, which had to be drafted to replace the treaty which expired (after being denounced by Austria) on July 15.　The Socialists accused the Austrian Government of truckling to Italy by discussing at the same time a secret political understanding with Hungary and Italy directed against Yugoslavia.　The new treaty was concluded on December 10 for one year, on the basis of a fixed ratio between the imports and exports of the two countries with one another. The Minister of Finance submitted estimates for 1933, in which expenditure and revenue balanced at the high figure of about 57,000,000*l*.　Among the fresh restrictions on Finance and Trade introduced during the year was a censorship of registered letters, instituted on February 29 (still in force at the end of the year), to prevent the export of foreign currency, and the issue on June 30 of a long list of import prohibitions, so extensive as to be calculated to reduce the standard of living even for the richest to a very low level.　The list of restrictions was later widened, but somehow or other Austrian importers managed, despite the Government, to secure at any rate a diminished supply of practically all the prohibited imports.　The various clearing agreements which Austria had made during the preceding year with other countries proved unsatisfactory, and were gradually dropped.

The Credit Anstalt problem remained throughout the year one of the most troublesome which the Government had to face.　By the end of the year no less than nine different Credit Anstalt reform Bills had been passed since the collapse of the bank in 1931.　The position regarding the former directors and high officials on the Credit Anstalt was never satisfactorily cleared up, although formal proceedings were taken against some of them. The Opposition always denied that the Government had ever had any sincere intention of exposing those culpable for the collapse. There were continued negotiations with the foreign creditors of the institution, to whose demands the Austrians maintained a steady opposition despite occasional concessions.　The Socialists particularly attacked the proposed term of settlements on various occasions on the ground that the creation of a holding company dominated by foreign interests, which should gradually close down industrial undertakings of the Credit Anstalt which were unremunerative, meant handing over a greater part of Austrian industry and industrial workers to foreign capitalists.　On June 13 representatives of the Government and the foreign creditors issued a joint statement saying that after long negotiations the latter had been unable to accept the Government programme, and that negotiations were interrupted.　The unacceptable

Austrian proposals were to pay in forty annuities a sum between 20 and 30 per cent. of the total in full settlement.   On July 27 it was announced that the Government had agreed with the National Bank to treat as a total loss " Financial bills " amounting to 16,000,000*l.* which had been discounted by the State for the Credit Anstalt.   In October the Credit Anstalt negotiations were resumed in London.

The so-called " Tardieu Plan " naturally attracted great interest in Austria, but on the whole the opposition to the scheme in the form in which the French put it forward was considerably stronger than the support.   It was felt in Austria that, highly desirable as was closer combination between the five Danubian States, French insistence that the principal customers and markets of most of these States individually—Germany and Italy—should be excluded, revealed the cloven hoof of French political intrigue.   The Opposition saw in the scheme proof that the French, in their determination to prevent Austria from joining Germany, had decided to support some form of a Danubian Federation which would be dominated by French financial, railway, and commercial influences, and might even lead some day to an attempted Habsburg restoration under French auspices.   Apart from political opposition, Austria found herself obliged to look askance at the plan because of the damage it would have inflicted on her very important trade with Germany and Italy.   In connexion with the Tardieu proposals, a very important conference of the International Chamber of Commerce (at which delegates of ten countries, including the Danubian States, Great Britain, France, Germany, Italy, and Poland, took part) was opened in Innsbruck on April 16.   It was intended that it should draw up some sort of more acceptable alternative to the Tardieu scheme, which though, of course, unofficial would be of assistance to the World Economic Conference later.   The result of the conference was to reveal the acuteness of the suspicions of one another entertained by the various States.   Broadly speaking, the delegates from the Little Entente countries ranged themselves on the side of France and the Tardieu Plan which Austria, Germany, and Italy strongly opposed.   The conference closed on April 20 without having done much more than demonstrate how impossible it was proving despite all attempts to separate economics from politics.

The economic and financial conference, which opened at Stresa on September 5, suggested another ray of hope for Austria and the Danubian States.   The Austrian representative pointed out that, compared with the first quarter of 1929, Austrian imports had decreased by 48 per cent. during the first quarter of 1932. The Stresa programme, said the President, M. Bonnet, affected economic, agricultural, and military problems of the States concerned.   The World Economic Conference, he said, could not be successful if Stresa failed.   The conference had to consider two main alternatives—the adoption by the Danubian countries of a system of preferential tariffs, or the concluding of agreements between the greater exporting and importing countries on the one hand and the individual hard-hit Danubian States on the other. France was opposed to loans as a remedy, and in favour of preferential tariffs, and submitted a scheme. Germany, without condemning the French scheme, put forward an alternative plan of her own, offering preferential tariffs but no money to the Danubian States. The British delegate pointed out that Great Britain, after herself abandoning the gold standard, could hardly be expected to lend money to enable other countries to maintain that standard. The French, Italian, and German delegates eventually approved a scheme whereby grain-exporting countries adhering to the Convention would be granted facilities on their exports up to the average of their exports in 1929, 1930, and 1931. States adhering to the Convention were to contribute annually to a common reconstruction fund. States importing cereals from the Danubian countries would make a reduced contribution. Germany would make no contribution, but would maintain existing and grant new bi-lateral preferences. In return, the Agrarian States should pledge themselves to reduce their Customs duties. Great Britain refused the contributory scheme. The conference concluded by agreeing on a number of recommendations to the Europe Commission of the World Economic Conference, but this outward agreement lost most of its value by the number of reservations made by most countries at a secret session preceding the last open session.

Although political differences were overshadowed in Austria by the alarming economic situation throughout the year, there were several violent clashes between Socialists and reactionaries, and continued bitterness caused by the one-sided policy of the Government in seizing the illegal armaments of Socialist and Republican organisations whenever they could be found, while leaving the reactionary and Fascist bodies in full possession of their far greater and equally illegal armaments. On January 12 a number of rifles, machine-guns, and other weapons were seized in the Vienna Socialist Secretariat. Immediately afterwards the Government promised yet another Bill, providing for the disarmament of both sides. Their failure to introduce it caused little surprise, as there were already laws enough for the purpose in existence, which the Government regularly enforced only against the Socialists. On April 24 the Provincial Diet elections were held, at which the Hitlerites made enormous gains at the expense of the Pan-Germans chiefly, then of the *Heimwehr* and Clericals, and lastly of the Socialists. In the Vienna Diet the National Socialists obtained 15 seats where they previously had none, wiping out the Pan-German Party. On May 6 Prince Starhemberg, Leader of the *Heimwehr*, had to apply to the courts for the appointment of a receiver owing to the debts which he had incurred by financing the *Heimwehr* movement. On May 26 the Hitlerites signalised their first appearance in the Vienna Diet by violent demonstrations. Anti-Semitic riots, organised by Hitlerites in the University, caused that institution to be closed on May 30 for a week. Similar disorders occurred several times during the year, notably in October and November. On June 29 the International Country Club was raided by Hitlerites in search of wealthy Jews. They smashed the furniture, and injured twenty persons, including several women and the diplomats of four States. On October 16 Hitlerites, marching through a Socialist quarter of Vienna, attacked the Socialist Secretariat. The latter unexpectedly produced rifles and started to shoot ; two Hitlerites and a policeman were killed, and forty-eight wounded on both sides, the Socialist casualties being mostly caused by the police shooting at their headquarters. Eighty rifles and twenty revolvers were seized from the Socialists by the police. On October 19 the Chancellor appointed Major Fey (a founder of the illegal *Heimwehr* organisation) as Secretary of State for Public Security. He immediately prohibited military marches, except by his own *Heimwehr*. This one-sided action resulted, on October 21, in violent scenes in the House when *Heimwehr* deputies hurled inkpots at the Socialists, hitting by mistake one of their own representatives in the Cabinet.

CHAPTER IV.

SOVIET RUSSIA — ESTONIA — LATVIA — LITHUANIA — POLAND — DANZIG — CZECHOSLOVAKIA — HUNGARY — RUMANIA — YUGO-SLAVIA — TURKEY — GREECE — BULGARIA — ALBANIA.

THE UNION OF SOCIALIST SOVIET REPUBLICS.

INDIFFERENT progress was made during 1932 with the prosecution of the Five-Year Plan for the industrialisation of Russia. Some industries, it is true, such as the electric, oil, and tractor and machine building, were ahead of their schedule, and had in fact completed the five-year programme by the beginning of the year. But the key industries, coal and steel and pig-iron, were considerably behindhand, and the unsatisfactory condition of transport also caused great retardation. There was much quantitative progress of industry as compared with the previous year, but this was offset by increasing qualitative defects, due to inefficiency and carelessness in the handling of plant and machinery. All the same, energetic preparations were made for launching a second five-year plan on the conclusion of the first.

In the industrial sphere, the year was notable for the completion of certain "giant" constructions, some of them said to be the largest of their kind in the world. These included the Nizhni-Novgorod motor works, opened on January 1, and blast furnace No. 1 of the metallurgic works at Magnitogorsk in the Urals, started soon after, the great dam across the River Dnieper which was finished in the spring, and the huge hydro-electric power station (Dnieprostroi) on the same river which was opened amid great celebrations on October 10. Both the motor works and the blast furnace, however, were soon reduced to idleness through lack of material, and the works which were to be fed from the power station had not yet started at the end of the year.

The problem of grain supplies caused the authorities great anxiety throughout the year. Early in the year the Government sent about 1,000,000 tons of grain supplies to the lower and middle Volga regions, the Urals, Kazakstan, and Western Siberia, to make up for a partial failure of crops due to drought. The spring sowing season opened under unfavourable conditions, the seed fund being considerably below the prescribed total and the peasants showing a marked reluctance to provide the necessary grain or to cultivate the full scheduled acreage. Fearing a bread shortage, the Government in May made a number of far-reaching concessions to the peasants. A decree of May 6 reduced by about 4,400,000 tons the quota of grain to be delivered to the State in 1932 by collective farms and individual peasants, and authorised them after January 15, 1933, to sell their grain produce surplus in the open market. A decree of May 10 reduced by one-half the quota of live-stock and meat to be delivered to the State, and allowed the disposal of all surplus cattle, fowls, and meat in the open market. Of special importance was a decree of May 20 by which extensive trading facilities were granted to collective farms and their members and to individual peasants, while the opening of shops by private traders was prohibited.

The official explanation of the complete change of policy evidenced by these decrees was that, in view of the successes of collectivisation, the Government could afford partially to substitute "Soviet trade in the open market" for centralised distribution, in order further to stimulate the energies of the peasants and increase their incomes while incidentally improving the food supply of the town population. These measures did succeed in producing a certain development of trade leading to a reduction of prices by 30 to 40 per cent. Prices still, however, remained exceedingly high, rye flour being quoted at 2l. per pood (36 pounds), meat at 8 to 12 shillings per kilo, butter 12 to 15 shillings per pound, milk 1 shilling and 8 pence to 2 shillings per litre, and eggs 5 to 6 shillings for ten.

Just before the harvest, it was announced that each peasant, instead of having to wait for the whole crop to be gathered in, as in the previous year, would be entitled to receive a certain percentage of grain and fodder, according to the work done by him, as it was being reaped. In spite of this encouragement, there was again much slackness, and work proceeded even more slowly than in the preceding year. There was much plundering of the corn in the fields by night, and the Government found it necessary to pass sentence of death on a number of " grain thieves." The amount of grain finally gathered was below the average, and a good deal of the autumn sowing was too late to be of much avail for the next harvest.

The agricultural policy of the Government was sharply criticised at the plenary session of the Central Committee of the Communist Party in October, and an agitation was started for the abandonment of the Soviet and collective farms. Stalin, however, retained his ascendancy, and about twenty members of the party, including Zinoviev and Kamenev, were expelled for " counter-revolutionary activities," for advocating a " surrender to the capitalist regime," and for associating with " class enemies " outside the party.

Towards the end of the year the Central Committee of the Communist Party announced that it intended to undertake a " general purge " of the party, similar to those which had been carried out in 1921 and 1929. The " purge " was to last for a year, during which time no new members or candidates would be admitted, and it was expected that as a result the numbers of the party, which now contained about 3,000,000 members and probationers, would be somewhat reduced.

The activities of Japan in Manchuria caused considerable anxiety to the Russian Government, which suspected that she was supporting Russian emigrés and " White Guards " in the neighbourhood of the Russian frontier. Friction became acute in March, when Japanese troops were moved to Pogranichnaia, the frontier station on the Chinese Eastern Railway, and the two parties accused each other of " war preparations." However, the importance of maintaining the peace was realised on both sides, and after the assassination of the Japanese Prime Minister in June, the excitement died down. The long-drawn-out dispute between the two countries over the fishing rights of Japanese nationals in Soviet territorial waters was at last settled by the signing in Moscow on August 13 of a new Fisheries Convention supplementing the Convention of 1928.

At the beginning of the year the negotiations which had been going on for some years between Russia and Great Britain for the settlement of inter-Governmental claims were broken off. This, however, did not prevent Russia from obtaining fresh credits to the amount of 1,600,000*l.* through the Export Credits Guarantee Department. During the six months ending April 30, Britain's visible adverse balance of trade with the U.S.S.R. was 4,500,000*l.*, against 14,000,000*l.* in the same period in the previous year. On October 17 Great Britain, as a result of the Ottawa Agreements, denounced the temporary Commercial Agreement concluded with Russia in April, 1930.

In the course of the year the U.S.S.R. made Pacts of Non-Aggression, accompanied in some cases by Conciliation Conventions, with Finland, Latvia, Estonia, and Poland. After two years of negotiation, the Franco-Soviet Pact of Non-Aggression, accompanied by a Conciliation Convention, was also signed at Paris on November 29. [See under Public Documents.] On December 12 diplomatic relations were formally re-established with China.

At the meetings of the League of Nations Disarmament Conference, M. Litvinoff, the Russian delegate, severely criticised the French proposals, as also the proposals of other Powers aiming merely at " moral " or even " qualitative " disarmament, maintaining that an immediate and drastic reduction all round was necessary.

ESTONIA.

At the end of March the Diet resolved that the post of State President should be created—the Prime Minister having hitherto acted in that capacity—and that the number of members of the Diet should be reduced from 100 to 80. In August the proposal was submitted to a referendum and was defeated by a small majority, so that the Constitution remained for the time being unaltered.

At the end of January the Prime Minister, M. Päts, resigned, and a new Ministry was formed by M. Teemant, which received a vote of confidence from the Diet on February 15. An election was held in May, which brought little change in the composition of the Diet. On July 20 M. Karl Einbund became Prime Minister, but he resigned on October 3. On November 1 a Coalition Cabinet was formed by M. Päts which obtained a vote of confidence from the Diet.

The Tartu (Dorpat) University celebrated its 300th anniversary on June 30. The ceremonies were attended by visitors from many countries, including the Crown Prince of Sweden.

A Non-Aggression Pact with the Soviet Government was ratified by the Diet at the end of July.

LATVIA.

Throughout 1932 the trade and finance of Latvia were subjected by the Government to drastic regulations, which inflicted great hardship on the population. Early in the year the quota system was extended to include coal, wheat, cotton, salt, and artificial silk yarn. In order also to enforce more strictly the restrictions on transactions in foreign currency, the authorities announced that correspondence, both ordinary and registered, would be liable to be opened and inspected, to see that it contained no currency or cheques. At the beginning of April a law was passed giving the Government a monopoly of the traffic in home and imported grain ; it came into force on June 15. On July 12 the duties on many classes of goods were further raised by 50-100 per cent.

On February 5 a Non-Aggression Pact between Latvia and Russia was signed at Riga, each party reserving the right to denounce the Pact without warning if the other party attacked a third State. The Pact was ratified at the end of July.

In May the Soviet representative at Riga gave six months' notice to terminate the Latvian-Soviet Trade Agreement concluded in 1927. Negotiations for a new agreement proved ineffectual, and in the latter half of the year trade between Latvia and Russia dwindled to a negligible quantity.

At the end of October the Government concluded an agreement with a company from New York for the construction of a hydro-electric power station across the river Daugava (Dvina), a few miles above Riga. The company undertook to finance the undertaking by means of a foreign loan of some 5,000,000 dollars. The Latvian Government reserved to itself the right to decide in what countries the orders for machinery should be placed. The work was expected to take five years.

LITHUANIA.

Lithuania in 1932 aroused considerable ill-will in various quarters by her proceedings at Memel. Early in February the Lithuanian Governor of Memel, Colonel Merkys, acting in accord with the Central Government at Kovno, dismissed the head of the locally-elected Directorate, Herr Boettcher, and placed him under arrest, on a charge of having entered into treasonable correspondence with the German Government. He also appointed a Directorate of strong Lithuanian sympathies, without consulting the inhabitants. Germany declared this to be a breach of the Memel Convention of 1924, and protested to the Powers signatory to the Convention—Great Britain, France, Italy, and Japan—who called on Lithuania to abide by the Convention. Soon afterwards, the Governor, in spite of the warning of the signatory Powers, dissolved the Diet, and they thereupon appealed for a ruling to the Permanent Court of International Justice at The Hague, much to the annoyance of the Lithuanian Government and people.

On May 4 and 5 an election for a new Diet was held at Memel, as a result of which the upholders of the autonomous regime somewhat strengthened their position. Colonel Merkys thereupon resigned, and after some interval was succeeded by M. Vytautas Gylys, hitherto Consul-General in London. At the end of May the Directory under M. Simaitis resigned, and a new Directory was formed by Herr Scheiber, which received a vote of confidence from the Diet. Thenceforth a calmer atmosphere prevailed in the city.

On August 11 the Permanent Court ruled, by 10 votes to 5, that the Governor of Memel had been justified in dismissing Herr Boettcher and replacing him with M. Simaitis, but that he had not been in order in dissolving the Diet on the advice of M. Simaitis before the Directorate had received a vote of confidence from the Diet. This decision was received with great gratification at Kovno, where it had been feared that the Court would rule against Lithuania on all points.

M. Valdemaras, the ex-Premier, was tried during September and October on charges which had been impending against him for some years, and was acquitted on all of them.

Towards the end of the year a railway line, about 50 miles long, from Tels to Kretina was opened, establishing through communication between Central Lithuania, Shavli, and Memel.

POLAND.

Throughout 1932 Poland was engaged in an arduous struggle to maintain her financial credit. For this purpose it was essential that she should keep up the exchange rate of her currency, which had already been devalued in 1919-24 and again in 1927, and she was thus precluded from abandoning the gold standard. This placed a severe handicap on her export trade, with the result that her production, both agricultural and industrial, fell off, revenue from taxation was greatly reduced, and unemployment and economic distress generally became rife. In consequence, the problem of balancing the Budget became one of increasing difficulty.

On February 13 the Seym approved a Budget showing an estimated revenue of 2,373,357,100 zlotys, and an estimated expenditure of 2,446,917,311 zlotys. There was still enough money in the Treasury reserves accumulated during the years 1926-30 to cover the estimated deficit of 73,560,211 zlotys. The Government was in addition given permission, as in the previous year, to make further reductions in expenditure at its discretion. It soon took advantage of this liberty by reducing pensions to the extent of 40,000,000 zlotys. Nevertheless, economic conditions continued to be so unsatisfactory that for the period April-September the Treasury had to record a deficit of 121,000,000 zlotys, largely due to the difficulty of collecting agricultural taxes. One result of this was that Poland was unable to pay its instal-

ment of 3,000,000 dollars for its debt to the United States in
December.

To guard against an unduly adverse trade balance, the Government sought to reduce the volume of imports, and on January 1
import prohibitions were imposed on some of the chief commodities
bought abroad, on the understanding, however, that generous
quotas would be allowed to countries having regular commercial
relations with Poland. Customs duties were also raised with
the proviso that goods entering the country by sea would be
granted special reductions. On March 26 a provisional Convention was signed between Germany and Poland by which both
countries agreed to moderate somewhat the extreme restrictions
placed upon each other's imports. The Commercial Treaty of
1930, however, which was to end the Customs war between the
two countries and which had been ratified by Poland, was still
unratified by Germany. An agreement with regard to import
quotas was also signed with Switzerland on May 8.

Before it adjourned, Parliament passed Bills making provision
for reforms in public and private schools, for the control of private
meetings, for inflicting penalties for tax evasion, and for the
unification of procedure in criminal cases. All these measures
were highly distasteful to the Opposition, as they placed greater
power in the hands of the Administration. In fact, the Seym
played a very secondary part in the conduct of affairs during the
year, and did not sit at all from May to November. Before
adjourning it conferred special powers on the President, in virtue
of which in April he prohibited the expulsion of defaulting tenants,
if unemployed and occupying not more than two rooms, and
issued a coal decree giving the Government large powers of interference in the production and the sale of coal. At the end of
April he held two conferences with the Prime Minister, Colonel
Prystor, and the ex-Prime Ministers Professor Bartel, M. Switalski,
and Colonel Slawek, with the object, according to the Press, of
seeking their assistance in dealing with the economic crisis and
in exercising his special powers.

Towards the end of March some changes took place in the
Ministry as a result of which it became slightly less military in
character, more prominence being given to the professional element.
This tendency was carried a step further in September, when
Professor Zawadski, who had been Deputy Prime Minister since
March, became, in addition, Minister of Finance, in succession
to M. Jan Pilsudski, brother of the Marshal, who was appointed
Vice-Director of the Bank of Poland. A sensation was created
in November by the resignation of M. Zalewski from the post
of Minister of Foreign Affairs, which he had held for six years.
His replacement by M. Beck, the Vice-Minister, was taken to
indicate that the Marshal desired to exercise a greater control
over foreign policy.

O

In August the Government published four decrees for affording relief to the farmers from their most pressing liabilities, by extending for them the period of payment of debts, obviating forced sales, establishing village arbitration courts, and lowering the rate of interest. Unfortunately, the chief effect of these measures was to dry up the supply of fresh credits for agriculture.

Early in the year Polish mine-owners and ironmasters demanded a reduction of wages by 21 per cent. in the coal-mines and 25 per cent. in the iron and steel works, nominally on account of British competition. The matter was referred to Government arbitrators, who awarded a reduction of 8 per cent. in the coal-mines, but opposed any reduction in the steel works. In the coal-fields of Cracow and Dombrowa, 20,000 miners struck work on February 18 as a protest against the award, but after remaining out for nearly a month they accepted the reduction of wages.

In May twenty-two members of the Left Wing of the Socialist Party were brought to trial on the charge of belonging to an illegal organisation, and three were sentenced to five years and three to three years' imprisonment. In the autumn, the "Camp of Great Poland," a chauvinistic organisation operating in the Western provinces, was declared illegal and broken up. About the same time, too, the Selrob, the Ukrainian Nationalist organisation in Wolhensa, was dissolved on the ground of carrying on anti-Government propaganda. On March 22 M. Czechowski, Commissioner of Police at Lwow, was shot dead in the street by East Galician terrorists. On March 25-26 the Ukrainian National Democratic Organisation held its annual congress at Lwow, and with difficulty avoided a split.

On January 25 a Polish-Soviet Pact of Non-Aggression was initialled in Moscow by M. Patek, the Polish Minister, and M. Litvinoff. The Pact was concluded in the first instance for three years and was to be renewable for another two years, and it was not to be signed until a similar instrument had been negotiated between the Soviet Government and Rumania. In fact, however, it was signed on July 25. On January 4 a Treaty of Conciliation, Arbitration, and Friendship was signed between Poland and Greece at Warsaw.

After consulting its Ministers in Austria, Czechoslovakia, Hungary, Rumania, and Yugoslavia at a conference held in Warsaw on March 7-10, the Polish Government gave its support to the Tardieu Plan for assisting the Danubian countries, on condition that Polish interests were fully safeguarded. In August a conference of Agrarian States, comprising Bulgaria, Czechoslovakia, Estonia, Latvia, Poland, Rumania, and Hungary, was held at Warsaw. The conference agreed that for the salvation of the Agrarian States it was essential that the Geneva Convention of November, 1927, for preventing the introduction of further restrictions on the exchange of goods, should be brought into force, with the proviso that it should apply to agricultural as well as to industrial products.

The census of 1931 showed the population of Poland to be 32,132,936, of whom 69·1 per cent. (22,308,936) had Polish for their native language. The increase on the population in 1921 was 10 per cent.

FREE STATE OF DANZIG.

The tension already existing between Danzig and Poland was aggravated during 1932 by a number of disputes which took place between them. On the ground that the Free City had long been systematically smuggling German goods into Poland, the Polish Administration, after vainly trying to arrive at an understanding, instituted in January a control of all goods crossing the Danzig frontier into Poland, in spite of the fact that there is a Customs Union between Danzig and Poland. Danzig appealed to the League Commissioner, who, on March 29, issued a provisional ruling in Danzig's favour. On October 25 the Polish Ministry of Communications announced that it would only accept Polish money for services rendered in Danzig, instead of Danzig gulden, as heretofore. The matter came before the League of Nations in November, but was eventually settled by direct negotiation in Danzig's favour. The Free City agreed, however, that at some future date they would negotiate on the question of a unified currency. The possession by Danzig, under the Warsaw Agreement of 1921, of special rights of importation from Germany was the subject of a conference at Warsaw in November which proved fruitless as the Free City refused to abandon any of its rights.

A violent anti-Danzig agitation was carried on at Gdynia in May, June, and July. It was eventually stopped by the Polish-Danzig Agreements of August, providing for a cessation of propaganda.

In April M. Strassburger was succeeded as Polish Commissioner at Danzig by M. Papee, who adopted a more activist policy. On September 15 Count Gravina, the League High Commissioner, died. He was succeeded temporarily by M. Elmer Rosting, of the League Secretariat at Geneva.

CZECHOSLOVAKIA.

The " Big " Coalition which was formed after the General Election of the autumn of 1929, and had been in office since the December of that year, maintained its position without any far-reaching change—only a small German fraction (four members in all) having seceded in 1930—until April, 1932, when the Czechoslovak Small Traders' Party seceded as a consequence of the

Government's decision to increase certain taxes which particularly affected the interests of small traders. The withdrawal
of the Small Traders' Party from the Government caused the
resignation of the Minister of Railways, a member of that party
(April 9). In order that the balance of party representation in
the Cabinet should not be disturbed, the Railways portfolio was
entrusted to a high official of the railways department who had
attracted considerable notice by a memorandum which he had
drafted and submitted to the Government on the subject of
a reorganisation of the railways, M. Hula, who became a non-
party member of the Cabinet like the Minister of Finance, M.
Trapl. Despite the withdrawal of the Small Traders' Party—
twelve members in all—from the Coalition, the Government
still possessed a secure majority in Parliament, having the support
of seven parties, Czechoslovak and German. In addition to
the Communist forty members, the Opposition consisted of the
Slovak People's Party under M. Hlinka (nineteen members),
and three minor German groups. Other changes in the Cabinet
took place in the autumn, but they were chiefly changes of personnel, the Coalition continuing.

The main task of the Government in 1932 was to combat
the consequences of the world economic crisis, which year by
year was becoming more seriously felt in Czechoslovakia also.
The Prime Minister declared that the outstanding task of the
Government was to maintain the country's favourable trade
balance, to balance the Budget, to retain the stability of the
Czechoslovak currency, and to revive production. The most
serious problem was that of the increase in unemployment.

The coalition system, in view of the unusual situation, was
universally regarded as essential, but it was also generally obvious
that the composition of the Government, formed, as it was, of
representatives of parties whose interests were frequently opposed,
made agreement difficult, and acted as a drag upon speedy decision even in the most urgent matters. Preliminary discussions,
both inside the Cabinet and within the ranks of the parties themselves, took up far too much time, and the actual work of Parliament was thus reduced to a minimum. The lack of initiative
with which the Premier was subsequently reproached very often
arose from divergencies of opinion among the parties constituting
the Coalition. For example, the attempts to institute an Unemployment Fund fell through, owing to the fundamental differences between the views of the Socialist and non-Socialist
parties. For similar reasons the question of housing and tenants'
protection could not be definitely settled, and this problem,
which had remained unsolved from the war years, had to be
regulated temporarily by a prolongation of the existing provisional
housing laws. There was also within the parties themselves a lack
of unanimity and of political discipline which had a most un-

favourable influence on the progress of Government activities ;
even the strongest Parliamentary party—that of the Czechoslovak
Agrarians—suffered from it, and thus the work of the Prime
Minister was greatly hampered.

In these circumstances it was found impossible to draw up
a comprehensive plan for dealing with the economic crisis, and
attention had to be confined to the most urgent matters, such as
the securing of economies in State expenditure and a balanced
Budget, leaving other matters to be postponed to a more favourable
financial future.

The unfavourable state of the country's finances soon made
it obvious that Budget equilibrium could not be maintained unless big cuts were made in expenditure, and unless the decline
in revenue, caused by the general economic stagnation, were
made good by opening up new sources of income. Of the fiscal
measures adopted, the most important was an increase in the tax
on turnover, a measure which led, as already stated, to a Cabinet
change in the resignation of the Minister of Railways.

Early in January a measure was passed authorising borrowing
up to the limit of 1,000,000,000 crowns. The purpose of this
was to secure a loan of 600,000,000 francs in France (repayable
in five years and bearing interest at 5 per cent.). The proceeds
of the French loan which, owing to a change of Government in
France, was not ratified by the French Chamber till the spring,
greatly strengthened the currency and exchange reserves of the
National Bank, and thus helped to stabilise the Czechoslovak
crown—in itself a most beneficial result, even though the liquidity
of the money market was not thereby substantially increased.
An equally important step was the new adjustment of the small
coinage. The bank notes for 10 and 20 crowns respectively were
now classified under the category of small currency, and the total
of this category was doubled from 600 to 1,200,000,000 crowns.
By this means the gold backing of the bank note circulation
was strengthened and the credit position of the National Bank
was improved. Thus, in 1932 also, the Czechoslovak crown
maintained its stability and was again one of the world's steadiest
currency units.

Another outcome of the economic crisis was the so-called
" Banking Act " passed after lengthy debates in the spring.
The banks were especially hit by the crisis, as the general lack of
confidence resulting in a withdrawal of foreign credits and the
fall of the English £, coupled with other serious features of world
finance, caused distrust to become widespread among the home
population, who withdrew their deposits from the banks and thus
aggravated the general feeling of insecurity. Despite the considerable resilience which the Czechoslovak banking system
manifested, the losses arising from the crisis were so large that the
State had to assist in the rehabilitation of several of the large

banks. Thus arose the Banking Act as a measure supplementary
to the Banking Acts of the year 1924, which adjusted the losses
of the banks resulting from the unprecedented conditions of the
early post-war years. The Banking Act of 1932 represented
also a certain measure of State control of banking, for it contained provisions increasing the responsibility of bank officials.

Among other measures of economic importance passed in 1932
was the Rural Districts Electrification Act, under which the
State is to contribute for seven years an annual sum of 25,000,000
crowns towards the electrification of the countryside. Among
other important laws was one shortening the period of army
conscription from eighteen to fourteen months.

The difficulties in the financial situation were by no means
removed by the measures which were taken up to the end of the
summer session of Parliament ; revenue failed to reach the level
anticipated in the Budget estimates, and so finance was still the
burning question in the autumn. As early as September the
Minister of Finance announced that new excise duties would have
to be levied, and emphasised particularly the necessity of economies
in administration—in effect, a reduction of the pay of the State
employees. Although the necessity of such a measure had been
the subject of public discussion for some considerable time and
it had the support of Dr. Englis, the former Minister of Finance,
the political parties nevertheless hesitated to take a step which
would so profoundly affect the standard of living of whole classes
of public servants, and the mere suggestion of which had evoked
great indignation in their ranks. The situation was further
complicated by the resignation of M. Udrzal, the Prime Minister,
whose serious state of health compelled him to abstain for the
time being from all political activities. M. Jan Malypetr, till
then the Speaker of the Chamber of Deputies, and a member
of the Czechoslovak Agrarian Party, succeeded in forming a new
Government, the twelfth since the establishment of the State
(October 29).

The Malypetr Government was like its predecessor a Coalition.
The only changes made were in respect of the portfolios held by
members of the Czechoslovak Agrarian Party. In addition to
the supersession of M. Udrzal by M. Malypetr, a new Minister of
Agriculture was appointed in the person of Dr. Hodza, who had
held the post in former years, while M. Bradác, till then Minister
of Agriculture, was transferred to the department of National
Defence, and M. Cerny, head of the Provincial Office at Brno,
who has twice held the Premiership as head of a Cabinet of
Officials, succeeded an Agrarian as Minister of the Interior.
Two of the three members of the second largest Czechoslovak
Party—that of the Social Democrats—retained the Cabinet
posts they had held under M. Udrzal, Dr. Meissner as Minister
of Justice, and Dr. Dérer as Minister of Education, while a third

member of the party, M. Bechyne, took over the Railways.
The post of Minister of Food Supply, hitherto held by M. Bechyne,
was left vacant, as it was intended to abolish the department. The
other Cabinet posts remained unchanged. Dr. Benes, who, once
more, was Minister of Foreign Affairs, and Dr. Franke, Minister
of Posts and Telegraphs, belonged to the Czechoslovak (National)
Socialist Party ; M. Dostálek, the Minister of Public Works, and
Monsignor Srámek, the Minister of Unification, to the Popular
(Catholic) Party ; the National Democrats were represented by
Dr. Matousek (Commerce), the German Agrarians by Dr. Spina
(Public Health), the German Social Democrats by Dr. Czech
(Social Welfare), while in addition to M. Cerny, the new non-
party Minister of the Interior, the non-party element of the Udrzal
Cabinet continued to hold office in the Malypetr Cabinet in
the person of Dr. Trapl, the Minister of Finance.

The new Government presented itself to Parliament on
November 3, and in its declaration of policy did not hesitate to
admit with the utmost candour the serious state of the country's
finances, at the same time declaring that the Government's
first duty was to secure financial equilibrium. Since, however,
the limits of taxation had been virtually reached, it would be
essential substantially to reduce State expenditure, and the
Government announced its intention of passing a Bill, the provisions of which would apply likewise to the local Government
authorities, to reduce expenditure on personnel by 600,000,000
crowns for two years as from January 1, 1933.

The Malypetr Government concentrated all its energies on
drafting the new Budget and, in contradistinction to previous
practice, called in the aid of Parliament in settling the estimates.
A special Parliamentary Budget Commission, composed of seven
members—one from each of the Coalition parties—studied the
preliminary draft of the Budget for 1933 as prepared by the
Government. The Budget for 1933, drafted on these lines,
could not be laid before Parliament until December 14, and as
there was not enough time to pass it by the close of the year
the Government was empowered to carry on the State's finances
for the first two months of the year on the basis of the 1933
Budget. The expenditure provided for in the Budget totalled
8,632,537,770 crowns, and the revenue was estimated at
8,634,170,060 crowns.

Realising the need of a still further reduction in State expenditure Parliament passed, just before Christmas, a measure providing for the appointment of an Economy and Control Commission
of twenty-four members, sixteen being chosen from the Deputies
and eight from the ranks of the Senate, to see that strict economy
is observed in the State administration and State undertakings,
and to supervise all expenditure, paying particular attention to
the allocation of Government contracts.

The unfavourable economic conditions were naturally exploited by the extreme elements of the Left as well as of the Right. The Communists took a big part in the miners' strike that broke out in North Bohemia in the spring. They also provoked local, and, in some cases, violent conflicts between the unemployed and the authorities, but the weakness of their party organisation prevented them from successfully undertaking any aggressive mass movement. Similarly their refusal to join in Parliamentary activities, and the poor quality of their Parliamentary representatives, condemned the Communist group in Parliament to complete impotence. The attempts to organise great demonstrations invariably ended in a complete fiasco. Realising their lack of influence, the Communist leaders attempted to transfer their centre of operations to Slovakia and Carpathian Ruthenia, where a lower standard of life and education makes the masses more susceptible to Communist agitation, and where it is therefore an easier matter to stir up strife. Numbers of Communists who had left or been expelled from the party and had formed a Communist Opposition returned to their former allegiance—the Social Democratic Party.

The authorities were compelled to take administrative measures also against the Czechoslovak Fascist organisations for infringement of the law relating to the formation of associations. Despite some local activity of a somewhat noisy nature the Czechoslovak Fascists remained numerically and politically an insignificant fraction. Of somewhat more consequence was the group headed by M. Stribrny, an ex-Cabinet Minister, and which, known as the " Liga " (League), had the support of a widely read sensational Press. As a result of the findings of a Parliamentary Committee of 1931, Deputy Stribrny was placed on trial on a charge of corruption, but though the evidence placed his activities in a very unfavourable light, he was acquitted. The verdict was quashed on appeal and a new trial ordered, but the Court again did not find the evidence against Stribrny sufficient.

The growth of radicalism was evidenced also in the German parties. The German National Socialist Party (Nazis), encouraged by the expansion of the Hitler movement in Germany, adopted a very aggressive attitude towards the two German parties represented in the Czechoslovak Cabinet, as well as towards the German opposition party—the German Nationalists—endeavouring to draw to themselves members from all three parties. Attention was further focussed on the Nazis by the trial of members of two organisations of youthful Nazis—the *Volksport* and *Jungsturm*—which ended in several of the officers of these associations being sentenced to various terms of imprisonment. The trials, based on the Defence of the Republic Act, amply substantiated the accusations. Bodies, registered as sport organisations, carried out, as was shown at the trial, military drill according to the regulations in force in the German Army, and conducted their exercises jointly with the Nazi organisations in Germany on either side of the Bohemian-German frontier, and so on. The German extremists endeavoured to create the impression that the trial was a species of persecution of the Germans as a body in Czechoslovakia, and that the matter was the common concern of all Germans in that country. The two German parties associated with the Czechoslovak Government, however, ascribed the responsibility for the misfortune of the condemned youths to the leaders of the German National Socialist (Nazi) Party who had led the young into lawless activities.

In the sphere of foreign affairs Czechoslovakia was most particularly concerned with the French proposals. Following upon the rejection in 1931 of the German scheme for a solution of the Central European problem by means of a Customs Union between Germany and Austria, France put forward in the spring of 1932 the suggestion that the States of Central Europe should arrange among themselves a close economic collaboration on the basis of preferential prices and quotas. This "Tardieu Plan," which obviously presupposed the active co-operation of the Great Powers of Europe, was frustrated by the opposition of Italy and Germany. The same divergence of opinion rendered fruitless the conference of the Powers convoked in London to discuss Danubian problems. The September conference at Stresa, where the Central European and the leading import countries met in the spirit of the Lausanne Conference to discuss the economic problems of Central Europe, concluded with a mere recommendation of agreements for the export of grain.

Through her spokesman Dr. Benes, the Minister of Foreign Affairs, Czechoslovakia registered her adherence to the Tardieu Plan before it was definitively thrown out by its opponents (May 22, 1932), regarding it as being in accord with the basic tendencies of Czechoslovakia's foreign policy.

The customary conferences of the Little Entente took place in 1932 in the months of May and December—on both occasions at Belgrade. The May meeting was held soon after the unsuccessful London Conference, and the deliberations were concerned in the main with Central European economic questions. In view of the disunion among the Great Powers in respect of this problem, and of the anarchy prevailing generally in the sphere of economic policy, the Ministers of the three Little Entente States were able to express only general opinions on the problem. They declared that in the prevailing circumstances the States of the Little Entente would abstain from all initiative, but were prepared to collaborate with all good-will in any step taken towards a better adjustment of economic relations in Central Europe. At the same time they expressed the opinion that a beginning must be made with regional agreements, and they therefore gave their approval to the French suggestion of an agreement among the Danubian States which could subsequently be expanded into a general agreement.

The second Little Entente conference held at Belgrade in the latter half of December was devoted to a discussion of the international situation as a whole arising from the Disarmament Conference and especially from the discussions of the Five Powers on the subject of disarmament, which to a certain extent signified a revision of the military provisions applied under the terms of the Peace Treaties. The conference also dealt with questions relating to events in Central Europe, and discussed the increased propaganda in favour of treaty revision—a question of vital concern to the Little Entente. In the matter of organisation the Belgrade Conference completed previous negotiations for a closer collaboration on the part of the allied States, and decided upon the establishment of a Standing Council of the Little Entente to be composed of the Foreign Ministers of Yugoslavia, Rumania, and Czechoslovakia, to meet three times a year.

HUNGARY.

The Károlyi Government was hampered from the outset by its legacy from the Bethlen regime, the consequences of which continued to unfold themselves with tragic effect throughout the year. The mere fact that Count Bethlen remained leader of the Government Party not only made any new departure impossible but also put the President of the Council in a sort of dependence upon him every time a necessary but unpopular measure had to be forced upon the reluctant assent of the ruling party. It was also on Count Bethlen's authority that the Premier had to lean for securing recognition for a number of unofficial foreign missions, such as the one to Italy (Jan. 18) and others.

The defection of Count Károlyi's supporters continued nevertheless, and increased more or less openly the ranks of the Opposition. Among those who deserted him were Baron Kray, T. Rakowsky (Feb. 1), A. Klein, A. Erdelyi, G. Farkas (Feb. 27), and Z. Meskó (March 17). This last-named, in imitation of Hitler, founded the Hungarian " Swastika " party, the introduction of which to the Lower House succeeded in provoking a good deal of hilarity (June 16). A more serious loss was the resignation of the Minister of Agriculture, B. Tvády (Feb. 4), to whom a successor was found, not without difficulty, in the person of Mr. E. Purgly.

The exceedingly unfavourable report of the League of Nations (Jan. 27) on the financial situation of the country could only aggravate the gloomy forebodings with which the year began. A very painful impression was therefore made on Liberal public

opinion when Count Bethlen found no better theme at the Szech-
enyi banquet (Feb. 1) than to claim the political leadership of
the country for the Aristocracy and Landed Gentry, in spite of
their large share of responsibility for the existing distressing
conditions.   One of his own relatives, Count F. Hunyady, evidently
did not share his views, as, in company with a group of friends, he
formed a new party (Feb. 3) with aims in direct opposition to
those of Count Bethlen.

Meanwhile political activity, both home and foreign, became
more and more a daily struggle for the economic survival of the
nation.   The first stage of this Calvary was the sitting of the
League of Nations (Jan. 17) at which the Chancellor of the
Exchequer, Baron Korányi, and Mr. Popovics, President of the
Hungarian National Bank, had to explain the financial situation
of the country and defend the measures taken to mitigate its
distress.   The next was the fight put up by the " financial
dictator " of Hungary, Mr. Teleszky, with the British creditors
assembled in London (Feb. 10) to obtain a postponement of the
interest payments on the Hungarian foreign loans, which was
eventually granted.   Similar conversations were initiated with
other countries (Feb. 11) with equal success.

But such temporary solutions were of no more help than the
recommendation of the League of Nations (April 2) to keep the
Budget under the figure of 800 million pengös, for, a few days
after (April 7), the Government had to grant a new subsidy of
42 millions to agriculture.   With such enormous and unexpected
outlays even the most draconic taxation was unable to keep pace,
and a new reduction of 6 per cent. of the salary of the members
of Parliament (April 9) and of 2 to 5 per cent. of those of Civil
servants (April 12) greatly increased the growing unpopularity of
Count Károlyi with this class of his supporters.   It also became
growingly difficult for him to retain the allegiance of the landowners without sacrificing to their insatiable demands the whole
State machinery.   In vain did Baron Korányi, Minister of Finance,
point out that in a period of seven years 1,500 million pengös
had been offered up for the relief of agriculture ; a slight misunderstanding over the question of the alcohol quota sufficed
to mass the greater part of the House against him (May 14).

This was a premonitory shock which was soon followed by
others, threatening the existence of the Government.   To make
matters worse, Count Bethlen, at this juncture, exasperated the
Opposition by returning to the defence of his ten years' rule.
The storm which he raised in the House of Commons (May 5)
had its repercussions in public opinion, which did not fail to
remember once more the solidarity declared by Count Károlyi
with this regime.   It also remembered the scandal of the former
Ministry of Public Welfare and the millions which it had
squandered, the question of the " Optants," the abuses connected

with the free distribution of products of the State Tobacco Monopoly and similar other legacies, the discussion of which gave rise to some tumultuous scenes in the House of Commons (Jan. 14, Feb. 11, May 18, etc.).

Meanwhile there appeared (April 30) the third report of the Commissary of the League of Nations, containing some extremely severe strictures on the State expenditure, and especially on the immense losses of the State enterprises (railways, agricultural properties, factories, etc.), and emphasising the necessity of transferring them to private hands. The report of the Ministry of Finance (June 8) regarding the first ten months of the budgetary year 1931-32, confirmed these conclusions, as the balance-sheet of the State expenditure proper showed a deficit of 69 million pengös and that of the State enterprises one of 27 millions.

Such being the results of a year's superhuman efforts on the part of the Government to re-establish the equilibrium of the Budget, the demands of the landowners (June 9) for the declaration of a new moratorium for the repayment of their debts came as a real calamity. But although the threat of the smallholders group of the Government Party to secede shook the party to its foundations, Count Károlyi had still enough strength of character to maintain his ground.

As a result of its precarious position, however, the Government displayed great vacillation, and so important an item as the " bonus " to producers of cereals—another legacy of the Bethlen regime—after being first withdrawn (May 1) was granted again (June 16). Yet nothing could satisfy the smallholders and the agricultural class generally, whose situation had really become desperate. In consequence, following upon a report of the Committee of the Government Party (June 17) and encouraged by Count Bethlen himself, this class formally declared a moratorium of agricultural mortgages and the reduction of interest to 4 per cent. as well as the extension of credits to be the conditions for its further support of Count Károlyi. A simultaneous audience (June 18) given by Admiral Horthy to the Premier and Count Bethlen no doubt contributed to the decision of Count Károlyi to give in at last and announce (July 1) that in a very large measure satisfaction would be given to the landowners. But in vain did the Liberal leader, K. Rassay, claim (July 8) similar concessions for other equally suffering sections of the population, for, as their political power was insignificant, Count Károlyi, being assured for the time being of the support of the agriculturists, could afford to disregard them, especially when Baron Sztereuyi assured him of the confidence of the House of Lords (June 24) and the Governor refused to accept his proffered resignation (July 30).

Meanwhile in the international sphere the Government could do no more than, by means of continuous haggling, secure general or partial moratoriums and the deferred payment or reduction of the interest of foreign loans. This was the limit of its success, and the request of Hungary for equality of rights put forward by Count Apponyi at the Disarmament Conference (March 13) was not taken seriously, nor did anything come of the project of M. Tardieu for a kind of new edition of a Danubian Confederation, in preparation for which Hungary was asked to conclude preferential Custom treaties with Austria and the Little Entente (March 1). On the other hand, every occasion was seized to strengthen the bonds between Hungary and Italy, and the noble gesture of the Duce in replacing the aeroplane " Justice for Hungary," which was destroyed along with the transatlantic flyer, Endresz, on Roman soil (May 20), was greeted with real enthusiasm by Hungarian public opinion. In contrast with this, an untimely article published by Lord Rothermere (Aug. 24), stating that the crown of Hungary had been offered to him by some Hungarian patriots, created a painful impression even amongst his warmest admirers and weakened the popularity of the cause he defended. Indignation was also aroused, not only in Hungary but among Liberal circles abroad which were favourable to a revision of the Trianon Treaty, by the execution of the Communist agitators, Sallai and Fürst, which took place (July 29) without their being allowed to communicate with the lawyers charged with their defence. A violent Press campaign and attacks upon the Hungarian legations in Brussels, Berlin, and elsewhere, followed, but left little impression on a Government solely occupied with the immediate *ad hoc* solution of the most urgent problems, and which had to rest satisfied with such negative results as the acknowledgment by the League of Nations of the necessity of a " transfer moratorium " (July 7) and a three months' prolongation of the credit of the Hungarian National Bank by the International Payments Bank of Bâle (July 11). The proposal of Mr. Walkó, Minister of Foreign Affairs, at the Lausanne Conference (July 8), for the creation of a market for fixed quotas of Hungarian cereals, was adopted, but its practical results were rather poor. All the more gratifying, therefore, were the very few positive measures carried through by the Government, such as the initiation of negotiations with Austria (July 19) with a view to a renewal of the commercial treaty. The Stresa Conference (Sept. 5-8), however, only brought to it new disillusions in spite of Mr. J. Teleszky's strenuous efforts.

During this period the Budget and the law of " incompatibility " having been voted (June 27 and 30), the House of Commons was adjourned (July 3-Oct. 26) and the Government was left free to devote the whole of its energy to the economic reconstruction of the country. But the results, according to the new report (July 28) of the Commissary of the League of Nations, were as unsatisfactory as ever, and the desertion of the Government by an ever-growing number of its own partisans continued. Moreover, in spite of the intimidation to which it resorted at the by-elections of Mezöcsát—for which Count Károlyi was called to account at a stormy sitting of the House of Commons, convened for the purposes of protest by the Opposition (Aug. 12)—the Governmental candidate, E. Purgly, Minister of Agriculture, was defeated (Aug. 28).

Neither could the financial report for the Budgetary year 1931-32 save the authority of the Government, showing as it did a deficit of 120 million pengös, of which 40 millions had to be put again to the account of the State enterprises. The long-term debts amounted to 1370·5 million pengös, the short-term debts to 433·4 millions, and miscellaneous debts to 188·6 millions. Even the promise of Count Károlyi to grant universal secret suffrage (Aug. 23) and the withdrawal (Aug. 31) of the much criticised decree imposing taxation according to visible signs of wealth—which made spying an institution—was of no help, and on September 9 G. Gaál, leader of the secessionist Independent Smallholders Party, announced that he was prepared to assume office.

From this point a crisis in the Government Party and with it the fall of the Government could no longer be arrested, and after a memorable meeting of the party (Sept. 14), at which some bitter criticisms were expressed, Count Károlyi was forced to tender his resignation (Sept. 21), after a year of self-sacrificing and honest endeavours.

After several vain attempts had been made by various party leaders, not excluding even Count Bethlen, General Gömbös, Minister of War of the Károlyi Government, and formerly known for his Fascist leanings, succeeded in forming a Cabinet (Sept. 30), composed as follows :—

Gy. Gömbös	-	-	-	-	Premier and President of the Council.
F. Keresztes-Fischer	-		-	-	Minister of the Interior.
A. Lázár	-	-	-	-	„ „ Justice.
T. Fabinyi	-	-	-	-	„ „ Commerce.
B. Tmrédi	-	-	-	-	„ „ Finance
B. Hóman	-	-	-	-	„ „ Public Instruction.
M. Kállay	-	-	-	-	„ „ Agriculture.
Gy. Gömbös	-	-	-	-	„ „ War
E. Puky	-	-	-	-	„ „ Foreign Affairs.

Public opinion soon expressed approval of the nomination of General Gömbös, whose dynamic personality was at least a refreshing change from the drabness of Count Károlyi. More-over, he was popular in the country—as proved by the sixty-five honorary citizenships conferred on him by provincial towns—and was still recognised as a leader of the nationalist extreme Right. He was also statesmanlike and courageous enough to abjure his antisemitic antecedents, and thus reconcile Liberal public opinion, and by disclaiming emphatically every dictatorial tendency, he pacified the upholders of a Parliamentary regime.

That General Gömbös was fully expecting to be called to office was proved by the fact that on the day following his nomination he was able to announce an imposing programme composed of ninety-five paragraphs. Pending the publication of this document, he considered it his first duty to proclaim his adherence to the policy of friendship with Italy, an overture to which the Duce answered with an assurance of his unalterable good-will towards Hungary.

The introduction of the new Premier to the Government Party (Oct. 5) provoked a marked display of enthusiasm. Similar manifestations accompanied his address at the banquet of the Association of Nationalist Societies (T. E. S. Z.) when he declared war on the abuses of bureaucracy and red tape and announced that a new leaf would be turned over in general governmental methods. The high hopes raised by these assurances were, however, considerably damped, when it was found that their first practical expression was a new increase of 20 per cent. in the income tax (Oct. 21). On the same day the publication of the Socialist newspaper, *Nepszava*, was suspended for eight days, on account of some criticism considered to be provocative by the Government.

Meanwhile General Gömbös had been discussing with his Ministers his great national programme, which was awaited by the nation with the utmost eagerness. Their curiosity was at last satisfied by its publication on October 25. Even the new Premier's political opponents had to admit it showed a praiseworthy effort towards a comprehensive understanding of the needs of the country, but doubts were expressed as to the possibility of realising the greater part of its proposals, owing to the general economic situation. Those points of the programme which were independent of finance were criticised by the Opposition for their lack of precision, especially the proposals regarding the reforms of the electoral law, the liberty of Press, the right of assembly and association, the question of the State enterprises, and the development of professional representation (on the Fascist model) with a corresponding social policy. However, as General Gömbös himself declared that the value of the most complete programme consisted in such parts as could be realised, public opinion declared its readiness to give him a fair chance.

On his side the Premier, realising that the execution of so ambitious a programme required the unconditional obedience of the Government Party and his direct control of it, proceeded at once to its reorganisation (Oct. 27). It was decided that the leader of the party should be henceforth General Gömbös in person, to whom the President appointed by him and an Executive Committee of six should be subordinated. Significantly enough Count Bethlen had to content himself with a place in this body. As great importance was also attached to an intensive

propaganda in the provinces, the party—henceforth designated the
" Party of National Union "—was equipped with an adequate
provincial organisation, the somewhat military character of which
was evidenced by the distinctive signs worn by its members.

Once more, however, the country was reminded by the usual
"memento " of the Commissary of the League of Nations that
it was not yet out of its troubles (Oct. 28). According to this,
the economic situation had grown still worse during the last three
months. The deficit had risen to 120 million pengös, and the
results of the Budgetary year beginning with July 1, pointed to
the necessity of a drastic reduction of the administrative expenses
resulting from an utterly disproportionate Civil service. The
Commissary also once more criticised the unbusinesslike management of the State enterprises and the lavish expenditure of the
municipalities. The report contained, moreover, a stern warning
with regard to the agricultural moratoriums, which, it said,
would close up all future sources of credit, and it concluded by
declaring that the extreme limits of taxation had been reached,
and even passed in Hungary. Yet in spite of these warnings the
Parliamentary Committee of thirty-three voted the new agricultural moratorium (Oct. 29).

Parliament reassembled on October 26, and the Government
was almost immediately assailed (Oct. 28) with tempestuous
protests from the Liberal Opposition on account of the antisemitic
brutalities at the Universities of Budapest and Pecs. In spite
of the formal promises of M. Hóman, Minister of Public Instruction, these were repeated in Debrecon, where a woman student
was also one of the victims, while the Jewish student who branded
such acts as cowardly and challenged their authors to a duel
was expelled from the University by decision of the Rector.
This time even the members of the Government Party joined in
the protests and demanded energetic measures (Nov. 18 and 29),
which were eventually applied.

Meanwhile General Gömbös had found time to make the usual
pilgrimage of Hungarian Premiers to Rome, where he was
received with high honours by Duce and King (Nov. 8). More
stress was laid this time on the necessity of strengthening economic
relations than on the pompous assurance of friendly feelings. As
a consequence of this, deliberations for the conclusion of a
Hungarian-Italian commercial treaty were immediately begun
(Nov. 10). It was also thanks to his quick decision and energy
that the commercial treaty with Austria was concluded (Dec. 11),
and that negotiations with Czechoslovakia were begun for the
same purposes (Dec. 13).

General Gömbös now entered on a campaign of feverish
activity in order to establish personal contact with his partisans
and to increase their number. Day after day he was to be seen
in some country-town or other addressing mass meetings (Dec.

10-22), with undeniable results for his popularity and the
strengthening of his party. Thanks to the devoted support of
his followers, he was also able to withstand the attacks of the
Opposition during the discussion of the final accounts (Dec. 12).
He also behaved with great coolness in face of the dastardly and
provocative attack of the Rumanian mob of Kolozsvar on the
Hungarian Consulate and theatre, and on Hungarian citizens.
The counter-demonstrations of the Hungarian patriotic societies
and students before the Rumanian Legation in Budapest were
happily kept within legal limits, and the formal apologies of
M. Titulescu, Rumanian Minister of Foreign Affairs, closed the
incident (Dec. 1) which might easily have become dangerous.

RUMANIA.

As in many other countries, and perhaps to a greater extent
than in most, finance was the burning question in Rumanian
affairs during 1932. To balance the Budget, to maintain the
value of the currency, and to pay the interest on the external
debt—these were the chief problems with which successive
Governments had to struggle throughout the year. Thanks to
the skilful management of M. Argetoianu, the Minister of Finance,
the position improved somewhat during the latter part of 1931,
and the Budget for 1932 drafted by him, which reduced expenditure from 32 to 25 milliards of lei, obtained the approval of
M. Auboin, the French official adviser of the Bank of Rumania.
The danger lay in the fact that, owing to economic depression,
the revenue was continually diminishing ; but this, in the opinion
of M. Auboin, could be partly counteracted by better methods
of collection.

By the end of February it was already clear that the amount
of revenue estimated for 1932 would not be forthcoming. M.
Argetoianu therefore decided to make further drastic cuts in
the expenditure, so as to bring it down to the figure of 20,000,000
lei. In spite of all his efforts, however, the financial stringency
became more and more acute, and early in May the Cabinet
thought it well to appoint a committee of French experts to advise
what measures should be adopted to cope with the situation.
The Commission consisted of M. Charles Rist, the author of the
scheme for the stabilisation of the lei, M. Auboin, and six others.
Their report, which was presented at the end of May, recommended
the appointment of a Standing Advisory Committee on Finance,
composed of foreign experts, and the overhauling of the whole
administration. It also advised the Rumanian Government to
apply to the League of Nations for assistance.

In the meantime the Government had taken measures of a somewhat panic character affecting the currency. On May 12 the

P

import of all foreign bank notes into Rumania was prohibited by Ministerial decree, which, however, was withdrawn early in June. On May 18 a further regulation was issued prohibiting the export of foreign and Rumanian currency from Rumania. These measures were taken in order to check speculation in foreign exchange, but they also tended to depreciate the Rumanian currency abroad, and so accentuated the economic crisis.

The financial situation reacted on the political, and brought about a change of Government. The King had long been anxious to create a "Government of National Concentration" under M. Titulescu, the Rumanian Minister in London, and his opportunity now seemed to occur. M. Argetoianu, having failed in his efforts to raise a foreign loan, had demanded that, until economic conditions improved, all State employees, including members of the Cabinet, should receive only a percentage of their salaries in proportion to the State revenue. At a meeting of the Cabinet on May 31, the King insisted that the Government should respect "at any price" their obligation to pay the salaries of the Army and the State officials. After a long discussion M. Jorga presented the resignation of his Cabinet, which was accepted. He had been in office over thirteen months.

The King immediately summoned M. Titulescu from London by telephone to come at once to Bucharest, and on June 3 he commissioned him to form a Government of National Concentration. This proved to be beyond M. Titulescu's powers, and the King thereupon asked Dr. Vaida-Voevod to form a temporary Cabinet from the National Peasant Party with a mandate to hold a General Election without delay. Dr. Vaida-Voevod succeeded in forming a Ministry with himself as Minister of the Interior and M. Mironescu as Minister of Foreign Affairs, and on June 13 a decree was issued dissolving Parliament and fixing the elections for the Chamber for July 17 and for the Senate for July 20.

The new Government obtained the necessary funds for paying the salaries of State employees by a loan of 70,000,000 lei from the National Bank. It further secured M. Auboin's consent to its using the balance of former loans for current needs and for diverting to its own use another 1,000,000,000 lei originally set aside for the State railways. It also invited the League of Nations to send experts to Rumania in order to prepare a scheme for the reorganisation of the State finances, a request which was complied with at the end of August.

At the elections for the Chamber of Deputies on July 17, the National Peasants polled about 45 per cent. of the votes, and consequently, in accordance with the electoral law of 1926, obtained 277 seats out of a House of 387. The Old Liberals secured 28 seats and the Young Liberals, under Professor Georg Bratianu, 13 seats. Professor Jorga lost his seat, and his party, the so-called National Union, obtained only 5 seats.

On August 10 the Provisional Government of Dr. Vaida-Voevod resigned, and the King invited M. Maniu, who had lately been elected once more Leader of the National Peasant Party, after living in retirement for more than a year, to form a Government. M. Maniu, however, preferred to stand aside in favour of Dr. Vaida-Voevod, who on August 11 formed a Cabinet with himself as Foreign Minister and M. Mironescu as Minister of Finance. In a statement made the next day in Parliament, the new Premier announced that his programme would include the modification of the law for the conversion of agricultural debts, the reduction of agricultural and direct taxation, and the abolition of useless State expenditure.

Parliament was in session from July 31 to October 10, and during that time passed a Finance Act limiting the salaries of State officials to 700*l.* as a maximum ; an Act amending the Act for the conversion of agricultural debts ; and an Act rendering present and past State officials liable to control of their property. During the same period, the Financial Delegation sent out by the League of Nations framed its report, on the basis of which the Financial Committee of the League early in October submitted certain proposals to the Rumanian Government. The Government found them unacceptable, as they entailed the appointment of four League controllers, and the League Committee thereupon consented to allow it further time for consideration. As the financial position continued to deteriorate, the Treasury early in October opened negotiations with its foreign creditors for a suspension of payments on their loans.

At the instance of France and Poland, Dr. Vaida-Voevod in September authorised the Rumanian Minister at Moscow to draw up a Soviet-Rumanian Pact of Non-Aggression. A strong protest was entered against this procedure by M. Titulescu in the Paris Press, and M. Vaida-Voevod accordingly tendered his resignation to the King on October 17. He was succeeded by M. Maniu, who formed a Cabinet with M. Mironescu as Vice-Premier, M. Titulescu as Minister of Foreign Affairs, and M. Madgearu as Minister of Finance. A few days later M. Maniu stated that he desired sincerely to conclude a Pact of Non-Aggression with the Soviet Government, but he could not sign an agreement that would put Rumania in a position less favourable than that created for her by the Kellogg Pact.

Negotiations with Russia continued for some time, but led to no result. On November 23 M. Titulescu, in a speech in the Chamber, stated that they had broken down chiefly because M. Litvinoff had desired to insert in the Pact a clause to the effect that the treaty should not affect standing disputes between the two countries—in other words, that Russia would be at liberty to reopen the question of Bessarabia. Rumania was also unable to accept a proposal of Russia that existing differences, as well as any that might arise in the future, should be brought before an International Arbitration Tribunal.

At the end of the year the country was anxiously awaiting the result of the negotiations with the League of Nations for securing financial support and with foreign creditors at London and Paris for securing relief in respect of debt and interest payments. Pending the conclusion of these latter negotiations, the current Budget was prolonged till March 31, 1933, and steps were taken to keep the inevitable deficit as low as possible, such as the imposition of new duties, reductions in expenditure, and administrative reforms.

A new trade agreement based on preferential tariffs was concluded between Rumania and France early in January.

YUGOSLAVIA.

The royal dictatorship established in 1929 remained in force without modification throughout 1932. Its unpopularity, already marked at the beginning of the year, continued to increase, and the history of the year is largely a record of the manifestations of public discontent and the steps taken by the Government either to allay or to stifle it.

On January 18 the new Parliament was opened with a Speech from the Throne which emphasised once more the dangers threatening the unity of the State and insisted upon the necessity which had arisen of proclaiming the new regime in January, 1929. The Parliament, packed as it was with the supporters of this regime, expressed its full approval of the Government's work "from January 6, 1928, to the present day." How little this piece of flattery represented public opinion was shown by the fact that in the latter half of January the students of Belgrade and Ljubljana Universities carried out violent demonstrations, demanding the abolition of the dictatorship and the restoration of public political liberties. The demonstrations were suppressed by the police with great brutality.

Shortly afterwards the King showed signs of a desire to place himself on a better footing with the population. Towards the end of February he received the Radical leader, M. Aca Stonajevitch, and also the Croat leaders, Mm. Matchek and Trumbitch. No result followed from these interviews, but a change in policy did seem to be foreshadowed by the sudden resignation, on April 4, of the Premier General Zifkovitch, who for three years had been the King's chief instrument in wielding his dictatorial powers. General Zifkovitch gave as his reason his belief that the mandate assigned to him by the King in 1929 had been fulfilled, that national unity was assured and the revival of the old political parties had been made impossible. He was succeeded as Premier by Dr. Marinkovitch, once a Radical and Democrat and now the most eminent supporter of the dictatorial regime, who retained in his hands the Foreign Office.

The change of Ministers made in fact very little difference to the internal policy of the Government, the old restrictions being maintained in full force. Early in April fresh disturbances occurred at Belgrade University, as a result of which it was closed for the whole summer term. Professor Dragoljub Jovanovitch, a well-known economist, and a number of teachers, writers, and co-operative leaders were thrown into prison and subjected to very harsh treatment for spreading " Peasant Agrarian " views in Serbia proper. At the end of May the official paper *Vreme* began to adopt a violently chauvinistic tone, attacking both Communism and Yugoslavia's neighbours—Italy, Hungary, Austria, and Bulgaria—and holding up Hitler as a model. The *Vreme's* articles were generally regarded as the prelude to the murderous attack which, on June 7, was made in Zagreb on Dr. Budak, one of the Croat Peasant leaders, and to similar attacks made shortly afterwards on other politicians of lesser note. It was openly alleged that the assailants were police agents, and protests were made even in Parliament against the activities of the police chief Bedekovitch.

During this period discontent began to show itself in quarters which hitherto had been regarded as immune—the Army and Slovenia. A great sensation was caused early in May by the discovery of a conspiracy among the officers of the garrison of Maribor, in Slovenia. An attempt to hush up the affair having failed, a court-martial was held at Belgrade as a result of which two officers were sentenced to death and four others and a N.C.O. to long terms of imprisonment. The charge brought against them was one of Communist propaganda in the interest of a Bolshevik revolution, but it was well known that none of the accused was a Communist and that their real aim was a federal republic.

M. Marinkovitch's chief object was to raise a loan at Geneva or Paris, the finances of the country being in a desperate condition. He was not successful, and being in a precarious state of health, he resigned on June 30. It was expected that, in consequence of the advent to power of the " Left " parties in France, the Government would now adopt a more liberal policy, in order to obtain the good opinion of the Herriot Government. The reverse, however, happened. M. Marinkovitch was succeeded by M. Srskitch, a strong Centralist, and with him were associated in the exercise of power M. Jevtitch, an uncompromising supporter of the King, and M. Zika Lazitch, who for twelve years had been largely responsible for the regime of repression in Macedonia. The appointment of men with such antecedents was taken to indicate a firmer adhesion than ever to a Centralist regime and a policy of the " strong hand " ; and indeed the attitude of the

Government was sufficiently shown by the appointment of Dr. Bedekovitch, the notorious Police Chief of Zagreb, to be Chief of the Department of Public Safety.

As was to be expected, the French Chamber was strongly averse to granting a loan to Yugoslavia under its present regime. Nevertheless, the Finance Minister, Dr. Gjorgjevitch, after long negotiations at Paris, was able to secure a sort of moratorium of one year for the debt payments, amounting to 630,000,000 dinars (2,700,000l. nominal), due on previous loans. The Government made the most of this qualified success and attributed its failure to secure a loan to the shortness of money even in France. Dr. Gjorgjevitch soon after announced that the revenue had fallen 15-20 per cent. below the preliminary Budget estimates, and that it would be necessary to raise 1,150,000,000 dinars by fresh taxation.

One of the reactionary steps of the new Government was to tighten the censorship of the Press, which had been somewhat relaxed under M. Marinkovitch, though his regime too had witnessed the expulsion of Madame Samsonova, the correspondent of *The Times* in Belgrade, and one of the best informed and most independent writers on Balkan affairs. In the summer a monopoly for the import and sale of foreign newspapers was granted to the " Avala " Press Agency, with the object of still further keeping from the public as far as possible a knowledge of foreign criticism of the regime.

During September and October there were a number of armed encounters between Croat peasants and the gendarmerie in the mountainous districts of Dalmatia. In September Dr. Jovanovitch was brought to trial and sentenced to a year's imprisonment and the loss of his Chair, and five of his associates received terms of imprisonment—one of the mildest set of sentences known under the dictatorship. Early in October the assailants of Dr. Budak were sentenced to three years' imprisonment. On October 17 Dr. Matchek and Dr. Trumbitch were arrested on account of some outspoken remarks of theirs on the Croat question reproduced in the *Manchester Guardian* of September 17. They were, however, almost immediately released.

On November 3 the Srskitch Cabinet suddenly resigned, without any apparent reason, but in a few days it resumed office with very little change. Some dissatisfaction at this time manifested itself in the Skuptchina, where about forty Deputies declared themselves dissidents, and a new electoral law was therefore introduced by M. Lazic to make it more amenable to Government control.

The close of the year witnessed the beginnings of a movement for closer union among the various elements of the population opposed to the dictatorship. Early in November representatives of the Croat Peasants, the Croat Clericals, the Serbian Democrats,

and other parties joined in signing a manifesto which also had
the sympathy of the Bosnian Moslems and the Slovene Clericals,
demanding a return to the year 1918 as the point of departure
for a reorganisation of the State by means of which the moral
and material life of the Serb, Croat, and Slovene nations should
be guaranteed. A copy of the manifesto, which was of course
confidential, fell into the hands of the Government and was
denounced as treasonable by the Government Press.

Early in December the mutilation by some young Dalmatian
Croats of two sculptured Venetian lions on the town wall of
Trogir (Trau), which were regarded as Italian symbols, led to
a diplomatic protest from the side of Italy and violent demonstrations against Yugoslavia in a number of Italian cities. On
December 21 M. Jevtitch in the Skuptchina expressed regret
at the act of vandalism committed at Trogir, to which he thought
exaggerated importance was attached, and declared that Yugoslavia was profoundly pacific, which, however, did not mean that
she would submit tamely to insult.

TURKEY.

In 1932 the Turkish people was called upon by its Government to make greater sacrifices than ever for the purpose of
maintaining the equilibrium of the Budget and the value of the
currency, and again it obeyed the call unflinchingly. Although
the tobacco harvest was excellent, there was owing to the world
depression almost no sale for the crop, and the same fate befell
other Turkish products. The result was that the value of exports
fell off considerably. Being determined not to let the country
incur an adverse trade balance, the Government imposed drastic
restrictions on imports, to the great inconvenience of the population. The decline in imports caused a corresponding decline in
Customs revenue, and to make this good further heavy taxation
was imposed. Thus the population was doubly hit.

In the Budget for the financial year which commenced in
June, 1932, expenditure was provisionally fixed in April at
173,000,000*l*.T. (10*l*.T. equals about 1*l*. sterling at par), which was
13,000,000*l*.T. less than in the preceding year, and nearly
50,000,000*l*.T. less than two years before. Estimated revenue
for the year did not exceed 149,000,000*l*.T., and to make up the
deficiency a " Budget balancing tax " was imposed on all salaried
workers—in the first place those employed by the Government—
increasing the deductions made under the " Crisis Tax " of the
preceding year to totals varying from 20 to 35 per cent. The
victims of this unparalleled load of taxation had the satisfaction
of knowing that they were enabling the Government to save
the Turkish currency, to keep clear of foreign loans, and, alone

of the Balkan States, to maintain a comparatively sound financial position. The Budget was ultimately balanced at round about 169,000,000*l*.T., the Vote for Defence being 19,000,000*l*.T. less than in the preceding year.

Economic conditions remained bad throughout the year, the purchasing power and the taxable capacity of the people continuing to decline. The strain proved almost too great even for Turkish patience, and an outcry was raised which led to the resignation in September of the Minister of Economy, and the withdrawal by his successor of some of the most drastic restrictions on imports.

On January 23 the Convention with Persia for rectifying the frontier near Mount Ararat was signed at Teheran. By obtaining a tract of country behind Mount Ararat into which Kurdish raiders were accustomed to retire, Turkey was able to defend the frontier against Kurdish raids much more effectively than heretofore.

On April 28 Ismet Pasha, the Turkish Prime Minister, and Tewfik Rushdi Bey, the Minister for Foreign Affairs, arrived in Moscow at the head of a large Turkish Delegation, partly to return the visit paid to Ankara a few months earlier by M. Litvinoff, the Soviet Commissar for Foreign Affairs, and partly in order to examine the economic position in Russia, and discuss with the Soviet Government the possibilities of increasing trade between the two countries. They were treated with marked consideration by the Soviet authorities, and remained in the country over a fortnight, during which they inspected a large number of factories and power-plants. The Turkish journalists who accompanied the Delegation were greatly impressed by the evidences shown to them of Russian industrial progress, and reported to the Turkish public that Russia was becoming a second America, in which no one suffered from hunger. But the Bolshevik political institutions they considered entirely unsuited for Turkey. The practical fruit of the visit was a credit granted by Russia to the Turkish Government of 1,600,000*l*. for the supply of machinery essential for the development of Turkish industry, in return for which Turkey was to furnish Russia with products of her own over a period of twenty years.

Another country which set equal store by Turkish friendship was Italy. On May 25 Ismet Pasha and Tewfik Rushdi Bey arrived in Rome, where they were received by the Government with every mark of honour. They signed there, along with Signor Mussolini and Signor Grandi, a renewal for five years of the Italo-Turkish Treaty of Friendship and Conciliation due to expire in July. They also obtained from the Italian Government a credit in favour of Turkey of 4,166,000*l*., one-third of which was to be devoted to wiping off Turkish indebtedness to Italian shipyards, one-third to the purchase of Italian machinery,

and the remainder to be paid in cash.   In effect, Turkey floated
a loan of 6,000,000*l.* with the Soviet and Italian Governments
on easy terms.

On July 6 the Assembly of the League of Nations passed
a resolution to invite Turkey to become a member of the League.
On July 10 the Grand National Assembly accepted the invitation
unanimously, and on July 18 Turkey was formally admitted to
the League.

On April 28 the Turkish delegate to the League of Nations
Advisory Committee on Opium Traffic announced that his Government had decided to subscribe to The Hague Convention of 1912,
the additional Protocol of 1914, and the Geneva Opium Convention
of 1925.

The exchange of Turkish and Greek minorities and the liquida-
tion of their properties, which had been commenced in 1923,
was completed in August of this year.

Further important steps were taken in 1932 for freeing Turkish
culture from Arabic and Persian influences.   On February 3—
the "Night of Power"—the Government caused the Koran to
be read and the prayers to be recited in Turkish instead of Arabic
in all the mosques of Constantinople.   And in September,
a "Kuriltai" (an ancient Turkish word used as a substitute for
"Congress" or "Assembly") attended by Turkish philologists,
historians, authors, editors, and politicians, was held at Ankara
to discuss and forward a movement, which had the enthusiastic
support of the Ghazi, for removing from the Turkish language all
words of Persian or Arabic origin—forming perhaps half of the
present vocabulary—and replacing them by words purely Turkish.

On May 22 Sir George Clerk, the British Ambassador at
Constantinople, visited Ankara, and on behalf of the British
Government presented to the Ghazi a richly bound copy of the
British Official History of the Gallipoli Campaign, in which full
justice is done to the decisive part played in the Turkish defence
by Mustapha Kemal, then only a Divisional General.   The
copy was inscribed : "To Ghazi Mustapha Kemal, a great Commander, a noble Adversary, a generous Friend, from His Britannic
Majesty's Government."   The thanks of the Ghazi were conveyed
to the British Ambassador at the end of May by the Turkish
Foreign Minister in a highly appreciative letter.   The Government
announced its intention of having the work translated into Turkish
for use as an official text-book in all colleges and schools.

GREECE.

In 1932 Greece, like many other countries, suffered acutely
from a shortage of foreign currency with which to meet her
external obligations.   Combined with the expenditure on undertakings which, while essential for the country's development,

were for the present unproductive, these obligations placed on
her resources a strain which, in the prevailing economic stringency,
they were unable to stand, and gravely compromised the country's
financial stability.

At the beginning of the year M. Venizelos, the Prime Minister,
took energetic steps for the purpose of enabling the Government
to cope with the financial crisis. The movement of capital into
and out of Greece was severely restricted. Exports were encouraged and imports discouraged, and where treaty obligations
permitted, a heavy duty was imposed on goods from abroad. The
Athens Stock Exchange was closed, and a system of bartering
goods with other countries was arranged. The Budget was
severely cut, and three meatless days a week were imposed on the
population.

On January 19 M. Venizelos left Athens on a visit to Rome,
Paris, and London for the purpose of explaining the financial
difficulties of Greece and obtaining assistance. At the same time,
the Bank of Greece, with the concurrence of the Greek Government, invited Sir Otto Niemeyer to visit Athens in order to study
the financial and economic situation and report upon it to the
League of Nations.

M. Venizelos sought to obtain from the Powers whom he
visited a loan of two-and-a-half million sterling a year for four
years, this being the sum which, on his calculation, was required
to enable Greece to balance her Budget, continue the services of
the external debt and stabilise the currency, and complete the
productive works which the Government had in hand. The
Powers in response instructed their representatives on the Financial
Committee of the League of Nations to go to Athens to report,
and with Sir Otto Niemeyer at their head, they arrived in Athens
on February 16.

While they were conducting their investigations, the position
of M. Venizelos became very precarious. Speaking in the Chamber
on March 5, he said that the fate of his Government was in the
hands of the Financial Committee of the League of Nations. If
they adopted his proposals, the Government would hold a General
Election, and, if returned to power, carry out their policy of
economic reconstruction. If, however, the League refused to
provide adequate assistance, the Government would resign and
leave it to the Opposition parties to adopt the inevitable alternative of repudiating public debts. His party would support a
Coalition Government, but he himself was precluded from taking
office in it by the pledges which he had given to foreign Powers
that he would never be a party to repudiation.

The recommendations of the League Financial Committee
were made known on March 23. They were that Greece should
meet her foreign payments due on April 3 ; that a loan of 2,000,000*l.*
for immediate needs should be granted her ; that sinking fund

payments on foreign debts should be suspended for a year ; and that the interest on foreign debts should be reduced to 25 per cent. of its amount for the same period. These recommendations fell so far short of the assistance asked for by M. Venizelos that on the next day he offered to resign in favour of a Coalition Government. M. Tsaldaris, however, the leader of the Royalists, refused his collaboration, and M. Venizelos thereupon decided to remain in office and postpone the elections till September or October.

On April 8 M. Venizelos left for Geneva in order once more to lay his case before the Council of the League of Nations. Addressing them on April 15, he pointed out that the single loan of 2,000,000*l.* which they contemplated, was quite inadequate for Greece's requirements, nor would it be sufficient to suspend sinking fund for one year, as there was no ground whatever for supposing that Greece would be able to resume payments on her debt at the end of one year ; a moratorium for five years was the indispensable minimum. The League, however, would not go beyond their previous offer. M. Venizelos thereupon, seeing that nothing more was to be obtained from the League, instructed the Greek Legations in London and Paris to approach the foreign bond-holders and ask them to agree to the suspension for five years of the sinking fund on Greek external debts, and to the postponement of the interest payments on them falling due on May 1 until the League had granted the promised loan of 2,000,000*l.*

On April 27 the Chamber passed a Bill enabling Greece to abandon the gold standard. On May 1, instead of remitting the interest due on the 7 per cent. Refugee Loan of 1928, the Government sent a request to the bond-holders not to press for payment and to defer negotiations until the next meeting of the League of Nations. The Budget for the year, introduced on May 20, made no provision for the sinking funds of foreign and external loans. It set aside, however, a sum of nearly 1,250,000*l.* for interest on foreign loans. This sum was to be treated as a special fund, not to be transferred out of the country until this could be done without depreciating the drachma. On July 30 a decree was issued, with retroactive force as from April 26, but applying to Greek subjects only, converting all foreign currency deposits in Greek banks into drachmas at the rate of 100 to the dollar and 385 to the pound, the ruling rates being 145 and 555 respectively.

One result of Greece's default was that the League of Nations withheld the promised loan of 2,000,000*l.*, so that Greece was unable to pay even the interest which had fallen due on May 1. Accordingly, early in June, the Government sent M. Drossopoulos, Director to the Greek Public Debt, to England to negotiate with the Greek Bond-holders' Committee and the Council of Foreign Bond-holders. He failed to obtain an agreement, and on August 17, M. Varvaressos, the Minister of Finance, arrived in London to take up the negotiations. In the second week of September an arrangement was reached by which Greece undertook during the financial year 1932-33, to remit payments in foreign exchange amounting to 30 per cent. of the total annual interest due on the foreign loans, at the same time recognising its full liability in respect of its external debts.

During the second half of the year, the centre of interest shifted from external finance to internal politics. In the middle of May violent controversy was aroused by two Bills brought forward by M. Venizelos, one for adopting proportional representation in the forthcoming elections, and one for restricting the liberty of the Press. The object of the former was to prevent the Royalist Party from obtaining a decisive majority, which otherwise M. Venizelos judged to be not unlikely. The Press Bill was declared by him to be necessary on account of the violent tone adopted recently by Royalist newspapers. The Proportional Representation Bill was eventually passed by the Chamber, but the Press Bill met with such determined opposition both from the Opposition parties and nearly the whole of the Press, that on May 21 M. Venizelos resigned.

Acting on the advice of M. Venizelos, the President entrusted the task of forming a Cabinet to the dissident Republican leader, M. Papanastassiou, who had been Prime Minister in 1924. M. Tsaldaris refused to co-operate with him, but he formed a Cabinet from his own group. His Ministry, however, was short-lived. He made his first appearance before the Chamber on June 3, was violently attacked, and resigned the same day. Thereupon on June 5 M. Venizelos again took office with a new Ministry.

At this juncture a number of Army officers of strong Republican sentiments formed a Military League to support the Republic. Opponents of M. Venizelos immediately alleged that he had himself created the League for purposes of his own advancement. A manifesto, signed by M. Tsaldaris, leader of the Popular Party, and MM. Kaphandaris, Papanastassiou, and Zavitzianos, leaders of the anti-Venizelist Republican groups, was published accusing M. Venizelos of having invented a fictitious danger to the Republic in order to justify his action in encouraging Army officers to form the Military League. They declared, too, that the Republican regime was in no danger except from a Government which " had already disgraced the regime by repeated violations and arbitrary acts," and " which had heaped ruin on the country." M. Venizelos retorted by challenging the Popular Party to give a pledge not to raise the question of the regime for ten years, asserting that if they would do so, the Military League would dissolve itself. The pledge was not taken up, and M. Venizelos, having thus defined the issue, dissolved the Chamber on August 18. In a final speech to it on that day, he passed in review his four years of office, pointing with pride to the immense improvements which had been effected by his Government in almost every sphere of national existence. The Public Debt had been redeemed to the extent of 4,600,000 drachmas; brigandage had been suppressed, order maintained, and great public works put in hand; cordial relations had been established with Turkey, and Pacts of friendship concluded with Italy and Yugoslavia; currency inflation had been avoided, and the purchasing power of the drachma largely regained.

On September 6 M. Tsaldaris complained to M. Zaimis, the President of the Republic, that in the course of his electoral campaign, M. Venizelos was both speaking and acting in a revolutionary manner, and he asked that a neutral Government should be formed to carry out the elections impartially. The President, however, managed to pacify him, and on the next day he declared that his party would not raise the question of the regime either during or after the elections, and that they would oppose any attempt to overthrow the Republic. Thereupon the campaign proceeded more calmly. Polling took place on September 25 without disorder, and produced the kind of result which M. Venizelos had anticipated. The Liberal Party, after losing 77 seats, retained 102, and the Popular Party, after gaining 76, obtained 96. The Progressive Republicans obtained 15, and other groups 40. The party situation, therefore, was one of stalemate.

The President was anxious to form a Coalition Government representing all parties except the Communists, and steps were taken on both sides to pave the way for this. On October 3 M. Tsaldaris, in a letter to the President, unreservedly recognised the Republic and expressed the hope that Greece would flourish under that regime. On October 5 the Military League announced its dissolution. In spite of this, however, M. Tsaldaris still refused to enter into a coalition with M. Venizelos. Thereupon, on October 28, the President convoked a conference of party leaders at which it was agreed that M. Tsaldaris should form a Cabinet from a coalition of the Opposition parties for a period of eight months, during which M. Venizelos and the Liberals would observe a truce and refrain from out-voting the Government, though they reserved the right to criticise Government policy and put forward amendments. Similar promises were given by the parties of MM. Kaphandaris and Papanastassiou.

On this basis M. Tsaldaris formed, on November 4, a Government which had 111 supporters in the Chamber against an Opposition of 129. At the beginning of December he asked for a "vote of confidence," but was accorded only a "vote of toleration." Some proposed economies of the new Government, including the abolition of the Ministry of Aviation and the placing of the Air Service under the control of the Army and Navy, soon met with uncompromising opposition from M. Venizelos; but the Chamber adjourned before the new arrangement could be really put to the test.

The Budget introduced in May had practically balanced (excluding a deficit from the past year of 390,000l.) at a figure equivalent to 15,500,000l. When M. Tsaldaris came into office, the deficit was already estimated at 700,000,000 drachmas, which by a revised estimate at the end of November became 1,200,000,000 drachmas (about 3,500,000l. at par). In spite of this the Cabinet on December 15 decided to pay 30 per cent. of the interest due to foreign bond-holders, according to the agreement made in September. M. Angelopoulos, the Finance Minister, opposed this decision on the ground that the payments could not be made without drawing on the country's resources of foreign exchange essential for obtaining food supplies ; and as the Cabinet would not give way he resigned.

At the end of November and beginning of December strikes, accompanied by violence, took place in Athens among the omnibus drivers and public servants. They were attributed to Communist incitement, and the Communist newspaper *Rizopastis* was suppressed and its premises raided.

On September 26 Thessaly and Greek Macedonia were shaken by a severe earthquake. The shocks continued for some days in Chalcidike, where great damage was done, 150 persons being killed and many hundreds injured. Relief was brought by five warships of the British Mediterranean Fleet, for which the Government conveyed the thanks of the Greek nation to King George and the Admiral.

BULGARIA.

Bulgaria in 1932 was greatly harassed by foreign debts on the one hand and internal dissensions on the other. On January 8 M. Mushanoff, the Prime Minister, declared that unless assistance were given from abroad, Bulgaria would be unable to meet her financial engagements. On January 20, in company with the Finance Minister, M. Stephanoff, he explained Bulgaria's position to the Finance Committee of the League of Nations, and on February 8 three Commissioners from the League arrived at Sofia to hold an inquiry there before action was taken at Geneva. While the matter was still undecided, M. Mushanoff announced that unless facilities were granted by her creditors, Bulgaria would be obliged to suspend all foreign payments as from March 15.

In spite of this declaration, the Government on March 15 met the loan payments falling due on that date, having received word that only so could they hope to receive any help. On April 15 the Council of the League of Nations adopted the recommendation made in March by its Financial Committee, that the foreign transfer in respect of Bulgarian loans should be reduced by half for six months from April 15, that the moiety retained in the country should be paid into a special account in

the name of the Bank Adviser, and that at the end of that period
the position should be reviewed. A similar recommendation
was made with regard to Bulgaria's pre-war loans. Taking advantage of this authorisation, the Bulgarian Government in June
announced that for the six months ending in September only
half of the interest on its foreign loans would be remitted. Shortly
afterwards too the Controller of the Bulgarian Public Debt stated
that unless economic conditions improved payments could not
be resumed even on the expiration of the partial moratorium.

The action of the League carried no weight with the bond-
holders either of its own loans or of the pre-war Bulgarian loans.
The trustees of the former were invited by the Government to
negotiate a new agreement, but they refused to be parties to any
variation in the terms of issue. The Delegate of the bond-holders
of pre-war loans at Sofia also demanded payment in full, appealing
to the Convention which guaranteed the receipts of the cigarette
monopoly for the service of the 1902 and 1907 loans. As the
Government persisted in its refusal to pay, the Delegate refused
to issue to it the banderoles in which the cigarettes had to be
sold, as proof that the tax had been paid. The Government
threatened to print and issue their own banderoles, but eventually
they consented to send a representative to Paris to negotiate.
The result of the negotiations was that on July 14 the bond-holders'
representatives declared themselves willing to accept the recommendations made by the League of Nations Financial Commission in March, on condition, however, that the untransferred
half of the interest payments should be paid in Bulgarian currency
into a special account in the name of the Counsellor of the National
Bank, so that the Bulgarian Government should be unable to
use the sums so deposited without the consent of the bond-holders'
Delegate.

In the autumn negotiations took place between the Bulgarian
Government and the newly formed League Loans Committee,
as a result of which it undertook to remit interest on the two
Bulgarian League of Nations loans—the Settlement Loan of 1926
and the Stabilisation Loan of 1928—for the six months ending
April, 1933, in foreign exchanges up to 40 per cent., the remaining
60 per cent. and sinking fund to be paid into a blocked account.

Internally Bulgaria was kept in a state of unrest by quarrels
between the Agrarians and the Government and of the Agrarians
among themselves, by the spread of Communism, and by a revival of the feud among the Macedonian revolutionaries. On
January 5 the Sobranje accepted the amnesty proposed by the
Government in the previous year, which permitted the return
to public life of most of the proscribed Agrarians (*vide* ANNUAL
REGISTER, 1931, p. 252). In the course of the year, however,
friction arose between the Agrarians and the Democrats, the
two chief parties in the Government *bloc,* the former alleging

that M. Ghirginoff, the Democrat Minister of the Interior, was showing great hostility to the Agrarian Party and individual Agrarians. Early in August, they formally demanded the resignation of this Minister, under threat of withdrawing their own Ministers from the Cabinet, but they were persuaded by the Premier to suspend action until the international discussion on Eastern reparations should have taken place. Soon after, however, dissension became acute between two Agrarian members of the Cabinet, M. Ghitcheff, the leader of the party, and M. Yordanoff, a strong partisan of the exiled Agrarians, whose amnesty had not yet come into force. In order to rid himself of M. Yordanoff, the Premier on September 7 resigned, and immediately reconstructed his Cabinet, replacing M. Yordanoff by M. Dimoff, the brother-in-law of M. Ghitcheff. On October 16 twenty-two Agrarian exiles from Sofia tried to enter Bulgaria in order to attend an Agrarian conference in Sofia, but their train was searched at the frontier, and six of them who were under sentence of death were sent back to Yugoslavia, while the rest were conveyed to Bulgarian prisons.

On December 26 the three Agrarian Ministers in the Cabinet resigned on account of the refusal of the Premier to dismiss the National Liberal Minister of Justice, who was accused of corruption. M. Mushanoff thereupon resigned, but he was invited by the King to resume office, and on December 30 he formed a Cabinet containing the same three Agrarian Ministers, but in different posts.

At the municipal elections held in February, the Communists obtained majorities in several towns, while the National *bloc*, which had gained an overwhelming victory in the rural (communal) elections held in the previous November, polled less than half the votes. The continued progress of Communism moved the powerful Union of Reserve Officers in the autumn to send a delegation to the Prime Minister and the heads of all political parties to warn them of the dangers which threatened from Communism and Bolshevism, to call for economic measures against these dangers, and to hint that neglect of this warning might cause the Army to intervene against the prospect of anarchy. That the danger was real was shown by the fact that soon after, on September 25, at the municipal elections in Sofia, the Communists won 19 out of 35 seats. Owing to its fear of Communism the Government would not allow a Soviet Legation in Sofia, and was therefore unable to renew commercial relations between Bulgaria and Russia, as recommended by a Bulgarian delegation which visited Russia in the summer.

The feud between the Mihailoffist and Protogueroffist factions of the Macedonian Revolutionary Organisation, which had been quiescent for a time, broke out again in May, and led to a number of assassinations on both sides in the course of the year.

On December 28 a street battle, in which a policeman was killed and eight persons fatally or seriously injured, was fought between thirty members of the two sections in a principal street of Sofia under the windows of the Royal Palace with King Boris as a spectator. The activities of the revolutionaries again caused considerable friction between Bulgaria and Yugoslavia, which complained on various occasions that the Bulgarian Government did not take sufficiently energetic measures to combat anti-Yugoslav demonstrations and propaganda.

At the beginning of the year Bulgaria made an unofficial agreement with Albania by which the two countries were to recognise the legal existence of the minorities of either country in the other. Bulgaria intended this as an example to other Balkan countries, especially Yugoslavia, but it produced very little effect. At the third Balkan Conference held at Bucharest in October, the Bulgarian delegation called for an immediate pronouncement on the question of Bulgarian minorities in the Balkans, and when the conference shelved the question it withdrew.

ALBANIA.

The rule of King Zogu became increasingly unpopular during the year among the educated class, chiefly on account of his Italian proclivities, and there was much plotting against him. In the summer he ordered the arrest of some two hundred persons from all parts of the country, among them several who had assisted him to rise to power in 1924. A number of them were tried by a special emergency Court at Tirana in September, and seven were sentenced to death, fourteen to imprisonment for life, and thirteen to fifteen and one to three years' imprisonment.

CHAPTER V.

LESSER STATES OF WESTERN AND NORTHERN EUROPE : BELGIUM — NETHERLANDS — SWITZERLAND — SPAIN — PORTUGAL — DENMARK—SWEDEN—NORWAY—FINLAND.

BELGIUM.

FINANCIAL anxieties weighed heavily on Belgium as on many other countries during 1932. The Belgian franc had successfully weathered a serious crisis in 1931, but the position at the beginning of 1932 was still difficult. According to a statement made by the Minister of Finance, Baron Houtart, in the Senate on February 2, the Hoover moratorium had deprived the Budget of 600,000,000 francs, and the deficit in consequence would be about 1,000,000,000. To provide this sum, reductions were made in the pensions and in

Q

the salaries of Civil servants and members of Parliament, certain
Customs were raised by 15 per cent., and taxes were increased by
one-tenth. A loan of 1 milliard of francs was also raised.

In spite of these steps the financial situation remained disquieting, and in July the Government seriously contemplated
asking the Chamber for dictatorial powers to deal with financial
matters during the Parliamentary recess. This proposal was
abandoned owing to the opposition of some of the party leaders,
but on September 6 the Cabinet drafted a special financial Bill
authorising the Government to issue at home or abroad a long-
term loan of 1,500,000,000 francs, and also to issue 500,000,000
francs' worth of bonds on account against the amount of credit
required by the Treasury, and to create bonds for the renewal or
reimbursement of 760,743,000 francs' worth of ten-year bonds
falling due on October 1. On September 7 the Chamber passed
this Bill by 98 votes to 57, the Socialists declaring that they did
not regard the proposals as a remedy. The Bill was passed by
the Senate on September 14.

Further drastic measures for the balancing of the Budget and
the rehabilitation of the public finances were sanctioned by the
Chamber on December 28. They included a national crisis levy
of from 1 to 4 per cent. on salaries, pensions, and allowances, and
on returns from capital and landed property, and a special tax on
goods requiring export or import licences. These imposts were
expected to bring in about 450,000,000 francs. Further economies
were also adopted, including a reduction in the pay of the militia
and the estimates for national defence, the suspension of all
recruiting for the public services, and the removal of certain
abuses in unemployment pay and old-age pensions. The Conservatives and Socialists, while not actively opposing the Bill,
tried to prevent its passage by walking out of the House, but
a quorum was obtained without them. On December 13 the
Cabinet decided that Belgium could not pay the debt instalment
due to the United States.

The economic troubles which were at the root of the financial
crisis led also to serious manifestations of Labour unrest in the
summer. On July 4 there were demonstrations of unemployed
throughout the country, and a procession of about 12,000 marched
through the streets of Brussels protesting against the proposal of
the Government to cut down the dole. On the same day a strike
broke out among the miners of the Mons basin on account of an
attempt of the mine-owners to reduce wages. M. Heyman, the
Minister of Industry and Labour, intervened, and a commission
of owners, miners, and officials was appointed to try to settle the
dispute. Meanwhile the Communists carried on an active agitation, which led to grave riots in the province of Hainaut. The
workers demanded the maintenance of the present wage rates,
notwithstanding the fall in the cost of living, until October 31,

the continuance of unemployment relief on the present scale, and a forty-hour week.   On July 13 M. Heyman announced that the delegates of the owners and miners had unanimously accepted the first demand and had recommended that the Government should appoint a Commission to examine the question of the length of the working day and the distribution of work among the employed and unemployed.   On the next day the National Congress of Miners decided in the face of very strong opposition to accept the agreement, but the order to return to work was disregarded by most of the miners, and in the first week of August there were still 100,000 on strike out of a total of 138,000.   There was a likelihood at one time also that the strike might spread to other industries.   However, on September 1, the coal-owners consented to increase wages by 1 per cent. and to consider a revision of the lower wages as soon as they had been able to estimate the results of the Convention about to be concluded between German and Belgian coal-owners.   Work was then generally resumed, but there was still considerable feeling in some districts.

The Government of M. Renkin, which had been originally appointed as a kind of stopgap, commanded more confidence than had been anticipated, and continued in office for the greater part of the year.   Its great achievement was to complete practically the official recognition of the Flemish language.   At the beginning of March the Chamber, by 120 votes to 19, approved a Bill laying down that the administrative language in Flanders should be Flemish, and in the Walloon provinces French, and that in Brussels and the Province of Brabant there were to be two sets of officials, one Flemish and the other French speaking, in the highest administrative departments.

Further steps taken by the Government in connexion with the language question led to disagreement between the Flemish Catholic and Liberal sections of its supporters.   The former desired that municipalities should have the option of either maintaining or suppressing minority classes with teaching in French in the Flemish section of the country.   To this the Liberals would not agree, and M. Renkin to get over the difficulty resigned on May 17, forming a new Government a few days later in which the Liberals were not so uncompromising.   The Flemish extremists were not satisfied with this, and in June violently attacked the Government for its educational policy, but the Chamber accorded it a vote of confidence.

In the autumn differences between the Liberals and the Catholics, chiefly over the question of educational subsidies, became more pronounced.   The Liberal Party was itself divided, a large section desiring it to ally itself with the Socialists, especially after the marked successes of the latter in the Communal elections on October 9.   At a Cabinet meeting on October 17 M. Hymans, on behalf of the Liberal Ministers, supported the

Socialist demand for a dissolution of Parliament and an early election. On the next day the Government resigned, and a temporary Government was thereupon formed with Count de Brocqueville as Prime Minister. On October 28 Parliament was dissolved, on the ground that it was necessary to have a Parliament fully representative of the nation and competent to undertake the financial and economic reconstruction of the country. The General Election held on November 27 resulted in slight gains for the Catholics and Socialists and a slight loss for the Liberals. At a meeting of the National Council of the Liberal Party on December 11, it was resolved by 227 votes to 139, on the proposal of the leader of the party, M. Devèze, to support the Catholics. Count de Brocqueville then formed a Catholic-Liberal Ministry in which M. Devèze was Minister of National Defence. On December 22 Count de Brocqueville outlined the programme of the Government, in which financial restoration occupied the first place, and on the next day the Government obtained a vote of confidence from 100 Catholics and Liberals against 80 Socialists, Communists, and Flemish extremists.

Great irritation was caused in Belgium throughout the year by the application by France of quota restrictions against Belgian imports. Negotiations conducted at the beginning of the year produced a certain improvement, but complaints continued to be made that the Belgian export of horses and vegetables was severely penalised. There was some talk of taking retaliatory measures, but M. Hymans, in a debate in the Senate on July 20, declared that it would be madness to attempt a Customs war with France.

On June 19 representatives of Belgium initialled at Lausanne a convention with Holland and Luxemburg " for the reciprocal and progressive reduction of economic barriers " between the three countries. The convention was officially signed on July 18.

At the end of July it was announced that the Minister of Defence had given instructions for the erection of fortifications on the high ground about seven miles from Aix-la-Chapelle, in order to protect the eastern frontier, and that the district north of Eupen would be similarly fortified.

THE NETHERLANDS.

As was to be foreseen a year ago, when the *corps electorate*, the Provincial States, were renewed, the composition of the First Chamber after the elections in the beginning of the summer remained nearly the same as before. A few Roman Catholic members only had incurred unpopularity on account of their opposition to a Bill providing that on the renewal of a lease, the rent should in certain cases be fixed by the district judge. They were ostracised by their party and were forced to resign their seats to more democratically minded co-religionists.

In the meantime the increasing depression in agriculture had led the Radical group of the Second Chamber to take a further step for relieving the farmers by introducing a Bill giving to the district judge the power to exempt the lessee, on his own request, from the payment, either wholly or in part, of his rent, on every occasion on which he proved himself unable to do so during the term of his lease.

The fact that the States-General sanctioned so far-reaching an infringement of the legislation which hitherto had governed the relations between landowner and leaseholder was clear proof of the desperate situation of these vital branches of industry. They had for many years been organised on a scale greatly transcending the wants of the home market and intended to cope with an un-restricted export to the surrounding and even to more distant countries. The raising higher and higher of all kinds of impedi-ments in almost all countries to the importation of products of the Dutch soil struck a heavy blow at the whole peasantry. Great quantities of rural, especially horticultural, products had to be destroyed as unsaleable, and the Government was forced by these occurrences to demand large credits from the States-General in order to prevent the complete collapse of such important branches of national industry.

The economic position of the country on the whole, and in consequence also the financial situation, deteriorated in the course of the year to such a degree that the Government in July con-sidered it expedient to make a direct appeal to the people, partly in order to meet the widespread discontent aroused by the pub-lication of the report of a State Commission containing elaborate proposals aiming at the reducing of the Budget by about 100 million guilders on a total of 600. The Prime Minister, Jhr. Ruys de Beerenbrouck, for this purpose broadcast a speech on the economic and financial difficulties of the country, in which he made an appeal to all classes of the population for their co-operation even at the cost of painful sacrifices.

The same ideas pervaded the Speech from the Throne with which the Queen on September 20 opened the new session of the States-General, and the "Millions Note," as the Explanatory Memorandum to the Budget is usually nicknamed. In preparing the Budget for 1933, the Government had adopted the view that the gold standard ought to be maintained. The safest way of meeting the financial crisis seemed to be to make sharp retrench-ments on all public services to a total amount of 66 million guilders ; the salaries of all public servants, which in the beginning of the year had already undergone a reduction, would have to be sub-jected to a fresh cut to a total amount of 17 millions.

The financial position indeed was in many regards alarming.

Whilst the ordinary service for 1929 had left a surplus of 58·2 and that for 1930 one of 27·9 million guilders, the provisional figures for 1931 indicated a deficit of nearly 50 millions. For 1932 also a considerable deficit, probably exceeding 40 millions, was to be expected. There was no hope that the economic situation would improve within a reasonable time, so that it seemed inexpedient to cover the deficit by way of a loan. In anticipation of a still further decline in the national income, the Budget for the ordinary service for 1933 expenditure was fixed at 572·8 and revenues at 518·2 millions, leaving an estimated deficit of 54·6 millions. To meet this deficit the Government proposed to draw 18 millions from the reserve fund and to raise temporarily by 30 per cent. the tariffs of the municipal fund, the property tax, the excise on beer, and the import duties.

In a country with so old and strong a Free Trade tradition as Holland it was naturally only with the greatest reluctance that both the Government and Parliament resorted to such measures as the imposition of quotas, the granting of State support of vital industries, and the raising of import duties to a level which was apparently protectionist. In June, on the occasion of the Lausanne Conference, in order to counteract this tendency, a Convention— the so-called Ouchy Convention—was initialled by Dutch, Belgian, and Luxemburgian representatives, in which the parties engaged themselves not to impose fresh duties in their mutual trade, by means of an annual reduction of 10 per cent. to bring down the existing duties to a certain figure, and to place no fresh restrictions on each other's imports. It was also provided that all other States should have the right to join the Convention on an equal footing with the original signatories.

The Government maintained that the proposed temporary surtaxes on all import duties had no protectionist character, about half of the estimated yield (11 millions out of 23 millions) being from goods not produced in the country. The Ouchy Convention also, not yet having come into force, did not, as far as its actual wording went, forbid an increase of tariffs. The spirit of the Convention, however, led the Government to refrain, from the day of its coming into force, from levying any surtaxes as far as the contracting parties were concerned.

In the Second Chamber the Bill nevertheless met with opposition from three sides—from the opponents of all protection, from those who feared that the ratification of the Ouchy Convention might be endangered, and from those who, like the Minister of State Dr. Colyn, did not desire an increase of the import duties all along the line. The tone of the debate made it fairly certain that the Bill would not be passed, in which case a Cabinet crisis would have been inevitable. To avoid this the Chamber adopted almost unanimously a motion introduced by Dr. Aalberse, leader of the Roman Catholics, proposing the adjournment of further debates on the Bill until after the general discussions on the 1933 Budget. In this way further deliberation between the Chamber and the Government was made possible, though the Minister for Finance, Jhr. de Geer, declared that it would prove impossible to find a majority in favour of any other means of increasing the revenue, such as a new or increased tax on tobacco or a tax on coupons, as suggested by Dr. Colyn. In order to secure agreement between the Government and the Chamber, however, Jhr. de Geer introduced a change in his proposal, restricting the increase of the import duties to those articles which are not produced in the country and thus eliminating all idea of protection. This modification rendered the increase permissible under all circumstances, even after ratification of the Ouchy Convention. As 21 millions would have been obtained from the original surtax while the increase in the tariffs would now produce only 10·5 millions, the Government proposed to levy an extra 20 per cent. in the sugar excise, the import duties on sacchariferous goods being proportionally increased. The Chamber agreed to these new proposals, and thus a serious Ministerial crisis was averted.

SWITZERLAND.

The dispute between Switzerland and France before The Hague International Court of Arbitration regarding the free zones of Upper Savoy and the Gex (*i.e.*, the free zones of Geneva) was at last terminated on April 30. The French contention was that Article 435 of the Treaty of Versailles abolished the free zones, the Swiss that it did not. The Hague Court in its decision fully upheld the Swiss view that Article 435 of the Treaty neither abolished the zones nor contemplated their abolition. France therefore had no right to levy Customs dues at the political frontier, as she had been doing since 1923. Since, however, the treaties of 1815, which created the zones, confer on France full sovereignty in other respects—as The Hague Court expressly recognised—France has the right to levy fiscal dues at the political frontier. Thus, though the legal dispute is settled, the prospects of an agreement between France and Switzerland, which the judgment of the Court calls on them to make, have become more remote, as fiscal dues may be levied in such a way as to frustrate the purpose of the zones, which is to leave to Geneva its natural market. The French Ambassador in Berne, on September 5, declared in the name of his Government that it was ready to obey the judgment of The Hague Court, but up to the end of the year, in spite of repeated invitations from the Swiss Government, no negotiations had been opened for regulating the zones question in accordance with the judgment of the Court, and France continued to levy Customs dues at the political frontier.

The temporary tension between France and Italy was followed in Switzerland with some anxiety. As the frontier between France and Italy is short and naturally strong, besides being fortified by art, Switzerland is threatened with the fate which befell Belgium in 1914 for similar reasons, especially as the Swiss Alpine passes lead straight to the economic heart of Italy—Milan and the Po valley. Switzerland, therefore, spares no effort to maintain its army in fit condition for defending the country, and preventing any attempt of a foreign army to march through. Heavy offensive weapons, however, are not kept by her, nor has she any bombing aeroplanes or long-range artillery. Parliament, however, in the face of Social Democratic opposition, voted a sum for the provision of gas masks.

At the Disarmament Conference, Switzerland, through its chief delegate, the Foreign Minister, M. Motta (who in 1932 was Federal President), actively supported the idea of qualitative disarmament. On account of her fixed policy of neutrality, Switzerland could be no party to a further extension of the " security system," nor had she any sympathy for the idea of a League of Nations army.

Official relations with Italy were throughout friendly. Among the public, however, there was some excitement when—not for the first time—it was discovered in the course of the year that the Italian police were maintaining spies in Switzerland, especially in the border canton of Ticino, in order to keep watch on the anti-Fascists who escaped from Italy. These spies also acted in some cases as *agents provocateurs*. Some were arrested, but the Federal Court ordered their release, as they were not liable to punishment either under the law of Ticino or that of the Federation. The Bundesrat finally expelled them by administrative order. The events in Ticino brought home to many people the need for making good the lack of a proper criminal code (a Federal criminal code has been in preparation for years, but is not yet in force), and for the cantons to maintain a better police force in order to combat the activity of spies, and themselves to keep watch on unruly foreign elements.

Taking advantage of the economic crisis, the Third International developed an activity in Switzerland which led to some highly regrettable incidents. On January 23, some Communists in Zurich, in order to liberate two soldiers—Communists—who had been placed under arrest, attacked the barracks, the police of the city being unable to stay their approach. The cantonal police, which occupied the (cantonal) barracks, found itself compelled to fire on the assailants, with the result that four persons were wounded. The disorders of November 9 in Geneva, in which thirteen persons were killed and seventy wounded, attracted the attention of the whole world, and in some places excited great indignation. They arose out of the quarrel between the " Union

Nationale," a middle-class party of Fascist leanings, and the Socialists and Communists. Instigated by a Socialist leader of extreme views named Nicole, a crowd tried to break up a meeting of the Union Nationale. It occupied the whole street, and Nicole openly preached revolution. In view of the weakness of its police force, the Geneva Government made a request for troops. Accordingly, a school of recruits just commencing training was transported from Lausanne to Geneva, and was now called on to clear the streets. It is established beyond question that the soldiers were first attacked by the crowd, which was provided with pepper, and were so hard pressed that they had to make use of their rifles. On November 11 the trade unions of the canton of Geneva, by 87 votes to 56, with 95 abstentions, declared a general strike on the next day, a Saturday. The Bundesrat declared Federal intervention in the canton of Geneva. A Wallis battalion was sent to Geneva, and Geneva itself called four battalions to the colours. The call for a general strike was only partially responded to. Fearing a spread of the disturbances, the Government of the canton Vaud had mobilised three squadrons of cavalry, and the Governing Council of the canton of Berne had issued an order forbidding all meetings and demonstrations, and stationed troops on the look-out. On the 13th a bomb exploded at the Rathaus in Lausanne, wounding five men. Otherwise order was not further disturbed. Protest demonstrations were arranged by the Social Democrats and Communists in several towns, but they were sparsely attended and passed off quietly, as a large section of the Socialists themselves did not approve of Nicole's proceedings. He himself had been arrested on the night of the 10th, but he was subsequently released on account of ill-health. His trial was to take place in 1933. Nicole's position as a Member of the National Council did not save him from arrest, as in Switzerland Parliamentary immunity holds good only while Parliament is sitting.

The half-canton Basel-Land celebrated, on June 19, the hundredth anniversary of its independence, having separated itself from Basel-City during the democratic movement of 1832. There is, however, a strong movement for reuniting the two halves, chiefly on economic grounds. A plebiscite has been initiated.

A reduction of wages in trade and industry, for the purpose of maintaining Switzerland's competitive power, took place during the year almost without a struggle. The attempt of the Federal Council, however, to reduce the salaries of the Federal officials (especially those belonging to the post and telegraph services, and the railways) led to violent disputes. The National Council finally decided on a reduction of $7\frac{1}{2}$ per cent., with a bonus of 30 francs for each child after the third. A movement is on foot for submitting this law to a referendum.

A plebiscite for a new tax is probably unique. It is a fact, however, that at the end of the year signatures were collected for a plebiscite having for its object the introduction of a direct Federal tax. As things are, the Federal Government can impose only indirect taxes and Customs duties, direct taxes being left to the cantons. The proposed tax was to be a crisis tax, for the purpose of raising means for mitigating the crisis. The idea of it comes from the Socialists and Radicals. Incomes below 7,000 francs (for married people 8,000, with 400 francs for each child) are to be free from the tax. A sufficient number of signatures had been collected by the end of the year, so that next year the people will decide on the crisis tax.

The economic crisis was felt more severely in 1932 than in 1931. At the end of December, 1932, there were 81,887 fully unemployed (compared with 50,570 at the corresponding period in 1931 and 23,045 in 1930) and about 20,000 partly unemployed. The trade balance, which is normally adverse to the extent of 500 million francs, showed for 1932 a deficit of 960 millions (in 1931 904 millions). In virtue of the extraordinary powers conferred on it at the end of 1931 for regulating the economic life of Switzerland, the Federal Council was able, chiefly by means of import quotas, to curtail imports by about half a milliard, as compared with the previous year. But exports also fell by about half a milliard. The balance of payments, which used to be highly favourable (from the interest of money loaned abroad and the tourist traffic), was by some reckoned to be barely favourable, by others strongly adverse. The State railways, in consequence of decline in traffic and competition of motor vehicles, showed a deficit of 50 million francs. The agricultural situation, especially with the smallholders, was serious. (On July 7 the Federal Parliament voted the establishment of a Federal loan fund, and in various cantons such funds were opened for small farmers.) The watchmaking, textile, and lace industries were the worst sufferers. Efforts were made to assist those belonging to the trades most hardly hit by teaching the unemployed new trades and starting new industries. In addition, emergency works were carried out by cantons and municipalities. The hotel keepers had a bad summer, but the winter season made some amends.

Against all this is to be set the fact that the consumption of coal, electricity, gas, and petrol, that is to say, the chief sources of power, sank little if at all below that of 1931 (3 per cent. at most) ; also that the capital invested in life insurance policies and savings banks increased considerably in 1932 also. The Swiss people has to-day about 10 milliards of francs invested in life insurance policies and savings banks (for a population of somewhat more than four million). The standard of living of the masses, compared with that of the neighbouring peoples, is still very high. The Swiss franc remained stable, and the notes in circulation were covered to the extent of 100 per cent.

SPAIN.

The year 1932 was one of unrest unparalleled in Spain since the times of the First Republic. It began under the shadow of the bloody riot at Castilblanco in Extremadura, where the mob had risen on New Year's Eve and put to death the small garrison of Civil Guard. The perpetration of a similar outrage five days later at Arnedo, in the upper Ebro valley, and the indignation aroused among the parties of the Left by its stern suppression showed how openly the principle of authority was flouted, even in the Cortes. That repression led to the outbreak of revolutionary strikes all over the country, which culminated in the rising of Communists and Anarcho-Syndicalists on January 20 in Catalonia. For several days the mining district of Llobregat was in the hands of the rebels, but the rebellion petered out upon the arrival of columns of troops rapidly concentrated from Barcelona, Lerida, and Saragossa, and under the wide powers granted by the Chamber, the ringleaders, to the number of 110, were deported on February 10 to Rio de Oro.

With the prestige gained by this success the Government now adopted a more radical policy towards the Church and the Right. The decree dissolving the Society of Jesus in Spain was signed on January 23, and by the end of February all the property of the Jesuits, including a number of schools and colleges, was confiscated. In some quarters it was alleged that in order to facilitate the enforcement of these and other sectarian measures, public opinion was effectively muzzled by the arbitrary suppression of the great Catholic newspaper *El Debate* from January 19 to March 26, and the wholesale prohibition of public meetings organised by the parties of the Right.

By its anti-clerical policy the Government sought to placate the extreme Left and divert attention from the series of ugly strikes that in reprisal for the deportations had been organised at Barcelona, Granada, Melilla, Valencia, Saragossa, Huelva, Murcia, and Madrid, and that threatened for a time to establish lawlessness. Indeed, the mob set fire to churches, shot at the few Holy Week processions that were held, or broke up by force such Traditionalist meetings as the authorities could not well forbid. But May Day was seized upon by Communists and Anarcho-Syndicalists alike to make a fresh bid for the hegemony of Labour, and in most large towns, except Madrid—the stronghold of organised Socialism—the day was marked by grave social disturbances. On May 19 the discovery of stores of bombs at Seville, Madrid, and Manresa put the authorities on the track of a revolutionary plot that was planned for the end of the month, but was revealed in time to prevent any but abortive risings in a number of cities.

More difficult than in the towns, however, was the maintenance of even a semblance of law and order in the open country;
there the brunt of the task fell upon the sorely tried Civil Guard.
In the towns Labour was organised, mostly socialistically, and
shared political responsibility, whereas the wretched agricultural
labourer had fallen a prey to Communism. The revolutionary
seed sown in former years now bore bitter fruit. The Socialists,
let alone the traditionally Republican Radicals, were regarded by
the masses as traitors, and a wave of anarchy swept over the
countryside from Andalusia through Extremadura and New Castile
to Old Castile and as far as Galicia and Catalonia.

In view of the chaotic condition of the country it is not
surprising that the saner elements among the Republicans, such
as Melquiades Alvarez, Ortega Gasset and Unamuno, should have
expressed dissatisfaction with the Government and even with
the regime. Educated opinion now swung sharply over to the
Right. In the elections held on June 1 in Madrid, and later
in the month in the provinces, for the renewal of the Governing
Committees of the semi-official Corporations of Doctors and
Lawyers, the Monarchists swept all before them; and June 4,
the festivity of the Sacred Heart, was made the occasion of
a striking display of Catholic sentiment.

General discontent was fanned by the unpopularity of two
measures which the Government brought before Parliament—
the so-called Agrarian Reform and the Statute of Catalan Autonomy. These proposals formed the main planks of the Government's programme, and for two months political attention was
concentrated on them, particularly on the Catalan question.
Opposition to the latter, led in the Cortes by Royo Villanova,
Miguel Maura, Melquiades Alvarez, and Sanchez Roman, grew in
strength and volume and was re-echoed in mass meetings throughout the country and reflected in incidents in the Army. At last
Lerroux, the Leader of the Radical Party, nominally in opposition,
in his speeches on July 10 and 11 at Saragossa, openly attacked
the Government as being completely estranged from the country
and called upon the Socialist Ministers to resign. This was the
beginning of the split between the Radicals and Socialists, and
the Government was expected to fall. The Socialists, however,
on July 14, threatened to make a fresh revolution in the event
of any change of policy and, after a further violent speech by
Lerroux in the Chamber on July 19, the Radicals abandoned
their official opposition fearful lest they should bring down the
Republic with the fall of the Government. The latter were now
anxious for a compromise, as they recognised the unpopularity
of the Statute, which was strikingly demonstrated at the monster
meeting of protest held on July 27 in the bull-ring at Madrid.
But compromise was impossible in view of the opposition in
Parliament and the temper of the nation. Nor was the outlook

more hopeful for Agrarian Reform, and by the first week in August
things had come to a deadlock.

Out of this dilemma the Government and the regime were
delivered by the rising of August 10. The confiscatory measures
of the Agrarian Reform had driven the aristocracy to desperation ;
the Socialists, in addition to arousing the bitter hatred of the
Radicals, had fallen foul of the Army by systematic attacks on
the Corps of Officers ; all this added fuel to the flame of indignation kindled by the proposed dismemberment of the country.
Thus, barred from all legal means of protest, the hotheads among
the Conservatives of Madrid in league with the Radicals, particularly in Seville, attempted a *coup d'état* with the idea of
setting up a Dictatorship. The Government had been warned,
however, and the rising, which broke out in the early hours of
August 10, was easily suppressed. On the same day General
Sanjurjo, backed by the garrison and population, seized the
Government of Seville, only to abandon it twenty-four hours later
on finding himself unsupported in the rest of the country and
left alone to face the columns hurried south by the Government
of Madrid. The movement at once collapsed, and General
Sanjurjo was captured near Huelva and taken to Madrid, where
he was tried on August 24, and though condemned to death
was reprieved and sent to the convict prison at Dueso.

The ignominious failure of this rash attempt left the Government master of the situation. Republican fervour was re-
awakened and Señor Azaña, supported by a vote of confidence
in Parliament, now set about the annihilation of his enemies.
Over a hundred newspapers in Madrid and the provinces were
suspended and seized ; hundreds of persons were thrown into
prison without trial, where they remained for many months, and
138 suspected of participation in the rebellion were deported to
Rio de Oro ; the estates of those implicated in the plot and of
the Grandees were confiscated in favour of Agrarian Reform ; and
the Army, the Bench, and the Civil and Diplomatic Services were
ruthlessly purged of all elements considered hostile to the regime.

In the Cortes everything was now plain sailing. The Bill
of Agrarian Reform and the Catalan Statute were passed on
September 9 and the latter signed at San Sebastian in honour
of the famous Pact on September 15 by the President of the
Republic ; it was handed over by Señor Azaña to the Catalan
authorities in Barcelona amidst great enthusiasm on September 25.

The elections held on November 20 for the first Catalan
Parliament, which was opened on December 5, gave an overwhelming majority for the Catalan Left, which obtained 67 out
of the 85 seats, and Señor Maciá was confirmed as President
of the Generalitat. On September 3 the International Congress
for Telegraphs and Wireless Telegraphy met at Madrid and came
to important decisions during its sessions.

On December 7 the Parliamentary Tribunal appointed to try the question of responsibility for the *coup d'état* of September 13, 1933, and for the ensuing Dictatorship, delivered its verdicts, condemning the Generals and civilian Ministers to varying terms of banishment with loss of civil rights.

On December 15 a Bill introducing income tax into Spain was passed, and on December 19 the Budget for 1933 was approved, having been balanced with the help of the 500,000,000 pesetas' worth of Treasury Bonds issued on April 1.

A bumper harvest went a long way to restore the economic situation so rudely shaken by the widespread lawlessness, but there was a recrudescence of strikes and anarchy towards the end of the year.

PORTUGAL.

Like other countries Portugal severely felt the world crisis in all branches of her internal and international economy during 1932. Nevertheless, the careful administration of her finances by the Finance Minister, Dr. Oliveria Salazar, enabled the country satisfactorily to weather the storm. The Budget for four consecutive years showed a considerable surplus, and at the end of the year there was a credit balance of considerably more than 5 million pounds in foreign banks. In his report on the 1931-32 Budget the Minister expressed the certainty that, should nothing unforeseen happen, the floating debt would completely disappear.

The Dictatorship continued during the year, but it was generally felt that the sooner it was ended and the country governed on constitutional lines the better. The projected New Constitution was published on May 28, 1932, and the country will have an opportunity of voting on it by plebiscite on March 26, 1933. It introduces an entirely new system of voting ; the voting unit, instead of being the individual, becomes the head of the family, man or woman. The heads of families elect the parish councils, these in turn elect the municipal councils, and the municipal councils the county councils. The National Assembly is elected by the parish, municipal, and county councils jointly.

Portugal's decision to follow Great Britain and abandon the gold standard resulted in British imports increasing. Furthermore, the whole of Portugal's new naval programme was placed with British firms, at a cost including armaments of over 3 million pounds.

The stability of the Exchange and the fact that the English pound has the same purchasing power as its Portuguese equivalent induced many British seekers after health and sunshine to visit Portugal, and the hotels of Mont Estoril—" the Costa do Sol "

or Sunny Coast—have never been so full as during the autumn
and winter months of 1932.

Politically the year was uneventful.   On June 20 the Ministry
resigned, and was succeeded by another on July 5, consisting
almost entirely of civilians with the Minister of Finance also
holding the portfolio of Prime Minister.   An event which
recalled political memories was the funeral, on August 2, of
ex-King Manuel, whose body was brought from England by
H.M.S. *Concord.*   The procession passed through the streets
of Lisbon to the Church of St. Vicente de Fora between respectful
and sympathetic crowds, and thence to the Pantheon of the
Braganzas.

On December 6 a general amnesty was granted to all political
prisoners with the exception of fifty of the most prominent and
active enemies of the Dictatorship, including Dr. Bernardino
Machado who has twice been President of the Republic.

During the summer the Minister of the Colonies, Dr. Armindo
Monteira, made a prolonged tour of all the Portuguese possessions
in Africa.

By decree, the term of office of General Carmona as President
of the Republic was extended for a further period of two years,
to expire in 1935.

DENMARK.

Denmark had two elections in the course of 1932, an ordinary
election in September of one-half of the members of the Upper
House (Landsting), and an extraordinary election (in November)
of the whole of the Lower House (Folketing).   These elections
did not bring about any change of Government.   The Stauning
Cabinet was maintained in office by a coalition of the Social
Democrats and Radical Left.   It continued also to command
a majority in the Lower House only (76 against 73), its supporters
being in a minority in the Upper House (34 against 41).   A
further result of the election was that the Government Coalition
in each House lost a seat, and that there was a certain gain for the
smallest parties, two Communists, for instance, being elected to
the Lower House for the first time.

Whereas for some years Denmark had the satisfaction of
showing a surplus on her State finances, and was even able to close
the one terminating on March 31, 1932, with a modest balance on
the right side, a considerable deficit was clearly foreshadowed for
the year 1932-33, and before the end of 1932 measures were already
proposed to cover it.   The number of unemployed at the end of
1932 reached a total of 180,000, or about 40 per cent. of all
organised workers—mostly owing to the fact that the falling
purchasing power of those engaged in agriculture was paralysing
industry more and more.   The crisis, in fact, weighed most heavily

upon the country's main occupation, farming, which, owing to the low prices obtainable for its products, had to operate at a loss to such an extent that Government measures were necessary to lend assistance to those most seriously hit.

The regulative measures taken to consolidate the krone when, in September, 1931, on account of her intimate association with the British market, Denmark found herself compelled to let her currency follow sterling away from gold, were crystallised in an Act of Parliament dated January 30, the main provisions of which were that all foreign exchange acquired by the sale of Danish commodities abroad was to be recalled and surrendered to the National Bank on terms fixed by the Bank, and that commodities from abroad were only to be imported on the production of certificates from the National Bank to the effect that there was nothing in the exchange position to prevent it. This Act did not operate without friction. It was passed for only short periods at a time, and therefore had to be renewed continually, with more or less important amendments ; one of the most far-reaching was introduced on August 27, when the obligation to surrender foreign currency at a fixed rate was rescinded, and at the same time a free list was issued, comprising about one-third of the country's normal imports, which for the future could be cleared without an exchange certificate. After the Folketing election, it was possible to pass an Act for the period of the whole of 1933 on very similar lines, the regulated commodities being specified in an annexe to the Act, and it is laid down that every importer has the right to import at least 45 per cent. of what he imported in 1931.

Side by side with these measures for stabilising the exchange, by means of which the krone was kept on a level with sterling throughout the year, corresponding efforts were made, in face of the steady decline of foreign trade, to maintain proportionately the same balance between imports and exports in relation to the various countries as prevailed in more normal times, but in such a manner that those countries which put least hindrances in the way of Danish export commodities should be given a correspondingly greater share in Denmark's imports.

In this connexion, mention should be made of the great exhibition of British goods which was held in Copenhagen in September and October under the patronage of the Prince of Wales and the Crown Prince of Denmark. By means of this exhibition Denmark desired to demonstrate her willingness to accede to England's wish that as far as possible the balance of trade between the two countries should be changed in England's favour, and, at a time when all countries were exclusively occupied in finding means of keeping foreign goods out, Denmark invited British manufacturers and merchants to try by means of this exhibition to expand their sales in Denmark. The exhibition attained its object to the satisfaction of most exhibitors.

The Oslo Convention, which was signed on February 7, 1932, bore definite fruit in the field of Denmark's secondary trade connexions, especially in her relations with Sweden and Belgium.

Outside of trade relations, the matter which in the field of foreign affairs occupied the mind of the nation most was the Danish-Norwegian dispute regarding certain parts of the east coast of Greenland. Whilst the process commenced by Denmark at The Hague International Court in consequence of Norway's occupation of the coast from lat. 71° 30′ to 75° 40′ N. in 1931 was still *sub judice*, Norway proceeded to a similar " occupation " in July, 1932, this time of a stretch more to the south (lat. 60° 30′ to 63° 40′ N.). This new Norwegian action resulted in both parties commencing a new process, as Norway, in accordance with the statutes and rules of procedure of the Court, requested the Court to make a pronouncement as quickly as possible to enable temporary protective measures to be taken to prevent the Danish Government from undertaking " any kind of forcible action against Norwegian subjects " in the new area of occupation. By its award on August 3, the Court dismissed the Norwegian request, but reserved its statutory right to examine later whether the circumstances should make protective measures necessary. After a voluminous exchange of pleadings in the first action, the verbal process was commenced in November. The case has been followed with keen attention by the public in both countries, and it is not to be denied that the unavoidable bitterness aroused by the dispute has been aggravated to some degree. Nevertheless, both parties have repeated the solemn promise that whatever decision the Court may arrive at will be loyally accepted.

Denmark's relations with her neighbour on the south were to a certain degree affected by conditions in North Schleswig during the year. The unrest that agitated Germany during the year spread to the German minority at Denmark's southern border. Whereas in the year before there had been a pronounced display of peaceable manifestations in the relations between the two peoples in the border region, in 1932 a sharper and more provocative tone on the German side was distinctly perceptible. The German agitation endeavoured to take advantage of the difficulties caused by the world crisis, difficulties which were particularly marked in places where the transfer of the land to the new sovereignty was still causing friction. This agitation culminated in a demand for North Schleswig's economic attachment to Germany by moving the Customs border northwards to the old national frontier along the river Kongeaa. This agitation gave rise to one or two regrettable incidents, but the General Election in November showed that while the German minority had maintained its total of votes, it had not increased them in proportion to the growth of the population and the higher total number of votes polled.

R

SWEDEN.

As a result of the decline in world trade and the heavy fall in the prices of agricultural products, unemployment and agricultural questions practically dominated political life during 1932. The Social Democratic Party put forward increased demands for measures of State help, and the needs of agriculture led to a more urgent call for protective tariffs from the parties of the Right. On grounds of economy the demands for increased outlay on social works were opposed by the parties of the Right, while the protectionist efforts of the latter were naturally opposed by the parties of the Left. The Ekman administration, which came into power in June, 1930, and which was in a marked degree a minority administration, constituted entirely from the People's Party, maintained itself in power by securing support alternately from the two principal parties, that of the Right and that of the Social Democrats—of the former, in defending its Budget against the heavy demands for social purposes made by the Social Democrats, and of the latter, in withstanding the special proposals of the Right.

For the relief of unemployment the Government had before the meeting of the Riksdag begun to adopt exceptional measures and had set aside for them a sum of 18,000,000 kronor taken from various reserve funds. In its Budget proposals it provided for a further sum of 20,000,000 kronor for the same purpose, i.e., twice as much as in the previous year, while other items of expenditure for combating unemployment were increased. Owing to the continued increase in unemployment, the Government was obliged later in the session of the Riksdag to propose substantial increases in the grants for these purposes, and these were agreed to.

Although the Social Democrats gave their approval to the Budget in other respects, they were not satisfied with these measures, and submitted instead a programme estimated to cost about 100,000,000 kronor for the relief of unemployment and of the agricultural crisis. This, however, was rejected, and the Government's own proposals were carried with the support of the parties of the Right. In regard to certain other social questions, however, the Government had to give way to a great extent to the wishes of the Riksdag for a substantial increase in the proposed outlays, although the equilibrium of the Budget was thereby threatened.

Included in the Social Democratic programme was the proposal, first put forward long before, for compulsory insurance against unemployment. While not objecting in principle to such a scheme, the Government opposed its immediate introduction on the ground of the Budget difficulties this year. In respect to the other great question which hitherto had divided parties, that of grants in support of agriculture, a compromise was arrived at which in great degree accorded with the Government's own policy.

The Government's industrial programme as set forth in the Speech from the Throne was on the whole the same as in the preceding year. Without definitely renouncing a tariff policy, the Government endeavoured to avoid as long as possible having recourse to it. It wished instead to support home industries by means of a system the chief features of which would be a minimum price and an import monopoly. Thus in order to further and support the cultivation of sugar, the Government proposed that the Swedish sugar manufactories should be granted an import monopoly, while minimum prices should be fixed for raw sugar and sugar-beet.

There were no proposals for purely protective tariffs in the Government's programme. Tariffs were, indeed, imposed on a number of luxury articles, but as these were of a kind not manufactured to any extent at home, the purpose of the taxes was only to provide an additional source of revenue to help to balance the Budget, and might be regarded therefore as purely revenue tariffs.

The Government's industrial policy met with sharp criticism from the side of the Right both in the Riksdag and in the Press. This criticism was of a strongly protectionist colouring, and was based on the growing excess of imports over exports, and the trade restrictions enforced by other countries. The Government was reproached for not having summoned an extraordinary session of the Riksdag in the autumn of 1931 for the introduction of the new tariffs now proposed, which were approved even by the Social Democrats, who recognised their necessity on economic grounds. The Social Democrats raised objections to the proposed increase in the tax on coffee, but the Government carried it through with the help of the other parties.

The Party of the Right demanded a protective tariff in place of the Government's proposals with regard to sugar, and the Social Democrats also preferred certain minor increases in tariffs to regulation of prices, considering that the minimum price arrangement was likely to benefit the sugar industry unduly. To save the industry from losing State support altogether, the Right voted in favour of the Government's proposals, which were thus carried without any difficulty.

As the session of the Riksdag proceeded, the demands for protective taxes grew in strength, and even within the ranks of the Ministerial Party, especially among the agriculturists, there was a gradual falling away from their original Free Trade convictions as a result of the agricultural crisis. The protective measures advocated, however, especially those emanating from the Right, were rejected by the Riksdag with a handful of exceptions, including taxes on eggs and potatoes, and the system of

compulsory milling of home-grown grain and of price regulation
introduced for the protection of grain cultivation was maintained.
The debates on these questions of tariffs showed that both the
Ministry itself and the Ministerial Party were divided into two
camps, for tariffs and against.

Other measures were also passed for the support of agricultural
industries. Thus the Government decided to establish a fund
of 15,000,000 kronor from which farmers could obtain loans free
of interest ; and when the Right demanded an import duty on milk
and an additional tax on butter, it submitted a proposal the essence
of which was that certain private dairy combines should levy
a special milk fee on all the country's dairies, for use in regulating
prices in the interests of those dairies, which produce butter for
export. These proposals of the Government were passed by the
Riksdag in the teeth of strong opposition from the Social Democrats, whose chief objection was against private concerns being
given the right to collect fees which bore a strong resemblance
to taxes. The Right, knowing that there was no prospect of
carrying through their own tariff proposals, supported the
Government's measure, which was of course, backed also by the
Farmers' Party.

These measures involved considerably increased grants from the
Treasury. There were differences of opinion among the parties
as to the way in which the money needed should be raised, but
the Government's proposal for increasing certain taxes on articles
of consumption (spirits, tobacco, motor cars), reducing the bonus
(the so-called *dyrtidstillägg ;* literally " expensive times supplement ") given to Government employés, and imposing an extra
income and property tax on persons with annual incomes of more
than 6,000 kronor was agreed to by the Riksdag.

The Minister of Finance when bringing forward the Budget
for the current year had reckoned on a deficit, as also in the Budget
to follow. These fears were realised, and in April he announced
that the Budget for the year would show a deficit of from 20 to 25
million kronor and that the Budget to follow would show a
deficit of from 15 to 20 million.

These Budget difficulties were certainly due in part to the
increased outlays which the Riksdag had sanctioned—to a certain
degree against the wishes of the Government—but they were
attributable mainly to the decrease in revenue due primarily to
the economic crisis. The effects of the crisis were intensified to
some extent by the notorious Kreuger " crash," following upon
Kreuger's suicide in March, 1932. This crash, however, was not
accompanied by anything like the calamitous consequences for
Swedish industry and State finance which at one time had been
feared.

The first step taken by the Government on hearing of Kreuger's
death was to bring in a Bill for a moratorium to relieve those

businesses whose position was threatened as the result of their relations with the Kreuger concerns. This Bill was passed by the Riksdag without opposition. Another Government measure put through with equal expedition and practically unanimously, was the one for a State loan of more than 200 million kronor to the Skandinaviska Kreditaktiebolag, one of the great commercial banks, which was involved in Kreuger's concerns to the extent of 158 million kronor. The Riksbank had lent this commercial bank large sums—according to the opinion of many without adequate security—and the Party of the Right criticised its credit policy severely. The Social Democrats, however, confined themselves to complaints regarding the means available for public control of the banks.

The immediate consequence of all this was that the question of the *décharge* of the Riksbank administration acquired a political character which had not previously marked it. Through the Riksbank's proceedings the State's credit policy assumed a new character and significance which it had not hitherto possessed. It turned out, however, that the Riksbank had acted on an understanding with the Government, which therefore shared the responsibility with it, actually if not formally. Accordingly the Premier declared himself in complete accord with the Riksbank authorities.

The action of the Riksbank directors was therefore sanctioned, but the Government's position was scarcely strengthened by this affair. The Government's currency policy and its measures in connexion with Sweden's departure from the gold standard also called forth criticism from the parties both of the Right and of the Left. Nevertheless, it may be said on the whole that all parties in general supported the Government loyally in its energetic efforts to solve the exceptionally difficult economic and financial problems which it had to face, not least that which resulted from the Kreuger crash.

The Government's position in fact had never been threatened, and evidently none of the chief parties harboured any intention of upsetting it. This was made clear in the Budget debate, and again in the customary so-called " Discharge " debate on the report made on the Protocol of the Cabinet by the Constitution Committee. Some change in the feeling of the Social Democrats towards the Government was noticeable, however, during the session. Their original attitude of benevolence changed to one of a certain coolness towards the close, especially owing to the Government's diminished opposition to the demand for tariffs, and the leading organs of the Social Democratic Party began to talk of the Government's " leaning to the Right." In spite of all this, however, the Government's position was quite strong at the close of the session.

The elections to the Second Chamber were now pending,

and it was expected that the parties which represented the classes hardest hit by the crisis, namely, the Social Democrats and the Farmers' Party, would benefit, especially as unemployment continued to increase despite the State's relief measures, while the measures for the support of agriculture also had brought about no immediate improvement. Suddenly, however, a month before the elections, something occurred which quite unexpectedly altered the whole outlook.

In the course of the inquiry into the irregularities in the Kreuger affair which were brought to light, it was discovered that the People's Party had received contributions from Mr. Kreuger. These had been made to the Premier himself, the leader of the Party, and his attempt to keep secret the latest of these contributions, which had been made in February, 1932, resulted in his being compelled to resign. The Ministerial crisis, however, did not spread further than this, and the Government remained in office under the leadership of the Minister of Finance, Mr. Hamrin, on the understanding that it would resign as soon as the election had taken place.

There could be no doubt that this incident was in some measure responsible for the defeat of the People's Party in the elections (held in September), in which their strength was diminished by nearly a third. The Farmers' Party, on the other hand, achieved the success which was expected, and the Social Democrats profited likewise. The successes of these two parties were made primarily at the expense of the Party of the Right, which absolutely, if not relatively, suffered the greatest losses. Their losses were about equivalent to the Social Democrat's gains.

The elections to the First Chamber, which took place soon after, and in which by reason of their indirect character the views of an earlier electorate were reflected, also resulted in gains for the Social Democrats and losses for the People's Party.

The result of the voting constituted in great degree a return to the situation before the election of 1928. The Social Democrats had their revenge for the victory of the Right on that occasion. The difference lay, however, in the fact that the Farmers' Party had now made an important advance, mainly at the cost of the People's Party. Herein was to be observed the effect in the political sphere of the agricultural crisis.

When the Hamrin Ministry retired, as soon as the election results were made known, it was expected that the Farmers' Party would seek to establish a majority Government in co-operation with the other bourgeois parties. After some negotiations between them, however, the task of forming a Government was entrusted by the King to Mr. P. A. Hansson, the Leader of the Social Democrats, who had his Ministry completed by September 24. This included the former Premier, Mr. Rickard Sandler, as Foreign Minister, and the former Foreign Minister,

Mr. Östen Undén, as Minister without portfolio. The Government was given an exceptionally favourable reception by the Press, and it was generally acknowledged that it appeared well fitted to cope with the heavy tasks confronting it. It soon showed its independence of the Communists by rejecting their demand for an amnesty for those prisoners who were sentenced for their share in the strike disturbances in Ådalen in 1931. It also proved that its election programme was not merely a bait for votes by putting this same programme forward as its Ministerial policy as soon as it was appointed.

In the field of foreign affairs the People's Party Government, like the Social Democratic Government, maintained the old tradition of Sweden by doing all in its power to promote peace and reconciliation through the League of Nations.

The so-called Oslo Convention for closer economic co-operation opened on February 7, after being ratified by Holland, the last of all the signatories. A series of conferences between representatives of the Governments of the States forming the Convention, took place during the year with a view to keeping each other informed as to what was happening in respect of trade policy, and officials were specially appointed by their respective Foreign Offices to maintain contact between the affiliated States. In December the delegates of the Oslo Powers met at The Hague to discuss the question of a common representation at the forthcoming World Economic Conference, and their deliberations on this subject are to be continued at Stockholm during the spring of 1933, shortly before the World Conference opens.

During the last months of the year important commercial treaty negotiations took place with Germany and with England. A number of measures taken by Germany had proved harmful to Swedish exports to that country, and discussions regarding them had been entered into on several occasions earlier in the year. In September an agreement was arrived at providing certain facilities for the exchange of goods in respect to currency. The Swedish-German commercial treaty of 1926 having been denounced by Germany as the result of pressure from German agriculturists, negotiations were entered into at Stockholm for a new treaty. Simultaneously negotiations of the same kind were entered into with England, which, after the Ottawa Conference had invited the Scandinavian States to take part in such deliberations. No result had been reached by the close of the year.

The growing importance of international understandings in respect to commerce found recognition in January in the appointment of a special Governmental Commission to study such matters, the Government securing authority from the Riksdag, when the Riksdag is not sitting, to impose temporary tariffs. The Government declared definitely that this decision did not mean any departure from Sweden's previous trade policy, but was intended only to provide a weapon of defence in any tariff war.

The difficulties resulting from the world depression which confronted Sweden's exports were considerable, and the attempt to modify them by the depreciation of the Swedish currency along with the departure from the gold currency was soon countered by new trade restrictions on the part of other countries, such as, for instance, additional taxes on goods from countries with weak currencies, new currency restrictions, etc. There was at no time, however, any State control over dealings in currency in Sweden. Conditions steadily worsened for Sweden's principal exports, timber and iron. Towards the close of the year the export market for the saw-mill trade improved somewhat. Agriculture and shipping also suffered badly from the effects of the depression, but home industries were less affected. The stone industry was specially hard hit. As regards agriculture, good harvests are to be recorded.

Unemployment was most widespread in the export industry. The percentage of unemployed was considerably higher at the end of 1932 than at the end of 1931. There were no serious industrial disputes. –

Owing to the deterioration of the economic situation, the apprehensions as to the State's finances which had been expressed in the Riksdag were realised. The current Budget (1932-33) showed a deficit reckoned at 140 millions at the close of 1932, a serious figure if we take into consideration the fact that the Budget total for the year, ratified by the Riksdag, amounts to 896,086,600 kronor.

NORWAY.

During the first months of the year the serious illness of the Premier, Mr. P. V. Kolstad, cast a shadow over the political life of Norway and caused grave anxiety. Mr. Kolstad's sudden removal from political activity was deeply regretted not only by his own party, but also by the Opposition, and it was earnestly hoped that he might soon recover. The illness, however, proved fatal. The Premier's death on March 5 was felt as a national loss, all parties and classes recognising his sterling qualities as a politician and a man.

The Minister of Foreign Affairs, Mr. Braadland, acted as Premier during Mr. Kolstad's illness. A new Farmers' Government was formed by the Parliamentary leader of the Party, Mr. J. Hundseid. All the members of the Kolstad Government remained in office with the exception of the Minister of Commerce, Mr. Per Larssen, who was replaced by Mr. Kirkeby Garstad, one of the leading farmer members of the Storting. The Minister of

Agriculture, Mr. Sundby, was appointed Minister of Finance, the Premier taking charge of the Ministry of Agriculture. The new Premier was born in 1883 and, like his predecessor, is a farmer and a prominent agricultural expert, the headmaster since 1915 of an Agricultural School in Talemark. Having shown his ability in municipal affairs, he was elected member of the Storting in 1925, and soon came to be recognised as the coming man of the Farmers' Party. He was elected Chairman of the National Executive of the party in 1929 and Parliamentary leader in January, 1931.

The new Premier made his statement of policy in the Storting on the day of the formation of the Government. He declared that the policy of the new Government was identical with that of the Kolstad administration. The Government intended to pay special attention to Norway's commercial relations with other countries.

The debate in the Storting on the Speech from the Throne and the declaration of the Premier took place in the first week of April. The Government was subjected to some sharp criticism, not only by the Leader of the Labour Party, Mr. Nygaardsvold, but also by the Conservative leader, Mr. Hambro, and the Radical leader, Mr. Mowinckel. The leaders of the bourgeois opposition parties specially criticised the refusal of the Kolstad Government to resign after its failure to carry out the policy of the Farmers' Party in regard to the concession to Unilever, the question which had caused the fall of the Mowinckel Cabinet in May, 1931 (*vide* ANNUAL REGISTER, 1931). The bourgeois Opposition leaders, however, did not desire a change of Government and expressed their willingness to co-operate with the Government and support it on its merits. The Premier, Mr. Hundseid, replying to his critics, stated that before forming his Government he had made inquiries with a view to forming a National Coalition Government and had ascertained that it was impossible. A vote of censure, proposed by the Labour Party, was rejected by 97 to 45 votes.

The growing hostility of the Labour and the Communist Parties to the Minister of Defence, Major Quisling, attracted considerable attention throughout the year. Major Quisling was Fridtjof Nansen's collaborator during his relief work in Russia. A couple of years ago he excited the wrath of the Communists by publishing a book on Russia, containing some very outspoken criticism of the Soviet regime. When he obtained office in Mr. Kolstad's Cabinet without having had any previous political experience, his appointment was characterised by the Labour papers as a challenge to Labour. On February 2 Major Quisling was the object of a mysterious assault in his office at the Ministry of Defence. In the afternoon, after office hours, he was attacked by one or more men who tried to stab him with a knife in the chest. The Minister succeeded in averting the blow, but during the

struggle he was blinded with pepper and received a serious blow
on the head, which rendered him unconscious.

The assailants were never found, and whether their object was
to steal secret military documents or revenge themselves on the
Minister for personal or political reasons remained an unsolved
mystery. Major Quisling was an invalid for several weeks after
the assault. He recovered in time to take part in the debate on
the Speech from the Throne, and caused a sensation by a speech
on April 7 in which he accused the Labour leaders of plotting
revolution. He said that the Ministry of Defence possessed
documents which were very compromising to some Labour
leaders. Two of the Labour politicians, who had been particularly
active in criticising him, were paid agents of a foreign country.

At the request of the Storting the documents which the
Minister of Defence had referred to were submitted to a special
Committee of the Storting for examination. The Labour leaders
implicated were heard by the Magistrate at Oslo in secret sittings,
the members of the Committee being present. The report of the
Committee was published in June. In the opinion of the majority
(all the bourgeois members) the documents showed that the
Minister of Defence was right in the main. The majority considered it to be proved that the Norwegian Communist Party
had received from the Communist International at Moscow
a subvention of about half a million crowns during 1928 and 1929
and 1½ millions later. The Norwegian Federation of Trade Unions
had received 800,000 crowns from the Russian Trade Union
Federation. The Leader of the Communist propaganda in Norway,
Mr. Arvid Hansen, was receiving a salary of 24,000 crowns a year,
and other Labour leaders had received smaller subventions. The
documents further made out that demonstrations of a seditious
character had been planned from Moscow during the labour
conflict in the Skien district in 1931, but there was no proof of the
existence of Communist stocks of arms and munitions.

The Labour members of the Committee dissented, being of
opinion that the accusations made by the Minister of Defence
had not been satisfactorily proved.

The report was dealt with by the Storting on June 30.
A motion, proposed by the Labour Party, demanding the resignation of the Minister of Defence, was rejected, all the bourgeois
members, with one exception, voting against it. The Storting
thereupon unanimously adopted a resolution to the effect that
the speech of the Minister of Defence on April 7 did not necessitate
any action on the part of the Storting.

The Greenland question continued to be the dominating
problem in the foreign policy of Norway, and was the cause of an
unexpected political move after the close of the Parliamentary
session. A second Norwegian occupation in East Greenland,
farther south than the occupation of 1931, was proclaimed by

the Government on July 12. The new occupation embraced the territory between 63° 40' and 60° 30' North latitude. Helge Ingstad, the Governor of Eirik Raudes Land, occupied by Norway in July, 1931, was appointed Governor of the new Norwegian territory also. In an official announcement the occupation was characterised as a defensive measure which Norway had found it necessary to take after Denmark had granted general magisterial powers (*i.e.*, also against Norwegian citizens) to its expeditions to East Greenland during the summer. It was evident that Denmark was planning the transfer of Eskimos to South-East Greenland, where there had never been any Eskimo colony previously, and where two Norwegian expeditions had built about 30 small houses and carried on trapping of fur-bearing animals and salmon fishing. Off the coast of South-East Greenland Norwegians had for many years carried on sealing operations. In the opinion of the Norwegian Government, Denmark was attempting to acquire sovereignty over the remainder of East Greenland before the judgment of the International Court as to Eirik Raudes Land had been pronounced. If Denmark succeeded in this, the Danish prohibition of foreign vessels would apply also to East Greenland, which would thus be closed to all non-Danish nationals. After the expiry of the East Greenland agreement in 1944, Norwegians would also be shut out. The Norwegian Government emphasised the fact that it was not Norway's intention to close any of the territories to which it had been compelled to raise the claim of sovereignty. The good harbours in South-East Greenland, which can serve as bases for both whaling and deep-sea fishing, might be used by Norwegian whalers and fishermen as well as by those of other countries, and would to a certain extent be independent of the Danish preserve in West Greenland. The basis of the Norwegian policy in East Greenland was to maintain the principle of the open door.

The Norwegian Government on July 18 informed the Permanent Court of International Justice of the new occupation, and requested the Court to pronounce its verdict, recognising Norwegian sovereignty over the occupied territory. At the same time the Norwegian Government asked the Court to enjoin the Danish Government to refrain from any use of force against Norwegian citizens in the occupied territory, its apprehensions having been aroused by the provocative statements made by prominent Danish politicians, especially the Leader of the Danish Conservative Party and the Chairman of the Greenland Committee of the Danish Parliament.

The Norwegian appeal was at once dealt with by the International Court. In its award on August 3 the Court declared that it did not consider it necessary for the time being to enact provisional measures to prevent the use of force against the

Norwegians in South-East Greenland, but it was ready to take up the question later if it did prove necessary.

Although the Court did not accede to the Norwegian request, the result did not cause any disappointment in Norway, mainly owing to the statements made by the Danish advocates before the Court, to the effect that Denmark did not intend to make use of force. The Norwegian Premier and the Minister of Foreign Affairs both declared themselves satisfied, Norway having in reality obtained what she wanted.

The oral pleadings at The Hague in the lawsuit concerning Eirik Raudes Land, the territory occupied by Norway in 1931, commenced on November 21. Norway was represented by the following counsel: Per Rygh, Arne Sunde, and the Frenchman, Professor Gidel. The proceedings were suspended on December 15 to be resumed in January, 1933.

In Norway, as in most other countries in 1932, special measures had to be taken to cope with financial difficulties. In February a special "Crisis Committee" of four members was appointed to advise the Government on financial matters. In April the extraordinary supplement to the existing import duty was prolonged until further notice, and on June 28 the Government was authorised, when the Storting was not in session, to increase rates of duty by as much as 400 per cent. and to impose a duty of 50 per cent. on goods on the free list, "when commercial or political circumstances should require it." The Budget for 1932-33 was balanced in January at kr. 364,300,000, but in August the Finance Minister estimated that at the end of the year there would be a deficit of 30-40 million kroner, against last year's deficit of kr. 8,500,000.

FINLAND.

Towards the end of 1931, members of the Lapua movement began to assemble at Mantsälä, about forty miles north of Helsingfors, and organise themselves there into a military force under the command of General Wallenius. They demanded the resignation of Baron von Born, the Minister of the Interior, and General Jalander, the Governor of Nyland County, two of their most active opponents. As they refused to desist from their threatening attitude, the Government decided, on February 29, to put into operation the National Security Law of 1929 prohibiting the movement of armed forces, and they also mobilised troops at Helsingfors, and set police and soldiers to guard the railways and the roads. At the same time, they issued orders for the arrest of General Wallenius and his chief associates. Thereupon two pro-Lapuan members of the Cabinet resigned. The determined attitude of the Government produced the desired effect, and on March 6 the rising collapsed. General Wallenius and other leaders were arrested, and the rank and file, to the number of five or six thousand, surrendered their arms and were allowed to return home. In a Ministerial statement made to the Diet on March 10, it was explained that the civil authorities had been unable to cope with the movement as many of the rebels were members of the Skyddskar organisation, a kind of militia.

On April 12 President Svinhufvud signed a Bill granting an amnesty to the rank and file of those who had taken part in the Mantsälä rising, on the ground that they had been misled by their leaders and had abandoned them as soon as they became aware of the real meaning of their actions. A hundred and two leaders of the movement were brought to trial on July 26. Their continued detention in prison during the trial led to popular protests, and in October they were all released. Judgment was pronounced on November 21, when fifty-two of the accused were sentenced to terms of imprisonment of from two to thirty months. Only twenty of these were obliged to serve their terms ; the rest, including General Wallenius, were in effect merely bound over for three years.

Following upon the result of the Referendum taken at the end of 1931 in favour of abolishing Prohibition, the Government in January brought forward a Bill containing elaborate provisions for regulating the manufacture, sale, and consumption of alcoholic liquor. The chief proposals were that a State-controlled liquor monopoly should be set up, and that of the annual earnings 30 per cent. should be used for temperance purposes and old-age pensions, 20 per cent. should be allotted to the Communes for various social purposes, and 50 per cent. should be used for general State expenditure. On January 31 the Diet passed the third reading by 120 votes to 45, the minority consisting chiefly of Socialists and Agrarians. The public sale of alcoholic drinks commenced on April 5, amid great popular excitement. On September 23 a Bill granting an amnesty to about 20,000 persons who were in prison for offences against the Prohibition Law before April 5 received the Presidential sanction.

When the Diet assembled on September 1 the Government of Dr. J. E. Sunila was somewhat severely criticised on a number of grounds, including the detention of the Lapuan leaders and the recent dismissal of General Jalander. As no other group, however, was anxious to take office, it was given a vote of confidence. Its fall, however, was not long delayed. A Bill was brought forward, on the demand of the Agrarian members of the Cabinet, to limit the interest on certain loans to 7 per cent. Opposition was offered from life insurance companies and other quarters, the President refused his approval, and the Government, in consequence, resigned on December 7. On December 14 a Coalition Government which was promised support from the Social Democrats was formed by the Progressive leader, Hr. T. M. Kivimäki.

The programme of the new Government gave the chief place to economic questions.

Early in April twenty Communists, including seven women, were arrested on charges of subversive propaganda, and eleven were sentenced to varying terms of imprisonment with hard labour. On September 3 twenty-one Communists, including three women, were sentenced to penal servitude for high treason.

A Non-Aggression Treaty was signed at Helsingfors on January 21 by the Finnish Foreign Minister and the Soviet Minister in Helsingfors, M. Maiski. The treaty was for three years, to be prolonged automatically for another two years unless denounced six months previous to its expiry. On April 22 a draft Conciliation Convention was attached to the Pact, which, after being approved by the Diet, was ratified by the President on July 7.

CHAPTER VI.

THE MIDDLE EAST : PERSIA—AFGHANISTAN—IRAQ—PALESTINE— SYRIA—ARABIA.

PERSIA.

THE Convention concluded at the end of 1931 between Persia and Turkey for the purpose of rectifying the frontier between the two countries in the neighbourhood of Mount Ararat (*vide* ANNUAL REGISTER, 1931, p. 263) was duly signed at Teheran in the last week of January. By this agreement, Persia ceded to Turkey Little Mount Ararat and the Agridagh in return for areas in Kotur and near the Bajvige Pass.

On April 26 King Feisal of Iraq, accompanied by several members of his Cabinet, arrived in Teheran to pay a State visit to the Shah. King Feisal remained in Teheran till May 1, and receptions were given in his honour by the Court and the resident Iraquis. He returned to Iraq by way of the new road through Luristan to Mohammerah and Basrah. The purpose of his visit was to cement the newly formed friendship between Iraq and Persia, and also to pave the way for closer economic co-operation between the two countries.

In October two motor gunboats and four motor launches, built for Persia in Italian yards, arrived in the Persian Gulf to constitute the Persian Fleet. On November 4 the Shah, attended by Jafar Gholi Khan Assad, his Minister for War and Marine, left Bushire in one of the gunboats, the *Palang*, and proceeded to Bandur Shapur, where he opened the new port—the terminus of the southern section of the State railway—and afterwards the regular service of trains between the port and

Salehbad. Celebrations in honour of the new fleet were also held at Mohammerah, Abadan, and Ahwaz.

In the autumn banditry again became rife in Luristan, and in September three American Consular officers were kidnapped on the main Bagdad-Teheran road. The Government took severe measures to restore order, and a number of bandits were hanged in the streets of Teheran.

At the end of March the Junkers Aircraft Company, of Dessau, discontinued its air services in Persia. The immediate reason was that the firm was in financial difficulties, but in addition the Persian Government had placed difficulties in the way of renewing its concession which expired at that date. During the five years of its operation, the Junkers service had carried 20,000 passengers and 800 tons of freight over 1,550,000 miles without injury to either passengers or cargo, and the proportion of Persian passengers had increased from 10 to 75 per cent. of the whole.

Later in the year another foreign concession—that held by the Anglo-Persian Oil Company—was cancelled in circumstances which led to international complications. This was a concession for exploiting the oil resources of Persia granted by the Shah to one William Darcy, in 1901, at a time when the existence of oil in Persia was still problematical. The concession was for sixty years and in 1909 had been taken over by the Anglo-Persian Oil Company. The Nationalist Government which came into power in Persia in 1925 had from the first looked with a jealous eye on the extensive privileges enjoyed by the Company and had desired a greater share in its profits. It had accordingly at an early period approached it with a view to altering the terms of the concession. The Company had shown itself not averse to discussing the matter, but no progress had been made towards an agreement till in the winter of 1931, the Persian Court Minister, H. H. Mirza Khan Timurtash, while on a visit to London, went into the matter thoroughly with representatives of the Company, and succeeded in drafting an agreement. When he returned to Persia, however, a hitch occurred, and no further progress was made. In the summer the Government began to contemplate the possibility of cancelling the agreement on its own responsibility, and its impatience was brought to a head when it was discovered that, owing to the fall in oil prices and the policy of restriction practised by the Company, the royalties for 1931 would amount to only 306,000*l.* against 1,300,000*l.* for 1930. On his return from the Gulf of Persia, the Shah himself went into the matter and, acting practically on his instructions, the Government on November 28 informed the Company that the Darcy concession was cancelled. At the same time, however, it declared its willingness to negotiate a new concession " based on the rights of both parties," and meanwhile the activities of the Company were allowed to continue unaltered. This action was made an occasion for national rejoicing, and by order of the police Teheran was illuminated on November 29 and 30 and the cinemas were open free.

The Company did not fail to protest vigorously against the high-handed action of the Persian Government, and it had the support of the British Government, which, apart from the question of maintaining the rights of British subjects abroad, was directly interested as the largest single shareholder in the Anglo-Persian Oil Company. Energetic representations were made by the British Minister at Teheran on December 2, but the Persian Government refused to make any change in its policy. On December 8 the British Government addressed a further Note to Teheran suggesting that the dispute should be referred to The Hague International Court. The Persian Government, however, refused to admit the competence of this Court to deal with a dispute between itself and a commercial company. It complained that the British Government was using "threats and pressure," and announced its intention of bringing this to The notice of the League of Nations. In this, however, it was anticipated by the British Government, which on December 14 formally requested the Secretary-General of the League to submit the matter to the League Council in accordance with Article 5 of the Covenant. Persia also consented to send special delegates to the League, but demanded a little time to prepare her case.

AFGHANISTAN.

Towards the end of February the new Fundamental Rules of the Afghan Government were promulgated in an issue of the *Islah*, of Kabul. These declared Afghanistan to be completely independent both in external and internal affairs, with Kabul for its capital. Islam was to be the religion of the country, and the Shariat (Islamic law) was to be binding. Afghan subjects were to enjoy liberty of the person and freedom in all matters of trade, industry, and agriculture, and slavery and forced labour were prohibited. There was to be a Council of State (*Majlis-i-Shora-Milli*) of elected representatives from the provinces, to which proposals for new laws were to be submitted, and a Chamber of Notables (*Majlis-i-Ayan*) selected and appointed by the King. Primary education was made compulsory, and foreign newspapers which did not offend against the religion and policy of the State would be free to enter Afghanistan.

At the end of September the Sardar Ala Gholam Nabi Khan, son of Abdurrahman's famous general, Haidar Khan Charkhi, who had himself been for many years Afghan Minister at Moscow under King Amanullah, and had made an abortive attempt to restore that monarch in May, 1929, with Russian assistance, returned to Kabul from Berlin, where he had been living since the accession of Nadir Khan. Early in November he was arrested on a charge of fomenting rebellion among the tribes of the south-east among whom his family had great influence, and of intriguing with the Soviet Government, with a view to procuring the restoration of King Amanullah. He was brought to trial before the Loe Jirga, or Great Assembly, early in November, and, incriminating documents being produced, he was condemned to death and shot. One of his brothers Gholam Jilani Khan, who had recently returned from Moscow, was also arrested, and another, Gholam Zaddiq Khan, who was Minister in Berlin, was dismissed from his post. The King's brother, the Sardar Shah Mahmud, took energetic steps to combat disaffection in the south, where one or two pretenders had appeared.

IRAQ.

The great event in the history of Iraq during 1932 was the consummation of the independence of the new State by its admission as a member to the League of Nations on October 3. Simultaneously the European Powers surrendered their privileges under the Capitulations and the Iraquian Government, in order to show that it was indeed independent, took steps to increase its armed forces. With the acquisition of independence the British Mandate over the State came to an end. Before the Council of the League agreed to the withdrawal of the Mandate certain guarantees had, however, to be accepted. The agreement on these was reached in May, and announced at the meeting of the Council of the League of the 19th of that month. The guarantees covered :

(1) The effective protection of racial, linguistic, and religious minorities ;
(2) The safeguarding of the interests of foreigners in the judicial sphere ;
(3) Freedom of conscience and the safeguarding of the activities of religious missions ;
(4) Rights acquired and financial obligations contracted by the Mandatory Power before the termination of the Mandate ;
(5) Respect for international conventions ;
(6) The concession to States members of the League under certain conditions of most-favoured-nation treatment, subject to reciprocity ; and
(7) The right of the members of the League represented on the Council to lay before the Permanent Court of International Justice any difference of opinion arising out of the interpretation or execution of the undertakings assumed by Iraq before the Council.

The official correspondence between the Governments of the United Kingdom and Iraq and the League of Nations was published (League of Nations Publications A. 17, 1932, VII.).

Even on this late occasion the question of the Kurdish minority arose, the French representative expressing regret that no provision had been made for the administrative autonomy of that

S

minority. This question had caused much trouble to the British and Iraquian Governments in the previous year, trouble which had culminated in the hopeless revolt of Sheikh Mahmud who abandoned the struggle and surrendered in May, 1931. The new year witnessed a new revolt under Sheikh Ahmed of Barzan which lasted but a short time. In the operations the British Air Force co-operated with the Iraquian Army. In the end the rebels surrendered to the Turks over the frontier in June, and after two years of almost continuous disturbance peace was restored to this wild region.

A few days before this source of trouble was removed, another one of a different character broke out among the Assyrians or Nestorian Christians, a community that looked with great misgiving on the proposed grant of independence to the kingdom without, as they considered, sufficient safeguards for their own security. This community supplied a force of levies that acted as auxiliaries to the British forces, and as the grant of independence came nearer they expressed their disapproval by a sudden resignation *en masse*. To replace them troops had to be sent by air from Egypt. The Assyrians had petitioned the League of Nations to safeguard them by providing for an autonomous enclave within the Iraquian State, but this prayer had been rejected in January. The movement of June was a consequent protest. It, however, did not last for long, and within three weeks the protest had ended and the British troops returned to Egypt.

Another preliminary to and concomitant of the admission of Iraq to the League was a final delimitation of the frontier between Iraq and Syria. This was satisfactorily arranged by a Committee of the League which visited the districts concerned.

Earlier in the year before the kingdom attained its independence the King of Iraq paid two visits to neighbouring States. In April he went to Teheran, and the friendly relations thus set up between the two kingdoms and their rulers are expected to be reflected in the settlement of several outstanding questions of a minor character. In September King Feisal was in Jerusalem in the course of a visit to his brother the Emir Abdullah in Transjordan. His visit to these two countries gave rise to many rumours, and advantage was taken of them by the advocates of a federation of Arab states to bring the attainment of their programme nearer.

The question of the Assyrians in Iraq, however, again came before the Council of the League of Nations in December. After an explanation by the representative of the Iraquian Government who said that while the desire of the Assyrians to live in mountainous country in a compact body in the Mosul Vilayet had made a settlement impossible up to the present, Iraq hoped to carry out next summer the recommendations of the Mandates Commission and provide settlement for the large proportion still

without land—care being taken to avoid a complete dispersion
of families. Iraq, while opposed to the granting to the Assyrians
of an administrative autonomy, had no objection to their settlement in their country of origin or in any other country near
Iraq.

This satisfied the Council of the League which resolved that
the demand of the Assyrians for administrative autonomy within
Iraq could not be accepted, but that the Council noted with
satisfaction the Iraquian Government's intention to select from
outside Iraq a foreign expert to assist them for a limited period
in the settlement of all landless inhabitants of Iraq, including
Assyrians, and in the carrying out of their scheme for the settlement of the Assyrians in Iraq under suitable conditions, and
so far as may be possible, in homogeneous units, it being understood that the existing rights of the present population should
not be prejudiced. If these measures did not provide a complete
solution of the problem, and there remained Assyrians unwilling
or unable to settle in Iraq, the Council trusted to the Iraquian
Government to take all possible measures to facilitate the settlement of such Assyrians elsewhere.

At the end of October the Cabinet of General Nuri Pasha
es Said resigned and later Parliament was dissolved.

PALESTINE.

The most important incident in the history of Palestine during
the year was probably the noticeable growth of anti-British feeling
among the Arabs. Until about the end of the year 1931 there
was no appreciable anti-Government or anti-British feeling.
There was considerable anti-Zionist, not in its essence anti-
Jewish, hostility, but the Government and the British were not
involved in this. For the Arabs, however, the past year has
been one of disillusionment, justified or unjustified, and disappointment, and the British are gradually coming to be held
responsible. The fear of and consequent hostility to Zionism
as interpreted by its spokesmen, have in the meanwhile not
abated, and to this is to be attributed much of the agrarian and
in some instances purely political crime that has been sporadic
throughout the greater part of the year, crime which has for
the most part gone undetected and unpunished. Economically
Palestine has occupied a very curious situation. With other
countries in sore economic and financial straits, the situation
in Palestine has at the same time been both favourable and
unfavourable. Agriculture in Palestine has felt the pressure no
less than in other countries, and in addition, in parts of the country
the crops on which much of the rural population depends for its
daily bread have failed in whole or in part. As a consequence

over two-thirds of the tithe had to be remitted.   Commerce and industry outside of the Jewish town of Tel Aviv and some. of the other Jewish settlements has been almost at a standstill. There has been much suffering among the professional and shop-keeping classes and their employees, and bankruptcies and compositions with creditors have been frequent.   On the other hand, the Government accounts showed a relatively large surplus, mainly due to import duties on goods consumed by newly arrived immigrants, and there was great activity in building and land purchase for orange growing, especially in Jewish circles. This was accounted for by the transference of a relatively large amount of money from America and Europe to Palestine in the course of the year by immigrants and others who, doubtful of the course of events elsewhere, thought their money safer in Palestine. In Palestine in the absence of more satisfactory employment, the money was invested in orange land or buildings or left on deposit in the banks, the owners living on capital while they looked around for means of employing it to advantage.   Great building activity on the part of Palestinians, especially in Jerusalem, was attributed to fear of a prospective income tax and belief that a tax on income derived from house property could be more easily evaded than bank interest.

Towards the end of the year two topics aroused considerable interest and apprehension.   Mr. Lewis French had been appointed Development Commissioner in July, 1931, with instructions to report on the situation of the agricultural population to which Sir John Hope Simpson had called attention, and to make proposals for remedying it.   Mr. French, however, laboured under one great handicap.   Sir John Hope Simpson, in his tentative suggestions for land development, had foreseen a fund of three or four million pounds to be obtained by loan, as capital for the undertaking.   Such a sum was still in the offing when Mr. French's appointment was made, but in the meanwhile came the financial crisis, and as time passed the possibility of any large sum being available became less and less.   Mr. French presented his final report in the course of the summer.   It was communicated in confidence to both the Executive of the Jewish Agency and the Arab Executive, the intention being to publish it in time for the meeting of the Mandates Committee of the League of Nations in November, together with the observations of these two Committees and the decisions of His Majesty's Government.   This plan was, however, not carried out, and Mr. French's conclusions and proposals had not been made public at the end of the year. In the meanwhile he had resigned his office which was always a temporary one.   Both Executives considered the proposals and denounced them whole-heartedly, apparently not so much for their expected influence on the fortunes of their own clientéle but because they were likely to benefit the other side.

The other topic of interest was that of the proposed Legislative Council. One attempt had been made in Sir Herbert Samuel's time to establish such a body with very limited powers. This attempt had been wrecked by the general hostility of the Arabs, who demanded a Council with far greater powers than those offered. Lord Passfield in his White Paper of 1930 revived the earlier proposal, and added at the same time that a Council would be established with or without the co-operation of one or other section of the population. It was on this occasion that the Jews opposed it tooth and nail, declining to have anything to do with it unless they were guaranteed at least an equality in membership with the Arabs. With other proposals made in the White Paper this fell for a time into the background. The Arabs gradually adopted an attitude of non-co-operation ; the Jews thought that all danger of a Legislative Council had been postponed indefinitely. Then suddenly, before the Mandates Commission, the High Commissioner announced that the proposal had been by no means shelved, and that early in the new year the question would be taken up in earnest. The Jews at once hailed the announcement as a betrayal of their cause and started an agitation not only in Palestine but throughout the Diaspora to prevent the feared step from being taken. This was the state of affairs at the end of the year.

Throughout the year the Arab or Palestine Arab national movement strengthened. As early as January the Moslem Youth Conference met and adopted a number of extremist resolutions, and above all the denunciation of all sales of land to Jews. Older Arab notables, despairing of the leisureliness of the Arab Executive, established a new party and a new organisation which was expected to be more active and more energetic in forwarding their aims. This movement resulted in the creation and celebration of a new national festival, Hattin Day, the anniversary of the Battle of Hattin at which Saladin finally destroyed the Latin Kingdom and drove out the European invaders. This celebration may have gone rather further than was intended, for it commemorated a victory of Moslems over Christianity and as such could not be celebrated as enthusiastically by Christian Arabs as the Moslem Arabs desired. It may have been from this cause that a certain rift was opened between Christian and Moslem Arab, which widened when the Moslems suddenly discovered that Christians had obtained a proportionately undue number of Government appointments at the expense of the Moslems. The Christians being on a higher plane than the Moslems naturally compete advantageously with them for Government appointments.

For one short period about Easter there was such tension that an outbreak might have been possible. An international sports meeting, and also an industrial exhibition at Tel Aviv, had brought to Palestine a large number of young Jewish visitors on whom the Arabs looked somewhat with suspicion. About the same time, there was a series of tragedies that almost created a panic. First, a Jewish tourist, immediately on his arrival, cut his own throat in a field in a Jewish suburb of Jerusalem. The Jews without awaiting an inquiry at once cried out this was another Arab outrage, and the following night an Arab was found with his throat cut in the same neighbourhood. Then a Jew travelling in an Arab omnibus to Jaffa fell out and was killed. Suspicion was again aroused of a racial crime, and within a few days an altercation at the gate of the Mosque between the gatekeeper and a tourist family who were, of course, announced as Jews, which they were not, excited the Arabs. The Government, however, treated these troubles suitably and the excitement, which for a time threatened to boil over, passed away.

King Feisal of Iraq, during his stay with his brother, the Emir Abdullah at Amman in September, paid a short visit to Jerusalem, and his visit was made a focus for Arab national activity. The newly formed Arab Independence Party utilised the occasion to advertise their ideal of a Pan-Arab State, comprising Palestine, Transjordan, Iraq, and Syria. The proclamation of the independence of Iraq about the same time, and the persistent rumour that Syria would shortly be given a similar status, gave them much encouragement.

At the end of the year a minor excitement was aroused by a visit of the ex-Khedive Abbas Hilmi, the second within the year, who was generally believed to be engaged in political activities, possibly to secure for himself a kingdom either in Syria or Palestine.

The agricultural depression was reflected in the remission by the Government of 70 per cent. of the tithes due by the cultivators, almost entirely Arabs. There was no alternative, for the cultivators after a series of bad harvests were quite unable to pay the tax. Not unrelated was the provisional settlement made in the matter of the Wady Hawareth lands. These had been acquired by the Zionist Organisation, which proposed to develop them and settle a relatively considerable Jewish population. No provision was, however, made for the scattered Arabs who had hitherto eked out a scanty living on them. They were forced off the land, but there was nowhere else for them to go. In the end the Government intervened and the Zionist Organisation granted the Government a lease of a part of the land for eighteen months, pending arrangements for settling the dislodged Arabs elsewhere.

The year passed without any settlement, or even prospect of a settlement, of the Orthodox Patriarchate tangle. At the end of the year 1931, despite the almost unanimous objections of the Orthodox community, including the lower religious orders, the

election of a new Patriarch was proceeding, and if there had
not been an interruption, the election of a Greek ecclesiastic
entirely out of sympathy with the overwhelming majority of his
flock would have been completed. This election would have
been held with the full approval of the Government, but an
interruption did occur. The objectors to the election appealed
to the Supreme Court and won their case. The ecclesiastical
authorities declined to appear before the Court on the ground
that the Patriarchate was not subject to its jurisdiction. This
plea was rejected. The proceedings for the election hitherto
taken were declared to be invalid on technical grounds. With
this judgment in January the election of a Patriarch came to a
sudden end, and the year passed without as far as was known
any further step being taken. In the Moslem Community also
there was talk of a reorganisation of the Supreme Moslem Council,
to the constitution of which a strong minority was hostile, and
of the holding of new elections. There were rumours and more
than rumours of impending changes, but nothing occurred during
the year. The Moslems of Hebron, however, took proceedings
against the Council on the ground that they had diverted certain
charitable funds from the purpose for which they were intended.
This case also came before the Supreme Court and the Petition
of the Hebron Moslems was dismissed.

SYRIA.

Although there was no change in the constitutional status
of Syria or the Lebanon during the year, the rumours that were
so persistent throughout the year 1931 continued in varying
form in its successor, and the belief that the French Mandate
over Syria was nearing its close and that it would be succeeded
by a treaty of alliance between France and Syria, was very
general. The constitutional developments in Iraq gave strength
to that belief which spread also to the neighbouring countries.
The year opened in the midst of a General Election in Syria. The
first stage of the elections was held in December, 1931, and led
to riots and bloodshed in several towns. So great was the
violence that in some centres the elections had to be suspended.
They were completed in due course, and under the pressure of
French officialdom, returned an overwhelming nominally moderate majority. It was said at the time that there was no real
difference between moderate and extremist in Syrian politics.
They were all Nationalists. The programme of the successful
party may be defined as a strong constitutional Government,
transformation of the Mandate into a treaty of alliance, the
admission of Syria to the League of Nations, and a united Syria
with a national army strong enough to enable the country to
dispense with a French army of occupation. However, the

relations between the French Government and the Syrian Parliament were not unsatisfactory during the year. In June a President of the Republic, who had been more or less nominated by the French, was elected in the person of Ahmed Ali Bek el Abed.

The one unsatisfactory spot in the Republic was Aleppo. This was one of the cities in which the elections had had to be postponed. In August the unemployed there, who were relatively numerous, caused a riot which evoked certain economic concessions or promises before it was suppressed. Later in the month there were a number of outrages, to counter which the French arrested most of the prominent Nationalists of the city.

In November the Council of the League of Nations adopted the frontier line between Syria and Iraq, suggested by the Commissioner of Enquiry it had sent out at the beginning of the year. The line chosen was a compromise between the Anglo-Iraqui and the Franco-Syrian one.

In the Lebanon State the Constitution was suspended in May, and the Government left in the hands of M. Dabbas, the President of the Republic, acting under the direct control of the High Commissioner. The change was not unpopular with the general population. The new regime showed a noticeable improvement in administration. Expenditure was greatly reduced, especially on staff.

In the Jebel Druse, whose administration is separate from that of Syria, the High Commissioner in November announced in the course of a visit to that territory that France intended to grant the Druses the independence for which they had in the past struggled in vain.

ARABIA.

On September 22 the name of the twin kingdom of Hedjaz and Nejd was changed to that of the Kingdom of Saudi Arabia (Saudieh).

The principal incident of consequence in the history of Arabia during the year was a revolt, or more properly invasion, of disaffected elements in June. The importance of this event was increased by the very strong suspicions that the Emir Abdullah of Transjordan was not altogether unsympathetic to the rebels, and in order that the trouble might not spread British forces temporarily occupied the Akaba region either to prevent further incursions from Sinai, whence the rebels had concentrated, or to keep the forces of the Nejd-Hedjaz and Transjordan apart. The revolt was headed by Sheikh Ibn Rafadah el Oar, an exile from the Hedjaz and a supporter of the Hashimite dynasty, who gathered round him a number of dissatisfied members of the Beni Ali and Howeitah tribes who had taken refuge in Trans-jordan and Sinai. With these he invaded the territory of Ibn Saud in May. In the Hedjaz, however, they failed to secure the welcome and support they expected. The adventure was short-lived. Before the end of July the invaders had been thoroughly defeated, and their leader and his two sons killed. With this defeat the movement came to an end. The incident was used by dissatisfied elements in Palestine to spread rumours to the effect that the British had seized and were occupying Hedjazian territory, and more or less detailed reports were actually given in the Arabic Press of battles between the British and the Hedjazian forces. In due course, however, as other excitements attracted the Arab man in the street and journalist the whole matter was forgotten, except probably by the maimed and the mourners.

At the end of the year a new trouble broke out in the south. The Emirate of Asir, which Ibn Saud had annexed, had been a cause of unpleasantness with the Imam Yahia of Sanaa in the previous year, and the strain in the relations between the two rulers which had at one time threatened had been avoided with some difficulty. At the end of the year a revolt broke out in this region. From the reports that were slowly coming in Ibn Saud had the situation well in hand before the year closed.

In November steps were taken to negotiate a treaty of friend-ship with the Imam Yahia, and six months earlier a similar treaty was signed between the Kingdom of Nejd-Hedjaz and that of Afghanistan.

The economic and financial state of the kingdom was not very satisfactory, although it was by no means as bad as rumours current in the neighbouring countries at the beginning of the year suggested. The prosperity of the people and of the Govern-ment suffered seriously from the reduced number of pilgrims on whom they both so largely depend, a reduction due mainly to the financial difficulties in other Moslem lands. The difficulties were enhanced by the drought from which Northern Arabia suffered for the second year in succession.

At the beginning of April the administrative status of Aden and Perim underwent another change. Hitherto the settlement and its dependencies had been administered jointly by the Govern-ment of Bombay and the Government of India. By the change these territories were formed into a Chief Commissionership directly under the Governor-General of India. The reasons for the change were merely administrative and financial. In May Arab-Jewish riots broke out in the town but were soon suppressed. A few of the foreign participants were deported.

CHAPTER VII.

THE FAR EAST : CHINA—JAPAN—THE DUTCH EAST INDIES.

CHINA.

THE year 1932 was notable for an attempt of the civilian elements to assert themselves in the face of military despotism, and for the manifestation of a somewhat heightened sense of public duty in those who were in control of the country's affairs. The feebleness of Chang Hsueh-Liang's resistance to the Japanese in Manchuria towards the close of the previous year discredited not only that general but also all the other " war lords," and emboldened the civilian authorities to set them at defiance. The depletion of the Treasury, while it removed the opportunities for peculation, impressed on the Government and its servants the necessity for a more careful management of the country's resources. Consequently in spite of, or perhaps because of, severe blows from without, China in 1932 enjoyed somewhat greater political stability and suffered somewhat less economic hardship than in previous years.

The opening of the year found the Government in the hands of Sun Fo and his Cantonese clique, with General Chiang Kai-shek in retirement, watching developments (vide ANNUAL REGISTER, 1931). These were not long in bringing him to the fore again. Faced with the problem of meeting an expenditure of 20,000,000 dollars a month with a revenue of 6,000,000, the Government became hopelessly divided against itself. Thereupon, towards the end of January, Wang Ching-wei made his peace with Chiang Kai-shek, whom he had driven out of office a few months before, and the two in conjunction forced Sun Fo and his clique to retire, and installed themselves with their own followers. From that time these two, with Mr. T. V. Soong as Minister of Finance, practically ruled the country for several months, the Kuomintang sinking into the background, and China enjoyed probably its best Government for years. To strengthen its position, the Government in April convened at Loyang a National Emergency Conference of two hundred notables, which passed a resolution demanding the abolition of party rule.

Immediately after the accession of the new Government to power, hostilities broke out between the Japanese and Chinese at Shanghai, near which the 19th Route Army was stationed. The Chinese public were delighted with the excellent stand made by their countrymen against the enemy, and were anxious that they should be supported until the Japanese should be forced to retire from Shanghai unconditionally. The Government, however, did not venture to break off diplomatic relations with

Japan, partly because of the pressure exercised on them by commercial and financial interests, partly because a Japanese demonstration against Nanking, which forced them to retire to Loyang, inspired them with caution. Though disappointed with the Government's inaction, the public regarded the armistice which was concluded in May as a diplomatic victory for China [*vide* Japan].

Chinese indignation with Japan for her conduct in Manchuria was expressed by an intensification of the anti-Japanese boycott. The Chinese delegate continued to protest to the League of Nations, but the Government made no attempt to enforce by arms its demands for the restoration of the province. The action of the Japanese in transferring to the Manchukuo Government the Customs receipts at the Manchurian ports added further fuel to Chinese irritation, besides depriving the Government of an important source of revenue, and in retaliation the Chinese Government announced on September 23 that the Customs houses at Harbin, Newchwang, Antung, and Lungchingtsun would be closed as from September 29 and the Customs duties legally collectable there would be collected temporarily at other Chinese ports. The Report of the Lytton Commission was welcomed in China for its condemnation of the Japanese military operations and its denial that the State of Manchukuo had been created in accordance with the wishes of the inhabitants. Its recommendations, however, were not received with favour, and its failure to instigate the Powers to stronger action was a great disappointment to the Chinese. At the third Plenary Session of the Central Executive Committee of the Kuomintang, held in December, a resolution was passed declaring that it was futile for China to depend on the League of Nations and the Western Powers, and advocating that China should concentrate troops in Jehol and other places to resist further Japanese advance and, if possible, to recover lost ground, and that the Government and Kuomintang should support Chinese volunteers and troops in Manchuria with supplies and encourage and direct the national boycott movement against Japanese goods.

If China for the greater part of 1932 was relieved from the depredations of the war lords, she suffered almost equal havoc from the exploits of the Communists in her midst. After the retirement of Chiang Kai-shek towards the end of 1931, there was a great development of Communist activity, and, acting under instructions from Moscow, they established " the seat of the Central Provisional Government of the Soviet Republic of China " in South Kiangsi. General Chiang Kai-shek took the field against them in the spring, but for a long time made little headway. In the middle of May they threatened the treaty port of Amoy, which, however, was relieved by the arrival of the 19th Route Army from Shanghai. In July they claimed to control

867 Hsien districts in the central provinces of China, and their armies in Kiangsi, the Honan-Hupei-Anhui border, and Hupei were stated by the Chinese Minister of War to have a strength of over 110,000 men, with about 80,000 rifles. The Government at length realised that they derived their strength largely from the agrarian discontent, and took measures to placate the farmers, with the result that towards the end of the year General Chiang Kai-shek was able to gain some marked successes against them and to clear them out of most of Central China.

In the summer, Wang Ching-wei, the President of the Executive Yuan, published an article attacking Marshal Chang Hsueh-liang for his conduct in Manchuria, and soon afterwards he resigned with all his Ministers, while Chang also resigned his position as Governor of Northern China, handing over control to a military council of which he remained a member. The resignation of the Cabinet was also withdrawn at the end of August. On October 22, however, Wang left for Europe, ostensibly to seek medical advice, and his place during his absence was taken by Dr. T. V. Soong. In the same period hostilities had broken out in Shantung between General Han Fu-chu, the Governor, and General Liu Chen-nien, who had his headquarters in Chefoo. There was also severe fighting between rival commanders in Szechuan. The Government succeeded at the beginning of November in effecting a reconciliation between the opponents in Shantung, and on the approach of winter a *modus vivendi* was also reached in Szechuan.

During the first half of the year efforts for the relief of the victims of the 1931 floods were actively carried on under the supervision of Sir J. Hope Simpson. It was estimated that at least 10,000,000 persons had been rendered destitute. To raise money for the relief, special taxes on railway fares and a Customs surtax were imposed, while to prevent further floods, 200 miles of dykes were built in Central China.

On December 12 diplomatic relations were resumed between China and Soviet Russia by an exchange of Notes at Geneva between Dr. W. W. Yen, First Chinese Delegate to the Disarmament Conference, and M. Litvinoff. Dr. Yen became Chinese Ambassador in Moscow and M. Bogomoloff, Soviet Ambassador to China.

The Plenary Conference of the Central Executive Committee of the Kuomintang in December passed a resolution that a National People's Congress should be convened in March, 1935, for the purpose of adopting a Constitution, and that the Legislature should begin immediately to draft such a Constitution. For the time being, however, Chiang Kai-shek was left in undisturbed possession of power. The Government about the same time returned to Nanking from Loyang.

Thanks to the rigid economy practised by the Finance Minister,

Dr. T. V. Soong, the Budget was balanced and the credit of the Government materially improved during the year, although Customs revenue declined considerably. The Government, however, came in for some adverse criticism for its decision towards the end of the year to take over the shares of the China Merchants Steam Navigation Company at a cash price of 50 dollars for each set of three. This price was said to be much less than the shares were worth and to be equivalent to confiscation.

JAPAN.

Throughout 1932 the wave of national and militarist feeling which towards the end of the previous year had led to the fall of the Minseito Ministry (*vide* ANNUAL REGISTER, 1931) continued to be the dominating factor in Japanese affairs. With the support of the great mass of public opinion, successive Governments embarked upon a " forward " policy in Manchuria, in spite of the fact that such a course antagonised a large part of the civilised world against Japan and caused grave dislocation in the finances of the country. Even so, their military efforts, great as they were, failed to satisfy the more ardent patriots, who did not hesitate to resort to assassination and similar terroristic acts in order to show their displeasure.

On December 29, 1931, Japan addressed a declaration to the League of Nations, pointing out that the bandit menace in Manchuria was so great that both for the protection of her nationals and for the restoration of tranquillity it was essential that the Japanese forces should cross to the west of the Liao river ; and on January 3 Chinchow was occupied. This step alarmed the United States Government, which on January 7 sent Notes to Japan and China stating that it would not recognise any agreement between them calculated to impair American rights or to threaten China's independence or territorial integrity or the principle of the " open door," and that it would not accept any agreement brought about by means contrary to the Kellogg Pact. At the same time, the British Government sought from Tokio confirmation of an assurance already given by Japan that the principle of the " open door " would be maintained. This was readily given ; while to America the Government replied that there was no intention of encroaching on American rights in Manchuria, and that the anarchy now prevailing in China had completely altered the situation existing when the Washington Treaties were signed.

At the end of January the Diet was dissolved, and in the election which followed the Seiyukai, who were the Government and also the war party, gained an overwhelming victory, securing 303 seats against 146 obtained by the Minseito. Labour secured five seats, polling only 200,000 votes, or half the number it obtained at the preceding election.

Such being the state of public opinion, the Government had no hesitation in taking the further steps which it deemed necessary for consolidating the Japanese position in Manchuria. Harbin having been occupied, on February 18 a Proclamation was issued at Mukden announcing the establishment of a Manchurian Republic to be known as Manchukuo, entirely independent of China and composed of the three Eastern provinces Fengtien, Kirin, and Heilungkiang, and part of Jehol. The capital was to be at Changchun, and the boy ex-Emperor Hsuan Tung (Pu Yi) was appointed dictator for life.

Although Japan was nominally at peace with China and in fact continued to maintain diplomatic relations with her, violent hostilities between the two countries took place early in the year in and around Shanghai. In consequence of various anti-Japanese demonstrations by the Chinese in Shanghai, the Japanese Admiral in Shanghai waters determined at the end of January to seize Chapei, the Chinese port near the town, nominally in order to protect the 30,000 Japanese in Shanghai. He met with un-expected resistance, and at his request reinforcements to the num-ber of 12,000 troops were sent out from Japan, under the command of General Ueda, who assumed control (February 14). General Ueda delivered an ultimatum to the Chinese which they refused to accept, and fighting was resumed on February 20. All the Powers which had settlements in Shanghai had from the first made strenuous efforts to restore peace, but for a long time they produced no effect. Fighting went on throughout February, and in the course of the operations the Japanese bombed from the air the Chinese settlement quarter in Shanghai, and attacked the Chinese fort of Woosung, twelve miles from the city, even-tually capturing it with the help of fresh reinforcements. At length on March 3, as a result of conversations held on board H.M.S. *Kent*, a truce was arranged, and at the end of April both sides accepted an agreement drafted by Sir Miles Lampson, the British Minister in China, by which the Chinese were allowed to retain their present positions, while the Japanese troops were to be withdrawn to the International Settlement or to Japan. The agreement was signed on May 5, and soon afterwards the bulk of the Japanese troops were withdrawn to Japan.

At the beginning of March the new Manchurian State issued a proclamation outlining its policy, which was briefly, respect for the policy of the " open door," the promotion of the welfare of the people on a basis of racial equality, the encouragement of education, the fulfilment of international obligations, and the acceptance of such international liabilities relating to Manchuria as existed before the foundation of the Chinese Republic. On March 9 Mr. Pu Yi was formally installed as Chief Executive.

All important posts were left in the hands of Chinese, who ostensibly governed the country, but behind them there was what a Japanese military writer, in an article in a Tokio magazine, called a " steel frame " in the shape of a Board of General Affairs, composed entirely of Japanese, which possessed complete control in matters relating to policy, personnel, and finance.

Notification of the establishment of the new State was sent to all the Powers, but all hesitated to recognise it. On the instigation of China, the League of Nations sent out a Commission headed by Lord Lytton to study and report on the situation. The Commission, after visiting Japan and China, arrived at Mukden on April 22. The authorities at first made difficulties about the admission of the Chinese assessor, Dr. Koo, but eventually waived their objections on obtaining an assurance from him that he would not engage in any political activity during his stay in Manchuria. Otherwise they placed no obstacles in the way of the Commission. On July 4 the Commission paid its second visit to Tokio and pressed the Government to effect a *modus vivendi* with China. The Government, however, refused to modify its attitude, which was that as a preliminary to any settlement the independence of Manchuria must be recognised, and that Japan would never consent to its being again placed under Chinese rule.

In Manchuria itself, the new regime was very far from being universally accepted. A great part of the province, particularly in the north, was seething with revolt. Armed bands, which the Japanese designated as bandits, but which often attained the size of considerable armies, infested the country and carried on a guerilla war against the Japanese troops. As the latter were not accustomed to this kind of warfare, and as the character of the country favoured the insurgents, little progress was made with the pacification of Manchuria in the course of the year, and trade and industry suffered considerably.

In May the Manchurian authorities, after vainly endeavouring to reach a *modus vivendi* with the Nanking Government on the subject, took control of the Customs service at the ports of Manchuria, in spite of the protests not only of China, but also of Great Britain and the United States. Part of the detained Customs revenues were subsequently remitted to Shanghai as a token of the willingness of the Manchukuo Government to contribute its *pro rata* share to the service of foreign loans secured on the Customs revenues. On September 15 the Manchukuo Foreign Minister announced that as from September 25, Manchukuo would treat China wholly as an alien nation in matters of Customs, tariffs, commerce, and navigation. Towards the end of the year, Mr. A. H. F. Edwardes, formerly Inspector-General of Chinese Maritime Customs, was appointed Adviser to the Manchukuo Government.

On May 15 the Prime Minister, Mr. Inukai, was assassinated

in Tokio by a band of young military and naval officers who immediately surrendered to the police. The Minister of War narrowly escaped a similar fate. At the same time, bombs were thrown at five of the principal buildings of the capital, and officers in uniform distributed in the streets handbills denouncing the Government's financial administration, the corruption of politicians, the conduct of the national diplomacy, and various high officials in the Army and Navy. The fate of Mr. Inukai had already earlier in the year befallen two other leading men who were obnoxious to the ultra-patriotic elements on account of their political or financial views—Mr. Inouye and Baron Dan. Though public opinion was shocked, it did not protest very vigorously. Mr. Inukai was succeeded after a short time as Prime Minister by Viscount Admiral Saito, who formed a Cabinet containing representatives of both the big parties. He himself at first acted as Minister for Foreign Affairs, but after a short time handed over that post to Count Uchida.

On August 25 Count Uchida, in a speech in the Diet, announced that it was Japan's intention to recognise the new State of Manchukuo in the near future. As a preliminary, the High Commissioner in Manchuria was replaced by a special Ambassador with much the same powers. The post was given to General Muto, and he was charged to negotiate a treaty with Manchukuo prior to recognition. The agreement finally took the form of a Protocol which was signed on September 15. Its chief provisions were that the new State should be recognised as the expression of the desire of the people of Manchuria for independence ; that it took over all existing obligations ; that it confirmed all the rights possessed by Japan or Japanese subjects in Manchuria ; and that its defence should be a common obligation on both parties. As the new State was unable to finance itself, a syndicate of Japanese banks towards the end of the year agreed to float on its behalf a loan of 30,000,000 silver dollars on the security of the Salt Gabelle and the Opium Monopoly.

The Lytton Commission Report, which was made public on October 2, met with a less hostile reception in Japan than had been anticipated, its general fairness and its value as a storehouse of information being recognised. Its proposed solutions were, however, regarded as no longer applicable, the independence of Manchuria being in the opinion of Japan an accomplished fact which could not be undone. Particular exception was taken, especially in military circles, to the description of China by the Report as " a nation in evolution," the Japanese view being that it was rather a country in chaos. Sooner than accept the recommendations of the Lytton Report, Japan declared herself ready to leave the League of Nations.

In spite of the rigours of the season, there was some severe fighting in Manchuria in November and December. Early in

November the insurgents captured the towns of Anta and Hailun, but they were defeated later in two engagements to the north and south of Harbin. At the beginning of December the Japanese launched an offensive against General Su, who was holding out with a large force in the western part of Heilungkiang, and forced him to retire with his troops into Russian territory, where he was disarmed and interned. At the end of the year it was reported that many of the insurgents were laying down their arms.

The financing of the operations in Manchuria laid a heavy burden on the Japanese Treasury. In January the Budget for the year was provisionally calculated at 1,397,095,000 yen, but by June the expenditure had been swollen by supplementary estimates to 1,544,244,000 yen; and to meet this sum 241,000,000 yen had to be raised by loans. In the Budget for 1933 drafted at the end of the year, expenditure was estimated at 2,239,000,000 yen, of which 447,000,000 yen was for the Army and 372,000,000 yen for the Navy, the Army estimate including 186,000,000 yen for expenditure in Manchuria. Revenue was estimated at only 1,341,000,000 yen, leaving a deficit of 898,000,000 yen.

Owing largely to the failure to balance the Budget, the value of the yen fell very considerably in the course of the year. While this caused a rise in the cost of living, it benefited the export trade, so that the adverse trade balance was considerably less in 1932 than in the preceding year. Nevertheless, there was much unemployment. In August a special session of the Diet was held to pass measures for the relief of agriculture and unemployment. These included the provision of funds for the use of farmers at a low rate of interest, the starting of public works, and grants to local authorities to enable them to pay the salaries of school teachers and to provide free meals for school children. The cost of these measures was about 175,000,000 yen, which was raised by public loans. In the session of the Diet in June, laws were passed to increase the note issue to 1,000,000,000 yen, to restrict dealings in foreign exchange, and to raise the tariff.

After the assassination of Mr. Inukai, the police authorities took vigorous measures to deal with so-called patriotic societies, and early in November they discovered a plot to destroy various power stations in Tokio and to assassinate the Prime Minister and other high officials. A number of persons were placed under arrest, including the son of one Toyama Mitsuru, the most notorious of the reactionary leaders.

On January 8, as the Emperor was returning from the annual New Year review, a bomb was thrown at him by a young Korean, but no one was injured. In accordance with precedent, all the members of the Cabinet at once submitted their resignations, but they were ordered to remain in office.

In October the trial of the Communists who had been arrested during the previous three years was concluded, and ninety-seven

T

persons were sentenced to terms of imprisonment varying from two years to penal servitude for life.

Early in December Japan submitted to the delegates of the Disarmament Conference proposals for naval disarmament of which the chief features were : the abolition of aircraft carriers, the fixing of the maximum tonnage of battleships at 25,000 and of gun calibre at 14 in., and the reduction of the maximum tonnage of submarines to 1,800 tons.

THE DUTCH EAST INDIES.

Bad as 1931 had been economically for the Dutch East Indies, 1932 was even worse. The value per ton of exported goods once more dropped considerably, and imports likewise decreased. The result was an adverse trade balance, with all the usual consequences.

The foreign trade of the colony was marked not only by a decrease in the imports from Holland, but by an increase in those from Japan, especially textiles, due in part to the fact that Japan had abandoned the gold standard, so that by December 31 the yen had depreciated to about 70 per cent. of its former value. On the other hand, the boycott of Japanese wares in China may have been of some influence, just as the impoverishment in Netherlands India, which obliged many who used to buy European goods of better quality to content themselves with the cheaper products of Japan. The drop of the index figure for the cost of living in general was responsible for the course taken by the Government at the end of the year of applying a 4 per cent. cut in the salaries of European, and a 7 per cent. cut in those of native Civil servants. The new retrenchment caused great discontent especially amongst the lower personnel of the Navy, which to a large extent is recruited from the native population.

The financial situation of the country was clearly explained by the Governor-General, Jhr. Dr. B. C. de Jonge, at the ceremonious opening of the new session of the " Volksraad " (People's Council) in June. He was of opinion that for 1933 the revenues could not be estimated at more than 331 million guilders, whilst the expenditure for the current year was still 507 millions. It was impossible to economise to the extent of 176 millions at a moment's notice for that reason efforts had been made to bring the estimates provisionally up to 400 millions. The retrenchment measures already taken or still to be taken included not only a sharp reduction of salaries, but also a decrease in the number of officials.

In the years 1931 and 1932 a certain number of public servants with incomes below 20,000 guilders had been discharged, and even 11 per cent. of those with incomes over 10,000 guilders. Since 1930 the expenditure for the Army had been reduced from 72 to

58 millions. In order to effect further economies, the existing
organisation was to be replaced by a smaller one, on a cost
basis of 50 millions. A reduced defensive army had, after
serious consideration, been found preferable to a police army. As
to the Navy, in February the Netherlands Minister for Defence,
Dr. C. N. Deckers, had paid a three weeks' visit to the Dutch
East Indies to inspect the naval institutions and to discuss the
question of the distribution of expenditure for the Navy between
the Home Country and the eastern part of the realm. For the
last few years this method had been followed, so that half the cost
of construction of ships for the East Indies was charged to the
Netherland India Budget.

At the end of the year the revenues yielded 262·1 million
guilders, so that the deficit could be estimated at 139·3 millions.
A 5 per cent. loan was issued to an amount of 106 million guilders,
the proceeds of which were intended for the redemption of the
floating debt. On December 31 the consolidated and the floating
debt totalled 1418 millions, and that of the provinces and communes, 100 millions.

CHAPTER VIII.

MOROCCO AND EGYPT.

MOROCCO.

EARLY in 1932 the operations which the French had been
carrying on for several months on the southern side of the High
Atlas were crowned with complete success. On January 15
French and Moroccan troops occupied without loss the oases
of Tafilet, a district covering about 115 square miles and with
a reputed population of 80,000. Some resistance was encountered
at Risan from the rebel chief Belkacem, but he was eventually
surrounded, and only escaped capture by abandoning his wives and
a great part of his arms and ammunition. Since the insurrection
of Moroccan tribes under Belkacem in 1917, Tafilet had been
a rallying ground for the dissidents, and raids had frequently been
made from it on French posts on the borders of Algeria and
Morocco. When M. Lucien Saint became the French Resident-
General in 1930, the idea of a frontal attack on the district was
discussed, but was dismissed as likely to be too costly. Instead
it was decided to proceed by means of a gradual military en-
circlement, while at the same time French political agents negotiated with the chiefs in order to detach them from their
allegiance to Belkacem. The occupation of Tafilet gave the
French for the first time a real control over the farther side
of the Atlas, and was expected to be followed by a complete

pacification of the Atlas district within a couple of years. Early
in April it was announced in Paris that Tarudant had been brought
into the safety zone, which now extended as far as Biugra, south
of Agadir.

At the end of 1931 a decree was published in Madrid reorganising the Spanish Protectorate in Morocco under a High
Commissioner, to whom both the armed forces and the Moorish
Khalifa were to be subordinated. Early in March the Republican Government of Spain declared that in no circumstances
would it abandon the Spanish Zone in Morocco. Conditions in
the Zone remained peaceful throughout the year, but owing to
disturbed conditions in Spain and the general economic depression, little progress was made with the economic development
of the country.

In Tangier the International Legislative Assembly early in
the year, in order to relieve the prevailing depression, voted a
sum for public works. On March 30 the Committee of Control,
consisting of the representatives of the Powers, exercising for
the first time the prerogative conferred upon it by the Constitution, vetoed the proposed expenditure as unduly extravagant.
Energetic protests were made against this decision, first by the
Legislative Assembly, which threatened to suspend its activities
if certain reforms were not granted, and then by a demonstration
representing all sections of the population, which on April 25
presented a number of demands for the redress of grievances to
the President of the Committee of Control and the Mendub.
The demands included, in addition to relief from insupportable
Budget charges, the construction of the necessary public works,
the authorisation of a casino, and a free port zone in the harbour
area. These demands were assented to, and the agitation sub-
sided. The proposal to open a casino once more failed to obtain
the assent of the Spanish representative. The only step taken
by the Committee of Control was to consult a financial expert,
who made a number of proposals. In November it called upon
the Administrator to make drastic changes in the proposed Budget,
which showed a grave deficit, and feeling again became excited.

The Sultan of Morocco in June signed a decree declaring
that Kenitra port should henceforth be known as Port Lyautey,
in honour of the former famous French Resident-General.

EGYPT.

Throughout the year Ismail Pasha Sidky retained office
and power, keeping Parliament suspended for the greater part of
the period. The main opposition, the Wafd, showed signs of
disintegration, and the Prime Minister's position was appreciably stronger at the end of the year than at the beginning.

First, in January, the Government decided to prosecute
Mohamed Pasha Mahmud, a former Prime Minister, and the
Leader of the Liberal Constitutional Party, whose alliance with
the Wafd was close, for certain intemperate passages in his
political speeches. The cleavage in the Wafd itself, however,
did not come to a head until October, when a definite split developed between the more reasonable and moderate members,
former stalwarts in the party, and Nahas Pasha, who considered
himself almost the divinely appointed successor of Zaghloul, and
as such the appointed dictator, and his following.   Nahas
Pasha secured the support of a majority in his organisation.
Attempts at reconciliation failed, and in the end several prominent Wafdists, who did not support their leader's dictatorial
claims, were expelled. The Government, of course, took no part
in this internal quarrel. Their action, in fact, if it had any
influence on it, would have tended to heal it. For in the midst
of the dispute the Prime Minister took the extreme step of in
effect closing "The House of the People." He called upon
Mme. Zaghloul, and impressed upon her the necessity, in future,
to use her house only as a private residence and not as the headquarters of the Wafd. At the same time the usual celebration
of the anniversary of Zaghloul Pasha's formal demand for independence for Egypt made in November, 1918, was prohibited
and prevented. There were disturbances also in November, when
the Wafdists tried to assemble in the Saadist Club in order to
elect successors to those members of the Executive Council
who had been dismissed by Nahas Pasha. In the course of the
disturbances the crowd, which included a number of Wafdist
ex-Cabinet Ministers, was forcibly dispersed and some of its
members injured.

Early in May an unsuccessful attempt was made to blow up
the Prime Minister's train. The Wafd was directly held responsible for the outrage, and a number of members of the party
were convicted and sentenced to imprisonment.

The Prime Minister's visit to Europe in the summer, in the
course of which he interviewed several European Ministers, raised
expectations of movements in the foreign political field and the
beginning of new negotiations for an Anglo-Egyptian treaty.
Sidky Pasha had been back in Egypt more than a month before
he made any statement on the subject. This was merely to the
effect that he had discussed with the British Foreign Minister
the question of a treaty, and that they were in agreement that
such a treaty should be negotiated. More important for
Sidky Pasha and his party was this acknowledgment by the
British Government that his Government was sufficiently stable
and well founded to justify its acceptance as representative of
the Egyptian people. It may be that it was this indirect support
given by the British to his Government that led to the very

mild bomb explosion at the British Residency in December.
The explosion did practically no damage, and was probably
intended to be a gesture rather than a serious attempt. An
attempt by young Wafdist hotheads to organise a boycott of
British goods in retaliation for supposed British support of the
Sidky Government fell noticeably flat.

At the end of the year Mohamed Pasha Mahmoud again took
formal steps to secure the dismissal of the Government. He
appealed direct to the King, citing in support the Badari affair,
which subsequently led to differences in the Cabinet. Two young
men of that district were convicted of murdering the local Mamur
or Sub-prefect, but were recommended to mercy because the
Mamur had persecuted and tortured them, apparently merely
because they were opponents of the Government. The affair had
its repercussions even outside the circles of the opposition. The
Minister of Justice ordered an inquiry, with a view to the abolition
of administrative practices to which the trial had drawn attention,
but the Prime Minister himself was less inclined to a change.

Finance and related matters were prominent in the history
of Egypt during the year. The detachment of sterling from gold
carried the Egyptian pound in its wake. Its effects, at any rate
in the first stages, were beneficial. The value of the staple
product, cotton, rose in terms of the Egyptian currency, yet fell
in those of the gold countries. As a consequence its export found
encouragement. The original Budget estimates showed a deficit
of 3,300,000l.E., but it was possible to suppress this, mainly by
economies, and the Budget was balanced without any appreciable
increase in taxation. There was, however, one cause for anxiety,
not very large, perhaps, but growing. The French and Italian
rentiers claimed that the Egyptian Debt was on a gold basis,
and that in consequence payments of interest and amortisation
should be in gold and not Egyptian pounds. They proceeded
to law in the matter, but the case had not been heard at the end
of the year. Meanwhile political negotiations were proceeding
in which the British Government, despite the number of British
creditors, was urging the Egyptian case on the other Governments. The sum involved was about 1,700,000l.E. for the current
year, with arrears of about two and a half millions.

Despite a certain increase in the export of cotton, the cotton
situation, in the past the source of the greater part of Egypt's
wealth, remained very unsatisfactory. With the fall in price
by two-thirds the volume of cultivation fell by a half. With
the encouragement of the Government, which hopes to make
the country largely independent of imports, wheat was extensively planted in place of cotton. But the cultivation of wheat
did not relieve the cultivators, and the Government had to step
in, and by means of loans and deferment of debt repayment
come to their assistance. To encourage the production of wheat

a heavy import duty was put on all foreign wheat. For twenty years the scheme for building the great Gebel Aulia dam across the White Nile had been under consideration, and in the later years the opposition had been not only economic, but as so often happens in the East, also political. Opposition to the project had become a cardinal principle among all true opponents of Sidky Pasha. The Government, however, in May, succeeded in getting the project through Parliament, and when the dam is completed, it is estimated that some 600,000 acres of agricultural land will benefit.

The one incident in the history of the Sudan during the year was an incursion of raiders from Abyssinia. After a conference between representatives of the Governments of the Sudan and Abyssinia, the latter undertook to return the captives and cattle taken and in addition to pay compensation.

CHAPTER IX.

AMERICA : THE UNITED STATES—ARGENTINA—BOLIVIA AND PARA-
   GUAY — BRAZIL — CHILE — MEXICO — PERU — ECUADOR—
   URUGUAY.

THE UNITED STATES.

THE " economic blizzard " which had begun to blow across the United States in the autumn of 1929, continued at almost " hurricane force " throughout the first half of 1932.

Then came a lull. Wholesale commodity prices which had been steadily falling, turned and climbed moderately upward for three months, and business followed. But in October a fresh decline of prices set in, the various indices reaching at the end of December the lowest levels since 1908. On November 3 wheat on the Chicago Board of Trade touched $41\frac{5}{8}$ cents—below the tariff of $42\frac{1}{2}$ cents a bushel—and the lowest recorded price in the history of the country. The country's foreign trade, both as to imports and exports, fell to the level of 1905. However, business activity held its very slight gains, despite the resumed fall in prices, and the year ended, like the two previous ones, with an immense question mark.

Unemployment, which had been estimated by the American Federation of Labour in 1931 at 7,000,000, reached—according to the same authority—a total of 11,000,000 in 1932 out of the 48,000,000 found " gainfully employed " in the 1930 census. Without minimising the almost impossible burden laid upon public relief and private charity by this volume of unemployment, perhaps the most remarkable phase of the situation was the rapid development of " barter " among the unemployed themselves as a method of relieving their destitution.

Since employment for wages was obviously not to be had, the unemployed in some 500 communities organised " barter exchanges " at which the enrolled members offered to do work in exchange for food, clothing, shelter " or what have you ? " In Los Angeles more than 200,000 thus found fresh resources ; in several of the rural States the movement spread to the professional classes, doctors accepting eggs, chickens, and other farm produce in exchange for their services. The movement in some communities spread so widely that local shopkeepers found business depressed still further by the " barter exchanges." In Hawarden, Iowa, and in Minneapolis, the exchanges issued engraved " scrip " to facilitate the exchange of goods and services —a device publicly approved by Dr. Irving Fisher, the economist. In all it is estimated that at least 2,000,000 out of the 11,000,000 unemployed were being more or less continuously assisted by organised exchanges of this type.

However, admirable as this was as an expression of American " individualism," there was not lacking, in other quarters, a determination to get direct Federal aid. The veterans of the World War, organised as the " American Legion," exerted political pressure upon Congress to force the passage of an Act which would provide 2,400,000,000 dollars in additional currency to be given outright to the veterans as a " bonus " for their services ; this was to be in addition to the heavy pension bill already assumed for those disabled in the war and for the dependants of those killed.

Banking circles were profoundly alarmed at this proposed " inflation " of the currency, and Mr. Hoover courageously opposed it, notwithstanding the possible or probable loss of the " veteran vote " at the forthcoming presidential election.

But the ensuing struggle was a remarkable chapter in the Republic's experience with the veterans of its various wars. After months of newspaper and platform agitation there rolled into Washington on May 29 some 16 truckloads of " bonus marchers," the first detachment of the self-styled " Bonus Expeditionary Force." In all there converged upon the Capitol some 20,000 ex-soldiers—many bringing their wives and children —who announced that they proposed to camp in Washington until their demand for that bonus was granted. They lived precariously in tents, rude " shacks," and unused Government buildings, furnishing the authorities serious problems in providing food and sanitation.

They successfully " stormed " the Lower House, that responsive body adopting their " bonus Bill " on June 14 amid cheers, but when the Senate rejected the Bill three days later, there were scenes of considerable disorder. Finally on July 28 troops were called out, the camps broken up and burned, and the "marchers" forcibly expelled from the Capitol. For this Mr. Hoover got both praise and censure.

But the President, having lost in large measure the confidence of the country and, very definitely, the co-operation of the Democratic Lower House, found the closing year of his administration a discouraging one.

The Treasury's deficit at the close of the calendar year 1931 had been 1,385,449,000 dollars, but the failure of Congress to agree either on economies in expenditures or on suitable fresh sources of revenue, brought it by June 30, 1932, to 2,885,000,000 dollars. However, by that time fiscal legislation of sorts had been adopted and the deficit at the close was down to 1,159,286,000 dollars, though the prospects are that June 30, 1933, will see the gap between revenue and expenditure widened rather than narrowed. Toward the close of the year the Democrats, conscious of their responsibilities as the party in power, seemed disposed to grant the new Democratic President, Mr. Franklin D. Roosevelt, very large powers in furthering Government economies.

But Mr. Hoover accomplished at least two things. In January Congress, at his request, set up the Reconstruction Finance Corporation, with a revolving fund of 2,000,000,000 dollars to be loaned to banks, building and loan associations, railways, and agriculture. The President signed the Bill on January 22 and the machinery started on February 2. At first the loans were made secretly, so as to relieve hard-pressed situations without causing local alarm, but Congress grew suspicious and demanded that it be furnished with full details as to the way the fund was being managed. Mr. Hoover refused, but finally gave way, and a policy of full monthly disclosures of amounts and beneficiaries was adopted. In the case of banks requiring assistance, this had the effect of immediately " broadcasting " their plight and frequently of increasing the " runs " upon them. However, the Reconstruction Finance Corporation was instrumental in rescuing many small banks and a few large ones, as well as in tiding various railroads over their emergencies.

Another Bill, the Glass-Steagall Bill, which was signed by the President on February 27, was designed to improve the borrowing powers of the member banks in the Federal Reserve system as well as to increase the system's reserve of " free gold." It proved of material assistance to the banking system. Theoretically or potentially it increased by some 800,000,000 dollars the gold available to meet any foreign drains upon the reserve.

But neither of these measures seemed to add anything to Mr. Hoover's popularity. As early as January he intimated his willingness to stand for re-election in November, and it was a foregone conclusion that the Republican Party would have to re-nominate him or confess at once that his administration had been a failure.   This they did, without much enthusiasm, at the party's convention in Chicago on June 16.

The Democrats, at their convention in the same city on July 1, nominated Governor Franklin D. Roosevelt, of New York, for President, and John N. Garner, of Texas, Speaker of the House of Representatives, as Vice-President.

Curiously enough, neither convention paid the slightest attention to the current depression, being completely absorbed in the perennial fight between the " wets " and the " drys." Mr. Hoover, although on record as a " dry," permitted the Republican Party to write a " damp " plank, promising " State option " on the enforcement of the 18th Amendment, but the Democratic convention, perhaps to the dismay of the leaders, was stampeded into adopting a clear-cut resolution demanding the repeal of the 18th Amendment by State conventions in the various States, and promising, in the interim, legislation permitting the manufacture and sale of " beer and other beverages." This was received with wild enthusiasm throughout the country, showing that the Democrats had successfully gauged the reversal of feeling regarding the " noble experiment." A poll of several million people, taken by the *Literary Digest* in May, had shown majorities against prohibition in all the forty-eight States except Kansas and North Carolina.

But the actual campaign swung back immediately to the realities of the depression.   Mr. Hoover, despite great physical fatigue, made some very strong speeches over the wireless, defending his record and painting rather alarming pictures of Democratic incapacity.   Mr. Roosevelt severely criticised Mr. Hoover's lack of real achievements, promised to remedy certain abuses connected with " big business " and Wall Street, but cautiously refrained from advancing any very radical programme.

The results were never in doubt after the Republican State of Maine, in September, went Democratic by a large majority. The election on November 8 was a history-making " landslide " for the Democratic Party.   Mr. Hoover, with a popular vote of 15,759,286, carried only six States with 59 votes in the electoral college, while Mr. Roosevelt, with a popular vote of 22,813,786, carried forty-two States with 472 votes in the electoral college. This is the first time that the Democratic Party has ever won a majority of the popular vote.   The Democrats captured the Senate and increased their majority in the Lower House.

The months which ensued before the President-Elect could take office on March 4, 1933, revealed as almost never before that undesirable feature of the American constitutional system by which the newly elected President was forced to wait four months before assuming office and the newly elected Congress (unless summoned in special session) was forced to wait eleven months. Mr. Hoover, his policies repudiated by the country and faced with a Congress which was not only Democratic but which included a large contingent of defeated Congressmen (popularly known as " lame ducks "), was forced virtually to mark time.

Fortunately this " interregnum " will be the last in American history. After ten years of discussion, Congress on March 2 submitted to the States, for ratification by the State legislatures, a proposed Amendment to the Constitution—the 20th—by virtue of which the incoming President assumes office at noon on January 20 and the newly elected Congress assembles on January 3, in both cases of the year following the November election. Public opinion was ripe for the change. Virginia ratified it on March 4, being the first State to do so, and by January 23, 1933, Missouri became the thirty-sixth State to ratify it, thus effecting its adoption by three-fourths of the States.

The new Amendment will not advance the date of Mr. Roosevelt's inauguration nor the convening of the 73rd Congress, but it will apply to all future Presidents, Vice-Presidents, and Congresses.

In the main the country was thoroughly preoccupied by the industrial and financial effects of the depression. Mr. Hoover set an example of economy by cutting his presidential salary 20 per cent. ; the Vice-President and members of the Cabinet reduced theirs 15 per cent. A New York magazine printed a detailed article—quite possibly emanating from the White House—showing in detail how Mr. Hoover's private fortune had melted during his presidency from 4,000,000 dollars to 700,000 dollars owing to the depression. The private fortune of Mr. John D. Rockefeller, Sr., according to a current biographer, had declined from close to 500,000,000 dollars to 150,000,000 dollars. Henry Ford, who startled the world in 1914 by establishing 5 dollars a day as the " minimum wage " for unskilled employees —a figure which, during the boom, had reached 8 dollars a day— cut the minimum wage to 4 dollars a day. The decline in stocks was picturesquely driven home by one of the big " chain store " systems which sold over the counter, for 100 dollars each, " assorted parcels, each containing twenty-five different leading shares."

There was widespread interest in the final report of Mr. Hoover's " Research Committee on Social Trends " which appeared at the close of the year. That report, a voluminous document heavily bulwarked with statistics, declared : " The American standard of living for the near future must decline because of lower wages caused by unemployment, the possible slowness of business recovery, and the weakness of mass action by employees." While disclaiming any " alarmist " views, the Committee declared it would be " highly negligent to gloss over the stark and bitter realities of the social situation and to ignore the imminent perils in further advance of our heavy technical machinery over crumbling roads and shaking bridges."

More sensational was the emergence in November of a gloomy analysis of the situation put forth by a group of engineers headed by Howard Scott of New York City, under the name of "Technocracy." This group blamed machine technique for the slump, pointing out that "technological unemployment" was bound to get worse, and proposing, in place of the conventional wages and price system which had "broken down," a new system based on "units of energy." This was a ten days' wonder, much exploited in the Press, but it got no organised following.

Strange as it may seem in the light of subsequent developments, public opinion at the beginning of the year showed a strong drift towards cancellation of the so-called "war debts."

This was earliest revealed in the South where cotton trade journals and newspapers began to point out that cotton was the chief export of the United States and that the cancellation of these international debts—which would cost the United States 268,000,000 dollars a year—might prove a small price to pay for the restoration of foreign markets for cotton. Exports of raw cotton had dwindled in 1931-32 to 340,000,000 dollars compared with average yearly exports, for the previous five years, of 611,000,000 dollars. "Forget the debts, and restore our foreign markets."

On April 13, at a Jefferson Day dinner in New York city, Mr. Alfred E. Smith—the unsuccessful Democratic candidate for the presidency in 1928 against Mr. Hoover—echoed and improved on this. He suggested that "we forget the debts for 20 years" and that the Government should write off from the principal of each debt annually an amount equal to 25 per cent. of the debtor country's imports from the United States. This had a very favourable Press, and in May the powerful Railroad Brotherhoods presented to President Hoover and Congress a joint memorandum pressing for debt cancellation as a short cut out of the world-wide depression.

Although Congress was silent, the tide seemed to be setting strongly.

Then came reversals. In the middle of May the French banks began hurriedly withdrawing their balances from New York in the form of gold. This was certainly due, at least in part, to general European alarm at the growing deficit of the United States Government, at Congress's apparent inability to face the need for severest economy, and perhaps to the fear that the United States was about to embark on an inflation of its currency. At any rate, the "gold drain" amounted to 1,000,000,000 dollars during the first six months, reducing the country's monetary gold stock on June 15, to 3,909,000,000 dollars, a new low level, and giving rise to widespread fears that the country was being forced off the gold standard. Intense resentment was felt especially towards France who was popularly regarded as having deliberately engineered the " dollar panic " in order to show her financial power.

But the Lausanne Conference from June 16 to July 9 was also unfortunate in its repercussions on American opinion. It had, in the main, a good Press until towards the close when it became apparent that a " gentleman's agreement " had been reached by the seven Powers that the Lausanne concord was to be contingent upon favourable action by the United States substantially reducing the international debts owed to it. This caused immediate resentment as, apparently a concerted European attempt to fasten upon the United States the sole responsibility for the perpetuation of German reparations or, alternatively, to face a general default on the " foreign obligations " owing to it.

The very words, " gentleman's agreement," were unfortunate, for Americans reserve the phrase almost exclusively for those underhanded and illegal agreements reached by " big business " in its efforts to circumvent the law ; its associations are entirely satiric. Thus Lausanne became, almost overnight, discredited in American eyes as simply a piece of low cunning aimed at the American taxpayer and nobody else.

On top of this came, to American astonishment, the Franco-British exchange of Notes pledging each other to " complete candour " on all questions " similar in origin to that now so happily settled at Lausanne." If this amicable exchange meant anything, it could only mean that Great Britain and France had decided to stand together in confronting the United States regarding the international debts. With the Presidential campaign already under way, President Hoover felt he could not let this pass without comment, and on July 13 he wrote to Senator Borah, Chairman of the Senate Committee on Foreign Relations, reiterating that the United States was not a party to the Lausanne Conference and could not be influenced on international debts by any " European agreement."

Furthermore, the Americans became vividly conscious at this juncture of the overwhelming burden of the domestic debt. Farm mortgages outstanding, for example, totalled 8,500,000,000 dollars (1,700,000,000*l*. at par), though the annual farm income had dropped from 11,000,000,000 dollars in 1929 to 5,300,000,000 dollars in 1932. Other debts of the farmers totalled 3,000,000,000 dollars, making a gross indebtedness more than twice the current income. Defaults on farm mortgages were widespread, leading in many States to mob intervention to prevent foreclosure sales. In Mississippi alone 16 per cent. of the farm acreage and 12 per cent. of the urban property were " sold for taxes " in April. Both New York City and Chicago were on the verge, apparently, of bankruptcy ; in New York City alone it was estimated that one resident out of every seven was being fed by private or public charity. Public opinion, conscious of the presence in

New York of 700,000,000 dollars in gold belonging to the Bank of
France and the other French banks, was inclined to ridicule the
plea of the French Government that it could not find 19,000,000
dollars with which to pay its instalment.

The first reaction in Congress was a general demand that
the debtors should be forced to default, facing the consequences
of their action in the delicate field of international credit. But
Senator Borah made steady headway with his contention that
the reduction or cancellation of the debts should be used to wrest
concessions from the debtors as to disarmament, the revision of
the Versailles Treaty and the promotion of world trade through
tariff reductions. The U.S. Chamber of Commerce held in
December a referendum of its members of the Borah proposals ;
the member organisations voted 7 to 1 in favour of making
European disarmament a condition, and 17 to 1 in favour of
making general tariff reductions a condition.

But the two major political parties avoided the question.
The Republican platform merely endorsed Mr. Hoover's handling
of the debt problem, and the Democratic platform simply said :
" We are opposed to the cancellation of the war debts " with
no reference to their possible modification.

It was not until the receipt of the British and French Notes
on November 10, asking postponement of the December 15 payment and the re-opening of the entire question, that the issue
became a leading one.

The Notes [1] were not of much assistance to the small American
group, headed by Dr. Nicholas Murray Butler and Mr. Newton D.
Baker, who were arguing for complete and generous cancellation.
American opinion, according to a writer in *Scribner's Magazine*,
crystallised more or less as follows : " These people, for their
own ends, mean to default on their debts, but in the meantime
they try to gloss it over by reading us a lecture on economics,
and to back up their demands by threatening ruin to our currency
and the loss of our European markets." An article by Mr. J. M.
Keynes, intended for English readers but reprinted in the New
York *Herald-Tribune*, caused considerable indignation by its
reference to the debts as " pure usury "—presumably in the
theological sense of that term.

As December 15 approached, when the resumed instalments
of principal and interest fell due, there was widespread curiosity
to see what course the debtor countries would pursue. Great
Britain got an enthusiastic Press when she "earmarked " 95,500,000
dollars in gold in payment of her instalment. Others who remitted were Italy (1,245,437 dollars), Czechoslovakia (1,500,000
dollars), Finland (186,235 dollars), Latvia (111,852 dollars), and
Lithuania (92,836 dollars).

---

[1] For the text of the principal British Note see under Public Documents.

France's decision to "postpone" payment of 19,261,432 dollars provoked indignation and a wave of anti-French sentiment in and out of Congress. She was, however, joined in this course by Poland (3,302,980 dollars), Belgium (2,125,000 dollars), Estonia (266,370 dollars), and Hungary (40,729 dollars). The "defaults," temporary or otherwise, amounted to 24,996,512 dollars compared with payments of 98,685,911 dollars.

Mr. Roosevelt, as President-Elect, held aloof from Mr. Hoover's handling of the November debt Notes, preferring to reserve his policy until after his inauguration on March 4, 1933. President Hoover, in accepting the British Government's invitation on August 2 to participate in the World Economic and Monetary Conference, had expressly stipulated that neither the international debts nor the American tariff should be on the agenda. It seems quite probable that Mr. Roosevelt, when he assumes office, may take a bolder line than that. At any rate, an influential group of industrialists as well as numerous economists, pressed him to seize the World Economic Conference as the occasion for a general settlement of both these questions.

The agitation to get rid of Filipino competition in sugar and tobacco by granting the Philippine Archipelago its "freedom" culminated in December in the passage of an Act to that effect by both Houses of Congress. President Hoover vetoed it promptly with a message declaring it to be an irresponsible measure, embodying a fallacious economic theory and representing the abandonment of the country's international and moral obligations. The House of Representatives was obstinate and re-passed the measure immediately, followed by the Senate on January 17, 1933.

However, as cables from Manila suggested that the Act was unacceptable to the Filipino Legislature, the outcome is by no means clear. The Act provides that the Filipino Legislature must approve of the terms offered within two years and call a Constitutional convention ; refusing or failing to do that, the offer becomes void. The Constitution, as drafted by the Filipino convention, must be approved by a plebiscite. If approved, a preparatory period of ten years must elapse at the end of which the islands become automatically free. During the ten years interim, Filipino immigration into the United States is to be shut off and imports are to be restricted, in part by quotas and in part by taxation ; the President during the interim retains control of constabulary and the Supreme Court retains the right of deciding appeals on constitutional points.

Although the drive behind the measure was very largely economic, there were not lacking those like Senator Borah who declared that "imperialism" and Republican institutions were incompatible. The Act, incidentally, pledges the Government to secure, if possible, an international treaty guaranteeing the independence of the islands, thus presumably disposing of the "Japanese menace."

In the Caribbean the year was fairly quiet, though the Haitian Legislature rejected the treaty signed on September 3 which would, in effect, have prolonged American " assistance " to 1952. There was some annoyance in September when Great Britain, France, Spain, and several other countries recognised the " insurrectionary " Government of President Martinez of Salvador, the State Department regarding it as a blow at the South and Central American Treaties refusing to acknowledge revolutionary Governments. General Martinez was Secretary of War, and these treaties all provide that no Secretary of War may be declared President. In Nicaragua the warring factions made peace, and on January 1, 1933, the last detachment of American Marines retired from the country.

Apart from the question of the international debts, referred to above, foreign affairs played but a small part in the year.

On January 7 the State Department sent identic Notes to China and Japan invoking its own rights and those of its nationals in Manchuria, under the Nine-Powers Treaty of 1922 and the Kellogg-Briand Pact, to " outlaw war," to which Japan replied on January 16 to the effect that the " open door " policy would be maintained in the new Manchurian State. The United States also signed the joint Note—along with Great Britain, France, and Italy—which was addressed to Japan and endorsed by the League Council on February 2. Perhaps the most significant development of the year, on this and similar issues, was the statement made by Mr. William R. Castle, Jr., the Acting Secretary of State, in an address to the Congress on International Justice in Washington on May 4 ; Mr. Castle declared that the United States had evolved a " new policy," that of not recognising any territorial gains made by any nation which violated the Kellogg-Briand Pact.

Disarmament fell into the background, though there was general support for Mr. Hoover's proposals, submitted to the Disarmament Conference at Geneva on June 22, that there be a limitation on the number of men under arms, total abolition of tanks, bombing planes, and mobile artillery, and a reduction in the tonnage of battleships by one-third and of aircraft-carriers, cruisers, and destroyers. But there was apparently not much confidence that any real disarmament programme could be carried during a period of rising international friction in Europe. The St. Lawrence Waterway Treaty with Canada, providing for the dredging and development of the St. Lawrence river by the two countries, was signed in Washington on July 18, but it awaits ratification by Congress.

Easily the most disturbing and sensational event of the year was one which brought home to the nation the growing lawlessness of the post-war period. On March 1 the nineteen-months-old son of Colonel Charles Lindbergh was kidnapped from the

Lindberghs new home in the Sourland Mountain region north-west of Princeton, New Jersey. The crime shocked the public profoundly, and a world-wide hunt for the kidnappers ensued. Night after night the clues were broadcasted and every agency, from that of the Federal Government downwards, was enlisted. Colonel Lindbergh paid 50,000 dollars to a heartless individual who falsely professed his ability to bring the distracted father into touch with the kidnappers. But every clue failed, and on May 12 the child's body, reduced almost to a skeleton, was found in a thicket by the roadside within five miles of home. Although a number of wealthy men had been kidnapped and held for substantial ransom, this case in particular brought home to the public the prevailing insecurity of life in the face of crime and lawlessness.

ARGENTINA.

The early part of 1932 was marked by the full return of the country to constitutional government, the way to which had been paved by the election in the previous November of General Agustin Justo as President, and of a new Congress (*vide* ANNUAL REGISTER, 1931). Congress was sworn in on January 20, and at once commenced its sittings. On February 18 the President-Elect made a statement of policy in which he said that he intended to conform strictly to the law, " the only sure way to protect citizens in their rights." In foreign affairs he would follow the traditional policy of peace and concord with all the world, and attempt to strengthen the moral and material ties which united Argentina with other countries, especially those with whom she had commercial treaties, or who sent her immigrants. He expressed the hope that his country would be represented at the next Assembly of the League of Nations. Referring to domestic affairs, he said that he could not co-operate with the Radical Party until it had re-organised itself and got rid of some of its obnoxious members —a reference probably to the ex-Presidents Irigoyen and Alvear. He concluded by saying that he intended to make in all departments the severe economies demanded by the situation of the Treasury, in order to balance the Budget and to enable the country to meet its international obligations.

General Justo was installed on February 20 with a minimum of ceremony. The occasion was taken throughout the country to pay homage to the retiring Provisional President, General Uriburu, who had established his title to be regarded as one of the greatest patriots, if not the greatest, in the history of the nation by his self-sacrificing efforts during his period of office, and not least by resigning his exceptional powers as soon as his work was completed—a proceeding rare indeed in South American history. He died soon after (April 28) in Paris [*vide* Obituaries].

U

President Justo, in his address to Congress, pleaded for harmony between Congress and the Executive, and emphasised the need for constitutional reform. His Cabinet comprised three anti-personalist Radicals, one Conservative, one Independent Socialist, and three non-party men. The Minister of Finance was Don Alberto Hueyo, well known for his work as president of the central produce market.

Financial questions at this period overshadowed all others. It was estimated that the Budgetary deficit for 1931 would be equal to about 23,000,000*l*., and on January 20 emergency taxation measures had been decreed which were to remain in force for five years and covered income tax, matches, cigarettes, cinematograph films, business licences, foreign exchange, landed property, securities, and insurance. General Uriburu, on the eve of his retirement from the Ministry of Finance, issued a memorandum in which he said that, while there had been no increase in the amount of currency in circulation, he had thought it necessary to establish a central bank and to pass new banking laws for the eventual stabilisation of the currency and control of exchange operations. His successor, Don Alberto Hueyo, was reported to share these views, and in his first message to the public he exhorted them to endure the recently imposed taxation with patience, as the object of it was to enable the Budget to be balanced on the basis of drastic economy. He followed this up by stating on March 10 that there was absolutely no intention to resort to the emission of a paper currency, and that the regularity of the service of foreign debts was fully assured, as was also the payment of arrears of salaries to Government officials.

One of the chief devices of Senor Hueyo for combating his financial difficulties was to institute a " Patriotic Loan " of 500 million pesos. This idea was well seconded in the country, and by August 150 million pesos had been raised. Thanks to this and to very careful management, including irksome restrictions on the movement of exchange, and economies representing about 30,000,000 pesos, Argentina was able to maintain the service on her foreign debts and to avoid inflation of the currency. In August the Finance Minister foreshadowed a Budget deficit which would be equivalent to about 8,000,000*l*. Towards the end of the year the Banco de la Nacion, with the approval of the Government, invited Sir Otto Niemeyer to visit Buenos Aires for the purpose of making an investigation of the financial and banking situation.

One cause of the Government's financial difficulties was a drop in revenue due to the decline in imports, in spite of the fact that the average rate of duty had been raised from 20 to 28 per cent. of the value of the imports. There was a strong feeling in the country in favour of encouraging imports from Great Britain—partly as a result of the Anglo-Argentine Exhibition of 1931. As a first step in this direction, the Government in the spring halved the duty on whisky, and in August it sent a commercial mission to England, presided over by Senor Malbran, the Argentine Ambassador in London, to negotiate a reciprocal trade treaty. The results of the Ottawa Conference, however, came as a severe disappointment to Argentina, which could not believe that Britain would ever impose food taxes, and there was a certain revulsion of feeling against England. It was thought that the restrictions on meat imports into England would deal a crushing blow to the Argentine cattle-raising industry. These fears, however, were to some extent allayed by the British Ambassador, Sir R. Macleay, who pointed out that the British restrictions were only tentative and might be modified as the result of further experience. In October the Argentine Rural Society urged the President to make without delay an agreement with Great Britain under which British imports should be treated with the same liberality with which Britain treated Argentine imports, as otherwise " the consequences of the Ottawa Conference might prove disastrous to Argentine trade." On the other hand, the Argentine Government towards the end of the year practised a discrimination against German goods which led to sharp protests from Germany, with the threat of retaliatory measures.

Resentment was also caused in Argentina by the efforts of the British Government to obtain more favourable treatment for the Anglo-Argentine Tramways Company, which had invested about 20,000,000*l.* in tram, omnibus, and subways services in Buenos Aires. Owing to the refusal of the authorities to allow a revision of the scale of fares, which had been fixed in 1908, the Company had paid no dividend for years, and in November, 1931, had been compelled to ask for a moratorium. On November 15 the Independent Socialist Party in the Buenos Aires City Council protested energetically against what it called the attempt of the British Government to dictate to the city, and their views found much sympathy.

Political conditions were fairly stable for the greater part of the year, and the Congress debates were on a higher level than usual. One of the last acts of General Uriburu's Government was to drop the charges which had been brought against Senor Irigoyen and to set him at liberty. This conciliatory gesture, however, failed to produce the desired effect. The ex-President demanded a full acquittal, and announced his intention of reorganising the Radical Party with a view to regaining power. Some excitement was caused in the summer by the sudden appearance in Buenos Aires of a " Fascist Party " which called upon the public to deliver itself from the thraldom of the banking institutions. The chief effect of this move was to cause a reaction towards the Left. Taking advantage of this, Dr. Irigoyen and Dr. Alvear—who had been allowed to return to Argentina—towards the end of the year formed a plot for overthrowing the Government and making

Senor Alvear President. The plot, however, was discovered, and the two ex-Presidents, along with over 100 of their followers, including many prominent Radicals, were placed under arrest on December 16. Martial law was declared for thirty days, although in many of the provinces the Governors declared that it was quite unnecessary. The country remained calm, and the bulk of the population rallied to the support of the Government.

Soon after the accession of the new Government to power, most of the Argentinian exiles who had taken refuge in Montevideo were allowed to return. An exception, however, was made in the case of General Toranzo, a notorious rebel. In July the cruiser *Uruguay* visited Buenos Aires to greet the Argentine nation on the anniversary of its independence. The Argentine authorities suspected that the vessel had General Toranzo on board and treated it in a manner which was resented by the Uruguayan officials. In consequence of the ill-feeling thus aroused, diplomatic relations between the two countries were broken off. It was soon recognised, however, that there had been a misunderstanding, and, the feeling between the publics of the two countries continuing to be most friendly, diplomatic relations were resumed on September 12.

Towards the end of December, Dr. Saavedra Lamas, the Minister for Foreign Affairs, published his draft of proposals for a Treaty of Non-Aggression and Conciliation between South American countries. The chief object of these was to eliminate the resort to force for the settlement of all disputes between the contracting parties. The new treaty was to supplement and not to suspend existing treaties. The draft was communicated to all South American States.

On September 28 the Chamber of Deputies authorised the Government to pay its dues to the League of Nations. At the same time it requested the Executive to explain to the League that Argentina considered the Monroe Doctrine, mentioned in Article 21, to be a unilateral political declaration which at one time rendered signal service to the cause of American independence, but did not constitute a regional agreement.

While economic troubles led to a certain amount of friction between England and the Argentine in the political sphere, cultural ties between the two countries were still further strengthened. On January 19 the Prince of Wales addressed the Argentine Chamber of Commerce in London, and laid special stress on this point, mentioning that the University of Buenos Aires had formed a committee for Anglo-Argentine cultural relations on which all faculties were represented. Later in the year scholarships bearing the name of the Prince of Wales were instituted at Oxford for two students from the University of Buenos Aires, on the lines of the Rhodes scholarships.

There was a good deal of Labour unrest during the year,

owing to reductions of wages or dismissals. At the end of May some men dismissed from the Union Telephone Company as a result of the financial crisis committed acts of sabotage which caused damage running into hundreds of thousands of pounds. At the end of the year the Buenos Aires Great Southern Railway announced its intention of reducing wages by 8 per cent., and it was feared that a strike would ensue.

BOLIVIA AND PARAGUAY.

Towards the end of 1931 a conference of neutral American States met in Washington to try to settle the long-standing dispute between Bolivia and Paraguay regarding the Gran Chaco. After sitting for eight months, it seemed to be within sight of bringing about an agreement when trouble again broke out. On June 29 and again on July 15 encounters took place between Bolivian and Paraguayan outposts in the disputed region, as a result of which the Bolivians first captured and then lost some forts. Immediately there was an outbreak of war fever in Bolivia, and the Government began to mobilise troops. Paraguay followed suit, and the danger of war again became imminent. Efforts at mediation were made by the neutral American States, by Great Britain, and by the League of Nations, and both sides expressed their willingness to submit the dispute to arbitration, but neither would consent to an armistice, save on terms unacceptable to the other. By September both sides had concentrated considerable forces in the Chaco district, and fighting took place in which the Bolivians were worsted, with some loss. Popular opinion in Bolivia, however, was still strongly in favour of continuing the war, and on October 28 the Chamber of Deputies in La Paz was mobbed because of its unwillingness to support the Government. Towards the end of November the League of Nations again made offers of mediation, as a result of which hostilities were suspended for the rest of the year.

BRAZIL.

During 1932 Brazil was kept in a state of unrest, culminating in a civil war, through the hostility of the State of São Paulo to the Provisional Government under President Dr. Getulio Vargas established in October, 1930. The leading politicians of São Paulo hankered after the old regime which had been overthrown by the revolution of that year, and which suited their interests better ; and they had sympathisers in the States of Matto Grosso, Minas Geraes, and Rio Grande do Sul. Early in the year dissension became acute between the Government and representatives of all these States, but it was temporarily composed as a result of a conference held in March at Petropolis, at which Dr. Vargas promised to hold General Elections at an early date, with a view to the restoration of what was called "constitutional" government.

On May 15 Dr. Vargas actually signed a Decree convoking a Constituent Assembly and fixing an election for it on May 3, 1933. Immediately after he delivered a Message to Congress in which, reviewing the work of his dictatorship, he showed that unprecedented economies had been effected in public expenditure, enabling the Budget to be balanced, and greater efficiency to be secured in the Civil Service at reduced cost. Dr. Vargas declared that he " neither was nor could be opposed to the return of Brazil to a constitutional regime," but that the greater part of the reforms carried out could not have been made during a regime in which party interests predominated. These claims, whatever measure of truth there might be in them, were not of a kind to recommend him to the Paulista leaders, who desired a return to " constitutional " government precisely because it would afford the governing clique greater opportunities of self-aggrandisement. Some of the President's measures also bore hardly on São Paulo, such as his increases of taxation, and his levying of the 2 per cent. gold tax on imports at Santos, the port of São Paulo, which hitherto alone of Brazilian ports had been exempt from this impost.

From an early point in the summer, preparations were made by the Paulista leaders with great secrecy for an armed rising. The unrest in São Paulo and other States was accentuated by the failure of the negotiations of the United Front (Frente Unica) with the dictatorship for the formation of a Government of National Concentration. Matters were brought to a head by the dismissal early in July of General Berthold Klinger, commanding the Federal troops in the State of Matto Grosso, for having protested against the appointment of General Espirito Santo Cardoso as Minister of War in place of General Leite de Castro, who resigned. On July 9 a revolt led by two regiments of the Fuerza Publica, or State militia, broke out in the city of São Paulo. The Federal Interventor, Senhor Pedro de Toledo, resigned his position and placed himself at the head of the revolt. A call for volunteers was responded to with the utmost enthusiasm, and in a short time General Klinger, who was placed in charge of the military operations, found himself at the head of an army said to number 150,000 men. A Provisional Government was installed at São Paulo, which conscribed practically the whole population for the making of munitions and similar services.

The Federal Government was taken completely by surprise, and had General Klinger acted with promptitude, he could probably have captured Rio. The Paulistas, however, dallied in the expectation that a number of other States would join them. In this they were disappointed. There were sporadic risings in Minas Geraes and Rio Grande do Sul, but the bulk of the

Federal troops in these States remained loyal to the Government, as did also the Navy. In Rio itself there were some demonstrations, mostly by students, against the Government, but they were soon suppressed. Apart from some small reinforcements from neighbouring States, the Paulistas were left to fight the battle by themselves.

The Federal Government was not long in taking the field with numbers and equipment which made its ultimate success only a matter of time. One of its first steps was to blockade closely the port of Santos. It also sent aeroplanes over São Paulo which bombed the aerodrome there but not the town itself. The Federal armies advanced towards the São Paulo frontiers both on the south and the north, and early in August severe fighting took place, with somewhat heavy losses on both sides. Various efforts were made at mediation, but the Federal Government insisted that the rebels should first lay down their arms, and to this they would not consent. Gradually the Federal troops obtained the upper hand. On September 14 they captured the important railway junction of Cruzeiro, near Campinas, in the north-western portion of the State of São Paulo, after a bombardment of nine weeks, and this opened the way to them to the interior of the State. On September 21 they took possession of the important military position of Cunha. Soon afterwards dissensions broke out among the Paulistas themselves, the bulk of the population realising that they had been deceived by the revolutionary leaders. On October 2 the insurgent Government fell and General Klinger took to flight, and Colonel Carvalho, who hitherto had been in command of the police force, assumed charge of the Government of the State in the name of the Federal Commander, General Monteiro, who soon after took possession of the town.

The rebel leaders were sent to Rio de Janeiro, and about a hundred of them were deported to places in the north of Brazil. The ex-President, General Bernardes, who was also among them, was exiled to Europe, along with Senhor de Toledo. Apart from this, the Federal Government did not carry out any reprisals against the population of São Paulo, though it kept martial law in force there for, a time. The only penalty which it laid upon the State was to insist that it should redeem the paper money which had been issued by the " Constitutionalist " Government, to the amount of 342,566 contos of reis, within forty-five days of October 15. To facilitate this operation, however, the Bank of Brazil agreed to advance to the State 150,000 contos. The total cost of the civil war to the State of São Paulo was estimated at between 160,000 and 170,000 contos of reis. Discontent continued to simmer in the city of São Paulo, and there were demonstrations against the Government.

The civil war placed a severe strain also on the finances of the Federal Government. On August 11 it raised an emergency

loan of 400,000 contos (about 8,500,000*l*.) at 7 per cent., repayable
in ten years. It also suspended for the time being redemption
and interest payments due in foreign currency. In the Budget
for 1933 which was issued on December 31, revenue was estimated
at 877,756 contos gold, and expenditure at 34,264 contos gold
and 1,861,975 contos paper. To assist the coffee industry, which
was severely affected by the world depression, the Government
in July, in conjunction with the Brazilian State Railways, arranged
with the Franz Haniel Company, of Duisberg-Ruhrort, for the
delivery to the Brazilian railways of 350,000 tons of Ruhr coal
in direct exchange for additional German imports of Brazilian
coffee.

A Commission was appointed in the autumn to prepare a new
Constitution, and commenced its labours on November 10.

At the end of the year the Brazilian Government addressed
a strongly worded Note to Peru and Colombia, threatening to
close the Amazon to traffic so far as those countries were concerned
if they persisted in using it for the movement of troops.

At the end of October the President signed a decree establishing
the eight-hour day in industry in Brazil.

CHILE.

The year 1932 in Chile was one of exceptional political unrest,
having its chief root in the economic distress of the country.
The export of nitrate, owing to the depression in world trade,
almost ceased, so that there was widespread unemployment
and great suffering among the working classes. A movement
for a Socialist Republic gained strength not only in civilian but
also in military quarters, and this, combined with previous political divisions, rendered stable government almost impossible.

The troubles of the year began with a forty-eight hours general
strike on January 11, the leaders of which put forward demands
of a highly Socialistic character. The Government managed to
keep the situation under control, but the Socialist agitation went
on unabated, its chief leader being Don Carlos Davila, a former
Chilean Minister at Washington. On April 7 a military plot to
capture the President, in which Señor Davila was implicated,
was discovered, and he and certain officers were placed under
arrest. The Ministry was reconstituted, and President Montero
obtained permission from Congress to place the country under
martial law for sixty days, at the same time issuing a manifesto
in which he charged his opponents with carrying on a subversive
propaganda based on the present financial difficulties of the country,
for which they themselves were to blame for having made promises
incapable of fulfilment.

For a few weeks longer Señor Montero maintained himself in

a precarious position. On June 3 he attempted to remove from office Colonel Grove, the Commander of the Aviation School, whom he distrusted on account of his Communist sympathies. This was the signal for a revolt, carried through by the garrison and air forces of the capital, as a result of which Señor Montero was driven from the Government palace, and power was seized by a Junta consisting of Colonel Grove, Señor Davila, and General Puga. A Cabinet was formed in which General Puga took the Ministry of the Interior and Colonel Grove that of Defence. A Socialist Republic was proclaimed, and a programme of an advanced Socialist colour was issued, including the increased taxation of large fortunes ; the confiscation of unproductive farm property in order to provide work for the unemployed ; the dissolution or reorganisation of Cosach (the Chilean Nitrate Company) ; the reopening of the smaller nitrate plants ; the confiscation of the sterling bank deposits at the rate of 40 pesos ; the establishment of State monopolies of iodine, petroleum, matches, tobacco, alcohol, and sugar ; and the Socialisation of the banks.

The installation of the new Government was accompanied by a good deal of disorder in the country, and for many days there were processions and demonstrations of workmen carrying red flags in the capital, and demanding the creation of a " Red " army. On June 11, however, Colonel Grove broadcast a warning that the Junta would not tolerate any subversive propaganda or any excesses either by Communists or by the Right, and this had a tranquillising effect. Within the Junta a cleavage almost immediately manifested itself between Colonel Grove and Señor Davila, whose Socialism was of a more moderate cast. On June 13 Señor Davila resigned, but three days later there was a military and naval counter revolution as a result of which Colonel Grove was deposed and imprisoned and a new Junta was formed with Señor Davila at its head. Its first public declaration was that it would convoke a Constituent Congress as soon as possible, with the object of adopting a new Socialist Constitution, and that in the meantime it would respect the present Constitution, would not interfere with the judicial authorities, and would respect international obligations.

The deposition of Colonel Grove caused a great ferment among the lower classes, and strikes and disorders took place throughout the country. On the other hand, it was received with relief by foreign countries, especially after Señor Davila announced that he would give full protection to the lives and property of foreigners. A few foreign countries, including the Argentine, Brazil, Italy, and Germany, recognised the new Government, but most reserved judgment. Early in July Señor Davila declared himself Provisional President. On August 21 the Government propounded an emergency plan for absorbing 100,000 unemployed by means of rationalising the mining, agricultural, and manufacturing industries out of a fund of 170,000 pesos to be raised by the issue of Treasury notes at 1 per cent. At the same time also it decreed the holding of General Elections on October 30.

Señor Davila held power for close on three months. On September 13 he was overthrown by a revolt of the garrison commanders of Santiago, led by Air Commodore Merino, because he would not give them an assurance that he would not be a candidate for the Presidency at the forthcoming elections. General Blanche became Provisional President in his place, and immediately issued a Decree for holding Presidential Elections on October 30. A fortnight later a revolt was raised by General Vignola, Commander of the Northern Military Headquarters at Antofagasta, in order to put down military interference in the civil Government. The civilian population rallied to his side, and General Blanche was forced to resign. His place was taken by Señor Oyanedel, of the Supreme Court.

Preparations were now actively made for holding the Presidential Election on October 30. The candidates who finally came forward were the ex-President Don Arturo Alessandri, who stood as a Radical and Radical-Socialist ; Colonel Grove, who stood as a Communist ; and Señor Zanartu, who had been Minister of Finance under Señor Davila. The bourgeois parties did not put forward a candidate, on the ground that Señor Montero was still President. The elections passed off without any disorder, and resulted in the victory of Señor Alessandri by a great majority. He was formally installed with much ceremony on Christmas eve. His first step was to place a number of generals on the retired list and to reorganise the secret service. General Vignola was appointed Commander-in-Chief.

A statement issued by Don Julio Canto, Minister of Finance, in October, showed that the Grove and Davila Administrations had cost the country between June 4 and the end of August 300,000,000 pesos. The statement estimated the Budgetary deficit to the end of 1932 at 156,000,000 currency pesos, apart from the service of the foreign debt.

Owing to the high duty placed in 1931 on foreign live cattle for the protection of the home breeder, the import of cattle from the Argentine came to a standstill. This caused such a loss to the Trans-Andine Railway that in April it suspended all its services. After much negotiation, an agreement was made to run three trains weekly for the carriage of mails and passengers from November 12. Owing to a disagreement about rates, however, there was no resumption of passenger service.

MEXICO.

The Mexican Government in May received a request from the Peruvian Government to withdraw its Legation from Lima on the ground that the Mexican Minister there had assisted the Aprista (Socialist) leader, Señor Haya de la Torre, in his efforts to overthrow the Government. The Mexican Government protested that the charge was quite unjustified and accused the Peruvian Government of acting with undue precipitation, but, while declaring that its feelings towards the Peruvian nation remained most friendly, found that it had no option save to hand their passports to the members of the Peruvian Legation in Mexico. Mexican interests in Peru were placed in charge of the Spanish Legation in Lima.

At the beginning of September Señor Ortiz Rubio resigned, and General Rodriguez became President in his place.

Great exception was taken in Mexico to a Papal Encyclical published soon after " on the distressing religious conditions in Mexico." For trying to defend it Archbishop Ruiz y Flores, the Papal delegate, was at the beginning of October expelled from Mexico by the President, on the request of the Chamber. An investigation was also ordered into the status and activities of Mgr. Pasqual Diaz, the Archbishop of Mexico City.

At the end of the year the President was granted special powers for rectifying the financial and economic position of the country.

PERU.

In the course of 1932 a number of attempts were made to overthrow by force the Government of Don Luis Sanchos Cerro, who had been elected President in 1931. Most of them were due to the Asociacion Popular Revolucionaria Americana, commonly known as Apra, an organisation with Communistic leanings founded by Victor Haya de la Torre, who had polled over 100,000 votes as candidate for the Presidency in the previous year. On March 6 an attempt was made on the life of the President in Lima, and he was somewhat seriously wounded. Two of his assailants were sentenced to death, and Señor de la Torre, who had gone into hiding after the affair, was also subsequently arrested on a charge of complicity.

On May 8 the crews of the cruisers *Almirante Grau* and *Coronel Bolognesi* mutinied, with the intention of sailing to the northern provinces and joining an insurrection there. The Government, however, was warned in time by a loyal sailor, who swam ashore, and was able to nip the attempt in the bud. Martial law was declared for fifteen days, and eight of the leaders of the mutiny were executed. The Government declared that it had been inspired by a Soviet committee in Montevideo, which had also many agents in the Apra party. The San Marcos University was also closed as a centre of Communist agitation. The Government further found evidence that the Mexican Minister in Lima had been intriguing with Señor de la Torre, and requested the Mexican Government to recall him.

In the early hours of July 2 an attempt was made by Communists and Apristas under Colonel Godos to seize the military aerodrome in Lima, but they were frustrated by the prompt action of the Minister of the Interior. A few days later a serious outbreak took place at Trujillo, the third city of Peru. Communists were in possession of the place for some days, during which they treated their opponents with unspeakable barbarity ; the Lima Press subsequently characterised their conduct as one of the blackest blots in the history of the Republic. Trujillo was recovered on July 11, after four days' fighting, and some of the victims of the massacres were brought to Lima and buried with military honours, the day of the funeral being observed as one of national mourning.

While still in ignorance of the fate of Trujillo, Major Lopez Mindreay, Governor of Cajamarca, raised the standard of revolt at Suaras, 180 miles north of Lima. He was defeated, however, by loyal troops, and was soon after captured and executed. After this the country remained comparatively tranquil till the end of the year.

On September 1 a representative group of Peruvians, mostly from Iquitos, entered the town of Leticia on the Amazon, in Colombian territory, hoisted the Peruvian flag, and imprisoned the Colombian officials. They claimed that the transfer of Leticia from Peru to Colombia in 1927 had been carried out against the will of the inhabitants, and that the town ought to be restored to Peru. The Peruvian Government considered the claim justified, and called upon the Colombian Government to revise the Treaty of 1924 under which the transfer had been made, at the same time suggesting that the matter should be submitted to the Washington Committee of Conciliation. Colombia did not accept the offer, and relations between the two countries became severely strained.

In September the Assembly authorised the Cabinet to contract an internal national defence loan of 20,000,000 soles (about 1,200,000l. at par). At the end of the year the President announced that bonds would be issued on January 1, 1933, to bear interest at 6 per cent., and that the proceeds of the loan would be devoted to the purchase of war material according to a plan drawn up by a technical commission.

ECUADOR.

At the end of August the partisans of Señor Neptali Bonifaz, who had been elected President in 1931, but had been disqualified on the ground that he was a Peruvian and not an Ecuadorian, seized the city of Quito and deposed the President, Dr. Alfredo Monteiro. The Congress fled to Riobamba. Loyalist troops marched on Quito from Guayaquil and other places, and after a few days' fighting, gained possession of the place, and installed Don Alberto Martinez, the President of the Senate, as Acting President of the Republic. It was estimated that 380 persons were killed and 732 wounded in the street fighting.

URUGUAY.

After much preparation, President Terra, on August 9, laid before the National Council a Tariff Plan providing on the one hand for a 10 per cent. reduction of the existing duties on goods imported from countries with which Uruguay had a favourable trade balance exceeding 1,000,000 pesos annually, provided that they conceded to Uruguay preferential treatment in return, and on the other hand, for increases up to 50 per cent. in the duties on goods from countries which exported more to Uruguay than they imported from her. The National Council subsequently increased the proposed reduction to 15 per cent. The Government was anxious to give Great Britain—whose trade with Uruguay showed a balance of 66,000,000 pesos over six years in favour of Uruguay— special preferential treatment, but were not able to do so on account of a most-favoured-nation agreement with France. Negotiations were opened with Britain with a view to surmounting the difficulty.

At the instigation of Señor Blanco, the Uruguayan Foreign Minister, a Meat Conference was held at Montevideo on November 4 and 5 between representatives of Uruguay, Argentina, and Brazil. It was unanimously resolved that the Governments of these countries should be advised to ask the British Government to allow them to distribute among themselves the meat quotas established under the Ottawa Agreements, as this would enable them better to control the operations of foreign firms.

After a most careful inquiry, the Uruguayan Government was able, in July, to deny emphatically the report disseminated in some countries that Communist activities in them were directed from Montevideo. It was pointed out that Communism had no hold in Uruguay, and that most of the agitators who came to the country soon left it.

PART II.

PART II.

CHRONICLE OF EVENTS

IN 1932.

JANUARY.

1. In the New Year Honours List Princess Mary, Countess of Harewood, was given the title of Princess Royal; Lord Sankey, the Lord Chancellor, had a Viscounty conferred upon him, and five new Barons were created— Mr. Clifford Allen [Baron Allen, of Hurtwood, in the County of Surrey]; Lt.-Col. William Ashley [Baron Mount Temple, of Lee, in the County of Southampton]; Mr. Walter Guiness [Baron Mayne, of Bury St. Edmunds]; Mr. Leif-Jones [Baron Rhayader, of Rhayader, in the County of Radnor]; and Sir William Mitchell-Thomson [Baron Selsdon, of Croydon, in the County of Surrey].

5. *The Times* announced that the Edinburgh College of Art had received a bequest of 350,000*l.* from the late Andrew Grant.

9. Heavy rains and severe gales swept the country; Monmouth was flooded owing to the rapid rise of the River Wye.

20. The first regular air-mail service opened between London and Cape Town; about 20,000 letters and 150 parcels were carried between the two points.

21. Two new Great Seals were prepared by the Royal Mint, one for Nova Scotia and the other for Northern Rhodesia.

22. Santa Lucia, Antigua, and Cotzumalhuapa, three towns in Guatemala, were destroyed by an eruption of the volcano Acatenango.

24. Two French airmen, MM. Codos and Robida, established a new record by flying from Paris to Hanoi (French Indo-China), a distance of 6,900 miles in 3 days 5 hours and 40 minutes.

FEBRUARY.

3. Santiago de Cuba was greatly damaged by an earthquake; the Cathedral was completely destroyed.

5. The Rev. Thomas Fitzpatrick, President of Queen's College, Cambridge, left 10,000*l.* to the College for the purpose of establishing Fellowships to bear his name.

A

7. By the death of Herr Gustav Benda, the Vienna Museum of Art became possessed of his valuable collection, principally of sculpture, and the Museum of Arts and Crafts of his rare porcelain and furniture.

8. George Eyston, driving an M.G. Midget car at Pendine Sands, beat the world's record for " baby " cars by reaching a mean speed of 118·38 miles an hour.

17. Sir Herbert Baker, A.R.A., architect, Mr. W. G. de Glehn, A.R.A., painter, and Mr. G. Spencer Watson, A.R.A., painter, were elected Royal Academicians.

24. At Daytona Beach, Florida, Sir Malcolm Campbell made a new record of 253·968 miles an hour, as compared with his previous record of 245·736 miles an hour on February 5, 1931.

MARCH.

14. Dr. John A. Venn was elected President of Queen's College, Cambridge.

15. Mr. Samuel Courtauld placed his residence, 20 Portman Square, in the hands of Trustees for the remaining fifty years of his lease, to become the temporary headquarters of the Courtauld Institute of Art.

17. The four-hundredth anniversary of the foundation of the Bristol Grammar School was celebrated.

19. Sydney Harbour Bridge was officially opened by Mr. Lang, the Premier of New South Wales.

— Cambridge won the University Boat Race (by five lengths) for the ninth time in succession.

23. *The Times* announced that Lord Wakefield had given 25,000*l.* as a contribution to the Imperial Institute.

28. Stype Grange, a Berkshire Mansion, was destroyed by fire.

— Mr. J. A. Mollison, flying alone from Lympne, reached Milverton Beach, near Cape Town, in 4 days and 17½ hours, and so set up a new record.

APRIL.

13. The University of Western Australia moved into its new home which includes the Winthrop Hall.

17. Summer time began.

22. At the Wakefield by-election, Mr. Arthur Greenwood captured the seat for Labour from the Conservatives.

— *The Times* reported that the Rockefeller Foundation had made a grant to the McGill University, Montreal, of 1,232,652 dollars for the establishment of a neurological institute.

23. Newcastle United won the Football Association Challenge Cup for the third time at Wembley, beating Arsenal by 2 goals to 1. King George and Queen Mary were present, accompanied by the Princess Royal and Lord Harewood.

— The new Shakespeare Memorial Theatre at Stratford-on-Avon was opened by the Prince of Wales.

25. Under the will of Mrs. Jane Edith Caulfield, whose estate was valued at 546,597*l*., over 85,000*l*. was left to various charities.

— Frankley Beeches, a property comprising beeches on a hill crest to the south-west of Birmingham, and the adjoining land to the extent of 24 acres, was presented to the National Trust by Cadbury Brothers Limited, in memory of the founders of the Bournville Works.

27. Mr. C. W. A. Scott flew from Lympne to Darwin, North Australia, in 8 days 20 hours 44 minutes.

29. Col. Wygin handed over 862 acres at Dunkery Hill and Beacon on Exmoor to the National Trust.

MAY.

7. *The Times* reported that the Pilgrim Trust, which had begun its work on October 1, 1930, had up to December 31, 1931, made grants totalling 115,321*l*.

— Mr. W. P. Crozier was appointed Editor of the *Manchester Guardian* in succession to the late Mr. E. T. Scott.

9. Piccadilly Circus first lit by electricity.

10. A Tablet was unveiled at Stoke-on-Trent in memory of Arnold Bennett.

— The centenary of the death of Jeremy Bentham was celebrated at Queen's College, Oxford.

14. The last programme was broadcast from Savoy Hill, in which the history of British broadcasting since 1922 was reviewed.

20. *The Times* announced that Mr. Percy Holt left all his property, to the value of 32,406*l*., to the Westminster Hospital.

22. Miss Amelia Earhart (Mrs. Putnam) established a record by flying across the Atlantic from Harbour Grace, Newfoundland, to Londonderry in 13½ hours. She is the first woman to have flown the Atlantic alone, and she has achieved the record time for an Atlantic flight.

24. The Benue Bridge, the longest in Africa (2,584 ft.), was opened by Sir Donald Cameron, Governor of Nigeria.

31. Rainfall figures for the month showed that this May was the wettest since 1878.

JUNE.

1. April the Fifth, a colt owned by Mr. Tom Walls, the actor and play producer, won the Derby at Epsom by three-quarters of a length. Dastur came second, and Miracle third. King George V. and Queen Mary were present at the race.

3. In the Birthday Honours List peerages were conferred on Sir Arthur Churchman [Baron Woodbridge, of Ipswich, in the County of Suffolk]; Mr. David Davies [Baron Davies, of Llandinam, in the County of Montgomery]; Mr. Henry Neville Gladstone [Baron Gladstone of Hawarden, of Hawarden, in the County of Flint]; the Rt.-Hon. J. F. Hope [Baron Rankeillour, of Buxted, in the County of Sussex]; Sir Robert Hutchison [Lord Hutchison of Montrose]; and Sir Frederick Lewis, Bt. [Baron Essendon, of Essendon, in the County of Hertford].

6. A Great Western Railway express broke the record for speed by travelling from Swindon to Paddington, a distance of 77·3 miles, in 56 minutes 47 seconds, or at an average rate of 81·6 miles an hour.

8. " Alexandra Day " : total amount collected was 52,404*l*.

11. A Dutchman, aged 51, crossed the Channel from Calais to Dover on a hydrocycle.

27. Tercentenary of the foundation of the University of Amsterdam celebrated.

JULY.

1. Celebrations to commemorate the third centenary of the University of Dorpat.

18. Kaye Don achieved a new motor-boat record by reaching an average of nearly 120 miles an hour.

— The " Flying Scotsman " beat its own record time to Edinburgh by covering the 392¼ miles in 7 hours 27 minutes without a stop.

— The fastest start-to-stop railway journey of over 150 miles in Europe was established by an L.M.S. train between Liverpool and Euston, which, timed to do the 152 miles from Crewe to Willesden in 142 minutes, finished several minutes before time.

19. King George V., accompanied by Queen Mary, opened the new Lambeth Bridge.

20. A gift of 20,000*l*. was made by Mr. Samuel A. Courtauld to increase the endowment of the Institute of Biochemistry in the Middlesex Hospital Medical School which bears his name.

25. Lord Chelmsford was elected Warden of All Souls College, Oxford, in succession to Dr. F. W. Pember who is retiring.

26. The Centenary Meetings of the British Medical Association began in London.

27. At the by-election at Wednesbury, Labour recaptured the seat from the Conservatives.

— A gift of 50,000*l*. was made by Sir John Priestman, of Sunderland, to the Monkwearmouth and Southwick Hospital.

— Lord Iveagh made another gift of 50,000*l*. to the Southend-on-Sea and District New General Hospital, thus raising his total gifts to 97,700*l*., beside his presenting the site of 12 acres.

29. *The Times* announced an offer by the Prudential Assurance Company to contribute 1,500*l*. a year for seven years to the funds of the London School of Hygiene and Tropical Medicine, to be used for the Chair of Public Health.

AUGUST.

1. The International Congress of Prehistoric and Protohistoric Sciences was opened at King's College, London.

7. Loud speakers were used in St. Paul's Cathedral in order to enable congregants sitting in the Choir to hear the preachers more clearly.

13. *The Times* reported that a mechanical device has been introduced at the Zoo, by which for 6*d*. placed in a slot, a fog-horn is sounded bringing the sea lions to the fore, and a fish is then thrown into the water.

17. Professor Piccard, the Belgian Scientist, made his second attempt into the stratosphere by means of a balloon, reaching a height of 16,700 metres.

19. The hottest day in the year in London, the temperature reaching 96 degrees.

24. The new Newspaper Library of the British Museum was opened at Colindale.

25. Mrs. Putnam (Miss Amelia Earhart) set up another record for women (see under May 22), by making a solo non-stop flight across the United States, in 19 hours 4 minutes.

SEPTEMBER.

2. Mr. Edwin Glasgow was appointed Keeper of the National Gallery.

12. " The World's Fastest Train," the Cheltenham Flier, completed the journey between Swindon and Paddington (G.W.R.) in 65 minutes, being an average speed of 71·3 miles an hour.

14. The charter incorporating Barnes as a borough was handed over to the local authority.

15. The British and Foreign Bible Society reported that in 1931 633,041 English Bibles were sold—a record number.

19. The Piccadilly Underground Railway extension from Finsbury Park to Arnos Grove was opened for traffic.

20. The Deed was signed uniting the Wesleyan Methodist, the Primitive Methodist, and the United Methodist Churches into the Methodist Church of Great Britain and Ireland.

22. *The Times* announced that the Corporation of London had decided to make a grant of 100,000*l.*, payable over a period of ten years in annual sums of 10,000*l.*, to the University of London towards the cost of the Great Hall in the new buildings of the University.

— At a General Court of the Bank of England certain old by-laws were amended, including one to increase the remuneration of the Governor and Deputy-Governor respectively.

26. The Charter of incorporation of Hendon as a borough was handed over to the local authority.

29. Alderman Sir Percy Greenaway elected Lord Mayor of London.

30. *The Lancet* announced that University College Hospital had been granted 48,000*l.* by the Rockefeller Foundation to be applied for the advancement of Clinical Research.

OCTOBER.

1. Summer time ended.

3. The Charter of incorporation of the new Middlesex borough of Heston and Isleworth was handed over to the local authority.

20. The University College of Wales, Aberystwyth, built for the most part by subscriptions from people all over Wales, celebrated the fiftieth anniversary of its opening.

— A special service was held in St. Paul's Cathedral in celebration of the tercentenary of the birth of Sir Christopher Wren.

21. The *Hereford Times* celebrated the centenary of its first issue.

24. *The Times* announced that Mr. Emslie J. Horniman had bequeathed 10,000*l.* to the London County Council for the extension of the Horniman Museum at Forest Hill.

27. The Nobel Prize for 1932 in Medicine and Physiology was awarded jointly to Sir Charles Sherrington and Professor Edgar Douglas Adrian.

29. The *Normandie*, the largest liner afloat, was launched at Saint-Nazaire.

NOVEMBER.

2. At the Mansion House, the Prince of Wales received from the Lord Mayor of London the grant of Livery to the newest of city companies—the Company of Master Mariners, of which the Prince is the first Master.

6. Details were published of a charitable trust for the benefit of Sheffield, amounting to over 400,000l., the gift of Alderman J. G. Graves.

8. Dr. Frederick Hicks, Lord Bishop of Gibraltar, was translated to the See of Lincoln, vacant by the resignation of Bishop Swayne.

10. It was announced that the Fishmongers' Company had made a gift of 10,000l. to the University of London, to be used in the erection of the central hall.

— The Nobel Prize for Literature for 1932 was awarded to Mr. John Galsworthy, O.M., and the Nobel Prize for Chemistry for 1932 to Dr. Irving Langmuir, Director of the General Electric Companies Research Laboratory at Schenectady.

14. The British Records Association, for the preservation of records, was founded.

— Mrs. Mollison left Lympne in an attempt to fly to the Cape.

18. Mrs. Mollison successfully landed at the Cape, having occupied 4 days 6 hours and 54 minutes on her journey, this being 10 hours and 28 minutes less than the last record (by Mr. Mollison, March 28, 1932).

23. It was announced that the estate of Muckross, near Killarney, comprising about 10,000 acres, is to be presented to the Irish Free State Government as a national park.

28. The two oldest skating clubs in the country, the Skating Club and the Wimbledon Skating Club, were amalgamated under the title of the Royal Skating Club, a name approved by King George V.

DECEMBER.

1. The National Gallery, Millbank, reverted to its original name, the Tate Gallery.

3. The *Field* Distemper Council announced that, as a result of ten years' research, a completely successful method of protecting dogs and other animals against distemper had been found.

— Mr. Stanley Spencer was elected an Associate of the Royal Academy.

7. The University of Birmingham received a gift of nearly 12,000l. from Lady Barber, to be devoted to the provision of an Institute of Fine Arts in the University; to the study of Fine Arts generally; and to the advancement of music and musical education in the University.

11. The University of Glasgow received a legacy of about 13,000*l.* from Dr. James Alexander Ure, to be used for scholarships and prizes in medicine.

16. The Colonial Office announced that, owing to the munificence of the Trustees of the Carnegie Corporation of New York, selected officers of the Colonial Service will be able to take a " refresher " year's absence from their ordinary duties, to be spent in study or research.

18. Mrs. Mollison completed her homeward flight from the Cape, having completed the journey of 6,200 miles in 7 days 7 hours and 5 minutes.

19. Heanton Satchville, Lord Clinton's North Devon seat, near Hatherleigh, was destroyed by fire.

22. *The Times* announced that the University of Liverpool had received a legacy of 20,000*l.* under the will of Mr. John Middlemass Hunt, for the endowment of the Chair of Tropical Diseases of Africa.

25. Cobtree Manor, an Elizabethan mansion, reputed to be Dingley Dell of the " Pickwick Papers," was partially destroyed by fire. The Maidstone Fire Brigade succeeded in saving two wings.

29. Work was commenced on the Bloomsbury site of the new buildings of the University of London.

30. The Lord Mayor of London assisted in the official opening of the Southern Railway Company's electrified line from London to Brighton and Worthing.

31. The year was deficient in sunshine ; only 1,386 hours of sunshine were recorded at the Rothamsted Experimental Station, the fifth lowest record since 1893. The total rainfall was 25·94 inches, being 2·79 inches less than the average. The year was also noteworthy for an almost entire absence of snow.

RETROSPECT

OF

LITERATURE, ART, AND SCIENCE IN 1932.

LITERATURE.

(Books marked with an asterisk are specially noticed at the end of this section.)

DURING 1932 some 10,500 new books and pamphlets appeared, of which about 1,900 were works of fiction, native and foreign. There were marked increases in the publication of poetry, drama, and history, and decreases in literature and science.

The increase in poetry was accompanied by some excellent achievement, and the year was important in that a definite direction, whatever its ultimate value may be, made its appearance. Mr. F. L. Lucas in his *Ariadne* (Cambridge University Press) complained that verse

> is grown
> The public place where epileptics moan,
> Dragging their sores like Lazarus to the gate
> For curs to lick, and fools to contemplate ;
> The stage for eunuchs imitating Donne
> Whose periwinkle minds in circles run,
> Blind, bloodless, tasteless, tortuous,

and thereby summed up the dissatisfaction of many older writers with an unrest they are unable to understand or share ; but this unrest has now apparently served its turn as an historical landmark and halting-place for the distresses and after-strains of the war, and a newer generation seems determined to have its revenge on its immediate seniors by taking the imagery and materials of those seniors' experience and using it for purposes more subversive than complaint. The Universities are always nurseries of singing-birds, and *Oxford Poetry, 1932*, edited by Mr. Richard Goodman (Blackwell), was dedicated to Wystan Auden, Cecil Day Lewis, and Stephen Spender, the three leaders of the new movement, although the poems in the volume seem to show an excessive and somewhat belated influence of Rupert Brooke. *New Signatures*, collected by Mr. Michael Roberts (Hogarth Press), is the repository of the new movement, and all three poets mentioned are to be found in it, together with Messrs. William Empson, Julian Bell, and A. J. Tessimond. It is not yet clear to what end they are working, but they are all alert and assured, alongside of a

9

fundamental groping. Their technical skill is almost frightening in accomplishment. They are satirists, they use the most contemporary of images, and have a thin spoken idiom which may be the voice of poetry to-morrow. At any rate, they are the only conscious group which in any way claims to deal with the problems of the poet's creative consciousness in terms of the sensibility and image-content of the age. Mr. Day Lewis published a volume in 1931. Mr. W. H. Auden issued his *Poems* in 1930, and in 1932 advanced an important step in * *The Orators : An English Study* (Faber & Faber), which presents a unity in verse and in very exactly controlled prose which displays a background of association built up from public-school procedure, O.T.C.'s, aviation, the world of mechanics, and tangential war-experience. There is considerable influence of Wilfred Owen, one of the two great poets killed in the war. Another new-comer was Mr. A. Abrahams, whose *Poems* (Heinemann) offered powerful imagery and concentrated and tensely knit passion in a field of expression of which the pioneer was the other dead war poet, Isaac Rosenberg. An excellent opportunity of surveying the contemporary field of established poets was to be found in Mr. J. C. Squire's selection from *Younger Poets of To-day* (Martin Secker), in which, with some important exceptions, most of the interesting poets writing to-day are represented by poems presented without any critical guidance. For American poetry there was the admirable guidance of Mr. Louis Untermeyer in *Modern American Poetry* (Jonathan Cape). This was the fourth revised and enlarged edition, and each author is provided with a neat biographical, critical, and bibliographical introduction of the utmost value for orientation. The volume begins with Emily Dickinson, and includes selections from one hundred and fifty-six poets. For English readers the most interesting poets are, of the older names, E. A. Robinson, Robert Frost, Carl Sandburg, Vachel Lindsay, Wallace Stevens, Ezra Pound, Sara Teasdale, John Gould Fletcher, Edna St. Vincent Millay, H. D., Robinson Jeffers, Conrad Aiken, and T. S. Eliot, and of those less well known in this country, William Carlos Williams, John Crowe Ransom, Maxwell Bodenheim, Archibald MacLeish, E. E. Cummings, Joseph Auslander, Allen Tate, and Hart Crane.

Mr. Arlington Robinson published a new volume, *Matthias at the Door* (Macmillan), and Mr. T. S. Eliot, in *Sweeney Agonistes* (Faber & Faber), released two highly complicated " Fragments of an Aristophanic Melodrama." Another interesting anthology was Mr. Sherard Vines' collection *Whips and Scorpions* (Wishart), which assembles a formidable array of contemporary satirists, and is indicative both of technical accomplishment in a not too easy art, and of the specific channels of unrest among contemporary poets. Mr. Richard Church published another volume, *News from the Mountains* (Dent), Mr. G. Rylands collected a few more delicate *Poems* (Hogarth Press), Mr. A. J. Young continued his even path of skilled craftsmanship and pleasant mood in *The New Shepherd* (Bumpus), and Mr. Padraic Colum collected all his *Poems* (Macmillan) after many years. The *Collected Poems* of the late D. H. Lawrence (Martin Secker) were made available in a single volume, while his *Last Poems* (Orioli) added no inconsiderable contribution to the canon of his poetry. Mr. William

Plomer published *The Five Fold Screen* (Hogarth Press) in a special edition. Mr. W. H. Davies presented his steady circle of admirers with his *Poems, 1930-31* (Jonathan Cape), and Mr. Edmund Blunden continued his firm progress of fine and dignified technical accomplishment and rich serious mood in *Half Way House* (Cobden Sanderson), and *To Themis*, a limited edition issued by the Beaumont Press. Of older poets the third volume of Mr. Sturge Moore's *Collected Poems* (Macmillan), the Poet Laureate's *Tale of Troy* (Heinemann), and Mr. Wilfrid Gibson's *Islands* (Macmillan), continued the Georgian tradition.

In many directions criticism was busy during the year, and though no new volume of fundamental importance appeared, there were some valuable explorations and collections. One of the most interesting volumes of the year was Mrs. Q. D. Leavis's *Fiction and the Reading Public* (Chatto & Windus), a serious and in many ways successful attempt to investigate the basis of contemporary taste in fiction, to assess the significance of the best seller, and to examine the growth of the reading public in the light of its cultural background and prejudices. It is a valuable diagnosis of the present disease of taste and should provide much material for the future historian of an age of unrest and critical disintegration. " A. E." 's *Song and its Fountains* (Macmillan) was that rare thing, a poet's attempt to display the psychical background of his poetry, and with a poet of such integrity the investigation is of great value in the sectional field explored. Mr. F. R. Leavis, in *New Bearings in English Poetry* (Chatto & Windus), forcibly reminded the reader of poetry that an old age is passing and a new age equipped with far different standards and background has taken its place. He writes persuasively of the later W. B. Yeats, of T. S. Eliot, and of Gerard Manly Hopkins as ingredients in the new poetical feeling. Mr. T. S. Eliot leaves the critical reader much in his debt by permitting the publication of his *Selected Essays, 1911-1932* (Faber & Faber), in which the whole course of his critical development from *The Sacred Wood* to *For Lancelot Andrewes* and beyond can be traced. A valuable feature of the volume is the inclusion of articles from the *Criterion*, *The Dial*, and some of his influential articles on Elizabethan drama from *The Times Literary Supplement*. Mrs. Virginia Woolf was also generous in her publication of an admirable and human second series of *The Common Reader* (Hogarth Press). Of the older critics Miss Vernon Lee, a contemporary of Walter Pater, wrote a penetrating volume on *Music and its Lovers* (Allen & Unwin), a study in psychological æsthetics dealing with emotional and imaginative responses to music. Mr. G. B. Shaw included three volumes of sprightly essays on *Music in London, 1890-94* (Constable), in his collected edition, and thereby provided a companion to his famous *Dramatic Opinions*. He also collected a volume of brilliant *Pen Portraits and Reviews* (Constable), which brought together much hitherto inaccessible material. Mr. Havelock Ellis collected for our delight some of his earlier *Views and Reviews* (Harmsworth), and Mr. Desmond MacCarthy's volume of *Criticism* (Putnam) was an admirably smooth and urbane volume of shrewd comment on past and present literature. Miss Edith Sitwell, in the third series of her *Pleasures of Poetry* (Duckworth), examined the

poetry of the Victorian Age with an exact and fascinating technical approach.
Professor Irving Babbitt, in *On Being Creative* (Constable), continued his
firm onslaught on the Rousseauistic Romantic position, while Mr. Herbert
Read, in a coolly conducted study of *Form in Modern Poetry* (Sheed &
Ward), helped to clarify one of the most pressing of present-day poetical
problems.

In the closely allied subject of art criticism, a really epoch-making
work has at long last been translated. Heinrich Wölfflin's *Principles
of Art History* (Bell) for nearly twenty years has dominated and vitally
affected European approaches to art. It is a work of fundamental pene-
tration, classification, and analysis. It examines the problem of Classical
and Baroque art by means of a rigorous examination of the inner nature
of style, analysing form into its central antitheses, linear and painterly,
plane and recession, closed and open form, multiplicity and unity, clarity
and unclearness, in such a way as to provide almost objective standards
of consideration for any serious student of art. It is profusely illustrated
with a masterly choice of examples, and the volume is probably the most
important cultural publication of recent years. Mr. E. F. Carritt tried
to answer the question *What is Beauty?* (Clarendon Press), Mr. R. H.
Wilenski wrote a provocative book on *The Meaning of Modern Sculpture*
(Faber & Faber), and Mr. Adrian Stokes endeavoured to alter our conception
of *The Quattro Cento* (Faber & Faber). English art was belatedly but well
treated by Mr. Charles Johnson in *English Painters from the Seventh Century
to the Present Day* (Bell), and Mr. John Rothenstein gave an account of
Nineteenth Century Painters (John Lane). A valuable and handy publication was *Greek Sculpture and Painting* (Cambridge University Press),
being the chapters, richly illustrated, contributed to the *Cambridge Ancient
History* by Messrs. J. D. Beazley and Bernard Ashmole. A valuable
reprint prepared by Mr. Herbert Read was L. March Phillips' illuminating
survey of *The Works of Man* (Duckworth). Mr. Robert Schmidt's *Porcelain
as an Art and a Mirror of Fashion* (Harrap) was an admirable contribution
to the materials for a history of taste. Mr. Roger Fry wrote an analytical
study of *The Characteristics of French Art* (Chatto & Windus), and a master
sculptor received sympathetic treatment in Mr. L. B. Powell's *Jacob
Epstein* (Chapman & Hall). One of the most beautiful of the year's books,
and one whose contents aroused strange and moving emotions, was Dr.
Karl Blossfeldt's superb photographs of further *Art Forms in Nature*
(Zwemmer), in which the beauty and human relevance of selected natural
forms were displayed in grandiose manner.

The year was unusually rich in the publication of plays of special and
outstanding interest. The most interesting single volume was the latest
series of experiments by Mr. Eugene O'Neill, * *Mourning Becomes Electra*
(Jonathan Cape), a trilogy of ominous grandeur. The sad and sudden
death of Ronald Mackenzie took from us the author of *Musical Chairs*
(Victor Gollancz). Mr. Gordon Bottomley's *Lyric Plays* (Constable)
reminded us of the continuance of a lofty strain of poetic drama. Mr.
Somerset Maugham published his ruthless contemporary study *For Services
Rendered* (Victor Gollancz), as well as the third and fourth volumes of his

Collected Plays (Heinemann). Mr. C. K. Munro collected *Three Plays* in one volume (Victor Gollancz), *The Rumour, At Mrs. Beam's, The Birth, Death, and Life of Mr. Eno.* Mr. Elmer Rice issued his amusing *See Naples and Die* (Victor Gollancz). Among important translations were Mr. Hans Chlumberg's moving *Miracle at Verdun* (Victor Gollancz), and Miss Christa Winsloe's delightful and successful *Children in Uniform* (Victor Gollancz). Mr. Carl Zuckmayer's *The Captain of Köpenick* (Geoffrey Bles) was also translated from the German. Mr. and Mrs. Granville Barker translated a further *Four Comedies* from the Spanish of the brothers Quintero (Sidgwick & Jackson), and the new Soviet classic, *Roar China*, by S. Tretiakov (Martin Lawrence), also received an English dress. Mr. Noel Coward's *Cavalcade* (Heinemann), and Mr. Rodney Ackland's *Strange Orchestra* (Victor Gollancz) represented more obviously modern moods ; while *Wings Over Europe*, by Messrs. Robert Nichols and Maurice Browne (Chatto & Windus), gave us one of the most serious of recent plays. The most sumptuous of modern books on the theatre was Mr. L. Moussinac's superbly illustrated *The New Movement in the Theatre* (Batsford), with its valuable survey of the most advanced achievements in European staging. Two delightful illustrated volumes, Max von Boehn's *Dolls and Puppets* (Harrap), and Mr. A. E. Wilson's study of the juvenile drama in *Penny Plain and Twopence Coloured* (Harrap), formed welcome additions to the theatrical library. Miss Winifred Smith went back to an important and little explored subject in the *Italian Actors of the Renaissance* (Coward McCann), and Mr. James Agate scampered through *The English Dramatic Critics, 1660-1932* (Barker). Messrs. Wishart's new *Adelphi Quartos* included two dealing with the theatre and its present enemy in Mr. Tyrone Guthrie's *Theatre Prospect*, and Mr. William Hunter's stimulating and independent *Scrutiny of Cinema*. Mr. Andrew Buchanan's *Films* (Pitman) gave an excellent practical survey and much inside information from the editor of the accomplished *Cinemagazine*. An unusual and attractive experiment was Mr. C. Dennis Pegge's *Bombay Riots—A Film Poem* (Scholartis Press), which treated the subject-matter with great force and subtlety in the form of a scenario for an unproduced and possibly unproduceable film.

In the history and appreciation of literature, its mapping and assessment, and particularly in the field of language studies, some important volumes appeared. One of the most serious books of the year was Professor Karl Vossler's *The Spirit of Language in Civilization* (Kegan Paul), a translation of a work indicative of the wide range in which philology may be regarded almost as one of the æsthetic sciences. As a philosophical study of the inner problems of language it deserves the fullest attention. A more methodical volume on a more limited scale was Mr. Willem L. Graff's survey of *Language and Languages* (Appleton). Mr. Ernest Weekley, in *Words and Names* (John Murray), contributed another volume of his fascinating studies of the private habits and family history of words. *A Dictionary of the Older Scottish Tongue*, under the veteran and expert editorship of Sir William Craigie (Oxford University Press), began its steady progress. This section, too, is most appropriate for a notice of

Mrs. E. M. Wright's fine biography of her husband, *Joseph Wright*, 2 vols. (Oxford University Press), philologist, inspired teacher, and heroic compiler of the English Dialect Dictionary, whose love for philology extended even to the naming of his two kittens, "Umlaut" and "Ablaut." In literature the year was noteworthy for the enterprise of the Cambridge University Press in issuing a handy, cheap edition of the *Cambridge History of English Literature* in 15 volumes. It is a monument to the English scholarship of the last generation. The newer generation should find stimulus from the bibliographies which are omitted from the present issue in view of their reorganisation and revision in special volumes to be issued shortly. Sir Paul Harvey edited a long-needed and useful *Oxford Companion to English Literature* (Clarendon Press) for those whose memories cannot be burdened with names, dates, and allusions. In older literature Professor H. M. Chadwick and his wife issued the first volume of a profound and important study of *The Growth of Literature* (Cambridge University Press), and Professor R. W. Chambers, the most eminent of Anglo-Saxon scholars, prepared an amply enlarged and up-to-date edition of his study of *Beowulf* (Cambridge University Press).

A series of important anthologies spanned nearly the whole field of English poetry. Professor Carleton Brown prepared the first collection of *English Lyrics of the 13th Century* (Clarendon Press), Sir E. K. Chambers a welcome *Oxford Book of 16th Century Verse* (Clarendon Press), Professor Ronald S. Crane, of Chicago, compiled an imposing *Collection of English Poems (1660-1800)* (Harpers), with a bibliographical appendix of the highest value, and Mr. John Hayward brought the admirable taste of a younger editor to his *Nineteenth Century Poetry* (Chatto & Windus). Mr. G. K. Chesterton approached the problem of *Chaucer* (Faber & Faber) in his usual provocative manner, and reminded us that his best gifts really lie in the direction of literary criticism. An important survey of *The Ballad Tradition* (Clarendon Press) was written by Professor G. H. Gerould, and the edition of Harpsfield's *Life of Sir Thomas More* by the Early English Text Society (Milford), with an ingenious piece of special pleading by Professor R. W. Chambers on *The Continuity of English Prose*, heralds the canonisation of a great English figure. In early drama John Bale's *King Johan* was reprinted by the Malone Society (Milford), and Dr. F. S. Boas's edition of *Doctor Faustus* continued the complete edition of Marlowe (Methuen). Shakespeare received some useful attention. Mr. A. Ralli compiled an invaluable * *History of Shakespearean Criticism*, 2 vols. (Oxford University Press), Professor Dover Wilson prepared a highly personal view of what he considered to be *The Essential Shakespeare* (Cambridge University Press), and Mr. G. Wilson Knight surveyed an aspect of dramatic imagery in *The Shakespearean Tempest* (Oxford University Press). The background of Shakespeare's time was penetratingly displayed in an unjustly forgotten volume of satire, *Skialetheia, 1598*, by Everard Guilpin, rescued by the Shakespeare Association (Milford). The magnificent and scholarly edition of Ben Jonson, by Mr. Percy Simpson, and the late C. H. Herford issued a fourth volume containing *Cynthia's Revels, Poetaster, Sejanus*, and *Eastward Ho* (Clarendon Press).

A much needed *Complete Works of Michael Drayton* (Blackwell) issued its first volume under the editorship of Mr. J. W. Hebel.

The seventeenth century continued to attract scholars and critics. Miss Elizabeth Holmes explored a profitable field in *Henry Vaughan and the Hermetic Philosophers* (Blackwell). The fifth and sixth volumes appeared of Dr. Keynes' definitive edition of *Sir Thomas Browne's Works* (Faber & Faber). Milton's *Paradise Regained* was newly edited by Mr. E. H. Blakeney (Scholartis Press), a translation of Milton's *Private Correspondence and Academic Exercises* (Cambridge University Press), and Miss Helen Darbishire's *Early Lives of Milton* (Constable) threw renewed light. Mr. W. P. Mitchell devoted important and comprehensive study to *English Pulpit Oratory from Andrewes to Tillotson* (S.P.C.K.). Miss Mary Sturt attempted a new biography of *Francis Bacon* (Kegan Paul), and *The English Newspaper*, a product of the century, was examined in masterly fashion throughout its whole physical course by Mr. Stanley Morison (Cambridge University Press). The *Works of Thomas Otway*, 2 vols. (Oxford University Press), received a stately edition. In the eighteenth century Richard Steele's *Christian Hero*, edited by Miss Rae Blanchard (Oxford University Press), dealt with a neglected aspect. Swift's *Satires and Personal Writings* were collected in a handy cheap volume by Mr. W. A. Eddy (Oxford University Press). Light on a changing epoch was thrown by *Richard Hurd and William Mason's Correspondence* (Cambridge University Press), and Mr. A. W. Evans' *Warburton and the Warburtonians* (Oxford University Press). Valuable work in a kind of which not enough is done, was seen in Mr. Harold Williams' study of *Swift's Library* (Cambridge University Press), and Mr. James Bonar's greatly augmented *Catalogue of the Library of Adam Smith* (Macmillan). A very welcome reprint of an almost inaccessible classic was the issue of Richardson's *Clarissa* in 4 volumes in the Everyman Library (Dent), and Mr. J. Y. T. Greig's collection of *The Letters of David Hume* (Clarendon Press), valuably supplemented his recent biography of the philosopher. A really important and extensive contribution to eighteenth century literature was the splendidly printed * *Letters of Chesterfield*, 6 vols. (Eyre & Spottiswoode), edited by Mr. Bonamy Dobrée with splendid industry and critical discernment. Dr. Johnson and his circle were generously treated. Letters from *Dr. Johnson to Queeney Thrale*, edited by the Marquess of Lansdowne (Cassell), and *French Journals of Mrs. Thrale and Dr. Johnson*, edited by Mr. Moses Tyson and Dr. Henry Guppy (Manchester University Press), threw much new light on the less formidable side of the doctor's life, while Mr. C. E. Vulliamy's life of *James Boswell* (Geoffrey Bles) dealt sympathetically with that romantic and often maligned biographer. The Romantic period offered rich fields for research. Miss Mona Wilson's *Life of Blake* (Peter Davies) was made available in an unlimited edition. Mr. J. W. Oliver studied the increasingly popular *William Beckford* (Oxford University Press). The intimate and social side of romantic literature was displayed by Mr. R. C. Bald in *Literary Friendships in the Age of Wordsworth* (Cambridge University Press), while an important aspect of contemporary criticism was assembled by Miss Elsie Smith in *An Estimate of Wordsworth* *by his Contemporaries* (Blackwell). Miss C. M. McLean increased knowledge in a study of the early years of *Dorothy Wordsworth* (Chatto & Windus), and a full life of *John Clare* was written by S. W. and Anne Tibble (Cobden Sanderson). Coleridge is still far from an exhausted subject, and Mr. E. L. Griggs gave a very valuable collection of *S. T. Coleridge's Unpublished Letters*, 2 vols. (Constable). Mr. Floyd Stovall wrote a suggestive study of *Desire and Restraint in Shelley* (Cambridge University Press), and Mr. H. R. James' *Mary Wollstonecraft* was issued by the Oxford University Press. One of the most readable works of the year was on a little-explored topic, *The Popular Novel in England, 1770-1800*, by Miss J. M. S. Tompkins (Constable), and a handsome and meticulously edited collection of *Jane Austen's Letters*, 2 vols. (Oxford University Press), was prepared by Mr. R. W. Chapman. The centenary of the death of Scott produced less serious work than might have been expected. A rounded biography of *Sir Walter Scott* was written by Mr. John Buchan (Cassell), the *Minstrelsy of the Scottish Border* was re-edited in 4 volumes by Mr. T. F. Henderson, several articles by the late Thomas Seccombe, W. P. Ker, and others, were reprinted from *The Times Literary Supplement* as *Scott Centenary Articles* (Oxford University Press), Professor H. J. C. Grierson edited a number of studies of varying merit in *Sir Walter Scott To-day* (Constable), but the most important contribution was the beginning of the publication of a standard edition of *Scott's Letters* by Professor H. J. C. Grierson (Constable). The nineteenth century in general received meagre treatment. Mr. F. V. Morley wrote a sympathetic study of *Lamb before Elia* (Jonathan Cape). Mr. E. F. Benson surveyed the life of *Charlotte Brontë* (Longmans), but the chief contribution to Brontë studies was *The Brontës : Their Lives, Friendships, and Correspondence*, edited by Messrs. T. J. Wise and A. J. Symington, 4 vols. (Blackwell). Mr. Osbert Sitwell's short study of *Dickens* (Chatto & Windus) was a tribute from a new generation, and Mr. M. Elwin's life of *Thackeray* (Jonathan Cape), the first serious estimate for some years. An interesting attempt by some fifty moderns to estimate the position of *The Great Victorians* (Nicolson & Watson) was edited by H. J. and Hugh Massingham, and Mr. Emery Neff's study of *Carlyle* (Allen & Unwin) produced much discussion. The Pre-Raphaelites and their allies were studied by Mr. R. D. Waller in *The Rossetti Family, 1824-1854* (Manchester University Press), by Mr. Francis Bickley in *The Pre-Raphaelite Comedy* (Constable), and by Mr. G. Lafourcade in an English abridgment of his voluminous French work on *Swinburne* (Bell). The Rev. Samuel Synge, in *Letters to My Daughter* (Talbot Press), gave some reminiscences of his brother, the dramatist, J. M. Synge. Of more recent writers the harvest was not very plentiful. *The Journals of Arnold Bennett (1896-1921)*, 2 vols (Cassell), threw much light on the literary world and the capacity for work of a considerable novelist. Increasing interest was taken in D. H. Lawrence, and Mrs. Catherine Carswell's *The Savage Pilgrimage* (Martin Secker) was issued in a version more acceptable to some than the edition so hastily withdrawn early last year. His sister, Miss Ada Lawrence, gave an account of the *Young Lorenzo* (Orioli), but the most important contribution, and one of the richest volumes of the year was * *D. H. Lawrence's Letters* (Heinemann), nearly 900 pages of fascinating revelation under the careful editorship of Mr. Aldous Huxley. Miss Winifred Holtby produced the first English study of *Mrs. Virginia Woolf* (Wishart), and *The Twentieth Century Novel* (Appleton) was studied in its technical aspects by Mr. J. W. Beach. Mr. Stuart Gilbert's analysis of *James Joyce's Ulysses* (Faber & Faber) was made more accessible in a cheap edition. *The Poetry of T. S. Eliot* (Hodder & Stoughton) was subjected to commentary by Mr. H. R. Williamson. Sir Henry Newbolt's reminiscences in *My World as in My Time (1862-1932)* (Faber & Faber), and Mr. John Drinkwater's *Recovery* (Ernest Benn), gave portraits of two poets in growth. Mr. Romilly John, a young poet whose first volume was noticed last year, wrote an unusually attractive account of his youth in *The Seventh Child* (Heinemann). Mr. A. Henderson's collections of over a quarter of a century were assembled into a huge biography of * *Bernard Shaw : Playboy and Prophet* (Appleton). The literature of the United States was lightly sketched from without by Mr. A. C. Ward in *American Literature (1880-1930)* (Methuen), and critically examined from within by Mr. V. F. Calverton in *The Liberation of American Literature* (Scribners). A wide ranging survey of social history and literature during five centuries was Mr. F. J. Harvey-Darton's *Children's Books in England* (Cambridge University Press).

In foreign literature the outstanding work, and one likely to become an English classic, was *The Odyssey* (Sir Emery Walker, Wilfred Merton, and Bruce Rogers), a superbly produced translation in powerful and crisp prose, by " Thomas Edward Shaw," formerly Colonel Lawrence of Arabia. A verse translation was also published by Mr. J. W. Mackail (Clarendon Press). Professor F. A. Wright wrote a readable history of *Later Greek Literature* (Routledge), Mr. Gilbert Norwood surveyed *Greek Comedy* (Methuen), and also wrote of our debt to *Plautus and Terence* (Harrap). In German literature the centenary of Goethe's death evoked very little of importance from England. Professor J. G. Robertson's *Life and Work of Goethe* (Routledge) was a balanced study, and Mr. Barker Fairley gave an account of *Goethe as Revealed in his Poetry* (Dent). Miss E. Purdie wrote a study of *F. Hebbel* (Clarendon Press), and a useful *Companion to German Studies* (Methuen) was edited by Mr. Jethro Bithell, but the most important publication on German literature was a translation of Professor O. Walzel's profound study of *German Romanticism* (Putnam). In French literature Professor E. R. Curtius's brilliant and understanding *Civilization of France* (Allen & Unwin) was translated from the German. Mr. Matthew Josephson compiled a biography of *Jean Jacques Rousseau* (Victor Gollancz), Mr. Henri Barbusse's *Zola* (Dent) was translated, and an analytical study of Verlaine entitled *Poet under Saturn*, by Marcel Coulon (Toulmin), was translated by Mr. Edgell Rickword. Mr. A. Kaun's *Maxim Gorki and his Russia* (Jonathan Cape) represented Russian studies. One of the most important of European literary histories was at last made available in a translation of Francesco de Sanctis's great classic, *The History of Italian Literature*, 2 vols. (Oxford University Press).

Historical studies were miscellaneous in quality and direction, though

B

a number of special studies stood out prominently. Of the major works of reference in course of publication several added to their stature. * *The Cambridge Ancient History*, issued Vol. IX., and * *The Cambridge Mediæval History* in its seventh volume (both from Cambridge University Press), gave an account of the decline of the Empire and the Papacy. *The Cambridge History of India* added a fourth volume and *The Cambridge History of the British Empire* achieved its fifth volume. In ancient history Mr. M. Cary gave the first volume of a new series in *A History of the Greek World from 323 to 146 B.C.* (Methuen), and a very important and readable continental study was translated from Professor Ulrich Wilcken's *Alexander the Great* (Chatto & Windus). A book of fascinating content was Sir Rennell Rodd's intimate topographical and historical picture of *Rome of the Renaissance and To-day* (Macmillan). Jewish history, ancient and more recent, received some study. A massive *History of Israel* in two volumes was written by Mr. T. H. Robinson (Clarenden Press), and Professor A. Lods issued a survey of *Israel from the Beginnings to the Eighth Century* (Kegan Paul). The late Dr. Israel Abrahams' rich study of *Jewish Life in the Middle Ages* (E. Goldston) receives a new and enlarged edition (by Dr. Cecil Roth), based on his own notes, while an intimate picture of life in the seventeenth century was given in Mr. Marvin Lowenthal's admirable translation of the *Memoirs of Glückel of Hameln* (Harper). The history of certain modern European countries was illuminated in Mr. W. E. D. Allen's *History of the Georgian People* (Kegan Paul), and in Dr. A. A. Stomberg's *History of Sweden* (Allen & Unwin). Much light was thrown on Russian affairs by translations of V. I. Lenin's studies of *The Paris Commune* and *The Revolution of 1905* (Martin Lawrence), and by the first volume of Mr. Leon Trotsky's monumental and vividly written *History of the Russian Revolution* (Victor Gollancz). A number of special studies of solid work appeared on problems of European and British history, Mr. R. G. Collingwood wrote on *Roman Britain* (Oxford University Press). Mr. G. Sheldon explored a difficult field in *The Transition from Roman Britain to Christian England, 368-664* (Macmillan), Mr. T. Alison illuminated cultural history in a picture of *Pioneers of English Learning* (Blackwell), and an important publication was a translation of *The Correspondence of Pope Gregory VII.* (Oxford University Press), while domestic problems in the same period were treated by Professor F. M. Stenton in *The First Century of English Feudalism, 1066-1166* (Clarendon Press). Miss H. M. Chew wrote an important study of the highly specialised topic, *The English Ecclesiastical Tenants in Chief and Knight Service* (Oxford University Press), and Miss May McKisack of *Parliamentary Representation of the English Boroughs during the Middle Ages* (Oxford University Press). A wider survey of European Life was given by Professor J. W. Thompson in *Economic and Social History of Europe in the Later Middle Ages, 1300-1550* (Appleton). Materials for a study of social life nearer home were found in *A Calendar of Select Pleas and Memoranda of the City of London, 1381-1412* (Cambridge University Press). Professor P. Geyl studied *The Revolt in the Netherlands, 1555-1609* (Williams & Norgate), and Spanish history received attention in Mr. David Loth's account of *Philip II. of Spain* (Routledge), and

Professor A. S. Turberville's concise "Home University" volume on *The Spanish Inquisition* (Thornton Butterworth). A topic of considerable importance and difficulty was explored in Mr. W. K. Jordan's *The Development of Religious Toleration in England from the Beginning of the Reformation to the Death of Queen Elizabeth* (Allen & Unwin), and another special study was prepared by Miss Agnes Conway on *Henry VII.'s Relations with Scotland and Ireland, 1485-1498* (Cambridge University Press). Seventeenth-century history received some attention in Mr. A. D. Innes' *Maritime and Colonial Expansion of England under the Stuarts, 1603-1714* (Sampson Low), and in Mr. Harold Acton's brilliantly written account of the decadence of a great family in *The Last Medici* (Faber & Faber). Mr. F. J. Varley studied *The Siege of Oxford, 1643-1646* (Oxford University Press), and Mr. A. A. Thomson set in order an important section of administrative history in *The Secretaries of State, 1681-1782* (Clarendon Press), while Mr. G. A. Jacobson, in a special study of *William Blathwayt* (Oxford University Press), gave detailed attention to a seventeenth century administrator. Sir Charles Petrie wrote on *The Jacobite Movement* (Eyre & Spottiswoode), and the eighteenth century was admirably approached in Mr. Basil Williams' important study of war and diplomacy in the career of *Stanhope* (Clarendon Press), and Professor G. M. Trevelyan's masterly account of * *Ramillies* (Longmans). Social history was explored in three widely different fields in Mr. T. S. Spear's *The Nabobs* (Oxford University Press), an account of the social life of the English in eighteenth-century India, in Mr. J. B. Chambers' *Nottinghamshire in the 18th Century* (P. S. King), and in Mr. Gilbert Armitage's lively picture of *The History of the Bow Street Runners, 1719-1829* (Wishart). Nineteenth-century history involves much reckoning with politics : the Congress of Vienna was examined by Mr. J. G. Lockhart in a study of *The Peace Makers, 1814-15* (Duckworth), and its effects in Mr. R. B. Mowat's survey of *The States of Europe, 1815-71* (Edward Arnold). The theoretical background of the same period was examined in a varied and brilliant series of lectures on *Social and Political Ideas of Some Representative Thinkers of the Age of Reason and Reconstruction* (Harrap), collected by Professor F. J. C. Hearnshaw, while Mr. G. F. H. Berkeley showed *Italy in the Making, 1815-46* (Cambridge University Press). Irish affairs were dealt with in Mr. R. W. Postgate's study of *Robert Emmett*, the Irish revolutionary of Napoleonic times (Martin Secker), and Mr. Dennis Gwynn's full *Life of John Redmond* (Harrap). The magnificent series of *Queen Victoria's Letters* were rounded off by the appearance of a final volume (John Murray). The first volume of *The Collected Papers of Thomas Frederick Tout* (Manchester University Press) was a splendid monument to a fine character and an enthusiastic teacher of History.

There seems no limit to the supply of general biography and memoirs, and many volumes of outstanding importance in various fields appeared during the year. Historical memoirs included an important study of *Metternich* by Arthur Herman (Allen & Unwin), and the first English study of *Monsieur Thiers*, by Mr. J. M. S. Allison (Allen & Unwin). Mr. Duff Cooper presented an account of *Talleyrand* (Jonathan Cape), and

Mr. Stephen Graham studied *Ivan the Terrible* afresh (Ernest Benn).   Mr.
Hilaire Belloc's *Napoleon* (Cassell) contained some fine descriptive writing
on a subject very dear to him.   Mr. G. O. Griffith wrote a life of *Mazzini*
(Hodder & Stoughton), and among earlier figures *Sir Christopher Wren*
received attention from Mr. C. W. Wilson (Methuen), while Mr.
Bonamy
Dobrée wrote a lively and well-documented study of *William Penn, Quaker
and Pioneer* (Constable).   Miss Elizabeth Jenkins turned her accomplished
pen from fiction to a brilliant portrait of *Lady Caroline Lamb* (Victor
Gollancz), and *Sarah Duchess of Marlborough* was treated by Mrs. Kathleen
Campbell (Thornton Butterworth) and Mr. F. Chancellor (Philip Allen).
Samuel Butler, the author of *Erewhon*, was given a welcome biography
by Mrs. C. G. Stillman (Martin Secker).   Of more recent figures *Prince
Von Bülow's Memoirs, 1819-89* (Putnam) were put into English by those
indefatigable translators Mr. G. Dunlop and Mr. F. A. Voigt.   The
romantic Nansen was presented in two forms, in a biography by Mr.
J. Sorenson, *The Saga of Fridtjof Nansen* (Allen & Unwin), and in a selection from his writings in Mr. E. G. Reynolds' *Nansen* (Geoffrey Bles).
The *Memoirs of Marshal Joffre*, in 2 vols. (Geoffrey Bles), and Mr. R. P.
Baker's *Woodrow Wilson*, Vols. III. and IV. (Heinemann), gave rich
materials for contemporary history.   A life of *Mendel* by Hugo Iltis presented part of a very important biographical study (Allen & Unwin).

Several politicians received biographical attention.   The official life
of * *Lord Oxford and Asquith* was written by Messrs. J. A. Spender and
Cyril Asquith (Hutchinson).   Mr. J. L. Garvin's first volume of his *Life
of Joseph Chamberlain, 1836-1885* (Macmillan) aroused considerable interest.
Sir Charles Mallet's *Herbert Gladstone* (Hutchinson) was a record of public
service.   The Marquess of Zetland gave a full account of *Lord Cromer*
(Hodder & Stoughton).   The late Mr. Edward Marjoribanks was able
to complete only Vol. I. of his *Life of Lord Carson* (Victor Gollancz),
and the Rt. Hon. Mr. Winston Churchill described his own *Thoughts and
Adventures* (Hodder & Stoughton).

A number of interesting figures in more creative callings left, or
formed the subject of, attractive memoirs.   Mrs. Charlotte Leaf wrote a
life of *Walter Leaf, 1852-1927* (John Murray).   Professor G. M. Trevelyan
wrote of his father, *Sir George Otto Trevelyan* (Longmans).   A well-known
Oxford figure was recalled in Mr. Laurie Magnus's life of *Herbert Warren
of Magdalen, 1853-1930* (John Murray).   Mr. J. McCabe wrote on *Edward
Clodd* (John Lane).   The world of the Arts contributed heavily.   Mr. V.
Dandré gave a memoir of *Anna Pavlova* (Cassell), Sir William Rothenstein's
Recollections, 1900-1922 (Faber & Faber), was a picture of artistic and social
life in the twentieth century.   Mr. Maurice Baring's *Lost Lectures* (Heine-
mann), Mr. W. S. Blunt's *My Diaries, 1888-1914* (Martin Secker), and
Mr. E. F. Benson's *As We Are* (Longmans) provided unusual good reading.
Miss Nina Hamnett, in *Laughing Torso* (Constable), fluttered the dovecotes.
Mr. Cedric Hardwicke gave an actor's reminiscences in *Let's Pretend*
(Grayson), and Mr. C. B. Cochran, in *I Had Almost Forgotten* (Hutchinson),
gave another picture of theatrical existence.   From America came two
volumes.   Mr. Theodore Dreiser's *A Hoosier Holiday* (Constable), and Mr.

Upton Sinclair's very *Candid Reminiscences* (Laurie) of his first thirty years.

Problems of our own time produced the usual flood of ephemeral pamphlets and plethora of prophecy or wisdom after the event, but of outstanding quality and stimulus were Mr. H. G. Wells' * *The Work, Wealth and Happiness of Mankind* (Heinemann), and a monumental survey by Dr. H. Finer of *The Theory and Practice of Modern Government*, 2 vols. (Methuen). The *Encyclopædia of the Social Sciences* (Macmillan) gave a seventh volume of concentrated and valuable material, and Sidney and Beatrice Webb, in *Methods of Social Study* (Longmans), gave the principle in which the new survey of London's poor is being achieved. Mr. C. H. S. Fifoot's study of *English Law and its Background* (Bell) was of special interest as a picture of underlying social forces, and Mr. J. G. Crowther conducted an important inquiry into *Industry and Education in Soviet Russia* (Heinemann).

Science and philosophy received considerable attention, but few works were of general enough interest to be included in a survey of literature. Dr. George Sarton's comprehensive and valuable *Introduction to the History of Science*, in its second volume (Bailliere, Tindall & Cox), surveyed the field from Rabbi Ben Ezra to Roger Bacon, while two special studies, for those who could follow them, seemed to be more than usually serious contributions to European Scientific theory : Mr. F. A. Lindemann's *The Physical Significance of the Quantum Theory* (Oxford University Press), and Mr. P. A. M. Dirac's *The Principles of Quantum Mechanics* (Oxford University Press). Mr. Jacques Maritain's *Introduction to Philosophy* (Sheed & Ward) represented an important strain in French Catholic thinking. Dr. Rudolf Otto's *Mysticism East and West* (Macmillan) was a well-considered contribution from Germany, and an important series of leaders of Philosophy, published by Messrs. Benn, included studies of *Berkeley*, by Mr. Dawes Hicks, of *David Hume*, by Mr. B. M. Laing, and of *Aristotle*, by Mr. G. R. C. Mure. *The Philosophy of Descartes* (Methuen) received an important analysis from Professor A. Boyce-Gibson, while the translation of three volumes of N. Hartmann's *Ethics* (Allen & Unwin) was of comparable importance with that of Husserl's volume of the previous year. Mr. George Bernard Shaw's * *The Adventures of the Black Girl in her Search for God* (Constable), though not exactly a philosophical work, was a stimulating book that caused much controversy.

An unusual number of excellent volumes eluded classification in the major groups. Mr. George Buchanan, in *Passage Through the Present* (Constable), gave a fascinating picture of day-by-day existence as mirrored in the mind of a poet and novelist of the youngest generation. Mr. J. R. Ackerley gave much delight and amusement in his *Hindoo Holiday* (Chatto & Windus). Mr. Bertram Thomas's *Arabia Felix* (Jonathan Cape) was declared in Colonel T. E. Lawrence's introduction to be in the great tradition of Arabian masterpieces. Mr. Edmund Blunden, with the subtlety and understanding of a poet and a nature lover, showed *The Face of England* (Longmans). Mr. David Garnett gave his flying experiences literary quality in *A Rabbit in the Air* (Chatto & Windus). Mr. Gerald Barry's

selection, *A Week-End Calendar* (Geoffrey Bles), made varied reading
for leisure moments. Mr. Wyndham Lewis, in *Doom of Youth* (Chatto &
Windus), made a penetrating and witty onslaught on all youth movements
of to-day, and in his *Filibusters in Barbary* (Grayson) wrote a travel book
of merciless exposure of romantic humbug. Miss Edith Sitwell gave a
picture of *Bath* (Faber & Faber) of outstanding personal quality. Mr.
D. H. Lawrence's *Apocalypse*, with an introduction by Mr. Richard
Aldington (Martin Secker), represented an important side of his thought,
while *Etruscan Places* (Secker) showed him at his best in estimating
a civilisation in emotional prose. Mr. Osbert Sitwell's *Winters of Content*
(Duckworth) was full of distinguished matter, while Mr. Yeats Brown's
Golden Horn (Victor Gollancz) and Mr. Peter Quennell's superficial
Journey through Tokyo and Peking (Faber & Faber) represented two different
attitudes towards experience. One of the most moving records of experience was Mrs. Anna Eisenmeyer's *Blockade*, the diary of an Austrian
middle-class woman from 1914 to 1924 (Constable). Two fascinating
surveys were *Fifty Years, 1882-1932* (Thornton Butterworth), being the
articles which attracted so much attention on their publication in *The Times*,
and Mr. Alan Bott and Mrs. Irene Clephane's anthology of quaint pictures
of *Our Mothers* (Victor Gollancz). Mr. Aldous Huxley's personal anthology,
Texts and Pretexts (Chatto & Windus), provided opportunity for comment
from one of our sensitive modern minds. Mr. F. S. Smythe's *Kamet
Conquered* (Victor Gollancz) was the record of one of the bravest feats of
endurance of recent years. The sad and untimely death of Mr. Paul
Cohen-Portheim removed the sensitive author of *The Discovery of Europe*
(Duckworth), an acute analysis of European tradition and mentality.
The vexed problem of *Religion in the U.S.S.R.* (Modern Books Ltd.) was
presented by Mr. F. Yaroslavsky, leader of the League of the Godless.
One of the most fascinating books of the year, and all the more interesting
as coming from one of the most accomplished of modern writers of fiction,
was Mr. Ernest Hemingway's vivid descriptive and technical study of
the art of bull-fighting in * *Death in the Afternoon* (Jonathan Cape).

New periodicals appeared to meet fresh needs and interests. The
New English Weekly, under the editorship of Mr. A. R. Orage, is a resumption
of *The New Age*, whose passing had been regretted by a generation of
grateful readers. *Character and Personality*, a quarterly, edited by Mr.
Robert Saudek, started in dignified fashion with contributions from
Professor William McDougall and Dr. C. G. Jung. The *Cinema Quarterly*,
edited by Mr. Norman Wilson in Edinburgh, is the first British periodical
to devote itself to serious discussion of the art of the cinema. The *Medical
Forum*, edited by Dr. Maurice Sorsby, was intended to record the transactions
of medical societies. *Town and County Planning* was the quarterly organ
of the Garden Cities and Town Planning Association. A new critical
Quarterly devoted to the serious study of literature and contemporary
culture was *Scrutiny*, edited at Cambridge by Mr. L. C. Knights and Mr.
F. R. Leavis, and *The Jewish Review* (Soncino Press), edited by Mr. Norman
Bentwich and Mr. Harry Sacher, was intended to supply a want in the
discussion of modern Jewish culture and civilisation. Another literary

review of advanced tendency was *Contact*, an American Quarterly, edited
by Mr. William Carlos Williams (Joiner & Steele), and among miscellaneous
new periodicals were *The Tree Lover* (Alexander Moring) and *The Straight
Thinker*, a fortnightly, edited by Miss Beatrice Hastings.

The task of selection among the year's novels is almost beyond human
power. Nearly two thousand works of fiction appeared, and several
hundred were worthy of attention in varying degree. It has been remarked
that the provision of a substantial monthly prize in the form of the Book
Society's choice, in practice the sale of at least 20,000 copies, has so highly
extended the possibility of financial reward for literary industry that
hundreds of writers have sprung up to join in the struggle for fictional
existence. Yet, despite the tendency to lower the tension and adjust
the tone of fiction to a broader and less exigent audience, a comfortingly
large proportion of new writers seem prepared to run the risk of making
no concessions, and to write with sincerity, economy, precision of notation,
and conscious attention to problems of form, on themes that do not always
make for complacency on the part of the reader. It is interesting, moreover, to notice that the choice of novels for translation from foreign
literature tends to emphasise the more serious side of European problems,
both social and technical. With the possible exception of the work of
Vicki Baum, the literature of colportage does not seem to be widely represented in the year's translations.

As in several fields of non-fictional writing a surprisingly large proportion of the most important books of the year came from abroad. The
most remarkable foreign novels were translations from the German.
Jacob Wassermann headed the list with his impressive *Wedlock*, a work
of incomparable sureness and grandeur of handling (Allen & Unwin),
and his bold study of the world of medicine in *Etzel Andergast* (Allen &
Unwin). Erich Kästner, the author of the charming and whimsical
Emil and the Detectives, turned to grimmer themes and problems in *Fabian*
(Jonathan Cape). The veteran Arthur Schnitzler, in *Flight into Darkness*
(Cassell), gave a masterly study of progressive mental disintegration,
and Hermann Broch achieved a trilogy of monumental proportions in
The Sleepwalkers (Martin Secker). Franz Werfel gave a wide sweep to
his study of *The Pascarella Family* (Jarrolds), and Lion Feuchtwanger's
study of the Jewish wars in *Josephus* (Martin Secker) was of epic proportion. A writer less well known in England than his brother was presented
in a translation of Heinrich Mann's subtle psychological study, *The
Blue Angel* (Jarrolds). Stefan Zweig's tense *Amok* (Cassell) and Arnold
Zweig's comprehensive *Young Woman of 1914* (Martin Secker) both stood
out. The German contribution was so rich that important and highly
competent works must be passed by hastily. Kurt Heuser's *Inner Journey*
(Martin Secker) and Karl Friedrich Boree's *Summer's Not Over* (Faber &
Faber) were fine psychological studies. Max René Hesse's *The White
Flame* (Faber & Faber) was a study of the borderline of human relationships.
Robert Neumann's *On the Make* (Peter Davies) was a rich comedy of ruthless feminine progress. Felix Salten's *The Hound of Florence* (Heinemann)
was a symbolic romance of Renaissance Italy. Heinz Liehmann's picture

of tragedy in evolution in *Peace Broke Out* (Chatto & Windus), Hans Gopsch's *Death Rattle* (Faber & Faber), Max Mohr's *Philip Glenn* (Sidgwick & Jackson), Erich Ebermayer's *The Great Gulf* (Sidgwick & Jackson), and Friedrich Torberg's *The Examination* (Chatto & Windus) were all full of important information about the German spirit. From France came very little. André Maurois sent *The Family Circle* (Cassell). Henri Barbusse's *Inferno* was translated by Mr. John Rodker (Joiner & Steele). Pierre MacOrlan's *One Floor Up* was translated by Mr. Vyvyan Holland (Hamish Hamilton). The winner of the *Prix Theophraste Renaudot*, Mr. Philippe Heriat's *The Lamb* (Obelisk Press), was given an English dress, and Colette's *Morning Glory* (Victor Gollancz) continued the series of new translations. A fine translation of an earlier novel, E. Fromentin's *Dominique* (Howe), was received with enthusiasm. Of newer writers Paul Morand's *Orient Air Express* (Cassell), and Antoine de Saint Exupéry's *Night Flight* (Harmsworth) made a vivid pair. Russia sent very little, a complete translation of Goncharov's great classic *Oblomov* was made available in the Everyman Library (Dent). Boris Pilnyak's compelling and tempestuous *The Volga Flows to the Caspian Sea* (Peter Davies) and Alexei Tolstoy's *Imperial Majesty* (Matthews & Marot), with Alexandra Kollontai's *Free Love* (Dent), complete the total of novels, though Mr. S. Konovalov, in *Bonfire* (Ernest Benn), collected a series of contemporary short stories. Spanish short stories were introduced in a *Spanish Omnibus*, translated by Mr. W. B. Wells (Eyre & Spottiswoode). From Scandinavia came the prize novel, *Two Living and One Dead*, by Sigurd Christiansen (Victor Gollancz), Knut Hamsun's *August* (Cassell) and Olle Hedberg's *Prisoner's Base* (Allen & Unwin). Czechoslovakia sent Karel Čapek's *Tales from Two Pockets*, brilliantly translated by Mr. Paul Selver (Faber & Faber). Hungary made a contribution in Lajos Zilahy's *The Deserter* (Nicolson & Watson). Holland contributed two works in Marie Schmitz's *The Infinite Longing* (Harrap), and Herman de Man's *Rising Waters* (John Lane). A brilliant Italian writer was translated for the second time in Italo Svevo's *As a Man Grows Older* (Putnam), with a prefatory account of the late author's relations with Mr. James Joyce.

Native fiction may be divided for convenience into four groups, the first consisting of work of real interest from writers of greater or less accomplishment, but all with a fresh and serious concern with the art of the novel and the problem of shaping experience, real or imaginary, into an art form of some contemporary relevance. The second group contains those well-known writers from whom, whether from long eminence or capitulation to the public taste, or clearly indicated capacity and direction, no surprises are to be expected. In the third category are included the large number of extremely competent writers, many of them with their own quite large public, who, in a ruthless selection and struggle for existence would not be too poignantly missed. The final category is that of new novelists who have given their first hostages to fortune, and who must be watched to see how they carry out their self-entrusted task. Of these last many must be considered without further investigation in the first group.

Very fortunately the first group was unusually large in 1932 and provided more than a regular book a week of distinguished fiction. Mr. Aldous Huxley opened the year with * *Brave New World* (Chatto & Windus), in which his satirical powers extended to a world of logical prophecy. Mr. William Faulkner, the closest to genius of all contemporary novelists, turned his attention in * *Sartoris* (Chatto & Windus) to the tragic decline of an old southern family. Mr. Somerset Maugham, a veteran who is perpetually in touch with contemporary sensibility, in * *The Narrow Corner* (Heinemann), presented a spiritual pilgrimage in Eastern waters. Mr. John Dos Passos, another of America's most accomplished novelists, in * *Nineteen Nineteen* (Constable), gave a distinguished and penetrating kaleidoscopic view of the war in its effect on representative human beings. Of the younger writers Miss Rosamund Lehmann continued her exploration of the feminine viewpoint in * *Invitation to the Waltz* (Chatto & Windus). Of distinguished writers of an earlier generation several maintained their triumphal progress. Mr. J. D. Beresford with his social analysis, *The Middle Generation* (Collins), and Mr. Frank Swinnerton's evocation of *The Georgian House* (Hutchinson), Mr. Ford Madox Ford with his customary adult treatment in *When the Wicked Man* (Cape), and Mrs. Edith Wharton with her sure distinction in *The Gods Arrive* (Appleton), and Miss Willa Cather in *Obscure Destinies* (Cassell), ably represented America. Of the established younger writers Mr. Liam O'Flaherty, in *Skerrett* (Victor Gollancz) and *The Puritan* (Jonathan Cape), gave ruthless portraits seen in an almost fevered vision of concentration. Mr. A. E. Coppard's whimsicality was doled out in smaller compass in *Crotty Shenkin*, expensively produced by The Golden Cockerel Press. Mr. Wyndham Lewis, in *Snooty Baronet* (Cassell), wrote one of the most piercing volumes of fictional satire in muscle-tight tension and control of prose, and Mr. James Joyce, in *Tales of Shem and Shaun* (Faber & Faber), released a fragment of his fascinating but difficult *Work in Progress*. D. H. Lawrence's *Lady Chatterly's Lover* (Martin Secker) was issued in a mutilated form which can mean nothing to any serious student of Lawrence's works, and Mr. Richard Aldington's volume of short stories, *Soft Answers* (Chatto & Windus), contained beauty, satire, and some fine analysis of contemporary existence. Some thirty or forty new or first novelists made brilliant and distinguished contributions to the year's fiction. Mr. James Cleugh made a startling entry with his alarmingly accomplished *Ballet for Three Masks* and *Inflictions, 1931* (both from Martin Secker). Mr. James Hanley continued his troubled and sombre view of life in *Aria and Finale* (Boriswood). Mr. L. A. G. Strong gave a lurid picture of primitive passion in *The Brothers* (Victor Gollancz), and a number of highly skilled short stories in *Don Juan and the Wheelbarrow* (Victor Gollancz). Mr. Geoffrey Dennis again exercised his control of human destiny in *Sale by Auction* (Heinemann). Mr. Alec Brown, in *Chadwick Roundabouts* (Jonathan Cape), surveyed murder with fine fantasy and speed control. Mr. Anthony Powell repeated the accomplishment of *Afternoon Men* in a different field in *Venusberg* (Duckworth). Mr. H. E. Bates goes from strength to strength, and in his short stories, *The Black*

Boxer (Pharos) and *The Fallow Land* (Jonathan Cape) raised himself to the forefront of the younger generation. Mr. Rhys Davies, in *The Red Hills* (Putnam), was another of the serious younger generation to prove his right to his critical position. Mr. Louis Bromfield gave a powerful and compressed picture of *A Modern Hero* (Cassell), and Mr. Robert Nathan supplied the opposite pole of fantasy in *The Woodcutter's House* (Elkin Matthews). Mr. Myron Brinig pursued his spacious chronicle in *Sons of Singermann* (Cobden Sanderson). Mr. William MacFee, in *Harbour Master* (Heinemann), made good use of the humours of the sea, and Mr. Richard Blaker raised historical fantasy to a very high pitch in *The Needle Watcher* (Heinemann). Mr. William Plomer's study of suburbia in *The Case is Altered* (Hogarth Press) was a new departure. Miss E. B. C. Jones' delicate handling appeared once more in *Morning and Cloud* (Victor Gollancz). Mr. Austin Clarke's *The Bright Temptation* (Allen & Unwin) was an unusual exercise in poetical legend, and Mr. Francis Stuart's *Pigeon Irish* (Victor Gollancz) attracted many by its fantasy. A large number of women writers of the younger or youngest generation dazzled with their brilliance and amazed by their control. Miss Yvonne Cloud's wickedly witty or wittily wicked *Nobody Asked You* (Willy Nilly Press) was of startling quality. Miss Mary Butts's short stories, *Several Occasions* (Wishart), aroused much strenuous controversy. Miss Malachi Whitaker's *Five for Silver* (Cape) collected several of her precise and forceful studies. Miss Lorna Rea, in *First Night* (Heinemann), fulfilled her earlier promise. Miss Ruth Holland, in *The Lost Generation* (Victor Gollancz), gave a grim picture. Miss Eleanor Reid's study of *A Wife and Child* (Ernest Benn) was of admirable observation and precision. Miss Maude Meagher's *Fortunate Traveller* (Heinemann) was a philosophical journey of unusual distinction. Among the younger men Mr. F. C. Boden's *Miner* (Dent) was one of the most vivid atmospheric studies of the year, and introduced a talent of which much may be awaited. Mr. Keith Winter's *The Rats of Norway* (Heinemann) justified the opinion his previous novel had raised, and Mr. John Hampson, in *O Providence* (Hogarth Press), was another who kept a promise. Mr. Graham Greene's *Stamboul Train* (Heinemann) received the reward of wide circulation. Mr. Francis Iles' *Before the Fact* (Gollancz) was of unusual treatment, and Mr. Adrian Alington's *Mr. Jubenka* (Chatto & Windus) was of a humorous quality rare in these days of grimness or heartiness. Mr. Sean O'Faolain's *Midsummer Night Madness* (Jonathan Cape) drew attention to a new writer of short stories. *The Saint and Mary Kate* (Macmillan) proved Mr. Frank O'Connor's power to continue the capacity of his previous year's stories, *Guests of the Nation*, into a full length novel. *The Best Short Stories of 1931*, edited by Mr. E. J. O'Brien (Jonathan Cape), gave its customary shrewd estimate and stocktaking of the shorter fiction of the year. An anonymous work of the highest distinction was *Memoirs of Other Fronts* (Putnam), a study of prison and passion during the war.

Of the second group a number of individual volumes stand out with distinction. Mr. Kipling's *Limits and Renewals* (Macmillan) proved that its author's powers were still capable of producing the effects which made his earlier reputation. The late Arnold Bennett left behind him two interesting studies in his *Dream of Destiny* and *Venus Rising from the Sea* (Cassell). Miss Rose Macaulay, in * *They Were Defeated* (Collins), turned with brilliant success to the field of intellectual and historical fiction. Mr. Louis Golding's * *Magnolia Street* (Victor Gollancz) was an epic attempted on the grandest scale. Mr. Galsworthy's * *Flowering Wilderness* (Heinemann) was the second volume of an important social survey. Mr. J. B. Priestley's *Faraway* (Heinemann) strengthened both admiration and suspicion in different quarters, and Mr. Hugh Walpole's further massive instalment in *The Fortress* (Macmillan) fully answered to expectation. Miss Sackville-West gave another result of her interest in *Family History* (Hogarth Press), and Miss E. M. Delafield, in *Provincial Lady goes Farther* (Macmillan) and *Thank Heaven Fasting* (Macmillan), poured out further treasures from her discriminating vision. Mr. Maurice Baring's *Friday's Business* (Heinemann) was of high distinction, and Mr. F. Brett Young's *The House Under the Water* (Heinemann) was agreed to be one of his richest achievements. Mr. Hilaire Belloc, in *The Postmaster-General* (Arrowsmith), imposed his scaffolds once more on the world's shoulders, and Miss Sheila Kaye Smith, in *The Children's Summer* (Cassell), and Miss G. B. Stern, in *Little Red Horses* (Heinemann), supplied their admirers with their awaited sustenance. Mr. T. S. Stribling, in *The Store* (Heinemann), maintained his hold on the affection of many readers grateful for fine feeling and distinguished descriptive movement.

The third group contains some very readable matter. At the very head was Mr. Charles Morgan with his widely discussed philosophical pattern * *The Fountain* (Macmillan). Miss Kate O'Brien achieved a best-seller in *Without My Cloak* (Heinemann), and Mr. James Laver, in *Nymph Errant* (Heinemann), reaped the reward of his daring and witty approach. Miss Phyllis Bentley's study of the generations in *Inheritance* (Victor Gollancz) received much praise, as did Miss Helen Ashton's *Bricks and Mortar* (Victor Gollancz) and *Belinda Grove* (Victor Gollancz). Mr. Ivor Brown's venture in fiction, *Marine Parade* (Victor Gollancz), was received with more than encouragement by his admirers, and popular writers such as Mr. George Preedy in *The Pavilion of Honour* (John Lane) and *Violante* (Cassell), Mr. Archibald Marshall with *The Lady of the Manor* (Collins), Mr. Stephen McKenna with *The Way of the Phœnix* (Chapman & Hall), Mr. A. E. W. Mason with *The Three Gentlemen* (Hodder & Stoughton), Mr. R. H. Mottram in *Home for the Holidays* (Chatto & Windus), Miss Margaret Kennedy in *A Long Time Ago* (Heinemann), and Miss Mazo de la Roche in *Lark Ascending* (Macmillan), gave full measure to their expectant clientele. A number of women writers consolidated their position. Mrs. Ruth Manning Saunders with *She was Sophia* (Cobden Sanderson), Miss Storm Jameson with *That was Yesterday* (Heinemann), Miss Helen Simpson with *Boomerang* (Heinemann), Mrs. Beatrice Kean Seymour with *Maids and Mistresses* (Heinemann), Mrs. Naomi Royde Smith with a volume of short stories, *Madam Julia's Tale* (Victor Gollancz), Miss Sarah Salt in *The Wife* (Victor Gollancz), Miss Hilda Vaughan in *The Soldier and the Gentlewoman* (Victor Gollancz),

and Miss Radclyffe Hall with *The Master of the House* (Jonathan Cape)·
A number of writers of special literary gifts pursued the path of fiction
with varying success: Mr. F. L. Lucas in *The Wild Tulip* (Joiner &
Steele), Mr. Edward Shanks in *Queer Street* (Macmillan), Mr. F. O. Mann
in *Grope Carries On* (Faber & Faber), and Mr. Harold Nicolson in *Public
Faces* (Constable). Several novelists stood out in a varied category for
the distinction of their purpose : Mr. Edwin Muir in *Poor Tom* (Dent),
Mr. Edward Thompson in *Lament for Adonis* (Ernest Benn), Mr. L. P.
Hartley in *The Killing Bottle* (Putnam), Mr. Gerald Bullett in *Helen's
Lovers* (Heinemann), and Mr. Martin Armstrong in *Lovers' Leap* (Victor
Gollancz). Mr. A. J. Cronin did not, in the opinion of everybody, equal
his previous achievement in *Three Loves* (Victor Gollancz). Work of
interest came from Mr. Ronald Fraser in *Marriage in Heaven* (Jonathan
Cape), from Mr. Alec Waugh in *Thirteen Such Years* (Cassell) and *No
Quarter* (Cassell), from Mr. Claude Houghton in *Chaos is Come Again*
(Thornton Butterworth), and Mr. C. S. Forester in *Death to the French*
(John Lane). Different kinds of humour and satire were to be found
in Mr. Denis Mackail's *David's Day* (Hodder & Stoughton) and *Ian and
Felicity* (Hodder & Stoughton), and Mr. Evelyn Waugh's *Black Mischief*
(Chapman & Hall).

The group of promising first novels include Mr. G. Scott Moncrieff's
picture of underworld life in *Café Bar* (Wishart), Miss Ann Bridge's witty
Peking Picnic (Chatto & Windus), Miss Margery Sharp's amusing *Fanfare
for Two Trumpets* (Barker), and Mrs. Nina Salaman's convincing picture
of adolescent experience in the Russian Revolution in *Two Silver Roubles*
(Macmillan). Mr. Bonamy Dobrée carried his critical accomplishment
into *St. Martin's Summer* (Hogarth Press). Miss Stella Gibbons' *Cold
Comfort Farm* (Longmans), though written at the expense of a very
easy subject, displayed considerable satirical gifts.

Two publishing ventures in fiction call for comment. Messrs. Benn
instituted a new series of short unpublished novels in paper covers at
ninepence per volume. It was justified by its inclusion of Mr. J. D.
Beresford's brilliant cameo survey of *The Next Generation*. A new series
of the highest importance for the destiny of English fiction on the Continent was *The Albatross Modern Continental Library*, a formidable rival
to the Tauchnitz edition, and under British control. The volumes are
of distinguished get-up, printed in beautiful modern versions of Garamond,
Baskerville or Elzevir types, on excellent paper and in attractive paper
covers. The first six volumes included works by Sinclair Lewis, Hugh
Walpole, and James Joyce, and the series is to include Conrad, Susan
Glaspell, Rosamund Lehmann, Katherine Mansfield, and Virginia Woolf.
With such evidence of careful choice it may be possible for Europe to be
in much closer touch than hitherto with the representative products of
contemporary English fiction.

Of the above books the following have been deemed suitable for special notice ; they are given in the order in which they happen to appear in the General Survey :—

GENERAL LITERATURE.

The Orators : An English Study, by W. H. Auden (Faber & Faber). In 1930 Mr. Auden's volume of *Poems* attracted the serious attention of those anxious for the present destiny of English poetry. He displayed technical mastery of a rare kind, seemed to be able to wield all the mechanism of emotion without too clearly indicating his own possession of it, and suggested under a difficult and almost obscure diction and imagery a traceable path of intellectual movement. In *The Orators* the technical accomplishment is even more surely fixed. Rhythms are handled with consummate skill, allusions are juggled with, and a whole world of experience called upon, modern machinery, aviation, the Officers' Training Corps, motor cars, chemistry, the Great War, the Great Strike, Edgar Wallace, sexual allusion, smoking-room bawdry, in a *Walpurgisnacht* of association. The influences are many and some are patent : Robert Graves, Wilfred Owen, Gerard Hopkins, Kaffka and Skelton merely head the list. By means of this alarming equipment ruthless satire of the English scene and of an earlier generation is hinted at, not merely in attack on institutions but on mentality, stance, intonation, habit, and vocabulary. All the materials of poetry are used, both in prose and verse, to display a poetical personality that does not as yet seem to include direct statement or melody, but nevertheless clearly embodies the conscience of a new generation that is grimly determined not to know Joseph. For many readers and many young poets Mr. Auden is the leader of the new movement.

Mourning Becomes Electra : A Trilogy, by Eugene O'Neill (Jonathan Cape).—Few modern dramatists have attempted high tragedy with all the paraphernalia of Greek drama transmuted to the purposes of modern situations. Mr. O'Neill takes a family in which passion, deeply corrupt and turning upon itself, employs jealousy, murder, incest, and suicide to rearrange the pattern of existence under an inborn curse which is Mr. O'Neill's temporary interpretation of Fate. Mr. O'Neill once said that he never went to the theatre because he could do a better production in his own mind. Something of that attitude is implied in the manner in which significant stage directions and interludes of descriptive emotion force upon the reader interpretations and dramatic direction which could be supplied in the theatre only by impeccable physical acting, superb stage control and timing, and speech-melody of an order never seen and scarcely demandable. The trilogy is an object lesson in dramatic craftsmanship in that the words are almost bare of dramatic emotion, and the tragedy of the play lies in the spaces and pauses and compelled linkings for which the dramatist has provided the masterly notations of a puppet wielder sure of his desired effects.

A History of Shakespearean Criticism, by Augustus Ralli, 2 vols. (Oxford University Press).—There is no more helpful way of estimating the movement of human intellect and taste than by tracing the fortunes of a great writer. Shakespeare transcends all ages and countries, and this survey of what has been said on the greatest of modern creative writers from the seventeenth century to our own time provides material of the highest significance for human history. The views and statements of every important critic in England and many in France and Germany are methodically presented in summary, and an index enables the reader to trace a topic such as characterisation, or the treatment of religion, society or evil, of love or friendship, of fools or women. The varied treatment of the problem of Hamlet is a chastening reminder of relativity in judgment. What emerges from a survey of this vast field, however, is the small attention that has been paid to Shakespeare's dramatic structure, his mental processes in poetry, and the problem of his staging, compared to the vast quantity that has been written on the assumption that Shakespeare's characters are objective realities. To the student these two volumes are invaluable in directing him to the full text of what has attracted him in summary. Fortunately the descriptions are never substitutes for the original. For the advanced student the volumes are a valuable release from the drudgery hitherto attendant on any attempt to write a synthetic history of Shakespeare criticism.

The Letters of Lord Chesterfield, 6 vols., edited by Bonamy Dobrée (Eyre & Spottiswoode).—This noble and definitive edition of the letters of Lord Chesterfield is an important enlargement of the shelf of English classics. It is meticulously edited, with a full understanding of contemporary affairs, and a substantial biography in the first volume which, for its elegance of writing and masterly summary of event and character, would by itself confer distinction on the work. So far as the main body of the edition is concerned, there is a total of 2,629 letters, of which some 1,400 are office letters given for the first time in full or summary for those whose interest in Lord Chesterfield is predominantly historical or administrative, but there is a further set of 158 letters never before published in any edition or in any form. The marshalling of the complete correspondence in chronological order enables the epistolary career of Chesterfield to be followed in full detail without any disturbance of emphasis in favour of the famous letters to his son. Alongside of the vast series of Horace Walpole's correspondence and the recently published letters of John Wesley, they give a picture of the eighteenth century of the highest value. Statesman, wit, moralist, and commentator on life and literature all appear in the letters and the life in complementary richness. As a specimen of stately printing and presentation, and of scholarly editing and humane comment, the work is deserving of the warmest welcome and highest esteem.

The Letters of D. H. Lawrence, edited by Aldous Huxley (William Heinemann).—It is seldom that so important a collection of material for the estimation of a literary figure is provided so soon after the author's death. But with D. H. Lawrence it was necessary, in view of the misunderstandings, the cross purposes, the misinterpretations of his philosophy, produced by friend and enemy alike, to provide authentic material of unimpeachable authority. An explanation of the cross purposes is to be found in the fact that each friend was a separate entity to Lawrence, and completely different persons were addressed in completely different terms. The chief impression that emerges is that of fundamental honesty and decency, of a weak spirit growing visibly to strength upon strength, of an organism becoming increasingly sensitive to the beauty and irritations of the world. As a literary man he practised what he demanded for human beings—direct action in the emotions and precise notation in expression. He almost welcomed the war because it " set a slump in trifling." Some of the most remarkable letters are to Lady Ottoline Morrell and to Mr. Middleton Murry, in which the direct and fearless man expresses himself without reference to conventional standards of politeness, of language or decorum. There may be more letters to come, but the present volume is an indispensable commentary and key to the works of a great man and writer.

Bernard Shaw : Playboy and Prophet, by Archibald Henderson (Appleton).—Professor Henderson has devoted twenty-five years to the study of Mr. Shaw's career, and in this massive volume of nearly nine hundred pages presents an authorised official biography of the last survivor of a generation of prominent writers. Mr. Shaw's activities as fiction writer, critic of art, music, and the theatre, as socialist politician, dramatist and publicist are displayed with a wealth of intimate detail no other person could have assembled. The volume is richly illustrated with photographs, cartoons, caricatures, portrait busts, reproductions of autograph letters and manuscripts, playbills, and stage photographs. There are printed many of the provocative and witty letters which prove Mr. Shaw a master of invective and amiable insult. The whole course of Mr. Shaw's growth and reputation is traced and a special appendix is devoted to the fortunes of his plays in other lands. A history of the modern theatre is contained between the lines. Obscure prefaces and addresses, private conversations, marginal notes, critical comment of friend and foe, combine to provide more material than Boswell would have known how to use, and make this biography indispensable for a serious study of the life, art, or the career of Mr. George Bernard Shaw.

The Cambridge Ancient History, Vol. IX., The Roman Republic 133-44 B.C. (Cambridge University Press).—As this splendid co-operative effort approaches completion, it seems to reach a higher and higher standard of achievement. The ninth volume is devoted to the last century of the Roman Republic, a period of storm and stress not unlike our own, a period which produced great leaders of men, among whom Julius Caesar stands easily first. Such an epoch demands adequate treatment ; even the most critical readers will not be disappointed with the volume. Here they will find the judgment of the latest and best scholarship as it modifies the standard authorities on the period ; they will find in particular two splendid studies—one on the Gracchi (by Mr. Hugh Last) and the other on Julius Caesar (by Mr. F. E. Adcock) which are not only informative but exceedingly

illuminating.   One cannot help being struck by the similarity of the outstanding problems of the period with those of our own—what to do with
the unemployed, the parcelling out of land among them, the utilisation
of the workless in military groups, and the outbreak of civil warfare.
Side by side with the economic difficulties a rich literary life flourished in
Rome ; the volume contains two very attractive chapters on life and
letters (the one by Dr. J. Wight Duff and the other by Mr. E. E. Sikes),
which read smoothly and entertainingly.

**The Cambridge Mediæval History, Vol. VII., Decline of Empire
and Papacy** (Cambridge University Press).—The fourteenth century is
the theme of this, the last volume but one of a splendid enterprise.   What
a canvas !   The Black Death, the Hundred Years' War, the Social up-
heavals in England, in France, and in Italy, the division of the Papacy,
the birth pains of the national states of Western Europe—to tell each of
these stories adequately requires not only specialised knowledge but the
pen of a ready writer.   It is not too much to say that in both respects
those who are responsible for the principal chapters in the book pass the
test brilliantly.   Consider, for example, Professor Mollart's short studies of
Venturino da Bergamo and of Giovanni Colombini, the late Professor
Waugh's picture of the Emperor Charles IV., or Mr. Manning's summary of
Wyclif's place in mediæval thought, and you have a few illustrations of
learning and sound judgment combined with an attractive style.   Not only
is the political and ecclesiastical history of the period described, but due
attention is paid to the social and economic history ; Dr. Eileen Power's
chapter on Peasant Life is one of the most fascinating in the volume.   When
we read of the exactions to which the peasantry were subjected, when we
consider the selfishness of lay and ecclesiastical lords alike, we realise the
more vividly the influences which in some measure at least were responsible
for the Peasant's Revolt in England in 1381 or the Jacquerie in France.
Dr. Cecil Roth's very competent chapter on the Jews in the Middle Ages
is also for the most part social history.   A word must be said about the
excellence of the bibliographies at the end of the volume.

Ramillies and the Union with Scotland., by G. M. Trevelyan
(Longmans, Green & Co.), is the second volume in the trilogy in which
Professor Trevelyan intends to give us a picture of England under Queen
Anne.   To say that the second volume is a worthy companion of the first
is to pay it the highest compliment.   Again we have beauty of writing
which carries the reader along, making him realise that truth is stranger
than fiction ; again we are treated to splendid descriptions of battle scenes :
the story of that Whit Sunday morning, May 23, 1706, will not easily be
forgotten, so vivid is every detail ; again we read with pleasure judiciously
chosen extracts from contemporary records which are valuable for the
pictures they convey.   As the author himself explains, three strands
combine in the texture of this book—the war, English politics, and the
Union with Scotland.   Over all three hangs the shadow of Marlborough,
who because he is something of a hero for the author is chiselled so skilfully
and clearly that he is made to live again before us, and we come to regard
him as a close friend.   Professor Trevelyan is an historical artist gifted in an

eminently high degree. His book will not only be the standard work on the reign of Queen Anne, but will rank as first-rate literature.

The Life of Lord Oxford and Asquith, by J. A. Spender and Cyril Asquith (Hutchinson).—A son who was in the fullest sympathy with his father and an intimate political confidant form an admirable combination as biographers of Lord Oxford. Though they are jointly responsible for the work as a whole, they have wisely decided on a division of labour, the more personal chapters being naturally entrusted to Mr. Asquith, while the political side of the story is left in the main to Mr. Spender, who contributes half the first volume, and all but one chapter of the second. Lord Oxford's rise to fame began with his sensational success as an advocate before the Parnell Commission in 1889. His public career came to a close with his resignation of the Liberal leadership in 1926. Between these dates, and especially between 1902, when he took the field as the protagonist of Free Trade in the fiscal controversy which has now come to seem so unreal, and 1916, when he was finally manœuvred out of office, he played a leading and eventually a predominant part in all the great transactions of his time. His Life, therefore, was bound to be in a measure a political history of modern England. The political background is admirably sketched ; indeed, the only criticism to be made is that there is, perhaps, too much background and too little Asquith— for though we do penetrate behind the scenes, the intimate personal revelations are fewer than might have been expected. We do not learn as fully as we should like to do what Asquith himself really thought and felt about it all. On the purely personal side the most striking feature of the book is the collection of extracts from Lord Oxford's letters to the lady who became his second wife. These reveal him in a new and unexpected light, and it is not too much to say that their romantic fervour and their intrinsic literary beauty may give some of them at least a place among the classic love-letters of all time. Mr. Asquith also contributes an illuminating study, which some readers will find more interesting than many of the purely political chapters, of his father's personality, character, and intellect. Perhaps because true biographical material was not abundant to begin with and had in part been used already by Lord Oxford himself, this can hardly be called a really great biography, but if " adequate " and " competent," rather than " great," are the epithets which suggest themselves, this is unquestionably a work of permanent value and importance.

The Work, Wealth and Happiness of Mankind, by H. G. Wells (Heinemann).—This was unquestionably one of the outstanding books of the year—judged by importance, excellence of production or popularity. Mr. Wells has already given his contemporaries an *Outline of History* and a *Science of Life*. In this book he furnishes a comprehensive account of economic life as only Mr. Wells can do it. Here we have a perfect treatise on Descriptive Economics—brimful of information, touched with imagination, and written in a style which interests the reader. The book is unique both as regards its authorship and its plan ; there is nothing like it. It should be the constant companion of every intelligent newspaper reader.

C

It will not only keep him informed ; it will also make him think. Mr.
Wells touches on (and illuminates) many of the problems of every day
—work and leisure, commerce and government, the wonders of communication, education (a magnificent chapter !), war and peace, and
the influence of women in modern life. Only Mr. Wells could have
covered so wide a field in so skilful a fashion. The book will long remain
the best account of the economic aspect of Western civilisation in the
year 1932.

The Adventures of the Black Girl in her Search for God, by
George Bernard Shaw (Constable), is a magnificent parable to show the
various conceptions of the Deity that are to be found in the world—the
phases of God in the Old and New Testaments, Mahomet's God, Voltaire's
God, the God of Natural Science. The story interested thousands of
people, for thousands read Mr. Shaw's parable. In a sense, are we not all
following in the footsteps of the Black Girl in that we are also searching
for God ? Needless to say, Mr. Shaw is not only serious ; he pokes fun at
many institutions and conceptions current in our Age—missionaries, for
instance, and the claim of every organised church that it alone possesses
divine truth. Needless to say, also, Mr. Shaw provides excellent reading
in that racy style of his which has won so many admirers among the
discerning. The story of the Black Girl is followed by an " Afterword "
in which Mr. Shaw provides a new evaluation of the Bible. The Bible,
according to Mr. Shaw, remains an interesting record of how the idea of
God developed from childish idolatry to the sublime notion of a loving
father. Mr. Shaw stresses the point that not one but many conceptions
of God are to be found in the Bible—Noah's, Job's, Micah's, for instance.
A word of special commendation should be said of the original illustrations
(by Mr. John Farleigh).

Death in the Afternoon, by Ernest Hemingway (Jonathan Cape).—
It is seldom that so fascinating a volume is written on a subject that fills
so many people with horror. It is a study, in full technical panoply and
richly restrained prose, of the art and practice of bull-fighting. It treats
the art as a tragedy, displays the nature and psychology of the participants,
gives a fascinating account of the recent history of the art, and for those
who have seen a bull-fight confirms the amateur's feeling, that it is an art,
not only of skill and daring, but of beauty. Mr. Hemingway is able, by
the sheer directness of his deliberately unflowery prose, to bring character
to the bulls themselves, to the bull-ring, and to the back-stage existence,
as well as the glory of the bull-fighter and his troupe, the sordid cafés,
and financial intrigues. The formal celebration of the Mithraic cult in
its last stages is given in the ordered succession, described with instructive
detail and hidden emotion, of work with the cape, the bandilleras, and the
sword ; tiring the bull until it is an even combat between man and animal,
ending in the death-thrust which, for its cleanness and direct beauty of
sculptured posture, is called by the Spaniards " the moment of truth."
There are passages of Bunyan-like simplicity and effectiveness which show
the result of a preoccupation with literary craftsmanship discussed constantly throughout the book, and the writing is reinforced with many

superb photographs of moments of technical significance in the ritual. The book adds to the essential information of the reader, a rare achievement.

FICTION.

Brave New World, by Aldous Huxley (Chatto & Windus).—This book is prefaced by a quotation saying that Utopias may be attained— the great problem is how best to avoid them. It is because he wishes us to concentrate all our energies on this great problem, that Mr. Huxley has forced himself to show us the Utopia inevitably reached, after development according to plan, by modern science, modern philosophy and modern a-morality. But the driving force that sweeps Mr. Huxley on to presenting every nook and cranny of his Brave New World to the fiercest light of inquiry is the heart-corroding disgust he feels for human society as it will become according to his vision. This vision is the logical result of the perfecting of our ideals of life to-day. It is as surely and clearly set up by Mr. Huxley as it is ruthlessly demolished by the battering ram of his hatred, defaced by the scorching acid of his satire, and left at last to lie forgotten and buried under the soot and smut that its own self-annihilation have caused. Like the ebb and flow of the tide we see the birth, growth, and maturity of beings in his world of machine-made humans. They are brought into existence in waves, they rise and fall, accomplish nothing more permanent than mechanised pleasure and its well-regulated satisfaction, then disappear and, unlike the waves, do not even leave a graceful fringe of sea-weed behind. From the point of view of science and engineering this " World " of Mr. Huxley's may be a consummation devoutly to be wished ; he himself, with the mocking humour of a Hogarth, draws a picture of so bitter a death in life that by contrast all the injustices, deficiencies, and lacunæ of the social and moral framework of our own day appear as desirable as Nirvana. With whips and scorpions are our aspirations chastised in this thought-provoking book lest for want of proper leading we go madly astray.

Sartoris, by William Faulkner (Chatto & Windus).—Mr. Faulkner is no ordinary novelist. He is the nearest to a genius among contemporary writers, and he shows that genius by his power of leaping over stepping-stones without the laborious snail-crawl of most ambitious and unsure writers. His descriptions are written in fever and provoke fever, his images unlock vast trains of association directed to a rigidly pre-arranged destination. For his present venture in creative virtuosity he has taken the old Southern family of Sartoris and displayed the action of war on the men and women of a decadent family. The characters leap into life at a phrase, the relationship between characters, frank or violent or sombre, emerge with sureness from the linking imagery ; even his animals have personality. Like Dostoievsky he has an overtone, but with him it is more æsthetic than mystic. The story, fascinating as its details are, is only an excuse for the pattern it helps to display, and Mr. Faulkner shows this by venturing wilfully to insert a descriptive moral. " He must have a name for his pawns. But perhaps Sartoris is the game itself, a game outmoded and played with pawns shaped too late to an old dead pattern, and of which the Player Himself is a little wearied," and lest he be thought incapable of compelling such a moral by purely fictional means he emerges deliberately from his interlude of reverie to say, in the last spoken sentence of the book, "'Do you think,' Miss Jenny repeated, 'that because his name is Benbow, he'll be any less a Sartoris and a scoundrel and a fool.'"

The Narrow Corner, by W. Somerset Maugham (William Heinemann). —Mr. Somerset Maugham has the power of satisfying completely without pandering to the mood of the moment. His *Liza of Lambeth* was a grim study in actuality, his *Of Human Bondage* one of the finest of contemporary Odysseys, and *Cakes and Ale,* one of the most welcome of exposures of human meanness. In *The Narrow Corner* he has taken a series of incidents and from them drawn a philosophy. Death, murder, and suspicion of murder are interwoven with suspense, tragedy, and precise character delineation in a story whose triumphant march is more the purpose of the novel than even the disposition of the incidents it contains. The novel is a minor epic of detachment which mirrors in concrete form the author's attitude to life, which has somehow earned him the label of cynic. Mr. Maugham's powers of descriptive manipulation, his use of the aroma of personality, and of the sub-grotesques of human oddity, make this a rich and a wise book.

Nineteen Nineteen, by John Dos Passos (Constable).—This is a continuation of the theme of *42nd Parallel* and deals with the war as seen by a number of American citizens behind the lines of war in Europe. The main characters are a soldier, an ordinary seaman, a middle-class girl, and the daughter of a business man, whose lives converge or approach in asymptotic detachment from time to time. The technique is already familiar. A thread of continuity is provided by the " Newsreel," a *montage* of newspaper clippings, headlines, popular songs and speeches arranged towards a specific emotional end, by intense close-ups of reality called " The Camera Eye," with all the flux of discontinuity to fix a moment in eternity, by select and splintered biographies of prominent rebels, critics, and acceptors of American life, such as John Reed, Randolph Bourne, Roosevelt, Woodrow Wilson, J. P. Morgan, Joe Hill, Paul Bunyan, and the Unknown Soldier. The war behind the war, the futility, the lechery, the hypocrisy of war, the degradation of character, the breaking of Nature's promises to youth, the spiritual blackmail and intimidation that accompany wars are displayed with an indignation that is never evangelist or explicit, but emerges from the cunning manipulation of objective statement in some of the most effective prose of our day.

Invitation to the Waltz, by Rosamund Lehmann (Chatto & Windus). —To take everyday interiors and by the magic of colour, technique and atmosphere so to present them that they become fascinating masterpieces was the aim and achievement of more than one now famous Dutch painter. Miss Lehmann has desired to follow their example, though her medium is the pen. Most successfully has she carried out her intention. She has opened a door, and for two short days she has allowed us glimpses, intimate and all-revealing, of the life of a country family. She has shown us each member of the group and his or her immediate reaction to the others and towards the humans, of high or of low degree, that go to make the small society in which all move. Had Miss Lehmann done this merely from the vantage-point of an outside observer, the result might have been photographically perfect and yet extremely dull. Instead, it is through the eyes and emotions of Olivia, a healthy, sensitive, not too confident, but mentally alert and acutely aware young girl of seventeen that we make the acquaintance, and in some cases even achieve the friendship, of the many figures that give this little world its inhabitants. There is no effect of overcrowding or artificiality, nor of triviality either. It is all as natural, busy, and important as one or two outstanding days in youth are, and persist in remaining even in long-after memory. The gradual perception by the young girl of the many intricate possibilities, and per-chance, even sordid problems that life, both familiar and strange, may hold, is so tenderly portrayed that there is a sense of shock neither to the reader nor to the rapidly developing personality. This is a simple story, but there is exquisiteness and liveliness in its simplicity, and boredom has been banished by the firm and artistic lines with which each individual, each incident has been limned in.

They were Defeated, by Rose Macaulay (Collins).—Miss Macaulay has achieved a new kind of historical novel. She has cut a cross-section through the raw material of English social and literary history at about the year 1640, and with ripe learning and sensitive time-feeling has manipulated personalities and atmosphere in an age of cultural transition. The first section, " Bucolick," is the world of Robert Herrick, the essence of English country life in a Devonshire scene, rustic and super-stitious. The second section, " Academick," turns to Cambridge with a group of fantastics, John Cleveland, Cowley, and Crashaw, and a world of political, religious, and poetical discussion founded on searching scholarship. The third section, " Antiplatonick," gives a moving account of the idealistic affection of a dainty child for the fantastic Cleveland, and its tragic conclusion. The book is written in delicately poised prose, walking with precision through the snares of modernity, and using only the words employed in the period of the novel. No stricter unity of diction could be imposed by a modern Aristotle of the novel, and with the exquisite balance between character and chronicle, archæology and artistry, sets a new standard for historical fiction.

Magnolia Street, by Louis Golding (Victor Gollancz).—Mr. Golding has attempted a vast panorama of history and human topography in this survey of the action of the war on two opposing, conflicting or coalescing camps of Jew and Gentile on either side of a street in Doomington. By means of a set of characters and caricatures every category of humanity, visionary, artist, lecher, hewer of wood and drawer of water, and a hundred others, is brought together in an ambitious pattern. Sometimes there is all the complexity of a Balzac human comedy, and sometimes, as in the coloured description of the brothel quarter of Salonika, and the return to a house burdened with mourning, there is tragedy of a restrained and measured quality hitherto unreached by Mr. Golding. Any attempt to break the bonds of fiction by extending the particularity of local description to the universality of a world problem is to be welcomed, and Mr. Golding deserves every encouragement in this vast breathing if it is to inform his next work with intensive rather than extensive power and control.

Flowering Wilderness, by John Galsworthy (William Heinemann). —This is the second volume of the last of Mr. Galsworthy's trilogies. It is the exploration of a mentality rather than a *milieu*, although every page is full of sociological documentation hurrying to keep pace with the fleeting generations. The Cherrells and distant ramifications of the Forsytes are harried from pillar to post as sacrifices to the world of the " pukka sahib." Wilfred Desart has been converted to Islam at the point of the sword and thereby smirched British prestige, and not content with apostasy has added the unpardonable sin of poetry to his crime sheet. The problem is based on the fatal flaw in Wilfred Desart, a secret doubt which forbids him to accept Dinny Cherrell's proffered loyalty. The characters are deployed with that urgent demand for sympathy so many readers are happy to grant ; and moments of beauty and poignancy enhance what in a lesser writer would be merely an academic discussion. It is good to hear that the final volume was ready for press before the last illness of the author.

The Fountain, by Charles Morgan (Macmillan).—The story of *The Fountain* is laid in Holland during the war. A handful of English officers are prisoners there ; a Dutch family of ancient lineage on their estate with an alien intruder in the heroine, an English girl, who is the step-daughter of the head of the house ; the interweaving of the threads of life between members of the little society, the passing of time bringing with it quiet contemplation, love with its calm deeps of friendship, beauty and possession, and as a resultant the agony of a great soul destined to be eternally denied and solitary. In bald outline this is the tale Mr. Morgan unfolds, but in essence it is as little like *The Fountain* as its chemical symbol is like an emerald. Mr. Morgan is the knight-errant who is in search of Beauty and on his quest he has achieved it. The rhythm, the harmony, the swelling chords, and all the deep spiritual movement of a great symphony are in this work, and its true appraisement will come when frequent re-reading have made of it an eagerly repeated joy.

ART, DRAMA, CINEMA, AND MUSIC.

I. ART.

EXCEPT for the success of the French exhibition, the season in London was of unexampled gloom, poor sales in the auction rooms, few commissions for artists, and bad business for nearly all the dealers. Two or three of the latter, however, effected a fair number of sales by exhibiting selections of drawings and small works in water-colour, some of them excellent, all of which were offered at or below ten or five guineas. The exhibition of French art, held at Burlington House, was most successful as far as attendance was concerned, for in the two months during which it remained open, more than 340,000 visitors passed through the turnstiles. But the attendance, great as it was, did not approach that of the Italian exhibition of two years earlier. The French exhibition, controlled by two committees, one presided over by Sir William Llewellyn, P.R.A., and the other by M. Paul Léon, Director-General of the Fine Arts in France, contained more than a thousand works of all kinds, and was, as might be expected, extremely interesting. Too much space was given, however, to the more modern developments of the art of France, and the work of some good men was but poorly shown. That remarkable painter of peasant life, Bastien-Lepage, whose influence on English artists was considerable, was represented by only one canvas, and that a portrait. Although France can claim in Fantin-Latour the greatest master of flower painting, not one of his works in this department graced the walls. The French exhibition was opened on January 4 and closed on March 5.

The works intended for the summer exhibition of the Royal Academy numbered 11,706, and the preliminary examination was so severe that not a single work was accepted outright, a thing unprecedented in the 164 years of the Academy's existence. Before the war it was not uncommon for a hundred or more to be accepted, and thus made certain of obtaining a good place in the exhibition. Of the 11,706 submitted on this occasion 9,601 were rejected outright, and from works selected from the remaining 2,015 the exhibition was composed, so far as the contributions of outsiders were concerned. The committee by which it was arranged was composed of Mr. L. Campbell Taylor, Mr. Oliver Hall, Sir E. L. Lutyens, Mr. A. J. Olsson, Mr. C. L. Hartwell, Mr. G. Harcourt, Mr. F. L. Griggs, Mr. Harold Knight, and Mr. F. Jagger.

The sales at the Royal Academy, though not to be compared with those customary before the war, were not bad, considering the general condition of affairs. Of the pictures that found purchasers the principal were the following: "Conversation Piece: Hilaire Belloc, G. K.

Chesterton, and Maurice Baring," by Mr. H. James Gunn (1,500*l.*) ; " Cagnes, France," by Sir H. Hughes-Stanton (700*l.*) ; " Girl Reading," by Mr. Harold Knight (120*l.*) ; " Riverbed " (210*l.*), " The Moorhen's Nest " (157*l.* 10*s.*), and " In Springtime " (84*l.*), by Mr. Adrian Stokes.; " Snowclad " (75*l.*) and " By the Lune " (75*l.*), by Mr. R. G. Brundrit ; " The Severn from the Forest of Dean " (75*l.*), by Mr. Charles M. Gere ; " The Sampler " (420*l.*), by Mr. Campbell Taylor ; " The Bridge of Gweek " (150*l.*), " The Old Barge " (125*l.*), and " At High Water " (105*l.*), by Mr. Stanhope Forbes ; " The Full River " (200*l.*), by Mr. A. J. Munnings ; " Old Mill House " (262*l.* 10*s.*) and " Marshland on the Moorish Coast " (78*l.* 15*s.*), by Mr. Oliver Hall ; " The Beach " (630*l.*), by Mr. Arnesby Brown ; " Diana " (85*l.*) and " Reflections in a Silver Ball " (145*l.*), by Mr. H. Davis Richter ; " A Psalm to Winter Skies, Pend-Vounder, Lands End " (300*l.*), by Mr. Lamorna Birch ; " The Family " (200*l.*), by Mr. B. Fleetwood Walker ; " Dampier Joins the Bucchaneers " (200*l.*) and " Saluting the Vanquished " (200*l.*), by Mr. J. D. McCormick ; " Czech Peasant Girl " (90*l.*), by Miss Phillis Dodd ; " The Young Menage " (150*l.*), by Mr. Harold Harvey ; " A Conversation in Aragon " (150*l.*) and " Spanish Gipsies' Winter Quarters " (150*l.*), by Mr. W. Russell Flint ; and " The Young Rower " (120*l.*), by Mr. L. M. Glasson. The prices of several of the pictures sold were not made public, and among these were, " The South Downs, Hikers Resting," by Mr. George Henry ; " Nancy " and " The Derbyshire Mill," by Mr. Sidney Lee.

Several works for the Chantrey collection were acquired before the exhibition opened, and places were given to them on the walls. They were " A Cotswold Farm " (350*l.*), by Mr. Gilbert Spencer ; a portrait by Miss Ethel Walker, " Miss Jean Werner Laurie " (68*l.* 5*s.*) ; and a clever still-life painting by Mr. Alan Beeton, " Decomposing " (100*l.*). No purchases were made from the Academy exhibition, but a fourth work for the Chantrey collection was acquired late in the year, a life-size self-portrait of Mr. Frederick Brown, for many years professor of drawing and painting at the Slade School, and the teacher of several artists now eminent.

Much attention was given in the summer to the work of that distinguished veteran sculptor, Mr. Alfred Gilbert, whose memorial to Queen Alexandra was unveiled in the garden of Marlborough House. Mr. Gilbert was invited to resume his seat among the Royal Academicians—a seat he resigned many years ago, and a knighthood was bestowed upon him by the King. An interesting collection of Sir Alfred's small works of all periods—bronze statuettes—was afterwards held at the gallery of the Fine Art Society, New Bond Street. Another sculptor to whom a compliment was paid was Mr. Alfred Drury, R.A., whose statue of Sir Joshua Reynolds was unveiled in May, in the courtyard of Burlington House. The statue, which shows the great first President of the Royal Academy standing with brush in hand and palette on thumb was awarded the silver medal of the Society of Sculptors, as being " the best work of the year by a British sculptor in any way exhibited to the public in London." Mr. Frank Brangwyn also received an honour, the Albert Medal " for services to decorative and commercial art," which the Royal Society of Arts awarded to him in June.

In the saleroom the centre of interest was at one time shifted from London to Durham, where at Lambton Castle the famous " Red Boy," perhaps the best-known work of Sir Thomas Lawrence, came under the hammer. This portrait has always been extremely popular, and a prodigious price might have been offered for it in normal times. As it was, the bidding was carried up to 95,000*l.* when the " Red Boy " was withdrawn, as the reserve price (the amount of which was not disclosed) had not been reached. In London business in the saleroom was limited, as collectors who wished to dispose of fine works were reluctant to offer them in such a gloomy period for trade. No really great price was realised for any picture, and the fall in the value of some of the works of Victorian painters was astonishing. Some that were sold half a century ago for hundreds of pounds were knocked down for merely nominal sums. On the other hand, a picture by a little-known eighteenth century artist, Arthur Devis, who exhibited only at the almost forgotten gallery of the Free Society, was bid up to 2,415*l.* The most important sale at Christie's, was a collection belonging to Sir John Ramsden, which included pictures, bronzes, furniture, and silver. The sum realised for the Ramsden collection was 49,644*l.* ; and for a collection formed by the late Sir Ernest Cassell, sold by Puttick & Simpson, 25,636*l.*

The exhibitions of the year, other than those at Burlington House, were numerous. Sir Philip Sassoon, whose efforts to raise funds for hospitals by means of exhibitions at his house met with much success in 1930 and 1931, showed a third collection in Park Lane, in which rare furniture, plate, jewels, and documents were more conspicuous than pictures, which were also represented. Another exhibition, somewhat similar in nature but different in motive, was held in the late autumn at Christie's auction rooms in King Street, St. James's. Here were displayed art treasures of nearly every kind, enamels, bronzes, pictures, furniture, musical instruments, jewels, arms, ivories, all for sale, and all lent by prominent English firms to show how fine and rare are the antiques they can offer to collectors. Nothing was admitted to the exhibition until its excellence had been certified by one of several committees of experts, and the profits from the charge for admission were divided equally between the National Art Collections Fund, the Artists' General Benevolent Institution, and the benevolent fund of the British Antique Dealers Association.

At the Burlington Fine Arts Club the summer exhibition was attractive, although the pictures on view were not collectively of the first rank. Described in the catalogue as composed of works by "neglected English masters," the collection contained paintings in oil or water-colour by John Downman, William Peters, and Wright of Derby, who are by no means neglected to-day, as well as by many obscurer artists. The work of some of the lesser men was attractive, but the most interesting picture in some respects was one described as " Portrait of an Artist and his Wife," the authorship of which could not be traced by any of the connoisseurs or critics who visited the exhibition. It was assigned by some to Arthur

Pond, a mid-eighteenth century painter. Messrs. Agnew showed at their gallery in Old Bond Street a valuable collection of Old Masters brought from the Continent, which contained paintings by Rembrandt, Memling, Lucas Cranach, Tiepolo, and Goya. A portrait of an elderly lady by Goya, the draperies of which were white, blue, and the palest pink ; the Rembrandt, and the Memling were among the most notable of the works shown. An exhibition of Old Masters was also held at Messrs. Colnaghi's Bond Street gallery, where also were shown in the summer Sir John Lavery's slight and rapid sketches in oil of ladies who figured in the artist's picture at the Academy, " His Majesty's Court." At the Leicester Gallery Mr. Glyn Philpot showed a collection of paintings and sculpture executed in his new manner ; and Mr. Peter Arno, the American caricaturist, a collection of his original drawings. Early English water-colours were on view at Walker's Gallery ; some strange works—so-called " spirit pictures "— by the late Charles Sims, R.A., at the Redfern Gallery ; and a collection of busts, by Rysbrach, at the rooms of Messrs. Spink.

Except for the much regretted resignation of the Keeper, Mr. C. H. Collins Baker, the year was uneventful at the National Gallery. At the National Portrait Gallery, in connexion with the centenary of the death of Sir Walter Scott, an exhibition was held of portraits of the great novelist and of certain of his friends and acquaintances in London and Edinburgh. Some interesting additions were made to the Gallery's collection of portraits, including a fine full-length of Thomas Day, the author of " Sandford and Merton," by Wright of Derby, and other presentments of interest by a famous portrait painter of the Victorian Era, Frank Holl, R.A., including one of himself when a youth, and one, executed in his prime, of his father, Francis Holl, A.R.A., the well-known engraver.

II. THE DRAMA.

Whatever may be said to the credit of the year 1932 in relation to theatrical happenings, it will probably be remembered more for the number of disastrous failures that marked its course than for its productions of really outstanding interest. Indeed, there can hardly ever have been a period in the annals of the London stage during which, out of a multiplicity of new plays, so small a proportion succeeded in drawing the public. Down to the middle of May there were no fewer than sixteen pieces presented in the West End that averaged only nine performances each, while in several cases plays were withdrawn within a week of production. Some of them, it must be admitted, hardly deserved a better fate. But there can be little doubt that bad times, heavy expenses of production and running, and the ever-growing competition of talking films, among other adverse factors, were to some extent responsible for an abnormal crop of failures.

To Somerset Maugham belongs the distinction of having made what many discerning theatre-goers must have considered the most significant contribution to the year's output. " For Services Rendered " (Globe, November 1) was too pessimistic in its reflection—from the author's standpoint—of post-war conditions, too undeviatingly sombre in atmosphere, to make a wide appeal to the public. Nevertheless, as a grim and relentless exposition of Mr. Maugham's views, the play, apart from its intrinsic qualities as such, could rightly be adjudged a masterpiece. Furthermore, if only for the superb acting of an admirably chosen cast, it deserved a far larger measure of success than it secured.

Curiously enough, the play which, after Mr. Maugham's, probably ranked higher in the estimation of connoisseurs than any other came from an author of very little stage experience. Mr. J. B. Priestley, it is true, had been partly responsible for the adaptation of his very popular novel, " The Good Companions." But " Dangerous Corner " (Lyric, May 17) was the first play he has written single-handed. Not one for all tastes, admittedly, and lacking—by reason largely of its peculiar theme—in variety of mood, it yet showed not only freshness of conception but a high degree of skill in the handling of an arresting, if unedifying, root-idea. It should be recorded here, as a somewhat curious coincidence, that another distinguished novelist, Hugh Walpole, made one of the few notable contributions to the list of the year's new plays. In his own version of " The Cathedral," the novel which a few years ago added appreciably to his reputation, Mr. Walpole came nearer to complete success as an adapter than the majority of dramatists who, unlike him, bring to such a task thorough experience of stage technique. The novel itself possessed all the elements of real drama, and these were effectively retained in the adaptation. Produced at the Embassy on November 21, the piece was afterwards transferred to the New, and if only for the fine acting of Baliol Holloway as the protagonist, certainly should have run longer than it did.

Apart from the works already mentioned, the year brought forth little enough of any genuine significance. Of the older generation of dramatists, indeed, Mr. Maugham alone may be said to have lived up to his reputation. Very few, even among the most enthusiastic of Bernard Shaw's admirers, would acclaim as a masterpiece " Too True to be Good." Produced originally in America, this play, like its author's " The Apple Cart," was first staged in this country (August 6) at Sir Barry Jackson's Malvern Festival. Both there and in London, to which the play was afterwards brought (New, September 13), it met with a very mixed reception alike from critics and the public. Some of the former, in fact, did not hesitate to describe the poorer of Mr. Shaw's quips as not only cheap but vulgar. The piece, as was only to be expected, had some compensating qualities, but these proved insufficient to secure for it more than a very brief run. An even less distinguished effort—though possessing at least the virtue of complete unpretentiousness—was Pinero's comedy, " A Cold June " (Duchess, May 20). A mere trifle, this, which contained hardly more than a hint or two of its veteran author's once brilliant craftsmanship.

On the other hand, it was pleasant to find John van Druten, perhaps the foremost of our younger playwrights, keeping up to form. For reasons difficult to explain, his play, " Somebody Knows " (St. Martin's, May 12), failed to obtain anything like a solid success, in spite of the fact that many who saw it considered it more interesting than any of his previous works. The acting, moreover, was on a very high level of excellence. Singularly enough, another play by Mr. van Druten, " Behold We Live " (St. James's, August 16), held the stage for a considerably longer period, notwithstanding its consistent adherence to a sombre and serious mood. In all probability the fine and polished acting of Gerald Du Maurier in association with Gertrude Lawrence (who rose well enough on the whole to the demands of a strenuously emotional part) contributed largely to the success of this play. The fact remains that it was one wherein the author displayed skill, insight, and high sincerity. To another young playwright, Ronald Mackenzie (whose career was cut short by a motor accident during the run of his play), fell the distinction of scoring one of the few notable successes of 1932. But as the piece in question, " Musical Chairs " (Criterion, April 1), dates from the previous year, when it was experimentally staged at the Arts, it does not claim discussion in the present record. Another play of unusual interest and quality was James Bridie's " Tobias and the Angel " (Westminster, March 9). In this play the author of " The Anatomist " gave us a skilful, and on the whole effective, paraphrase of the story from the Apocrypha, bringing a good deal of humour at times to his treatment of the theme. Henry Ainley gave a superb performance in the part of the Archangel. Considerably less successful was Mr. Bridie with his version of " Jonah and the Whale," presented at the same theatre on December 12.

A play luckier than most was " Evensong " (Queen's, June 30), an entertaining version by Edward Knoblock and Beverley Nichols of the latter's novel of the same title. A good deal of the popularity won by the play may be attributed to the brilliant acting of Edith Evans in the part of the prima donna whose identity Mr. Nichols in his novel had not even thinly disguised. Another play that at once caught the public's fancy was " Service " (Wyndham's, October 12), in which " C. L. Anthony " (Miss Dodie Smith) clearly showed that the remarkable success she had secured with her first essay, " Autumn Crocus," was no mere fluke. For, whatever its artistic shortcomings, her second play was dramatically interesting and thoroughly competent in its technique. A far less happy fate fell to the work of a considerably more experienced playwright, J. Hastings Turner, whose " Punchinello " (Globe, February 12), in which he recreated the immortal Punch characters, was withdrawn after a very few performances. On the other hand, notwithstanding the young author's emancipation from stage artifices, Rodney Ackland's " Strange Orchestra," first seen at the Embassy in 1931, obtained quite a good run when it was put on at St. Martin's (September 27). Among native playwrights must also be included Clifford Bax, whose historical play, " The Rose Without a Thorn " (Duchess, February 10), was a work of characteristic charm and distinction, while, in a totally different category, the late Edgar Wallace's " The Green Pack " (Wyndham's, February 9) also claims mention as that highly popular author's last contribution to the stage. And to the list might also be added Sutton Vane's " Man Overboard." This play, produced by Leon M. Lion at the Garrick (May 6), had something of the eerie atmosphere of the same author's " Outward Bound," but proved far less arresting in theme and treatment.

Two foreign plays of serious interest that were seen in English versions call for special mention. First Hans Chlumberg's " Miracle at Verdun," which, although many who saw it were genuinely impressed by its originality and power, failed on its transference from the Embassy to central London to appeal to the public in general. The other was " Children in Uniform " (Duchess, October 7), which secured no little success as an adaptation— beautifully produced by Leontine Sagan—of the German play on which one of the most popular of recent films, " Mädchen in Uniform," was founded.

Of plays in very light vein there were any number ; yet few that either deserved or achieved success. Among very rare exceptions was " While Parents Sleep " (Royalty, January 19), a farce by a young and unknown author, Anthony Kimmins, which had the luck to survive all its competitors. Also successful, " Road House " (Whitehall, October 6) was a typical Walter Hackett mixture, somewhat extravagant both in its elements of comedy and melodrama. Typical enough, also, was Eden Phillpott's " A Cup of Happiness " (Royalty, December 24). Frederick Lonsdale's " Never Come Back " (Phœnix, October 28), though witty and amusing enough, somehow missed fire, whereas Benn W. Levy's " Springtime for Henry " (Apollo, November 7), a gay and somewhat audacious trifle, appeared not unlikely to repeat the success it had won in America. In " Dr. Pygmalion " (Playhouse, March 30) Harrison Owen, an Australian author, came near to achieving complete success with a play fundamentally reminiscent of Molière. Gladys Cooper and Ronald Squire were his chief interpreters. Ivor Novello's " Party " (Strand, May 23) was a by no means unamusing exercise on a satirical note, which gave Lilian Braithwaite and other clever players an opportunity of poking fun at their own profession, while an agreeably light-hearted affair upon more or less familiar lines was " Orders are Orders " (Shaftesbury, August 9), in which Ian Hay and Anthony Armstrong collaborated. Infinitely better, however, than most of the plays of light texture in a very long list was " See Naples and Die " (Little, March 22), by the American author, Elmer Rice. This was a very happy piece of absurdity in a delicate vein of extravaganza. Among other plays brought from America one of the best was Rose Franken's " Another Language " (Lyric, December 1), in which Herbert Marshall and Edna Best made a welcome return to the London stage.

Notable revivals were " Julius Cæsar " (His Majesty's, February 8), with a star cast in which Godfrey Tearle particularly distinguished himself as Mark Antony ; and " Twelfth Night " (New, May 24), in which Phyllis Neilson-Terry was a superb Olivia. An extremely elaborate production in a setting far more opulent than that of Max Reinhardt in 1911 was " The Miracle," as revived by Charles B. Cochran at the Lyceum (April 9). This venture, however, failed to realise the expectations of its promoters. There was also a very welcome series of revivals of Galsworthy's plays, under the auspices of Leon M. Lion, at the Garrick.

III. THE CINEMA.

Economy was the keynote of film production during 1932. The financial depression, especially in America which sets all film fashions, became a serious factor in the studios, and though film stars were still very highly paid, yet there were all-round salary cuts. Moreover, very few spectacular pictures were made, though Cecil de Mille was allowed to run riot with a talking version of "The Sign of the Cross." Otherwise the tendency was to substitute good acting and smart dialogue for colossal sets, a tendency which greatly helped the cinema in its long and painful progress towards maturity. Pictures became steadily more sophisticated, despite the censorship which was particularly active. It was also a hopeful sign that in many of the recent comedies the film folk were ready to satirise themselves.

The standard of pictures during the year was remarkably high, and many which in normal years would have been outstanding were only a little better than their competitors.

The best picture of 1932 came from Germany in " Mädchen in Uniform," a study in adolescence under Prussian regime in a girls' school. It is interesting to note that this was the work of a woman director, Leontine Sagan, for women screen directors have so far been few and unimportant. The picture made a great impression wherever it was shown. English appreciation was demonstrated in a practical manner. Leontine Sagan was invited over to make a picture of Oxford undergraduate life. The result was surprisingly successful, and " Men of To-morrow " was a much better picture than was expected. It certainly seemed a dangerous experiment to put the picturisation of anything so traditional, so masculine, and so essentially English, as Oxford into the hands of a foreigner and a woman.

America showed her appreciation of " Mädchen in Uniform " by taking the leading lady to Hollywood.

Another German actress, Leni Reisenstahl, scored a big artistic success as director, author, and star in an imaginative production called "The Blue Light," based on a legend of the Dolomites.

Both these pictures had long runs and frequent revivals at the little specialised London cinemas which cater mainly for an educated public. Three such houses in the West End did excellent business.

The best pictures still came to us from the Continent, and with " A Nous La Liberté " René Clair made another stride forward. This time he combined his gay method of fitting movement and music with keen political satire, of which the moral reduced to its simplest terms was that there is very little difference between the restrictions of the factory and the restrictions of prison, and that only the vagabond knows real liberty.

It was in comedy that the English specialised during the year. The standard showed distinct advance, and " Jack's The Boy " and " There Goes The Bride " proved popular medleys of fun and rhythm. At the close of the year Walter Forde—ex-comedian—jumped into the front rank of directors with " Rome Express." Technically this picture was as good as anything out of Hollywood, the acting was first-rate, and it was only the story that left something to be desired. It gave the British film industry new self-confidence and had a highly successful pre-release run at the Tivoli.

One of the tragedies of the British studios was their continued inability to recognise the talent in their midst ; they continued to pay high salaries to imported stars rather than risk giving their own people a long-time contract and building them up in the public favour. During the year Hollywood took and made, or was making, star material of Charles Laughton, Colin Clive, Herbert Marshall, Elizabeth Allen, Heather Angel, Diana Wynward, Ursula Jeans, Lawrence Olivier, Jill Esmond, and Benita Hume. Another American capture was the screen version of Noel Coward's " Cavalcade," which was made on a big scale with a largely imported cast. From Germany, America took Anna Sten, after her success with Emil Jannings in " The Tempest," and Ufa's little English star, Lilian Harvey.

Gangsters have declined in popularity. " Scarface," which was shown early in the year, established Paul Muni as a great screen actor, gave George Raft his first big chance, and proved the zenith of gangster melodrama.

There has been no particular tendency in type of production ; the only experiment was in bringing Eugene O'Neill's " Strange Interlude " to the screen. (The censor insisted that for film purposes the title should be "Strange Interval.") To represent O'Neill's device of the players "thinking aloud " you hear the voice but the lips do not move. Norma Shearer and Clark Gable shared the acting honours.

One of the most expensive of the year's productions was " Grand Hotel," which had a showy all-star cast including Greta Garbo, Joan Crawford, John Barrymore, Lionel Barrymore, Wallace Beery, Lewis Stone, and Jean Hersholt.

Ronald Colman did not add to his laurels with " Arrowsmith," which was a travesty of Lewis Sinclair's realistic novel.

One of the best sentimental pictures of the year was " Emma," which gave Marie Dressler a particularly good part, with plenty of natural comedy and pathos.

" Shanghai Express " showed Marlene Dietrich to advantage, and Ernst Lubitsch held his directorial place with " Trouble in Paradise." Douglas Fairbanks produced a breezy South Seas fantasy in " Mr. Robinson Crusoe," and Mary Pickford spent the year trying to decide on a story for her next picture. Several were accepted and later rejected.

The most elaborate of the open-air pictures was " Tarzan the Ape Man," with Johnny Weismuller, the swimming champion, in the leading part.

Walt Disney's " Mickey Mouse " was rivalled in popularity by Walt Disney's " Silly Symphonies." In November these appeared for the first time in colour. Disney's imagination never seems to flag, and he appears to be on the verge of creating a new form of film art, which will owe nothing to the stage and nothing to the photo plays of the last twenty years.

During the year 641 films were trade shown, of which 449 were American and 153 were British. America imported twenty-two British features.

The biggest financial deal of the year was concluded in October, when British Gaumont bought sufficient ordinary shares in Moss Empires to have voting control in thirty-nine theatres. Four of these were cinemas. They made no change in the policy of the others, and now hold a monopoly of the music halls of the country. In December they acquired the " Dominion," and by the close of the year owned the biggest cinema circuit in Europe.

Outside the London County Council area the fight for " Sunday Opening " was pursued with vigour. As matters stood at the end of the year, apart from London proper, only about 500 cinemas opened on Sunday throughout England.

Since October it has been necessary for the local Councils to apply for permission to the Home Secretary. At Croydon, Dartford, Maidstone, and Walthamstow, where the Town Councils were divided, the matter was submitted to a local plebiscite, with the result in every case of an overwhelming majority in favour of Sunday opening.

IV. MUSIC.

To the prevailing economic conditions may be chiefly attributed the fact that, apart from orchestral enterprises, 1932 was remarkable for the very small number of musical events that marked its course. As a rule, even in seasons hardly memorable, London has experienced a glut more or less of vocal and instrumental recitals. For once, however, there was an almost unprecedented dearth of activities of this kind, and it is probably no exaggeration to say that during the summer months there were not more recitals of any real musical interest than would formerly have taken place within a fortnight.

Of opera on the " grand " scale London had very little. At Covent Garden there was a short German season officially described as a Wagner Festival. This opened on May 9 with a performance of " Die Meistersinger," under the conductorship of Sir Thomas Beecham, and lasted until June 3, the works given, in addition to the usual two cycles of " The Ring," being " Tristan und Isolde," " Der Fliegende Holländer," and " Tannhäuser." Except for the appearance of one or two newcomers of no special distinction, the performances of the Nibelungen dramas, as of the other operas, ran on such long familiar lines that no detailed comment seems called for. A word, however, should be said in praise of the uncommon sensitiveness and finish of the orchestral playing—notably as regards " Tristan " and " Meistersinger "—when Beecham assumed control. The other conductor, as in previous years, was Robert Heger. A certain melancholy interest attached to this brief season from the circumstance that it brought a stage nearer the day, now close at hand, when Covent Garden will no longer possess an opera house. For it has been more or less definitely decided that after the next summer season of opera the site will be required in connexion with a big scheme projected by the owners of the property which will involve the demolition of the historic theatre.

It appears likely, indeed, in whatever direction the Royal Opera Syndicate may look for a home, that opera enthusiasts will have to rely more and more for their pleasures on the joint enterprise of the Old Vic and the re-created Sadler's Wells. In alternate weeks during the winter months operas, mostly from the standard repertory, are staged at those theatres at " popular " prices, under the management of Lilian Baylis. As given in English, these performances in recent times have shown a very marked advance, from almost every standpoint, on those of previous seasons at the Old Vic. Notably, with Aylmer Buesst and other conductors in control, the playing of the orchestra has improved out of all knowledge, while in their work as producers, Sumner Austin, Clive Carey, and their colleagues have revealed a welcome tendency to rid some of the operas of outworn conventions. An interesting addition to the well-stocked repertory was an excellent revival of Verdi's too long neglected " Ballo in Maschera." Worth recalling, also, is the increasing importance devoted by the Vic-Wells organisation to the staging of ballet, under the super-vision of Ninette de Valois. A ballet entitled " Douanes," with music by Geoffrey Toye (who conducted), was among the new productions of the kind presented during the season.

As already indicated, orchestral concerts were exceptionally numerous. An interesting feature in this connexion was the advent of the London Philharmonic Orchestra, which proved to be an important addition to the list of those already in existence. The new organisation was sponsored by Sir Thomas Beecham, who conducted on the occasion of the orchestra's début at a concert of the Royal Philharmonic Society on October 7. From the first it was clearly apparent that the L.P.O. was destined to play a valu-able part in the musical life of London. In a programme of familiar classics, reinforced by Delius and Strauss—whose " Heldenleben " was superbly played—the new orchestra made a fine impression, fully confirmed at their later appearances. A series of Sunday afternoon concerts at which they played in Queen's Hall received, nevertheless, a measure of public support by no means commensurate either with the interest of the programmes as a whole or the high quality of the performances. It should be noted here that the London Symphony Orchestra appointed as permanent chief for their twenty-seventh season Sir Hamilton Harty, who, with one or two exceptions, conducted at all their concerts. At the first one a much dis-cussed feature was the performance, under Hans Weisbach, of Bach's mighty " Kunst der Fuge " in an orchestral version, new to this country, by Wolfgang Graeser. But, while giving him due credit for the skill re-vealed in his translation of Bach's great work from one medium to the other, the general impression conveyed, perhaps inevitably, was of an experiment only partially successful. In addition to the symphony con-certs of the L.S.O. there was a generous series of programmes (of which Adrian Boult and Sir Henry Wood were conductors-in-chief) given under the auspices of the B.B.C. So that, what with the foregoing enterprises,

D

the seasons of the Royal Philharmonic Society, the Courtauld-Sargent Concert Club, and one or two less representative organisations, lovers of orchestral music enjoyed many and varied experiences.

Nevertheless, there was very little to chronicle in the way of performances of new or unfamiliar music. This applies to native, no less than to foreign, compositions. In the former category, indeed, novelties claiming any real importance were singularly few. One notable exception was the first performance in London, under the direction of Malcolm Sargent, of Arnold Bax's fourth Symphony. In this work the composer, whilst hinting at a greater appreciation of classical form than in some of his earlier scores, does not allow that tendency to fetter his imagination. Of remarkable simplicity and directness—for Bax—is the slow movement, appealingly lyrical in style and feeling. There are fewer traces in this symphony of over-elaboration than in some of its predecessors, and as a whole it conveys a sense of vigour, even at times of brightness, that distinguishes it from those that have shown the composer in a more characteristic mood. Two other works of his were new to London. One of these, an " Overture to a Picaresque Comedy," revealed in its gaiety and almost rollicking spirit unsuspected traits in the composer's temperament. But, in his " Winter Legends," described as a Sinfonia Concertante for piano and orchestra, played under Boult at a B.B.C. concert, Bax returned to a typically serious mood. Alike in thought and craftsmanship the work (in which Harriet Cohen was the soloist) deserves an honoured place in the list of his more mature compositions.

Another new native work given a hearing was Dr. George Dyson's " Canterbury Pilgrims," which owed its first London performance to the Philharmonic Choir, conducted by C. Kennedy Scott. Dr. Dyson's setting was confined to a selection of " Portraits from the Prologue " to Chaucer's poem, and if it lacked the asset of a purely personal style, the score was at any rate characteristic in the undeviating respect shown by the composer for the finest models. So far as concerns the older generation of native composers, the year was singularly barren. From Elgar, the doyen among them, came nothing new. But reference must be made to a very fitting celebration of the composer's seventy-fifth birthday in the form of a series of concerts at Queen's Hall, under the auspices of the B.B.C., Elgar himself participating at two of them as conductor. The only new work by Delius was a setting for double choir and orchestra of some poems of Walt Whitman. In these " Songs of Farewell," as he calls them, Delius found good scope for the expression of that mood of quiet, dreamy ecstasy of which he has given us so many examples. Listening to this work, one could but marvel that the composer, incapacitated by grievous physical afflictions, should have been able to dictate a score so rich in intricate patterns and delicately blended orchestral hues. With the foregoing works the slender list of representative British novelties produced during 1932 is practically completed.

For that matter, London concert-goers heard very little new music from the Continent that proved of any particular account. A couple of pieces for various combinations of instruments from the pen of Paul

Hindemith did not bring that astonishingly prolific composer any nearer to the affections of the public. Nor was the reputation of Maurice Ravel enhanced by either of the new Piano Concertos of which performances were given. But to one of them attached the element at least of novelty in the fact that the difficult solo part was written for one hand only, being dedicated to Paul Wittgenstein, the one-armed Austrian pianist, by whom it was brilliantly played. Of greater musical value was Sibelius's symphonic poem, " Pohjola's Daughter," played by the L.S.O. under Robert Kajanus, a Finnish conductor (new to this country), who made an excellent impression. But the work in question was composed many years ago.

For the rest, notable occurrences included visits from the Berlin Philharmonic Orchestra (conducted by Furtwängler), Stravinsky, and Rachmaninov, both of whom were heard as soloists in concertos of their own ; Artur Schnabel, who gave a memorable series of Beethoven recitals, and that marvellously gifted boy violinist, Yehudi Menuhin, who on one occasion, in association with the London Philharmonic Orchestra, played no fewer than three concertos—an unfamiliar one by Mozart, Bach's in E major, and that of Elgar. His readings of these widely contrasted works showed him to be, notwithstanding his youth, a fine interpreter as well as the possessor of an uncannily advanced technique. Finally, mention should be made of the bi-centenary of Haydn's birth, which was observed notably by a performance of his seemingly immortal " Creation " in which the Royal Philharmonic and Royal Choral Societies joined forces under the direction of Malcolm Sargent.

SCIENCE OF THE YEAR.

THE BIOLOGICAL SCIENCES.

Evolution and Genetics.—1932 was a year of enormous activity in Biology. Further skeletal fragments of Sinanthropus were found and, in the Choukoutien cave, 30 metres of strata with remains, indicate that it was occupied probably over thousands of years. The associated fauna was upper Lower Pleistocene and the artefacts show that, culturally speaking, Sinanthropus was right-handed and possessed a nervous mechanism for articulate speech. In these matters a warning was sounded by Kappers that mechanical as well as functional characters influence the surface anatomy of the human brain ; and Lotsy pointed out that hybridisation has played so important a rôle and followed so circuitous a route that it seems hopeless to reconstruct the past.

Hill showed that the earlier stages of placental development in Primates exhibits Lemuroid, Tarsioid, Pithecoid, and Anthropoid stages suggestive of four actual phyletic steps in the evolution of the order ; a scheme agreeing well with those of Elliott Smith based on the brain of living and fossil primates, and of Gregory based on morphological and palæontological evidence. Note may be made here of Bingham's psycho-biological study of mountain gorillas in the Belgian Congo.

The method of evolution received attention especially by palæontologists who mainly adopted a Lamarckian position. Broom, in " The Mammal-like Reptiles of South Africa," concluded that all the steps by which mammals have arisen from the reptiles seem to be connected with change of habit and change of diet ; and further that evolution is by almost imperceptible slight modifications along definite lines from small generalised forms to large highly specialised types. Interpretations on a basis of statistical and experimental genetics were supported by Morgan in " The Scientific Basis of Evolution," Haldane in " The Causes of Evolution," and Hurst in " The Mechanism of Creative Evolution," but in the more philosophical treatises by Johnstone, " The Essentials of Biology," and Woltereck, " Grundzüge einer allgemeiner Biologie," this interpretation is found inadequate. Generally, it would seem that modern genetics is satisfactory in relation to speciation but fails to explain adaptive evolution. Woltereck supports the theory of orthogenesis, but Crampton, studying the " Variation, Distribution, and Evolution of Partula," found no evidence of this, but merely a local differentiation among members of ancient stocks disseminated by their own unaided movements.

Numerous genetic analyses of animal and plant species were made ;

perhaps the most striking results of this mass of work being the comparative rareness of complete dominance of any character, and the remarkable correlation of cytological results with breeding experiments and taxonomic studies. These researches were synthesised by Sansome and Philp in " Recent Advances in Plant Genetics."

Durham and Woods could not confirm Stockard's findings on the deleterious effect of alcohol on the genetic behaviour of guinea-pigs ; and Eaton, reviewing twenty-five years inbreeding of guinea-pigs, found no evidence of decline due to this process. It looks as though devices to ensure exogamy in living things are to ensure the well-being of the immediate progeny and not the species ; to guard them against recessive defects lying latent in parents.

Much work was done on the induction of sports by exposure of organisms to high frequency radiation, perhaps the most striking outcome being the remarkable capacity of germplasm to sustain and perpetuate extreme quantitative alterations and reorganisations.

The Sixth International Congress of Genetics at Cornell University, U.S.A., was made notable by Emerson's maps of the loci of genes in maize.

Zoology.—There appeared the usual flood of morphological and systematic researches covering all animal groups. Systematic and faunistic work is essential, as the basis of all zoological investigations, and detailed morphological study produces the data of animal science. Such publications added voluminously to zoological literature, but it is difficult to see any new or major issues arising from them during 1932. An interesting volume which may be mentioned here is Sunamoto's " Zo " (Elephant).

Important developments were made in ecology, and signalised by the publication of a new *Journal of Animal Ecology.* Pure Zoology having largely lost physiology and genetics has for many years appeared quiescent, but it looks as if the ecological viewpoint may be a most potent influence in its revitalisation. It is striking to see how ecology is acting as a catalyst and crystallisation point in all branches of Zoology. The conservation of wild life and the control of pests received much attention, an interesting paper being Dearborn's " Foods of some predatory fur-bearing animals in Michigan." It would seem that destruction is apt to reach far beyond the pests at which it is aimed. Investigations on the part played by light in controlling the periodic recurrence of breeding seasons in certain birds and mammals may be capable of important practical application.

In fisheries research attention was chiefly paid to estimation of stocks, to the underlying causes of fluctuations and the possibility of prediction, to the distribution and migration of fish in relation to environmental factors, and to food chains. Paulsen's investigations of the Cod in Danish waters showed a distinct correlation to exist between the water temperature and larval numbers, and between the salinity of the water and the numbers of fry. Bhatia's interesting researches showed that food supply and not temperature is primarily responsible for the development of broad " summer " and narrow " winter " rings of the scales of certain teleostean fishes.

Students of insects and related forms published a vast amount of work, and attention can only be drawn to typical investigations showing the main lines of study. Shelford, from the ecological aspect, published an important study of the records of the abundance, migration, and decline of the chinch bug in Illinois in relation to climate and weather since 1840. The need for work on particular pests, such as the locust, was shown by the issue of the "4th Report of the Commission on Locust Control," in which it was estimated that during 1927-31 this pest in Africa and Western Asia caused damage of over 6,000,000*l.* in value. Faure, studying the locust in South Africa, experimentally produced the solitary locust phase from the gregarious phase, thus confirming the general truth of Uvarov's phase theory. As examples of biological control may be mentioned the control of bramble, rose, ragwort, and other weeds in New Zealand and Australia, and Compere and Smith's work on mealy bug, a serious pest which has been reduced in California to negligible proportions by the introduction of internal parasites. Work on biological strains is illustrated by the findings of Painter, Salmon, and Parker that the hard and soft wheat belts in Kansas harbour distinct biological strains of the Hessian Fly. On the other hand, Huxley's studies on relative growth showed that forms of male Lucanids distinguished by the coleopterist are purely growth forms without systematic significance. Investigating the water conservation of insects Wigglesworth found that in larvæ and adults of all the main orders the osmotic pressure of the blood is maintained during life at a constant level, the rectal glands and epithelium reabsorbing water from the excrement before discharge. Further, the mechanism regulating the extent of air in the tracheoles of aquatic insect larvæ is the same as that in terrestrial insects. The biological trend of studies in this branch of Zoology is shown by Nielson's " Biology of Spiders " and Metcalfe and Flint's " Fundamentals of Insect Life." Important works on the lower invertebrates were Germain's " Molluscan Fauna of France," Wilson's " Copepods of the Woods Hole Region," and Sprehn's " Lehrbuch der Helminthologie." Attention may be drawn to the important series of investigations on the bottom fauna of Japanese lakes published by the National Research Council of Japan; Mortensen's work showing the modern prevalence of certain families of sea urchins previously thought to be scanty remnants of tribes dominant in the Jurassic and Cretaceous epochs; Naumann's " Die Binnengewasser," in which the ecological and physiological basis of regional limnology is emphasised; and to Wilson's investigation of the cataclysmic metamorphosis of the Mitraria larva of *Owenia fusiformis,* one of the most remarkable phenomena in invertebrate development.

General Physiology.—A. V. Hill sounded the keynote of general physiology and biochemistry when, at the Fourteenth International Physiological Congress, he referred to "the intolerable burden of the accumulating literature "; and the most significant thing about the 400 papers read at that congress was the absence of any advance of a notable kind. On the other hand, physiology is influencing in a most fundamental way the whole of biological science : physiological ideas and data of apparently small intrinsic value, when applied to some other branch of biology, often have an astonishing catalytic influence.

Most attention during 1932 was given to work of a chemical or physical nature, and Gowland Hopkins sounded a not unneeded warning when he said that " biochemical events are of course limited by chemical possibilities, they are not safely to be predicted by chemical probabilities, even when these are strong." More philosophically, Woltereck regards the organism not as a substance, but as an activity, and the activity to a large extent controlling the constitution of the substance. Much attention was paid to human blood groups. The characters that differentiate blood are also present in all the cells and secretions of the body, and even in its excreta, and their investigation has changed from a qualitative to a quantitative aspect. Important monographs were Lattes' "Individuality of the Blood in Biology " and Steffan's "Handbuch der Blutgruppenkunde." Interesting work was also published by Benedict on heat production of large reptiles, as compared with warm-blooded animals, and its relation to metabolism ; and by Hukuda, who showed that the isotony of the body fluids of marine invertebrates to sea water is maintained by diffusion of salts through bounding membranes and that of the blood of Elasmobranchs by diffusion of water. Attention may be drawn here to Bolani's monograph on " The Donnan Equilibrium." In an important work on the " Physiologie des Höhenklimas," Loewy showed that the causes of many of the main physiological effects at high altitudes are referable to a compensating response of the organism to the low oxygen tension in the atmosphere.

The chemistry and physics of development received much attention. Creatine phosphate, which plays an important part in muscular contraction in vertebrates, seems to be represented by arginine phosphate in invertebrates. Work on hormones revealed the great complexity of the relation between the pituitary secretions and the functional activity of the ovary. The chemical composition of Oestrin, an ovarian hormone, was elucidated. Steady advance was made in knowledge of vitamins. Vitamins A, D, and B have been isolated, and the small quantities in which they are effective— in certain cases less than $1/10,000$ milligram—seem to call for considerable revision of conceptions regarding the possibilities of drug action. Six factors are known in the vitamin B complex which seems to be capable of extensive division. It is important that Perry and Zilva found the vitamin content of butter (A and D) to be practically unaffected by cold storage ; and it may be noted here that certain factors affecting milk yield in cows have proved to be sex-linked. Vitamin A is probably one of the alcohol series with a formula $C_{20}H_{29}OH$; vitamin B seems to be a fairly simple sulphur compound with the formula $C_{12}H_{17}N_3OS$; vitamin C seems to be a hexuronic acid, a simple glucose derivative ; and vitamin D, obtained from pure irradiated ergosterol, has the formula $C_{27}H_{41}OH$.

Sheldon and others gave attention to the part played by metallic elements in physiology, and found that copper is an essential factor in the formation of hæmoglobin ; whilst manganese seems to be essential to the proper functioning of the endocrine organs, especially those concerned directly with reproduction.

Progress was made in knowledge and methods of tissue culture. Waddington cultivated *in vitro* entire blastoderms of chick and duck removed from the egg during the first two days of incubation ; and, looking more generally at this kind of work, it seems that the course of metabolism of tissues *in vitro* during extensive periods of survival need differ in no way from that of tissues *in vivo*.

The nature or even existence of Gurwitsch's mitogenetic rays is still a subject of controversy. It is claimed that their emission from active cells has been conclusively demonstrated by Geiger's counter, that their wavelength has been measured, and specific spectra in various cases duly mapped ; but Richards and Taylor and other workers discredit the methods used to demonstrate their very existence. The present position was summarised in Gurwitsch's "Die mitogenetische Strahlung" and Stempell's "Die unsichtbare Strahlung der Lebewesen." In an interesting investigation Lepeschkin showed that visible rays of light decrease the stability of protoplasm which is, therefore, more stable by night than by day ; and that ultra-violet rays increase stability but are harmful if the exposure is for too long a period. At the centenary meeting of the British Medical Association a discussion on senescence suggested little more than that senescence is the result of the continued action of the regulator after growth is stopped. Of more importance is work by Baly, which gave evidence of the evolution of heat by dying organisms, *e.g.*, poisoned plants ; the amount of energy given out depending directly upon the length of time the plant had been plucked. The same phenomenon was also found with oysters, and recalls American work showing that the anti-rachitic value of freshly cut leaves gradually disappears after twenty-four hours, but can be restored on exposure to ultra-violet radiation. An interesting investigation was also published by Becquerel who argues that since certain fungus and bacterial spores can germinate after exposure to − 192° C. for 492 hours, or − 253° C. for 77 hours, or *in vacuo* can withstand 135° C. for 5 minutes or 100° C. for 15 minutes, therefore their outer integuments must be impermeable, and the latent life must be anærobic. Researches in cold- and gas-storage of animal and plant foods has now progressed to such an extent that the results obtained can be transferred to the full commercial scale.

Attention may be drawn to important monographs by Blanchard, Penau, and Simonnet on "La Thyroide" ; Atkinson on "Acromegaly" ; three volumes on "The Cytology and Cellular Pathology of the Nervous System," edited by Penfold ; Tzanck on "Immunité—Intolerance—Biophylaxie" ; Whitnall on "The Anatomy of the Human Orbit and Accessory Organs of Vision," and by Needham on "The Biochemistry of Muscle."

Botany.—Numerous floras were published, of which may be mentioned those by Craib on Siam, by Port on the Near East, by Burt Davy on the Transvaal, and Druce's "Comital Flora of the British Isles." Volumes also appeared by Lloyd Praeger on the Sempervivums, by Brown, Tischer, and Karsten on Mesembryanthema, by Keller on Roses, by van Hall on Cacao, by Rechinger on Rumex, by Sirjaev on Ononis, by Chalk and Burt Davy on East African Forest Trees, and by Chittenden on Conifers. A volume of general interest was that by Nelmes and Cuthbertson containing portraits and bibliographical notes to the dedications of a century of Curtis's *Botanical Magazine*. Two important studies in the application of epidermal anatomy to systematics were those by Prat on the Grasses, and by Ohki, who confirmed the value of the spodogram method in his studies on the Bambusaceæ. Of more general morphological interest were the volumes by Goebel on " Die Samenpflanzen," and Haidenhain on " Die Spaltungsgesetze der Blätter." Attention may also be drawn to Bernbeck's studies of the floral morphology of the Urticaceæ and Moraceæ; to Goldsmith's and Hafenrichter's " Anthokinetics " ; to Taushin's anatomical study of Philippine Mangrove woods, and to Burgeff's " Saprophytismus und Symbiose."

In plant physiology and ecology the nutritive, light, and more especially the water relations of plants occupied attention ; the principal result being the increasing recognition that none of these relationships can be fitted by simple formulæ unless artificial restrictions are imposed. Osborne stated the position in saying that " Transpiration is no criterion of a Xerophyte unless we follow Maximov and make higher transpiration rate a mark of the Xerophyte," and the actual experimental position is shown, for example, by Mittmeyer's findings that although light is the determining factor in evaporation from Xerophytes, yet saturation deficit also has an influence. It was also very generally recognised that the complex of forces concerned in the absorption of water by plants in which little transpiration is taking place differs from that concerned in water absorption by an actively transpiring plant. Considerable attention was paid to the relative water conductivity of higher plants, the interesting fact being discovered by Malhotra that the tracheæ of apples are 26·4 per cent. more efficient than those of plum. Attention may be drawn to the interesting researches by Bergdolt on the physiology and experimental morphology of the Genus Viola ; and of Chazé on tobacco alkaloids ; and to the volumes by Lundegardh on " Die Nahrstoffaufnahme der Pflanze," by Boysen-Jensen on " Die Stoffproduktion der Pflanzen," and by Pringsheim on " Julius Sachs."

In Palæobotany the most notable work was Florin's comparative anatomical studies of the epidermis and stomata of recent and fossil species of Coniferales and Cordaitales ; and Seward's description of a Sigillaria from Persia, which marks the first recognition of the carboniferous flora in this region.

In cytology the outstanding events were the appearance of Guilliermond, Mangenot, and Plantefol's monumental " Traité de Cytologie Végétale " and the smaller, but very important work by Darlington, " Recent Advances in Cytology," in which the view is put forward that meiosis is mitosis with delayed division of the chromosomes, chiasmata result from crossing over, and metaphase pairing is due to chiasmata that prevent separation of divided homologues. Most attention was paid to chromosome numbers and cytogenetics ; and attention may be drawn to Bruun's study of the cytology and taxonomy of the Primulas ; to Eichhorn's interesting study of the comparative nuclear structure in Gymnosperms and Angiosperms ; to the discovery by Pastrana that the egg nucleus of *Begonia Schmidtiana* contains an accessory sex chromosome ; and to Wakayama's demonstration that the chromosome numbers in thirty-four Autobasidiomycetes are either two, four, or six.

Bryologists showed great activity, but attention can only be drawn to Verdoorn's "Manual of Bryology," to Casares-Gil's volume "Bryophyta" in the *Flora Ibirica,* and to Helmut's revision of "Plagiochila." Zahlbruckner issued Vol. VIII. of his "Catalogus lichenum universalis"; and monographs appeared by Czurda on the "Zynemales," by Hawlitschka on "Tribonema," by Geitler on "Der Formwechsel der pennaten Diatomaceen"; and by Newton on "British Seaweeds." Skinner, following Bristol-Roach's lead, showed that green algæ multiply in soil under conditions of darkness and moderate moisture; and Hartmann showed that even in extreme isogamous types of algæ, the gametes, though morphologically and physiologically similar, yet exude different substances according to whether they are + or —, and that only gametes of these opposite kinds will copulate.

Mycology is one of the most actively developing fields of Botany. Systematic treatises appeared, of general nature such as Butler and Bisby's "The Fungi of India," or restricted such as Singer's "Monograph of the Genus Russula"; and a notable event was the publication of Grove and Buller's translation of Tulasne's "Selecta Fungorum Carpologia." Genetics continued to be the main focus of attention and was marked by the finding of the heterothallic state in numerous fungi, by the extension of Buller's diploidisation process to the rust fungi, and by an increasing recognition of hybridisation and hyphal fusion as the basis of genetic variation. Attention may be drawn to the researches of Christensen and Sleumer on maize smut, and of Drayton on the sexual function of microconidia. The relation of bacteria to higher plants received considerable attention, and note may be made of Aldridge-Blake's discovery of the fixation of atmospheric nitrogen by bacteria in the root nodules of Casuarina, and of the researches of Starkey and of Thom and Humfield showing that roots tend to maintain their own reaction in the immediate vicinity, thus establishing an environment favourable to micro-organisms. Fred, Baldwin, and McCoy published an encyclopædic treatise on "Root Nodule Bacteria and Leguminous Plants."

Important volumes on soil were Russell's "Soil Conditions and Plant Growth," Robinson's "Soils," Blanck's "Der Kulturboden und die Bestimmung seines Fruchtbarkeitszustandes," and Weis's fine researches on Danish podsols, showing that all these must be considered sick and degenerate forms. A paper of unusual interest published by Hoyt and Troxall calls in question the long and widely-held assumption of the usefulness of forests in maintaining and regulating water supplies.

Microbiology and Disease.—In plant pathology, two outstanding publications were Appel and Reh's Vol. III., Part II., of "Sorauer's Handbuch der Pflanzenkrankheiten," and G. and M. Arnaud's "Traité de pathologie végétale." Great attention was paid to fungicidal dusts, especially sulphur, and to morphological, physiological, and genetic studies of disease resistance. In relation to the latter, it was claimed by Leemann that fungus secretions can be incorporated into the host protoplasm and actively modify its susceptibility to pathogenic invasion. Considerable advances were also made in knowledge of the animal mycoses.

In bacteriology important monographs were published by Ellis on
" The Sulphur Bacteria," and by Rahn on " The Physiology of Bacteria."
Much attention was paid to dissociation phenomena, and Read showed that
in *Mycobacterium lepræ* the rough may revert to the smooth form.   The
outstanding event, however, was Stoughton's discovery of conjugation in
Bacterium malvacearum.   A notable volume was Dobell's " Leeuwenhoek."
Virology attracted increased attention.   Laidlaw and Dunkin's protective
inoculation for dog distemper proved successful in a high percentage of
cases, only one dose being required of a vaccinating mixture of blood
serum of an immune animal and live virus.   True distemper was found in
silver-fox, fitch, mink, and fisher.   The number of virus diseases previously
attributed to other causes is increasing, and Gordon showed that Lympha-
denoma is probably to be included in this category.   Ledingham showed
that the tissue changes produced by virus are the same as those due to
ordinary bacteria, and regards the visible intracellular inclusion bodies as
the real virus, a conclusion agreed in by Bedson working on Psittacosis.
German workers, in contrast with English, Dutch, and American workers,
still tend to regard plant viruses as unorganised and not living autonomous
organisms, and important researches supporting this viewpoint were published by Thung on tobacco virus diseases, and by Marx and Merkenschlager
on potato virus diseases, whilst the general position was reviewed in
Esmarch's " Die Blattrollkrankheit der Kartoffel," and by Rivers in an
important paper in Physiological Reviews.   Plant virology during 1932
dealt chiefly with the composite nature of plant viruses and their classification, the value of X-bodies as a diagnostic character, and the carrier
problem in relation to host development and environmental conditions.
Storey made the important discovery that in *Cicadulina mbila* ability or
inability to transmit maize streak is inherited as a simple dominant sex-
linked Mendelian factor.

In cancer research valuable results were obtained by Crabtree, Cramer,
and others in following up Warburg's ideas regarding the exceptional
character and magnitude of cancer metabolism, on the underlying assumption that the intensity of metabolism of a cell is an index of its vitality.
Moppett published interesting researches on the differential action of
X-rays on tumour tissues ; and Cloudman succeeded for the first time in
obtaining successful transplants of tumour tissues from one mammalian
species to another.

Important work was done on mineral-deficiency diseases, and on the
relation between the composition of herbage and the health of grazing
animals ; and Kintner and Holt showed that equine Osteomalacia in the
Philippines appears to be solely due to a mineral imbalance of calcium to
phosphorus.   Barger published a valuable monograph on " Ergot and
Ergotism " ; and from South Africa came notable books by Henning on
" Animal Diseases in South Africa," and by Mitchell, Watt, and Breyer on
" The Medicinal and Poisonous Plants of Southern Africa."

General.—In more general biological matters 1932 was chiefly marked,
firstly by an increased recognition of the cultural value of biology and the
great need for its inclusion throughout the educational curriculum, and

secondly by the attention given to biology in its human and social applications. Attention may be drawn to Bavink's remarkable work on "The Anatomy of Modern Science."

THE PHYSICAL SCIENCES.

First place in the records of a year of quite unusual scientific achievement must be given to the discovery of the *neutron*, a particle of mass 1·0067 and charge 0 consisting of a proton (*i.e.*, the positively charged nucleus of a hydrogen atom) and an electron in close union—much closer than in the ordinary hydrogen atom which has, otherwise, the same constitution. The possibility of the existence of such particles was pointed out by Lord Rutherford in 1920, but the history of their discovery begins with the observation, by Bothe and Becker in 1930, that beryllium emits a radiation of great penetrating power when it is bombarded by α particles from polonium. In 1931 Mme. Curie-Joliot (the daughter of Mme. Curie) and M. Joliot observed that the ionisation produced by this radiation is much increased when the radiation passes through matter containing hydrogen, *e.g.*, paraffin wax. This ionisation appeared to be due to protons ejected from the hydrogen and they suggested that the beryllium radiation consisted of photons (*i.e.*, quanta of electromagnetic radiation) which reacted with the hydrogen in a manner analogous to the Compton effect.

The problem was investigated in the Cavendish Laboratory and, in a letter published in *Nature* (Feb. 27), Dr. Chadwick stated that he had been able to show that the particles ejected from hydrogen molecules (and molecules of other light elements) are recoil atoms and that observations of their range and the number of ions which they produce were best explained by the hypothesis that the radiation from the beryllium consisted of neutrons projected from its surface with a velocity about one-tenth that of light. Further experimental work by Chadwick, by Feather and by Dee (*Proc. Roy. Soc.*) supported this explanation, but showed that the processes involved are by no means simple. Much experimental confirmation was quickly forthcoming from the Continent. It was shown (Becker and Bothe, Rasetti, Auger) that γ rays are emitted from beryllium along with the neutrons : that neutrons are emitted from boron (Chadwick, Joliot, Becker and Bothe) and lithium (Joliot). Joliot and Joliot showed also that the neutrons emitted from beryllium fall into two groups, one with an air-range of 28 cm. and the other with an air-range of 70 cm.

Feather placed a polonium source and a beryllium plate in the expansion chamber of a Wilson condensation apparatus containing oxygen or nitrogen and by studying the ionisation tracks was able to show that, very occasionally, the impact of the neutrons and gas molecules produced an atomic change. For example, the impact of a neutron and an oxygen atom produced one carbon atom and one helium atom.

The phenomenon of atomic disintegration has been familiar since 1922, but the honour of effecting it for the first time by artificial means fell to

Cockcroft and Walton (*Proc. Roy. Soc.*). Working in the Cavendish Laboratory they developed a technique whereby they could produce steady potentials as great as 600,000 volts and use them to accelerate a stream of protons. These protons they used to bombard lithium and, as soon as their energy exceeded a certain critical value, some of the lithium atoms disintegrated, forming helium, as might be expected from the hypothetical equation : 1 lithium atom (mass 7) + 1 proton (mass 1) = 2 helium atoms (each of mass 4). The result was of great interest for two reasons. In the first place, the type of disintegration was new in that atoms of smaller mass were formed. Previous disintegrations by α-particles from radioactive bodies resulted in the ejection of a proton from the bombarded atom which at the same time captured the α-particle (mass 4), forming an atom of greater mass. Secondly, it provides a means of disintegrating atoms in relatively large numbers. At 250,000 volts 1 atom was disintegrated for every 10^9 protons striking the lithium and it was possible to produce a stream of 5×10^{13} protons per sec. The rate of disintegration was therefore at least fifty times greater than that obtainable with radioactive sources. The same process effected the disintegration of atoms of beryllium, boron, and carbon : results with nitrogen fluorine and aluminium were uncertain.

The structure of atomic nuclei was discussed by Lord Rutherford, Ellis and others at a meeting of the Royal Society in April. It is supposed that the emission of a β-ray from the nucleus of a radioactive atom (*e.g.*, radium C) causes a violent disturbance in the nucleus so that some of the α-particles which it contains are raised to higher energy levels. After a short interval they fall back and the energy released is emitted as γ radiation. During the short interval, however, these high level α-particles have a chance of escape from the nucleus and on rare occasions a particle does escape, carrying with it energy characteristic of the level from which it comes. Measurement of this energy therefore gives an indication of the levels within the nucleus. Tarrant and Gray (*Proc. Roy. Soc.*) obtained further information concerning these levels from an examination of the secondary radiation from lead and tin when they are excited by γ-rays from thorium C''.

The announcement by Urey, Brickwedde and Murphy (*Phys. Rev.*) that they had discovered an isotope of hydrogen created considerable surprise. However, Bleakney (*Phys. Rev.*) confirmed their result and found the isotope to be present in commercial electrolytic hydrogen to the extent of 1 atom in 30,000. Later Bainbridge (*Phys. Rev.*) found that its atomic weight is $2 \cdot 0135 \pm 0 \cdot 0002$, so that its nucleus probably consists of one proton and one neutron—a combination which Perrin (*J. Physique*) called a *demihelion*.

The nature and place of origin of the " cosmic " radiations (ANNUAL REGISTER, 1931, p. 60), still remain quite unknown, although several hundred papers dealing with them have already been published (see Hoffmann, *Phys. Zeits.*, September). At the International Electricity Congress, held at Paris in July, Millikan adhered to his view that they are photons and originate in interstellar space as a consequence of atomic reconstruction.

A. H. Compton (*Phys. Rev.*) measured the intensity of the radiation at different stations in the northern and southern hemispheres and found marked changes of intensity with locality, especially for the less penetrating components of the rays, greater values being observed at places where the dip is greater. His observations were confirmed by Clay and Berlage on a voyage from Amsterdam to Batavia. Compton and his collaborators found also that the ionisation produced by the radiation is at least 1 per cent. greater between 8 a.m. and 4 p.m. than between 8 p.m. and 4 a.m. These results are in direct conflict with those obtained by Millikan and others in 1931 and would be expected only if the radiations consist of charged particles.

Regener observed the variation of intensity with altitude up to heights of about 28 km., and Piccard states that the observations he made during his balloon ascent on August 10 are in agreement with Regener's results and *might* be explained if the rays originate in the upper atmosphere. Schonland in S. Africa and Rizzo at Naples observed a diminution in the intensity of the radiations during thunderstorms. The most striking observations, however, were those made by Hoffmann, Steinke and Schindler and also by Blackett, namely, that when the rays pass through a Wilson chamber they produce a burst of ionisation much more intense than that given by the swiftest α-particles.

It appeared that both Einstein and de Sitter (*Proc. Nat. Acad. Sci.*) agree that the observations which indicate that distant nebulæ are receding from us at a rate proportional to their distance can be explained by supposing them fixed in a quasi-Euclidean space which is itself expanding with time. Milne put forward a much simpler explanation based on the kinematics of an unenclosed system with an initial central condensation. Jeans was unable to agree with this explanation. Hubble, at Mount Wilson, photographed a cluster of nebulæ in Gemini whose distance is estimated to be 135 million light years and whose recessional velocity is 24,000 km. per sec.—nearly one-tenth that of light. The possibility of another explanation of the displacement of the spectral lines on which the estimates of these velocities depend cannot be overlooked.

The angular deflection of light rays by the sun's gravitational field is still uncertain. As stated last year (ANNUAL REGISTER, 1931, p. 60) the Potsdam observations of the 1929 eclipse gave 2″·24, and a recalculation at Potsdam of the Lick observations in 1922 gave 2″·2. These calculations were attacked by Trumpler (*Zeit. für Astrophysik.*) who deduced the value 1″·75 in agreement with Einstein's prediction. Freundlich and others at Potsdam maintained that the higher values are correct.

Two minor planets were discovered, both with diameters less than 3 miles. Delporte discovered the first on March 12 ; its minimum distance from the earth is only 10 million miles, its period is $2\frac{3}{4}$ years and its eccentricity 0·45. The other was found by Reinmuth on April 27 ; its period is 1·8 year, its eccentricity exceeds 0·5 and it should approach to within 2 million miles of the earth every 11 years. It is not known whether these and other asteroids are solid bodies or aggregates of solid particles, observations at Johannesburg having shown elongations in the shapes of both Eros and Pallas.

Three British expeditions travelled to Canada to observe the total eclipse on August 31. A party from Greenwich, including Dr. Jackson and Mr. Davidson, established itself at Parent on the C.N.R., north of the St. Lawrence, for work on the coronal spectrum. Dr. Dingle went to Montreal to study the spectrum of the limb, and a Cambridge party under Professor Stratton set up instruments at Magog in S. Quebec to study the polarisation of light from the corona and the ultra-violet spectrum of the chromosphere. Weather conditions were very cloudy and only the Greenwich party was able to make any observations. The Lick and Harvard expeditions and a French expedition were more fortunate.

Radio observations during the eclipse period, in England, Canada, and the United States, indicated that ultra-violet light is the principal ionising agent in the Kennelly-Heaviside layer of the atmosphere (region E, height about 100 km.) as it almost certainly is in the Appleton region (height about 200 km.). There was no evidence of any change in ionisation due to an eclipse of particles from the sun, but the conditions for such observations were very unfavourable.

Notable progress was made in short-wave wireless transmission. The Post Office used five metre waves to connect the land lines terminating at Hutton and Lavernock on either side of the Bristol Channel. Still shorter waves were used for telephonic communication between the Vatican and the Pope's palace at Castel Gandolfo, 20 km. away, while the Marchese Marconi established communication with 57 cm. waves between Rocca di Papa and Cape Figari, Sardinia—a distance of 168 miles. This result was of great interest, for it showed that such waves follow, at least to some extent, the curvative of the earth.

In April the Baird Television Co. used waves 6·1 m. long for a transmission between their premises in Long Acre and Selfridge's store in Oxford Street. In May the Company gave a demonstration of two-way television and ordinary telephony at Paris, and on June 1 the Derby was televised and shown on a translucent screen $10' \times 8'$ at the Metropole Cinema.

The Empire Broadcasting Station at Daventry was completed. It was equipped with two 20 kilowatt transmitters arranged to operate on any one of eight selected wave-lengths between 14 and 50 metres. Directional aerials were provided for transmissions to different zones of the Empire.

Lecturing at the Royal Institution in April, Professor H. Hartridge discussed the various theories which have been proposed to explain auditory phenomena and concluded that only the resonance theory is capable of accounting satisfactorily for all the known facts. On June 3, in the same lecture room, Professor McLennan exhibited, for the first time in this country, a superconductive lead ring carrying a current. This was a remarkable achievement, for the ring was cooled in liquid helium and a current induced in it at the Cryogenic Laboratory, Leiden, that morning, it was then conveyed in the helium cryostat to London by aeroplane and arrived just in time for the lecture.

Possibilities of an era of cheap illumination were opened by a new type of lamp devised by Pirani in Berlin and in the laboratories of the General Electric Co. of America. The lamps are in fact discharge tubes fitted with electrically heated electrodes composed of alkaline earth oxides and filled with suitable gases or vapours. The emission of electrons from the heated cathode permits the passage of large currents through the gas when a potential is established across the electrodes. Lamps containing sodium, and emitting therefore a yellow light, were made on a commercial scale and used experimentally for street lighting in Croydon, Zurich, and in Holland. They gave about 500 C.P. for 100 watts. An efficiency of 30 C.P. per watt is possible, a figure which must be compared with 2 C.P. (or less) per watt obtainable with the ordinary 100 watt lamp.

The Committee on Atomic Weights of the International Union of Chemistry, in its second report, recommended two changes in the International Table, *viz.*, krypton to be 83·7 instead of 82·9 and xenon 131·3 and not 130·2. The values of the atomic weights of selenium and tellurium deduced by Aston from their mass-spectra differ appreciably from those given in the International Table, and Hönigschmid (*Naturwiss.*) redetermined their values by chemical methods. For selenium he obtained 78·962 $\pm$ 0·002, agreeing with Aston's value, while for tellurium his value was 127·587 $\pm$ 0·019, which was lower than Aston's result but agreed with the figure obtained by Bainbridge (*Phys. Rev.*), using Aston's method.

Aston (*Nature*) found traces of two additional isotopes of mercury (197, 203) but an investigation of niobium and tantalum showed one isotope only to be present in each (93 and 181). Murakawa (Tokyi) confirmed the existence of the isotope 204 of lead and found indications of another (210). Hertz (*Naturwiss.*) prepared an almost pure sample of the lightest isotope of neon (20) by differential diffusion and discovered a fourth (23—the others being 22 and 21).

Hevesy and Pahl (*Nature*) found that samarium has marked radioactive properties. It appeared to emit α-particles and to have an activity about one-third that of potassium. Whether the radioactivity is due to a radioactive isotope (as in the case of potassium) or to traces of another element (*e.g.*, No. 61) was not ascertained.

A feature of *The Times* and other illustrated papers was the reproduction of photographs of distant scenery obtained by using plates stained with xenocynanin. This dye makes the plates sensitive to infra-red rays ($\lambda\lambda$ 8,600-10,600 Å) which do not affect the eye. Such rays pass through the air with much less loss from scattering than visible rays of shorter wave-length and photographs taken with a telephoto lens and a suitable screen show objects twenty and more miles away which may be quite invisible to the eye, even when vision is aided by a telescope.

The annual meeting of the British Association was held at York during the period August 31 to September 7. The president, Sir Alfred Ewing, devoted his address to a review of the physical sciences as they appear to an engineer and was thereby led to deplore the all too obvious fact that progress in those sciences has given man powers which he is morally quite unfitted to handle. Professor A. O. Rankine, president of Section A, discussed geophysical prospecting for minerals and oil. Dr. Mills, in his presidential address to Section B, dealt with stereochemistry, especially in relation to the optical activity of living matter.

The Physical Society of London and the Optical Society were amalgamated under the title of the Physical Society. An Institute of Physics was formed in the United States to correlate the work of the various societies concerned with physics. One of its first acts was the publication of a new journal entitled *Chemical Physics* and intended for papers too chemical for physical journals and too mathematical for journals of physical chemistry. The need for such a journal became urgent owing to the wide application of quantum principles and wave mechanics to chemical problems.

Among the more important congresses held during the year were the International Electrical Congress at Paris, the International Astronomical Union at Cambridge, Massachusetts, and the International Conference on Radio-communication at Madrid. The Physical and Optical Societies held a joint discussion on Vision in London, and the Faraday Society discussed the Colloid Aspects of Textile Materials at Manchester.

A new Indian society, the Academy of Sciences of the United Provinces of India, held its inaugural meeting on March 1, with Professor M. N. Saha as president.

Sir F. Gowland Hopkins was re-elected President of the Royal Society at the anniversary meeting on November 30, and Royal medals were awarded to Professor R. Robinson and Professor E. Mellanby.

Dr. P. A. M. Dirac was chosen to succeed Professor Larmor as Lucasian Professor of Mathematics in the University of Cambridge—the chair held by Newton.

E

FINANCE AND COMMERCE IN 1932.

THE world economic crisis became more intense in 1932, and at home as well as abroad prodigious efforts were made to overcome its angrier features. Exceptional success, however, attended the British effort, and as a result the prestige of Great Britain stood higher than that of any other of the leading nations at the close of the year. Great Britain of course was helped by the possession of resources and reserves which other countries did not possess in so large a measure. Some of these reserves she had not touched before, that is to say, having pursued a Free Trade policy down to the last moment, she could fall back upon the device of Protection, in order to assist the recovery of her domestic industries. Further, Great Britain alone amongst the European belligerents in the Great War had not devalued her currency in terms of gold, and her departure from the gold standard in September, 1931, was followed by depreciation of the pound in terms of gold currencies of such an amount as to give British export trade and industries a substantial advantage. Imports from gold countries were checked because they cost 50 per cent. more in Britain ; exports to gold countries became 33 per cent. cheaper than before the departure from the gold standard, and were therefore stimulated. The combination of a depreciated pound and the general tariff became such an enormous factor—representing an advantage estimated at an average of about 70 per cent.—in British trade and industries that domestic business could not fail to improve. The improvement was gradual but progressive ; there was a marked increase in the building of factories, the amount spent on them being, in the latter part of the year, nearly double as much as in 1931. Imports were drastically reduced mainly by the tariff, but exports were surprisingly well maintained with the aid of the cheaper pound, with the result that the visible adverse balance of trade was improved by about one hundred and twenty millions sterling. By the close of the year there was a more confident feeling in business circles than had been known for some years, which was due not only to the action of the Government in balancing the Budget, converting the 2,000,000,000l. 5 per cent. War Loan into a $3\frac{1}{2}$ per cent. stock, imposing a tariff, but also to an improvement in the relations of labour and capital. This was notably the case in the Lancashire cotton industry, where after much opposition the workers agreed to operate more looms per weaver, in order to reduce the costs of production. While the signs of recovery in domestic trade were unmistakable in the latter months of the year, over 200 new enterprises being started, in international trade the outlook remained black, owing to

66

the breakdown in the previous year of the international financial machinery, the virtual stoppage of foreign lending, the suspension of the gold standard in many countries, and the drastic restrictions which in consequence had to be imposed by them on foreign payments, including some of the so-called gold countries, like Germany. Default by foreign debtors, Government, municipal, and private, became the more numerous during the year, and even at the close of the year the scaling down of debtors' obligations was still in progress in one form or another. A notable event of the year was the suspension of gold payments by the Union of South Africa in the last week of December. The South African £ fell from a premium of about 30 per cent. above sterling to par. The blackness of the international trade outlook, especially in America, cannot be relieved until the world restores the gold standard or discovers a better standard of value and a medium of settling international transactions to take its place. Before this can happen, however, the war debts and reparations payments must be ended. At Lausanne in July the European nations agreed to do this, but America refused to participate. If America does not cancel the debts due to her the debtors will default through sheer inability to make the payments. It can certainly be said that so far as the European nations are concerned the debts were dead by the end of 1932. In complying with America's request for payment on December 15, the British Government plainly indicated that they regarded it as part of a final settlement to be reached later, when the new president of the United States of America, Mr. Roosevelt, took office in March, 1933.

Forced to reduce their purchases abroad, because of the breakdown of the international financial machinery, practically every country in the world had a more even trade balance ; that is to say, exports and imports were more evenly balanced than in previous years. But the process of balancing meant further restrictions of the volume of world trade. This coming at a time when the world was better equipped to produce material wants for the satisfaction of mankind than at any other time inevitably caused a substantial increase in unemployment, which is only likely to be cured if individual working hours are shortened, which means more leisure, or the world develops new wants the satisfaction of which will rapidly renew the demand for labour. Indications in 1932 pointed to the possibility of both of these factors operating to an increasing extent in succeeding years. The League of Nations, in its review of world trade in 1931-32, showed a very startling decline in the three years 1929-32. In 1930 world trade in terms of gold was 19 per cent. less than in 1929. In 1931 there was a further decline of 28 per cent., and in the first six months of 1932 there was a further fall of 33 per cent. ; prices fell about 50 per cent. on the average in the three years 1930-32. The United States, because she was the largest holder of gold, was affected more severely by the trade depression than the other internationally trading and financing countries. The reduction in the value of her trade amounted to 67 per cent. compared with 60 per cent. for Germany, 57 per cent. for the United Kingdom, and 54 per cent. for France.

Conversion Operations.—The monetary expression of trade stagnation was the abundance and cheapness of money, due to the difficulty of employing it profitably. This was true of every country in the world in greater or lesser measure. It enabled the British Government to carry through in the second half of the year with marked success the greatest loan conversion scheme in history. The way was prepared by the issue in April of 3 per cent. Treasury bonds redeemable by equal annual amounts at par in ten years. They were offered for tender at a minimum price of 97¾*l*. Tenders for 110,000,000*l*. were accepted, which was a great deal more than was needed to pay off 65,000,000*l*. of 4 per cent. Treasury bonds. These bonds were sold on an average price of about 6*d*. over the minimum price. At the end of June the Government startled the world by announcing that 2,085,000,000*l*. of 5 per cent. War Loans would be repaid on December 1 in cash; at the same time holders were invited to continue the stock at 3½ per cent., receiving a bonus of 1*l*. per cent. if they notified acceptance of the invitation by the end of July. By the end of July 1,850,000,000*l*. had been converted and by the end of September, when the conversion operation ceased, 1,920,000,000*l*. had been converted, leaving about 165,000,000*l*., or 8 per cent. of the total, to be paid off in cash. The result was practically equal to Goschen's great achievement. Encouraged by its success the British Government, in October, for the first time in British history, made an issue of bonds bearing 2 per cent. interest, 150,000,000*l*. of such bonds redeemable in three to five years, being sold at par. In November 300,000,000*l*. of 3 per cent. stock were sold at 97½, to provide the money to pay off the balance of the unconverted war loans and other liabilities.

Banking.—For the third year in succession the turnover of money at the London Bankers' Clearing House was lower than in the preceding year. For 1932 the total was 32,111,959,000*l*., a decrease of 4,123,910,000*l*., or 11·3 per cent. on 1931. The total shows a decrease of 12,784,718,000*l*., compared with the record year of 1929. The decrease of course is the reflection of the world-wide financial and commercial crisis, but the decline in London was quite small last year compared with the enormous falling off in New York, where the decrease was 39·4 per cent., the total being 32,886,872,000*l*., a decrease of 21,391,914,000*l*. The greater part of the shrinkage in London was in the city, which reflected the falling off in financial transactions. Although there was a decrease on the year, in the fourth quarter there was actually an increase, while in the provinces there was an increase on the year of 38,587,000*l*., which was due partly to trade improvement.

The year was the leanest the banks had known for many years; not since the nineties had the discount rate fallen so low, while the yield from investments fell to the lowest point since 1913. The average rate for Treasury bills during the year was 1*l*. 13*s*. 2·9*d*. per cent. per annum, but this was very much above the rate in the last half of the year, when it never exceeded 1 per cent. The fall in the rate was due to the great difficulty that the banks had in employing their funds, which at the same time were increased by the operations of the Exchange Equilisation Fund, which was established by the Finance Act of 1932 for the purpose of giving the Bank of England resources with which to control the exchange and prevent undue fluctuation. There was one pleasant side to low money rates, and that was the great appreciation in investment securities. This greatly improved the balance sheets, but brought no benefit to the profit and loss accounts. Some of the banks reduced their dividends, but most of them maintained them, although they did so knowing that 1933 was likely to be a poorer year even than 1932. At the beginning of the year bank rate stood at 6 per cent. ; on February 18 it was reduced to 5 per cent. and after that was gradually lowered until it reached 2 per cent. on June 30, this being the lowest rate for thirty-five years. During the year the Bank of England bought 18,956,495*l.* of gold, raising its stock to 140,305,216*l.*, then 19,677,185*l.* was sold in December to America to pay the War Debt instalment. The last return of the year of the Bank of England is shown in the subjoined table :—

	Dec. 30, 1932.	Dec. 30, 1931.	Dec. 31, 1930.
	£	£	£
Coin and bullion - - - -	120,593,672	121,348,721	148,271,371
Note circulation - - - -	371,193,057	364,150,042	368,801,566
Public deposits - - - -	8,865,481	7,732,655	6,580,599
Other deposits :—			
Bankers' - - - -	102,409,590	126,397,730	132,449,330
Other accounts - -	33,760,123	40,341,083	36,159,228
Reserve (notes and coin) -	24,400,615	32,198,679	39,469,805
Ratio - - - - -	16$\frac{13}{16}$ per cent.	18$\frac{7}{16}$ per cent.	22$\frac{1}{2}$ per cent.
Government securities - -	102,371,824	95,340,906	81,021,247
Other securities :—			
Discounts and advances -	18,509,400	27,290,602	48,962,458
Securities - - - -	17,738,428	37,612,864	23,690,166

The next table shows the average money rate for the last five years :—

1928	1929	1930	1931	1932
BANK RATE AVERAGE.				
£ s. d.	£ s. d.	£ s. d.	£ s. d.	£ s. d.
4 10 0	5 10 0	3 8 4	3 19 0	3 0 4
DISCOUNT RATE (THREE MONTHS BANK BILLS) AVERAGE.				
4 3 4	5 5 2	2 12 6	3 11 9	1 17 3
BANKS' DEPOSIT RATE AVERAGE.				
2 10 0	3 10 0	1 8 4	2 0 10	1 5 4
TREASURY BILL (TENDER) RATE AVERAGE.				
4 2 9	5 5 1·7	2 10 10·31	3 10 2·08	1 13 2·9
SHORT LOAN RATE AVERAGE.				
3 12 9	4 12 0	2 9 0	3 1 9	1 17 3

In the following table is shown the figures of the London Bankers' Clearing House :—

	1932.	1931.	Decrease.
	£	£	£
Grand total - - -	32,111,959,000	36,235,869,000	4,123,910,000 (or 11·3 per cent.)
Town clearing - - -	27,833,633,000	31,815,808,000	3,982,175,000 (or 12·5 per cent.)
Metropolitan clearing -	1,610,407,000	1,667,852,000	54,445,000 (or 3·4 per cent.)
County cheque clearing -	2,667,919,000	2,752,209,000	84,290,000 (or 3 per cent.)

The totals of the eleven provincial clearings for 1932 are compared with those for 1931 in the following table :—

Town.	Amount.		
	£		£ per cent.
Birmingham - - - - -	112,969,000	+	2,543,000 (2·3)
Bradford - - - - -	40,108,000	+	1,844,000 (4·8)
Bristol - - - - -	60,255,000	+	3,303,000 (5·7)
Hull - - - - -	36,067,000	—	708,000 (1·9)
Leeds - - - - -	42,584,000	—	642,000 (1·4)
Leicester - - - - -	32,497,000	+	549,000 (1·7)
Liverpool - - - - -	300,826,000	+	9,957,000 (3·4)
Manchester - - - - -	487,894,000	+	21,310,000 (4·5)
Newcastle-on-Tyne - - - -	65,856,000	+	1,348,000 (2)
Nottingham - - - - -	22,550,000	+	317,000 (1·4)
Sheffield - - - - -	36,550,000	—	1,245,000 (3·2)

The next shows the deposits, discounts, advances and investments of the ten London Clearing Banks for each month of the year :—

	(000's omitted.)			
	Deposits.	Bills discounted.	Advances.	Investments.
1932	£	£	£	£
January - -	1,713,996	239,294	904,916	283,372
February - -	1,658,551	207,543	902,278	279,607
March - -	1,676,418	216,789	902,074	281,885
April - -	1,680,525	240,076	881,009	287,544
May - - -	1,698,969	246,498	871,447	300,204
June - - -	1,764,365	277,658	852,210	339,728
July - - -	1,803,886	317,432	836,228	348,776
August - -	1,850,620	374,354	816,213	363,534
September -	1,864,918	392,226	802,690	382,980
October - -	1,893,409	390,463	795,149	411,572
November -	1,989,415	391,211	785,054	424,973
December -	1,983,075	407,892	773,373	472,389

At the end of the year the total of deposits was lower than it had ever been. The advances on the year were heavily reduced, but both investments and bills discounted rose very considerably. The reduction in advances was due to trade depression. The increase in bills was wholly in Treasury bills, for commercial bills decreased further in volume. The next table shows the composition of the Floating Debt, from which it will be seen that Treasury bills were increased by 263,776,000l, mainly for the purpose of providing an investment for foreign monies sent to London :—

Floating Debt.	Dec. 31, 1932.	Dec. 31, 1931.
	£	£
Ways and Means Advances :—		
From the Bank of England - -	9,250,000	14,000,000
From Public Depts. - - -	40,475,000	49,000,000
Treasury Bills - - - -	928,250,000	664,480,000
Total - - -	977,975,000	727,480,000

Foreign Exchanges.—Thanks to the operations of the Exchange Equalisation Account, which was established by the Finance Act of 1932 to stabilise the pound with resources of 150,000,000l., the £ was kept fairly steady, although in April the New York Exchange for sterling rose to $3·80, falling towards the end of the year to $3·14½. The operation of the fund prevented considerable speculation, but it resulted in much contraction of the foreign exchange business on the London market. Following Britain's departure from the gold standard, foreign exchange dealers were driven more and more to rely upon the dollar and the franc exchanges to cover their transactions. At the end of the year there were only five countries, the United States, France, Holland, Belgium, and Switzerland which were on a free gold standard. About forty countries had exchange restrictions in force, which meant that there was an official market and an unofficial one, rates in the two varying considerably. South Africa left the gold standard on December 29 and reduced the value of her £ to that of sterling. New Zealand after the turn of the year put her exchange (formerly at a 15 per cent. premium) at a parity with Australia. The Japanese yen dropped from ½ to ⅓. These were the outstanding events in a memorable year in the foreign exchanges, and taught a signal lesson to those who believed that world trade could go on as well off the gold standard as on it. The agreement to suspend the collection of German debts known as the Standstill Agreement was renewed and worked satisfactorily.

The following table of the foreign exchanges is taken from *The Times Annual Financial Review* :—

Place.	Par of Exchange.	Dec. 31, 1932.	Dec. 31, 1931.	Highest, 1932.	Lowest, 1932.
New York	4·86$\frac{2}{3}$	3·32$\frac{3}{4}$	3·39	3·83$\frac{1}{2}$	3·14$\frac{1}{2}$
Montreal	4·86$\frac{2}{3}$	3·77	4·01$\frac{1}{2}$	4·29	3·58
Paris	124·21	85$\frac{1}{4}$	86$\frac{1}{2}$	97$\frac{3}{8}$	80$\frac{3}{8}$
Brussels	35·00	24·05$\frac{1}{2}$	24·40	27$\frac{3}{8}$	22$\frac{11}{16}$
Milan	92·46	64$\frac{7}{8}$	66$\frac{7}{8}$	74$\frac{1}{4}$	61$\frac{3}{4}$
Switzerland	25·22	17·30	17$\frac{3}{8}$	19$\frac{13}{16}$	16$\frac{5}{16}$
Athens	375	625	265	660	250
Helsingfors	193·23	228	235	250	200
Madrid	25·22	40$\frac{13}{16}$	40	50$\frac{7}{8}$	38$\frac{1}{2}$
Lisbon	110	109$\frac{1}{4}$	109$\frac{3}{4}$	110$\frac{1}{2}$	104
Amsterdam	12·11	8·28	8$\frac{15}{32}$	9$\frac{1}{2}$	7$\frac{13}{16}$
Berlin	20·43	13·96$\frac{1}{2}$	14$\frac{5}{16}$	16$\frac{1}{8}$	13$\frac{3}{16}$
Vienna	34·59	28$\frac{1}{2}$ ‡	29$\frac{1}{2}$ ‡	39	26
Budapest	27·82	19	28 ‡	21	17
Prague	164·25	112$\frac{1}{4}$	114$\frac{1}{2}$	129	106
Warsaw	43·38	29$\frac{11}{16}$	30$\frac{1}{2}$	35	27$\frac{3}{4}$
Riga	25·22	17	18	21	15$\frac{1}{2}$
Bucharest	813·60	565	570	660	525
Constantinople	110	690 §	705 §	780	660
Belgrade	276·32	245	190	280	180
Kovno	48·66	32$\frac{1}{2}$	34	40	30
Sofia	673·66	465	460 ‡	550	400
Reval	18·16	12·50	13·00	15$\frac{1}{2}$	11
Oslo	18·16	19·40	18$\frac{1}{4}$	20$\frac{7}{8}$	18$\frac{1}{8}$
Stockholm	18·16	18·31	17$\frac{7}{8}$	20$\frac{7}{8}$	17$\frac{1}{2}$
Copenhagen	18·16	19·29$\frac{1}{2}$	18$\frac{1}{8}$	19$\frac{3}{4}$	18
Alexandria	97$\frac{1}{2}$	97$\frac{1}{2}$	97$\frac{1}{2}$	97$\frac{5}{8}$	97$\frac{3}{8}$
Bombay	18*d.*	1/6$\frac{3}{16}$	1/6$\frac{5}{32}$	1/6$\frac{1}{4}$	1/5$\frac{7}{8}$
Calcutta	18*d.*	1/6$\frac{3}{16}$	1/6$\frac{5}{32}$	1/6$\frac{1}{4}$	1/5$\frac{7}{8}$
Madras	18*d.*	1/6$\frac{3}{16}$	1/6$\frac{5}{32}$	1/6$\frac{1}{4}$	1/5$\frac{7}{8}$
Hong-Kong	—	1/3$\frac{1}{4}$	1/5$\frac{5}{8}$	1/6$\frac{3}{4}$	1/2$\frac{3}{8}$
Kobe	24·58*d.*	1/3	2/0$\frac{1}{2}$	2/2$\frac{1}{2}$	1/2$\frac{1}{2}$
Shanghai	—	1/7$\frac{13}{16}$	1/11$\frac{1}{2}$	2/0$\frac{9}{16}$	1/7$\frac{1}{4}$
Singapore	2/4	2/3$\frac{29}{32}$	2/4$\frac{1}{8}$	2/4$\frac{1}{4}$	2/3$\frac{11}{16}$
Batavia	12·11	8·25	8·52$\frac{1}{2}$	9·50	7·84
Rio de Janeiro	5·90*d.*	5$\frac{3}{8}$*d.* ‡	4$\frac{1}{4}$*d.*	5$\frac{3}{4}$*d.*	3$\frac{7}{8}$*d.*
Buenos Aires	47·62*d.*	42$\frac{1}{2}$*d.* §	40$\frac{5}{8}$*d.*	44$\frac{13}{16}$*d.*	34$\frac{1}{4}$*d.*
Valparaiso †	40	‡	28·40	65	58
Montevideo	51*d.*	30*d.* ‡	31$\frac{1}{2}$*d.*	32*d.*	28*d.*
Lima †	17·38	18·70 ‡	12·07$\frac{1}{2}$	20·80	11·85
Mexico	9·76	10·67$\frac{1}{2}$	8·50	20·70	8·25
Manila	24·66*d.*	3/0$\frac{1}{4}$	2/10$\frac{1}{2}$ ‡	3/2	2/9

Stock Exchange.—It was a remarkable year on the Stock Exchange, with an increase of capital values extending practically throughout the list. It was essentially, however, a year for Gilt Edged securities, the *Bankers' Magazine*, index number of Stock Exchange values, the basis of which is 100 in December, 1921, at the end of December, 1932, stood at 109 after having fallen to the record low level of 98·5 at the end of 1931. At the end of December the value of 365 securities was 6,079,756,000*l.*, an increase on the year of 612,264,000*l.*; 87 fixed interest-bearing securities rose in value by 520,193,000*l.* or 13·5 per cent., while 278 securities of the variable dividend class rose by 92,071,000*l.* or 5·6 per cent. Some British Government securities rose by as much as 50 per cent. during the year, and all fixed interest-bearing securities closed at a higher level than they

† 90 days. ‡ Nominal. § Sellers.

had done since 1913.   German bonds, which had suffered a heavy fall in
the early part of the year, practically doubled in value by the end of the
year ; the German 5½ per cent. Young Loan, after dipping into the thirties,
rising into the eighties.   British railway stocks alone showed a fall on
the year, this was due to a further falling off in revenue, which in the case
of the four main groups amounted to 13,500,000l., making a total of
37,500,000l. loss of traffic in three years.   In spite of big economies, not only
ordinary stocks but some preference stocks failed to earn a dividend, and
only one railway, the Great Western, remained in the trustee list as a result
of the dividends declarations for 1932.   The rise in securities was due
primarily to cheap money, which caused bankers and other large holders of
funds to buy securities in order to find profitable employment for their
money.   Brewery shares declined, over-taxation of beer reducing earnings ;
shipping shares were also very flat, the P. and O. Company for the first
time failing to pay a dividend on its deferred stocks.   Oil shares were rather
dull, partly owing to the action of the Persian Government in annulling
the concession of the Anglo-Persian Oil Company.   The gold mining
companies had a record year ; the Rand production was 11,553,565 fine
ounces and the price of gold shares rose considerably during the year.

New Capital Issues.—Issues of new capital in 1932 were slightly larger
than in the previous year, when they were actively discouraged because of
the financial crisis.   The public issues amounted to 113,038,000l., against
88,666,000l. ; this figure, however, was still far below normal, the average
for the ten years down to 1930 having been 252,000,000l.   The amounts
and the destinations of new capital issues for the past three years are shown
in the following table :—

	1932.	1931.	1930.
	£	£	£
United Kingdom - -	83,817,000	42,588,000	127,356,000
India and Ceylon - -	6,390,000	22,469,000	28,661,000
Other British countries -	22,483,000	14,363,000	41,385,000
Foreign countries - -	348,000	9,246,000	38,757,000
Total - - -	113,038,000	88,666,000	236,159,000

Empire Governments raised 24,642,000l., domestic municipalities and
other public authorities borrowed 32,611,000l., and British railways borrowed 8,524,000l., all in debentures, for their low credit prevented them
raising money in any other form.   Electric light, gas and water companies
took between them about 18,000,000l., or more than double the amount
raised in the preceding year.

Commodity Prices.—Wholesale prices finished the year 5·2 per cent.
below the level of December, 1931, following a fall of 3·6 per cent. in 1931
and of 19·9 per cent. in 1930.   The index number on December 31, 1932,
was 94·3, but the average for the whole year was 95·9, against 98·3 in 1931.
The index number fluctuated during the year between 100 (the same as
in 1913) and 90·3.   The average level of wholesale prices of food during the

Commodities.		Dec. 30, 1932.	Dec. 31, 1931.	Average, 1913.
FOOD.				
Wheat, Eng., Gaz. Av.	112 lb.	5s. 4d.	6s. 1d.	7s. 5d.
„ No. 2, N. Man.	496 lb.	25s. 9d.	33s. 3d.	37s. 3d.
Flour, Ldn. Straights	280 lb.	22s. 6d.	25s.	27s. 6d.
Barley, Eng., Gaz. Av.	112 lb.	6s. 11d.	8s. 3d.	7s. 8d.
Oats, Eng., Gaz. Av.	112 lb.	5s. 9d.	6s. 8d.	6s. 10d.
Maize, La Plata, ex-ship	480 lb.	18s.	17s. 3d.	24s. 3d.
Rice, No. 2, Burma	cwt.	9s.	9s. 9d.	9s. 9d.
Beef, English sides	8 lb.	4s. 6d.	4s. 5d.	4s. 3d.
„ S.A., chilled hqr.	8 lb.	3s. 6d.	3s. 11d.	3s. 5d.
Mutton, N.Z. frozen	8 lb.	3s.	2s. 10d.	3s. 3d.
Bacon, Irish lean	cwt.	66s.	64s.	77s.
„ Amer. Cumb.	cwt.	49s.	45s.	68s. 3d.
Fish *	stone	5s. 9d.	5s. 5d.	3s. 3d.
Eggs, English	120	16s.	14s. 6d.	12s.
Sugar, Eng., ref., cubes	cwt.	22s. 9d.	24s. 3d.	18s. 3d.
„ W. Ind. cryst.	cwt.	17s. 6d.	19s. 6d.	16s.
Tea, N. Ind., Auctn. Avg.	lb.	$7\frac{1}{2}$d.	$10\frac{1}{4}$d.	$9\frac{1}{8}$d.
Cocoa, f.f. Accra, f.o.b.	cwt.	22s. 9d.	23s.	55s.
Cheese, Eng., Cheddar	cwt.	80s.	86s.	73s. 9d.
Butter, Danish, fine	cwt.	116s.	136s.	125s.
Lard, Amer., ref., boxes	cwt.	47s.	47s. 3d.	56s. 3d.
Potatoes, English, good	ton	5l. 10s.	10l.	79s. 3d.
MATERIALS.				
Pig iron, Hemt., M'bro'	ton	59s.	65s.	72s. 8d.
„ Cleve'd, No. 3	ton	58s. 6d.	58s. 6d.	58s. 2d.
Iron, marked bars, Staff.	ton	12l.	12l.	9l. 12s. 6d.
„ Com. bars	ton	9l. 5s.	9l. 15s.	7l. 15s.
Steel, rails, heavy	ton	8l. 5s.	8l. 5s.	6l. 12s.
„ boiler plates	ton	8l. 7s. 6d.	9l.	8l. 16s. 3d.
„ galvzd. sheets	ton	10l. 10s.	9l. 5s.	11l. 7s.
„ tinplates	box	15s. 9d.	14s. 3d.	13s. 6d.
Copper, electrolytic	ton	34l. 5s.	45l. 10s.	71l. 15s.
„ strong sheets	ton	61l.	77l.	85l.
Tin, stand., cash	ton	149l.	141l. 2s. 6d.	200l. 2s. 6d.
Lead, English	ton	12l. 10s.	16l. 15s.	19l. 2s. 6d.
Spelter, foreign	ton	15l.	14l. 6s. 3d.	22l. 10s.
Coal, Lge. steam, Cardiff	ton	19s. 6d.	19s. 6d.	20s. 6d.
„ best gas, Durham	ton	14s. 6d.	14s. 9d.	15s. 3d.
„ best hse., Yorks	ton	23s.	24s.	17s. 6d.
Petlm., Amer., rfd., brl.	gal.	$9\frac{1}{2}$d.	$9\frac{1}{2}$d.	$8\frac{1}{2}$d.
Cotton, Am., mid.	lb.	5·29d.	5·39d.	7·12d.
„ Egypt, f.g.f. Sak.	lb.	7·27d.	7·05d.	9·84d.
„ yarn, 32's twist	lb.	$8\frac{1}{2}$d.	$8\frac{3}{4}$d.	$10\frac{1}{8}$d.
„ „ 60's „ Egp.	lb.	$13\frac{3}{4}$d.	15d.	$17\frac{1}{2}$d.
„ shirtings, $8\frac{1}{4}$ lb.	piece	8s. $9\frac{1}{2}$d.	9s.	8s.
„ prnt., 17 × 17·32 in. 125 yards	piece	20s. $10\frac{1}{2}$d.	22s. 3d.	19s.
Wool, gsy., merino, 60's	lb.	$9\frac{3}{4}$d.	$9\frac{1}{4}$d.	$10\frac{3}{4}$d.
„ gsy., crossbd., 46's	lb.	$5\frac{1}{4}$d.	$5\frac{3}{4}$d.	$11\frac{1}{2}$d.
„ tops, 64's	lb.	$23\frac{1}{4}$d.	24d.	29d.
„ tops, 40's	lb.	$8\frac{1}{4}$d.	10d.	$15\frac{3}{4}$d.
Flax, Livonian, Z.K.	ton	55l.	41l.	38l.
Hemp, Grade K	ton	16l. 7s. 6d.	18l. 15s.	29l.
Jute, first marks, shipmt.	ton	15l. 5s.	19l. 7s. 6d.	30l. 15s.
Hides, Eng., Ox, first	lb.	$4\frac{5}{8}$d.	$5\frac{3}{4}$d.	$7\frac{1}{2}$d.
„ Cape, dry	lb.	$6\frac{3}{8}$d.	$7\frac{1}{8}$d.	$11\frac{1}{2}$d.
Timber, gd. deal, 3 × 9	stand	19l. 10s.	19l. 10s.	15l.
„ W'cot oak, 1 in.	foot	1s. 3d.	1s. 3d.	10d.
Cement, best Portland	ton	2l. 4s. 9d.	2l. 2s.	36s.
Rubber, Plant, sheet	lb.	$2\frac{7}{16}$d.	$3\frac{5}{16}$d.	3s. 1d.
Linseed oil	ton	19l. 10s.	16l. 10s.	24l. 15s.
Soda crystals, bags	ton	5l. 3s. 9d.	5l. 5s.	2l. 2s. 6d.
Index number, Food		97·4	108·1	100
Index number, Materials		92·8	94·6	100
Total index number		94·5	99·5	100

* Average price of plaice, cod, and haddock.

year was 103·1, against 105·1 in 1931, while the average for raw materials was 91·6, against 94·4.   It must be borne in mind that since September, 1931, prices are sterling paper prices instead of gold prices.   The Ministry of Labour index number of the cost of living dropped during the year from 147 to 142.   The table on p. 74 of commodity prices is taken from *The Times Annual Financial Review*.

Industrial Profits.—The profits of industrial companies again underwent a heavy shrinkage.   The calculations made by the *Economist* shows that 1,998 companies earned a total net profit, as disclosed by reports published in 1932, of 143,315,094*l*., against 174,993,061*l*., a decrease of 31,677,967*l*., equal to 18·1 per cent.   The average rate of dividends on preference capital was 4·2 per cent., against 5·2 per cent. in 1931, and on ordinary capital 5·9 per cent., against 7·2 per cent.

Unemployment.—The total number of insured persons in work on December 19, 1932, was 9,457,000, compared with 9,605,000 in December, 1931.   The total figure of unemployed on the same date was 2,723,287, against 2,509,921 on December 19, 1931.

Foreign Commerce.—British overseas trade suffered a further shrinkage in 1932.   Imports amounted to 703,133,000*l*., a decrease of 158,120,000*l*., following a decrease of 181,800,000*l*.   British exports were 365,138,000*l*., a decrease of 25,484,000*l*., following a decrease of 181,600,000*l*. in 1931.   Re-exports dropped by 12,954,000*l*. to 50,914,000*l*., following a decrease of 23,000,000*l*. in 1931.   The excess of imports over exports was thus 287,081,000*l*., against an excess in 1931 of 406,763,000*l*.   The big decrease in imports was the result of two factors, namely, the protective tariff and the depreciation in the £ sterling, which increased the price of imports. In the latter part of 1931 the imports of manufactured goods were greater than the exports, but this position was reversed in 1932.   A larger proportion of the total trade was done with countries within the British Empire.   In the first nine months imports from British countries was 35·26 per cent. of our total imports, against 29·11 per cent. in 1931, while exports of British products to Empire countries rose from 44·21 per cent. to 45·55 per cent.

The table on p. 76 is that compiled by the Board of Trade on the foreign balance of payment for the year 1932, and the preceding two years.

Iron, Coal, and Steel.—Great Britain's production of pig iron was 3,570,000 tons, a decrease of 5·5 per cent., but steel production at 5,260,000 tons was 1 per cent. more.   On an average iron and steel works operated at not more than 40 per cent. of capacity.   Thanks to protection imports of iron and steel dropped from 2,844,800 tons to 1,592,200 tons.   Exports were 1,888,600 against 1,979,000 tons.   Prospects for the industries are better for 1933 than for four years.   World production of pig iron in 1932 amounted to 38,750,000 tons, or 30 per cent. less than in 1931, and the steel output was 28 per cent. less at 49,200,000 tons.   The output of coal in Great Britain was the smallest since 1898, conditions remaining unfavourable throughout the year.   The total output was 209,200,000 tons, against 219,460,000 tons in 1931.   Exports dropped from 42,750,000

BALANCES OF CREDITS AND DEBITS IN THE TRANSACTIONS (OTHER THAN THE LENDING AND REPAYMENT OF CAPITAL) BETWEEN THE UNITED KINGDOM AND ALL OTHER COUNTRIES.

Particulars.	In Million £'s.		
	1930.	1931.	1932.
Excess of imports of merchandise and silver bullion and specie - - - - - - - -	386	408	289
Estimated excess of Government payments made overseas * - - - - - - - -	—	—	25
Total - - - - - - - -	386	408	314
Estimated excess of Government receipts from overseas * - - - - - - - -	19	14	—
Estimated net national shipping income † - -	105	80	70
Estimated net income from overseas investments -	220	170	140
Estimated net receipts from short interest and commissions - - - - - - -	55	30	30
Estimated net receipts from other sources - -	15	10	15
Total - - - - - - - -	414	304	255
Estimated total credit or debit balance on items specified above - - - - - - -	+ 28	− 104	− 59

to 38,900,000 tons. There was much criticism of the quota system, although this brought steadier prices. The profits of the industry for the whole year are reckoned at between half a million and a million.

Shipping and Shipbuilding.—New ships launched in 1932 numbered only 104, of 191,866 gross tons. Compared with 1913, the pre-war record year, this shows a decline of about 1,740,000 tons. The capacity of the yards to-day is about 1,500,000 tons. Last year's tonnage compares with 502,487 tons in 1931. World tonnage of new ships was 720,390 gross tons, against 1,617,115 in 1931. Last year therefore was the worst year the shipbuilding industry here and abroad has ever known. The shipping industry had another lean year, especially in the North Atlantic, where rates were further reduced. The average level of freight rates was 71·28, compared with 100 in 1913, and was the lowest level ever touched. The amount of idle tonnage in this country was over 2,000,000 tons.

Textiles.—The most remarkable development in the textile industry occurred in Rayon. Consumption surpassed all previous years by a big margin, and improvements of a revolutionary character in the production of yarns greatly reduced the cost of production. The year began with the industry very actively employed; February had the highest figure of production, the total being 6,520,000 lbs. The introduction of " cake " washing has saved both time and labour and produces a more efficient fibre. The introduction of the Rayon duties in May gave a further stimulus to business. Prices were lower but more stable. The production for

* Including some items on loan accounts.
† Including disbursements by foreign ships in British ports.

1932 was about 72,500,000 lbs., against about 54,500,000 lbs. in 1931. World output was 504,705,000 lbs., against 470,790,000 lbs.

The downward movement in the cotton industry, which began in 1920, was checked in 1932. Raw material was very cheap and that helped. Middling American fell from 5·53d. per lb. to 4·97d. per lb. by the end of the year, while Fair Egyptian fell from 7·13d. to 6·82d. Cotton re-established its reputation as the cheapest and most durable of light fabrics, but the industry suffers from over-production. This has been the case particularly in the Lancashire industry, for cost of production there has been higher than that of its competitors, in some cases by 25 per cent. After protracted negotiations labour agreed to a reduction of wages for both spinners and weavers, while ultimately the weavers agreed to operate more looms as they do abroad, an advantage which the foreign competitors have enjoyed for some years. Certainly the year closed with the industry in a more hopeful frame of mind than it had known for a long time. The woollen industry enjoyed twelve months work under a tariff system and was well satisfied with its experience. Imports of woollen and worsted tissues dropped from 48,600,000 square yards to 6,600,000 square yards. The price of raw material showed little change, and although exports were lower than in the preceding year the domestic trade was fairly active, especially for hosiery.

Motor and Film Industries.—1932 was a notable year in the motor industry, for it brought out the predominance of the small car, and put Britain in the very front rank as the most efficient producers of these cars. As a result British cars made a bigger entry into the foreign markets than in any previous year. Towards the end of the year the number of cars exported was nearly twice as large as in 1931. Exports amounted to about 7,000,000l., compared with about 6,000,000l. in the preceding year. The British film industry made very notable progress in production. Under the quota act the production of British films has increased from 202 to 242, the increase in long films being from 91 to 156, short ones being reduced from 111 to 86. Foreign films have decreased by about 114 long and 100 short.

Oil and Rubber.—Consumption of oil in the country was well maintained, amounting to 2,087,732,000 gallons, against 2,063,139,000. The production of oil, however, was unprofitable, prices being too low. The rubber industry had another bad year owing to low prices; producers, however, reduced the cost of production to a very low level, and it may be assumed that production to-day does not exceed consumption and that the price just covers the cost of such as is produced.

LAW.

THE year 1932 saw a continuance of the movement towards the reform of legal procedure and the cheapening of litigation and, what was more, the taking of practical steps to secure these ends. Heavy arrears in the King's Bench Division of the High Court were again a feature of the year, and at its close the lists showed little improvement, in spite of the appointment in the spring of an additional judge and frequent resort to the expedient of appointing Commissioners of Assize.

Both junior counsel and solicitors suffered a reduction in remuneration ; the two-thirds rule, hallowed by long usage, was modified by the General Council of the Bar so that, where a silk's fee exceeds 150*l*., the amount by which the junior's exceeds 100*l*. may be matter of arrangement, and the Law Society acceded to the suggestion of the Lord Chancellor that the $33\frac{1}{3}$ per cent. increase over the scale fees paid to solicitors should in the case of litigation costs be reduced to 25 per cent., the increase on non-contentious work to be 20 per cent. No step was taken to compensate junior counsel for the modification of the two-thirds rule by revision of the remuneration for preliminary work, as had been suggested in several quarters would be equitable.

With a view to the simplification and greater expedition of litigation in straightforward matters affecting more particularly the commercial community, the Lord Chancellor, Lord Sankey, and the Rule Committee put into operation as from May what are still known in the profession, and are likely long to be known as the " New Procedure " Rules, framed more or less on the analogy of the Commercial Court, under which witnesses may be reduced in number and facts proved by affidavit. This procedure applies only to a limited class of actions in King's Bench not unsuitable by reason of complexity or otherwise, and those in which the parties are entitled to a jury as of right are not covered by it. Thus, actions to which it is inapplicable are those for libel or slander and any action in which fraud is alleged. Within its limited sphere the experiment would seem to be proving successful.

Six months or so later, when the New Procedure was well established, the Lord Chancellor took a further step, and official announcement was made of the appointment of a thoroughly representative committee of judges, barristers, and solicitors, presided over by the Master of the Rolls. This body was given terms of reference wide enough to justify a general overhaul of procedure and organisation, extending to reorganisation of the divisions of the Supreme Court, to which were added certain specific minor matters such as the length of the Long Vacation. Invitation was given to submit suggestions for the improvement of Circuit arrangements, provided they did not extend to the abolition of the system.

The year which brought about these changes, each of them affecting intimately a section or sections of the profession as well as the public, saw comparatively few changes in the higher judicial offices.   Purely temporary expedients having failed ignominiously to cope with the position as regarded King's Bench arrears, Parliament agreed, in February, to a motion for the appointment of an additional judge, the appointee being Mr. du Parcq, K.C., who had been charged with the duty of reporting on an outbreak at Dartmoor Prison in the early days of 1932.   The retirement of Lord Dunedin and of Mr. Justice Rowlatt were announced in March. Mr. Justice Wright was promoted from King's Bench direct to the House of Lords in place of Lord Dunedin, and the two vacancies in that Division were filled by the elevation to the Bench of Mr. Rayner Goddard, K.C., and the Hon. Geoffrey Lawrence.

Death with great suddenness deprived the County and Metropolitan Police Courts of well-known figures in Judge Turner and Sir William Clarke Hall respectively.   The latter, whose knighthood had been conferred on him in the January honours in recognition of his work for children, was one of the four Metropolitan magistrates expressly selected to preside in the Juvenile Courts, and had made a special study of juvenile delinquency. Mr. Konstam, K.C., was a new recruit to the County Court Bench, and Judge Holman Gregory, K.C., became Common Serjeant on the retirement of Sir Henry Dickens, K.C.   Other consequential promotions were those of Sir Cecil Whiteley, K.C., to be judge of the Mayor's and City of London Court and of Sir Percival Clarke to the Chairmanship of the London Quarter Sessions.

In the autumn of 1932 final reports, with precise recommendations for future legislation, were submitted by the Gregory Committee on Unemployment Insurance and the Rent Restriction Committee, both set up in 1930.   The gist of the recommendations of the former was the reconstitution of the scheme on *bona fide* insurance lines, the period of benefit to range from thirteen to thirty-nine weeks in the year according to the contributions paid, and the appointment of a permanent statutory committee to have it constantly under review.   An important recommendation, only to take effect *pari passu* with similar action in regard to Health Insurance, was the raising of the income limit to 350*l*.   Of the Rent Restriction Report more will be said later.   The powers of Government Departments were reviewed in the constructive report of the Committee on Departmental Powers.   The Committee expressed the view that the delegation of legislative powers was inevitable, the dangerous tendencies being due to absence of system, and amongst several recommendations, they endorsed the suggestion put before them that there should be a Standing Committee of the House of Commons charged with the duty of investigating the relevant sections of Bills and putting clearly before Parliament exactly what was involved in each case.   In the domain of Criminal Law, also, the Persistent Offenders Committee dealt both boldly and practically with a problem of growing urgency, reporting in favour of prolonged detention for the "professional" criminal, and advocating for others of the class detention for a period sufficient to permit of reform, prisoners to be subjected to discipline on the general lines of Borstal training adapted to the more adult offender, with emphasis on the element of personal interest in the individual delinquent. They made the important recommendation that, before a court passed a sentence of " detention "—to be imposed in lieu of and not in addition to imprisonment or penal servitude—the prison authorities should be under statutory obligation to submit to it a report from their medical officer on the mental condition of the offender, information as to his history and circumstances, and observations as to his suitability for such a sentence.

The great development of Irish sweepstakes and greyhound betting in particular was responsible for the appointment in the spring of the year of a Commission on Lotteries and Betting to consider the highly anomalous gaming and betting laws, Sir Sidney Rowlatt accepting the office of Chairman. Another problem of social as well as legal interest entrusted to a Departmental Committee was the question of appeals from courts of summary jurisdiction.

In the not very interesting legislation of 1932 first place must be given to the Children and Young Persons Act, which, in addition to extending in several other directions the legal protection afforded to the child and young person, raised the age of criminal responsibility from seven to eight, and that at which the death sentence may be passed from sixteen to eighteen. Only a small part of the statute, including that raising the age for the passing of the death sentence, but excluding the provision as to the age of criminal responsibility, was in operation at December 31. A more technical matter of international importance was the theme of the very bulky Merchant Shipping (Safety and Load Line Convention) Act, giving effect to international conventions on these subjects and introducing uniformity of practice in regard to the use of certain familiar expressions. The title of the important Town and Country Planning Act, which carried further the process of subordinating landowners' interests to those of the community, is self-explanatory. The Rights of Way Act, which comes into operation on January 1, 1934, only, gave the public in effect a title to a right of way after twenty years' uninterrupted use. The Import Duties Act, by imposing duties on all imported goods save those placed on a free list kept constantly under review by a statutory Advisory Committee, wrought a significant change in fiscal policy, while the Ottawa Agreements Act gave legislative sanction to the arrangements for Imperial preference come to at the Imperial Economic Conference. The Solicitors Act codified merely the law as to solicitors, and the Patents and Designs Act amended the law as to patents in several important particulars. The Transitional Payments (Determination of Need) Act imposed a certain degree of uniformity on the " needs test " practice of Local Authorities, the variation in which was disquieting. Of legislation on the stocks when Parliament adjourned in December, mention must be made of the Rent Restriction Bill, based on the final report of the Rent Restriction Committee. It classifies, according to rateable value, houses affected by the present Acts, providing that control cease immediately in the case of the most highly rented, the second class being subject to decontrol under the 1923 Act on the landlord's obtaining possession or granting a lease, and the third being absolutely incapable for five years of further decontrol. Another significant item was the London Passenger Transport Bill providing for the co-ordination of services in and around the Metropolis.

During the year several decisions of general as well as professional interest have been given by the courts. In *Donoghue* v. *Stevenson*, where the plaintiff had the misfortune to find a decomposed snail in an opaque gingerbeer bottle, part of the contents she had already drunk, the House of Lords broke new ground by holding that the manufacturer of an article of food sold by him *in circumstances which prevent the distributor or the ultimate consumer from discovering by inspection any defect* is under a legal liability to take reasonable care that the article is free from defect likely to cause injury to health. The supreme importance of the qualification in italics above was exemplified in the later case of *Farr* v. *Butters* (Court of Appeal), where judgment was given in favour of the manufacturers of a crane sold in parts and assembled under the superintendence of the purchaser's skilled foreman, who, continuing the assembling of the parts after himself noting a defect, was killed by a collapse of the crane due to that very defect.

Rex v. *Manley* was a test case which " made legal history." It turned on the question whether a criminal offence had been committed by the fabrication of a " hold-up," as a result of which the police were diverted from their due activities and certain individuals exposed to danger of arrest. The court held that an offence coming within the category of a " public mischief " was involved, the Lord Chief Justice remarking in his judgment that *Rex* v. *Higgins* (1801) was still good law. In that old case it was held that " all such acts as tend to the prejudice of the community " are indictable. Of equal public interest was *Shuttleworth* v. *Leeds Greyhound Association, Ltd.*, in which a Divisional Court of King's Bench held that the keeping of a totalisator, while it was not, on the authority of the House of Lords decision in *Attorney-General* v. *Luncheon and Sports Club* (1928), an offence against the well-known sect. 1 (1) of the 1853 Betting Act, nevertheless infringed the second subsection, which prohibits the keeping of a place for the purpose of money being received by or on behalf of the occupier as consideration for a promise to pay thereafter on a racing contingency.

Another case with a flavour of the past, but decided under the New Procedure, was *Lavell & Company* v. *O'Leary*. There it was sought, under an old statute nearly 250 years old—the Sale of Distress Act, 1689—to recover treble damages for " pound breach " from contractors who, on the tenant's instructions and without knowledge of the circumstances, removed from a café goods on which a distress had been levied, but of which, following a common modern practice, " walking possession " only had been taken. It was laid down that, as between the landlord and strangers, the former could not in such circumstances be heard to say that he had complied with

F

the Distress for Rent Act, 1737. This hardly less ancient Act, while modifying that of the seventeenth century, where public pounds were in question, allowed the goods to be left on the premises but required the person distraining to " impound or otherwise secure " the distress.

Oliver and Another v. *Birmingham Motor Omnibus Company* is of special interest, because it destroyed the last vestiges of the doctrine of negligence by identification, the court holding that the contributory negligence of the grandfather of a child injured by an omnibus while in his charge could no longer be imputed to the infant so as to disentitle him to recover damages against the negligent driver. *Sutton* v. *Dorf* was also notable as confirming the trend of more recent judicial opinion towards regarding a statutory tenancy as a personal right. It established that such a tenancy was not " property " of a tenant passing to the trustee in bankruptcy under sect. 167 of the Bankruptcy Act, 1914. Professional interest attaches strongly, also, to the House of Lords judgment in *Re Cockell : Jackson* v. *Attorney-General.* There an executrix claimed to be entitled to retain out of an insolvent estate her own simple contract debt as against a Crown debt for taxes, and their Lordships, reversing the Court of Appeal, held that to the extent to which the Crown's claim was given priority in bankruptcy by sect. 33 of the Act of 1914 it was a debt of higher degree than that of the executrix. Other House of Lords decisions of importance were given in *Greenwood* v. *Martin's Bank* (ratification and estoppel) and two Workmen's Compensation cases—*McCullum* v. *Northumbrian Shipping Co.* (Workman or Seaman ?) and *Thomas* v. *Ocean Coal Co.* (Added Peril). In the sphere of motor insurance, also, a decision of considerable value was *Morgan* v. *Provincial Insurance Co.*, which emphasised the distinction between terms in policies which are conditions and those which are merely descriptive of risk.

Finally, the *Stedeford* v. *Beloe* case calls for a word of comment, greatly on account of his history. Early in the year the House of Lords, confirming Mr. Justice Rowlatt and the Court of Appeal, held that a pension in no way enforceable by the payee was not subject to income tax in the hands of the holder. The reaction of the Government to this decision was to alter the law in its own interest by inserting in the Finance Act a section enacting that pensions accorded voluntarily be assessable to tax.

PUBLIC DOCUMENTS.[1]

I.

IMPERIAL ECONOMIC CONFERENCE AT OTTAWA.

(JULY 21, 1932.)

SUMMARY OF CONCLUSIONS.

The conclusions of the Conference may be summarised as follows :—
(a) RESOLUTIONS AND STATEMENTS REGARDING THE PROMOTION OF TRADE WITHIN THE COMMONWEALTH.

(i) *Empire Content.*

With regard to the determination of the percentage of Empire Content necessary to secure preferential tariff treatment, the Conference draws the attention of the several Governments of the Commonwealth to the importance of this subject, and recommends that each of the Governments of the Commonwealth should investigate, as rapidly as possible, the standard of Empire Content which should be required by them for the import under preferential rates of the different classes of goods, bearing in mind the following principles :—

(a) That though it must rest with each Government to decide what standard it will require, a greater degree of uniformity throughout the Commonwealth is desirable ;

(b) The standard required should not be such as to defeat or frustrate the intention of the preferential rate of duty conceded to any class of goods.

(ii) *Export Bounties and Anti-Dumping Duties.*

With regard to the question of export bounties and anti-dumping duties within the Commonwealth, the Conference adopted the following resolution :—

This Conference, recognising that export bounties and exchange depreciation adversely affect the value of tariff preferences within the Commonwealth, expresses the hope that with a rise in the level of commodity prices and with stabilised exchanges such bounties and the special duties which have been adopted as a means of adjusting the situation so created, may be withdrawn.

[1] Document No. I. is reprinted from Cmd. Paper 4174, and Document No. II. (p. 92) from Commons Papers 4210 and 4211, by kind permission of the Controller of H.M. Stationery Office.

(iii) *Trade Agreements.*

With regard to the conclusion of certain Agreements for the extension of mutual trade by means of reciprocal preferential tariffs, the Conference adopted the following resolution :—

The nations of the British Commonwealth having entered into certain Agreements with one another for the extension of mutual trade by means of reciprocal preferential tariffs, this Conference takes note of these Agreements and records its conviction :

That by the lowering or removal of barriers among themselves provided for in these Agreements, the flow of trade between the various countries of the Empire will be facilitated, and that by the consequent increase of purchasing power of their peoples, the trade of the world will also be stimulated and increased ;

Further, that this Conference regards the conclusion of these Agreements as a step forward, which should in the future lead to further progress in the same direction, and which will utilise protective duties to ensure that the resources and industries of the Empire are developed on sound economic lines.

The Agreements referred to are annexed hereto and the Conference commends them to the Governments of the several parts of the Empire.*

(b) RESOLUTIONS REGARDING CUSTOMS ADMINISTRATION.

The Conference recommends that the aims to be kept in view should be :—

(i) The avoidance of uncertainty as to the amount of duty which would be payable on the arrival of goods in the importing country ;

(ii) The reduction of friction and delay to a minimum ;

(iii) The provision of facilities for the expeditious and effective settlement of disputes relating to all matters affecting the application of the Customs tariff ;

and that any measures which Customs Administrations might take to safeguard themselves against evasion should be consistent with these principles.

(c) STATEMENT REGARDING COMMERCIAL RELATIONS WITH FOREIGN COUNTRIES.

The Conference considered two broad groups of questions affecting the commercial relations of the several members of the Commonwealth with foreign countries.

In the first place, the Conference discussed the general question of the relationship between inter-Commonwealth preferences and the most-favoured-nation clause in commercial treaties with foreign Powers. Each

---

* The texts of the Agreements between the United Kingdom and the Dominions, India, and Southern Rhodesia are given in Appendices I. to VII. in Cmd. 4174.

Government will determine its particular policy in dealing with this matter, but the representatives of the various Governments on the Committee stated that it was their policy that no treaty obligations into which they might enter in the future should be allowed to interfere with any mutual preferences which Governments of the Commonwealth might decide to accord to each other, and that they would free themselves from existing treaties, if any, which might so interfere. They would, in fact, take all the steps necessary to implement and safeguard whatever preferences might be so granted.

In the second place, attention was drawn to recent tendencies in foreign countries to conclude regional agreements between themselves for the mutual accord of preferences which were designed as being exclusive, and not to be extended to countries which were not parties to, or did not adhere to, the agreements. On this point there was a general agreement that foreign countries which had existing treaty obligations to grant most-favoured-nation treatment to the products of particular parts of the Commonwealth could not be allowed to override such obligations by regional agreements of the character in question. Particular reference was made in this connection to the question of the Danubian States in regard to which preferential treatment was in contemplation for the cereal exports of the States concerned—exports which constitute a substantial proportion of the world's exports of the cereals in question. The Conference was, however, informed that in the discussion which took place at Lausanne on the matter, the rights of third countries had, at the instance of the United Kingdom, been expressly reserved.

The Conference recognised that the fact that rights are accorded by most-favoured-nation treatment does not preclude a foreign country from seeking the consent of the various Governments of the British Commonwealth to the waiver of their rights in particular cases, and that these Governments must be guided by consideration of their individual interests in deciding whether or not to meet the wishes of the foreign country concerned, so long, however, as the general principle that rights of this kind cannot be arbitrarily withdrawn is fully and carefully preserved.

The Conference would, however, recommend that where two or more Commonwealth Governments share a common interest in any proposal for the waiver of particular treaty rights, they should consult together with a view to arriving, in so far as possible, at a common policy.

(d) RESOLUTIONS AND STATEMENTS REGARDING MONETARY AND FINANCIAL QUESTIONS.

I.

(a) A rise throughout the world in the general levels of wholesale prices is in the highest degree desirable. The evil of falling prices must be attacked by Government and individual action in all its causes, whether political, economic, financial or monetary.

(*b*) For dealing with the problem in its widest aspects the Governments represented at this Conference record their conviction that international action is urgently necessary, and announce their desire to co-operate with other nations in any practicable measures for raising wholesale prices.

(*c*) The Conference has considered what action can be taken by the nations of the Commonwealth to help towards raising prices.

As regards monetary factors, the Conference recognises that the central position of the United Kingdom, not only among the countries of the Commonwealth but in world trade and finance, makes the United Kingdom a main factor in anything that can be done. The Conference, therefore, welcomes the following statement made on behalf of the United Kingdom by the Chancellor of the Exchequer :—

"His Majesty's Government desire to see wholesale sterling prices rise. The best condition for this would be a rise in gold prices, and the absence of a rise in gold prices inevitably imposes limitations on what can be done for sterling. A rise in prices cannot be effected by monetary action alone, since various other factors which have combined to bring about the present depression must also be modified or removed before a remedy is assured. His Majesty's Government, nevertheless, recognise that an ample supply of short-term money at low rates may have a valuable influence, and they are confident that the efforts which have successfully brought about the present favourable monetary conditions can and will, unless unforeseen difficulties arise, be continued."

(*d*) The Conference recommends the other countries of the Commonwealth represented here to act in conformity with the line of policy as set out in the statement of the Chancellor of the Exchequer, so far as lies within their power.

In the monetary sphere the primary line of action towards a rise in prices should be the creation and maintenance, within the limits of sound finance, of such conditions as will assist in the revival of enterprise and trade. Among these conditions are low rates of interest and an abundance of short-term money. While regard must be had to the different conditions applying to various types of loans, the rate of interest for all purposes should be kept as low as financial conditions permit. At the same time it is necessary that these favourable monetary conditions be achieved, not by the inflationary creation of additional means of payment to finance public expenditure, but by an orderly monetary policy, safeguarded, if the necessity should arise, by such steps as will restrain and circumscribe the scope of violent speculative movements in commodities or securities.

It must be kept in mind, however, that the success of any such policy will be hampered and might be nullified by the failure to modify or remove important non-monetary obstacles. Of the non-monetary factors which are depressing the level of prices many are of international character and require an international remedy. The nations of the Commonwealth should, nevertheless, take all steps that lie in their power to increase public confidence, especially in the field of business enterprise, and to facilitate trade.

(e) The Conference recognises the great importance to traders of stability of exchange rates over as wide an area as possible. The complete solution of this problem must await the restoration of conditions for the satisfactory working of an international standard as referred to below. In the meanwhile, and pending such a solution, this Conference has considered the possibility of achieving valuable results in two directions—first by creating an area of stability among countries regulating their currencies in relation to sterling; and, secondly, by avoiding wide day-to-day fluctuations between sterling and gold.

As regards the latter, the Conference has noted with satisfaction that the United Kingdom has already established machinery aimed at preventing wide fluctuations in the gold value of sterling caused by speculative movements. As to the former, the Conference recognises the value of the countries within the Commonwealth whose currencies are linked to sterling maintaining stability between their exchange rates and looks to a rise in the general level of wholesale prices as the most desirable means for facilitating this result.

II.

The Conference recognises that the ultimate aim of monetary policy should be the restoration of a satisfactory international monetary standard. Such a standard should so function as not merely to maintain stable exchange rates between all countries, but also to ensure the smooth and efficient working of the machinery of international trade and finance.

This postulates international agreement among the great trading nations of the world, and while certain of the States here represented hold very definite views on the question of the most desirable standard, the Conference refrains from making any recommendations on the subject in view of the fact that the question is shortly to be discussed at an international conference. There are, however, several conditions precedent to the re-establishment of any international monetary standard. The most important among them are : a rise in the general level of commodity prices in the various countries to a height more in keeping with the level of costs, including the burden of debt and other fixed and semi-fixed charges ; and an adjustment of the factors political, economic, financial, and monetary, which have caused the breakdown of the gold standard in many countries, and which, if not adjusted, would inevitably lead to another breakdown of whatever international standard may be adopted.

It is also, in the view of the Conference, of the utmost importance to the future working of any international standard that international co-operation should be secured and maintained with a view to avoiding, so far as may be found practicable, wide fluctuations in the purchasing power of the standard of value.

(e) Resolutions and Statements regarding Methods of Economic Co-operation.

(i) General Resolutions.

This Conference, having discussed the question of Economic Consultation and Co-operation within the Commonwealth, and having considered the report prepared for it on the constitution and functions of existing agencies operating in these fields :

Recommends that a committee should be appointed forthwith, consisting of not more than two representatives of each of the participating Governments, to consider the means of facilitating economic consultation and co-operation between the several Governments of the Commonwealth, including a survey of the functions, organisation, and financial bases of the agencies specified in the annexed report, and an examination of what alterations or modifications, if any, in the existing machinery for such co-operation within the Commonwealth are desirable.

The Conference further recommends that it shall be an instruction to the Committee to elect their own Chairman from among their members, and to report to the several Governments represented thereon not later than the 31st May next, with a view to the consideration of their report by the several Governments not later than September, 1933.

The Conference was given to understand by the representatives of the United Kingdom that, in order that the necessary time might be available for the preparation and consideration of the report of the Committee concerning the existing and future machinery for economic co-operation within the Commonwealth, the Government of the United Kingdom would continue to furnish any funds which may be required to finance essential work of the Empire Marketing Board down to the end of September, 1933. The Conference records its deep appreciation of the action of the United Kingdom in this respect.

With regard to the above recommendations reservations were made by Mr. Havenga, for the Union of South Africa, and by Mr. Lemass, for the Irish Free State, respectively, in the following terms :—

(Mr. Havenga) : " While not wishing to object to the acceptance of the report of the Committee on Methods of Economic Co-operation, I desire, in order to remove any ground for misapprehension, to record the following reservations on behalf of the Union of South Africa :

" 1. While not generally adverse to the institution of ad hoc bodies for economic investigation and preparation, the Union Government will not associate itself with any scheme for the erection of any organisation in the nature of a permanent secretariat or preparatory committee to Commonwealth conferences, whether economic or otherwise.

" 2. That portion of the report which introduces the draft resolutions relating to the appointment of a committee to consider the means of facilitating economic consultation and co-operation, must not be read in the sense that the Union Government is committed in principle to give financial support to Commonwealth Economic Organisations."

(*Mr. Lemass*) : " I do not object to the adoption of this report and the accompanying resolutions, but I wish it to be made perfectly clear in the published records of the Conference that the Government of the Irish Free State are not prepared to contemplate the setting up of an Imperial Economic Secretariat or of any similar organ of centralisation."

(ii) *Resolution concerning Industrial Standardisation.*

I. The Conference recommends that, with a view to assisting the co-ordination of the work of national standardisation, the following principles, as far as practicable, be observed :—

(*a*) That the specifications should be in accordance with the needs of industry and fulfil a generally recognised want ;

(*b*) That the community interest of producer and consumer should be maintained throughout ;

(*c*) That the specifications should be arrived at by general consent ;

(*d*) That periodical review and revision should be undertaken to prevent crystallisation and keep the specifications abreast of progress ;

(*e*) That full information regarding the initiation of any specification and progress in its preparation should, without delay, be circulated by the originating body to the corresponding bodies in other parts of the Commonwealth.

II. Having regard to the disadvantages which are apt to occur when a statutory provision embodies a standard specification verbatim, whether in whole or in part, instead of confining itself to a reference to a national standard specification, the Conference recommends that each Government of the Commonwealth, in co-operation with its central standardising body, should bring under review the position with regard to such statutory provisions, in order that it may be possible to keep these standards in line with industrial and scientific progress without the necessity of fresh legislation.

III. With a view to facilitating the general adoption of standard specifications throughout the Commonwealth, the Conference recommends that the Governments concerned take into favourable consideration the provision of free entry to standard specifications and other documents circulated between the central standardising bodies.

IV. In order to provide the various parts of the Commonwealth with an accurate means of exchange of colour information and to secure a basic standard in trade practice, the Conference recommends that each central standardising body should at an early date consider the issue of a standard schedule of colours.

V. As an immediate step towards the promotion of intra-Commonwealth trade through the adoption of commercial standard specifications, the Conference recommends that, in respect of steel, timber, industrial chemical products and replaceable parts of agricultural implements and machinery, immediate steps be taken by the central standardising bodies in those parts of the Commonwealth affected to secure a greater degree of uniformity in standard specifications and trade practices.

VI. With a view to the employment of common standard specifications for aircraft materials and component parts, and particularly the method of testing therein specified, the Conference recommends that the national standardising bodies in those parts of the Commonwealth particularly concerned, should co-operate directly with this object in view.

VII. The Conference, taking note of the observation contained in the last paragraph of the Report of the Conference on Standardisation accepted by the Imperial Conference of 1930, which reads as follows :—

"Apart from day to day consideration of matters of detail, we are impressed with the desirability of readier means of consultation on questions of policy than are afforded by the past, or by occasional conferences such as the present,"

is impressed with the desirability of obviating the difficulties and delays which inevitably occur under existing conditions in conducting consultations between the central standardising bodies in the various parts of the British Commonwealth of Nations, and the misunderstandings which occasionally arise due to the distances between the correspondents and to the subject-matter of the communications.

The Conference recommends that for the purpose of maintaining closer liaison in these matters the central standardising bodies in the different parts of the Commonwealth should be authorised to call together, periodically or otherwise, representatives in their respective countries of the corresponding bodies, or persons otherwise designated for the purpose.

The Conference further suggests that such an arrangement might include a provision whereby the Trade Commissioners maintained in different parts of the Empire by the several Commonwealth Governments should, as occasion requires, be available to act as Liaison Officers for this purpose. The Conference considers that it should be made clear that such consultations are purely supplementary to, and not intended in any way to supplant, the method of direct communication already established between the central standardising bodies.

(iii) *Grading and Standards of Agricultural Products.*

The report of the Sub-Committee on this subject, which is set forth as Appendix 2 to the Report of the Committee on Methods of Economic Co-operation,* was approved by the Conference.

(iv) *Resolutions Concerning Industrial Co-operation.*

This Conference, having examined the Report of the Imperial Economic Committee on Imperial Industrial Co-operation, finds itself in general agreement with the tenor of the Report.

* See p. 45 of Cmd. 4175.

The Report makes it clear that industrial production has developed and will continue to develop in the less industrialised parts of the Commonwealth. These developments involve changes in the economic structure both of the more industrialised and of the less industrialised countries ; and the Conference notes with approval the view of the Committee that : " the object of co-operation is not, and must not be, to arrest change, but wisely to direct and facilitate its course."

It should, in the opinion of the Conference, be the object of any policy of industrial co-operation within the Commonwealth to secure the best division of industrial activities among the several parts of the Commonwealth and the ordered economic development of each part, with a view to ensuring the maximum efficiency and economy of production and distribution.

It is further the view of the Conference that the precise nature and extent of the co-operation to be achieved in any particular industry must largely depend upon effective consultation between those engaged, or proposing to engage, in that industry in any two or more parts of the Commonwealth.

The Conference therefore recommends to the various industries in which conditions are suitable for the purpose, the desirability of making arrangements for such consultation at the earliest possible date ; but it records its belief that such consultation, to be fully effective, should be conducted between responsible persons or bodies adequately representative of the industry in each part of the Commonwealth concerned.

The Conference further recommends that the Governments concerned facilitate and assist such consultations by all available means.

The Conference further recommends that, without prejudice to their liberty to determine their own general economic policies, the Governments of the Commonwealth should give sympathetic consideration to any proposals which may be directed towards giving effect to the principle of industrial co-operation and which may be put before them by responsible parties representing similar industrial interests in the parts of the Commonwealth affected. In this connection the Conference would draw attention to the importance of taking into consideration the interests of other parts of the Commonwealth which might be affected by such proposals.

(v) *Resolution concerning Films and Radio.*

The Conference takes note of the suggestions contained in the Report upon Films and Radio submitted to it by the Committee on Methods of Economic Co-operation, and commends them for the consideration of the Governments represented at the Conference.

II.

NOTE ADDRESSED BY HIS MAJESTY'S GOVERNMENT IN THE UNITED KINGDOM TO THE UNITED STATES GOVERNMENT RELATING TO THE BRITISH WAR DEBT.

(WASHINGTON, DECEMBER 1, 1932.)

1. *Sir R. Lindsay to the United States Secretary of State.*

Washington, December 1, 1932.

Sir,

In the Note of the 10th November, His Majesty's Government put forward a request to the Government of the United States of America to enter upon discussions with a view to the adjustment of the British war debt, and at the same time they suggested a suspension of the payment due on the 15th December, their purpose being to avoid the financial and political unsettlement which must follow a resumption of war debt payments, to avert the intensification of the present world depression by further disturbance of the exchanges, to foster the revival of commercial confidence, of which some hesitating signs have recently appeared, and, finally, to allow of a close examination between the United States and this country of the whole subject in preparation for the International Economic Conference.

2. His Majesty's Government warmly welcome that part of the reply of the United States Government in which they express their willingness to facilitate such discussions, and noting that it does not appear to the United States Government that sufficient reasons have been given for their request for the suspension of the December instalment, they now propose to set out in greater detail the considerations which actuated them in presenting their previous note.

I.

3. The war produced a profound disorder in the course of international trade, and after fourteen years this disorder has culminated in a crisis of unparalleled severity. It has resulted in a general collapse of trade throughout the civilised world, with widespread unemployment and a disastrous fall in all national incomes, including those both of the United States of America and of the United Kingdom.

The causes of the depression may be manifold, but it has been generally recognised that war debts and reparations have been one of the major causes, and that a settlement of these debts, which will relieve the world of anxieties under this head, is an indispensable condition of a revival of general prosperity. As the Basle Committee declared in December last the " adjustment of all reparations and war debts to the troubled circumstances of the world is the only lasting step capable of re-establishing confidence, which is the very condition of economic stability and real peace."

The Committee proceeded : " We appeal to the Governments on whom the responsibility for action rests to permit of no delay in coming to decisions which will bring an amelioration of this grave crisis, which weighs so heavily on all alike." While in some respects it may be difficult for Governments to remedy the troubles of the world, there are certain steps which it is clearly within their powers and their responsibility to take.

4. The system of war debts was called into being by the war requirements of the belligerent nations. The resources in man power and production of the Allied countries had from 1914 been wholly employed in the prosecution of the war ; their normal trading activities were to a large extent suspended, and they had therefore less than their normal resources available for purchases abroad. But the vast requirements for war purposes in any case far exceeded any normal means of payment, and could only be financed by means of loans from the producing countries. The loans raised, whether they were market loans or Government loans, were taken, not in the form of money, but in the form of goods, and enormously augmented the volume of exports of the lending countries. For example, before 1915 the United States' export surplus normally varied from 200 million dollars to 600 million dollars. In 1917 and 1918 it exceeded 3,000 million dollars, and in 1919 it was about 4,000 million dollars. The United States made loans to the Allies (including the United Kingdom) totalling approximately 10,000 million dollars (2,055,000,000l. at par) ; the United Kingdom made loans to its European Allies amounting to 1,600,000,000l., equivalent (at par) to 7,800 million dollars ; the French Government had made similar loans equivalent (at par) to 2,237 million dollars. In the aggregate these loans reached the colossal total of approximately 20,000 million dollars (equivalent at par to over 4,000,000,000l.).

5. If the course of commerce were deflected to the extent required to repay these war-time debts, it would entail a radical alteration in the economy both of the debtor and of the creditor countries. During the first few years after the war this was recognised and no attempt was made to collect them. But it proved impossible to secure a general agreement for their remission, and the debtor Powers were called upon to fund their engagements. From 1923 onwards a series of agreements were concluded providing for their repayment on varying terms, and in 1924 a provisional settlement was reached of German reparations on the basis of the Dawes Plan. The annuities provided for in most of these agreements were low during the earlier years, and their payment was rendered possible by the flow of investment capital from the United States of America to Continental Europe, which was then taking place. But the prosperity of the period from 1923 to 1929 was to a large extent illusory and the seeds of future trouble had already been sown.

6. In the summer of 1929 the storm that was brewing was not yet visible, and it was hoped that conditions were sufficiently stabilised for a final settlement of reparations in the form of the Young Plan, under which Germany undertook to pay annuities of about 500 million dollars (100,000,000l. at par), of which the major part was passed on as war debt payments. Unhappily, almost before the ink had dried on the agreements

embodying the Young Plan, the storm had burst upon the world. Startled and alarmed, the lenders who had for five years so liberally poured their capital into Continental Europe withdrew such funds as were immediately recoverable. The debtors made desperate efforts to meet their liabilities, but confidence became more and more shaken and towards the middle of 1931 something like a panic prevailed. Since then the world has been living under the stress of repeated shocks, which have completely undermined the confidence on which the system of private investment depended. The process of disintegration has been pursued to the point where it has become an attempt to liquidate, not only private fortunes and industries, but whole countries. Currencies are threatened with instability, if not with collapse, and the controls and restrictions intended to remedy the trouble have merely aggravated it. Everywhere taxation has been ruthlessly increased and expenditure drastically curtailed, and yet budgets are in deficit or are balanced with ever-increasing difficulty. In all directions there are signs of the paralysis of trade, and the threat of bankruptcy and of financial collapse. The international monetary mechanism without which the modern world cannot effectively conduct its daily life is being broken into pieces with all the manifold forms of privation and distress which this involves. The countries of the world cannot even begin to consider how to restore this mechanism until the causes which undermine confidence have been removed. One of the most important of these is the system of inter-governmental debts.

7. These inter-governmental debts are radically different from the commercial loans raised by foreign Governments on the markets for productive purposes. Such commercial loans are normally self-liquidating. The market loans thus raised during the last hundred years have converted whole territories from desolate swamps or uninhabited plains to flourishing provinces teeming with human life and producing great additions to the real wealth of the world. Such productive loans directly afford the means whereby the borrower can repay them with interest and at the same time become more prosperous. But reparations and war debts represent expenditure on destruction. Fertile fields were rendered barren and populous cities a shattered ruin. Such expenditure, instead of producing a slow and steady accumulation of wealth, destroys in a few hours the stored up riches of the past. Like the shells on which they were largely spent, these loans were blown to pieces. They have produced nothing to repay them and they have left behind nothing but fresh complications and perplexities.

8. The repayment of these war debts necessitates unnatural transfers which provoke widespread economic evil. In so far as they have been paid in the past, their payment was made possible, directly or indirectly, by further foreign lending on the part of the creditor countries, which temporarily concealed but eventually aggravated the difficulties. In the long run, international debts can only be paid in the form of goods or services. But as the Basle Report of the 18th August, 1931, truly pointed out, " In recent years the world has been endeavouring to pursue two contradictory policies in permitting the development of an international

financial system which involves the annual payment of large sums by debtor to creditor countries, while at the same time putting obstacles in the way of the free movement of goods. So long as these obstacles remain, such movements of capital must necessarily throw the world's financial balance out of equilibrium."

9. The creditors in so far as they have refused to accept payment in goods have compelled their debtors to pay in gold. This has led to a drain on the gold reserves of many countries and this in turn has forced up the price of gold in terms of commodities or, in other words, has forced down the price of commodities in terms of gold currencies. This fall in prices has caused widespread ruin to producers in debtor and creditor countries alike and threatens disastrous social and political repercussions. It has seriously increased the burden of commercial debts ; but it has rendered intolerable the peculiar burden of unproductive war debts.

10. The difficulties in maintaining the payments fixed under existing agreements first became acute in the case of Germany, and despite the moratorium adopted as the result of President Hoover's initiative last year, the apprehensions created by the situation in that country caused large withdrawals of credits which, in turn, involved London as a leading international centre. The consequent movements of capital forced the United Kingdom to abandon the gold standard and, while sterling has remained more stable in terms of goods than the gold currencies, the events of September, 1931, gave a profound shock to confidence in the monetary system throughout the world. Thus the baneful effects of these unnatural transfers in respect of reparations and war debts have gravely accentuated the difficulties of all five continents, including many countries which were neither debtors nor creditors in " the tragic book-keeping " which resulted from the war. Confidence and credit cannot revive until an end has been put to these attempts to force the stream of capital to flow uphill.

11. In this connection, it is pertinent to recall the statement made by the Secretary of the United States Treasury in his Annual Report for 1924-25, that the principle of capacity to pay does not require the foreign debtor to pay to the full extent of its present or future capacity. The debtor Government must, he continued, " be permitted to preserve and improve its economic position, to bring its budget into balance, and to place its finances and currency on a sound basis and to maintain and, if possible, to improve the standard of living of its citizens. No settlement which is oppressive and retards the recovery and development of the foreign debtor is to the best interests of the United States or of Europe." A resumption of war debt payments in the present circumstances appears altogether inconsistent with the principles here laid down.

Experience has, in fact, shown that when dealing with international transfers of the character and of the unprecedented magnitude of the post-war inter-governmental obligations, the principle of " the capacity to pay " of the debtor—even if thus applied—can only be regarded as of secondary importance compared with an even wider principle, viz., that of the capacity of the world to endure the economic and financial consequences which those transfers would involve.

12. It is in the light of these wider economic and financial consequences that successive British Governments have framed their well-known policy on this question which is referred to in a later passage of this Note.

His Majesty's Government are aware that any remission of war debts may be criticised as merely transferring the liability from the taxpayer in the borrowing country to the taxpayer in the lending country, and in this respect the taxpayers in the United Kingdom and in the United States of America are in much the same position. Both are already bearing a large share of the burden of war debts and would continue to bear it, even if all the existing war debt arrangements between the Governments could be maintained. For example, in the case of the United Kingdom the effect of its reparation and war debt arrangements was to provide a sum sufficient to cover the current payments to the United States Government. But this does not mean that the British taxpayer was relieved from his burdens in respect of the advances made to the Allies during the war ; on the contrary, he was left to find over 80,000,000*l*. a year (390 million dollars at par) for interest on the internal loans out of which those advances had been made. For all the reparation and war debts receipts of the United Kingdom are required to cover the current payments due on its own war debt to the United States Government, and the United Kingdom taxpayer has had each year to find from his own resources the amount required for the interest on the advances made by the United Kingdom to the Allies, which, as stated above, amounted to a total of about 1,600,000,000*l*. (7,800 million dollars at par). In the case of the United States of America, the amount due from foreign Governments in respect of war debts is now 270 million dollars a year, and if this is not received, it would increase by that amount the burden on the American taxpayer. It will be seen, therefore, that the policy which His Majesty's Government have consistently advocated is one which, if it involves sacrifices on the part of the American taxpayer, has involved similar sacrifices on the part of their own taxpayers. The interests of the two countries looked at from this standpoint are the same. But it would be taking altogether too narrow a view to regard those interests as being limited to securing payment of these war debts from the borrowing Governments.

13. Payments across the exchange, restricted as they are by the effect of tariffs and trade barriers, are essentially different from payments made by the taxpayer in his own currency, and the burden of these vast inter-governmental debts must be judged by comparison not with the volume of internal revenue, but with the balance of trade. So long as debtor nations are compelled by every means to augment their export surpluses, in order to meet these inter-governmental debt burdens, they cannot play their part in the normal economic operations of commerce, and their diminished purchasing power will reflect itself in diminished receipts for the producers in the creditor country, with consequent fall in prices, depression of industry and unemployment. Even a partial recovery of business activity in the creditor countries as a consequence of the removal of these abnormal conditions would result in additional receipts from taxation on the existing scale which would compensate the exchequers

of the creditor countries many times over for the loss of revenue involved in the revision of the war debt settlements.

14. The immediate loss which both the United Kingdom and the United States of America taxpayers would suffer from a reconsideration of war debts cannot be measured in the same scales as the untold loss of wealth and the human misery caused by the present economic crisis. The value of international trade had already, six months ago, decreased in three years by 50 per cent., or by the equivalent of 5 million dollars for every hour, night and day, that passes, and the situation has since deteriorated even further. It will not profit a creditor country to collect a few million pounds or dollars if it thereby perpetuates a world disorder which, reacting on itself, involves losses of revenue many times greater ; and a settlement, however generous it may seem, which relieves the economic machinery of the world by clearing up these inter-governmental payments would be repaid again and again by the contribution which it would make to world revival.

15. For this loss and suffering is not due to the niggardliness of nature. The triumphs of physical science are ever growing and the vast potentialities of the production of real wealth remain unimpaired. It is in the power of the Governments of the world, and particularly of the United States of America and of the United Kingdom as the two greatest creditor nations, if they unite in co-operation, to make the first and essential step towards averting disaster, financial, economic and political.

II.

16. For the reasons given in the preceding paragraphs, His Majesty's Government base their request for a re-examination of the whole situation on the fact that the payment of war debts has in their view been proved to be inconsistent with the present economic organisation of the world, and that any resumption of these payments is bound to accentuate gravely the present crisis and to compromise fatally all efforts to counteract it. But apart from these general considerations, His Majesty's Government hold the sincere conviction that this request is fully justified on the grounds of the past record of the United Kingdom in the matter of inter-governmental debts, and of their present position.

17. In the first place, they would draw attention to the unprecedented efforts which have been made by the United Kingdom. The total British war expenditure in the United States of America amounted to approximately 12,000 million dollars (2,400,000,000l. at par). Of this total only about one-third was financed by borrowing from the United States Government. Approximately 3,000 million dollars (600,000,000l.) was obtained by the sale of gold and of securities representing the available capital assets which His Majesty's Government had at its disposal, the transfer of which has, of course, reduced permanently the wealth of this country. In addition, His Majesty's Government raised commercial loans on the United States market before the entry of the United States into the war, to the amount of about 1,480 million dollars (304,000,000l.

G

at par). The balance of British war expenditure in the United States of America was financed by the export of British goods, and by the reimbursement on the part of the United States Government of expenditure incurred by His Majesty's Government on behalf of the Allies and of sterling supplied by His Majesty's Government to the United States troops.

Of these market borrowings 1,340 million dollars (275,000,000*l.*) have been repaid. In respect of the debt to the United States Government payments have been made amounting to 1,352 million dollars (278,000,000*l.* at par), of which 202 million dollars (42,000,000*l.* at par) were in respect of the principal of the debt as funded. Furthermore, in addition to the payments under the Funding Agreement, His Majesty's Government have paid 233 million dollars (48,000,000*l.*) in respect of the war debt before funding, and they have repaid in full both the loan for the purchase of silver, amounting to 122 million dollars, and the debt of 16 million dollars for relief supplies to Austria. The total of these debt payments which His Majesty's Government have made to the United States since the war amount to the sum of 3,063 million dollars (629,000,000*l.*).

18. Meanwhile, the United Kingdom had claims on its Allies in respect of the war loans it had made. The advances made by this country amounted, as stated above, to 1,600,000,000*l.* (7,800 million dollars), and had increased subsequently by the addition of unpaid interest to capital. Shortly after the war His Majesty's Government offered to join in any equitable arrangement for the reduction or cancellation of inter-allied debts, provided it was of an all-round character. That proposal was not accepted, and His Majesty's Government were called upon to fund their debt to the United States of America. They then announced that they would limit their demands on their own debtors to the amount that they were themselves required to pay to their creditor. The fact that His Majesty's Government were the first to fund their debt to the United States of America, and that some time elapsed before their debtors completed funding agreements with them, has resulted in their receipts from their debtors being less than half their payments to their creditor. The relative position is that the United States of America made loans amounting to 10,000 million dollars (2,055,000,000*l.*), and the United Kingdom made similar loans amounting to 7,800 million dollars (1,600,000,000*l.*) ; the United States of America have received for the benefit of their taxpayers 2,112 million dollars (434,000,000*l.*), and the United Kingdom have received for the benefit of their taxpayers nothing, have passed on all their receipts to the United States of America, and have paid out of the pockets of their taxpayers to the United States of America 651 million dollars (134,000,000*l.*). In fact, when interest has been taken into account some 200,000,000*l.* (973 million dollars at par) has been found by the British taxpayer. It may be observed that, while the British share of the total indebtedness to the United States of America is only 40 per cent. of the total debt payments made to the United States of America, 80 per cent. has come from Great Britain. The efforts which this has involved to the British nation, coming as they did after the losses resulting from the war, constitute, in the view

of His Majesty's Government, a strong claim to consideration on the part
of the United States Government.

19. Moreover, His Majesty's Government feel justified in calling
attention to the changes of circumstances which have increased the burden
of their obligations.

In the first place, the British debt is expressed in terms of gold, but
the burden on the British people is measured in terms of sterling. The
payment due on the 15th December is, owing to this circumstance, increased
from 19,750,000,000*l.* to approximately 30,000,000*l.* The importance of
this from the national standpoint needs no emphasis.

In fact, however, as already stated, the discharge of all international
debts must in the long run take the form of a transfer of goods or services.
The average wholesale price index in the United States of America, during
the period when the debt was incurred, was 189 and is now under 94 (taking
1913 as a basis in each case). The debt therefore represents to-day in
terms of goods not less than twice the amount which was borrowed.

In this connection, His Majesty's Government would point out that
the effect of the American tariff has been to restrict rather than to facilitate
the import of the manufactured goods which the United Kingdom produces and the difficulties in this respect have not decreased in recent years.
In 1923, when the British war debt was funded, the war debt annuity
amounted to 33,000,000*l.*, or approximately half the value of the British
domestic exports to the United States (60,000,000*l.*).

From 1933 onwards the annuity which we should have to pay in
respect of the war debt would amount at present rates of exchange to
approximately 60,000,000*l.*, whereas the British domestic exports to the
United States of America amounted to only 18,000,000*l.* in 1931 and are
not likely to exceed 16,000,000*l.* for 1932.

The imports into the United Kingdom from the United States show
an equally remarkable fall from 211,000,000*l.* in 1923 to 104,000,000*l.* in
1931 and 59,000,000*l.* in the first nine months of 1932. The total trade
between the two countries from the time of the Funding Agreement has
fallen from about 300,000,000*l.* a year to 100,000,000*l.*

20. If, therefore, war debt payments had to be resumed, it is apparent
that the exchange position of this country would need to be strengthened
by a reduction of the very heavy adverse balance of visible trade between
the United Kingdom and the United States of America, which amounted
to 79,000,000*l.* in 1931. In present circumstances this could only be done
by adopting measures which would further restrict British purchase of
American goods. The United Kingdom has up to the present generally
been the best customer of the United States, and the result of such restrictions would inevitably be to reduce specially the market in the United
Kingdom for American farm products. To the extent therefore that
payments were resumed to the United States Treasury, a definite and
unfavourable reaction must follow to the United States producer.

Moreover, His Majesty's Government would also have to guard against
the effects which would follow if the facilities offered by the British market
were used by the other debtors of America to obtain sterling which they

would then sell across the exchange in order to meet their obligations to the United States Government. After the war, the United Kingdom attempted to maintain its traditional system of free imports, with the result that debtor countries throughout the world sold their goods on the British market and took the proceeds away over the exchange or in gold to meet their obligations elsewhere. Under the stress of the present crisis His Majesty's Government have had to modify their system and to adopt tariffs ; but the United Kingdom still imports from abroad goods to the value of several hundreds of million pounds in excess of what it exports, and it would be necessary to consider what action could be taken to secure that the sterling proceeds of these imports were used more largely for the benefit of the British market.

III.

21. President Hoover, in explaining his proposal for a suspension of inter-governmental payments for the year beginning 1st July, 1931, stated that its object was " to relieve the pressure of the difficulties resulting from the fall in prices and lack of confidence in economic and political stability, and to assist in the re-establishment of confidence, thus forwarding political peace and economic stability in the world."

The action then taken gave a much needed respite, but it was not sufficient to restore confidence. The depression still continues and a resumption of war debt payments to-day would, for the reasons outlined above, involve economic reactions which must intensify the instability of the world. If President Hoover's hopes are to be realised, definite remedial action requires to be taken to deal not merely with the British war debt to America, but with the whole system of inter-governmental obligations with which it is related.

22. The initiative in devising a settlement of reparations was taken by the creditor Governments of Germany at Lausanne, with the cognisance and approval of the United States Government. An arrangement was there signed, under which Germany would be substantially relieved of a burden which had become intolerable, and the participating creditors agreed provisionally among themselves to a waiver of their inter-governmental debts. It was in the nature of things inevitable that the settlement was provisional, and that its completion was dependent upon a satisfactory settlement in respect of the debts for which the creditor Powers themselves were liable to the United States Government.

23. The United States Government have frequently reiterated that they do not admit any connection between reparations and war debts ; but this differentiation in the matter of inter-governmental obligations arising out of the war is not accepted by other countries which have creditor claims on the German Government and whose ability to meet their own debt payments to the United States of America and to the United Kingdom is undoubtedly affected by the extent to which they are themselves paid by Germany. Whichever view is academically correct, there is a *de facto* connection between these two sets of inter-governmental

obligations, and this was by implication admitted by the United States Government when they proposed a moratorium on all inter-governmental obligations last year. Moreover, His Majesty's Government take it for granted that preferential treatment would never be claimed for the war debts due to the United States of America as compared with those due to this country ; and a situation in which this country was required to continue war debt payments while forgoing the war debt payments due to it would be admitted at once to be unthinkable. Thus, if the payment of the sums due in respect of the British war debt to the United States Government were to be resumed, His Majesty's Government would be obliged to reopen the question of payments from their own debtors—France, Italy, Portugal, Yugoslavia, Rumania and Greece, and also the British Dominions. The debtor countries would, in turn, have to demand the payment by Germany of her obligations under the Young Plan, and the United Kingdom would have to do likewise. Without a readjustment of war debt obligations the Lausanne Agreement could not be ratified ; the question of reparations would remain unsettled ; the improvement in confidence which followed the Lausanne Agreement would be undone, and fatal results might well be found to have accrued to the solution of many grave political, as well as financial, problems now under discussion.

24. His Majesty's Government understand that the Government of the United States of America have already appreciated the force of these considerations, in the light of which they have recognised the desirability of a discussion of the major point stressed in a previous communication, namely, the revision of the existing debt obligations. But His Majesty's Government wish to emphasise their conviction that their proposal for a suspension of the December payment, a proposal which would in no way affect any ultimate settlement, is necessary in order to create the conditions favourable to a successful issue of the subsequent conversations. The difficulties of making the transfer in present circumstances are so great and would involve such far-reaching reactions, both financial and political, that the resulting doubts and anxieties in regard to the immediate situation would distract the attention of the Governments and peoples when the chief need was an objective and systematic approach to the problem to be solved.

25. Allusion has been made in the last paragraph to the difficulty of any attempt to meet the payment on the 15th December by transfer across the exchange. It has been the object of His Majesty's Government to take all possible steps to mitigate the fluctuations in the relative value of sterling and gold currencies. To this end, having in the first place repaid in full large temporary credits borrowed in connection with the financial crisis of the preceding year, they have acquired certain reserves in gold and in foreign exchange, but though these reserves are adequate for the purpose for which they were designed they were not intended and would not suffice to cover, as well, the payment of $95\frac{1}{2}$ million dollars due on the 15th December. The exchange difficulty would remain even if the device were adopted of payment in sterling to a blocked account ;

for the existence of a large sum awaiting transfer would affect the market almost as seriously as an actual purchase of exchange.

The only remaining alternative would be payment in gold. Such a method of payment would involve the sacrifice of a considerable part of the gold reserves of the Bank of England, which are widely regarded as no more than sufficient for the responsibilities of London as a financial centre.

26. His Majesty's Government trust that the full statement of their views which they have now made will demonstrate clearly the ground upon which their request was based, namely, their own profound conviction that a resumption of war debt payments as they existed before the Hoover Moratorium would inevitably deepen the depression in world trade and would lead to further falls in commodity prices, with disastrous consequences from which no nation would be exempt.

They believe that a discussion between the United States Government and themselves upon these matters might bear fruitful issue for the revival of world prosperity. They are convinced that the prospects of success would be materially improved by the postponement of the December instalment and they are prepared to consider with the Government of the United States of America any manner in which that postponement might be most conveniently arranged.

I have, etc.,

R. C. LINDSAY.

2. *The United States Secretary of State to Sir R. Lindsay.*

Washington, December 7, 1932.

Excellency,

My Government has considered with the greatest care the Note of the 1st December, 1932, from the British Government, in which it has set forth at length the reasons which it advances for a reconsideration of the whole question of inter-governmental war debts, and for the postponement of the payment due by the British Government to the Government of the United States on the 15th December next.

Whatever part the debt payments may have played in the economic history of the post-war years, it is clear that in the present conditions of world-wide depression, accompanied by a sweeping fall of prices, their weight has greatly increased, and that they have a very definite relationship to the problem of recovery, in which both the British and the American people have so vital an interest.

The President of the United States is prepared, through whatever agency may seem appropriate, in co-operation with the British Government, to survey the entire situation and to consider what means may be taken to bring about the restoration of the stability of currencies and exchange, the revival of trade, and the recovery of prices.

I welcome the suggestion contained in the Note of your Government of a close examination between the United States and Great Britain of the whole subject in preparation for the International Economic Conference, for I believe that there are important avenues of mutual advantage which should be thoroughly explored.

Such an examination does not imply cancellation. In such an examination there would necessarily be consideration of other forms of tangible compensation available for the expansion of markets for the products of American agriculture and labour. And you will understand that the problem of foreign debts has in the American mind a very definite relationship with the problem of disarmament and the continuous burden which competitive armament imposes upon the entire world.

In order that you may understand more fully the attitude of the American people, I feel I should refer briefly to certain implications in your Note as to which the facts are viewed by our people differently from the understanding set forth by you.

Your Note seems to carry the thought that the loans made by the United States Government represent in their entirety expenditures on destruction ; that the payments heretofore made to the United States have been largely responsible for the existing world depression and the concentration of a large amount of gold in the United States, and that complete cancellation of war debts, as indicated in the Balfour Note, is essential to world recovery. We cannot agree with these conclusions.

Many of the loans made before the armistice, and substantially all the loans made after the armistice, were not for destruction. Of the amount expended in the United States by our debtors after we entered the war, both before and after the armistice, most of which was borrowed from the United States Government on war and relief loans, less than a third was spent for munitions and remounts. Very large amounts were spent for food, tobacco, etc., for cotton and exchange, for relief and surplus supplies sold on credit for repayments of commercial loans and for interest. Much of the food, tobacco, cotton, relief and other supplies sold on credit were resold by the Governments for use of their own civilian population. In certain cases these supplies were actually resold and the funds turned into the Treasury of the debtor Governments. The amounts used to purchase exchange were in reality loans by the United States to Allied countries which were no doubt expended by them, in part at least, in countries other than the United States ; they served to maintain the value of Allied currencies. Some of the loans made after the armistice were vital to the recovery and indeed to the very existence of the borrowing nations.

It does not seem accurate, therefore, to treat all of what are in the United States of America " war debts " as representing sums devoted in their entirety to expenditures on destructive and totally unproductive objects in so far as the borrowing Governments are concerned. The United States Government, in reaching settlements with its debtors, has combined loans made during the war period and loans made after the armistice, including commercial credits, funding all in debt agreements. It is our understanding that a different practice has prevailed in Europe. The figures cited in the Note of the British Government covering advances made by the United States of America and advances made by the United

Kingdom, as well as receipts to date on these advances, are not, therefore, strictly comparable.

The Note of the British Government also seems to us to over-emphasise the influence which war debt payments may have had in the past on world economy. With the various observations and figures presented by the British Government in that regard the American Government is not in accord, but it does not desire to enter into detailed discussion in face of larger immediate issues. In general, it is our view that the causes of this depression lie in much more potent forces than these debts transactions. We notice similar conclusions have been indicated in the careful study published by the League of Nations entitled " The cause and phases of the world economic depression."

Furthermore, in its inferences as to difficulties of payment, the British Government treat merely some of the items of payments, leaving out of account service items. It may be pointed out that expenditure of American tourists in foreign lands during the period 1924 to 1930 have totalled approximately 3 milliards 900 million dollars, and that during the period immigrant remittances have aggregated net 1 milliard 495 million dollars.

This is in comparison to total receipts of 1 milliard 673 million dollars on account of debt settlement during the same period. Again, in measuring the transfer question, account must be taken not only of trade directly with the United States of America but of the whole area of international dealings. In the total of receipts and outgo arising from international transactions of both our debtors and ourselves, debt payments have been a relatively minor item.

The argument that payment of these debts to the United States of America has drained gold reserves of other countries to the United States of America does not seem to us borne out by actual experience. The gold holdings of the United States of America at the time these payments upon debts began were about 4 milliard 28 million dollars, and they stand now at about 4 milliard 338 million dollars. It is true that our gold supply has at times exceeded this sum, but this extra gold was demonstrably temporary deposits by other nations not related to debt payments.

The main fault in distribution of gold supplies seems to us to have occurred as between the different countries of Europe, as gold supplies of Europe increased from about 3 milliard 18 million dollars on the 1st January, 1924, to about 6 milliard 963 million dollars at present, the distribution of which as between the countries of Europe cannot be attributed to forces originating in the United States of America.

I feel I must also call attention to the misunderstanding which might arise from the following statement in your Note :—

" The initiative in devising a settlement of reparations was taken by the creditor Governments of Germany at Lausanne, with the cognisance and approval of the United States Government."

The facts in this connection were more accurately set out in a statement issued by the British Treasury on the 14th July last :—

" Misunderstanding has arisen regarding Mr. Chamberlain's reference in his speech to the House of Commons on Monday referring to conversations with representatives of the United States. He did not suggest, and of course had no intention of suggesting, that representatives of the United States had approved, either tacitly or explicitly, what was done at Lausanne. The proceedings there were throughout on the basis that the right course was to seek a European solution of reparations without involving the United States in discussion."

In 1923, when the British Government sent a mission to settle the debt of Great Britain to the United States, the United States Treasury held demand obligations of Great Britain calling for interest at rate of 5 per cent. As a result of negotiations these obligations were re-funded on an interest basis of 3⅜ per cent., which was a lower rate of interest than credit of either country at that time commanded. The policy adopted by the United States in its settlement was stated by the Debt Funding Commission :—

"The Commission in its settlement with Great Britain made on the 19th June, 1923, and in subsequent negotiations or settlements has adhered to the principle that adjustments made with each Government must be measured by the ability of the particular Government to put aside and transfer to the United States the payments called for under the funding agreement. Nor does the principle of the capacity to pay require the foreign debtor to pay to the full limit of its present or future capacity. It must be permitted to preserve and improve its economic position, to bring its budget into balance, and to place its finances and currency on a sound basis, and to maintain and, if possible, to improve the standard of living of its citizens. No settlement which is oppressive and retards recovery and development of the foreign debtor is to the best interest of the United States or of Europe."

The representatives of no country have set their hands to any agreement which they believed at the time did not fulfil this policy.

While it seems desirable to state these facts from the standpoint of historical accuracy and as a necessary explanation of the point of view of the American people towards these obligations, the real question raised by the British note is : How can the problems which arise from the existence of these obligations best be dealt with under conditions in the world to-day ? As to the payment due on the 15th December I appreciate the cogency of the difficulties which you present as to the transfer of these monies in the present state of foreign exchanges. In an endeavour to meet this situation it already has been suggested to you that the President might be willing to recommend to Congress the acceptance of deposits in sterling in England to be guaranteed as to dollars value and transferred at such time as would not interfere with the stability of the exchange. This I understand your Government has declined in the belief that the existence of a large sum of sterling awaiting transfer would affect the exchange markets almost as seriously as the actual purchase of exchange. Accordingly further informal suggestions have been made to your Government of methods of meeting these difficulties which it has not been able to find acceptable.

Recognising these difficulties of effecting the transfer, I am confident that Congress will be willing to consider any reasonable suggestion made by your Government which will facilitate the payment of the sum due on the 15th December.

Accept, etc.,

HENRY L. STIMSON.

III.

NON-AGGRESSION PACT BETWEEN THE U.S.S.R. AND FRANCE.

(NOVEMBER 29, 1932.)

The following is the text of the Non-Aggression Pact signed between the U.S.S.R. and France on November 29, 1932 :—

Article 1.—Each of the High Contracting Parties undertakes under no circumstances to declare war on the other party either alone or with other Powers, nor to participate in attacks on land, sea or air, and to respect the inviolability of the territories under her sovereignty as well as of those territories for which it has undertaken the representation and control of its administration.

Article 2.—If one of the High Contracting Parties is attacked by one or more Powers, the other High Contracting Party undertakes not to accord any assistance or support whether direct or indirect to any of the attacking Powers.

If one of the High Contracting Parties is attacking a third Power then the other High Contracting Party will have the right to denounce the present Agreement without notice.

Article 3.—The undertakings above described in Articles 1 and 2 shall in no way limit or change the rights or duties of each of the High Contracting Parties in Agreements concluded by the parties before the present Agreement comes into operation. Each of the parties declares that she is not tied by any agreements which would make it necessary for her to participate in attacks undertaken by other Powers.

Article 4.—Each of the High Contracting Parties undertakes not to participate in any international agreement during the operation of this agreement which would practically lead to the prohibition of purchase from the other party or the sale to her of goods, or the granting of credits to her and to undertake no measures which would lead to the exclusion of the other party from any participation in her foreign trade.

Article 5.—Each of the High Contracting Parties undertakes to respect in every way the sovereignty or rule of the other party over all the territories determined in paragraph 1 of the present agreement, in no way to interfere in their internal affairs, especially to refrain from any kind of action leading to incitement or encouragement of any kind of agitation, propaganda or attempts at interference which aims to undermine the territorial unity of the other party or to change by force the political or social order of the whole or part of their territories.

Each of the High Contracting Parties undertakes also not to create, not to support, not to supply, not to subsidise, and not to allow on its territories military organisations which aim to fight with arms against the other party nor organisations which claim to be the Governments or representatives of the whole or parts of its territories.

Article 6.—The High Contracting Parties, having already in the General Non-Aggression Pact of August 27, 1928, recognised that the decisions on all quarrels and conflicts which may occur between them whatever their nature and origin must always be settled only by peaceful means, they now confirm this decision and in order to make it more effective include in the present Agreement a Convention about conciliation arrangements.

Article 7.—The present Agreement of which the Russian and French texts have equal power will be ratified and on its ratification will be exchanged in Moscow.

The Agreement will come into force immediately on the exchange of ratifications and will remain in force up to one year after one of the High Contracting Parties will inform the other of its desire to denounce it. The announcement of a desire to denounce can only take place two years after the present agreement has come into operation.

Signed in Paris in two copies on November 29, 1932,

DOVGALEVSKY.
HERRIOT.

OBITUARY

OF

EMINENT PERSONS DECEASED IN 1932.

JANUARY.

1. Charles Prestwich Scott, editor of the *Manchester Guardian*, was born at Bath, October 26, 1846, of an old Somersetshire family of Dissenters. He was educated privately and at Corpus Christi College, Oxford, of which he was later elected an honorary Fellow. In 1872, three years after leaving Oxford, where he had taken a first class in classics, he became editor of the paper with which he was to be connected for the rest of his life. He attracted to his staff a group of writers who raised his paper to the first rank of English journalism. After three unsuccessful attempts on the parliamentary seat of North-East Manchester, C. P. Scott was returned, in 1895, for the Leigh Division of Lancashire, which he represented until 1906. He denounced the South African War, as he opposed Britain's entry into the Great War. In 1905 he became governing director of a privately formed company which acquired the *Manchester Guardian*, and from then onwards controlled the paper virtually as proprietor as well as editor. He championed the cause of Home Rule and woman's suffrage, and looked with favour on the growth of political Labour. He resigned his editorship to his son in 1929, but remained governing director of his paper until shortly before his death. In 1929 he was made a Freeman of the City of Manchester ; he was a governor of the University of Manchester and of the Manchester Grammar School. His wife, daughter of Professor John Cook, and a leader in the movement for higher education for women, died in 1905. Two sons and a daughter survived him.

6. George Forrest, botanist and explorer, received his training at the Royal Botanic Gardens, Edinburgh. He spent twenty-eight years in plant collecting, making valuable additions to horticultural knowledge, his discoveries of new varieties of rhododendron being especially notable. Burma, Indo-China, and Tibet were his chosen fields, and he was the first to explore thoroughly the great divide between the Mekong and Salween rivers, a district rich in botanical specimens. The field notes made on his eight collecting expeditions numbered over 30,000. He died of heart failure at Tengyueh, in the Chinese province of Yunnan, while operating for the Edinburgh Botanical Gardens, and seeking the geographical matrix of the rhododendron genus.

7. André Maginot, French politician, was born on February 17, 1877, in Paris, of Lorraine parentage. Beginning his career as a civil servant in Algeria, he was elected, in 1910, a Deputy for Bar-le-Duc, which he represented almost continuously until his death. In 1913 he was appointed Under-Secretary for War, and after the fall of the Briand Cabinet formed a new political group, the *Entente Démocratique et Républicaine ;* but this attempt to form a Centre Party of the French Chamber was not successful. At the outbreak of war in 1914 he

was called to the colours as a private, was promoted to sergeant, received severe
wounds before Verdun in 1916, and left the service with a permanent limp, the
Cross of the Legion of Honour and the Médaille Militaire. He held successively
the posts of Minister for the Colonies under Ribot in 1917, and Minister of
Pensions under Millerand in 1917, and under Leygues, Briand, and Poincaré, and
the portfolio of War in the short-lived Ministry of François-Marsal in 1924. He
returned to the Ministry for the Colonies in the Poincaré Government of November,
1928, retaining it in Briand's twelfth Cabinet of 1929. In that year he made a
tour of the French possessions embodying his impressions in a report recommending a larger measure of self-government for the colonies of the Republic. He was
again Minister of War in the Tardieu Cabinet of the winter of 1929-30, and in
the Laval Ministry of January, 1931.

7. **Sir Muhammad Shafi, K.C.S.I., C.I.E.,** lawyer, and leader of the Indian
Moslems, was born March 10, 1869, in Lahore, and educated at the Government
and Christian Colleges in that province. Called to the Bar by the Middle Temple
in 1892, he returned to India to practise at the Punjab High Court. He was a
member of the All-India Mohammedan deputation to the then Viceroy, Lord
Minto, in 1907, and founder and general secretary of the All-India Moslem
League. He wrote on the Law of Compensation for Improvements in British
India, the Provincial Small Cause Courts Act, and a text-book on the Punjab
Tenancy Act; selections from his speeches and writings were published under
the title " Some Important Indian Problems." He was active in the founding
of the University of Delhi, of which he was Pro-Chancellor, and an honorary
LL.D. He became Minister of Education in the Viceroy's Executive Council in
1919, Law Member in 1923, and was Leader of the Council of State. He was
created C.I.E. in 1916, and K.C.S.I. in 1922. He represented India at the
Imperial Conference of 1930, and was a delegate at the first and second Indian
Round-Table Conferences of 1930 and 1931, and was a member of the Federal
Structure and Minorities Committees. His widow and daughter, the Begum
Shah Nawaz, survived him.

8. **William Graham,** politician and economist, was born at Peebles, July 29,
1887. He spent most of his early life in Edinburgh, where he attended George
Heriot's School, and later the University, where he read economics and law,
eventually graduating M.A. with honours in economics and LL.B. with honours
in statistics, mathematical economics, forensic medicine, and administrative law.
He studied for these degrees in his spare time, after spending two years as a
junior clerk in the War Office, and while working as a free-lance journalist, which
profession he followed for twelve years. He was one of the first lecturers in
Scotland for the Workers' Educational Association, and later lectured at Ruskin
College, Oxford. At 26 he became a member of the Edinburgh Town Council.
He was returned to Parliament in 1918 as a Labour member by Central Edinburgh,
for which constituency he sat continuously for thirteen years. He was a member
of several Royal Commissions, and on the fall of the Labour Government in
1924, he was made a Privy Councillor. In the second Labour Government, he
became President of the Board of Trade, winning the respect of all parties in
the House for his efficiency as a Minister and his skill as a debater. On the
resignation of the Labour Government in 1931, he went into Opposition with
other Labour Ministers, and was elected a Deputy-Leader of the party. Losing
his seat in the General Election of 1931, he went into the City. His death, after
a short illness, was due to pneumonia. His wife survived him.

13. **The Hon. Vicary Gibbs,** banker, antiquary, and gardener, was born at
Hampstead, May 12, 1853, the second son of the first Lord Aldenham. Educated
at Eton and Christ Church, Oxford, he was called to the Bar by Lincoln's Inn in
1880, and became a partner in the family business of Anthony Gibbs & Sons,
merchants, founded in 1808. He was Conservative member for the St. Albans

Division of Herts from 1892 to 1904. With his uncle, George Edward Cokayne, Clarenceux King of Arms, he brought out the second edition of "The Complete Peerage." His active connexion with this work continued from 1910 to 1929. He was a keen horticulturist, and his gardens at Aldenham, near Elstree, contained a remarkable collection of flowering trees and shrubs. He was also an authority on the growing of fruits and vegetables, which he exhibited with success.

13. **Sir Sidney James Mark Low,** distinguished journalist and writer, was born January 22, 1857, of Jewish stock. Educated at King's College School, London, Pembroke and Balliol Colleges, Oxford, he took a first class in modern history in 1879, and was called to the Bar by the Inner Temple. Entering the field of journalism, he rose rapidly in his profession, and was made editor of the *St. James's Gazette* in 1888, holding that position till 1897. Later he became a leader-writer on the old morning *Standard*, and subsequently literary editor. He was special correspondent during the royal visit to India, 1905-6, the coronation of King Haakon of Norway, and The Hague Conference of 1907, also in America, Germany, and Egypt. During the Great War he worked in France, 1915, and with the Italian Army, 1916, and was editor of the Wireless Service at the Ministry of Information in 1918, in which year he was knighted. His writings were marked by a keen historical sense and a lively style, and included "The Governance of England," "The Political History of the Reign of Queen Victoria," "The British Constitution," and the "Dictionary of English History." He lectured for some years on Imperial and colonial history at King's College, London, and was a member of the Imperial Studies Committee. He was an Alderman of the London County Council from 1901 to 1905. Sir Sidney Low was twice married.

17. **Dr. Charles Gore,** one of the best-known theologians in the Anglican Church of his day, was born January 22, 1853, a grandson of the fourth Earl of Bessborough. Winning a scholarship to Balliol from Harrow in 1870, he took a first class in Classical Moderations in 1872, and graduated with a first in *Literæ Humaniores*, 1875, being elected a Fellow of Trinity College, with which he was closely connected for twenty years. He took Orders in 1876, and for four years (1880-84) he was vice-principal of Cuddesdon (theological) College, and from 1884 to 1893 librarian of Pusey House, Oxford. His contribution in 1890 of an essay entitled "Inspiration" to the famous symposium "*Lux Mundi*" created a stir in ecclesiastical circles owing to its support of the school of higher criticism. He was Vicar of Radley, 1893-94, and appointed Hon. Chaplain to the Queen in 1898, and Chaplain-in-Ordinary to the King three years later. He was Canon of Westminster from 1894 to 1902, when he was consecrated Bishop of Worcester. He was active in the creation and endowment of the diocese of Birmingham, and became its first bishop in 1905. He was translated to the bishopric of Oxford in 1911, resigning his See in 1919 owing to differences on public questions with his laity. The most notable of his many theological works and treatises was the trilogy "Belief in God," "Belief in Christ," and "The Holy Spirit and the Church."

20. **Dame Bertha Surtees Newall,** aged 54, educationist and authority on Scandinavian languages, better known until her marriage in 1931 as Bertha Phillpotts, was educated at Girton College, Cambridge. She was placed in the first class of the Mediæval and Modern Languages Tripos in 1901, and was awarded a Pfeiffer Research Studentship at Girton, and later made librarian of the college. From 1910 to 1913 she devoted herself to archæology, publishing the results of her researches under the title "Kindred and Clan," which procured her the Lady Carlisle Fellowship at Somerville College, Oxford. From 1916 to 1919 she was private secretary to the British Minister at Stockholm, and made six visits to Iceland, becoming a pre-eminent authority on the language and customs of that island. From 1919 to 1921 she was Principal of Westfield

College, University of London, and from 1922 to 1925 was Mistress of Girton College. In 1923 she was appointed to the Statutory Commission for Cambridge University, being the only woman member, and in 1926 to a similar Commission on London University ; the same year she was made director of Scandinavian studies at Cambridge. She wrote " The Elder Edda and Ancient Scandinavian Drama," and was Litt.D. Dublin, and Fellow of the Royal Society of Antiquaries, Copenhagen. She was made O.B.E. in 1918, and D.B.E. in 1929. Her husband, Professor H. F. Newall, F.R.S., survived her.

21. **Giles Lytton Strachey,** man of letters, and famous in his generation as a biographer, was born March 1, 1880, and educated at Trinity College, Cambridge. In 1912 he wrote " Landmarks in French Literature," but it was not until 1918 that he made his mark in letters ; his " Eminent Victorians " of that year provoked widespread interest and amusement on account of its witty and satirical biographical sketches of Florence Nightingale, Dr. Arnold of Rugby, General Gordon, and Cardinal Manning. His " Queen Victoria," 1921, in the same vein, produced equal interest and discussion. His romantic biography, " Elizabeth and Essex," written in 1928, was a popular favourite. He also wrote critical studies of Voltaire, Gibbon, and Pope. He was considered by many the founder of the new biography. Lytton Strachey, as he was generally known, held the honorary degree of LL.D., Edinburgh University. He was unmarried.

22. **Leopold James Maxse,** trenchant journalist, was born in 1864 and educated at Harrow and King's College, Cambridge. In 1893, seven years after he came down from the University, he bought the *National Review,* of which he was editor and the largest shareholder until his death. After a visit to Germany in 1899, he began to denounce the nationalistic ambitions of that country ; in 1915 he published a pamphlet setting forth his own repeated warnings of the imminence of a world war side by side with the sceptical repudiations of his opponents. In 1913 his paper excited attention by an issue devoted exclusively to an examination of the celebrated " Marconi Case." He was known as a vigorous controversialist and a staunch Conservative Imperialist, but he was also keenly interested in tennis, music, and ornithology. In 1890 Leo Maxse married Miss Katharine Lushington, who died in 1922.

24. **Sir Alfred Fernandez Yarrow, Bart.,** industrialist and inventor, was born January 13, 1842, of Scottish and Jewish extraction. On leaving University College School, London, where he had been educated, he erected, at the age of 18, the first private overhead telegraph in England, and a year later built and drove one of the first steam road-cars. In 1866 he founded the engineering firm of Yarrow & Hedley (now Yarrow & Co. Ltd.), with works in the Isle of Dogs, where they remained for forty years, until in 1908 a new shipbuilding yard was established at Scotstoun on the Clyde. Yarrow was prominent in the development of high-speed craft, building destroyers and torpedo-boats for the Royal Navy, and producing many notable inventions and improvements in the construction of ships. He made liberal endowments to the British Association, Girton College, the National Physical Laboratories, and the Royal Society, of which last he was elected a Fellow in 1922. At the age of 88 he made a tour of Europe by monoplane. He was twice married : first, in 1875, to Miss Minnie Florence Franklin ; secondly, in 1922, to Miss Eleanor Barnes. He was made a baronet in 1916. His second wife, two sons and three daughters survived him.

FEBRUARY.

6. **Augusto Leguia,** four times President of Peru, was born February 19, 1863. Educated at a commercial school in Valparaiso, he engaged in business until, in 1903, at the age of 40, he entered politics. He was elected President of

the Republic in 1908, and in the revolution of 1909 was rescued from the insurgents in the nick of time, after he had decided to die rather than resign his office. He initiated irrigation and sanitation schemes and educational reforms, besides founding a national bank. He was defeated in the presidential election of 1912, and after his arrest had been ordered retaliated by an attack on the residence of his successor. First imprisoned and then exiled, he went to London, where he became well known in the City. In 1919 he organised a *coup d'état*, and returning to Peru installed himself as President with the aid of the army, promulgating a new Constitution the next year, which legalised his position. In 1925 he was re-elected for a further term, and in 1929 had himself " re-inaugurated," rather than face an election. On Good Friday, 1930, he narrowly escaped assassination, but, on August 24, driven from office by revolutionaries, he spent the last eighteen months of his life in confinement, the prisoner of the military Junta which super-seded his regime. He was made an honorary G.B.E. in 1922.

9. **Junnosuka Inouye,** Japanese banker and politician, was born in 1869, and graduated in law at the Tokio Imperial University in 1895. He entered the Bank of Japan the same year, and was its London agent from 1908 to 1911. Returning to Japan, he became vice-president, and two years later President of the Yokohama Specie Bank, retiring in 1919. He exercised considerable influence on Japanese finance during the war, and established his own reputation as a banker. In 1923 he became Minister of Finance, and piloted his country through the financial and economic crises following upon the earthquake of that year. He was Governor of the Bank of Japan in 1924, and again in 1927-28. He was again Finance Minister in 1929, and in the face of strong opposition secured the return of Japan to the gold standard. But the opponents of his monetary and economic policies proved triumphant and forced the resignation in December, 1931, of the administration of Mr. Wakatsuki, of which he was a member. He was generally held to have done more than any other to relate Japanese post-war financial policies to international movements. While in charge of the Minseito party's election campaign he was shot by an assassin outside a political meeting, and died within ten minutes.

10. **Edgar Wallace,** journalist, novelist, and dramatist, was born in East London of unknown parentage in 1875. At 9 days old he was adopted by a Billingsgate fish porter, and attended a Board School in Peckham. He first earned his living by selling newspapers in the street, and later as a factory hand, on a trawler, on a milk round, and as a builder's boy. He enlisted in the army and went to South Africa as a private in 1896, and wrote in his spare time. At the outbreak of the Boer War he became war correspondent for Reuter's, then for the *Daily News* and the *Daily Mail*. At the conclusion of peace he joined the *Rand Daily Mail* as Editor, and later returning to London became a reporter on the *Daily Mail*. In 1906 he made his first attempt at writing detective fiction, his " Four Just Men " meeting with instant success. Thereafter a continuous stream of novels flowed from his pen, some 150 in all. His vivid stories of crime and adventure became known and widely read all over the English-speaking world. He also wrote fourteen plays, which enjoyed great popularity in England and America; many of them, like several of his novels, were translated into foreign languages. He was keenly interested in the production of plays and the making of films, and was Chairman of the British Lion Film Corporation. He wrote dramatic criticism and racing articles, and was himself the owner of race horses. He fought a parliamentary election in Blackpool as a Liberal in 1931, but was defeated. His second wife, and two sons and two daughters survived him.

12. **John Cooke,** aged 66, painter, was trained in Paris. He first exhibited at the Royal Academy in 1887, and thereafter his pictures were hung regularly for nearly forty years. He was well known as a portrait painter, but his most

characteristic work was figure compositions of mythological or historical subjects, his " Bathing Nymphs," " An Idyll," " Viking Wives," " The Three Graces," and " Aristæus and Proteus " being particularly noteworthy.   He was an expert on frescoes and the use of tempera ; and a ceiling painting from his brush was commissioned for the new Lloyds building as well as stained-glass windows from his designs.   He did much to relieve distress among artists, being deputy chairman of the Artists' Annuity Fund.   He was a member of the Art Workers' Guild, and a good speaker and debater.   He was twice married, having a son and daughter by his first wife.

14. **Sir Arthur McDougall Duckham,** industrialist and inventor, was born July 8, 1879, and educated at a private school at Blackheath, later attending evening classes at King's College, London.   He obtained his technical training in engineering workshops under Sir George Livesay, specialising in furnace work, coal carbonisation and engineering connected with chemical developments.   He became assistant engineer to the Bournemouth Gas and Water Company, resigning his post to develop a patented method of his own for the continuous carbonisation of coal.   After six years of struggle he won recognition for several of his inventions and formed an industrial group known as the Woodall-Duckham companies. During the war he was Deputy Director-General of Munitions Supply, Chairman of the Advisory Committee of the Ministry of Munitions, and later Director-General of Aircraft Production and a member of the Aircraft Council.   In 1928 he was appointed to a Commission which went to Australia to advise on trade opportunities in that country.   In 1929 he represented other industries on the Coal Commission and presented a report favouring the State ownership of mineral rights, but opposing the nationalisation of mines.   He was a founder of the Institution of Chemical Engineers, president of the Society of British Gas Industries, and at the time of his death President-elect of the Federation of British Industries.   He was made K.C.B. in 1917, G.B.E. in 1929.   His wife, a son and two daughters survived him.

15. **Professor Robert Hatch Kennett, D.D.,** noted Hebraist and Canon of Ely, was born at Ramsgate, the eldest son of the town's first mayor, on September 9, 1864.   Entering Merchant Taylors' School in 1878, he won a scholarship for Hebrew at Queens' College, Cambridge, and was a member of that college from 1882 until his death.   He was the sole recipient of first-class honours in the Semitic Languages Tripos of 1886, and was ordained in the following year, becoming chaplain of his college, and a Fellow in 1888.   He held lectureships in Hebrew and Syriac at Queens' and Caius Colleges, and was University Lecturer in Aramaic from 1893 to 1903.   In 1903 he became Regius Professor of Hebrew to which Chair was then attached a Canonry at Ely Cathedral.   He was examining chaplain to the Bishops of Ely and Manchester, and proctor in Convocation. But he was more celebrated as a scholar than as an ecclesiastic, and perhaps more successful still as a teacher.   He made important contributions to the *Journal of Theological Studies*, the " Encyclopædia of Religion and Ethics," the " Encyclopædia Britannica," the *Interpreter* and the *Hibbert Journal.*   His separately published works included " The Composition of the Book of Isaiah in the Light of History and Archæology " (Schweich Lectures), " Deuteronomy and the Decalogue," " Old Testament Essays," " In Our Tongues," and " The Servant of the Lord."   He did much for the advancement of Hebrew and Old Testament Studies, and was one of the best-known figures at Cambridge for over forty years.   His wife, two sons and a daughter survived him.

17. **Sir William Somerville,** agricultural expert and Professor of Rural Economy at several universities, was born in 1860 and educated at the Royal High School and University of Edinburgh, and at Munich.   In 1889 he began his teaching career as Lecturer in Forestry at Edinburgh University, and in 1891 became Professor in Agriculture and Forestry at Durham University.   In 1899 he was

H

elected Professor of Agriculture at Cambridge, and Fellow of King's College, retaining his Chair until 1902, when he left Cambridge to become assistant secretary to the Board of Agriculture. Four years later he was elected to the Sibthorpian Chair of Rural Economy at Oxford, and, resigning in 1925, was made Emeritus Professor and elected an honorary Fellow of St. John's College. His principal work was the improvement of pasturage, and he did no less to convert the farmer to the use of artificial fertilisers on grassland than to establish the faculty of agriculture in the older universities. In both endeavours he was singularly successful, overcoming the farmer's suspicion of the academic theorist and the don's scepticism of the introduction of agriculture into university curricula. He was the author of treatises on various botanical, agricultural, and horticultural subjects, and was also an authority on forestry. He was made K.B.E. in 1926. His wife and a daughter survived him.

21. **Sir Maurice de Bunsen,** distinguished diplomat, was born in January, 1852, and educated at Rugby and Christ Church, Oxford. After entering the Diplomatic Service in 1877, and holding junior posts in Tokio and Siam, he became Secretary of Embassy at Constantinople, where he remained five years. After three years in Paris, he was appointed Minister to Portugal in 1905, and became Ambassador in Madrid in 1906, retaining that post until 1913, when he was transferred to Vienna. His second despatch from there contained the news of the assassination of the Archduke Francis Ferdinand and his wife at Serajevo on June 28. He kept his head in the crisis that followed, and was careful to inform Sir Edward Grey at the Foreign Office of every development in the hardening attitude of the Austro-Hungarian Government. On Britain's declaration of war against Austria, de Bunsen left for London, and his diplomatic career was virtually ended. His short term at Vienna was regarded as remarkably successful, and he was as well liked there as he had been at Madrid. He was Chairman of the Anglo-Austrian Society, and organised the Retrospective Exhibition of English Art in Vienna in 1927, and the Austrian Economic Exhibition in London. His last diplomatic mission was as Special Ambassador to the South American Republics in 1918, which achieved notable success. He was made G.C.V.O. and K.C.M.G. and a Privy Councillor in 1906, G.C.M.G. 1909, and baronet in 1919. His wife and four daughters survived him.

24. **Sir Frederick William Andrewes, F.R.S.,** pioneer of bacteriology in this country, was born March 31, 1859, and educated at Oakley House School, Christ Church College, Oxford, and St. Bartholomew's Hospital. After a distinguished academic career he was elected to a medical Fellowship at Pembroke College, Oxford, in 1886, and graduated M.D. in 1895, when he was also made a Fellow of the Royal College of Physicians of London. He was for a short time assistant physician to the Royal Free Hospital, but, deciding to specialise in pathology, was appointed lecturer in that subject in the medical school of St. Bartholomew's Hospital. As sanitary officer there he was able to avert the epidemics then prevalent, while he and his pupils did much to advance the new science of bacteriology. His work in this field was recognised by his election to a Fellowship of the Royal Society in 1915, and by his appointment to the Medical Research Council. He was Croonian Lecturer of the Royal College of Physicians in 1910, and Harveian Orator in 1920, in which year he was knighted. He served during the war as consulting pathologist for the London district, with the rank of major in the R.A.M.C., and received an O.B.E. for his services. A son and a daughter survived him.

27. **Dr. Frank Theodore Woods,** Bishop of Winchester, was born January 15, 1874, and educated at Marlborough, Trinity College, Cambridge, and Ridley Hall. He was ordained in 1897, and held curacies at Eastbourne and Huddersfield. After four years as vicar and rural dean of Bradford, during which his vigorous and sympathetic personality marked him for promotion, he was made Bishop of

Peterborough in 1916 at the age of 42. It was for pastoral leadership rather than scholarly or homilectical work that he was fitted, and he instituted the innovation of making long tours of his diocese on foot, his great stature and shepherd's crook making him a striking figure. In 1923 he was translated to the See of Winchester. At the Lambeth Conference in 1930 he stimulated much interest by the report issued by the committee on problems of marriage and sex, of which he was Chairman. His wife was Nina Katherine Thornton.

29. **Dr. George Claridge Druce,** noted botanist, was born at Potters Pury, Northants, May 23, 1850, and, educated privately, qualified with honours as a pharmaceutical chemist. In 1879 he opened a chemist's shop at Oxford, and taking an active part in municipal affairs, became a city councillor, sheriff, and mayor. In 1879 he published his " Flora of Northamptonshire," to be followed by companion works on the plant life of four other counties, as well as " Comital Flora of the British Isles," " Dubious Plants of Britain," and " North African Experiences." In 1895 the University of Oxford recognised his achievements by appointing him Curator of the Fielding Herbarium ; at the same time, he was attached to Magdalen College as an Hon. M.A. With the Professor of Botany he published in 1907 " The Dillenia Herbaria," in 1914 an account of the Morisonian Herbarium, and in 1897 and 1914 general accounts of the Fielding Herbarium. He was elected F.R.S. in 1927, having already received honorary degrees from Oxford and St. Andrews. He made many discoveries of new plants, and was regarded as one of the first of English field botanists of his day. He had one of the largest collections of plant specimens in the country, and was secretary of the Botanical Society and Exchange Club of Great Britain, and President of the Ashmolean Natural History Society.

MARCH.

3. **Dr. Ernest Howard Griffiths, F.R.S.,** physicist, was born June 15, 1851, and educated at Owens College, Manchester, and Sidney Sussex College, Cambridge, of which he became a Fellow in 1897. After graduating without taking an honours degree, he worked for some time as a coach while carrying on research in his private laboratory. In 1890 he published an important paper in the " Transactions of the Royal Society " on the comparison of the mercury and platinum resistance pyrometers, and in 1892, with Professor Callendar, issued a paper on the boiling-point of sulphur. In 1903 he went to Cardiff to become Principal of the University College of South Wales and Monmouthshire. For three periods of two years he was Vice-Chancellor of the University of Wales, and for three periods Fellow of Jesus College, Oxford. In 1906 he was president of Section A of the British Association, and in 1913 president of the Section on Educational Science. He took a keen interest in education, and especially educational movements for working men. He was on the Council of the Royal Society from 1909 to 1911, and was awarded the Hughes gold medal by that body for contributions to exact physical measurements. He was elected general treasurer of the British Association after he had resigned his principalship and returned to Cambridge.

— **Professor George Gregory Smith,** authority on Scottish literature, was born June 20, 1865, and educated at Edinburgh University and Balliol College, Oxford. After taking his degree at Oxford in 1888, he became Lecturer in English Language and Literature at Edinburgh. In 1905 he was appointed Professor of English Literature and librarian at Queen's College, Belfast (afterwards the Queen's University of Belfast), a position he held until 1930, when he retired. He specialised in the linguistic and historical aspects of literature ; for seven years he was general editor of the Scottish Text Society, and devoted special attention to the works of lesser known writers. His own most important contribution to learning was the editing of Robert Henryson's works in three volumes. He was also the author of " Scottish Literature : Character and Influence." He was regarded as an excellent teacher, and one of the foremost Scottish scholars of his day. In 1896 he married Mary, daughter of Colonel R. Cadell, who predeceased him in 1909. He left one son.

7. **Aristide Briand,** aged 69, famous French statesman and diplomatist of European fame, Foreign Minister and eleven times Premier of France, was born at Saint-Nazaire in 1862, the son of an inn-keeper, and educated there and at the Lycée de Nantes. His earlier years were devoted to the study of law and to journalism ; he contributed to anarchist papers, and founded the journal, *Humanité.* At the age of 35 he was engaged in organising labour unions, and became prominent in the Socialist party ; it was not till 1902, after several unsuccessful attempts, that he was elected to the Chamber of Deputies, being returned for Saint-Etienne. He did much in the preparation and passing of the law for the separation of Church and State, and became Minister of Public Instruction and Worship in the Sarrien Ministry of 1906, for the acceptance of which post he was excluded from the Unionist-Socialist Party. In 1908 he was appointed Minister of Justice, and a year later became Prime Minister, the first Socialist to hold that office in any country. His Government fell in 1911, and a year later he joined Poincaré's administration as Minister of Justice. In 1913 he was again Premier, holding too the portfolio of the Interior. He joined Viviani's war Cabinet in August, 1914, as Minister of Justice, and succeeded him as Premier in October, 1915. From then onward he turned his attention especially to foreign affairs, becoming the most notable Foreign Minister of his day. He played an active part in the prosecution of the war, but resigning in 1917, filled a minor rôle in negotiating the peace. Returning to office in 1921, he brought about the Wiesbaden Agreement with Germany, and made a series of defensive treaties with the States of the Little Entente. He put the French case at the Washington Disarmament Conference in November, 1921, but was unsuccessful in gaining acceptance of his country's proposals, and on his part refused to agree to the abolishing of submarines. He resigned in January, 1922. In 1924 he represented France on the League of Nations, and in 1925 played a leading part at the Locarno Conference, which guaranteed the frontiers between Germany and France and Germany and Belgium. In that year he again became Prime Minister, as well as Minister for Foreign Affairs. He resigned in 1926 during the financial crisis, but almost at once joined Poincaré's Ministry of National Union as Foreign Minister. He received the Nobel Peace Prizes of 1925 and 1926, and in 1927 formulated the proposals which developed into the Kellogg Pact for the outlawing of war, signed by fifteen nations the following year. In 1929 a substantial measure of agreement was reached between Germany and the Powers on the contentious questions of reparations and the evacuation of the Rhineland, a tribute to Briand's policy of conciliation. In July, 1929, he became Prime Minister of France for the eleventh and last time, and was chief delegate of his country at The Hague Conference on reparations ; his Government was defeated in the Chamber immediately afterwards. Briand, however, remained Foreign Minister in the Tardieu Cabinet, and in the succession of ephemeral ministries which followed. In 1930 he envisaged the formation of a United States of Europe by issuing his " Memorandum on the Organisation of a Régime of Federal Union in Europe." [See Public Documents, in ANNUAL REGISTER, 1930.] He played a leading part at the London Naval Conference, but there and in succeeding Franco-German discussions his peaceful policies received something of a check. His prestige also suffered from his unsuccessful candidature for the French Presidency. But he represented France at Geneva during the discussions on the proposed Austro-German Customs Union, securing the reference of the scheme to The Hague Court. He resigned from the Laval Cabinet in January, 1932, and went into retirement. M. Briand, who was unmarried, was regarded as one

of the most dexterous parliamentarians of his generation, as a great diplomatist, and one of the most successful and devoted workers for international peace.

10. **Paolo Boselli,** politician, economist, and historian, was born at Savona, July 8, 1838. After graduating in law at the University of Turin, he entered the Italian Civil Service, and in 1867 represented his country as Secretary-General at the Paris Exhibition. In 1870 he was returned to Parliament, appointed a member of the Permanent Committee on Finance, and made Professor of Public Finance in the University of Rome. In 1881 he became President of the Council for the Mercantile Marine, a body which he had helped to create, and in 1888 entered Crispi's first Cabinet as Minister of Public Instruction. He held in turn the portfolios of Agriculture and Finance in the Government of 1893-96, returning to the Treasury in Pelloux's Ministry of 1899 to 1900. He published many works on legal, scientific, economic, and historical subjects, and was honoured by many learned bodies. As the oldest member of the Chamber of Deputies, it fell to him to move the resolution in May, 1915, in favour of Italy joining the Allies. In June, 1916, at the age of 77, he headed a " National Government," which remained in office until October, 1917. He became a Senator in 1921, and received one of the few honorary memberships of the Fascist Party. He held the Collar of the Annunziata, the highest decoration conferred by the Italian Crown.

11. **Hermann Gunkel,** aged 70, well-known Bible Commentator, was born in the manse at Springe, near Hanover. Deciding on the academic career, he began teaching at Göttingen (1888), and moved from there to Halle (1889), Berlin (1894), Giessen (1907), ending up in Halle once more as full professor (1920). Gunkel won international renown for his commentaries on books of the Bible ; his " Genesis " (1901) was particularly successful, and his " Psalms " (1904) no less. His aim in his studies was to discover the environment in which the literature and civilisation of Israel flourished ; accordingly his researches led him to Babylonian and Egyptian sources. Gunkel was one of the editors of the theological encyclopedia, " Religion in Geschichte und Gegenwart." He was also an authority on the New Testament ; a valued contribution in this field was his commentary on the First Epistle of Peter. Gunkel retired in 1927.

12. **Ivar Kreuger,** aged 53, financier, was born at Kalmar, in south-east Sweden, and educated as a civil engineer. After working in New York as a real estate salesman, and for construction firms, he spent some time in South Africa in the employ of Waring & Gillow, and, returning to Sweden in 1907, established in the following year, the firm of Kreuger & Co., contractors. In 1913 he founded the United Swedish Match Co., and in 1917 amalgamated it with several other match companies, under the title of the Swedish Match Co. The same year Kreuger & Co. was divided into two parts, one of which became one of the largest and most important financial institutions in the world. Between 1922 and 1930 he played an active part in the financial reconstruction of Europe by obtaining loans in New York and re-lending the money to impoverished states in need of capital for development schemes. In this way he lent 6,000,000 dollars to Poland for the rehabilitation of agricultural sufferers from floods, 22,000,000 dollars to Yugoslavia, 36,000,000 dollars to Hungary to finance land reform measures, and 6,000,000 dollars to Latvia for farm relief. He also helped France to obtain a stabilization loan of 75,000,000 dollars when all other channels were closed to the Government, and by lending Germany 125,000,000 dollars, averted a probable major financial catastrophe. He played a prominent part in the Young Loan negotiations at The Hague. His death by his own hand made a deep impression on world opinion, but it was followed by the discovery of the most serious irregularities in the affairs of his companies, including the falsification of balances and the forging of bonds for use as spurious assets.

13. **John Atkinson** (Lord Atkinson), eminent jurist, was born December 13, 1844, and educated at the Belfast Academy and Queen's University. Called to the Irish Bar in 1865, he became a Q.C. at the age of 35. He joined the English Bar in 1890 as a member of the Inner Temple, being elected a Bencher in 1906. In 1889 he was appointed Solicitor-General for Ireland, but did not obtain a seat in Parliament until 1895, when he was returned as Conservative member for the North Division of Londonderry, and was made Attorney-General for Ireland. In 1905 he was made a Lord of Appeal in Ordinary with a life peerage, being the first Irish barrister to attain that office without preliminary service on the Bench. As a member of the Judicial Committee of the Privy Council, his judgments on Indian appeals became noted. He was one of the Law Lords who handed down the famous decision in the case of the Attorney-General *v.* De Keyser's Royal Hotel Ltd., which asserted the rights of the subject as against the Crown. Though sometimes obscure owing to a lack of literary style, his judgments were known for their common sense, discrimination, and independence of thought. His wife and three sons predeceased him, but one son survived him.

— **Charles Gide,** French economist, of international repute, was born June 29, 1847, in Uzès. He began his academic career at Bordeaux (1874-80) ; migrated to Montpellier (1880-98), and thence to the *Collège de France* in Paris. As a teacher of economics Gide obtained world-wide fame through his " Principles of Political Economy " which went through twenty-three editions and was translated into many European languages. Gide was also a passionate advocate of Co-operation ; " La Co-opération " appeared in 1900. He was also the founder of the *Revue d'Economie politique* (1887).

14. **George Eastman,** inventor and philanthropist, was born at Waterville, in New York State, on July 12, 1854. While working as a bank clerk, he devoted his spare time to amateur photography. He soon left the bank, and in 1880 perfected a process for making sensitive gelatine dry plates, and also the first plate-coating machine, and in 1884 he patented the first commercially successful rollable film. In 1888 he produced the original Kodak camera, and two years later the first machine for making rollable transparent films. Experimenting for five years in conjunction with Edison, he produced a celluloid film through which light could be passed, while Edison perfected the first film projector ; these inventions made possible the moving picture industry. Eastman became Chairman of the Eastman Kodak Company of America, and a member of the Board of Kodak Ltd., of London ; he had eighty-five subsidiary companies in all parts of the world. In 1924, having already given away half of his stock in his company, he gave away the remaining half to various educational institutions. His charities included £300,000 for a dental clinic associated with the Royal Free Hospital, London ; he endowed similar clinics in Rome, Paris, Brussels, and Stockholm. In 1930 he established a visiting professorship at Oxford, to be held by an American citizen. He set up a symphony orchestra in his native town of Rochester, N.Y. After several years of poor health, he committed suicide, leaving a note which read " My work is done. Why wait ? "

16. **Harold Monro,** aged 53, poet, publisher, and bookseller, was born in Brussels and educated abroad, at Radley, and at Caius College, Cambridge. He published volumes of poems in 1906-7, and in 1909, in prose, " The Chronicle of a Pilgrimage," an account of a walking tour from Paris to Milan. In 1911 he founded in conjunction with the Poetry Society the *Poetry Review,* the editorship of which he held for a year. In 1913 he issued under his own direction another periodical, *Poetry and Drama,* to which almost every young man of poetic or literary talent contributed. He then started in a small street off Theobald's Lane, near Gray's Inn, his Poetry Bookshop, where poetry readings by himself or well-known poets became an established and quite celebrated institution. He published further volumes of verse under the titles " Strange Meetings "

(1917), " Real Property " (1922), and " The Earth for Sale " (1928). But he was more concerned with helping able writers in difficulties, and with an increase in the reading and writing of good poetry than in the success of his own works. His home became the centre of an informal circle of poets and writers who frequently met there for talks and discussions. He was twice married, and had a son by his first wife.

20. **Dr. Louis Claude Purser,** noted Irish classical scholar, was born September 28, 1854, and educated at Middleton College, Co. Cork, Portora Royal School, Enniskillen, and Trinity College, Dublin, to which he was to devote his whole working life. He was a Classical Scholar, and First Classical Moderator at Trinity in 1875, and was elected a Fellow in 1881. From 1898 to 1904 he was Professor of Latin, his services to Latin scholarship being particularly noteworthy ; with the late Professor Tyrrell he brought out a comprehensive edition of Cicero's Letters, and also edited the Latin text of the letters. Besides filling the offices of Junior Bursar, Auditor, Bursar Registrar and Vice-Provost of Trinity, he was secretary of the Council of the Royal Irish Academy from 1902 to 1907 and from 1908 to 1914. He became a member of the British Academy in 1923. He received honorary degrees from the Universities of Oxford, Glasgow, and Durham. Dr. Purser was unmarried.

24. **George Robert Canning Harris** (fourth Baron Harris), politician and Indian administrator, perhaps better known as a cricketer, who won wide renown as a player and organiser of that game, was born February 3, 1851, at Trinidad, where his father was Governor. He was educated at Eton and Christ Church, Oxford. As a Freshman he scored a century against the University. In 1872 —the year he succeeded to his title—he played for the Gentlemen of England in Canada and the United States. In the 'varsity match of 1874 his brilliant play, both in fielding and batting, did much to secure Oxford's victory. He captained Kent from 1875 to 1889, and played for it until 1906, when it became champion county. In 1878-79 he took an eleven to Australia, and captained England in the Test Matches of 1880 and 1884. He played for I Zingari and the Eton Ramblers, and joined the committee of the M.C.C. in 1875, later becoming a trustee and treasurer ; he was president of the club in 1895. Harris was Under-Secretary of State in 1885-86, while Lord Randolph Churchill was at the India Office, and Under-Secretary for War from 1886 to 1889. In 1890 he became Governor of Bombay, where he succeeded in popularising cricket among the Indians. Returning to England in 1895 he was appointed a Lord-in-Waiting to Queen Victoria, and was A.D.C. to the two succeeding Sovereigns. He saw service in the South African War. He spent thirty-five years in the City, being Chairman of the Consolidated Goldfields of South Africa, and on the Boards of other companies. He was made C.B., G.C.I.E., and G.C.S.I. His wife, a daughter of Viscount St. Vincent, died in 1930 ; their only son survived him.

26. **Sir Horace Curzon Plunkett,** pioneer of the co-operative movement in Irish agriculture, was born October 24, 1854, third son of the sixteenth Lord Dunsany. He went to Eton in 1868, and then to University College, Oxford. At the age of 25 he bought a ranch in Montana, and in ten years acquired a fortune ; he returned to Ireland in 1889, impressed with the methods and ideas of American agriculturists. There the collapse of Parnellism was followed by the beginning of the Irish Revival. Plunkett took advantage of the growth of this cultural and economic movement to found in 1894 the Irish Agricultural Organisation Society, a non-political body, of which he was elected president. He resigned in 1899 on becoming vice-president of the Council of Agriculture, an advisory body formed to assist the Department of Agriculture and Technical Instruction, established by Act of Parliament in that year. Plunkett's work for the rehabilitation of Irish rural life was recognised by the conferment upon him of an Irish Privy Councillorship in 1897 ; he was elected an F.R.S. in 1902, and

made K.C.V.O., 1903 ; he had had a seat in Parliament as Unionist member for South County Dublin since 1892, but was defeated in 1900. He continued his work for the co-operative movement, and reported in his " Ireland of the New Century," 1904, that the turnover of the rural societies had reached 2,000,000*l*. His pamphlet, " The Better Way," 1914, proposed an agreed settlement of the Irish problem by inviting Ulster to accept a tentative period of Home Rule. He endowed and created in 1919 the Horace Plunkett Foundation for the promotion of agricultural development. In 1920-21 he advocated Dominion Home Rule for Ireland, and he was in the Senate of the Irish Free State from 1922 to 1923. He received honorary degrees from Oxford and Dublin, and an honorary Fellowship from University College, Oxford. Sir Horace was unmarried.

27. **Dr. Lionel George Bridges Justice Ford,** educationalist and Anglican divine, was born September 3, 1865, and educated at Repton, where he distinguished himself both as scholar and athlete. At Cambridge, where he won a scholarship to King's College in 1884, he obtained a first class in classics, won the first Chancellor's medal, was president of the Union and captain of the University golf team. In 1888 he became a master at Eton, where he remained thirteen years ; he took Orders in 1893, after studying at Cuddesdon Theological College. He was appointed headmaster of Repton in 1901, and instituted fundamental reforms in every branch of the school regime. After nine years at that school, he left to become headmaster of Harrow, where he remained for fifteen years. Here, too, he introduced many innovations into the life of the school, which prospered under his rule. In 1926 he was appointed Dean of York, where he did much for the improvement of the ceremonial of the Minster. He married, in 1904, a daughter of Bishop Talbot (of Winchester), by whom he had six sons (of whom one predeceased him) and two daughters.

29. **Norman McKinnel,** distinguished actor, was born at Maxwelltown, Kirkcudbrightshire, February 10, 1870, and educated as an engineer at Edinburgh and Leipzig. At the age of 24 he went on the stage, appearing at Her Majesty's Theatre under Beerbohm Tree in 1898. During his thirty years on the stage, he filled many parts with great success. He played with Irving in " Dante " in 1903, and had the rôle of the Devil in Shaw's " Don Juan in Hell " in 1907. A famous character study of his was the part of " John Anthony " in Galsworthy's " Strife " (1909). The same year he became stage director of the Haymarket Theatre, and appeared there as " King Lear." In 1914 he became manager of the Vaudeville Theatre. He became known for his restrained, but powerful, interpretation of old men's parts, his " Sylvanus Heythorp " in Galsworthy's " Old English " (1924), being especially notable. He was the author of several plays, and Chairman of the Actors' Association. His wife, known on the stage as Miss Gertrude Scott, survived him.

30. **Filippo Turati,** aged 75, at one time leader of the Italian Socialist Party, was born in Lombardy in 1857. Educated for the Bar, he soon adopted politics and was elected to Parliament as a Socialist. In the interest of that party he edited *La Critica Sociale*, and later the *Avanti*. Though by temperament a moderate, he was in 1899 sentenced to twelve years' imprisonment on a charge of provoking the riots at Milan in the previous year. He was released after two years, and resumed the seat in Parliament which he occupied through seven changes of Government. He was invited to join Giolitti's Ministry of 1903, but declined. In 1922, after the split in the Socialist Party, he joined the Unitarian wing. Refused permission by the Fascists, to whom he was opposed, to leave Italy, he escaped by motor launch to Corsica in 1926 ; for this act he was sentenced in his absence to ten months' imprisonment. He spent the remainder of his life in Paris.

31. **The Rev. Frank Edward Brightman, D.D.,** noted liturgical scholar and historian, was born at Bristol, June 18, 1856. From Bristol Grammar School

he went, in 1875, to University College, Oxford, where he gained distinctions in mathematics, classics, and theology. After having been ordained deacon in 1884 and priest in 1885, he became librarian of Pusey House, Oxford, and chaplain of his college. In 1903 he was elected a Fellow of Magdalen College. He published " Liturgies Eastern and Western " and " English Rite " (1915), and those works made his reputation pre-eminent in the field of liturgical scholarship. His editions of Bishop Andrewes' " Preces Privatae " (1903), and " Manual for the Sick " (1909), were accepted as standard works. He contributed valuable articles on the Anglican Prayer Book and on Bishop King of Lincoln to the " Dictionary of English Church History " (1912). His essay " Terms of Communion and the Ministration of the Sacraments in Early Times " (contributed to Dr. Swete's volume of essays on Early Church History, of 1918), was considered a masterly work. He was appointed Prebendary of Carlton-cum-Thurlby in Lincoln Cathedral in 1902, and was elected a Fellow of the British Academy in 1926. He was examining chaplain to successive Bishops of Oxford, and honorary chaplain to the Bishop of Gloucester. He contributed, in 1927, to the *Church Quarterly Review* a severe criticism of the Deposited Prayer Book, during the controversy over Prayer Book Revision. He was a co-editor of the *Journal of Theological Studies*, author of many theological works, and was honoured by several Universities.

APRIL.

4. **Sir Frederic de Waal**, politician, lawyer, and administrator, who played a prominent part in the problems of government arising from the conversion of the four South African colonies into the Union of South Africa, was born in Holland, July 8, 1853, and educated in Brussels. After studying languages and travelling in Europe and America, he went to South Africa in 1880, and settling at Middelburg, Cape Colony, practised law there for twenty-eight years. He became secretary of the Afrikander Bond, and in 1898 was returned to the Cape Parliament, representing the Bond interest there until the Union. In 1908 he was appointed Colonial Secretary in the Merriman Cabinet. On the establishment of the Union in 1910, he became the first Administrator of the Cape Province, and as for some fourteen years his Executive Council consisted of two Nationalists and two members of the South African Party, his casting vote made him virtually dictator. He initiated and carried through the Provincial Council measures for the consolidation of local government, the provision of free primary education for European and coloured children alike, improvement in the pay and status of teachers, and the establishment of boarding-houses for poor European children otherwise unable to attend school. He was twice reappointed Administrator, resigning in 1925, and was made K.C.M.G. in 1911. He had a son and a daughter.

— **Wilhelm Ostwald**, aged 79, a distinguished authority on physical chemistry, was born in Riga, and educated at Riga and Dorpat. In 1887 he received a call to Leipzig, where he became Director of the Institute for Physical Chemistry. Scholars from all over the world flocked to Leipzig to sit at his feet ; his researches won for him the 1909 Nobel Prize for Chemistry. In 1905 Ostwald became Visiting Professor at Harvard and Columbia Universities ; in 1906 he retired from academic work to devote himself to research. In the field of dyes Ostwald achieved great distinction ; in the sphere of thought he devoted himself to preaching the doctrine of the importance in life of human energy. He founded the *Zeitschrift für physikalische Chemie* and the *Annalen der Naturphilosophie*.

8. **Dr. Karl Hermann Breul**, distinguished as a teacher of German in the University of Cambridge, was born in Hanover, August 10, 1860. He studied at Tübingen, Strasburg, and Berlin. After taking his degree in 1883, he went to Paris and Cambridge, where he was appointed University Lecturer in German

(1884). Two years later he became a member of King's College, where he was subsequently elected a Fellow. In 1896 he obtained the degree of Litt.D., Cambridge, and in 1899 he was made University Reader in Germanic. In 1910 he was elected to the newly founded Schröder Chair of German at Cambridge. He was one of the founders of the English Goethe Society and of the *Modern Language Quarterly*, and was President of the Modern Language Association in 1910. He was the author of " The Teaching of Modern Foreign Languages in our Secondary Schools " (1898), and " A Handy Bibliographical Guide to the Study of the German Language and Literature," besides bringing out a revised edition of E. Weir's German Dictionary. His " Cambridge Songs " (1915), a unique collection of mediæval Latin poems, was a notable contribution to scholarship. One son survived him.

8. **(Albert) Eustace Short,** aged 62, was a pioneer in the construction and flying of the first aircraft. In 1897, with his brother Oswald, he took up balloon flying as an amateur ; within five years they were making balloons for the Indian Government. In 1907, with information supplied by the Wright brothers, and with the assistance of the third brother, Horace Short, an engineer, they began the construction of heavier-than-air and power-driven machines. Their first product, built in 1908, contained an engine taken from a motor-car. Their works, moved from Battersea to the Isle of Sheppey, provided in 1909 the machine for the first flight of a British pilot. In 1912 a seaplane from Short Bros.' factory was included in a Royal Naval Review. Their plant was moved to Rochester in 1913, and constructed many seaplanes during the war. In 1916 they built four airships for the Admiralty, and in 1926 the first all-metal flying-boat. Short Bros. were also the first firm to make aircraft from steel and duralumin. At the age of 58 Eustace Short began flying himself, and at the time of his death, which occurred in the cockpit of a seaplane after landing, he was preparing, with his brother Oswald, to make an ascent in an enormous specially constructed balloon to carry out scientific experiments in the stratosphere at a height of fifteen miles.

10. **Albert Goodwin,** aged 87, painter, was better known for his water-colours than his works in oils. With the encouragement of Ruskin, he began to exhibit as early as 1855, and from 1860 onwards he contributed pictures regularly to the Academy and the Royal Society of Painters in Water-Colours, of which he was later elected a member. He travelled widely, in India, Egypt, and the South Seas, as well as in Europe, finding subjects for his brush in all these places. Two of his best-known pictures were " Benares " and " Moonlight on the Citadel." His works were marked by careful observation and a delicate rendering of effects of light. He was honoured by a special exhibition of 150 of his pictures at the Birmingham Art Gallery in 1926. His " Sinbad the Sailor " and " Ali Baba and the Forty Thieves," as well as five water-colour drawings of cathedrals, were accepted by the Tate Gallery. Other pictures of his found a place in the galleries of Melbourne, Sydney, and Johannesburg.

11. **Professor Maxim Nikolayevitch Pokrovsky,** aged 64, Soviet historian, was born in 1868, and educated at the University of Moscow, where he taught for a time after graduating in 1891. Being interested in the revolutionary movement, he joined the Bolshevist wing of the Social Democratic Party in 1905, working for its journals, addressing workers' meetings, and joining the local Bolshevist directorate. He was a delegate to the London Conference of 1907, and while there was elected to the Bolshevist Central Committee. Returning to Moscow, he was arrested for engaging in illegal propaganda, but succeeded in escaping to Finland and thence to Paris, where he joined the " Forward " wing of the Bolshevists, and began his serious historical work. He returned to Russia after the amnesty of 1917, and was elected Chairman of the Moscow Soviet, and later Deputy Commissar of Education under Lunacharsky, a post he held until

his death. His outstanding work as a department head was his foundation of the Workers' Faculties. He was President of the Institute of Red Professors, and as an acknowledgment of his work was nominated in 1929 to the controlling organ of the Academy of Sciences. His principal scholarly works were his " History of Russia " and his " Russian History in Brief Outline," both recognised for their accuracy and depth of learning. He also edited and published, in *Red Archives*, valuable excerpts from State papers dating from the Napoleonic period to the Revolution of 1917. He was regarded by the Bolshevists as the foremost Marxist historian in the world.

17. **Sir Arthur Theodore Thring,** parliamentary draftsman and formerly Council to the Treasury, was born February 7, 1860, of an old West Country family distinguished in public life. He was educated at Winchester and New College, Oxford, where he was a scholar, and was called to the Bar by Lincoln's Inn in 1887. He practised for some years, chiefly before Parliamentary committees and Local Government inquiries. In 1902 he was appointed Second Parliamentary Counsel to the Treasury, and in 1903 First Counsel. Upon him fell the onus of drafting into intelligible legal form much important legislation initiated in political strife. His best work was probably the Merchant Shipping Act. In 1917 he became Clerk of the Parliaments, which office he held until 1930, and was also Registrar of the House of Lords in its judicial capacity. He was an active member of the Statute Law Revision Committee, and he was said to have guided the Upper House in all matters concerning the Standing Orders or rules of debate. He was a Deputy Lieutenant of Somerset, and Deputy Chairman of Quarter Sessions. Thring was made a C.B. in 1902, K.C.B. in 1908. He married, in 1902, Miss Georgina Bovill, and had one son.

— **Professor Sir Patrick Geddes,** aged 78, distinguished biologist and sociologist, was born in 1854, and educated at Perth Academy, the Royal School of Mines, University College, London, the Sorbonne and the Universities of Edinburgh and Montpellier. He was successively Demonstrator of Physiology at University College, London, of Zoology at the University of Aberdeen, and of Botany at Edinburgh, where he also lectured on Natural History in the School of Medicine. In the intervals of his academic work he travelled widely, paying visits to Continental Universities, zoological stations and botanic gardens ; he also visited the United States and Cyprus, and carried out exploration work in Mexico. He was for some years Professor of Botany at University College, Dundee, and Professor of Sociology and Civics at the University of Bombay. He caused to be built on Castle Hill, Edinburgh, the Outlook Tower, a regional geographic and synthetic type-museum, and he did much in the sphere of town-planning and city improvement. Personally gifted with quickness of thought and the quality of close observation, he made many educational experiments, including the founding of university hostels in Edinburgh, Chelsea, and India. Among his works were " The Evolution of Sex," " Chapters in Modern Botany " and " City Development." He was associated with the publishing house of Geddes and Colleagues, which issued books on geography and education, Celtic and general literature and art. He died at Scots College, Montpellier, of which he was a Director. He was knighted in 1932. His second wife, and two children by his first wife, survived him.

19. **Sir William Watson Cheyne, Bt.,** eminent surgeon, was born December 14, 1852, in the Shetland Isles. Educated at the University of Edinburgh, where he graduated with first-class honours in 1875, he visited Strasburg and Vienna, and on his return became house surgeon to Lister at the Royal Infirmary, and demonstrator of anatomy in the University. In 1877 he went to London as house surgeon to Lister on the latter's appointment as Professor of Surgery at King's College Hospital. In 1880 he was appointed assistant surgeon at King's College Hospital, and later surgeon, Professor of Clinical Surgery, and Emeritus-Professor.

He was Hunterian Professor at the Royal College of Surgeons, 1888-90. He was elected F.R.S. in 1894, and was appointed a civil consulting surgeon to the forces during the South African War, receiving a mention in despatches and a C.B. for his services. After the war he settled in London again, and his professional worth was recognised by election to the presidency of the Pathological, Harveian, and Medical Societies. He was appointed Surgeon-in-Ordinary to the King in 1908, and served as President of the Royal College of Surgeons of England from 1914 to 1916. His services in the Great War were acknowledged by his being made Surgeon Rear-Admiral for his work with the Navy. Retiring from practice in 1917, he was returned to Parliament as member for the Universities of Edinburgh and St. Andrews ; in 1918 he became M.P. for the combined Scottish Universities. He retired from the House of Commons in 1922, and in 1924 was awarded the Lister Memorial Medal and Prize. Among other medical works, he wrote a manual of surgical treatment in seven volumes. He received a baronetcy in 1908, a K.C.M.G. in 1916, and from 1919 to 1930 was Lord-Lieutenant of Orkney and Shetland. He was twice married, and two sons and a daughter survived him.

22. **Edward Taylor Scott,** journalist, was born November 15, 1883, and educated at Rugby, Corpus Christi College, Oxford, and the London School of Economics. From 1907 to 1909 he was private secretary and A.D.C. to the Governor of Jamaica. Returning to England, he acquired experience in financial journalism before joining the staff of the *Manchester Guardian* in 1911. After serving in the R.F.A. during the Great War, he returned to his father's (C. P. Scott's) paper, where for three years he was chief leader writer. On his father's retirement in July, 1929, he was appointed editor. Scott met his death by drowning when his boat capsized on Lake Windermere. His wife (a daughter of J. A. Hobson, the economist), two sons and two daughters survived him.

26. **Sir Adrian Knox,** former Chief Justice of Australia, was born November 9, 1863, in Sydney. Educated at Harrow and Trinity College, Cambridge, he was called to the Bar by the Inner Temple in 1886. Returning to Australia he was called to the New South Wales Bar, and practised for twenty years, taking silk in 1906. From 1894 to 1898 he sat in the State Legislative Assembly, and, after refusing more than once the offer of a seat on the High Court Bench, he was appointed Chief Justice of the Commonwealth in 1919, being the second holder of that office. He was sworn of the Privy Council in 1920, and made K.C.M.G. in 1921. In 1924 and 1925 he sat several times on the Judicial Committee of the Privy Council, and in 1924 he was a member of the Board which decided as to the constitution of the tribunal which fixed the boundary between Northern Ireland and the Free State. His judgments were marked by directness, clarity, and a certain circumspection. In 1930 he resigned his Chief Justiceship on inheriting one of the richest collieries in Australia. Apart from the law, his chief interest was the turf ; he was several times Chairman of the Australian Jockey Club, and won the Sydney Cup in 1910. His wife, a son and two daughters survived him.

28. **Sir David Drummond, M.D.,** distinguished brain specialist, was born in December, 1852, and educated at private schools and Trinity College, Dublin. After studying medicine at Prague, Vienna, and Strasburg, he settled in Newcastle in 1876, and became assistant physician at the Children's Hospital there. Before long he was associated with the Durham College of Medicine at Newcastle, a connexion which was to last for fifty years ; first as lecturer on therapeutics, then on physiology, and finally as Professor of the Principles and Practice of Medicine. He served a term as Vice-Chancellor of Durham University, and was physician to the Royal Victoria Infirmary. He developed a large consulting practice, especially of brain and spinal cord cases. During the war he was senior physician to the Northumberland War Hospital, and received a C.B.E. in 1920 and a knighthood in 1923. He was president of the British Medical Association in 1921, and also of the Association of Physicians of Great Britain and

Ireland ; he was a Fellow of the Royal Society of Medicine and of the Royal
Academy of Medicine of Ireland. He published several important papers on
diseases of the brain and spinal cord in *Brain.* In 1924 he was appointed a
member of the Royal Commission on Lunacy Law. He received honorary
degrees from Durham and Glasgow Universities. Four sons and two daughters
survived him.

28. **General José Uriburu,** aged 54, former President of Argentina, was born
of a family distinguished in Argentine history. Educated at the Military School
at Buenos Aires, he rose to become Colonel of the 8th Regiment of Cavalry, and
served for three years with the German Army. He was appointed to the
command of the 1st Division of the Argentine Army, and later was made Inspector-
General. He came to England as Military Attaché in the special embassy sent
by the Argentine Government. He was made a K.B.E. during the Prince of
Wales's visit to Argentina in 1925, and in 1931 he became G.C.B. When
President Irigoyen was deposed in 1930, after some years of misgovernment,
Uriburu became provisional President, announcing that he intended to restore
constitutionalism as soon as the country had returned to a stable footing. His
Government was promptly recognised by Great Britain and the United States,
and the general confidence in his regime was manifested by the offer of a loan of
10,000,000*l.* by British, Argentine, and American bankers. The period of his
dictatorship was marked by peaceful government, and in spite of the prevailing
trade depression, his administration succeeded in balancing its budgets, and
enabled the republic to meet its commitments. Uriburu had announced that
neither he nor any of his colleagues would be a candidate for the presidency ;
at the elections held early in 1932 he kept his word.

MAY.

7. **Paul Doumer,** President of the French Republic, was born of working-class
parents at Aurillac on March 2, 1857. Educated in the national schools, he began
to earn his living at the age of 14, working in a metal foundry during the day
and attending lectures in his spare time. He took his degree at an early age,
and obtained a professorship in mathematics at Laon. But he soon gave up his
academic work to enter political journalism in Paris, where his articles in the
Radical press attracted much attention. While still under 30 he was appointed
Chef de Cabinet by the President of the Chamber of Deputies. He was elected
to Parliament in 1888, at the age of 31, as Deputy for the Aisne, and in 1895 was
given the portfolio of Finance in the Ministry of Léon Bourgeois. He was
appointed Governor-General of Indo-China in 1897, and during his five years'
tenure of office proved an able administrator ; he reorganised the Civil Services of
the colony, restored its finances and carried out a comprehensive scheme of public
works. On his return to France he was included in the Combes Cabinet of the
Socialist-Radicals, and headed the Radical-Republican section of the Government's supporters in opposition to the Socialists. On the resignation of this
Ministry Doumer was elected President of the Chamber of Deputies. He was an
unsuccessful candidate for the Presidency of the Republic in 1906, being defeated
by Fallières, the President of the Senate. In 1912 he entered the Senate, and was
a member of several of the Ministries formed during and after the Great War.
In 1925 he was invited to form a Government but was unsuccessful, and shortly
after was appointed Minister of Finance by Briand. After various political
vicissitudes connected with the fall of the franc and the hostility of the *Cartel des
Gauches,* Doumer was elected President of the Senate in 1927, thus holding the
second highest position in the Republic. In the Presidential elections of 1931
he became the candidate of the parties of the Right, and defeated Briand by a
narrow margin ; at the latter's withdrawal he secured a large majority over
Pierre Marraud, the candidate of the Left. He proved an active head of the

State, in spite of his 74 years, and gained a reputation for his impartial arbitration between the various political parties. He met his death at the hands of a half-crazed political fanatic. Four of his sons were killed in the Great War ; his widow and two daughters survived him.

7. **Albert Thomas,** French politician and Director of the International Labour Office, was born at Champigny-sur-Marne, near Paris, July 16, 1878. The son of a baker, he was educated at the Ecole Normale Supérieure and at the University, where he took his degree with the highest honours. After winning scholarships which enabled him to travel in Germany, Russia, and Turkey, he published in 1903 his " Le Syndicalisme Allemand," a treatise which won him recognition as a Socialist thinker. A year later, at the age of 26, he was made sub-editor of the newly founded *L'Humanité*. He entered the Chamber of Deputies in 1910 as a leader of the *reformiste*, or Right, wing of the Socialist Party. After a few weeks' service at the front, he became Under-Secretary of State for Munitions in May, 1915, and a year later was appointed Minister for that Department. He continued in that post until 1917, when he was sent on a special mission to Petrograd, where he succeeded in persuading Kerensky to undertake the great offensive of that year. He was returned to the Chamber as a Majority Socialist in the elections of 1919, but resigned when, in 1920, at the International Labour Conference in Washington, he was appointed Director of the International Labour Office. During his twelve years at Geneva he saw the International Labour Organisation under his direction become a great agency of inquiry into industrial conditions, and he was tireless in his efforts to secure the raising of industrial standards by international methods. He travelled widely for the office, and took part in many conferences of workers' organisations. He left a wife and children.

— **Sir Thomas Morison Legg,** authority on industrial diseases, was born at Hong-Kong, January 6, 1863. He was educated at Magdalen College School and Trinity College, Oxford, and took his degree in medicine in 1886. After serving as secretary to the Royal Commission on Tuberculosis, he was appointed Senior Medical Inspector of Factories at the Home Office (1898), a position he filled for nearly thirty years. He was called upon to tackle the new problems presented by the passing of the Workmen's Compensation Act, and he worked to secure the control of factories by the State and for public recognition of the need for industrial hygiene. He represented the British Government at Geneva in 1921 at the drafting of the international convention prohibiting the use of white lead for the internal painting of buildings ; when six years later the time came for putting the instrument into force, he felt that the regulations issued by the Home Office fell short of the policy he had helped to formulate, and he consequently resigned his position. In 1930 he became medical adviser to the social insurance section of the Trade Union Congress, and by lectures and articles worked to keep the trade union movement informed on questions of health in industry. He received his knighthood in 1925. His wife, two sons and a daughter survived him.

13. **Dr. Paget Jackson Toynbee,** distinguished student, editor, and translator of Dante, was born at Wimbledon, January 20, 1855, and educated at Haileybury and Balliol College, Oxford. After taking his degree in classics, he became a private tutor, and in that capacity went round the world. He gave up teaching in 1892, and devoted the rest of his life to scholarship, and especially to the study of Dante. He compiled a " Dictionary of Proper Names and Notable Matters in the Works of Dante," and in 1900 published his " Life of Dante," which went through four editions, and was translated into Italian. He produced a popular edition of Cary's translation of the " Divine Comedy " and a volume of selected translations from Dante, entitled " In the Footprints of Dante." His most important work was " Dante in English Literature " ; this was amplified in

1921, the Dante centenary year, when the British Academy, of which he was a Fellow, published his " Britain's Tribute to Dante in Literature and Art : A Chronological Record of 540 Years (1380-1920)." He was editor of the Oxford Dante which appeared in 1924. He married, in 1894, Miss Helen Wrigley, who edited the best edition of Horace Walpole's letters in sixteen volumes. After her death in 1910 he finished her " Lettres de la Marquise du Deffand à Horace Walpole," and later published three supplementary volumes to his wife's edition of the letters. He also edited the correspondence of Gray, Walpole, West, and Austin, and published Mason's anonymous satirical poems with Horace Walpole's notes. Paget Toynbee, who was a brother of Arnold Toynbee, was an honorary Fellow of Balliol, D.Litt. Oxford, honorary LL.D. Edinburgh, and a Fellow of the Royal Historical Society.

15. **The Hon. William Pember Reeves,** eminent New Zealand politician and sociologist, was born in Canterbury, N.Z., February 10, 1857, educated at Christ's College Grammar School, Christchurch, and called to the New Zealand Bar. Preferring journalism to the law, at an early age he became editor of the *Canterbury Times* and the *Lyttelton Times.* In 1887 he entered the Dominion Parliament, and soon became known both as a redoubtable debater and as the initiator of much important legislation. He was mainly responsible for the Industrial Conciliation and Arbitration Act, 1894, which encouraged trade unionism and made compulsory State intervention in industrial disputes ; a Factories Act and an Undesirable Immigrants Bill. He was also connected with measures designed to tax absentee landlords, and to encourage the smallholder. In 1896 he laid down the portfolios of Education, Labour, and Justice to became Agent-General for New Zealand in London, and subsequently High Commissioner. In 1908 he was appointed Director of the London School of Economics, which flourished under his rule. He resigned in 1919, having become Chairman of the National Bank of New Zealand in 1917. He was the author of " State Experiments in Australia and New Zealand," " An Introduction to the History of Communism and Socialism," " The Long White Cloud : A History of New Zealand," as well as pamphlets on Near Eastern questions, and a volume of New Zealand verse. As Chairman of the Anglo-Hellenic League, he received a Greek decoration. He was survived by his daughter, Mrs. Blanco White, a novelist of note (under the name of Amber Reeves).

22. **Lady Augusta Gregory,** aged 73, was not only herself a playwright and poet of distinction, but by her foundation and control (with W. B. Yeats) of the Irish Players and the Abbey Theatre, Dublin, did much to foster a drama unique in the history of the English-speaking peoples. The daughter of Dudley Persse, in her childhood she learned to love the Irish people and their history and language, going about among her father's tenants in Roxborough, Co. Galway, and collecting folk-tales and legends with some idea that they should be acted by the peasants and their children. Her marriage, in 1881, to Sir William Gregory, P.C., F.R.S., a former Governor of Ceylon, gave her the opportunity to take a full share in the Irish renaissance then taking place. She first began to write in prose, then proved herself a talented poet, and finally reverted to prose. Her most distinctive plays were the one-act comedies of modern Irish life, such as " Hyacinth Halvey," " The Workhouse Ward," and " Spreading the News." The best known of her tragedies were " The Gaol Gate " and " The Rising of the Moon." For her plays, both comic and tragic, she used the Anglo-Irish speech of the peasants, to which she gave the name " Kiltartan." She even translated some of Molière's plays into this dialect. Besides folk-plays and tragedies of Irish legend, she wrote a " Book of Saints and Wonders," " Cuchulain of Muirthemne," and " Gods and Fighting Men," and also a description of her home at Coole Park, which she made a gathering place for poets, novelists, and playwrights. Her son, William Robert, a painter of promise, was killed in the war. Her husband, a noted Oriental scholar and art collector, died in 1892.

23. **James Lyle Mackay, Earl of Inchcape,** merchant shipper, was born at Arbroath, September 11, 1852. After a scanty schooling there and at Elgin, while still in his teens he entered the office of a ropemaker and canvas manufacturer at a salary of 5*l.* a year for a twelve-hour day, with annual increases of 5*l.* Obtaining a post with the shipping firm of Mackinnon, Mackenzie & Co., he went out to Calcutta in 1874, and soon made his mark, being taken into partnership and made Calcutta manager of the associated British India Steam Navigation Co. In 1889 he was Chairman of the Bengal Chamber of Commerce, and in 1892-93 also represented that body in the Viceregal Legislature. As President of the Indian Currency Association, he did much to bring about the decision of 1893 to close the Indian mints to free coinage of silver, and to establish the gold standard at 16*d.* ; this service earned him a K.C.I.E. He returned to England to become managing director, and later Chairman, of the British India S.N. Company. In 1897 he was chosen to represent commercial interests on the Council of India. He was appointed Special Commissioner and Plenipotentiary for the negotiation of a commercial treaty with China, signed in 1902, and received a G.C.M.G. He served on numerous official boards of inquiry, and in 1907, with Lord Morley, represented India at the Imperial Conference. In 1911, the year he received his peerage, he was given plenary powers by the Secretary of State to settle disputes between the Indian railway companies and the Railway Board. He had previously gone into banking as a director of the National Provincial Bank of England and of the Royal Bank of Scotland, and later he was a Government-nominated director of the Anglo-Persian Oil Co. and on the Board of the Great Western Railway. In 1920 the P. & O. Banking Corporation was formed under his chairmanship. In 1919 he liquidated the Government's holdings of merchant ships, disposing of vessels of an aggregate total displacement of 1,400,609 tons, which realised 35,000,000*l.*, at a total administrative cost of 850*l.* Similarly, he disposed of German shipping, to the extent of 2,530,016 tons, surrendered under the Treaty of Versailles. He was President of the Chamber of Shipping in 1903, 1918, and 1919, and of the Shipping Federation in 1926. In 1921-22 he was a member of the National Economy (" Geddes axe ") Committee, and in May, 1922, accepted the chairmanship of the Retrenchment Committee appointed by the Government of India, which effected economies to the extent of some 8,000,000*l.* and enabled India to balance her Budget. On his return, he was made G.C.S.I., was advanced to a viscounty in 1924, and to an earldom in 1929. Inchcape married Jane Patterson Shanks in 1883, and had one son, Viscount Glenapp, and four daughters, all of whom survived him, with the exception of the Hon. Elsie Mackay, who was lost in attempting an Atlantic flight in 1928.

27. **Heinrich Herkner,** aged 69, distinguished German economist, was born in Reichenberg, in Bohemia, and educated at the Universities of Vienna, Berlin, and Strasburg. Of a studious disposition Herkner early decided on the academic career ; he was in Freiburg in Breisgau (1889-92), in Karlsruhe (1892-98), in Zürich (1898-1907), and in Berlin, as successor to Schmoller (1912-32). Herkner's main interest was in social questions ; his best-known work, "Die Arbeiterfrage," which first appeared in 1894 as a small book of a couple of hundred pages, grew into two stout volumes, and was translated into several European languages. This has become a standard work on all aspects of the Labour Movement. Herkner was a great believer in Social betterment ; to this theme he devoted learning and research of a high quality. He was a successful teacher ; and for many years he was President of the "Verein für Sozialpolitik." His wife pre-deceased him, and his only son was killed at Cambrai in 1917.

28. **Edward Fordham Spence, K.C.,** noted advocate and dramatic critic, was born October 18, 1860, in Liverpool, and educated at Charterhouse. While still an articled clerk, he cultivated his taste for art and letters, as well as music and chess. He was admitted as a solicitor in 1882, and in 1884 became managing

clerk to the firm of Chapple, Welch & Chapple. He also began to contribute dramatic criticisms to *The Artist* and *Society*. He was called to the Bar by the Middle Temple in 1890 ; from 1890 to 1892 he was dramatic critic for the *Daily Graphic*, and wrote also for the *Pictorial World* and the *Pall Mall Gazette*. He joined the staff of the *Westminster Gazette* in 1892, and shortly afterwards was on the *Sketch* and the *Scotsman*. He was almost alone among his contemporaries in praising the plays of Ibsen. J. A. Spender, editor of the *Westminster Gazette*, described him as " a critic of rare acumen, courage and honesty." He attended almost every important first night performance in London for thirty-three years. As a pleader he appeared for the *Globe* and the *People* in libel actions, and he represented the Grand Trunk and the Grand Trunk Pacific before the Privy Council. He took silk in 1925, and retired three years later. He published his reminiscences under the title of " Bar and Buskin " ; others of his works were " A Freak of Fate," " Our Stage and its Critics," " The Crime of Sybil Cresswell," and " The Pike Fisher." His wife, who was Miss Grace Katherine Caspar, died in 1926.

29. **Dr. Cuthbert Christy,** aged 68, explorer and expert on tropical diseases, was born in 1863, and educated at Scarborough and the University of Edinburgh, where he was Mackenzie bursar in anatomy. From 1892 to 1895 he travelled widely in South America and the West Indies, and from 1898 to 1900 he was senior medical officer of the 2nd battalion West African Field Force, in Northern Nigeria. He was appointed special medical officer for plague duty in Bombay, and worked in the plague laboratory there. In 1902 he went to Africa as a member of the first Sleeping Sickness Commission sent out by the British Government, and later joined the sleeping sickness expeditions organised by the Liverpool School of Tropical Medicine and the Sudan Government. After seven years of extensive travel, he led expeditions in the Congo for the Belgian Government (1911-14), devoting his researches mainly to sleeping sickness ; in 1915-16 he explored the Nile-Congo divide with the same objective ; he also collected rare, and in some cases discovered new, kinds of animals and fishes. He was appointed Adviser for Malaria to the East African Expeditionary Force in 1916, and had charge of the military hospital at Dar-es-Salaam and later in Mesopotamia. From 1920 to 1923 he explored the Bahr-el-Ghazal, and from 1925 to 1928 the Tanganyika lakes and Nyassa for the Natural History Museum. In 1919 he was awarded the Gill Memorial by the Royal Geographical Society. He was appointed chairman of the International Commission established by the League of Nations to inquire into the existence of slavery in Liberia. Both the Council of the League and the Liberian Government accepted the recommendations of the Commission, while the publication of its report in 1931 shocked the civilised world by its exposure of conditions in the negro republic. Christy's death in the Belgian Congo followed upon his being attacked and gored by a wounded buffalo. His publications included " The Birds of San Domingo," " Mosquitoes and Malaria," " The African Rubber Industry," and " Big Game and Pygmies."

JUNE.

2. **Professor John Walter Gregory,** noted geologist and explorer, was born January 27, 1864, the son of a wool merchant, and educated at Stepney Grammar School. Entering his father's business at the age of 15, he continued in it for eight years until, in 1887, he was appointed an assistant in the Geological Department of the British Museum, where he remained till 1900. He travelled for geological purposes in the Rocky Mountains in 1891, and in East Africa in 1892-93. He organised single-handed an expedition to the Rift valleys, and his work there was the foundation of all subsequent geological exploration in Eastern Africa. He was naturalist to Sir Martin Conway's expedition across Spitzbergen in 1896, and in 1900-1 he was director of the civilian scientific staff of the Antarctic

expedition, while he headed the Lake Eyre expedition of 1901-2. He was Professor of Geology in the University of Melbourne from 1900 to 1904, being for part of that time Director of the Geological Survey of the Mines Department of Victoria. In 1908 he undertook a journey in Cyrenaica to report on its suitability as a Zionist colony. From 1904 to 1929 he was Professor of Geology in the University of Glasgow. He explored Southern Angola in 1912, while his expedition of 1922 to the Alps of Chinese Tibet proved of great scientific value. In January, 1932, Gregory, who was one of the foremost authorities on earthquakes, headed an expedition for the Peruvian Government to explore and study the volcanic and seismic centres of the Andes ; the journey was to include crossing the Andes, continuing along the headwaters of the Amazon, the examination of the geological structure of coast and desert, visiting the Inca ruins, and travelling across Brazil. But Gregory was drowned when his canoe overturned in the rapids of the River Urubamba. He was elected F.R.S. in 1901, and was president of the geological section of the British Association in 1907, and of the geographical section in 1924. He was joint author of the minority report of the Calcutta University Commission of 1917. The best-known of his many scientific works were those on the Great Rift valleys. He had a son, also a geologist, and a daughter.

3. **Harriette Emily Colenso,** aged 85, was known for her unremitting efforts on behalf of the Zulus. Born in 1847, the eldest child of Bishop Colenso, of Natal, she accompanied her father when he went out with his family to Pietermaritzburg to take up his new bishopric. At their mountain home, Bishopstowe, she shared the strenuous labours of the bishop—his strong protests on behalf of Langalibalele and Cetewayo, his varied theological controversies (which brought him excommunication and attempted removal by the Metropolitan), and his exacting diocesan labours. At her father's death in 1883 she continued his work for redressing the wrongs of the Zulus ; after the Natal Rebellion of 1906, when their Paramount Chief, Dinzulu, was put on trial for high treason, she procured distinguished counsel for his defence ; she was equally active on behalf of the rebel Cakijana. Although her efforts were regarded by South Africans generally as misguided and fanatical, she enjoyed the highest respect of the colony, which finally accepted her standards for the treatment of the native races.

14. **Arthur Lawley, sixth Lord Wenlock,** distinguished colonial administrator, was born November 12, 1860, and educated at Eton and Trinity College, Cambridge. After serving with the 10th Hussars at Suakin in 1884, he retired from the Army, and in 1896 was appointed Secretary to the Administration of Southern Rhodesia. Two years later he was made Administrator of Matabeleland, and then Acting Administrator of Mashonaland. By 1901 he had acquired a reputation for efficient administration, and he was appointed Governor of Western Australia and made K.C.M.G. A year later Lord Milner asked him to return to South Africa as Lieutenant-Governor of the Transvaal ; there he had to grapple with the complicated problems arising from the Boer War—questions of reparation and compensation, agricultural settlement, the restarting of the mining industry, and the movement for representative institutions. In 1906 he was appointed Governor of Madras, where it fell to him to initiate the Morley-Minto reforms. He was already known as an accomplished speaker, and his candour, tact, and sincerity stood him in good stead as President and leader of the Legislature, through which he carried the important Land Estates Act. On leaving India, in 1911, he entered the City, and became a director of several important companies. Before the Great War he was active in Lord Roberts' campaign for national training, and after the outbreak of hostilities he went to France and later to the East as Commissioner of the British Red Cross Society. As chairman of the Child Emigration Society he devoted himself almost single-handed to the maintaining and development of the work for the Fairbridge Farm Schools, where children from the slums were trained for agricultural life in Australia ; the

progress of the scheme was largely due to Lawley's efforts. He was created
G.C.I.E. in 1906 and G.C.S.I. in 1911 ; he succeeded to his brother's peerage in
1931. His wife and two daughters survived him.

15. **Sir Donald Maclean, M.P.**, aged 68, a leader of the Liberal Party and
President of the Board of Education in the " National " Government of 1931-32,
was born in 1864, the eldest son of John Maclean, of Kilmoluag, Tiree. Admitted
a solicitor in 1887, he practised in London and Cardiff, and was a member of the
Faculty of Procurators in Glasgow. He won a remarkable parliamentary victory
at Bath in 1906, following an unsuccessful attempt on the seat in 1900, and
quickly made his mark in the House of Commons, where, after serving in the
Whips' office, he was appointed Deputy Chairman of Ways and Means. He
was defeated at Bath in January, 1910, but secured a seat for Peebles and Selkirk
in the following December. In 1916 he was sworn of the Privy Council, and was
made chairman of the Treasury Committee on Enemy Debts, and of the London
Military Appeal Tribunal. In 1917 he was chairman of the Reconstruction
Committee on the Poor Law, and received a K.B.E. He became something of
a national figure when, after the " coupon " election of 1918 and Asquith's defeat,
he assumed the leadership of the 28 Independent Liberals. In 1924 he was
appointed chairman of the Committee on the Registration of Dock Labour, and
in 1926 of the Inter-Departmental Committee on the Effect of Social Insurance
on Migration. He lost his seat in 1922, and remained out of Parliament until
May, 1929, when he was returned for North Cornwall. In the first " National "
Government of 1931 he took office as President of the Board of Education, and
after the General Election of that year he retained that post, being given a seat
in the Cabinet. He was president of the National Liberal Federation from 1922
to 1925, and was one of the founders of the National Society for Prevention of
Cruelty to Children. His wife, with four sons and one daughter, survived him.

26. **Sir Gilbert Garnsey,** chartered accountant, was born March 21, 1883,
and educated at Wellington School. After being first in honours in the final
examination of the Institute of Chartered Accountants, in 1905 he joined the
firm of Price, Waterhouse & Co. as a clerk, becoming a partner in 1913. He
took a leading part in the reorganisation of the finances of many important
companies, such as Marconi's Wireless Telegraph and Spillers. During the Great
War he served without salary in the Finance Department of the Ministry of
Munitions in 1916, became Director of Internal Audits in 1917, and Controller
of Munition Accounts, and then chairman of the Finance Committee and Finance
Member of the Munitions Council in 1918. Among his many subsequent public
appointments, he was chairman of the Finance Committee of the Ministry of
Health in connexion with the Government Housing Scheme in 1919, and vice-
chairman of the Committee on Army Expenditure, 1922, a member of the
Treasury Committee on the accounting methods of public government depart-
ments, of the Board of Trade Committee on the Assurance Companies Acts, and
of the Court of Inquiry into the remuneration of doctors under the National
Health Insurance Acts, 1924. In 1930 he was chairman of the Marketing and
Distributing Consumable Commodities Committee of the Economic Advisory
Council, and of the British Industries Fairs Sites and Buildings Committee in
1931. He investigated the complicated affairs of the Hatry group and the
Royal Mail Steam Packet Co. He was created K.B.E. in 1918. His wife, son
and daughter survived him.

27. **(John) Arthur Godley, Lord Kilbracken,** a distinguished civil servant,
was born in London, June 17, 1847, the only son of John Robert Godley, at one
time Assistant Under-Secretary for War. When only two years old he accompanied his parents to New Zealand, where his father was one of the founders of
the Canterbury Settlement. Educated at Radley and Rugby—of which he was
later chairman of Governors—he proceeded to Oxford in 1866 as an exhibitioner

of Balliol College. After a singularly successful academic career, which included the winning of the Hertford and Ireland Scholarships, he began to read for the Bar, but in 1872 Gladstone chose him as his private secretary. On the defeat of his chief in the General Election of 1874, he was elected a Fellow of Hertford College, Oxford, won the Eldon Law Scholarship, and was called to the Bar by Lincoln's Inn in 1876. He became private secretary to Lord Granville in 1875, but returned to work for Gladstone when the latter became Prime Minister for the second time in 1880. Two years later, believing that Gladstone's final retirement was imminent, he reluctantly accepted an appointment as a Commissioner of Inland Revenue. In 1883 Godley was chosen in the face of some criticism to be Permanent Under-Secretary for India, a post he filled with distinction until 1909. He served under, and enjoyed the confidence of, seven Secretaries of State, while he exercised influence in the general sphere of politics outside, as well as within, his own department. He was intimate with most of the political leaders of his day, which facilitated his rôle—as described by himself—of defender, go-between, and interpreter of the Indian Government with successive Secretaries of State and with Parliament. He was a power at the India Office, of which he greatly improved the quality of the personnel. He was a member of the sub-Committee formed to advise the Government on the famous Curzon-Kitchener controversy, and he played his part in shaping the Morley-Minto reforms. He was made a C.B. in 1882, K.C.B. in 1893, and G.C.B. in 1908, and was raised to the peerage on his retirement in 1909. He was a member of the Royal Commission on Indian Finance and Currency in 1913, and became a Trustee of the British Museum. He was a finished classical scholar, and published privately, in 1924, a small volume of translations into Greek and Latin verse ; while still in the Civil Service, he had been approached to write Gladstone's biography. His wife, a daughter of the first Lord Northbourne, died in 1921 ; their son, Hugh John Godley, K.C., third Parliamentary Counsel to the Treasury, and two daughters, survived him.

29. **William Humble Ward, (second) Earl of Dudley,** a former Lord-Lieutenant of Ireland and Governor-General of Australia, was born May 25, 1867, son of the first Earl and a daughter of Sir Thomas Moncrieffe, Bt. After being educated at Eton, he made a three-years' world tour ; he succeeded to the earldom in 1885 and in 1891 married Miss Rachael Gurney. Largely through his wife's influence he gave up the pursuits of a country gentleman and entered public life ; he became a good and frequent speaker in the House of Lords, and was Mayor of Dudley in 1895 and 1896. Lord Salisbury made him Parliamentary Secretary to the Board of Trade. He went out to South Africa with the Worcestershire Yeomanry and served during the campaign on Lord Roberts' staff as Assistant Adjutant-General of the Imperial Yeomanry. In 1902 he was appointed Lord-Lieutenant of Ireland ; while the Viceroy and Vicereine entertained magnificently at Dublin Castle, they also took a small house in Connemara and made friends with the peasantry of the district ; Lady Dudley instituted district nurses in the poorest parts of the country. Dudley supported the policy of "devolution" of the then Chief Secretary, George Wyndham, and his political career in Ireland was by no means smooth. His period of office terminated at the fall of the Conservative Ministry in 1905. He was chairman of the Royal Commission on Congestion in Ireland from 1906 to 1908. He was appointed Governor-General of Australia in 1908 and represented the Crown there until 1911. He commanded the Worcestershire Yeomanry in Egypt and Gallipoli in 1915, and was Commandant at East Mudros. He owned about 30,000 acres rich in coal and minerals, as well as estates in Jamaica. He was made G.C.V.O., 1903, G.C.M.G., 1908, and G.C.B., 1911. The first countess died in 1920 ; his second wife, with four sons and two daughters by the first Lady Dudley, survived him.

JULY.

2. Dom Manoel de Bragança, formerly King of Portugal, was born November 15, 1889. Bearing the title of the Duke of Beja the young prince was trained for the navy, though his tastes were literary and musical. He succeeded to the throne at the age of 19, on February 3, 1908, after seeing his father, King Dom Carlos and his elder brother, the Duke of Bragança, shot before his eyes. Saddled with a legacy of unpopularity, his youth and inexperience of statecraft made him little fitted to cope with the prevalent political conditions and the general hostility to the monarchy. In 1909 he escaped for a time from the distasteful atmosphere of Lisbon by paying a state visit to England, where he celebrated his twentieth birthday and was invested with the Order of the Garter. Less than a year later local rioting by Republicans in Lisbon developed into open revolution ; the King was advised to withdraw to the Northern Provinces, but on his way thither fell into the hands of the insurgents, who put him on board the royal yacht and deported him to Gibraltar. After a reign of only thirty-two months, he settled down in exile at Twickenham, where he spent the rest of his life. He achieved a reputation as a musician, historian and bibliophile, and a patron of athletics and the arts. He became the leading private collector of works of the Portuguese Renaissance and one of the foremost bibliographers of the publications of the Peninsula. In 1929 and 1932 the first two volumes of the catalogue of his collection of incunabula and other Portuguese sixteenth-century works appeared under his own editorship. He was a member of the council of the British Academy. The thirty-fifth of his line, he married in 1913 Princess Augusta Victoria of Hohenzollern, who survived him.

6. Kenneth Grahame, aged 73, formerly secretary of the Bank of England (1898-1908), was better known as the author of books on child-life. Born in Edinburgh in 1859, the son of an advocate, he was educated at St. Edward's School, Oxford, and entered the Bank of England in 1878. His first published work appeared in 1890, a short satirical tale called " The Headswoman " ; this was followed in 1893 by " Pagan Papers," a little book of essays of considerable merit and charm, reprinted from W. E. Henley's *National Observer.* Two years later " The Golden Age " was published, eighteen sketches which quickly won acceptance as a classic, and which appeared in a list of the five best books about children in the Lewis Carroll exhibition of 1932. It was followed in 1898 by " Dream Days," dealing with the same characters ; both were written when Grahame was still a bachelor and engaged in routine work in the City. While these two books were rather studies of childhood for adult consumption, his " The Wind in the Willows " (1908), describing the adventures of the denizens of a stream, was definitely a book for children ; it was dramatised by A. A. Milne in 1930 under the title of " Toad of Toad Hall," and enjoyed considerable success. Grahame married Miss Elspeth Thomson in 1899 ; their only child died while still a young man at Oxford.

12. Professor Gerard Baldwin Brown, an authority on the history of art, was born in London, October 31, 1849, and educated at Uppingham and Oriel College, Oxford, of which he was a scholar and later an honorary Fellow. In 1874 he won the Chancellor's prize with an essay on " The Short Periods during which Art has remained at its Zenith in Different Countries," and was elected a Fellow of Brasenose College. After leaving Oxford he studied painting in London, and in 1880, at the age of 31, he was appointed first Watson-Gordon Professor of Fine Art in the University of Edinburgh, a Chair which he occupied for fifty years until his retirement in 1930, when he was made Emeritus-Professor.

His special subject, which was also the title of his *magnum opus*, published in six volumes between 1903 and 1930, was the Arts in Early England. Though considered by some critics to stress unduly the Teutonic contribution to our civilisation, this monumental work is still the standard authority on such subjects as East Anglian remains, Saxon churches and Northumbrian crosses. When nearly eighty he visited the caves of France and Spain to collect material for his Munro Lectures, afterwards published as " The Art of the Cave-Dweller." His archæological publications included " From Schola to Cathedral," " The Care of Ancient Monuments," and " Anglo-Saxon Architecture," while his other writings included " William Hogarth," " Rembrandt," and " The Glasgow School of Painters." He was a Fellow of the British Academy and an honorary LL.D. and D.Litt. of Edinburgh. He was married, but left no children.

16. **Herbert Charles Onslow, first Viscount Plumer,** distinguished soldier and colonial administrator, was born on March 13, 1857, at Torquay, of an old Yorkshire family. Educated at Eton and Sandhurst, he was gazetted to the York and Lancaster Regiment in 1876, soon became adjutant of his battalion, and was promoted captain in 1882. After seeing service in the Sudan campaign of 1884, he spent two years at the Staff College at Camberley. From 1890 to 1893 he was Deputy Assistant Adjutant-General in Jersey, and then going to South Africa with the rank of major, raised and commanded a corps of mounted rifles during the Matabele and Mashona rising of 1896. Returning to England with the brevet of lieutenant-colonel in 1897, he was appointed garrison instructor at Aldershot. Proceeding to the Cape at the outbreak of war in 1899, he was given command of the Rhodesian Frontier Force, attempted to relieve Mafeking, and generally distinguished himself in the various engagements of the South African campaign. For his services he was appointed A.D.C. to the King, received the C.B., and was promoted major-general at the early age of forty-five. In 1904 he was made quartermaster-general, and thus became the third military member of the newly-formed Army Council. Resigning in 1905, owing to differences with the Secretary for War, he was sent to Ireland to command the 7th and 5th Divisions. In 1906 he was created K.C.B., and in 1908 was promoted lieutenant-general. Plumer was appointed General Officer Commanding-in-Chief, Northern Command, in 1911, and was holding this post at the outbreak of the Great War. He went out to France on January 1, 1915, to command the newly constituted Fifth Corps, and held the southern end of the Ypres Salient during the German offensive of the second battle of Ypres. Given the command of the Second Army he was largely responsible for the British success at Messines in June, 1917, and also played a redoubtable part in the three-and-a-half months' Flanders offensive, which culminated in the capture of Passchendaele. In November, 1917, he was sent to Italy, after the disaster at Caporetto, in command of the four British divisions. Recalled to France in March, 1918, Plumer with his Second Army again took over the defence of the Ypres front, and took part in the final advance, forcing the German evacuation of Lille, and reaching the Scheldt just before the conclusion of hostilities. After the Armistice he went to Germany in command of the British Army of Occupation, and remained there until April, 1919. On his return to England he received the thanks of Parliament, a grant of 30,000*l.*, and a barony ; he had previously been decorated with the G.C.M.G., G.C.V.O., and G.C.B. He was promoted Field-Marshal in July, 1919. From 1919 to 1924 he was Governor and Commander-in-Chief of Malta ; he inaugurated and successfully put into force the Island's new Constitution of 1920, abrogated many social barriers, and did much for education. He was appointed High Commissioner and Commander-in-Chief in Palestine in May, 1925, and before the end of his term in July, 1928, showed much tact and skill in reconciling Jews and Arabs. He was made a G.B.E. in 1924, and a viscount in 1929, in which year he was president of the M.C.C. His widow, with three daughters and one son, survived him.

18. Jean Adrien Antoine Jules Jusserand, diplomat and man of letters, was born at Lyons on February 18, 1855, and educated there and in Paris. At the age of 21 he entered the French Consular service, gathering experience in many responsible posts both in Paris and in different parts of the world. In 1898 he was accredited Minister to Denmark, where he remained for four years. From 1903 until 1925 he was Ambassador at Washington, being retained in that post by numerous French Ministries and under succeeding American Presidents. His contributions to scholarship were several and noteworthy, both in English and French. His best-known work was perhaps that translated into English as " English Wayfaring in the Middle Ages." Shakespeare also interested him ; among his most important studies being " Le Roman au temps de Shakespeare " and " Shakespeare in France." He wrote also " English Essays from a French Pen," and another volume of essays, " The School for Ambassadors." On post-Renaissance English literature he wrote a " Literary History of the English People " and " Le Roman Anglais : Origine et Formation des Grandes Ecoles de Romanciers du XVIIIᵉ Siècle." He was also well read and deeply interested in the literature of his own country, and while still a young man founded the well-known series " Les Grands Ecrivains Français," to which he contributed the volume on Ronsard and also edited Scarron. He was honoured by many universities and learned societies, French, American and British, and held the Grand Cross of the Legion of Honour.

20. René François Nicolas Marie Bazin, French novelist, was born December 26, 1853, at Angers. There he attended the Lycée, studied law at the seminary of Mongazon, and took his doctorate of laws at the Catholic University of Angers, subsequently becoming Professor of Criminal Law there. During the holidays he wrote his first stories, " Stéphanette," " Ma tante Giron," and " Une Tache d'Encre," all published between his thirty-first and thirty-third year. Through the good offices of Ludovic Halévy, who also brought Bazin in touch with the *Journal des Débats* and the *Revue des Deux Mondes*, " Une Tache d'Encre " was " crowned " by the Academy, as was also his " Sicile," published in 1893. Between 1890 and 1900 he wrote a series of novels and sketches of travel, including " La Sarcelle Bleu," " Madame Corentine," and " La Terre qui Meurt." But it was not till 1901 that he really established his reputation as a novelist of the first rank with " Les Oberlé," an intimate study of the Alsace of the German occupation. In similar vein, and equally successful, was his " Roi des Archers," depicting life in the textile districts of French Flanders. In 1929 he was fêted by the Académie Française in celebration of the twenty-fifth anniversary of his election.

23. Alberto Santos-Dumont, aged 59, pioneer of aviation and aeronautical inventor, was born on a coffee plantation at Sao Paulo, Brazil, in 1873. He first became interested in balloons in 1892 during a visit to Paris, and proved by severe tests that Japanese silk, bamboo and piano wires could safely bear the weights he intended to put upon them. After five attempts with five different models he won the prize offered for the first airship flight from St. Cloud, round the Eiffel Tower and back within thirty minutes. He then built his first cylindrical balloon from which hung a basket containing the 3½ h.p. engine, weighing 66 lb., and the propeller. By 1900 he had constructed a balloon with a capacity of 15,000 cubic feet and a 7 h.p. engine, and with it had won the Paris Aero Club's prize. In 1901 a still bigger airship covered the prize course of about 11 kilometres in 40 minutes ; but a month later it came to grief on the roof of the Trocadéro, leaving Santos-Dumont hanging high above the courtyard until rescued. The same year his next airship, built in twenty-two days, with a capacity of 22,000 cubic feet and a 12 h.p. engine made the flight round the Eiffel Tower in a wind of about thirteen miles an hour, an event which created world-wide interest. In the next two years he built three more airships, in one of which he sailed up the Avenue de Bois de Boulogne, and alighted at his own front door. Turning his attention to aeroplanes, after a series of experiments, he made a flight of 17 kilometres in fifteen minutes in a tiny monoplane with a span of only 18 feet and an engine of 30 h.p. But his real contribution to aviation was his proof of the practical possibilities of the airship.

28. **Sir William Willcocks,** aged 80, famous engineer, was born in India in 1852. After passing out of the Thomason Civil Engineering College, Roorkee, with distinction, he served eleven years and made his mark in the Irrigation Department of what are now the United Provinces. At the age of 31 he left India for service in Egypt, and was soon made Inspector of Irrigation of the Central Provinces of the Delta. While Director-General of Reservoirs he drew up the designs and estimates for the famed Assuan Dam and the Assiut Barrage, works which on their completion had a capacity of 594,000 million gallons and which enormously increased the fertility of Lower Egypt. Willcocks also carried out experiments which led to the abolition of the *corvée* and made a survey of the rental value of all land in Egypt. For his services in connexion with the dam he received a C.M.G. He was sent to Africa in 1901 to report on the possibilities of irrigating 3,000,000 acres in the Cape, the Orange Free State and the Transvaal ; for his work on this mission he was made a K.C.M.G. Retiring from the Egyptian service in 1911 he became head of the Turkish Irrigation Department and drew up an elaborate report on irrigation in Mesopotamia, as a result of which the Hindiya Barrage on the Euphrates was constructed. After conducting an evangelising mission in Egypt he returned to India in 1926, and at the age of 74 submitted a scheme for the modernisation of the irrigation system of Bengal at an estimated cost of 12,000,000*l*. His technical works included " Egyptian Irrigation," in two volumes, " The Irrigation of Mesopotamia," and " From the Garden of Eden to the Crossing of the Jordan," the last named being a statement of his scheme for the revival by irrigation of the ancient fertility of Chaldea. He was married, but without children.

AUGUST.

2. **Mgr. Ignaz Seipel,** Catholic prelate and Austrian statesman, was born in Vienna on July 19, 1876, and ordained in 1899. After occupying for nearly ten years the Chair of Moral Theology at the University of Salzburg, he became professor of the same subject at Vienna in 1917. The same year his book on the Austrian constitution caused the Christian Socialist Party to make him their adviser on constitutional questions. Towards the close of the year 1918 he accepted the portfolio of Social Welfare in the newly formed Lammasch Cabinet, and thus became a member of the Ministry which counselled the abdication of the Emperor Charles. The revolution at first placed Austria in the hands of a Social Democratic Government, and Seipel soon came to the fore as the leader of the Christian Socialists of the Conservative and Church parties of the Opposition. When his party came into power, Seipel at first refused to take office but remained the guiding hand behind the Governments of Mayr and Schober. But in the summer of 1922, with the crown steadily falling, after Schober had failed to form a Ministry, Seipel agreed to take the Chancellorship. In August his final appeal to the Allies for more credit was refused and Austria's case was referred to the League of Nations. On June 1, 1924, Seipel was shot at and dangerously wounded. He made a partial recovery, but the appearance of a second economic crisis and a threatened strike of railwaymen led to his sudden resignation in November, 1924. He was Chancellor again from 1927 till his resignation in 1929, after the Vienna riots. In 1930 he was Foreign Secretary in the Vaugoin-Starhemberg Government ; he represented his country several times at Geneva and remained to the end the political adviser of the Christian Socialist Party.

3. Goldsworthy Lowes Dickinson, scholar and writer, especially on philosophical subjects, was born on August 6, 1862, the son of a portrait painter, and educated at Charterhouse and King's College, Cambridge. After appearing in the first class of the classical tripos of 1884, he was elected a Fellow of King's in 1887, and was librarian of the college from 1893 to 1896, when he was appointed a lecturer in history. He then devoted himself to his teaching and still more to a kind of Socratic inquiry. His philosophical and other works of the next two decades included " The Meaning of Good," the " Letters of John Chinaman " (a criticism of the crudeness of Western civilisation), " The Greek View of Life," " A Modern Symposium," " Religion and Immortality," and " Religion : a Criticism and a Forecast." In " Appearances," written in 1914, after a year of travel in America and the East, he stated his conclusion that the hope of the world lay in the development of souls. His later books were of a political nature —" Revolution and Reaction in Modern France " and " Justice and Liberty " being written shortly before the war. In 1916 he published his first big book on the causes of the war—" The European Anarchy " ; it was followed by " War : Its Nature, Cause and Cure," and " The International Anarchy, 1904-14." He did much for the cause of international peace and wrote profusely and often in support of the League of Nations. In 1923, with Miss Stawell, he published a commentary on Goethe's " Faust," held to be the best work on the subject in the English language, and in 1930 he produced a dialogue entitled " After Two Thousand Years," being a discussion between Plato and a modern young man. He was an accomplished musician and a poet of talent ; his love of Mozart inspired his allegorical fantasia, " The Magic Flute." His last work of importance was the life of McTaggart, written in collaboration with mutual friends.

9. Graham Wallas, aged 74, Emeritus-Professor of Political Science at London University, was born in Sunderland in 1858. Educated at Shrewsbury School and Corpus Christi College, Oxford, he first took to teaching (1881) and then to University Extension lecturing (1890). In 1886 he had joined the Fabian Society and was one of the contributors to " Fabian Essays " (1889). Wallas was keenly interested in education ; he was a member of the old London School Board from 1894 to 1904, and chairman of the School Management Committee from 1897 to 1904, when he became a member of the London County Council in the interest of the " Progressive " Party. In 1897 he brought out a biography of Francis Place, the Radical Reformer, and in 1908 produced his first important study, " Human Nature in Politics." From 1895 till his retirement in 1923 he was associated with the London School of Economics, first as lecturer (1895-1914) and then as University Professor of Political Science (1914-23). He acted as deputy for the Gladstone Professor of Political Science at Oxford in 1931, and received the honorary degree of D.Litt. His " Great Society " (1914) was a psychological analysis of the general social organisation of the modern State, and he also published " Our Social Heritage " (1921) and " The Art of Thought " (1926). He married Ada Rockford, author of " Before the Bluestockings," and their daughter survived him.

19. Edward Schröder Prior, A.R.A., Slade Professor of Fine Art at Cambridge, was born on June 4, 1852, and educated at Caius College, Cambridge. After leaving the University, where he was a noted athlete, he became a pupil of Norman Shaw, the architect. Prior's activities in the field of architecture were mainly divided between domestic work and the designing of buildings for schools and universities ; examples of the latter are Mount Lodge and the Music School at Harrow and the Medical School at Cambridge, and of the former, The Barn, Exmouth, and the house called Kelling Place, near Holt, Norfolk. Appointed in 1912 Slade Professor of Fine Art at Cambridge, he made his Chair, in itself something of a sinecure, the means of founding a school of architectural studies at the University, and succeeded in making architecture a recognised course of study with a school under his direction and a degree course. He was one of the founders of the Art Workers' Guild, and from 1902 to 1917 was secretary of the Arts and Crafts Exhibition Society. By his writings and lectures he helped the understanding of the mediæval art of this country ; his " History of Gothic Architecture in England " (1900) gave a continuous survey from the Norman period to the late fifteenth century, while " The Mediæval Figure Sculpture of England " (1912), written in collaboration with Arthur Gardner, was the first complete and authoritative work on the subject. His architectural style was simple to the point of severity. Two daughters survived him.

19. **Dr. Johann Schober,** twice Chancellor of Austria, was born on November 14, 1874, at Berg, in Upper Austria. After a short period in the service of the City of Vienna, he found employment in the Government police, and later was entrusted with important work in the Ministry of the Interior. In 1914 he was made head of the State Police Department, and the Emperor Charles appointed him Police President of the capital, a post which he retained after the revolution which converted the Empire into a Republic. In June, 1921, at the request of the Central Committee of Parliament, then the governing power in Austria, Schober accepted the Chancellorship, though with reluctance ; after eleven months of office he resigned and returned to his former post. During the following years he reorganised the police force from top to bottom, and his reforms attracting considerable attention abroad he was made head of the international police commission, which took permanent headquarters in Vienna. While he was head of the police force there occurred the July riots of 1927 in which some ninety lives were lost, and this did not enhance his popularity. Nevertheless, two years later, with the menace of the Fascist Home Guards upon the country, Schober was felt to be the man to save the constitutional regime. He again accepted office as Chancellor, and taking a middle course amended the Constitution. His greatest political *coup* was the cancellation of reparation payments and the loan of 1930, both of which he secured for Austria at The Hague Conference. But he remained in office for only a year. In December, 1930, he became Vice-Chancellor and Foreign Minister in the Ender Cabinet, and in that capacity attempted unsuccessfully to effect a Customs Union with Germany. He was married but childless.

20. **Henry George Watkins,** noted Arctic explorer, was born on January 29, 1907, and educated at Lancing and Trinity, Cambridge. There he soon showed a keen interest in natural science and remarkable qualities of leadership, so that in 1927, though only 21, he was chosen to head the University expedition to Edge Island, Spitzbergen. The following year he carried out the more ambitious task of exploring and surveying the almost unknown interior of Labrador. The success of this enterprise led to the forming of the Arctic Air Route Expedition of 1930, and the choice of Watkins as leader ; its object was to explore the Arctic ice-cap of Greenland with a view to the establishment of an all-British air route across the Arctic to Canada, by way of the Faroes, Iceland, Greenland, and Baffin Land, and in this the expedition was mainly successful. On his return to England Watkins lectured before the Royal Geographical Society, and received its Founder's Medal, being probably the youngest recipient of that award. He considered the possibilities of a journey across the Antarctic continent, but was compelled to abandon the project for lack of financial support. In July, 1932, he went to Greenland again to continue his survey for an air route ; he met his death by drowning when his canoe overturned some distance from land, and he attempted to swim ashore in the Arctic waters.

SEPTEMBER.

4. Sir Charles John Stewart, the first holder of the office of Public Trustee, was born at Rock Hill, Co. Donegal, on June 28, 1851, and educated at Harrow. His career was to be something of a *mélange* of lawyer, business man and public servant, and he began by entering the office of Deloitte, Plender, Griffiths & Co., the accountants. He was then called to the Bar by the Inner Temple ; in 1884 he was appointed an Assistant Official Receiver in Bankruptcy, being promoted to be Senior Official Receiver (1890) and entrusted with the setting up of the new Department of the Companies in Winding Up. Seven years later he was appointed Clerk of the London County Council ; he played a leading part in the organisation of the City Imperial Volunteers. In 1900 he became chairman of S. Allsopp & Sons. After twenty-one years of discussion and preparation, in 1906 an Act was passed empowering the State to offer its services as an executor and trustee under wills, or as a trustee under settlements, and the office of Public Trustee was created ; it was to charge in fees only sufficient to pay its way, and Stewart was chosen for the post. Starting in 1907 with five assistants, his staff eventually expanded into a Department of 800. The war brought him many extra responsibilities, including much work in connexion with the Trading with the Enemy Acts and the chairmanship of the United Workers. He was made a K.B.E. in 1918 and resigned the Public Trusteeship in 1919. He left three daughters.

6. Sir Gilbert Parker, novelist and politician, was born in Canada on November 23, 1862, and was educated at Trinity College, Toronto. After studying for Holy Orders and even being admitted a deacon, he changed his mind and accepted a lectureship in English literature at Trinity College, Toronto. Taking up journalism, in 1886 he became associate-editor of the *Sydney Morning Herald.* After travelling widely, the outcome of his journeyings was his first book, " Round the Compass in Australia," soon followed by a novel, " Pierre and his People," both published in 1892 ; thereafter he was set upon the paths of fiction, and for some time turned out two novels a year. His first noteworthy success was " When Valmond came to Pontiac," an historical romance appearing in 1895. His best-known book, " The Seats of the Mighty," a story of old Quebec, was published in 1896, and dramatised the following year for the opening of Her Majesty's Theatre by Herbert Tree. Two other popular stories, " The Pomp of the Lavillettes " and " The Battle of the Strong " followed in 1897 and 1898. Turning his attention to politics, he was returned to Parliament as Unionist member for Gravesend, a seat which he held from his election in 1900 until 1918. He received a knighthood in 1902. In 1903 he originated and organised the first Imperial Universities Conference in London, while for nine years he was chairman of the Imperial South African Association. He was founder and chairman of the Small Ownership Committee, and in 1909 published a pamphlet, " The Land for the People : Small Ownership and Land Banks," with a preface by A. J. Balfour. Between 1900 and 1914 Parker wrote eight more books with various settings, while for the first two and a half years of the war he was in charge of American publicity, and issued in 1915 " The World in the Crucible," an explanation of " the origins and conduct of the Great War." In the same year he was made a baronet, and in 1916 he was sworn of the Privy Council. Between 1915 and 1919 he wrote three more novels on Canadian themes, while his last books included " No Defence " and " The Promised Land." While the plots of his stories were laid in many different countries, it was as an interpreter of Canada and her history that he was most successful. His wife predeceased him ; they had no children.

14. Sir Charters James Symonds, a great teacher, and one of the earliest practitioners of abdominal surgery, was born at Dalhousie, New Brunswick, on July 24, 1852, a descendant of some of the first settlers of Massachusetts. Coming to London when he was 17, he began to study medicine at Guy's Hospital. He won distinctions both at Guy's and at the University of London, and though his inclination originally was towards medicine, in 1879 he was appointed Surgical Registrar, and in 1882 assistant surgeon to Guy's, and surgeon in 1902. With the introduction of anæsthetics and the development of the use of antiseptics, Symonds took the opportunity of doing pioneer work, especially in the surgery of the abdomen and the ear, nose, and throat ; he was one of the first, if not the first, successfully to remove the appendix. During his period as assistant surgeon he had charge of the throat department, and from 1882 to 1888 he was surgeon to the Evelina Hospital for Children. He was especially respected for his patience and kindliness as a teacher, and for his power of arousing the enthusiasm of his pupils. He was in turn president of the Hunterian Society, the Laryngological Society, the Medical Society of London, and the clinical section of the Royal Society of Medicine. He was a member of the Council of the Royal College of Surgeons from 1907 to 1923, and vice-president in 1916. On his retirement from the active staff of Guy's in 1912 he was appointed consulting surgeon, and continued with his large private practice. During the war he served in England, Malta, and Salonika, and was consulting surgeon also at Netley and to the Southern Command ; he was invalided home from the Near East with dysentery. For his war services he was mentioned in despatches, and created C.B. and K.B.E. Two sons survived him.

16. **Sir Ronald Ross,** the pioneer of the conquest of malaria, was born on May 13, 1857, at Almora, India, where his father held a high command in the Indian Army. After attending a private school, he studied medicine at St. Bartholomew's Hospital, and soon after qualifying, entered the Indian Medical Service in 1881. He became deeply interested in malaria, which the prevailing theory of the time attributed to a kind of miasma from marshes. After a visit to England and consultation with Sir Patrick Manson, Ross returned to India to pursue a new line of investigation. His first great discovery was that a particular species of mosquito absorbed malaria germs when it sucked the blood of patients, and these germs went through definite and hitherto unknown stages in their life history within the body of the insect. After further protracted research, he showed precisely how the mosquito acted as the carrier, and what changes in the germ took place in the insect. But his remarkable scientific success was followed by a long period of scepticism and official delay. In 1899, when the scientific side of his discoveries had been completed and acknowledged, Ross left the Indian Medical Service, and after a journey to West Africa, arranged by the Liverpool School of Tropical Medicine, in the course of which he identified the malaria parasite in malaria patients and mosquitoes, became Professor of Tropical Medicine in the University of Liverpool, from which he retired in 1917. In 1900 the Liverpool School issued its first memoir, " Instructions for the Prevention of Malarial Fever, for the use of residents in malarious places," largely the work of Ross himself, which went through many editions. In 1901 he went to the United States to lecture on malarial fever and mosquitoes, the first of a number of similar visits to malarious districts in many parts of the world in which he advised and reported on the control of malaria. In 1901 he was elected a Fellow of the Royal Society, receiving later the Royal Medal, and in 1902 he was Nobel laureate and prizeman for medicine. Among other distinctions British and foreign, he was made C.B. in 1902, K.C.B. in 1911, and K.C.M.G. in 1918. He founded the Ross Institute and Hospital for Tropical Diseases at Putney Heath, and became its Director-in-Chief after its opening in 1926 ; he also undertook the editorship of *Science Progress.* Ross achieved some success as a poet and writer of romance, his published verse including " Poems," 1928, " Fables and Satires," 1930, " Lyra Modulata," 1931 ; and his prose works, " Spirit of Storm," " Child of the Ocean," and " The Revels of Orsera," besides his " Memoirs," issued in 1923. His scientific work was regarded as of the greatest benefit to humanity. His wife pre-deceased him in 1931 ; he left a son and a daughter.

22. **Admiral John Luce,** who played a leading part in the actions of Coronel and the Falkland Islands, was born on February 4, 1870, at Malmesbury, Wiltshire, and educated at Clifton. He entered the *Britannia* as a cadet in 1883, and after receiving his commission saw service on the Mediterranean, America, and West Indies Stations. He was given several appointments in command of small craft before going to the Admiralty in the Naval Intelligence Department. In 1909 he was promoted Captain, and then appointed Flag-Captain to Rear-Admiral Patey, of the Home Fleet. In 1912 he took command of the *Glasgow* as Senior Naval Officer, South-East Coast of America. At Coronel, on November 1, 1914, after the loss of the flag-ship *Good Hope* and of the *Monmouth* with all hands, Luce became the senior officer and extricated his ship with skill. He again commanded the *Glasgow* at the battle of the Falkland Islands, where Admiral von Spee, the victor of Coronel, met defeat, the *Leipzig* being engaged and sunk by the *Glasgow*. On March 14, 1915, the *Glasgow* sank the *Dresden*, the last survivor of the German Asiatic Squadron, at Juan Fernandez ; for these services Luce received the C.B. On his return home in 1916 he was appointed commodore of the Royal Naval Air Service station at Cranwell. In 1919 he resumed sea service, and was appointed A.D.C. to the King. His last appointment was as Rear-Admiral in Charge and Admiral-Superintendent, Malta, from 1921 to 1924. He was promoted Vice-Admiral in 1925, when he retired; in 1930 he was advanced to Admiral on the retired list. He was joint-author of the Official History of the Russo-Japanese War (Naval Section). He married in 1902, and had four sons.

24. **Rear=Admiral Sir Charles Langdale Ottley,** formerly secretary to the Committee of Imperial Defence, was born on February 8, 1858, at Richmond, Yorkshire, the son of a Canon of Ripon. He entered the Navy in 1871, being appointed to the *Monarch*, in which he was present at the bombardment of Alexandria. After further service afloat, he became Naval Attaché for five years at Washington, Tokio, Rome, St. Petersburg, and Paris. In 1903 he was adopted as parliamentary candidate for Pembroke Boroughs. On the formation of the Committee of Imperial Defence he was appointed an assistant secretary, and in 1905 he became Director of Naval Intelligence. From 1907 to 1912 he was secretary of the Committee of Imperial Defence, and he was the principal British naval delegate to the Peace Conference at The Hague in 1907, when, largely through his efforts, rules were drawn up prohibiting the indiscriminate use of mines. In 1908 Ottley was a naval delegate to the International Maritime Conference which produced the Declaration of London. He did valuable work in transforming the Imperial Defence Committee into the War Council of the Empire. He was created K.C.M.G. in 1907, and C.B. in 1911 ; he had previously received the M.V.O. He was the inventor of the Ottley submarine mine. In 1908 he was promoted Rear-Admiral and automatically retired, since lack of the necessary " sea time " disqualified him for further promotion. He then became a director of Armstrong, Whitworth & Co., of Newcastle-on-Tyne, the armament manufacturers, superintending the firm's war output. Sir Charles married in 1902 a daughter of Colonel Alexander Stewart, R.A. ; their only son died of wounds in the first months of the war.

26. **Colonel Sir (Edouard) Percy Cranwill Girouard,** railway engineer and colonial governor, was born at Montreal on January 26, 1867, the son of a French Canadian Judge of the High Court of the Dominion. He was educated at the Royal Military College at Kingston, Canada, and graduated in 1886. After some eighteen months in the service of the Canadian Pacific Railway, he was gazetted to the Royal Engineers in 1888, and in 1890 became Traffic Manager at the Royal Arsenal, Woolwich. After five years in this post, he was seconded for service with the Egyptian Army, and was given the task of constructing and managing the Nile railway, whereby the reconquest of the Sudan was to be effected by Kitchener. With the end of the campaign in 1898 Girouard returned to England,

decorated with the D.S.O. At the outbreak of the South African War, now Brevet-Major, he was appointed Director of Railways, and his work did much to make possible Lord Roberts's march on Pretoria. After the peace he was appointed Commissioner of Railways in the Transvaal and Orange River Colony, a position he held until 1904. He had been made K.C.M.G. in 1900. In 1907 he was appointed first High Commissioner, and then Governor, of the Protectorate of Northern Nigeria. In his short term in this office he did much to advance the prosperity of the Protectorate, constructing the Baro-Kano Railway, ruling the country through the medium of the natives themselves, and instituting a new system of land tenure. In 1909 he was transferred to the Governorship of the East Africa Protectorate, which made marked progress under his administration, which lasted until 1912. He published a " History of the Railways during the War in South Africa." In 1903 he married the only daughter of the late Sir Richard Solomon. One son survived him.

OCTOBER.

1. **William Gershom Collingwood,** talented artist, writer, and antiquary, was born in Liverpool on August 6, 1854, the eldest son of the landscape painter, William Collingwood. After taking a first in " Greats " at Oxford in 1876, he studied at the Slade School, and exhibited his first picture at the Royal Academy in 1880. At Oxford he came under the influence of Ruskin, and the two became close friends. Collingwood travelled abroad with Ruskin, and then settled down at Gillhead, by Windermere, editing Ruskin's works, painting, and lecturing on the history and theory of art. In 1891 he moved to Coniston ; in that year he published " The Art Teaching of John Ruskin," followed in 1893 by " The Life and Work of John Ruskin." Turning his attention to historical studies in the form of fiction, he produced " Thorstein of the Mere," dealing with the Norse settlement at Coniston, and " The Bondwomen," of the same period, his best piece of imaginative work, which was scathingly attacked in the Press for its " immorality." After Ruskin's death he became for a time Professor of Fine Art at University College, Reading, where he proved himself an eloquent and enlightening teacher. Returning to his natural home, the Lake District, he was first editor and then president of the Cumberland and Westmorland Antiquarian Society, whose publications, chiefly due to his skill with pen and pencil, became known as a model of their kind. He also organised a society of Lake District artists, and took the lead in all matters connected with the art and history of the Lake country. His other works included " Dutch Agnes, her Valentine," " Northumbrian Crosses," and " The Lake Counties," his last book. His son Robin, philosopher and archæologist, Fellow and Tutor of Pembroke College, Oxford, and three daughters survived him.

4. **Rudolph Carl von Slatin,** generally known as Slatin Pasha, and formerly Inspector-General of the Sudan, was born on June 27, 1857, at Ober St. Veit, near Vienna, and educated for a military career. When only 17 he joined an expedition to the Egyptian Sudan, and conceived the ambition of entering the service of General Gordon. After returning home and serving as a lieutenant in the Bosnian campaign, he received and eagerly accepted the offer of a post under Gordon. He reached Khartoum in 1879, and was made Financial Inspector, and later Governor of Dara, South-West Darfur, where he remained for five years. In 1881 he was promoted to the governorship of the whole Province, and was made Bey. In 1882 the Arabs of Southern Darfur joined the Mahdi Revolt, and Slatin took the field against them, but after the destruction of Hicks Pasha's army, he was forced to surrender to the Mahdi's troops. While a prisoner of the Dervishes Slatin was brought the bloody and dissevered head of Gordon. After ten years of captivity, he succeeded in escaping across the desert to Egypt, where he was received with honour, given by the Khedive the title of Pasha, promoted colonel, and posted to the Egyptian Intelligence Department. During the campaigns of

1897-98, which culminated in Omdurman and the reconquest of the Sudan, he
served on Kitchener's staff, and after the peace the post of Inspector-General
was specially created for him.   His unrivalled knowledge of the land and understanding of the people were of great value in the work of reconstruction.   At the
outbreak of the Great War, as an Austrian he felt it his duty to resign his post
under the Sudanese Government and to return home, where he became president
of the Austrian Red Cross, and had charge of relief work for prisoners of war.
He published his memoirs under the title of "Fire and Sword in the Sudan."
During the course of his career he was made a Baron of the Austrian Empire,
a lieutentant-general in the Egyptian Army, an honorary major-general in the
British Army, and was decorated with the K.C.M.G., G.C.V.O., and C.B.   He
married, in 1914, the Baroness Alice von Ramberg, by whom he had a daughter.

7. **Dr. Florence Ada Stoney,** a pioneer in X-ray and ultra-violet light treatment, was born in 1870 of a family distinguished in scientific work.   Educated at
home and at the London School of Medicine for Women, she graduated M.D. in
1898.   She was for some years demonstrator of anatomy at the London School
of Medicine for Women till she began to specialise in the practice of X-rays.   At
a time when apparatus and facilities were still at a primitive stage and protection
for the operator was hardly considered, she started X-rays at both the Royal
Free and the Garrett Anderson Hospitals.   On the first day of the Great War,
with thirteen years' experience as an X-ray specialist, she offered her services in
London, but they were declined.   She thereupon organised, as head of the medical
staff and radiologist, the medical part of a surgical unit entirely staffed by women ;
with her section she went through the siege and bombardment of Antwerp, and
succeeded in getting out all the patients before their own escape to Holland.   The
band of women workers was then given the organisation of a small military
hospital near Cherbourg.   In March, 1915, Dr. Stoney was one of the first women
doctors to be accepted for full-time work under the War Office, when she was
appointed head of the radiological department of the Fulham Military Hospital
of 1,000 beds, 15,000 cases passing through her hands.   She published several
papers on the X-ray treatment of fibroids, exophthalmic goitre, and "soldier's
heart" and on the ultra-violet light treatment of rickets and osteomalacia.   She
received an O.B.E. in 1919.

19. **The Hon. Henry Charles Hull,** South African politician, was born at
Caledon, Cape Colony, on November 21, 1860.   At the age of 19 he received a
Civil Service appointment at Kimberley, and qualifying in law practised there
as a solicitor.   After the discovery of the Main Reef, in 1889 he joined the gold
rush and, negotiating and adjusting deals and claims, worked up an immense
practice in the promotion and flotation of companies.   On the failure of the
Jameson Raid in 1896 with other Johannesburg Reformers and protagonists of
the *Uitlanders'* rights he was tried, fined 2,000*l.*, and sentenced to two years'
imprisonment, penalties which were later remitted by Kruger.   After the Boer
War, in which he saw service with the British troops, he became a member of the
Transvaal Legislative Assembly, and the Inter-Colonial Council, and was chairman
of the Railway Committee of the Central South African Railways.   In the agitation for responsible government, despite his British origin and associations, he
joined the Dutch national movement, and when General Botha became the first
and last Transvaal Premier, Hull was appointed Treasurer in his Cabinet.   In
the National Convention which met in 1908 to consider the formation of the
Union of South Africa, he put before the delegates cogent arguments in favour
of unification.   He became Minister of Finance in Botha's first Union Government of 1910, but resigned and left politics two years later.   He had four sons
and one daughter.

23. **Sir Herbert Stephen, Bart.,** Clerk of Assize on the Northern Circuit from
1889 to 1927, was born on June 25, 1857, of a family long distinguished in law,

letters, and the public service. Educated at Rugby and Trinity, Cambridge, he was called to the Bar by the Inner Temple in 1881 and joined the Northern Circuit. In 1889 he was appointed Clerk of Assize for the circuit, and came to be recognised as one of the leading authorities on criminal law and practice. In collaboration with his brother, Sir Harry Stephen, he re-edited several times some of the works of his father, Mr. Justice (James Fitzjames) Stephen, including " A Digest of the Criminal Law," and " A Digest of the Law of Evidence." He also wrote " The Law Relating to Malicious Prosecution," " A Digest of the Law of Criminal Procedure in Indictable Offences," " Prisoners on Oath," and a book upon County Council Law. In his early days he did a good deal of journalism, writing for the old *Saturday Review*, and for Henley in the *Scots* (afterwards *National*) *Observer*. He was also a large contributor of legal biographies to the " Dictionary of National Biography." He wrote numerous articles on criminal law for magazines and newspapers, was a frequent correspondent of *The Times*, and was noted as an incisive and trenchant controversialist. He succeeded to his father's baronetcy in 1894. He married in 1927 his cousin, Mary Hermione, daughter of the late Sir Henry Stewart Cunningham.

28. **Sir Mervyn Edmund Macartney,** eminent architect, was born at Rose-brook, Co. Armagh, in 1853, and educated at Lincoln College, Oxford, taking his degree in 1877. Entering the office of Norman Shaw, with two others of his pupils, the late Ernest Newton, R.A., and the late Sir Ernest George, he initiated the revival of English Renaissance in domestic architecture. His first commission was for a block of studios in the West End of London, and this was followed by an important series of country houses, including " Frithwood House," near Pinner, where his taste in the architectural planning of gardens, in which he led the revival, was shown to advantage. From 1906 to 1930 he was surveyor to the Dean and Chapter of St. Paul's, and was one of the five experts forming the commission set up in 1921 to advise on the dangerous condition of the Cathedral. After the collection by public subscription of a St. Paul's Cathedral Preservation Fund of over 250,000*l.*, the commission's final report issued in 1925 recommended extensive measures for the consolidation of the piers, the support of the dome, and the general preservation of the fabric. At the completion of the work in 1930, Macartney received a knighthood. He was also partly responsible for the Lord Kitchener Memorial Chapel in St. Paul's, regarded as one of the finest combinations of architecture and sculpture of recent years. His publications included " English Houses and Gardens of the Sixteenth and Seventeenth Centuries " and " Later Renaissance in England," written in conjunction with the late John Belcher, R.A. Between 1905 and 1920 he edited the *Architectural Review*. He was married but had no children.

— **Sir Bernard Mallet,** distinguished statistician, was born on September 17, 1859, eldest son of Sir Louis Mallet, Permanent Under-Secretary for India, and a member of an old Huguenot family. Educated at Clifton and at Balliol College under Jowett, he entered the Foreign Office in 1882 and was transferred to the Treasury in 1885. From 1886 to 1891 he was private secretary to the Parliamentary Secretary of the Treasury, and then an assistant private secretary to the First Lord (Mr. A. J. Balfour). In 1897 he was made a Commissioner of Inland Revenue, in which post he produced a " multiplier," designed, when applied to the yield of estate duty for the year, to bring out the approximate total wealth of the country. In 1909 he was appointed Registrar-General of Births, Deaths, and Marriages. His term of office covered the period of the war, so that upon him fell the application of the National Registration Measure of 1915 as well as the registration of Belgian refugees. He was created K.C.B. in 1916, and retired in 1920. He was the biographer of an ancestor in " Mallet du Pan and the French Revolution," and of his father in " Sir Louis Mallet : a Record of Public Services and Political Ideals." He also wrote a life of Lord Northbrook, and produced two volumes on " British Budgets." From 1916 to 1918 he was president of the Royal Statistical Society, and later of the Eugenics Society. He married, in 1891, the Hon. Marie Constance Adeane, for a time Maid of Honour to Queen Victoria, who with two sons survived him.

30. **Paul Sanford (third Lord) Methuen,** distinguished soldier, was born on September 1, 1845, of a family prominent in public life since the seventeenth century. From Eton, where he went in 1858, he proceeded to Sandhurst; in 1871 he was appointed Brigade-Major, Home District. He first saw active service in the Ashanti expedition of 1873-74. In 1876 he was promoted lieutenant-colonel, and after six months as Assistant Military Secretary in Dublin was transferred to Berlin as Military Attaché, remaining there until 1881. On his return to London he was appointed A.A. and Q.M.G., Home District. On the outbreak of the Egyptian War he obtained the post of Commandant of Sir Garnet Wolseley's headquarters, and was present at the battles of Mahuta and Tel-el-Kebir. In 1884 he went out to Bechuanaland, where he raised and commanded Methuen's Horse during the native rising. He went out to South Africa as D.A.G. in 1890, but relinquished the appointment on his promotion as major-general. Succeeding to his father's barony in 1891, he was chosen to command the Home District in 1892. After five years in this post and some service in India, he was promoted lieutenant-general (at the early age of 53), and on the outbreak of the South African War was selected to command the 1st Division of the Field Force. He inflicted minor defeats on the Boers at Belmont, Enslin, and the Modder River, but failed to achieve his main objective, the relief of Kimberley. He suffered a severe reverse at Magersfontein, where the Highland Brigade under his command was all but annihilated. After the relief of Kimberley by General French and his cavalry, he was made administrator of the district ; later he was given charge of the Mafeking area, and commanded a mobile column in the Western Transvaal. There he was surprised and overpowered at Tweebosch by a superior force under the Boer leader De la Rey, his troops routed, and himself wounded and captured. In 1904 he was given the command of the IVth Army Corps, soon after reconstituted as the Eastern Command. He was sent to South Africa in 1908 as General Officer Commanding-in-Chief, and assisted the Government to set up a scheme for the defence of the Union. In 1911 he was promoted Field-Marshal. From 1915 to 1919 he was Governor and Commander-in-Chief of Malta, and on his return home was appointed Constable of the Tower. His decorations included the G.C.B., G.C.V.O., and the G.C.M.G. He was appointed Colonel of the Scots Guards in 1904. Lord Methuen was twice married, and had three sons and two daughters by his second wife.

NOVEMBER.

1. **Dr. William Garnett,** noted educationist, was born at Portsea on December 30, 1850, and educated at the City of London School, the Royal School of Mines, and St. John's College, Cambridge. He was bracketed 5th Wrangler in 1873, and the next year was elected a Fellow of his college. He was the first demonstrator of physics in the Cavendish Laboratory, where he worked under James Clerk Maxwell, of whose biography he was later a joint-author. After five years at Cambridge, in 1879 he was appointed to the Chair of Mathematics, Physics, and Mechanics at the University College of Nottingham, and in 1881 Professor of Mathematics and Principal of the Durham College of Science, which he helped to plan and build. In 1893 he became secretary and adviser to the newly formed Technical Education Board of the London County Council, which was responsible for the organisation of specialised studies in London and the correlation of the work of the polytechnics, art schools, and technical institutes. Retiring in 1915, he was chairman of the Education Reform Council in 1916-17, and he also organised the technical training of interned British prisoners of war in Switzerland. From 1919 to 1923 he was secretary to the London District

K

University Committee for the higher education of ex-Service students. Two of his sons fell in the war; his wife, with their eldest son and two daughters, survived him.

1. **Thomas Sexton,** noted parliamentarian and Irish Nationalist, was born at Waterford in 1848, the son of a constable in the Royal Irish Constabulary. At the age of 12 he became a railway clerk, and at 19 joined the editorial staff of the famous Nationalist weekly, the *Nation.* In the General Election of 1880 he contested County Sligo as a Parnellite and won a notable victory. In the new House of Commons Sexton's penetrating intellect and oratorical powers soon made an impression. In the session of 1881 Gladstone announced that a Bill for the suppression of the Land League agitation would be introduced, and Parnell and his followers pledged themselves to resist its passing with all the obstructive tactics they could devise. In the course of a continuous sitting of 41½ hours—the longest in the annals of Parliament—Sexton's contribution to the debate was a speech lasting 3½ hours. His speech on the debate on the Home Rule Bill of 1886 was described by Gladstone as the finest he had ever heard in the House. In the course of his Parliamentary career he also sat for the constituencies of West Belfast and North Kerry. He was High Sheriff of Dublin in 1887, and Lord Mayor in 1888-89. After his retirement he became chairman of the Nationalist paper, the *Freeman's Journal.*

3. **Brien Ibrican Cokayne, first Lord Cullen of Ashbourne,** who was Governor of the Bank of England from 1918 to 1920, was born July 12, 1864, the son of G. E. Cokayne, Clarenceux King of Arms. After leaving Charterhouse, he entered the firm of Antony Gibbs & Son, merchants (his mother was a Gibbs), and from 1883 to 1886 was in their London office and then worked in the firm's Chilean branches until 1900. On his return to England he was made a partner. In 1902 he succeeded his uncle, Lord Aldenham, on the Court of Directors of the Bank of England. He was Deputy Governor from 1915 to 1918, and Governor from 1918 to 1920, and so exercised an influence over the financial affairs of the country during the critical war and post-war period. He was chief representative of Great Britain at the International Financial Conference at Brussels in 1920. He was made K.B.E. in 1917, and raised to the peerage on his retirement in 1920, taking the title of an ancestor ennobled in 1642. He married in 1904 the daughter of the Rev. the Hon. John Marsham, by whom he had three sons and three daughters.

4. **Salomon Reinach,** distinguished archæologist, was born at Saint-Germain into a Jewish family on August 29, 1858. Educated at the Lycée Condorcet and the Ecole Normale, he took his degree as Doctor of Law and Doctor of Letters of the University of Paris. In 1879 he became a member of the French School of Athens, and after a term of service as secretary to the Archæological Commission of Tunis was appointed an attaché on the staff of the national museums. Between 1882 and 1884 he published a manual of classical philology, reprinted in 1907, and in 1885 appeared his "Traité d'Epigraphie Grecque," a Latin grammar and a handbook of advice to archæological field research workers. He spent the next years in compiling a monumental catalogue of the prehistoric museum at the Château of Saint-Germain, through which he became recognised as a leading authority on prehistoric archæology. In 1902 he became keeper of the museum and titular professor at the Louvre School, and also undertook the direction of the *Revue Archéologique.* He had become a member of the Académie des Inscriptions et Belles Lettres in 1896, and was president in 1906. His archæological researches took him far afield, his travels including visits to North Africa and South Russia, the Mediterranean fringe and the shores of the Bosphorus. His publications comprised more than seventy volumes and about 5,000 articles, and included a short history and a chronology of the Great War and a history of the Russian Revolution. His most popular works

were general histories of art, philosophy, and religion.   He married in 1891 Mlle. Margoulieff, M.D.   He was an hon. D.C.L., Oxford, and a member of the Institut de France.

12. **Sir Dugald Clerk,** noted engineer and inventor, was born on March 31, 1854, the son of a Glasgow machinist, and educated at the West of Scotland Technical College, Anderson College, Glasgow, and the Yorkshire College, Leeds.   After obtaining technical experience at his father's works, in 1877 he joined Thomson, Sterne & Co., the Crown iron works, Glasgow, and began his experiments on the gas engine.   From 1892 to 1899 he was scientific director of Kynoch's, Birmingham.   In 1881 he discovered an alternative to the Otto cycle, followed by the construction of a two-stroke engine, but the importance of this invention was not recognised until some thirty years later, when the Clerk cycle was generally adopted.   For his researches on the specific heat of gases and on explosive pressure he was elected in 1908 a Fellow of the Royal Society ; he served on the Council and received a Royal medal in 1924.   He was president of the Engineering Section of the British Association at the Dublin meeting in 1908, and was Watt medallist, Telford prizeman, and gold medallist of the Institution of Civil Engineers.   Besides being president of several engineering institutions, he was for a term chairman of the delegacy of the City and Guilds Engineering College, and Prime Warden of the Goldsmiths' Company.   During the war he served as director of engineering research at the Admiralty, and as member of the Advisory Committee for Aeronautics at the Air Ministry.   He was created K.B.E. in 1917 and received honorary degrees from five universities.   Since 1888 he had been in partnership with Sir George Croydon Marks (afterwards Lord Marks) as consulting engineer and patent expert.   His wife died in 1930.

20. **George Batley Scott,** veteran cartographer, was born on July 31, 1844, educated at the Lawrence Military Asylum (now the Royal Military School) and as a boy saw something of the second Sikh War and went through the Indian Mutiny.   In 1863 he entered the Survey of India as a sub-assistant and was posted to the North-Western Frontier Survey.   The work was not merely arduous, but dangerous, and on at least two occasions, with a handful of Sepoys, he had to withstand the attacks of fierce tribesmen and to fight his way back to safety. In the course of mapping and surveying he was in the Black Mountain, the Jowaki-Afridi, and the Zhob Valley expeditions and the prolonged Second Afghan War.   After twenty-one years' service he was promoted assistant superintendent, and six years later deputy superintendent.   His work in compiling a military and railway map of India led to his recommendation in 1885 for the C.I.E., but he did not receive that decoration until 1914.   After five years of survey work in Upper Burma he was appointed in 1894 Superintendent of Land Record Surveys in the United Provinces.   He was responsible for the cadastral survey in the Bundelkhand States of Central India, a survey of the Anglo-Persian oil-fields of South-West Persia, and in 1912-13 a contour survey of the tin mines of South-East Burma.   He published several works, including a Pushto vocabulary, " Twenty Years on the North-West Frontier " and " Religion and Short History of the Sikhs."   He had six children and thirteen grandchildren.

23. **Edward Stanley Roscoe,** Registrar of the Admiralty Court, historian and writer, was born at Chester in 1849 and educated at Radley.   He was called to the Bar by Lincoln's Inn in 1871 and joined the Northern Circuit, besides practising in the old Admiralty Court.   In 1883 he was appointed official reporter in that court after the move to the new Law Courts in the Strand and its becoming a branch of the High Court ; in 1890 he became Assistant Registrar, and in 1904 Registrar.   At the outbreak of the Great War he naturally became also Registrar of the Prize Court, a branch of law which many years of peace had rendered practically obsolete, but of which Roscoe had a special and extensive knowledge. In 1924 he published a " History of the English Prize Court " and in 1931 " Studies

in the History of the Admiralty and Prize Courts." His " Admiralty Law and Practice " and his " Measure of Damages in Actions of Maritime Collision " are standard works on the subjects. His biographical and general writings included " The English Scene in the Eighteenth Century," " Penn's Country," " Aspects of Doctor Johnson," and the lives of Robert Harley, Earl of Oxford, and Lord Stowell, the great Prize Court Judge of the Napoleonic era. He was joint editor of George Selwyn's " Letters and Life " and of the " Speeches and Addresses of the 15th Earl of Derby," a frequent contributor to, and for a time editor of, the *Edinburgh Review.* In 1905 he was an Assessor at the North Sea inquiry into the firing on English trawlers by the Russian fleet. Roscoe married a daughter of the Speaker of the House of Keys, and had two sons and five daughters.

23. **Percy Pitt,** noted musician, was born on January 4, 1870, and educated in France and Germany. He was associated with the early period of the Symphony and Promenade Concerts at the Queen's Hall, where he was organist, piano accompanist, and for a time writer of the programme notes. In 1902 he was appointed musical adviser to Covent Garden, and in 1907 musical director to the Grand Opera Syndicate. He worked in a similar capacity for the Beecham Opera Company, the British National Opera Company, and the B.B.C. ; in the early years of wireless entertainment he did useful work in indicating the lines on which the broadcasting of music should develop, besides doing a great deal of conducting in the studio. His many compositions included his " Symphonic Prelude " and " Ballade for Violin and Orchestra," 1900 ; " Five Poems for Baritone and Orchestra," 1902 ; and a " Concerto for Clarinet and Orchestra." His symphony, composed for and produced at the Birmingham Festival of 1906, was repeated with some success at the Queen's Hall. His lighter works of the dance suite type showed his sense of orchestral effect at its best. But he was most generally known, perhaps, for his work for the British Broadcasting Corporation. He married Miss Ivy Margaret Bruce, of Sydney, N.S.W.

30. **Dame Elizabeth Wordsworth,** first Principal of Lady Margaret Hall, Oxford, was born at Harrow in 1840, the eldest child of Dr. Christopher Wordsworth, headmaster of Harrow School, and was a great-niece of the poet. She was educated at home by governesses under her father's supervision, and after a year at a school in Brighton rejoined her family, taught her younger sisters, and took part in parish work. At Lincoln, of which her father became Bishop in 1868, she began the Bible classes for young women which were one of the most distinctive features of her thirty years' rule of Lady Margaret Hall (1868-1908). The latter was founded in 1878 on Church of England lines, when Miss Wordsworth became its first Principal. Her method of governing the college was intensely personal and individual, with a comprehensive absence of rules and regulations. Her force of character did much for women's education in Oxford, as her influence established the place and reputation in the University of the college in her charge. When she retired from the principalship in 1908 she continued to serve on the council, and was elected an honorary Fellow both of Lady Margaret and of St. Hugh's College. She founded the Lady Margaret Hall Settlement in Kennington Road. Her chief intellectual interests were in classics and in English literature of the eighteenth century, and her publications included " Thoughts for the Chimney Corner," " The Snow Garden and other Stories," " St. Christopher and other Poems," and " Essays, Old and New." But her principal work was the biography of her father which appeared in 1888. In 1928 she was created D.B.E., and received the honorary degree of D.C.L. from Oxford University.

DECEMBER.

3. **Miss Clotilde Inez Mary Graves,** journalist, novelist, and dramatist, was born on June 3, 1863, at Buttevant Barracks, County Cork, third daughter of an army major and a member of a well-known Irish family. While still a

girl she determined to write for the stage, and prepared herself by taking small parts in travelling companies. Her first play, " Nitocris," a tragedy in blank verse, was produced by Augustus Harris at Drury Lane in 1887. The next few years she devoted to current journalism, contributing to *Judy* (long since defunct), *Punch*, *Fun*, *The Gentlewoman*, *The Sporting Times*, and Tom Hood's " Comic Annual," besides illustrated weekly papers and monthly magazines. She also wrote dramatic criticisms. She resumed her work as a playwright in 1894 with " Dr. and Mrs. Neill," followed two years later by " A Mother of Three," which achieved some success. Between 1887 and 1913 sixteen of her plays were produced in London and New York, including " The Bishop's Eye," " A Maker of Comedies," and " The Bond of Ninon," several of them with distinguished castes. In 1910 she published " The Dop Doctor," a novel, the scene of which was laid in South Africa during the Boer War. The book, which was reprinted some thirty times, appeared over the name of Richard Dehan, a *nom de plume* which Miss Clo Graves (as she was generally known) used thenceforward. Some sixteen novels and volumes of short stories followed, the best known being " Between Two Thieves," " The Man of Iron," " Gilded Vanity," and " The Lovers of the Market Place." Miss Graves joined the Roman Catholic Church in 1896, and her last years were passed in a convent.

6. **Eugène Brieux,** distinguished dramatist, was born in Paris on January 19, 1858, the son of a carpenter. After leaving school he took to journalism, became editor of the *Nouvelliste de Rouen* and also started to write plays. In 1890 his " Ménage d'Artistes " was accepted by Antoine and produced at his Théâtre Libre. It was followed by " Blanchette " and " L'Engrenage," the latter dealing with political corruption and universal suffrage. In 1897 the Gymnase put on his play, " Les Trois Filles de M. Dupont," a study of womanhood crushed by social conditions which attracted the serious attention of the critics, and which, like its forerunners and successors, marked its author as moralist as much as dramatist. " La Robe Rouge " appeared at the Vaudeville in 1900, and was adapted for the London stage and produced by Arthur Bourchier as " The Arm of the Law " ; the original play was directed against certain failings of the French judicial system. The Stage Society produced an English version of " Maternité " in 1906 and in 1907 " Les Hannetons." " La Foi," produced in London by Beerbohm Tree in 1909 as " False Gods," was a study of dogmatic religion and priestcraft in an ancient Egyptian setting. " La Femme Seule " (1912) treated of the problem of the woman in France with her own living to make. " Les Avariés " (1901), on the subject of venereal disease, was widely known in England, being produced in London in 1914 under the title of " Damaged Goods." Though some of his less didactic plays showed a dramatic force and a mastery of detail, Brieux openly regarded the drama first and last as a medium for social reform. He was a member of the Académie Française and a Commander of the Legion of Honour.

8. **Miss Gertrude Jekyll,** one of the two leading authorities on gardening in England, was born on November 29, 1843, in London, the fourth child of Captain Edward Jekyll, of the Grenadier Guards. In 1848 the family moved to Bramley House, Surrey, where she developed a strong interest in painting and in all country pursuits. About 1861 she began to study in the art schools of South Kensington, and received help and encouragement from Watts, Leighton, and other painters, friends of the Jekylls. While on a visit to Italy she obtained instruction in several handicrafts, and became a skilled and expert craftsman in various media. After Captain Jekyll's death the family returned to Surrey, and the house they built on Munstead Hill, above Godalming, in 1878 became the meeting-place of a group of enthusiastic gardeners, while Miss Jekyll also acquired a professional knowledge of house decoration and furnishing. In 1882 she met William Robinson, with whom she joined forces in a common championship of the hardy flower border as against the stiff formality of the bedding-out

school. As her sight became worse and she was prevented from continuing her painting, she devoted more attention to horticulture. Her books on the subject included " Wood and Garden," " Home and Garden," " Wall and Water Gardens," " Children's Gardening," " Colour Schemes for the Garden," " Flower Arrangements," besides one entitled " Old West Surrey," re-issued in 1925 under the title of " Old English Household Life " ; all were illustrated with photographs, taken and developed by the author. For two-and-a-half years she was joint-editor of *The Garden*. In 1895 she was awarded the Victorian Medal of Honour by the Royal Horticultural Society. Her brother was Colonel Sir Herbert Jekyll, formerly Assistant Secretary to the Board of Trade.

13. **Edward Treacher Collins,** eminent ophthalmic surgeon, was born in London in 1862, and educated at University College School and the Middlesex Hospital. He was admitted a member of the Royal College of Surgeons of England in 1883 and elected F.R.C.S. in 1890. He was house surgeon at the Royal London Ophthalmic Hospital (Moorfields) from 1884 to 1887, pathologist and curator of the museum from 1887 to 1894 ; was elected surgeon in 1895, and became consulting surgeon in 1922. In 1894 he combined his honeymoon with a professional visit to Ispahan, where he had been summoned to treat the eyes of the Shah's eldest son. He recorded his experiences in Persia in a book entitled " In the Kingdom of the Shah." He soon built up a large consulting practice in London. He was Hunterian Professor at the Royal College of Surgeons in 1893-94 ; Bowman Lecturer in 1921, and Montgomery Lecturer in 1924 at the Royal College of Surgeons of Ireland. He was president of the Ophthalmological Society of the United Kingdom in 1917, and again in 1924, and honorary chairman of the International Ophthalmological Council. He was consulting surgeon to Charing Cross Hospital and to the Eye Hospital at Oxford. From 1923 to 1926 Collins was President of the Council of British Ophthalmologists. He was awarded the Middlemore prize by the British Medical Association in 1914. His published works included " Researches into the Anatomy and Pathology of the Eye," and " Arboreal Life and the Evolution of the Human Eye." He had a son and daughter who survived him.

16. **Vaughan Nash,** formerly private secretary to two Prime Ministers, was born at Clifton in 1861, and educated privately. From 1893 to 1899 he was on the editorial staff of the *Daily Chronicle*, for which he reported the dock strike of 1889. Joining the staff of the *Manchester Guardian*, he was sent to India by his paper during the famine of 1900. His accounts of these two events were published under the titles of " The Story of the Dockers' Strike " (written in collaboration with Sir Hubert Llewellyn Smith) and " The Great Famine " ; he also wrote various papers on industrial questions, on which during the course of his journalistic work he had made himself expert. He was for a time on the staff of the *Daily News*. In 1905 Mr. Campbell-Bannerman, then Prime Minister, appointed Nash his private secretary, and when in 1908 Mr. Asquith became Premier, he retained him in the post, which he occupied until 1912. In that year he was made vice-chairman of the Development Commission, continuing until 1929, when he resigned the vice-chairmanship, but remained a Development Commissioner (unpaid). During the war he was chairman of the Retail Coal Prices Inter-Departmental Committee, and a member of the Departmental Committee on the Settlement of Soldiers on the Land. He was secretary of the Ministry of Reconstruction from 1917 to 1919. He was made C.B. in 1909 and C.V.O. in 1911. His wife and his elder son survived him.

18. **Eduard Bernstein,** a pioneer of German Socialism, was born in 1850, one of ten children of a Jewish engine-driver, who became a minor State official. Joining the Socialist Party in his early twenties he had to give up his position as a bank clerk on account of his political views, and in 1878 was compelled to leave Germany. Settling in Switzerland he became editorial secretary of the Socialist

periodical *Zukunft*, and then editor of *Der Sozialdemokrat* at Zürich, since the paper was banned in Germany. Expelled from Switzerland also, he came to London, where he remained for thirteen years. In 1902, at the instance of Bülow, he was allowed to return to his native land, and, elected to the Reichstag by a large majority, became a leader of the Revisionist section of the Socialist Party, then rent by dissension, and played an important part in the conflict of the rival factions. He sat in several pre-war Parliaments, and during the war went over to the Radical wing of the party. He was arrested in 1914 for protesting against the invasion of Belgium, and belonged to the anti-war group of Socialists who in 1917 formed the secessionist Independent Socialist Party, which after the war partly reunited with the main body and partly went to form the nucleus of German Communism. Bernstein himself was among the first to return to the Socialist Party proper, and after the war he sat as a deputy in several Reichstags. In 1930 he received the tribute of the Conference of the German Social Democratic Party and acknowledgments of his life-long work for the movement.

18. **Harold Arthur Lee=Dillon, seventeenth Viscount Dillon of Costello Gallen,** Co. Mayo, in the peerage of Ireland, antiquary and expert on arms and armour, was born in Westminster on January 24, 1844, of a family notable in history since the twelfth century. He entered the army as an ensign in the Rifle Brigade in 1862 and was afterwards major in the 4th (Militia) Battalion, Oxfordshire Light Infantry. From 1892 to 1913 he was curator of the Tower of London Armouries, and did valuable work in reorganising and rearranging the collection. He was a Trustee of the British Museum from 1905 to 1912, and from 1894 to 1928 was chairman of the Trustees of the National Portrait Gallery, to which in 1925 he presented in memory of his wife portraits of Archbishop Warham, Sir Philip Sidney, and of his ancestor, Sir Henry Lee, K.G. ; all three from his own collection of Old Masters at Ditchley, Oxon., where he had an estate of 3,000 acres. He was made Antiquary of the Royal Academy in 1903, and was a Trustee of the Wallace Collection from 1918 till 1931 ; he was President of the Royal Archæological Institute from 1892 to 1898, and of the Society of Antiquaries from 1897 to 1904. Lord Dillon was a member of the Royal Commission on Historical Monuments, and secretary of the Royal Commission on Westminster Abbey (1890). He was made C.H. in 1921, and received the honorary degree of D.C.L. from Oxford in 1914. Lord Dillon was twice married ; his only son, also an antiquary, died in 1923 ; his daughter survived him.

— **Herbert Ainslie Roberts,** for over thirty years secretary of the Cambridge University Appointments Board, was born on February 13, 1864, at Swineshead, Lincolnshire, and educated at Christ's Hospital and Gonville and Caius College, Cambridge, where he was a mathematical exhibitioner and foundation scholar. He was 22nd Wrangler in 1886, and for ten years was senior mathematical master at Bath College. Returning to Cambridge in 1898 for four years he was a mathematical coach. In 1899 the Cambridge University Appointments Board was formed, and Roberts became its secretary in 1902. In itself something of an experiment, within ten years he had built up an organisation and a connexion, the results of which justified the board to its critics. In his evidence before the Royal Commission on the Civil Service in 1912 Roberts was able to report that in the preceding five years he had placed 420 men in business, administrative and technical careers, besides an almost equal number of teaching appointments, and of these 97 per cent. were found to be in the right jobs. Altogether he was instrumental in placing some 6,000 men in positions. He was for many years also secretary of the Cambridge University Association, the Board of Indian Civil Service Studies, and the Foreign Service Students Committee, retiring from these offices in 1932. After the war he became a member of the Resettlement of Officers Committee. He was elected a Fellow of his college in 1927. He married in 1894 and had one son, who survived him.

INDEX.

The figures between [ ] refer to PART I.

PRINTED IN GREAT BRITAIN BY THE UNIVERSITY PRESS, ABERDEEN